THE
BALLAD
BOOK

THE BALLAD BOOK

Edited by **MacEdward Leach**

A. S. BARNES & COMPANY, INC. • NEW YORK

THOMAS YOSELOFF LTD • LONDON

THE BALLAD BOOK

Library of Congress catalog card number: 55–6778

To

Donald and Douglas

CONTENTS

Ballads of England and Scotland with American and Danish Variants

American Ballads by Origin or Adoption

PREFACE

THE ballad is a fascinating type of literature. Extending from medieval times to the present, and ranging in space from Ireland to Russia, from Italy to Finland, they belong to no specific time or place. Ballads hold interest for students of literature, of song, of folklore, of social custom, of history. Many ballads contain lines of incomparable poetry; many of them give succinct readings of life. Truly they are universal. England, Scotland, and America are especially fortunate in their rich store of ballads.

It is the purpose of this book to bring together a wide selection of these English and American ballad texts with enough editorial apparatus to make them understandable. The primary considerations governing the choice of texts are intrinsic worth and historical importance. In addition, I have tried in the selection of texts and text variants to show the ballad in all of its aspects. Some ballads like "Colonel Sharp" are included because the stories they made popular have been used later in novel, play, or short story. Scandinavian variants of some of the "international" ballads are given for comparison with the native texts.

Since ballads are folksong, many will wonder why no music is included here with the texts. The most important reason is that no system of musical notation that I am aware of can indicate accurately the music of the ballads; especially is this true of the systems that reduce the melody of the whole ballad to that of the first stanza. Folk singing shows subtle variations in pitch, rhythm, phrasing, accentuation that cannot be captured by conventional notation; moreover, variations appear from stanza to stanza. Even the refrain of a given ballad may not be sung in exactly the same way throughout. Listening to field recordings of the ballads is the best way, short of listening to folk singers themselves, to come to knowledge and appreciation of the

music of folksong. No teacher of ballad teaches from a
score. He teaches by demonstration if he has the gift of
song, or, failing that, from field and authentic recordings
such as those listed below, starting on page 834.

Further reasons for omitting music scores involve space
and expense. I feel that it is more desirable to have an ade-
quate representation of texts than an inadequate representation of texts with music scores. The texts are more important
because they are basic. Melodies drift. Many ballads are
sung to several different melodies. Very often in many regions, like Newfoundland and parts of New England, melody practically disappears and ballads are "sung" to a kind
of parlando. It is my hope that those using this book will
familiarize themselves with the text of a given ballad, becoming acquainted with its story, feeling its drama, and that
then, to get its full flavor, they will listen to an authentic
recording of it.

I am indebted to authorities of the Bodleian, of Trinity
College, Cambridge, of the British Museum, of the Society
of Antiquaries, and of Harvard University for permission
to use manuscript material. I wish to thank the following
persons for permission to use ballad texts from their various
collections: Alan Lomax, Louis Chappell, Harold Thompson, Guy B. Johnson, George Korson, Paul Brewster, Vance
Randolph, Horace Beck, A. K. Davis, Maud Karpeles,
Henry Goddard Leach, and the late Fanny Eckstorm. Copy-
right ballad texts from Sharp's *English Folksongs of the
Southern Appalachians* are used by permission of Maud
Karpeles and the Oxford Press; from A. K. Davis' *Traditional Ballads from Virginia* by permission of A. K. Davis
and Harvard University Press. I am especially indebted to
Samuel Bayard for reading the Introduction and giving me
many helpful suggestions. I wish also to thank Dorothy
Thompson of Harper & Brothers for her help at every turn
and her patience with a long and difficult text.

MacEdward Leach

THE
BALLAD
BOOK

.

INTRODUCTION

I

WHAT IS A BALLAD?

In the Middle Ages in Europe there appeared a form of story-song which in English has come to be called ballad. From their beginnings these story-songs had certain definite characteristics, three of which are primary characteristics in that they are always found, and two are secondary in that they frequently appear. The primary characteristics are as follows: (1) The ballad tells a story; (2) it tells its story in song, in simple melody; (3) it is *folk* story-song since it has the unmistakable qualities of treatment, of style, and of subject matter that come only from folk culture. The two secondary characteristics—impersonality and concern with a single situation rather than with a developmental series of events—are not integral, but expected. Each of the primary characteristics is equally important, for each complements the others to make ballads what they are.

The ballad tells a story. But of the elements that go to make up a story—action, characters, setting, and theme— the ballad is mainly concerned with action. Characterization is conventional and general; setting is likewise general and static; theme is implied. But the action is always vivid and dramatic and often romantic as well. Often it is sensationalized into the melodramatic. The analogy between ballad story and modern newspaper story is valid, for many ballad stories would settle down in such pages and be at home: A girl murders her sister by pushing her into the millstream. Two famous rivals, an Englishman and a Scotchman, meet in battle and fight to the death. A brother kills his sister on her wedding day because she had not asked his permission to be married. An outlaw robs a priest and gives the money to a poor woman. A girl, abandoned by all her family, is about to be executed when her lover appears and saves her. These are all characteristic of the dramatic and romantic nature, and also of the generalized nature, of ballad stories.

1

Such stories have an appeal to the folk over the generations, for in basic form they occur over and over in real life. Always there are sensational deeds of violence, jealous lovers, family and tribal feuds, men against society. The situations are timeless.

Of the two common types of action in narrative, plotted and episodic, the ballad invariably uses plotted action. Or perhaps it would be better to say that the ballad maker chooses a plotted story around which to compose his ballad. The typical action is consequently twofold: the unstable situation and the solution. Hence ballad story is suspenseful and climactic. A girl's dead lover returns on horseback to carry her away to the land of the dead. A mermaid revenges herself on her mortal lover, when he deserts her, by casting a spell over him; he dies from the spell in spite of his wife's attempts to save him. A knight plays such beautiful music that the king's daughter falls in love with him and invites him to her bower for the night. He tells his page boy and orders the boy to awaken him in time. The boy promises, but instead goes to the lady himself in the guise of his master. When the page returns, he awakens the knight, who then goes to the princess. She receives him in consternation and surprise. All is discovered. Such is the unstable situation in "Glasgerion." Various resolutions of this unstable situation have been worked out by different balladists: (1) The princess kills herself, the knight kills the page and then himself; (2) she taunts the knight for being hoodwinked and passes it all off as a good joke; (3) she discovers that she has come to love the page and sends the knight on his way.

"Glasgerion" illustrates beautifully the lack of characterization in the ballad and the lack of connection between character and action; that is, the action is not motivated through character. We know nothing at all about this lady except that she is fond of music and is a princess. Therefore the unstable situation can be resolved logically in any of the three ways indicated above. A modern story writer, however, would be inclined to draw the character of the lady so particularly that we would expect her to act only in a certain way.

Another conspicuous difference between modern story and

ballad story is the tendency in the ballad to pass quickly over the first half of the plot—the unstable situation—to come to the second—the solution. It is somewhat like beginning a play in the last act, and it often leaves the modern reader bewildered, feeling that he has not been given enough information to know what is happening and why it is happening. "Lord Randal" begins with a dialogue between a boy and his mother which reveals that he has been poisoned and is dying; from what follows we surmise that his betrothed has poisoned him. But why should she kill him? The ballad does not tell us; rather it skips over such explanatory material to linger on the climax. "The Cruel Brother" likewise begins with John stabbing his sister when she bends over to kiss him as she starts to ride away after being married. Again, what is the situation? We are told only that she had asked all of her relatives for permission to marry, but not her brother John. Why did she not ask him? We have no clue. Perhaps this originally was an incest ballad. Perhaps it recapitulates a period in history when the brother had the disposal of his sister's hand, since her children would inherit his possessions. One version of the story would seem to suggest that the stabbing was instigated by John's wife because she hated the sister.

This tendency to concentrate on climactic action is a contribution of the folk to ballad style and form, for it develops in a given ballad as that ballad comes down in time from folk singer to folk singer. Ballads are things of growth; in their earliest forms many, but certainly not all, of the ballads probably told stories as detailed as any conventional narrative; but as they are re-created by the folk, the slow elements and the undramatic elements are dropped and only the hard core of tension remains—the moment of drama.

In one way this is the ultimate in dramatic expression, for here is the universal. Here is man in his dramatic moment. Here is *a* man becoming man and facing the one moment in life that destroys all or reveals all. What matter the details that bring this moment about? They are all different and yet all the same in that they bring man to his dramatic moment. The folk are not concerned with why, for they are not introspective or analytical. Rather they are concerned with the drama of the moment and the character's reaction to it. This, then, is the important difference between ballad story and sophisticated narrative with its emphasis on motivation.

Almost any of the nonhistorical ballads will illustrate this. "The Maid Freed from the Gallows," for example, in both British and American tradition is little more than a formula, so stereotyped that those who would see communal composition use it as evidence of how easy it would be for a group to compose it. A girl is about to be hanged. (Why? Where? By whom?) She asks the hangman to stay his hand for she sees her father coming. Then she addresses the father, asking if he has brought her "fee." He answers no. Follows the same routine with mother, brother, sister, and finally true-love, who has brought the fee and so saves her. This ballad, unlike most, has survived in an early form which is as detailed and circumstantial as one could wish. It tells of a girl who was stolen from her husband by pirates and held for ransom. She appeals to her various relatives in vain, being taken by the pirates to the home of each. Each incident is developed in detail by dialogue, and the reactions of the girl as each one turns her down are indicated. Finally her husband ransoms her and all is well. As this ballad was handed down, time and the folk gradually discarded details—local details—and kept the dramatic pattern and the climax. The ballad gains in intensity as the early clutter of details disappears and the point—that her lover does not desert her, though blood relatives do—is dramatically focused. It is interesting to compare ballad practice such as this with the similar technique Hemingway uses in short stories like "The Killers" in which, in striving for universality, he passes over the exposition and plunges into the climax, directing the reader to the significant. The historical ballads, those based on well-known historical events like "Chevy Chase" and composed near the time of the action, are exceptional, for they tell a more circumstantial and connected story.

Akin to the technique under discussion is the one in the ballad happily known as "leaping and lingering." This means simply that the ballad passes from scene to scene in the narrative without filling in the gaps, leaping over time and space and lingering on those scenes that are colorful and dramatic.

Almost any ballad will yield instances of this technique. "Hind Etin" is a good example.

Throughout we have been stressing the narrative nature of the ballads, and rightly so; but we must not fail to note that many of them have pronounced lyrical elements as well. Ballads are poetic and are written to be sung—two factors that would tend to bring lyricism in. We consequently find such lyrical qualities as we do in narrative poems like "The Highwayman" and "The Road to Mandalay": emotion, direct or evoked, sensuous and figurative language, musical lines. But categories cannot be hard and fast; some ballads are on the border between lyric and narrative. Often too we find that a ballad changes in form as it comes down through the years, following some such pattern as this: straight narrative > dramatic narrative > lyrical-dramatic narrative > lyrical narrative > lyric. "The Unquiet Grave," for example, is very close to lyric with its strong evocation of loneliness and sorrow, its beauty of language. The first two lines are perfect lyrical expression. So also is the "Twa Corbies." Although it tells a story, the whole is an evocation of powerful emotion that overwhelms the simple narrative and leaves the listener (reader) tremendously moved. Where in English will you find two lines more terribly final than the words pronounced over the dead knight (and all dead) at the end:

> O'er his white banes, when they are bare,
> The wind sall blaw for evermair.

Here compacted is the expression of the transitoriness of life, the inevitability of the march back to the elements.

Further illustration is afforded by contrasting "The Lyke-wake Dirge," a lyric containing many narrative elements, with the ballad "Willie's Lyke-Wake." This latter is the story of a man who feigns death in order to lure the girl he is in love with to his home to attend the lyke-wake (body watching). It is a humorous story developed through anecdote, with dialogue and suspense, to the happy ending. For the text see page 110. Note the difference between it and "The Lyke-wake Dirge," which follows. "The Lyke-wake Dirge" is a folk song—it was collected from oral tradition by John Aubrey in the seventeenth century—but it is not a ballad, for it is subjective rather than objective, lyric rather than narrative.

> This ean[1] night, this ean night
>   Every night and awle,[2]
> Fire and fleet[3] and candle-light
>   And Christ receive thy sawle.
>
> When thou from hence doest pass away
>   Every night and awle
> To whinny[4]-moor thou comest at last
>   And Christ receive thy sawle.
>
> If ever thou gave either hosen[5] or shun[6]
>   Every night and awle,
> Sitt thee down and putt them on
>   And Christ receive thy sawle.
>
> But if hosen nor shoon thou never gave nean
>   Every night and awle,
> The whinnies shall prick thee to the bare beane
>   And Christ receive thy sawle.
>
> From whinny-moor that thou mayst pass
>   Every night and awie
> To brig[7] O dread[8] thou comest at last
>   And Christ receive thy sawle.
>
> If ever thou gave either milke or drinke
>   Every night and awle,
> The fire shall never make thee shrink
>   And Christ receive thy sawle.
>
> But if milke nor drinke thou never gave nean
>   Every night and awle,
> The fire sall burn thee to the bare bane
>   And Christ receive thy sawle.

There is drama here and a bit of story, but the emphasis is on the lyrical elements. It evokes the scene: the dead body lying exposed, eyes closed, hands folded on its breast, the old women sitting around chanting this solemn song to the dead, and the flickering candlelight making weird shadows over all. These two songs illustrate how easy it is to pass from

[1] ean = one.
[2] awle = all.
[3] fleet = water.
[4] whinny = covered with furze.
[5] hosen = stockings.
[6] shun = shoes.
[7] brig = bridge.
[8] dread = dead(?).

narrative to lyric, especially when the medium of both is music.

The ballads have yet another quality that puts them in objective literature and marks them as essentially dramatic and not lyric, and that is their impersonality. The ballad is objective; the action is allowed to unfold of itself, without comment or expressed emotion of the author. The stage is set, the actors come on and go through their parts with no direction or comment. Moreover, the action is related throughout on the same level of tension. The most brutal or exciting detail is related in the same casual, unconcerned manner as a bit of explanation. Consider, for example, the beginning of one version of "The Twa Sisters":

> There were two sisters, they went playing,
> To see their father' ships come sayling in.
>
> And when they came to the sea brim
> The elder did push the younger in.
>
> O sister, O sister, take me by the gowne,
> And draw me up upon the dry ground.
>
> O sister, O sister, that may not be,
> Till salt and oatmeal grow both of a tree.

Note the lack of emphasis, as well as the lack of comment, in the second line of the second stanza. In "Lord Thomas and Fair Annet" (Pepys' *Ballads,* iii, 316) Lord Thomas' wife has stabbed his sweetheart:

> 17. "Oh art thou blind, Lord Thomas?" she sayd,
> "Or canst thou not very well see?
> Oh dost thou not see my own heart's blood
> Run trickling down my knee?"
>
> 18. Lord Thomas he had a sword by his side,
> As he walked about the hall;
> He cut off his bride's head from her shoulders,
> And he threw it against the wall.
>
> 19. He set the hilte against the ground,
> And the point against his heart;
> There was never three lovers that ever met
> More sooner they did depart.

The understatement of the last two lines reinforces this

sense of casualness, the supreme taking for granted, no matter what the action or the circumstances.

Even when the story is related from a first-person point of view, it is an impersonal kind of *I* that tells it. One does not get the feeling that the experience of a particular individual is being related, or that the experience is particularly a subjective one. "The Wee Wee Man" is told in the first person, but the effect is not one of personal revelation but rather simply one of immediacy and of credibility. Such first-person ballads suggest comparison with Poe's stories of incredible adventure. On the whole, the effect of impersonal presentation of action is intensely dramatic. The action unrelieved by comment stands starker, more emphatic, leaving the reader or listener to reconstruct the scene, to let his emotion run without curb of author's comment. Comment and explanation would *relieve* the terribleness of the scene in "Lamkin" in which Lamkin and the nurse stab the baby and then sit, one rocking the cradle and the other singing a lullaby as the blood runs out of the cradle and the baby frenziedly cries.

Then Lamkin's tane a sharp knife, that hang down by his gaire,[9]
And he has gien the bony babe a deep wound and a sair.[10]

Then Lamkin he rocked, an the fause nourice sang,
Till frae ilkae[11] bore o the cradle the red blood out sprang.

A ballad, then, tells a story, tells it dramatically with emphasis and focus on the climax, and treats it with complete detachment, objectively and impersonally.

The fact that the ballad is *folk* song and that the folk ultimately make a ballad what it is partly accounts for the qualities of narrative mentioned above, but the folk contribute much more. For these reasons discussion of ballad folk is necessary. Who are the ballad folk? There is a general impression that they are illiterate hillbillies, wandering around barefoot and smoking corncob pipes. The evidence from numerous records as far back as the Middle Ages points rather to the middle class: small farmers, shoemakers, village schoolteachers, nursemaids, tinkers, wives of small trades-

9 gaire = gore, side.   11 ilkae = each.
10 sair = sore.

men, innkeepers, drovers. Among these too are the itinerant singers of songs who go from village to village plying a small trade but concerning themselves largely with singing their stores of songs. Here and there members of the gentry and of the professional and book-educated class became interested in ballads and sang them or wrote them down. Mrs. Brown of Falkland, who lived in the latter half of the eighteenth century, had a great store of fine ballads which had come down in her family. Her father was an Aberdeen professor and her husband a clergyman.

One discovers that ballad singing and collecting run in families, that in a given community most of the people were listeners or at best participated only to the extent of singing the refrains, that keeping ballads alive was the business of the few, the few with a natural bent for singing and with a good memory for the old songs. Often such folk transmitted their talents and interest to their children, and for several generations a family might be famous as ballad singers. Today the Gaelic people of Cape Breton exhibit a culture analogous to the folk cultures of the past. The people are lumbermen, farmers, fishermen; it is largely a homogeneous classless society. They are completely literate; very occasionally they get to the movies; they do listen to radios, but they still believe in the fairy folk and they harbor many more superstitions than do people belonging to the general culture. There is much interest in folk songs and folk singing. In every community one person, usually a man, is the recognized folk singer of the community. A collector of songs upon inquiring about them is immediately referred to this person. Most of these singers also compose songs, turning the dramatic events of every day into local songs. Such a one is H.C., a farmer who lives beyond St. Anne. He has a large gift for singing and for making songs. He has composed over fifty songs, all dealing with local events. Many of these songs have passed into tradition and are now found far from St. Anne. Men frequently gather at the corner store in the evening as H.C. sings in Gaelic the songs he and others have made. And on certain Sundays when the old style of singing is used, it is H.C. who acts as precentor and lines out the Psalms for the congregation.

It is people like him who are the folk, people like him who, from the fifteenth century if not earlier, have carried these story-songs in memory and have sung them and had their way with them. They have had their way with them by singing them to simple and obvious melodies, by keeping alive the most dramatic and most romantic and most melodramatic of them, by working into them certain qualities of style, such as repetition, simple and incremental.

The difference between folk-song composition and the composition of songs and stories of art is one of individual consciousness. The musician and storyteller on the conscious level intellectualizes his material and method by trying them against aesthetic principles already codified and drawn up for him. The folk, on the other hand, accept, reject, modify, augment their songs and stories through unconscious subjective processes; and what one generation accepts, another may change or reject entirely. So we hit on beauty, or pathos, or sense of tragedy not exactly by chance but nearly so.

At best a definition of ballad must be approximate, for much overlapping occurs between ballad and lyric, ballad and carol, ballad and epic lay, ballad and narrative song. As a general and working definition, however, we may in summary say that a ballad is a narrative folk song that fixes on the most dramatic part of its story and impersonally lets the story move of itself, by dialogue and incident, quickly to the end. But really to know ballads is to hear them sung by people of whose culture they still form a part. Such an experience gives one the necessary synthesis of poetry, music, and dramatic story with folk background and culture. Next best is to hear records of ballads sung by real folk singers, and last to read them in books like this. Such activity, even this last one, will give one a subjective knowledge of ballad that will transcend definition.

II

BALLAD SUBJECTS

What are ballads about? Where do ballad stories come from? Answers to these questions will help to throw light on the origin and authorship of ballads and on the nature of the ballad audience. Since the ballad originated in the late Middle Ages we would expect its subject matter to be drawn largely from medieval story, but reading through the great Child collection reveals at once that we have in ballad form little material from medieval literature of record. Much of medieval culture is concerned with religion and as a consequence religious stories abound; the number of saints' lives alone is overwhelming. Yet fewer than a dozen ballads on religious subjects survive; two of these are as much carol as ballad. This is astonishing when we remember medieval folk drama and its wealth of Biblical stories.

The same situation obtains with romance story. Through the Middle Ages the great cycles of romance developed, each with hundreds of stories; but although ballads teem with knights and kings and princes and ladies, few make use of romance story. Romance in general has given only one important ballad, "Hind Horn," based on the romance story of King Horn. The great body of Arthurian romance is represented by only three or four ballads, such as "The Boy and the Mantle" and "The Marriage of Sir Gawain." Many romances treat of lovers and many ballads do, but nowhere in ballad do we find love stories from romance; there are no ballads of Tristan and Isolde, of Lancelot and Guinevere. Likewise we find few allegorical or satiric ballads, though both allegory and satire were extraordinarily popular in the Middle Ages. Even exempla, short pithy anecdotes to be used largely in sermons, and fabliaux, both widely found in medieval literature, are hardly found in ballad, though both contain much the sort of material that went into ballad. The historical chronicles contributed more, but in general the ballad seems to get its historical stories not from written records, but from floating legend and tradition as today we might know of Valley Forge and Bunker Hill. In short, there is little in the English and Scottish ballads that suggests material from the portfolio of the professional poets of the Middle Ages, for such a poet would most certainly draw upon his knowledge of romance, religious literature, satire, allegory, chronicle for themes and materials.

What then is the source of ballad subjects? Ballads are of the stuff that was the general concern of people living in homogeneous, semi-isolated groups: the folk of the glens and of the rural parishes. Ballads were made of the intellectual and emotional stock of lore of such people and were made because such people were interested in this stock of lore. In other words, the ballads are local and realistic in their content, no matter how romantic they may be in treatment. One of the largest groups of ballads is that embodying old oral tales, folk tales, old beliefs and superstitions. Some of the oldest ballads are to be found in this group. The belief in fairies was common among the folk through the eighteenth century; in fact, stories of fairies are still told and evidently half believed in, as witness one old man in Cape Breton who in 1949 remarked, "No, I don't think there were ever any fairies here in Cape Breton, but they were very common in Scotland." The folk, our ballad folk, had quantities of fairy lore, accounts of activities of the fairies, explanation of natural phenomena in terms of fairies. A good bit of this lore falls into the form of story. These folk told (and still tell) stories of fairy lovers enticing mortals, of the fairy court half-glimpsed in the wood and vanishing as one looks. Naturally such fairy lore found its way into ballad as did the lore of other supernatural creatures like the *etin,* mermaid, Billie Blin, the laily worm. Allied to these are the stories of the revenants, the dead who return. As so often in medieval and in sixteenth- and seventeenth-century lore, the revenant is simply a dead man given temporary animation. He can speak and he remembers, but he must hasten back to his grave by the time the black cock crows. He is so of the dead that the touch of his lips is fatal. Some of the most moving ballads tell of the return of revenants to bring messages to the living, or to warn the living of their excessive grief, or to ask back the troth plighted so the dead can be free of all earthly ties. Belief in transformation was also a general part of folklore; consequently ballads tell of human beings transformed by wizards, witches, or cruel stepmothers into various loathsome creatures to be restored by one who dares to kiss them or perform other unspelling deeds. Belief in the magic power of certain plants was likewise common and continues so among present-day folk. The rowan, the willow, the ash, the juniper, gentian, and rosemary are among the plants most frequently mentioned in the ballads. Part of folk culture was the riddle; constantly told and retold, it has come down in English from Old English times. In the later Middle Ages, stories of riddles were made into folk songs; from these it was an easy step to riddle ballads by making answers to riddles a means of solving a plot. Some riddle ballads were perhaps simply the versifying of riddle folk tales. All this great stock of lore not only furnished the ballad maker with active ballad story but graced and motivated many other ballad stories. Such lore and such stories were part of the general knowledge of everyone in any folk community.

Such folk knew too the countryside legends, stories like St. George and the Dragon, Lady Godiva, and Dick Whittington. Here belongs one of the most popular of England's legends and one of the most popular ballad subjects, Robin Hood. Robin Hood is the only character who appears in a considerable number of ballads, making him a kind of ballad hero. The earliest references to him are in *Piers Plowman* (1377), B Text, Passus v. 401, where the character Sloth says, "But I can (know) rymes of Robyn Hood and Randolf, erle of Chestre." During the fifteenth-century Robin Hood is mentioned in chronicles along with Little John. One of the most interesting is that in Bower's *Scotichronicon;* Bower refers to Robin Hood as a robber, mentions Little John as his man, and remarks that "the foolish vulgar in comedies and tragedies make lewd entertainment and are delighted to hear the jester and minstrels sing them above all other ballads." Another chronicle of this period, that of John Mairs, places Robin Hood in the reign of Richard I.

About this time it was, as I conceive, that there flourished those most famous robbers Robin Hood, an Englishman, and Little John, who lay in wait in the woods, but spoiled of their goods those only who were wealthy. They took the life of no man, unless either he attacked them or offered resistance in defence of his property. Robin supported by his plundering a hundred bowmen, ready fighters every one, with whom four hundred of the strongest would not dare to engage in combat. The feats of this Robin are told in song all over Britain. He would allow no woman to suffer injustice, nor would he spoil the poor, but rather enriched them from the plunder taken from abbots. The robberies of this man I condemn, but of all thieves he was the prince and the most gentle thief.

Such chronicle accounts attest to a general Robin Hood legend. Whether or not it was a real Robin Hood whose romantic and dramatic life started a legend makes little difference; the legend began and grew and spread over England. Outlaws have always been romanticized and dramatized by the folk and still are, as witness Jesse James. The Robin Hood outlaw legend was so popular that it begot a flock of ballads, plays, novels, short stories, juveniles. The ballad is the folk expression of the Robin Hood legend and evidently the earliest expression of it. Some forty ballads are concerned with Robin Hood; in addition, there is a long poem (456 four-line stanzas), "The Geste of Robin Hood," which tells of Robin Hood's various exploits in much detail. This poem is a kind of popular epic, unique as to type in English literature. It was made by a skillful artificer who pieced old ballads of Robin Hood together to tell a connected story. It dates from the last half of the fifteenth century. There is no evidence that the Geste as such was ever in oral tradition or that it was ever sung; all surviving texts are from printed sources except three manuscript fragments. The Robin Hood ballads are not the only outlaw ballads, for the outlaw tradition in general has always been popular among the folk, resulting not only in the Robin Hood ballads but also in such ballads as "Johnnie Cock" and "Robyn and Gandeleyn."

Among other legends known to the folk was that of Gilbert Becket, which certainly influenced "Young Beichan." This legend tells of the Saracen princess who set free one of the Crusaders, Gilbert Becket, and then followed him home to London, where, after she had embraced Christianity, they were married. Equally popular was the legend told in the ballad "King Edward the Fourth and a Tanner of Tamworth." This legend tells of a king in disguise meeting one of his subjects and the humorous situation that develops out of the encounter. The legend was popular in England as early as Old English times.

Historical events that caught the attention of the folk were often celebrated in ballads. "Chevy Chase" and "The Battle of Otterburn" are very fine examples. Probably both celebrate the Battle of Otterburn (1388), an account of which can be read in Froissart's *Chronicles*. But neither of these ballads, in spite of the fact that they are considerably more detailed, developed, and episodic than ballads usually are, was made by a professional poet working from a copy of Froissart. They come rather out of tradition, as do such other ballads that deal with history, like "The Battle of Harlaw," celebrating another battle between Scots and English (1411), "The Battle of Philiphaugh," "Durham Field," and "Flodden Field." The last one is a poor account of the battle but a spirited ballad. It is characteristic that the ballad is as much concerned about the quarrel between King James and the Queen (five of the twelve stanzas) as it is about the battle in general. Many more ballads tell of the perennial fighting between England and Scotland; these battles were largely local affairs and consequently became part of the folk tradition. Ballads are rarely concerned with the great battles; the Battle of Agincourt, for example, was celebrated in poetry and song, but, unless they have completely perished, no ballads tell of it. Such battles, it would seem, were too far away, too much a part of state affairs, to catch the imagination of the people.

Fully half the ballads can be classified under the next subject category, local happenings of a dramatic character. A stirring event occurs in a community; it forms the subject matter for a ballad, a ballad which at first is sung locally but which, because of its good story or fetching melody, gradually makes its way from glen to glen, parish to parish, and may in time become national. And such a ballad extends not only in space but also in time; that is, it is sung from generation to generation, often changing by being adapted to new local situations. Such ballads concern themselves with human relations: love, fidelity, jealousy, adultery, incest, murder, theft, betrayal, pride, honor, courage, seduction, elopement, horror, rape. These are the main themes of the "local" ballads. They read like the front page of a tabloid newspaper. Here are the bits of drama in the routine lives of commonplace folk. Two brothers fight over a girl and one kills the other. A man elopes with the girl he loves and spares the old white-haired man who discovers them; her father's men come in

hot pursuit and he kills them all. Then the old man whom
he had spared slips up and gives him a mortal wound in the
back. A Scotch prisoner is set free by the Earl's daughter,
and she elopes with him to Scotland. Safely across the border he tells her that he already has a wife and he offers to
make her his mistress. In despair, she appeals to two knights
of England who rescue her. A young man is poisoned by his
sweetheart. A girl about to have an illegitimate child elopes
with her lover. Her child is born in the wood while her lover
is absent. When he returns he finds her dead. After he
smooths the grave he discovers the child was buried alive,
for the ground moves and then is still. A woman alone in a
wood bears two illegitimate children. She kills them and buries them there. As she is about to go into her father's castle,
the children, revenants, appear there and greet and reproach
her. A girl sits weeping because she is pregnant by her
brother. When her brother discovers it, he kills her. Questioned by his mother, he confesses and announces that he is
going away, never to return. A sailor in the lateness of the
year gets a letter from the king ordering him to take his
boat over the seas, and though he knows what it probably
means, he obeys. All are lost. A girl is to be married to an
old French lord, although she is in love with Willie, whose
child she carries. On the day of the wedding the child is born
and spirited away by Willie to his mother. The girl dies that
night after her wedding as she dances with Willie at the
nuptial ball. Willie commits suicide. Young Hunting jilts his
lady; she stabs him, weights his body, and throws it in the
river. But Young Hunting returns as a bird and reveals the
details of the crime and the lady is burned. A girl admits her
lover to her bed, but her seven brothers discover them sleeping there and stab the lover. She awakens to find the bed
running blood, and her lover dead beside her. Two lovers
are to be separated for seven years, but the lady cannot endure the separation and dies; her lover returns as her funeral is being held and dies when he discovers the truth. A
girl with her baby goes over the sea to her lover to find his
gates closed. Her mother, impersonating him, refuses her
admittance, whereupon she goes out into the night and is ac-

cidentally drowned. Ballads on such subjects as these have a long life, for they are continually being adapted to local events or sung about such events.

Under this category of local events of a dramatic character we can appropriately classify the Border ballads. The Border is the debatable land between England and Scotland, the land where the men of free spirit of England and Scotland constantly roamed, raiding and fighting. It was a glorious life of adventure and high daring. The swift night ridings, the raids, the falling on a farmstead or village across the Border, the driving out of the cattle, the wild ride back, all made for dramatic story. Many ballads celebrating the exploits of individual heroes keep this life alive. Often such ballads were family ballads, like the stories of the Scotts sung by the Scotts, or of the Armstrongs sung by the Armstrongs, in their snug keeps in the hills.

Finally, a goodly number of ballads were drifters, ballads that wandered over Europe, international ballads. They were brought into both England and Scotland by sailors, travelers, and wandering singers. Scotland especially seems to have been very receptive, for many of her ballads are close analogues to ballads found in Denmark and Norway; and significantly enough, most Scottish ballads, other than the Border ballads, are from Aberdeenshire, the center of shipping across to the Scandinavian countries. Scottish ballads too are structurally closer to those of Denmark and Norway than are the English. But among our international ballads are many variants from both England and Scotland. "Lord Randal" is found in Italy and on the Continent; "Edward," all over north Europe. "Kemp Owyne," "The Maid Freed from the Gallows," "The Suffolk Miracle," "Sweet William's Ghost," "The Clerk's Twa Sons o Oxenford," "The Gay Goshawk," "The Twa Knights," "The Baffled Knight," "Fair Annie," "Earl Brand," "The Twa Sisters," —all of these are found among the Scandinavian countries as well as in England and Scotland.

The subjects of the English and Scottish ballads are those that would appeal to the middle classes, people closely grouped by physical boundaries and emotional and cultural ties, people with traditions and good taste and strong views, and people who savor life and the drama of life.

III

BALLAD STYLE

Ballads are conventional in style, as folk songs and folk stories usually are. They tend to tell the same kinds of story in the same way, developing them through stereotyped incidents and expressing them in the same language. The result is often identity of line, repetition of figures of speech, use of the same story devices, and the same manner of grouping details.

One is immediately struck in reading ballads by the repetition of lines and phrases in a given ballad. This is, of course, a general characteristic of folk literary style. It is used for emotional effect, for emphasis, and for melody. Often probably it is the natural consequence of oral expression and oral presentation. Sometimes it is echoic, serving to tie lines or stanzas, or in dialogue to indicate a speaker's attitude. Many times it serves only to fill out a line. The general effect of such constant repetition is to keep the narrative running; it certainly is a factor in creating vigorous and spirited narrative. The following stanzas from three very different ballads illustrate these points.

> "O waly, waly my gay goss-hawk
> Gin your feathering be sheen!"
> "O waly, waly, my master dear
> Gin ye look pale and lean!"

> "Gae, hame, gae, hame, gae hame, brother
> Gae hame and lie with yer wife;
> And I wish that the first news I may hear
> That she has taen your life."

> As she sailed upon the low and the lonesome low,
> As she sailed upon the lonesome sea.

Not only is such simple repetition commonly used in ballads, but repetition of a more complicated sort is skillfully employed. This is incremental repetition, repetition with an

addition that advances the story or contributes more information. This too gives the effect of running, fast-moving action, and furthermore it ties the elements of the story into
an integrated whole that helps to counteract the effect of
disunity which the leaping and lingering technique tends to
create.

> "Gar saddle me the black, the black
> Gar saddle me the brown
> Gar saddle me the swiftest steed
> That ever rode to town"

> "Oh ye hae poisoned your ae[1] son, mother
> Your ae son and your heir
> Oh ye hae poisoned your ae son, mother
> And sons you'll n'er hae mair"

> And as he rode thorow the wood
> Where trees and hearts and all were good
> And as he rode o'er the plain
> There he saw a knight lay slain.
> And as he rode still on the plain
> He saw a lady sit in a graine.[2]

A reading of "Child Waters" will show the overall effects
of incremental repetition. "Edward," "Randal," and "The
Maid Freed from the Gallows" admirably demonstrate the
use of incremental repetition in building to a climax—the
constant repetition of a familiar line of verse, with a new
element coming as a mild surprise at the end of each, creating a kind of minor climax, and then the last line that releases tension and resolves all. Detailed study of this device
will show that it is very effective and most artistically used.

Two elements found frequently as a part of folk song are
the refrain and the burden or chorus. The refrain is a line
repeated after each narrative line or each two narrative
lines. Sometimes the refrain lines rime.

> There is a feast in your father's house
> *The broom blows bonny and so it is fair*
> It becomes you and me to be very douce
> *And we'll never gang up to the broom ne mair.*

---

[1] ae = only.   [2] graine = fork of a tree.

There were three ladies lived in a bower.
Eh vow bonnie
And they went out to pull a flower
On the bonny banks o Fordie.

Refrains may be mere nonsense syllables, such as "With a High Down Downe a Downe, a." Some of these nonsense refrains become fantastic.

"Fa, fa, fa, fa, lilly
With my glimpy, glimpy glimpy eedle
Lillun too tee a ta too A tee a ta a tally"

Such nonsense syllables often result from the distortion of actual words. *Lilly,* for example, is Old English *leoflic,* lovely. Many medieval lyrics had Latin refrains, some of which in distorted form may have drifted to ballad. There is also the suggestion that elements in nonsense refrains may have come from singing notes of the musical scale. Refrains may echo words from the narrative or be directive expressions or terms of address. "Edward" with its alternating refrain, *Edward, Edward; mither, mither,* is an example.

A few ballads use a burden rather than a refrain, the burden being a lyrical stanza sung after each narrative stanza, somewhat like the chorus of a modern song. "Captain Car" has such a burden:

Syck, sike, and to-towe[3] sike,
And sike and like to die;
The sikest nighte that euer I abode,
God lord haue mercy on me!

The use of burden may be an influence from the carol, since burdens are very common in this type of folk song.

There is little evidence to indicate that the narrative element in the ballad was sung by a leader and the refrain by a group. Work songs were sung in that fashion; even today the milling songs are sung thus among the Gaelic people. The evidence shows that the ballad, both story and refrain, was sung by one person. And if we can argue from the practice of many folk singers of today, not only was the ballad sung by one individual (and without instrumental accompaniment), but the refrain was often sung in a different way

[3] to-towe = too, too.

after each stanza, tending to give a subjective interpretation of the story or arouse an emotional reaction to it. The method of singing the narrative never varied. Never did a traditional folk singer use the dramatic technique of the modern "folk singer" of radio and night club. Refrains are not necessarily a mark of primitivism, as some have tried to make out. Many European ballads did not have them at all. On the other hand, almost all the Danish ballads did. This suggests that the presence or absence of a refrain is conventional and local. It is interesting that most of our oldest ballads, those in couplet form, have refrains; this may indicate a long-ago drift of the Scandinavian ballad to Scotland and England.

The refrain, at any rate, should be looked on as a stylistic device and perhaps as a means of getting the singer's interpretation of the story and his reaction to it. In many cases the refrain obviously belongs to the ballad by artistic integration. The *glimpy* nonsense above, for example, belongs to one of the humorous ballads. The *plaid awa* burden and refrain of "The Elfin Knight" are certainly in keeping with the spirit of that ballad. Proof of this is the fact that the refrain degenerates when a ballad degenerates. A comparison of the old version of "The Three Ravens" and its American descendants, or "Sir Lionel" and the American "Old Bangum" will demonstrate this. Refrain is not accident.

Partly stylistic and partly structural are the allied ballad devices, the climax of relations and the testament. The climax of relations is the mustering of the relatives of a character in a ballad to show their importance to him personally and to the elucidation and resolution of the story. We discussed this technique in the first section in connection with "The Maid Freed from the Gallows" in which each relative is appealed to in turn: Father, have you brought me gold? Mother? Brother? Sister? All answer no. True-love? Yes. This device is frequently combined with the testament, the latter being a dramatic way of identifying the villain in the ballad story. What do you leave to your mother? Houses and lands. Father? Brother? Sister? All something desirable. Your sweetheart? A rope for to hang her. Both of these conventional devices are dramatic, tending to knit the story, build its suspense, and resolve it with the dramatic naming in the climax which releases the emotion and gives the information. Both devices are found widely in folk story and in other types of folk song. They are constantly used today in the Negro songs of America.

More ornamental is the "rose and brier" ending. Lovers must die, but out of the grave of one springs a rose and out of the other grave a brier which twine together in a true lover's knot. Many of the love ballads end thus. The device is also common in the romances (cf. the Tristan story) and in folk tales, where it usually takes the form of trees growing up from the bodies of the dead lovers. In one version of the Deirdre story, for example, two trees spring up from the graves of the two lovers and their branches join. The folk belief behind this is that the souls of dead lovers pass into the trees or plants that spring from the graves and so the lovers are united after death in a kind of physical way. Note the reading of one version of "Earl Brand":

> The one was buried in Mary's kirk
> The other in Mary's quire;
> The one sprung up a bonnie bush
> And the other a bonnie briar.

In ballad use this device is probably little more than a graceful and poetic means for closing a story of love tragedy, a device that mitigates the tragedy by symbolizing the reunion of the lovers after death.

To the superficial reader nothing is more distinctive about a ballad than the "quaint" expressions: lily white hand, red roan steed, wan water, yellow hair, white as milk, sewing a silken seam, and so on. This is conventional ballad diction. It comes from a variety of sources. Some of it certainly goes back to Old English alliterative poetry. Much of it, is probably derived from romance where such commonplaces abound. It is constantly employed as metrical and musical filler, for such tags are often fitted in to piece out a line when memory fails the singer. To the folk the familiar is pleasing and this partly accounts for the constant repetition of these commonplaces just as it does for the repetition of line and situation. The ballad of "Sir Patrick Spens" proves that these commonplaces can be manipulated to produce highly artistic effects.

IV

READING OF BALLADS : BALLAD METER

Ballad rhythms and rhythmical patterns are intimately connected with ballad music; in fact, we now realize that ballad structure cannot be studied accurately without constant reference to the music. Phrases and lines that seem awkward and crude when read are usually effective and right when sung. One used to the conventional poetry of conscious art who turns to ballad poetry is bound to find it crude, childish, and irregular, for his experience with poetry leads him to try to read a ballad as he would conventional narrative poetry. But he finds that accents do not always fall where expected, that too many syllables often crowd a foot, that elisions occur frequently, that stanzaic patterns change within a poem, that all the stresses are not of the same weight. However, the student of the ballad should never forget that ballads are texts of songs and that a line of verse sung to a melody and the same line spoken may produce quite different effects. Music adapts language to its needs by syncopating or resolving syllables, by shortening or lengthening syllables, by eliciting subtle connotations of sound. The result is that a stress falling on an unimportant word like an article or on the unaccented element in a word—each very awkward when read—can become effective or is at least unnoticed when sung.

This close connection between the line of poetry and the accompanying music is not accidental but integral. This can readily be seen by checking the melodic unit against the language unit. The smallest melodic unit beyond the note is the phrase; this is very important in folk song. Ballad melodies are commonly built up of four short phrases (frequently two measures) in which one or more of the phrases is repeated. Indicating phrases by capital letters, one can describe typical ballad melodies as AABA, ABBA, ABAC, AAAB. Some more complicated melodies exist, such as ABCBC. Also common is the two-phrase melody. This melody is built up of two long phrases (often four measures), but the long phrase is usually logically divisible into two short ones.[1]

The point to be made here is that these phrasal units correspond exactly to the natural sense units of the verse. Repetition of a phrase very often represents repetition of material or the statement of similar material. The pattern of the music is reflected in the word units. Or should we say that the word units reflect the musical pattern? Moreover, this close relationship exists between notes and syllables. It is impossible to tell which is the dominant member in this synthesis of melody and verse form, or which is the earlier. When we know more about the combination of poetry and music working together to produce the ballad form, then will the problem of origins be nearer solution. In the opening of one version of "The Twa Sisters" note the four musical phrases arranged on the pattern AABA; each corresponds to a natural unit in the verse. Note also the close relation between notes and syllables; there is no slurring, but rather almost direct translation. Note too the values of the notes in relation to the words and the functioning of the rests as marks of musical punctuation.

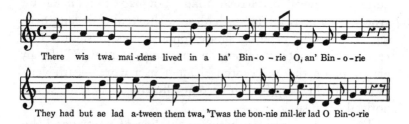

There wis twa mai-dens lived in a ha' Bin-o-rie O, an' Bin-o-rie

They had but ae lad a-tween them twa, 'Twas the bon-nie mil-ler lad O Bin-o-rie

Stress or accentuation is not as simple as some of the critics would lead us to believe. In general, ballad verse follows the iambic pattern, but the ballad poet like any good poet varies his pattern when it is effective to do so. Verses may begin on an accented syllable; constant use is made of the

[1] For a detailed discussion of ballad music, see Cecil J. Sharp, *English Folk-Song: Some Conclusions*, especially Chapters V, VI, VII; Phillips Barry, "The Music of the Ballads," in Barry, Eckstorm and Smyth, *British Ballads from Maine*, pp. xxi–xxxvii.

feminine ending—the unaccented syllable at the end of a line: caddie, laddie. Shifted accents likewise occur, usually, it would seem, as a result of conscious planning. "And the truth tell thou me." The placing of the accents is meaningful here, not accidental. The music that accompanies this line carries a rest between "truth" and "tell." In reading the line one should likewise come to a full stop; the infelicity of the two accents coming together is thus eliminated and the emphasis the author intended made manifest. Many instances of "hovering" accent and "wrenched" accent are felicitous enough when sung and can be made so in reading if one lets the text lead him rather than himself imposing strict usage on it. The following selected at random will illustrate: róse wáter; pený, lordýnge, ladíe, lemán. And finally the modern reader must not forget that many of the ballads are old and that their words may have different values from those of today. The final inflectional *e* had disappeared in pronunciation before most of the ballad texts were recorded, but it often influenced meter long after it had disappeared in pronunciation; in like manner the possessive often has the force of an extra syllable: "I am your bairn's father."

Carefully reading ballads aloud and listening to them sung in the traditional manner will show that the proper accentuation is not the regular succession of primary accents as usually indicated:

> He sét her ón a mílk white steéd, and himsélf upón a gráy;
> He húng a búgle róund his néck and só they róde away.

This is an oversimplification. What we really have is an alternation of primary (´) and secondary stresses (`). Not only do the sense and natural language rhythm favor such a reading, but the music indicates it as well. The accent coming at the beginning of each measure is primary by virtue of its position; that falling within the measure is less important and hence secondary:

> He sét her òn a mílk white stèed and himsélf upòn a gráy;
> He húng a bùgle róund his nèck and só they róde awày.

Examine the lines quoted above (p. 24) from the "The Twa Sisters" to see the relation of the primary and secondary accents to each other and to the music.

There wís twa maidens lived in a hà, Bin-ó-rie O, an' Bin-ó-rie;
Théy had bùt ae lád a-tween them twa, 'Twas the bónnie miller làd
   o Bin-ó-rie.

The English ballad is always divided into stanzas, as are
the Danish and those of other closely allied peoples. Other
ballads, especially those of eastern countries, use an un-
broken, more epic-like form. In English the most common
stanza is the one conventionally written as a quatrain, the
second and fourth lines riming:

O little did my mother think,	(a)
When first she cradled me,	(b)
That I was be sae far frae home,	(c)
And hang on gallows tree	(b)

Verses 1 and 3 carry four accents; verses 2 and 4, three.
This has come to be known as the ballad stanza; it is also
called common meter, fourteener, septenary. When such a
stanza is studied in relation to its music, it is soon discovered
that this arrangement of fours and threes is probably not
accurate. The music pattern tends to favor a stanza of seven-
stress couplets. One immediately suspects that the quatrain
came by way of the first collectors writing the poem in this
manner to avoid lines too long for the usual copybook. Evidence of a different sort comes from the fact that "Judas,"
the earliest poem in ballad form that we have, has a seven-
stress line and is so written in the manuscript. The whole
question is a bit academic since it does not affect the singing
of the ballad in any way. Here are lines from a version of
"The Lass of Roch Royal." Note that there is no musical
punctuation (longer note, rest, etc.) to suggest a break after
the fourth foot, and that such punctuation does appear after
the seventh. The two long phrases, too, favor a stanza of
couplets. In most cases the music should be the final arbiter.

In ballads in which the melody is broken into four phrases, one would naturally set down the verses in quatrains; on the other hand, when the melody consists of two long phrases, the couplet is clearly indicated.

The next most common stanza in ballad use is the four-line, four-stress quatrain; its rime scheme varies between abab and aabb. Again the music determines its nature, for the music is invariably composed of four distinct and equal phrases.

This long meter and the common meter discussed above account for three-fourths of all the ballads. The remainder have a variety of metrical forms. Several ballads use six-stress couplets. There are also stanzas of four seven-stress verses that rime in couplets; quatrains the first three lines of which are seven-stress and the fourth line three-stress; and various others. In some cases the stanzaic form shifts within the ballad; one version of "Childe Maurice" and one of "Tam Lin," both usually seven-stress couplets, admit occasionally a stanza containing three seven-stress lines all riming. Such stanzas are apparently used for emphasis; the "Tam Lin" stanzas, for example, seem to mark a change in the movements of Janet and are introduced when she leaves one place for another:

> Janet has kilted her green kirtle a little aboon her knee
> And she has broded her yellow hair a little aboon her bree
> And she's awa to Carterhaugh as fast as she can hie.

Further detailed analysis will show that ballad stanzaic forms and meters are by no means as simple as the early critics, in their efforts to prove that ballad is primitive poetry, would lead us to believe.

V

THE ORIGIN OF BALLADS

To discuss intelligently the origin of the ballad, one must first fix it in time. That is difficult to do with precision, for few ballads in the Middle Ages strayed into manuscript or into print and few references to ballads are to be found. It is conventional for scholars to accept "Judas" as the earliest ballad on record in English. It is to be found in a manuscript of the thirteenth century. Its first editor, Kenneth Sisam, pointed out that it is the "only example before 1400 of the swift and dramatic movement, the sudden transitions and the restrained expression charactristic of ballad style." All this is true, and one should note in addition that "Judas" is in couplets, often the seven-stress couplets so characteristic of ballad. On the other hand, there is much more of the scholarly cleric in "Judas" than of the folk, and there is no association with music and no evidence that the poem was in oral tradition. In the same thirteenth-century manuscript with "Judas" and in the same hand is another lyric-narrative, "Twelfth Day." It also shows evidence of ballad technique and form. These poems, though literary, are extremely important, for they prove the existence of ballad form and technique as early as the thirteenth century.

If we accept "Judas" as authentic narrative folk song, i.e., ballad, we still cannot say that its manuscript date represents the date of its composition or that it was the first ballad. Nor are we any better off when we examine the ballads of other European countries; German, French, Italian ballads all date from the late Middle Ages. Those of Denmark are earlier—1200, or thereabouts. If we can trust the accounts of the narrative folk poems of Greece as being ballads in our sense of the term, they are still earlier—the tenth or eleventh century. The whole matter is uncertain and probably it will never be fully determined when the type of narrative we know as ballad was first put to music and so became narrative folk song. At any rate, the ballad form as we know it emerged toward the end of the Middle Ages. There is no evidence whatever that would put ballads in England back in the Old English period. Epic lays like the "Battle of Brunanburgh" and the "Battle of Maldon" are not ballads, although some scholars have confused them with this form. There is a strong possibility that the Scottish and English ballad was an import from Denmark. Many of the Danish ballads did drift into Scotland. More "international" ballads are to be found in Scotland than in England, suggesting a general drift from the Continent to Scotland and thence to England.

But enough of speculation. We know that ballads about Robin Hood were being sung in the fourteenth century—if we can trust the references in *Piers Plowman*. We have texts of Robin Hood ballads from the fifteenth century. A few other ballads were written down in that century, but most of the English ballads—the texts—belong to the sixteenth, seventeenth, eighteenth, or even nineteenth centuries. What should be stressed here is that the ballad as a form, as a distinct genre, with the characteristics we have outlined above, emerged in England and in most of western Europe in the late Middle Ages and that in this form the ballad continued to be composed and to exist in diminishing numbers through the nineteenth century and into the twentieth. New versions of the oldest ballads are still being found today in America.

Many nineteenth-century scholars, basing their ideas on the fact that the ballad embodies folklore and old folk culture and that it uses techniques of old folk poetry, such as iteration, assumed that it originated in a primitive state of society. As a result, there developed first in Germany the communal theory of ballad origin, the belief that the folk as a group composed ballads as a kind of general group activity and hence that group improvisation is the key to ballad origin.

Today, however, most students of the ballad, realizing that the ballad is by no means primitive but late medieval, believe that it originated pretty much like any other form of art, by creation of individuals. The communal theorists were constantly led astray by lack of precise definition. When they found refrain and iteration in a savage song that asked the local god for rain, they noted that the ballad also had the refrain and iteration and hence they were inclined to see this as a mark of primitivism in ballads, a suggestion that the ballad was a remnant of primitive culture. Basically the difficulty probably stemmed from the fact that most of these theorists were studying the ballads in terms of a romantic philosophy, instead of studying them realistically in the field.

The best argument against the communal theory is the

body of facts that support individual authorship. We have quantities of analogical evidence of the individual composition of ballads. In sections where ballads are being made today, such as Cape Breton, the southern Appalachian Mountains, the Hebrides, Newfoundland, it is invariably a community singer who makes the story-song. We have considerable evidence too of the origin of American ballads, those narrative folk songs that have spread all over the country: "Springfield Mountain," "Young Charlotte," "Casey Jones," and the like. All without exception were composed by individuals and bequeathed by them to the folk. This is what one would expect. Even a primitive community very soon develops the song and story specialist; in the heroic age the making of song and story was firmly in the hands of the most competent individuals. The scop creates; the gleeman carries the song; and people receive it. What we have said about ballad meter, style, subject matter, and treatment should indicate that no group of people could be so skillful, so integrated as to produce such song poetry. One needs only to read "Mary Hamilton" or "The Unquiet Grave" or "Child Waters" or "Sir Patrick Spens" to know that poets and skillful artificers were behind these ballads.

But how can these be folk songs if they were composed by individuals? They are folk songs because the folk take them and make them their own. Generations of singers slowly, subtly, absorb them. A process of communal re-creation sets in. Lines in the original are given new emphasis. A word drifts in; a stanza is omitted. The ballad grows and with growth comes change, and change may bring beauty and power or buffoonery and degeneration. We have two old versions of "The Three Ravens" ("The Twa Corbies"). Each is great poetry, a dramatic reading of life. Each was probably taken down at the moment of perfection, but they must both stem from an archetype. We would guess that the archetype was more detailed and carried less impact. The difference between the "original" and these fine seventeenth-century versions is to be accounted for by the work of the folk poets. But these seventeenth-century versions have in turn continued to develop until now they have reached the extreme in corny humor and buffoonery—and all because the folk poets of America became self-conscious about these songs of crows talking and reacted to them literally.

The process of communal re-creation of course does not mean that a group of people get together at one time and re-create a song; rather it is the individual folk poets like James Rankin in Scotland who work a ballad into new patterns and new language. Years ago, in one of the high valleys of the Great Smokies, there lived a ballad singer and fiddler by the name of John Snead. John had a unique version of "Barbara Allen" in which the lady not only forgave her young man for slighting her but cured him by feeding him herb tea and then married him. When questioned about where he got such a version, John answered that he had never liked the usual one and had changed it himself. It is interesting to note that the people around, although they knew and sometimes sang John Snead's version, preferred the conventional one, saying about the other, "John Snead is always trying to excuse women. That Barbara Allen was a bad one." But in that valley John Snead alone was capable of changing a song; working with old songs and making new ones was his business, since he was the local fiddler, singer, and dance caller. Relevant here is the observation that folk songs were sung not by the folk *en masse* but rather by individuals and by families. Fortunate indeed was a folk center which could call upon a half dozen singers with a full repertoire of songs.

X The complete process, then, by which a folk song is created involves four steps: the original composition, the acceptance of the original composition by the folk, the re-creation by the folk of the original song into a folk song or folk songs to express local culture, history, emotion, and finally the socialization of the song(s) among the folk. A song like "My Old Kentucky Home," for example, has been sung in America for many years and very widely, sung by all groups, folk and professional, but it has never become traditional; nowhere have folk singers re-created it in terms of a local or individual culture. It remains simply a popular song. By contrast, Thomas Bailey Aldrich's "Ballad of Nantucket" did go into folk tradition. It was set to music; several variant tunes were developed for it; folk poets here and there changed the text. What emerged is by complete communal re-creation a new folk song bearing the ineffable touch of folk tradition. This is typical of the process of ballad making, typical of the process of making any folk song or folk story.

We have been discussing thus far the oldest traditional ballads. In the sixteenth century there developed a type of verse that came to be known as the broadside ballad or stall ballad. These are closer to professional poetry than to folk poetry, though many of them go into tradition eventually. The broadside ballads were so named because contemporary printers printed them on single sheets of paper; they were fly sheets that sold for very little and made their appeal through a journalistic style. Consequently, the "ballads" appearing on the broadsides are in large part far removed from those we have been talking about. Broadsides include songs, lyrics, dirges, elegies, long narratives, as well as narrative songs of a ballad character—but all were referred to as ballads. They were composed by hack writers in the employ of the printers. Such writers got their stories where they could, wrote them in the accepted poetic style of the day, cast them in ballad form, set them to tunes, and launched them forth into the semiliterary world. Most of them were set to old tunes, traditional tunes long associated with ballads. It is very possible that a new broadside would kill an old ballad to whose tune it was sung.

The names of a number of these ballad makers have survived. One of the most prolific and famous was Thomas Deloney, who flourished around 1580. Deloney was a silk weaver, his literary work being a side line. He wrote realistic prose tales concerning the clothiers, the weavers, and the shoemakers of London, and numerous broadsides and journalistic ballads. These latter are on every conceivable subject that might be popular; three, for example, tell the story of the Spanish Armada. Deloney's background and activity are typical of those of the makers of broadsides in general. Soon there arose the practice of making small pamphlets of these broadside ballads and other folk songs; these bore the general designation of "garlands." In England and

America both broadsides and garlands continued to be issued to the end of the nineteenth century.

By and large, the broadsides are far inferior to the old traditional ballads. They are frequently mawkish, sentimental, melodramatic, vulgar—the kind of poetry that skillful versifiers of little taste would write. The difference between the originators of the broadsides and the originators of the traditional ballads lies usually, it would seem, in the fact that the originators of the traditional ballads had no literary pretensions, no literary sophistication; as individuals they were part of a folk milieu. Pope's "A little learning is a dangerous thing; Drink deep or taste not . . ." can likewise be applied to art. A little art is a dangerous thing, much worse than none at all.

The printers sometimes published the traditional pieces in broadside form. "Barbara Allen," for example, appeared very early as a broadside. This practice, to a certain extent, established a fixed text, a text that seemed to discourage growth in tradition. That "Barbara Allen" was thus printed and, as a consequence, got into the song books early probably accounts for the fact that its story has changed very little. But this practice of printing old ballads in broadside form saved for posterity many that otherwise would have been lost.

In spite of the tendency of a printed version to fix the text of an old poem, many broadside texts did drift back to the folk and the process of re-creation started all over again. This, of course, was continually happening with new ballads printed as broadsides. Over the years the folk rejected far more than they accepted, in spite of the fact that they were rather inclined to look upon these broadside songs as finer because they were in print, because they were sung in music halls, and because they often bore the names of recognized song writers. But there has not been enough "folk time" for many great and fine ballads to emerge by folk re-creation of original broadsides, though many very good ballads have done so.

VI

HOW BALLADS WERE RECOVERED

Ballads have been recovered by two methods: Old manuscripts, daybooks, family lists, broadsides, and the like have furnished many texts; and since the eighteenth century collectors have taken ballads directly from oral tradition. "Judas," our oldest ballad-like narrative, is to be found in a thirteenth-century manuscript in Trinity College, Cambridge; Sloan MS. 2593, British Museum, contains two ballads, "Saint Stephen and Herod" and "Robyn and Gandeleyn." MS. Ashmole 48, Bodleian, Oxford, contains "The Hunting of the Cheviot." These are a few examples of the ballads which got written down more or less accidentally. The oldest deliberate collections of ballads are of broadsides. One such collection, that of Shirburn Castle, is an outstanding example. Samuel Pepys (1633–1703) became interested in ballads and built up a collection of about 2000, basing it on an earlier one by John Selden. The most important of these collections were made in the seventeenth and eighteenth centuries. John Bagford made one, almost entirely from broadside sources. It was later edited in the Ballad Society Publications, 1878.

The most important of all the early collections were those of Bishop Percy and Sir Walter Scott. Percy accidentally discovered a manuscript containing old ballads and lyrics in the house of William Pitt where he was a guest. He rescued it from the maids, who were using it to kindle fires. He found 191 poems, lyric and narrative, still remaining; the manuscript had been copied about 1650. Fired by this discovery and the encouragement of friends like William Shenstone the poet, Percy became interested in the old songs and eventually edited them, together with other pieces sent in by various friends, in the famous *Reliques of Ancient English Poetry* (1765, 1767, 1775, 1794). Percy tampered with many of his texts, even adding lines and "improving" the diction. The original manuscript was reëdited by J. W. Hales and F. J. Furnivall in 1867, with restoration of the original readings.

Sir Walter Scott's interest in early songs and lore in general led him to organize a corps of helpers who sent him much traditional material. Like Percy, he often "touched up" an original or "restored" lost stanzas. But his collection, published in 1802 as *Minstrelsy of the Scottish Border,* remains one of our most valuable sources. Scott's enthusiasm and his wide knowledge of folklore and history made his collection and comments of great critical worth.

Through the eighteenth century the interest in ballads and ballad collection was stronger in Scotland than in England. Allan Ramsey's *Ever Green* (1724) and the *Tea Table Miscellany* (1724) were so popular that they were issued in several editions during the century. David Herd, *The Ancient and Modern Scotch Songs and Ballads* (1769; 2nd ed., 1776); James Johnson, *The Scots Musical Museum* (6 vols., 1789), which Burns largely edited; Robert Jamieson, *Popular Ballads and Songs from Tradition* (1806); George R. Kinloch, *Ancient Scottish Ballads* (1727)—these are among the most important ballad collections, for they furnish many texts not only of broadsides but of traditional ballads. Any account of early activity in ballad publication must include the work of Joseph Ritson. Between 1787 and 1795 Ritson published several volumes concerned directly or indirectly with the ballad. Among these are collections of ballads—one work is devoted to Robin Hood exclusively—with notes and glossaries. In a spirited introduction to one of these collections Ritson takes various editors to task for "improving" and otherwise tampering with traditional material. He insists on the adoption of the word ballad to mean a narrative folk song in distinction to lyric, a suggestion that William Shenstone had made earlier to Percy.

In addition to those already mentioned, many of which were reissued and augmented as they went into successive editions, the collections of Peter Buchan are notable. Buchan himself collected from tradition in Scotland, and he also secured a great many texts from James Rankin, a folk singer whom he hired to collect for him. Both—but especially Rankin, who was paid by the piece—have been accused of much tampering with their texts, though later collectors have partly authenticated much of Buchan's work.

The great collection of ballad texts and study of individual ballads appeared at the end of the nineteenth century in F. J. Child's *English and Scottish Popular Ballads* (Boston, 1882–1898). It contains 305 ballads, with many variant versions, copious notes, extensive bibliographies, and other critical apparatus. Child's book is still the most important collection of English and Scottish ballads in English.

Inspired by Child's teaching at Harvard and by the example of the *English and Scottish Popular Ballads,* many scholars and collectors during the past fifty years have busied themselves with ballad collecting and study. A detailed account of this activity will be found in the Bibliography. These collections and studies have served largely to augment and illustrate the work done by Child and to establish the general validity of the criteria he used.

VII

BALLADRY IN AMERICA

Ballads have been sung and composed in America since the time of the first settlements and often in the face of opposition from the church. Cotton Mather in his diary inveighed against the singing of ballads: "I'm informed that the minds and manners of many people about the country are much corrupted by foolish songs and ballads which the hawkers and peddlers carry to all parts of the country." The Pentecostal preachers of today preach against ballads as "sinful songs" and forbid the members of their congregation to sing them. But they sing them just the same, as they did in Cotton Mather's time, for they drift unconsciously into ballads after a preliminary warming up on hymns. One of our largest collections of fine ballads comes from Puritan New England.

Ballads in America fall into three groups: (1) the traditional English and Scottish popular ballads (the Child ballads), (2) the broadside or stall ballads imported largely from England and Ireland, and (3) original ballads that in style, technique, and form imitate those in the first two groups.

Collectors have recovered from oral tradition in America over 100 of the 305 Child ballads. That is about the number that have survived in England and Scotland. It would seem that transplanting a ballad has little to do with its survival; survival both in the center and on the periphery of the culture depends rather upon the nature of the ballad itself. For example, historical ballads to survive must be very good or reflect a general pattern of behavior or be identified with an emotion still felt. Most of the Border ballads are completely lost; "Chevy Chase" is the exception. The Robin Hood ballads too are now practically extinct, although earlier they were very popular in America. Benjamin Franklin attests to the early demand for them: "I have known a very numerous impression of Robin Hood songs go off in this province at two shillings per book in less than a twelfth month; when a small quantity of David psalms have laid on my hands above twice that time." In the same passage Franklin advances the opinion that these are "vicious and silly things not worth reading," and that the people approve of them because they are "viciously and corruptly educated that good things are not encouraged." We can hardly argue that the Robin Hood ballads are not sung today because we are now less viciously or corruptly educated. Rather, it must be that these particular ballads, like the historical ballads, are hardly relevant to present folk society. That the Robin Hood stories survive in opera, movies, and juvenile literature illustrates a common attitude toward this ballad material: relegation to the nursery, to the picturesque, to the consciously romantic, to the quaint. "Robin Hood" has become a fairy tale; and in a less sophisticated society Robin Hood the character would merge with Robin Goodfellow to become a full-fledged fairy. Other types of ballads that are likely to die out or be rationalized into new patterns are the supernatural ballads, the ballads whose action is based on obsolete folk practices, and the ballads concerned with local affairs.

Those that do survive are simple ballads of romantic tragedy, such as "Lady Margaret," "Bonnie Barbara Allen," and "James Harris"; sentimental ballads like "Lord Lovel"; humorous ballads like "The Wife Wrapped in the Wether's

Skin" and "Get Up and Bar the Door"; ballads of happily
ending love like "Young Beichan." Of course the music is an
important factor in the preservation of a ballad; a good tune
can keep almost any ballad alive, though tunes are constantly
transferred from one ballad to another.

What kinds of change do the ballads undergo when they
come to America? The change that occurs, it will be discovered, is a consequence more of time than of place. English
ballads today show the same types of change as do American
ballads. A comparison of the older ballads and their American counterparts in this book will show that the changes are
due more to differences in culture and in taste than to en-
vironment.

The ballad stories tend to be rationalized in terms of the
later culture. The supernatural tends to disappear except in
ballads dealing with death, and even in them the revenant
is likely to be rationalized into a ghost. "Sir Lionel," for example, is a weird mythological tale concerned with the slaying of a great boar, a tale that goes back perhaps to the cult
of the Great Mother; its Amercian counterpart, "Old Bangum," is a rollicking song of a wild and woolly mountain
hunter who kills a wild pig. Ballads whose subjects shock
modern sensibilities are toned down. Incest as a motive is
likely to disappear, though it is kept in one version of "Lizie
Wan," but that ballad is rare in America, probably because
of its incest theme. Incest has completely disappeared from
the American "The Twa Brothers." Earlier manners and
customs no longer current are rationalized and made familiar: "tirled at the pin" becomes "knock on the ring"; Lord
Randal in Virginia becomes Lord Randolph. The refrain
made up of names of three plants—Jennifer, gentle (gentian), and rosemary—becomes three girls, Jennifer, Jennie,
and Rosemary. The cliches of the older ballads, such as lily
white hand and red roan steed, become sources of constant
variation. They are so common in ballads and fit the meter
of so many ballads so aptly that they constantly drift around.
When a singer has forgotten a line or part of a line, he is
likely to substitute such a cliché, often to the destruction of
rime and meaning. Whole stanzas become stereotyped like

the testament stanzas in "Edward" or "Randal" and so drift to any ballad that can possibly receive them. The "Who-will-shoe-your-pretty-little-feet" stanza is a constant drifter. The rose and brier verses found at the end of the early tragic love ballads are likely to be attached later to any such ballad.

Changes of this sort, and the additional changes that result from just plain forgetting, may affect the entire structure of the ballad and the ballad story. More and more explanatory detail is dropped; singers subconsciously are led to forget such material in favor of dramatic and climactic elements. So ballads become less meaningful, more skeletonized, until in some instances little is left but outline. Often, however, this process results in an improved ballad by focusing on the climax of the action and bringing more comprehension and unity of effect. This tendency can go on until most if not all of the story elements are eliminated, leaving only the lyrical elements that are kept alive by the music. The familiar folk lyric "On Top of Old Smoky" and various other versions of "The Unconstant Lover" are derived largely from the stall ballad "The Wagoner's Lad." The song "The False True-lover" is largely a detritus of the ballad "The Lass of Roch Royal." In both America and England "Mary Hamilton" tends to lose the story but keep the poignantly haunting stanza, the most lyrical in the ballad, "Last night there were four Maries . . ."

Stories not only lose elements but also gain them. The most obvious way is by borrowing a whole motive or section from another ballad. New material is also constantly introduced by sheer invention. "The Twa Sisters" ends in a variety of ways. The ending may tell of the punishing of the elder sister; it may focus on the miller and his actions; it may concern itself with a minstrel who makes a harp out of the tree that grows from the girl's grave; it may develop fantastically the story of the musical instrument made from various parts of the girl's body.

"The Maid Freed from the Gallows" has become a story with a variety of changes. For example, it may be a "golden ball" which is lost and which the various relatives must bring to set the girl free. The Negro folk make a kind of spiritual of it:

> I call to my father—
> My father, harken to me
> And the last word I heard him say
> Was, save me lord, save me.

Then follows: I call to my sister, brother, children, preacher, elder, etc. The Negroes also made a play of the ballad, with characters acting out each part.[1] They also made it into a children's game, "The Golden Ball." The action in the game centers around the recovery of the "golden ball" by the main character; she sings in turn to the players representing father, mother, brother, sister, etc., the proper adaptation of the following:

> Captain, captain hold the rope
> I hear my mother's voice.
> Mother, have you come to set me free
> Or have you come to see my hang
> On yonder rusty gallery?
> No, I have come to see you hang
> On yonder rusty gallery.

Finally, in Jamaica Mrs. Beckwith discovered the ballad made into a sort of *cante-fable,* partly sung and partly narrated, with much expansion of the story in the prose sections. These variant versions of "The Maid Freed from the Gallows" are reproduced on pages 295–300.

Occasionally the tone of a ballad is completely changed as it comes down. An excellent example of this is the humorous versions of "The Three Ravens." Self-conscious at singing a serious story about birds talking, the folk made over the song as a humorous one. Likewise a tragic story or a cynical one may be sentimentalized into one with a happy ending.

An absolutely new ballad may grow from a primary one through the use of only the basic idea, theme, or situation. Such ballads Barry has happily called secondary, ballads. "The Gallows Tree" is close to, but not derived from, "The Maid Freed from the Gallows." Likewise "The Yorkshire Bite" is related to "The Crafty Farmer"; "High Barbary" to "The George Aloe and the Sweepstake."

In general, time is not kind to ballads in either England or America, for by and large the ballad tends to degenerate.

[1] See Parsons, *MAF,* 13:152.

The folk of the past two hundred years are not the folk of Sir Walter's time. Some seem to think that the more illiterate and "hillbillyish" the folk are, the finer will be their ballad product. This is not true; the best ballads are found not among the uneducated and vulgar but among people of intelligence and taste. Ballads degenerate only when those who have them in their keeping degenerate. One incapable of appreciating the power and tragedy of "The Three Ravens" is likely to make it buffoonery or not to sing it at all. It is people like Mrs. Brown of Falkland from whom the best ballads come, both in the eighteenth century and in the twentieth. Unfortunately few Mrs. Browns of the twentieth century know ballads.

The second large class of ballads in America is the broadside—English and Irish broadsides brought here and circulated directly or reprinted in this country in broadside form or in the various songsters. The printed texts were sold for a few cents, and such was the demand for them that they were turned out by the hundreds. Many traditional ballads as well as the late products of the poetasters found their way into broadsides. "Barbara Allen" is more popular in America than in England largely because it was printed here early in broadside and song book. Many ballads, of course, drift from print into tradition and eventually become real folk songs and ballads. Some of the best of these are the Irish ballads and songs—the "Come all ye's." They often have a spirit and a liveliness that the English ballads lack, and musically they are excellent. It is these broadside imports which we are concerned with here and from which we have selected those reprinted in this book. In general, their quality is mediocre; but they do not have so far to fall as the older ballads had. They are important largely for the light they throw on the development of American civilization. Most of the broadside imports have had a considerable development in American tradition, so they can really be claimed as American ballads. Presenting these brings forth constant apologies, for in place of the deep emotion in the old ballads there is sentimentality; instead of tragedy there is melodrama; instead of poetry, verse. There are exceptions.

Of the ballads that originated in America, "Springfield

Mountain," "Young Charlotte," "Little Mohee," "The Jam on Gerry's Rock," "Casey Jones," "The Buffalo Skinners," "Jesse James," the John Henry ballads, the Frankie and Albert (Johnnie) ballads, and "Stagolee" are the most interesting in that they are the most original and most common in tradition. From an artistic point of view, the finest of these are the Negro ballads. They have a spontaneity and a seriousness that the others lack. Too, they have a deep folk quality, a quality that comes from a close-knit, homogeneous folk, united by common experience and by common emotion. These are the only ballads that show the virility of luxuriant growth; over 150 versions of Frankie and Albert exist, and over 50 of John Henry.

The phenomenon of the development of ballads among the various "folk occupations" in America—lumbering, cattle herding, mining, sailing—represents a new turn in folksong making. Here are artificial folk groups, that is, groups thrown together by accident of activity, living closely integrated lives, sharing the same experiences, and reacting emotionally as a group. Out of such conditions come folk songs and ballads. That no great body of fine ballads has appeared is accounted for by the fact that these groups are ephemeral after all. To produce fine ballads, such unified folk must develop through several generations and build common tradition and lore over several generations.

Lumbermen are likely to turn to local events and sing songs of actual happenings at camp. No one doubts for an instant that the jam on Gerry's Rock actually took place, even though no one knows where Gerry's Rock is located. The lumberman's songs are likely to be realistic in terms of everyday activity. The lyrical element is at a minimum; the narrative predominates.

Sailor songs are of two sorts: the work songs and the forecastle songs. The work songs were functional; they were sung to bring about concerted effort in group labor. Few of them had narrative elements. The forecastle songs were sung for entertainment. Usually they were brought on board from shore and consequently almost any type of folk song is to be found. But the sailors made their own songs too. Sailor ballads are likely to be lusty, ever ribald, and their stories are likely to be highly exaggerated and heroic.

Cowboys are a sentimental and happy-go-lucky lot. Their songs are lyrical. It would be difficult to find many real cowboy ballads. "The Old Chisholm Trail" perhaps comes closest but it really does not tell a story. Lyrical rather than narrative elements dominate. Many of the so-called cowboy ballads, such as "Laredo," are reworkings of eastern songs and ballads. "Laredo" ultimately goes back through various songs to the broadside "The Irish Rake." The solitary life of the cowboy tended to make him sentimental and so turned his folk songs to the lyric pattern rather than the narrative.

The best mining ballads are tragedies—stories of cave-ins and blackdamp, and stories of strikes. Among the miners, more than any other group, the folk song has developed as a song of social protest. "The Avondale Mine Disaster," included here on page 783, is one of the best, and it is typical of the kind of ballad miners sang. In most of them a pronounced element of didacticism is likely to be added to the narrative; that is, they become stories with a purpose, stories with a decided stress on theme. It was easy for these ballads to take on a note of protest. Often the conditions in the mine accounted for the explosion or fire that happened there and consequently the ballad recounting that disaster was likely to inveigh against such conditions. Thus, as their note of dissent became more pronounced, there developed ballads and general songs of social protest.

We have had ballads before which carried a moral; a good example is "The Irish Rake" just mentioned. It details the terrible story of the sinner from the time he left home and mother until, disgraced, diseased, he lies dead on a slab in the morgue after begging for a Bible at his head and a prayer book at his feet. Such ballads are late broadsides, for the didactic has no part in the old traditional ballad; there the moral is only implied. But with the miners' songs more and more of a didactic element crept in until we are likely to find that in such songs today the story is told merely to point up the note of protest. When this happens with narrative song, when idea becomes more important than the story, the narrative tends to disappear entirely and the song becomes completely lyric. Note that this is the tendency too in the moral ballad like "The Irish Rake." From that ballad have stemmed not only "Laredo" but also "St. James's Infirmary Blues." Typical of these didactic lyrics are the union songs, and the political songs engendered by a depression. But only one of these, "Joe Hill," has narrative and dramatic elements in as large a proportion as it has didactic.

The ballad has come a long way and over a difficult road from "Judas" and Robin Hood to "John Henry." Many scholars are pessimistic about its future. The old ballads are no longer being sung, they say, and the new ones are poor stuff. And when one goes among the folk in search of the ballad he is met constantly with the statement: "You should have come twenty-five years ago; everybody sang ballads then." But twenty-five years ago he would have heard the same thing: "You should have come twenty-five years ago." The ballad has survived much: pseudo-scholarly manipulation, an overload of sentimentality, moralizing, and antiquarianism. Today the greatest threat to its survival is the changed ways of folk life. Automobiles and concrete roads, radio, phonograph, and juke box are doing much to break up old folkways. And when the old culture goes, its elements may die with it or, changed and adapted, be taken over by the new culture. There is evidence in the pages that follow that this is what may happen to ballad.

BALLADS OF ENGLAND & SCOTLAND

WITH AMERICAN & DANISH VARIANTS

Ballads in the first section bear the numbers given them by Child in his *English and Scottish Popular Ballads.*

Original spellings are retained in texts from manuscript and printed sources; this accounts for the wide variation in spelling often found not only from ballad to ballad but also within a given ballad. Þ is Middle English *th;* 3 is the spirant *g(y).*

Occasionally passages in ballads long in oral tradition are so corrupted that they are meaningless.

Refrains when sung are repeated after each stanza; but here to conserve space they are printed only once, usually after the first stanza.

Major breaks or omissions amounting to a stanza or more are indicated by asterisks. The omission of words or lines in a stanza is indicated by a series of periods.

The following abbreviations are used in the headnotes:

Barry   Barry, Phillips, Eckstorm, Fannie, and Smyth, Mary, *British Ballads from Maine,* New Haven, 1929.

Belden   Belden, H. M., *Ballads and Songs Collected by the Missouri Folklore Society,* Columbia, 1940.

Buchan   Buchan, Peter, *Ancient Ballads and Songs from the North of Scotland,* Edinburgh, 1828.

Bulletin   Bulletin of the Folksong Society of the Northeast, Cambridge (Mass.), 1930–1937.

Child   Child, Francis J., *English and Scottish Popular Ballads,* Boston, 1882–1898.

Dixon   Dixon, James H., *Ancient Poems, Ballads and Songs of the Peasantry of England,* etc., Percy Society Publ. xvii.

Herd   Herd, David, *Ancient and Modern Scots Songs,* etc., Edinburgh, 1776.

JAF   Journal of American Folklore, Philadelphia, 1888–   .

JFSS   Journal of the Folk Song Society, London, 1889–1931.

Jamieson   Jamieson, Robert, *Popular Ballads and Songs from Tradition,* etc., Edinburgh, 1806.

Kinloch   Kinloch, George, *Ancient Scottish Ballads,* London, 1827.

MAF   Memoirs American Folklore Society, Philadelphia, 1894–

Motherwell   Motherwell, William, *Minstrelsy, Ancient and Modern,* etc., Glasgow, 1827.

Percy   *Bishop Percy's Folio Manuscript,* ed. Hales and Furnival, London, 1867.

Percy Papers   Percy MSS., Harvard.

Percy Reliques   Percy, Thomas, *Reliques of Ancient English Poetry,* ed. Wheatley, London, 1886.

Pepys   Broadsides, Pepys Collection, Magdalene College.

Prior   Prior, R. C. A., *Ancient Danish Ballads,* London, 1860.

PMLA   Publications of the Modern Language Association, 1884–   .

Randolph   Randolph, Vance, *Ozark Folksongs,* Columbia, 1950.

Scott   Scott, Sir Walter, *Minstrelsy of the Scottish Border,* 3 vols., Edinburgh, 1802–1803.

Sharp   Sharp, Cecil J., *English Folk Songs from the Southern Appalachians,* New York, 1917.

RIDDLES WISELY EXPOUNDED (1)

Riddles have been popular from earliest times. In the ballad they take several forms: a story in which one must guess riddles to win a spouse; a story in which one must guess riddles to avoid being carried away by a supernatural being, such as a fairy or the devil; a story embodying a riddle contest in which two persons ask riddles successively of each other, rewards or punishments adding suspense and drama. It is interesting to note that most of the riddles in the ballads are found widely in Europe.

Text A, Rawlinson MS.D. 328, Bodleian Library, 15th century; B, broadside, Pepys, iii, 19, 17th century; C, Maine, printed in *Bulletin*, 10:8.

A.

INTER DIABOLUS ET VIRGO

1.   Wol 3e here a wonder thynge
     Betwyxt a mayd and þe fovle fende?

2.   Thys spake þe fend to þe mayd,
     "Beleue on me, mayd, to day.

3.   "Mayd, mote y thi leman be,
     Wyssedom y wolle teche the:

4.   "All þe wyssedom off the world,
     Hyf þou wolt be true and forward holde.

5.   "What ys hyer þan ys þe tre?
     What ys dypper þan ys the see?

6.   "What ys scharpper þan ys þe þorne?
     What ys loder þan ys þe horne?

7.   "What ys longger an ys þe way?
     What ys rader þan ys þe day?

8.   "What ys bether than is þe bred?
     What ys scharpper than ys þe dede?

9.   "What ys grenner an ys þe wode?
     What ys sweetter an ys þe note?

47

10. "What ys swifter an ys the wynd?
     What ys recher an ys þe kynge?

11. "What ys ʒeluer an ys þe wex?
     What ys softer an ys þe flex?

12. "But þou now answery me,
     Thu schalt for soþe my leman be."

13. "Ihesu, for þy myld myʒth,
     As thu art kynge and knyʒt,

14. "Lene me wisdome to answere here ryʒth
     And schylde me fram the fovle wyʒth.

15. "Hewene ys heyer than ys the tre;
     Helle ys dypper þan ys the see.

16. "Hongyr ys scharpper than þe thorne;
     Þonder ys lodder than ys þe horne.

17. "Loukynge ys longer than ys þe way;
     Syn ys rader þan ys the day.

18. "Godys flesse ys betur þan ys the brede;
     Payne ys strenger þan ys þe dede.

19. "Gras ys grenner þan ys þe wode;
     Loue ys swetter þan ys the notte.

20. "Þowt ys swifter þan ys the wynde;
     Ihesus ys recher þan ys the kynge.

21. "Safer is ʒeluer than ys the wexs;
     Selke ys softer þan ys the flex.

22. "Now, thu fende, styl thu be;
     Nelle ich speke no more with the!"

B.

1. There was a lady of the North Country,
        Lay the bent to the bonny broom;
   And she had lovely daughters three.
        Fa la la la, fa la la la ra re.

2 There was a knight of noble worth,
        Which also lived in the North.

3. The knight, of courage stout and brave,
        A wife he did desire to have.

4. He knocked at the ladie's gate
        One evening when it was late.

5. The eldest sister let him in,
   And pin'd the door with a silver pin.

6. The second sister she made his bed,
   And laid soft pillows under his head.

7. The youngest daughter that same night,
   She went to bed to this young knight.

8. And in the morning when it was day
   These words unto him she did say:

9. "Now you have had your will," quoth she,
   "I pray, sir knight, will you marry me?"

10. The young brave knight to her replyed,
    "Thy suit, fair maid, shall not be deny'd.

11. "If thou canst answer me questions three,
    This very day will I marry thee."

12. "Kind sir, in love, O then," quoth she,
    "Tell me what your questions be."

13. "O what is longer than the way,
    Or what is deeper than the sea?

14. "Or what is louder than the horn,
    Or what is sharper than a thorn?

15. "Or what is greener than the grass,
    Or what is worse then a woman was?"

16. "O love is longer than the way,
    And hell is deeper than the sea.

17. "And thunder is louder than the horn,
    And hunger is sharper than a thorn.

18. "And poyson is greener than the grass,
    And the Devil is worse than woman was."

19. When she these questions answered had,
    The knight became exceeding glad.

20. And having surely try'd her wit,
    He much commended her for it.

21. And after, as it is verifi'd,
    He made of her his lovely bride.

22. And now, fair maidens all, adieu,
    This song I dedicate to you.

23. I wish that you may constant prove
    Vnto the man that you do love.

C.

1. Twas of a gay young cavalier
    Of honor and renown;
   All for to seek a lady fair,
    He rode from town to town.

2. Twas at a widow woman's door,
    He drew his rein so free;
   For by her side the knight espied
    Her comely daughters three.

3. Small marvel if his gallant heart
    Beat quick within his breast;
   Twas hard to choose, yet hard to lose,
    Which might he wed the best.

4. "Come, maidens, pretty maidens,
    Come read my riddles three;
   And she who reads the best of all,
    My loving bride shall be.

5. "Oh, tell me what is longer
    Than the longest path there be;
   And tell me what is deeper
    Than is the deepest sea.

6. "And tell me what is louder
    Than is the loudest horn;
   And tell me what is sharper
    Than is the sharpest thorn.

7. "And tell me what is greener
    Than the grass on yonder hill,
   And tell me what is crueller
    Than a wicked woman's will."

8. The eldest and the second maid,
    They sat and thought a while;
   The youngest she looked up to him,
    And said with a merry smile:

9. "Love, surely it is longer
    Than the longest path there be;
   And Hell, they say is deeper
    Than is the deepest sea;

10. "Thunder, I know is louder
    Than is the loudest horn;
   And hunger it is sharper
    Than is the sharpest thorn;

11. "I know a deadly poison, greener
         Than the grass on yonder hill;
     And a foul fiend is crueller
         Than a wicked woman's will."

12. Now scarcely had she spoke those words,
         When the youth was at her side;
     Twas all for what she answered him
         He claimed her for his bride.

13. The eldest and the second maid,
         They pondered and were dumb;
     And they, perchance, are waiting yet,
         Some other one to come.

14. Now maidens, pretty maidens,
         Be neither coy nor shy,
     But always, when a lover speaks,
         Look kindly and reply.

THE ELFIN KNIGHT (2)

Here in ballad form is the world-wide folk tale of the impossible
tasks. The variations of this ballad over Europe and America are
many. In general, the story element tends to disappear and the lyric to
become more dominant; the supernatural character of the elf knight
becomes rationalized into a mortal lover; the refrain becomes more
and more nonsensical as the ballad turns to humor. The four-line burden is unique in English balladry. It was not sung after every stanza
but as an accompaniment and at the beginning. The last line of such
a burden often, as here, becomes the refrain.

Text A, 17th Century broadside, and Webster, *A Collection of Old
Ballads*, p. 3; B, American, Vermont via Missouri, *JAF*, 23:430.

A.

My plaid awa, my plaid awa,
And owre the hills and far awa,
And far awa to Norrowa,
My plaid shall not be blawn awa.

1. The Elphin knight sits on yon hill,
        Ba, ba, ba lillie ba
    He blaws his horn baith loud and shrill.
        The wind hath blawn my plaid awa.

2. He blaws it east, he blaws it west,
    He blaws it where he liketh best.

3. "I wish that horn were in my kist,
   Yea, and the knight in my arms niest."

4. She had no sooner these words said,
   Than the knight came to her bed.

5. "Thou are o'er young a maid," quoth he,
   "Married with me that thou wouldst be."

6. "I have a sister, younger than I,
   And she was married yesterday."

7. "Married with me if thou wouldst be,
   A curtisie thou must do to me.

8. "It's ye maun mak a sark to me,
   Without any cut or seam," quoth he.

9. "And ye maun shape it, knife-, sheerless,
   And also sew it needle-, threedless."

10. "If that piece of courtisie I do to thee,
    Another thou must do to me.

11. "I have an aiker of good ley land,
    Which lyeth low by yon sea strand.

12. "It's ye maun till 't wi your touting horn,
    And ye maun saw 't wi the pepper corn.

13. "And ye maun harrow 't wi a thorn,
    And hae your wark done ere the morn.

14. "And ye maun shear it wi your knife,
    And no lose a stack o't for your life.

15. "And ye maun stack it in a mouse hole,
    And ye maun thrash it in your shoe sole.

16. "And ye maun dight it in your loof,
    And also sack it in your glove.

17. "And thou must bring it over the sea,
    Fair and clean and dry to me.

18. "And when that ye have done your wark,
    Come back to me, and ye'll get your sark."

19. "I'll not quite my plaid for my life;
    It haps my seven bairns and my wife."

20. "My maidenhead I'll then keep still,
    Let the elphin knight do what he will."

B.
THE CAMBRIC SHIRT

1. "Can you make me a cambric shirt
    Fluma luma lokey sloomy—
    Without seam or fine needle work?
    From a teaslum tasalum templum
    Fluma luma lokey sloomy.

2. "Can you wash it in a well
    Where water never run nor water never fell?

3. "Can you dry it on a thorn
    That never was since Adam was born?"

4. "Can you buy me an acre of land
    Between the salt water and the sea land?

5. "Can you plow it with a hog's horn,
    And seed it all down with one pepper corn?

6. "Can you put it in a horn
    That never was seen since Adam was born?"

7. When the fool has done his work,
    He may come to me and have his shirt.

LADY ISABEL AND THE ELF-KNIGHT (4)

This ballad is found in practically every language of Europe. Its varying forms indicate a long period of development. The German scholar Bugge made the suggestion that the ballad is a folk reworking of the widely known Judith and Holofernes story, but it does not seem necessary to try to derive it from such a general source when many Bluebeard types of folk tales were generally known. The basic story must have told of a supernatural being who lured girls, perhaps by his seductive music, to his realm and there destroyed them. Finally he met one who was his match and who by tricking him succeeded in killing him.

The ballad has been very popular in America; here the supernatural element has tended to disappear and the story to become largely one of thwarted murder. Some versions are strongly influenced by "Young Hunting."

Text A, Buchan, i, 22; B, Buchan, ii, 45; C, Maine, printed by Barry, p. 26.

A.

1. Fair lady Isabel sits in her bower sewing,
     Aye as the gowans grow gay
   There she heard an elf knight blawing his horn,
     The first morning in May.

2. "If I had yon horn that I hear blawing,
   And yon elf knight to sleep in my bosom."

3. This maiden had scarcely these words spoken,
   Till in at her window the elf knight has luppen.

4. "It's a very strange matter, fair maiden," said he,
   "I canna blaw my horn but ye call on me.

5. "But will ye go to yon greenwood side?
   If ye canna gang, I will cause you to ride."

6. He leapt on a horse, and she on another,
   And they rode on to the greenwood together.

7. "Light down, light down, lady Isabel," said he,
   "We are come to the place where ye are to die."

8. "Hae mercy, hae mercy, kind sir, on me,
   Till ance my dear father and mother I see."

9. "Seven king's-daughters here hae I slain,
   And ye shall be the eight o them."

10. "O sit down a while, lay your head on my knee,
    That we may hae some rest before that I die."

11. She stroakd him sae fast, the nearer he did creep,
    Wi a sma charm she lulld him fast asleep.

12. Wi his ain sword belt sae fast as she ban him,
    Wi his ain dag-durk sae sair as she dang him.

13. "If seven king's-daughters here ye hae slain,
    Lye ye here, a husband to them a'."

B.

1. O heard ye of a bloody knight,
     Lived in the south country?
   For he has betrayed eight ladies fair
     And drowned them in the sea.

2. Then next he went to May Collin,
     She was her father's heir,

The greatest beauty in the land,
  I solemnly declare.

3. "I am a knight of wealth and might,
      Of townlands twenty-three;
    And you'll be lady of them all,
      If you will go with me."

4. "Excuse me, then, Sir John," she says;
      "To wed I am too young;
    Without I have my parents' leave,
      With you I darena gang."

5. "Your parents' leave you soon shall have
      In that they will agree,
    For I have made a solemn vow
      This night you'll go with me."

6. From below his arm he pulled a charm,
      And stuck it in her sleeve,
    And he has made her go with him,
      Without her parents' leave.

7. Of gold and silver she has got
      With her twelve hundred pound,
    And the swiftest steed her father had
      She has taen to ride upon.

8. So privily they went along,
      They made no stop or stay,
    Till they came to the fatal place
      That they call Bunion Bay.

9. It being in a lonely place,
      And no house there was nigh,
    The fatal rocks were long and steep,
      And none could hear her cry.

10. "Light down," he said, "fair May Collin,
      Light down and speak with me,
    For here I've drowned eight ladies fair,
      And the ninth one you shall be."

11. "Is this your bowers and lofty towers,
      So beautiful and gay?
    Or is it for my gold," she said,
      "You take my life away?"

12. "Strip off," he says, "thy jewels fine,
      So costly and so brave,
    For they are too costly and too fine
      To throw in the sea wave."

13. "Take all I have my life to save,
    O good Sir John, I pray;
Let it neer be said you killed a maid
    Upon her wedding day."

14. "Strip off," he says, "thy Holland smock,
    That's bordered with the lawn,
For it's too costly and too fine
    To rot in the sea sand."

15. "O turn about, Sir John," she said,
    "Your back about to me,
For it never was comely for a man
    A naked woman to see."

16. But as he turned him round about,
    She threw him in the sea,
Saying, "Lie you there, you false Sir John,
    Where you thought to lay me.

17. "O lie you there, you traitor false,
    Where you thought to lay me,
For though you stripped me to the skin,
    Your clothes you've got with thee."

18. Her jewels fine she did put on,
    So costly, rich and brave,
And then with speed she mounts his steed,
    So well she did behave.

19. That lady fair being void of fear,
    Her steed being swift and free,
And she has reached her father's gate
    Before the clock struck three.

20. Then first she called the stable groom—
    He was her waiting man—
Soon as he heard his lady's voice
    He stood with cap in hand.

21. "Where have you been, fair May Collin?
    Who owns this dapple grey?"
"It is a found one," she replied,
    "That I got on the way."

22. Then out bespoke the wily parrot
    Unto fair May Collin:
"What have you done with false Sir John,
    That went with you yestreen?"

23. "O hold your tongue, my pretty parrot,
    And talk no more to me,

And where you had a meal a day
O now you shall have three."

24.   Then up bespoke her father dear,
From his chamber where he lay,
"What aileth thee, my pretty Poll,
That you chat so long or day?"

25.   "The cat she came to my cage-door,
The thief I could not see,
And I called to fair May Collin,
To take the cat from me."

26.   Then first she told her father dear
The deed that she had done,
And next she told her mother dear
Concerning false Sir John.

27.   "If this be true, fair May Collin,
That you have told to me,
Before I either eat or drink
This false Sir John I'll see."

28.   Away they went with one consent,
At dawning of the day,
Until they came to Carline Sands,
And there his body lay.

29.   His body tall, by that great fall,
By the waves tossed to and fro,
The diamond ring that he had on
Was broke in pieces two.

30.   And they have taken up his corpse
To yonder pleasant green,
And there they have buried false Sir John,
For fear he should be seen.

C.

THE FALSE-HEARTED KNIGHT

1.   I'll tell you of a false hearted knight
Who courted a lady gay,
And all that he wanted of this pretty fair maid
Was to take her sweet life away.

2.   "Go bring me some of your mamma's gold,
And some of your daddy's fee,
And away we'll ride to some foreign country
And married we shall be."

3.   She brought him some of her mamma's gold,
       And some of her daddy's fee,
     And two of the best horses in her father's stable,
       Where there stood thirty and three.

4.   She then mounted the milk-white steed,
       And he upon the grey,
     They rode till they came to a fair river side,
       Six hours before it was day.

5.   "Alight, alight, my pretty fair maid,
       I have something to tell unto thee;
     For it's six maidens fair I have drowned here
       And you the seventh shall be."

6.   "Some pity, some pity, my own true love,
       Some pity show unto me,
     For of all the gold that I ever gave to thee,
       I will double it over three."

7.   "Take off, take off your satin gown,
       And give it unto me,
     For I do think that your clothing is too gay
       To rot in the watery sea."

8.   She then took off her satin gown
       And laid it upon the ground,
     And out of this fair lady's pocket
       He took ten thousand pounds.

9.   "Go bring me the sickle, that I may crop the nettle
       That grows on the river's brim,
     That it may not entangle my curly, curly locks
       Nor nettle my milk-white skin."

10. He brought the sickle, that she might crop the nettle
       That grew on the river's brim,
     And with all of the strength that this fair maid had,
       She pushed the false knight in.

11. "Lie there, lie there, you false hearted knight,
       For I think that you've got your doom,
     And I do not think that your clothing is too gay
       To rot in a watery tomb."

12. "Some pity, some pity, my pretty fair maid,
       Some pity show unto me:
     For of all the vows that I ever made to thee,
       I will double them over three!"

13. "Lie there, lie there, you false hearted knight,
       Lie there instead of me,

For it's six maidens fair you have drowned here,
And the seventh hath drowned thee."

14. She then mounted the milk-white steed,
     And home she led the grey,
 She rode till she came to her father's stable door,
     Three hours before it was day.

15. The parrot being up in the chamber so high,
     Hearing the mistress, did say:
 "What is the matter, my own mistress,
     That you tarry so long before day?"

16. The maid being up in the chamber so high,
     Hearing what the parrot did say:
 "O! What is the matter, you silly parrot,
     That you prattle so long before day?"

17. "The cat she came to my cage door,
     And would not let me be,
 And I was obliged my own mistress to call
     To drive the cat away."

18. "Hold your tongue, my own parrot,
     And tell no tales on me,
 And your cage shall be made of the finest of gold,
     And doors of ivory."

GIL BRENTON (5)

This ballad is pan-Germanic. It has elements that suggest a fairy
background, and that the hero may be of the nature of the elf knight
in the preceding ballad. He appears before the lady when she pulls
the nut and the sloe in the greenwood—a common method of summoning the fairy folk (see "Tam Lin")—and he has married seven
kings' daughters and "cutted the paps from their breast bones and
sent them home again."
    Text from recitation of Mrs. Brown of Falkland, 1783; Jamieson-
Brown MS. No. 16.

1. Gil Brenton has sent o'er the fame,
     He's woo'd a wife an brought her hame.

2. Full sevenscore o ships came her wi,
     The lady by the greenwood tree.

3. There was twal an twal wi beer an wine,
     And twal an twal wi muskadine,

4. An twall an twall wi bouted flowr,
    An twall an twall wi paramour,

5. An twall an twall wi baken bread,
    An twall an twall wi the goud sae red.

6. Sweet Willy was a widow's son,
    An at her stirrup-foot he did run.

7. An she was dressd i the finest pa,
    But ay she loot the tears down fa.

8. An she was deckd wi the fairest flowrs,
    But ay she loot the tears down pour.

9. "O is there wate i your shee?
    Or does the win blaw i your glee?

10. "Or are you mourning i your meed
    That e'er you left your mither gueede?

11. "Or are ye mourning i your tide
    That ever ye was Gil Brenton's bride?"

12. "There is nae water in my shee,
    Nor does the win blaw i my glee:

13. "Nor am I mourning i my tide
    That e'er I was Gil Brenton's bride;

14. "But I am mourning i my meed
    That ever I left my mither gueede.

15. "But, bonny boy, tell to me
    What is the customs o your country?"

16. "The customs o't, my dame," he says,
    "Will ill a gentle lady please.

17. "Seven king's daughters has our king wedded,
    And seven king's daughters has our king bedded.

18. "But he's cutted the paps frae their breast-bane,
    An sent them mourning hame again.

19. "But whan you come to the palace yate,
    His mither a golden chair will set.

20. "An be you maid or be you nane,
    O sit you there till the day be dane.

21. "An gin you're sure that you are a maid,
    Ye may gang safely to his bed.

22. "But gin o that you be na sure,
    Then hire some woman o youre bowr."

23. O whan she came to the palace yate,
    His mither a golden chair did set.

24. An was she maid or was she nane,
    She sat in it till the day was dane.

25. An she's calld on her bowr woman,
    That waiting was her bowr within.

26. "Five hundred pound, maid, I'll gi to the,
    And sleep this night wi the king for me."

27. Whan bells was rung, an mass was sung,
    An a' man unto bed was gone,

28. Gil Brenton an the bonny maid
    Intill ae chamber they were laid.

29. "O speak to me, blankets, an speak to me, sheets,
    An speak to me, cods, that under me sleeps.

30. "Is this a maid that I ha wedded?
    Is this a maid that I ha bedded?"

31. "It's nae a maid that you ha wedded,
    But it's a maid that you ha bedded.

32. "Your lady's in her bigly bowr,
    An for you she drees mony sharp showr."

33. O he has taen him throu the ha,
    And on his mither he did ca.

34. "I am the most unhappy man
    That ever was in christend lan.

35. "I woo'd a maiden meek an mild,
    An I've marryed a woman great wi child."

36. "O stay, my son, intill this ha,
    An sport you wi your merry men a'.

37. "An I'll gang to yon painted bowr,
    An see how't fares wi yon base whore."

38. The auld queen she was stark an strang;
    She gard the door flee aff the ban.

39. The auld queen she was stark an steer;
    She gard the door lye i the fleer.

40.   "O is your bairn to laird or loon?
       Or is it to your father's groom?"

41.   "My bairn's na to laird or loon,
       Nor is it to my father's groom.

42.   "But hear me, mither, on my knee,
       An my hard wierd I'll tell to thee.

43.   "O we were sisters, sisters seven,
       We was the fairest under heaven.

44.   "We had nae mair for our seven years wark
       But to shape an sue the king's son a sark.

45.   "O it fell on a Saturday's afternoon,
       Whan a' our langsome wark was dane,

46.   "We keist the cavils us amang,
       To see which shoud to the greenwood gang.

47.   "Ohone, alas! for I was youngest,
       An ay my wierd it was the hardest.

48.   "The cavil it did on me fa,
       Which was the cause of a' my wae.

49.   "For to the greenwood I must gae,
       To pu the nut but an the slae;

50.   "To pu the red rose an the thyme,
       To strew my mother's bowr and mine.

51.   "I had na pu'd a flowr but ane,
       Till by there came a jelly hind greeme,

52.   "Wi high-colld hose an laigh-colld shoone,
       An he 'peard to be some kingis son.

53.   "An be I maid or be I nane,
       He kept me there till the day was dane.

54.   "An be I maid or be I nae,
       He kept me there till the close of day.

55.   "He gae me a lock of yallow hair,
       And bade me keep it for ever mair.

56.   "He gae me a carket o gude black beads,
       And bade me keep them against my needs.

57.   "He gae to me a gay gold ring,
       An bade me keep it aboon a' thing.

58. "He gae to me a little pen-kniffe,
    An bade me keep it as my life."

59. "What did you wi these tokens rare
    That ye got frae that young man there?

60. "O bring that coffer hear to me,
    And a' the tokens ye sal see."

61. An ay she ranked, and ay she flang,
    Till a' the tokens came till her han.

62. "O stay here, daughter, your bowr within,
    Till I gae parley wi my son."

63. O she has taen her thro the ha,
    An on her son began to ca.

64. "What did you wi that gay gold ring
    I bade you keep abbon a' thing?

65. "What did you wi that little pen-kniffe
    I bade you keep while you had life?

66. "What did you wi that yallow hair
    I bade you keep for ever mair?

67. "What did you wi that good black beeds
    I bade you keep against your needs?"

68. "I gae them to a lady gay
    I met i the greenwood on a day.

69. "An I would gi a' my father's lan,
    I had that lady my yates within.

70. "I would gi a' my ha's an towrs,
    I had that bright burd i my bowrs."

71. "O son, keep still your father's lan;
    You hae that lady your yates within.

72. "An keep you still your ha's and towrs;
    You hae that bright burd i your bowrs."

73. Now or a month was come an gone,
    This lady bare a bonny young son.

74. An it was well written on his breast-bane,
    "Gil Brenton is my father's name."

WILLIE'S LADY (6)

Danish versions of this ballad are common, though only two versions have been found in English. Stories and songs telling of someone putting a spell on a woman in childbed so that she cannot deliver her child are common everywhere. The use of a wax figure to cause a spell or to break one is common folklore. Billie Blin is found in four English ballads: "Gil Brenton" (one version), "Young Beichan" (one version), "The Knight and the Shepherd's Daughter," "King Arthur and the King of Cornwall." He is a kind of household familiar, a sort of grown-up brownie. His origin is obscure; Child suggests that he is derived from Bilvis, an aged counselor in Saxo Grammaticus who contrasts with his blind brother Bolvis, a strife breeder. Then somehow the characteristic of blindness (blin=blind) becomes attached to the good brother.

Text, Jamieson-Brown MS. No. 15.

1. "Willie has taen him o'er the fame,
    He's woo'd a wife and brought her hame.

2. He's woo'd her for her yellow hair,
    But his mother wrought her mickle care.

3. And mickle dolour gard her dree,
    For lighter she can never be.

4. But in her bower she sits wi pain,
    And Willie mourns o'er her in vain.

5. And to his mother he has gone,
    That vile rank witch of vilest kind.

6. He says, "My ladie has a cup,
    Wi gowd and silver set about.

7. "This goodlie gift shall be your ain,
    And let her be lighter o her young bairn."

8. "Of her young bairn she'll ne'er be lighter, ,
    Nor in her bower to shine the brighter.

9. "But she shall die and turn to clay,
    And you shall wed another may."

10. "Another may I'll never wed,
    Another may I'll ne'er bring home."

11. But sighing says that weary wight,
    "I wish my life were at an end."

12. "Ye doe ye unto your mother again,
That vile rank witch of vilest kind.

13. "And say your ladie has a steed,
The like o'm's no in the lands of Leed.

14. "For he's golden shod before,
And he's golden shod behind.

15. "And at ilka tet of that horse's main,
There's a golden chess and a bell ringing.

16. "This goodlie gift shall be your ain,
And let me be lighter of my young bairn."

17. "O her young bairn she'll ne'er be lighter,
Nor in her bower to shine the brighter.

18. "But she shall die and turn to clay,
And ye shall wed another may."

19. "Another may I'll never wed,
Another may I'll ne'er bring hame."

20. But sighing said that weary wight,
"I wish my life were at an end."

21. "Ye doe ye unto your mother again,
That vile rank witch of vilest kind.

22. "And say your ladie has a girdle,
It's red gowd unto the middle.

23. "And ay at every silver hem,
Hangs fifty silver bells and ten.

24. "That goodlie gift has be her ain,
And let me be lighter of my young bairn."

25. "O her young bairn she's ne'er be lighter,
Nor in her bower to shine the brighter.

26. "But she shall die and turn to clay,
And you shall wed another may."

27. "Another may I'll never wed,
Another may I'll ne'er bring hame."

28. But sighing says that weary wight,
"I wish my life were at an end."

29. Then out and spake the Belly Blind;
He spake aye in good time.

30. "Ye doe ye to the market place,
    And there ye buy a loaf of wax.

31. "Ye shape it bairn and bairnly like,
    And in twa glassen een ye pit,

32. "And bid her come to your boy's christening;
    Then notice weel what she shall do.

33. "And do you stand a little fore bye,
    And listen weel what she shall say."

34. "Oh wha has loosed the nine witch knots
    That was amo that ladie's locks?

35. "And wha has taen out the kaims of care
    That hangs amo that ladie's hair?

36. "And wha's taen down the bush o woodbine
    That hang atween her bower and mine?

37. "And wha has killd the master kid
    That ran beneath that ladie's bed?

38. "And wha has loosed her left-foot shee,
    And lotten that ladie lighter be?"

39. O Willie has loosed the nine witch knots
    That was amo that ladie's locks.

40. And Willie's taen out the kaims o care
    That hang amo that ladie's hair.

41. And Willie's taen down the bush o woodbine
    That hang atween her bower and thine.

42. And Willie has killed the master kid
    That ran beneath that ladie's bed.

43. And Willie has loosed her left-foot shee,
    And letten his ladie be.

44. And now he's gotten a bonny young son,
    And mickle grace be him upon.

EARL BRAND (7)

This story is complete in the English-Scottish versions except for one detail. When Earl Brand must fight the brothers and the father of the girl, he tells her that she must not under any circumstances speak his name. She, of course, forgets as he is about to kill her youngest brother, and calls on him to spare the boy. Earl Brand then gets a mortal wound. This is a remnant of the belief that a man's soul is bound up with his name as well as with parts of his body, and revealing of the name could work death or harm against him. This ballad is general in America, though it is considerably changed in some versions.

Closely associated with Earl Brand is the ballad "Erlinton" (Child, 8). It is likewise an abduction story, but this time with a happy ending. In America a number of ballads variously titled ("The Soldier's Wooing," "The Valiant Soldier," etc.) seem to be remote variations of the "Erlinton," since they end happily and possess here and there little details in common. A soldier would marry a rich girl, but her father objects. They elope but are overtaken by the father and seven men. The soldier fights and is about to kill them all when the father agrees to the marriage and adds an offer of a sum of money if the soldier lets them go unhurt. The girl makes the soldier continue the fight until the father agrees to give them all of his wealth. The text here printed is typical.

Text A, "Scotch Ballads, Materials for Border Minstrelsy," No. 22b; B, North Carolina, *JAF*, 28:152.

A.

1. Did ye ever hear o guid Earl o Bran
   An the queen's daughter of the southlan?

2. She was na fifteen years o age
   Till she came to the Earl's bed-side.

3. "O guid Earl o Bran, I fain wad see
   My grey hounds run over the lea."

4. "O kind lady, I have no steeds but one,
   But ye shall shall ride, and I shall run."

5. "O guid Earl o Bran, but I have tua,
   An ye shall hae yere wael o those."

6. The're ovr moss an the're over muir,
   An they saw neither rich nor poor,

7. Till they came to ald Carl Hood,
   He's ay for ill but he's never for good.

8. "O guid Earl o Bran, if ye loe me,
   Kill Carl Hood an gar him die."

9. "O kind lady, we had better spare,
   I never killd ane that wore grey hair.

10. "We'll gie him a penny-fie an let him gae,
    And then he'll carry nae tiddings away."

11.   "Where hae been riding this lang simmer-day?
       Or where hae stolen this lady away?"

12.   "O I hae not riden this lang simmer-day,
       Nor hae I stolen this lady away.

13.   "For she is my sick sister
       I got at the Winchester."

14.   "If she were sick an like to die,
       She wad na be wearing the gold sae high."

15.   Ald Carl Hood is over the know,
       Where they rode one mile, he ran four.

16.   Till he came to her mother's yetts,
       An I wat he rapped rudely at.

17.   "Where is the lady o this ha?"
       "She's out wie her maidens, playing at the ba."

18.   "O na! fy na!
       For I met her fifteen miles awa.

19.   "She's over moss, and she's over muir,
       An a' to be the Earl o Bran's whore."

20.   Some rode wie sticks, an some wie rungs,
       An a' to get the Earl o Bran slain.

21.   That lady lookd over her left shoudder-bane;
       "O guid Earl o Bran, we'll a' be taen!

22.   "But if ye'll take my claiths, I'll take thine,
       An I'll fight a' my father's men."

23.   "It's no the custom in our land
       For ladies to fight an knights to stand.

24.   "If they come on me ane by ane,
       I'll smash them a doun bane by bane.

25.   "If they come on me ane and a'
       Ye soon will see my body fa."

26.   He has luppen from his steed,
       An he has gein her that to had.

27.   An bad her never change her cheer
       Untill she saw his body bleed.

28.   They came on him ane by ane,
       An he smashed them doun a' bane by bane.

29. He sat him doun on the green grass,
   For I wat a wearit man he was.

30. But ald Carl Hood came him behind,
   An I wat he gae him a deadly wound.

31. He's away to his lady then,
   He kissed her, and set her on her steed again.

32. He rode whistlin out the way.
   An a' to hearten his lady gay.

33. Till he came to the water-flood:
   "O guid Earl o Bran, I see blood!"

34. "O it is but my scarlet hood,
   That shines upon the water-flood."

35. They came on 'till his mother's yett,
   An I wat he rappit poorly at.

36. His mother she's come to the door:
   "O son ye've gotten yere dead wie an English whore."

37. "She was never a whore to me;
   Sae let my brother her husband be."

38. Sae ald Carl Hood was not the dead o ane,
   But he was the dead o hale seeventeen.

B.

1. "Rise up, you seven bretherens,
       And bring your sister down;
   It shall never be said that a steward's son
       Had taken her out of town."

2. "I thank you kindly, sir," he says;
       "I am no steward's son,
   My father is of a regis king,
       My mother's a quaker's queen."

3. He mound her on a milk-white steed,
       He rode the dapple gray,
   He swung a bugle horn all round about his neck,
       And so went blowing away.

4. He had not got three mile of town
       Till he looked back again,
   And saw her father and seven bretherens
       Come tripling over the plain.

5. "Sit you down, fair Ellender," he said;
   "And hold this steed by the rein,
   Till I play awhile with your father
   And your seven bretherens."

6. Fair Ellender she sat still;
   It wasn't long till she saw
   Her own dear seven bretherens
   All wallowing in their blood.

7. Fair Ellender she sat still;
   She never changed a note,
   Till she saw her own dear fathere's head
   Come tumbling by her foot.

8. Saying, "Love runs free in every vein
   But father you have no more;
   If you're not satisfied with this,
   I wish you were in your mother's chamber
   And me in some house or room."

9. "If I was in my mother's chamber,
   You'd be welcome there;
   I'll wind you east, I'll wind you west,
   I'll wind along with you."

10. He mound her on a milk-white steed,
    He rode the dapple gray,
    He swung a bugle all round about his neck,
    And so went bleeding away.

11. As he rode up to his father's gate,
    He tinkled at the ring,
    Saying, "O dear father, asleep or awake,
    Arise and let me in."

12. "O sister, sister! make my bed;
    My wounds are very sore."
    Saying, "O dear mother! oh, bind up my head,
    For me you'll bind no more."

13. It was about three hours till day
    The cocks began to crow;
    From every wound that he received
    His heart blood began to flow.

14. Sweet William he died like it might be to-day
    Fair Ellender to-morrow;
    Sweet William died for the wounds he received;
    Fair Ellen died for sorrow.

15. Fair Ellender was buried by the church door;
       Sweet William was buried by her;
     And out of her breast sprung a blood red rose,
       And out of his a briar.

16. They growed, they growed to the top of the church,
       Till they could grow no higher,
     And there they tied a true lover's knot,
       And the rose ran round the briar.

THE FAIR FLOWER OF NORTHUMBERLAND (9)

Other European ballads agree with this in general, but in its specific detail it is a local English-Scottish ballad, with no American versions.

The oldest text is in Deloney's *Peasant History of John Winchcomb,* 1633, here reprinted.

1. It was a knight in Scotland borne
      Follow, my love, come over the strand
    Was taken prisoner, and left forlorne,
      Even by the good Earle of Northumberland.

2. Then was he cast in prison strong,
    Where he could not walke nor lie along,
      Even by the good Earle of Northumberland.

3. And as in sorrow thus he lay,
    The Earle's sweete daughter walkt that way,
      And she the faire flower of Northumberland.

4. And passing by, like an angell bright,
    The prisoner had of her a sight,
      And she the faire flower of Northumberland.

5. And loud to her this knight did crie,
    The salt teares standing in his eye,
      And she the faire flower of Northumberland.

6. "Faire lady," he said, "take pity on me,
    And let me not in prison dye,
      And you the faire flower of Northumberland."

7. "Faire Sir, how should I take pity on thee,
    Thou being a foe to our countrey,
      And I the faire flower of Northumberland."

8. "Faire lady, I am no foe," he said,
    "Through thy sweet love heere was I stayd,
      For thee, the faire flower of Northumberland."

9.   "Why shouldst thou come heere for love of me,
      Having wife and children in thy countrie?
          And I the faire flower of Northumberland."

10.   "I sweare by the blessed Trinitie,
      I have no wife nor children, I,
          Nor dwelling at home in merrie Scotland.

11.   "If curteously you will set me free,
      I vow that I will marrie thee,
          So soone as I come in faire Scotland.

12.   "Thou shalt be a lady of castles and towers,
      And sit like a queene in princely bowers,
          When I am at home in faire Scotland."

13.   Then parted hence this lady gay,
      And got her father's ring away,
          To helpe this sad knight into faire Scotland.

14.   Likewise much gold she got by sleight,
      And all to helpe this forlorne knight
          To wend from her father to faire Scotland.

15.   Two gallant steedes, both good and able,
      She likewise tooke out of the stable,
          To ride with this knight into faire Scotland.

16.   And to the jaylor she sent this ring,
      The knight from prison forth to bring,
          To wend with her into faire Scotland.

17.   This token set the prisoner free,
      Who straight went to this faire lady,
          To wend with her into faire Scotland.

18.   A gallant steede he did bestride,
      And with the lady away did ride,
          And she the faire flower of Northumberland.

19.   They rode till they came to a water cleare,
      "Good Sir, how should I follow you heere,
          And I the faire flower of Northumberland?

20.   "The water is rough and wonderfull deepe,
      And on my saddle I shall not keepe,
          And I the faire flower of Northumberland."

21.   "Feare not the foord, faire lady," quoth he,
      "For long I cannot stay for thee,
          And thou the faire flower of Northumberland."

22. The lady prickt her wanton steed,
     And over the river swom with speede,
         And she the faire flower of Northumberland.

23. From top to toe all wet was shee:
     "This have I done for love of thee,
         And I the faire flower of Northumberland."

24. Thus rode she all one winter's night,
     Till Edenborow they saw in sight,
         The chiefest towne in all Scotland.

25. "Now chuse," quoth he, "thou wanton flower,
     Whe'r thou wilt be my paramour,
         Or get thee home to Northumberland.

26. "For I have wife, and children five,
     In Edenborow they be alive;
         Then get thee home to faire England.

27. "This favour shalt thou have to boote,
     Ile have thy horse, go thou on foote,
         Go, get thee home to Northumberland."

28. "O false and faithlesse knight," quoth shee,
     "And canst thou deale so bad with me,
         And I the faire flower of Northumberland.

29. "Dishonour not a ladie's name,
     But draw thy sword and end my shame,
         And I the faire flower of Northumberland."

30. He tooke her from her stately steed,
     And left her there in extreme need,
         And she the faire flower of Northumberland.

31. Then sate she downe full heavily;
     At length two knights came riding by,
         Two gallant knights of faire England.

32. She fell downe humbly on her knee,
     Saying, "Courteous knights, take pittie on me,
         And I the faire flower of Northumberland.

33. "I have offended my father deere,
     And by a false knight that brought me heere,
         From the good Earle of Northumberland."

34. They tooke her up behind them then,
     And brought her to her father's againe,
         And he the good Earle of Northumberland.

35.   All you faire maidens be warned by me,
    Scots were never true, nor never will be,
      To lord, nor lady, nor faire England. ·

THE TWA SISTERS (10)

This ballad is found throughout the Germanic regions and here and there among the Slavs; it is widely current in England, Scotland, Ireland, and America. The text tends to break down into many different versions as one element of the story rather than another is stressed. Some versions stress the murder, some the miller's part in the story, some the fantastic instrument made from the girl's body, some the revealing of the murder through the singing of the harp. The refrains of this ballad are interesting. The most common are: Edinburgh, etc.; Bow down, bow down, bow down. I'll be true to my love, if my love'll be true to me; Binnorie, O Binnorie. By the bonny milldams of Binnorie. In addition there are a group of nonsense refrains. The bow-down refrain is characteristic of a large group of American versions; the Binnorie may be a corruption of a Scottish refrain found in one version: The Bonny Milldams o Balgonie. Cf. The Irish, Oh and ohone, and ohone and aree! On the banks of the Banna, ohone and aree! Many folk tales as well as folk songs tell of a murdered person's body speaking or emitting music, or of a musical instrument made from the wood of a tree growing out of the body and singing the story of the murders.

Text A, Jamieson, i, 48; B, West Virginia, printed in *Bulletin*, 9:4, 10:10; C, Danish, Prior, i, 381.

A.

1.   There was twa sisters in a bowr,
    Edinburgh, Edinburgh,
There was twa sisters in a bowr,
    Stirling for ay,
There was twa sisters in a bowr,
There came a knight to be their wooer.
    Bonny Saint Johnston stands upon Tay.

2.   He courted the eldest wi glove an ring,
But he lovd the youngest above a' thing.

3.   He courted the eldest wi brotch an knife,
But lovd the youngest as his life.

4.   The eldest she was vexed sair,
An much envi'd her sister fair.

5.   Into her bowr she could not rest,
Wi grief an spite she almos brast.

6. Upon a morning fair an clear,
   She cried upon her sister dear,

7. "O sister, come to yon sea stran,
   An see our father's ships come to lan."

8. She's taen her by the milk-white han,
   And led her down to yon sea stran.

9. The youngest stood upon a stane,
   The eldest came an threw her in.

10. She tooke her by the middle sma,
    And dashd her bonny back to the jaw.

11. "O sister, sister, tak my han,
    An Ise mack you heir to a' my lan.

12. "O sister, sister, tak my middle,
    An yes get my goud and my gouden girdle.

13. "O sister, sister, save my life,
    An I swear Ise never be nae man's wife."

14. "Foul fa the han that I should tacke,
    It twin'd me an my wardles make.

15. "Your cherry cheeks an yallow hair
    Gars me gae maiden for evermair."

16. Sometimes she sank, an sometimes she swam,
    Till she came down yon bonny mill-dam.

17. O out it came the miller's son,
    An saw the fair maid swimmin in.

18. "O father, father, draw your dam,
    Here's either a mermaid or a swan."

19. The miller quickly drew the dam,
    An there he found a drownd woman.

20. You coudna see her yallow hair
    For gold and pearle that were so rare.

21. You coudna see her middle sma
    For gouden girdle that was sae braw.

22. You coudna see her fingers white,
    For gouden rings that was sae gryte.

23. An by there came a harper fine,
    That harped to the king at dine.

24. When he did look that lady upon,
    He sighd and made a heavy moan.

25. He's taen three locks o her yellow hair,
    An wi them strung his harp sae fair.

26. The first tune he did play and sing,
    Was, "Farewell to my father the king."

27. The nextin tune that he playd syne,
    Was, "Farewell, to my mother the queen."

28. The lasten tune that he playd then,
    Was, "Wae to my sister, fair Ellen."

B.

1. There was an old woman lived on the sea shore,
       Hey oh, my Nanny!
   She had some daughters, some three or four,
       And the swim swom bonny.

2. He gave to her a guinea gold ring,
   And to the other, much nicer thing.

3. "Dear Sister, dear Sister, let's take a walk
   X To see the ships a-sailing o'er.

4. As they were walking along the sea shore,
   The oldest pushed the youngest o'er.

5. It's first she sank and then she swam.
   And she swum till she come to the miller's dam.

6. The miller's daughter a-being at need
   For to get some water to mix her bread.

7. (Crying) "Miller, oh miller, it's stop your mill,
   For yonder comes a swan or a milk white maid."

8. The miller threw out his old grab hook;
   He fetched her safely from the brook.

9. The miller got her pretty gold ring,
   And pushed her back in the brook again.

10. It's first she sank and then she swam.
    Till she came to her eternal home.

11. The miller was hung in his own mill-gate,
    For drowning of my sister Kate.

No mention of harp.

C.

THE CRUEL SISTER

1. There lived an honest man and true,
     O might I follow thee!
   And daughters had but only two;
     So dupest thou not me!

2. The younger bright as is the sun,
   But black as dirt the elder one.

3. The younger suitors came to woo,
   With th' elder none would have to do.

4. The younger loom and shuttle plied,
   The elder slept at chimney side.

5. The elder took her sister's hand,
   "Come let us go to younder strand.

6. "To yonder strand let us repair,
   And wash ourselves so clean and fair."

7. As on the younger stepp'd so gay,
   The wind would with her ringlets play.

8. The elder follow'd close behind,
   And anger fill'd her sullen mind;

9. As on a stone the younger trod,
   She thrust her into the rushing flood.

10. "O hear me, sister, let me live,
    And thee my best gold cup I give."

11. "I'll get thy best gold cup, and more,
    But thou shalt never com ashore."

12. "O hear me, sister, let me live,
    And thee my buckle of gold I give."

13. "Thy buckle of gold I'll have, and more,
    But thou shalt never come ashore."

14. "O hear me, sister, let me live,
    And thee my trulove I will give."

15. "Thy trulove I shall get, and more,
    But thou shalt never come ashore."

16. By God's high will a tempest blew,
    And on the coast her body threw.

17. Two minstrels walked along the strand,
    And saw the maiden float to land.

18. They took her golden hair so long,
    And therewithal their fiddle strung.

19. "To yon great house we'll now repair,
    Their merry wedding-feast to share."

20. The first string sang a doleful sound,
    "The bride her younger sister drown'd."

21. The second string, as that they tried,
    "In terror sits the youthful bride."

22. The third string sang beneath their bow,
    "And surely now her tears will flow."

23. The bride stripp'd off her golden band,
    And laid it on the minstrel's hand.

24. Tuesday began her heart to ache,
    And Thursday night smoked at the stake.

THE CRUEL BROTHER (11)

This ballad also is very popular in England and Scotland; it occurs here and there in Germanic tradition, especially in Danish; it is found in America but is not at all common.

The motivation for the brother's action is difficult. It has been suggested that this was originally an incest ballad, but the occurrence of close analogues in Danish and other Germanic languages suggests that this is rather a remnant of the brother-sister relation that exists in a matriarchal society in which a man's closest ties are with his sister's children and consequently the brother's consent must be obtained before a sister can marry. Note that the American version here printed puts the blame on the sister-in-law.

The "testament" ending of this ballad, in which the girl reveals by her bequests the author of the evil done to her, is a ballad commonplace.

Text A, Jamieson, i, 66; B, *JAF,* 28:300.

A.

1. There was three ladies playd at the ba,
    With a hey ho and a lillie gay,
   There came a knight and played oer them a'.
    As the primrose spreads so sweetly.

2. The eldest was baith tall and fair,
   But the youngest was beyond compare.

3. The midmost had a graceful mien,
   But the youngest lookd like beautie's queen.

4. The knight bowd low to a' the three,
   But to the youngest he bent his knee.

5. The ladie turned her head aside,
   The knight he woo'd her to be his bride.

6. The ladie blushed a rosy red,
   And sayd, "Sir knight, I'm too young to wed."

7. "O ladie fair, give me your hand,
   And I'll make you ladie of a' my land."

8. "Sir knight, ere ye my favor win,
   You maun get consent frae a' my kin."

9. He's got consent frae her parents dear,
   And likewise frae her sisters fair.

10. He's got consent frae her kin each one,
    But forgot to spiek to her brother John.

11. Now, when the wedding day was come,
    The knight would take his bonny bride home.

12. And many a lord and many a knight
    Came to behold that ladie bright.

13. And there was nae man that did her see,
    But wishd himself bridegroom to be.

14. Her father dear led her down the stair,
    And her sisters twain they kissd her there.

15. Her mother dear led her thro the closs,
    And her brother John set her on her horse.

16. She leand her o'er the saddle-bow,
    To give him a kiss ere she did go.

17. He has taen a knife, baith lang and sharp,
    And stabbd that bonny bride to the heart.

18. She hadno ridden half thro the town,
    Until her heart's blude staind her gown.

19. "Ride softly on," says the best young man,
    "For I think our bonny bride looks pale and wan."

20.   "O lead me gently up yon hill,
      And I'll there sit down, and make my will."

21.   "O what will you leave to your father dear?"
      "The silver-shod steed that brought me here."

22.   "What will you leave to your mother dear?"
      "My velvet pall and my silken gear."

23.   "What will you leave to your sister Anne?"
      "My silken scarf and my gowden fan."

24.   "What will you leave to your sister Grace?"
      "My bloody cloaths to wash and dress."

25.   "What will you leave to your brother John?"
      "The gallows-tree to hang him on."

26.   "What will you leave to your brother John's wife?"
      "The wilderness to end her life."

27.   This ladie fair in her grave was laid,
      And many a mass was o'er her said.

28.   But it would have made your heart right sair,
      To see the bridegroom rive his haire.

B.

1.   Three Ladies played at cup and ball,
          With a hey and my lily gay.
      Three Knights there came among them all.
          The rose it smells so sweetly.

2.   And one of them was dressed in green;
      He asked me to be his queen.

3.   And one of them was dressed in yellow;
      He asked me to be his fellow.

4.   And one of them was dressed in red;
      He asked me with him to wed.

5.   "But you must ask my father the King,
      And you must ask my mother the Queen,

6.   "And you must ask my sister Anne,
      And you must ask my brother John."

7.   "Oh, I have asked your father the King,
      And I have asked your mother the Queen,

8.   "And I have asked your sister Anne,
      And I have asked your brother John."

9. Her father led her down the stairs;
   Her mother led her down the hall.

10. Her sister Anne led her down the walk;
    Her brother John put her on her horse.

11. And as she stooped to give him a kiss,
    He stuck a penknife into her breast.

12. "Ride up, ride up, my foremost man,
    Methinks my lady looks pale and wan!"

13. "Oh what will you leave to your father the King?"
    "The golden coach that I ride in."

14. "And what will you leave to your mother the Queen?"
    "The golden chair that I sat in."

15. "And what will you leave to your sister Anne?"
    "My silver brooch and golden fan."

16. "And what will you leave to your brother John?"
    "A pair of gallows to hang him on."

17. "And what will you leave to your brother John's wife?"
    "Grief and misfortune all her life."

LORD RANDAL (12)

This is a genuine international ballad, for it is found from Italy to
Iceland and from the Slavs to Ireland. The basic story of a young
man poisoned and coming home to die varies little, but the names and
details constantly change. Instead of Randal, the hero is called also
Donald, Randolph, Terence, Lord Lantoun, Riller, John Willow,
Ramsay, Dear Willie, Uriar, Ransome, Durango, Anzo, Tyranty, etc.
He is poisoned consistently by eating eels, fish, or snakes, and usually
his sweetheart is responsible. The form of the ballad is very consistent.
Almost all have the dialogue plus the testament construction.

Text A, Macmath's MS. No. 5, c. 1800; B, Kinloch, p. 110; C,
Motherwell's MS., from tradition, p. 238; D, Massachusetts, from
tradition, *JAF*, 18:202.

A.

1. "O where ha you been, Lord Randal, my son?
   And where ha you been, my handsome young man?"
   "I ha been at the greenwood, mother, mak my bed soon,
   For I'm wearied wi hunting and fain wad lie down."

2. "An wha met ye there, Lord Randal, my son?
   And wha met you there my handsome young man?"

"O I met wi my true-love, mother, mak my bed soon,
For I'm wearied wi huntin an fain wa lie down."

3. "And what did she give you, Lord Randal, my son?
And what did she give you, my handsome young man?"
"Eels fried in a pan, mother, mak my bed soon,
For I'm wearied wi huntin, and fain wad lie down."

4. "And wha gat your leavins, Lord Randal, my son?
And wha gat your leavins, my handsome young man?"
"My hawks and my hounds, mother, mak my bed soon,
For I'm wearied wi hunting and fain wad lie down."

5. "And what becam of them, Lord Randal, my son?
And what becam of them, my handsome young man?"
"They stretched their legs out an died, mother, mak my bed soon,
For I'm wearied wi huntin and fain wad lie down."

6. "O I fear you are poisoned, Lord Randal, my son.
I fear you are poisoned, my handsome young man."
"O yes, I am poisoned, mother, mak my bed soon,
For I'm sick at the heart and I fain wad lie down."

7. "What d' ye leave to your mother, Lord Randal, my son?
What d' ye leave to your mother, my handsome young man?"
"Four and twenty milk kye, mother, mak my bed soon,
For I'm sick at the heart and I fain wad lie down."

8. "What d' ye leave to your sister, Lord Randal, my son?
What d' ye leave to your sister, my handsome young man?"
"My gold and my silver, mother, mak my bed soon,
For I'm sick at the heart, an I fain wad lie down."

9. "What d' ye leave to your brother, Lord Randal, my son?
What d' ye leave to your brother, my handsome young man?"
"My houses and my lands, mother, mak my bed soon,
For I'm sick at the heart, and I fain wad lie down."

10. "What d' ye leave to your true-love, Lord Randal, my son?
What d' ye leave to your true-love, my handsome young man?"
"I leave her hell and fire, mother, mak my bed soon,
For I'm sick at the heart and I fain wad lie down."

B.

1. "O whare hae hae ye been a' day, Lord Donald, my son?
O whare hae ye been a' day, my jollie young man?"
"I've been awa courtin, mither, mak my bed sune,
For I'm sick at the heart and I fain wad lie doun."

2. "What wad ye hae for your supper, Lord Donald, my son?
   What wad ye hae for your supper, my jollie young man?"
   "I've gotten my supper, mither, mak my bed sune,
   For I'm sick at the heart and I fain wad lie down."

3. "What did ye get for your supper, Lord Donald, my son?
   What did ye get for your supper, my jollie young man?"
   "A dish of sma fishes, mither, mak my bed sune,
   For I'm sick at the heart and I fain wad lie doun."

4. "Whare gat ye the fishes, Lord Donald, my son?
   Whare gat ye the fishes, my jollie young man?"
   "In my father's black ditches, mither, make my bed sune,
   For I'm sick at the heart and I fain wad lie doun."

5. "What like were your fishes, Lord Donald, my son?
   What like were your fishes, my jollie young man?"
   "Black backs and spreckld bellies, mither, mak my bed sune,
   For I'm sick at the heart and I fain wad lie doun."

6. "O I fear ye are poisond, Lord Donald, my son!
   O I fear ye are poisond, my jollie young man!"
   "O yes! I am poisond, mither, mak my bed sune,
   For I'm sick at the heart and I fain wad lie doun."

7. "What will ye leave to your father, Lord Donald, my son?
   What will ye leave to your father, my jollie young man?"
   "Baith my houses and land, mither, mak my bed sune,
   For I'm sick at the heart and I fain wad lie doun."

8. "What will ye leave to your brither, Lord Donald, my son?
   What will ye leave to your brither, my jollie young man?"
   "My horse and the saddle, mither, mak my bed sune,
   For I'm sick at the heart and I fain wad lie doun."

9. "What will ye leave to your sister, Lord Donald, my son?
   What will ye leave to your sister, my jollie young man?"
   "Baith my gold box and rings, mither, mak my bed sune,
   For I'm sick at the heart and I fain wad lie doun."

10. "What will ye leave to your true-love, Lord Donald, my son?
    What will ye leave to your true-love, my jollie young man?"
    "The tow and the halter, for to hang on yon tree,
    And lat her hang there for the poysoning o me."

C.

1. "O whare hae ye been a' day, my bonnie wee croodlin dow?
   O whare hae ye been a' day, my bonnie wee croodlin dow?"
   "I've been at my step-mother's; oh mak my bed, mammie, now!
   I've been at my step-mother's; oh mak my bed, mammie, now!"

2. "O what did ye get at your step-mother's, my bonnie wee croodlin
        dow?" (Twice.)
    "I gat a wee wee fishie; oh mak my bed, mammie, now!"
        (Twice.)

3. "O whare gat she the wee fishie, my bonnie wee croodlin dow?"
    "In a dub before the door; oh mak my bed, mammie, now!"

4. "What did ye wi the wee fishie, my bonnie wee croodlin dow?"
    "I boild it in a wee pannie; oh mak my bed, mammy, now!"

5. "Wha gied ye the banes o the fishie till, my bonnie wee croodlin
        dow?"
    "I gied them till a wee doggie; oh mak my bed, mammie, now!"

6. "O whare is the little wee doggie, my bonnie wee croodlin dow?
    O whare is the little wee doggie, my bonnie wee croodlin doo?"
    "It shot out its fit and died, and sae maun I do too;
    Oh mak my bed, mammy, now, now, oh mak my bed, mammy,
        now!"   *doesn't continue.*

D.

1. "Oh, where have you been to-day, Terence, my son?
    Oh, where have you been to-day, my pretty little one?"
    "I have been to see my grandame, mother make my bed soon,
    For I'm sick at the heart and I fain would lie down."

2. "Oh, what did she give you to eat, Terence, my son?
    Oh, what did she give you to eat, my pretty little one?"
    "Fresh-water potted eels, mother make my bed soon,
    For I'm sick at the heart and I fain would lie down."

3. "Oh, what will you give your father, Terence, my son?
    Oh, what will you give your father, my pretty little one?"
    "One half of my fortune, mother make my bed soon,
    For I'm sick at the heart and I fain would lie down."

4. "And what will you give your mother, Terence, my son?
    And what will you give your mother, my pretty little one?"
    "Ten thousand sweet kisses, mother make my bed soon,
    For I'm sick at the heart and I fain would lie down."

5. "And what will you give your brother, Terence, my son?
    And what will you give your brother, my pretty little one?"
    "'T other half of my fortune, mother make my bed soon,
    For I'm sick at the heart and I fain would lie down."

6. "And what will you give your sister, Terence, my son?
    And what will you give your sister, my pretty little one?"

"A thousand kind wishes, mother make my bed soon,
For I'm sick at the heart and I fain would lie down."

7. "And what will you give your grandame, Terence, my son?
And what will you give your grandame, my pretty little one?"
"A rope for to hang her, mother make my bed soon,
For I'm sick at the heart and I fain would lie down."

EDWARD (13)

This famous ballad is found in the Germanic countries and in Finland. It is consistent in keeping the dialogue-testament form of construction, but generally the crime is fratricide and usually the mother is not implicated. The American versions follow the English. Of the two versions here given, the first is English and the other Scottish. The Scottish, contributed to Percy by Sir David Dalrymple, may have been edited a bit and the spelling antiqued, but basically it is certainly genuine. As in the "Cruel Brother," we may have here the remnant of an incest ballad. Note the close association with "Lizie Wan," certainly an incest ballad.

Text A, Motherwell's MS., p. 139; B, Percy Reliques, 1794, i, 59; C, Missouri, traditional, Randolph, i, 69.

A.

1. "What bluid's that on thy coat lap,
    Son Davie, son Davie?
   What bluid's that on thy coat lap,
    And the truth come tell to me."

2. "It is the bluid of my great hawk,
    Mother lady, mother lady.
   It is the bluid of my great hawk,
    And the truth I have told to thee."

3. "Hawk's bluid was ne'er sae red,
    Son Davie, son Davie.
   Hawk's bluid was ne'er sae red,
    And the truth come tell to me."

4. "It is the bluid of my greyhound,
    Mother lady, mother lady.
   It is the bluid of my greyhound,
    And it wadna rin for me."

5. "Hound's bluid was ne'er sae red,
    Son Davie, son Davie.
   Hound's bluid was ne'er sae red,
    And the truth come tell to me."

6. "It is the bluid o my brither John,
       Mother lady, mother lady.
   It is the bluid o my brither John,
       And the truth I have told to thee."

7. "What about did the plea begin,
       Son Davie, son Davie?"
   "It began about the cutting of a willow wand
       That would never been a tree."

8. "What death dost thou desire to die,
       Son Davie, son Davie?
   What death dost thou desire to die?
       And the truth come tell to me."

9. "I'll set my foot in a bottomless ship,
       Mother lady, mother lady.
   I'll set my foot in a bottomless ship,
       And ye'll never see mair o me."

10. "What wilt thou leave to thy poor wife,
        Son Davie, son Davie?"
    "Grief and sorrow all her life,
        And she'll never see mair o me."

11. "What wilt thou leave to thy old son,
        Son Davie, son Davie?"
    "I'll leave him the weary world to wander up and down,
        And he'll never get mair o me."

12. "What wilt thou leave to thy mother dear,
        Son Davie, son Davie?"
    "A fire o coals to burn her, wi hearty cheer,
        And she'll never get mair o me."

B.

1. "Why dois your brand sae drap wi bluid,
                          Edward, Edward,
   Why dois your brand sae drap wi bluid,
   And why sae sad gang yee O?"
   "O I hae killed my hauke sae guid,
                          Mither, mither,
   O I hae killed my hauke sae guid,
   And I had nae mair bot hee O."

2. "Your haukis bluid was nevir sae reid,
                          Edward, Edward,
   Your haukis bluid was nevir sae reid,
       My deir son I tell thee O."

"O I hae killed my reid-roan steid,
       Mither, mither,
O I hae killed my reid-roan steid,
    That erst was sae fair and frie O."

3. "Your steid was auld, and ye hae gat mair,
        Edward, Edward,
Your steid was auld, and ye hae gat mair,
    Sum other dule ye drie O."
"O I hae killed my fadir deir, *Brother.*
       Mither, mither,
O I hae killed my fadir deir,
    Alas, and wae is mee O!"

4. "And whatten penance wul ye drie, for that,
        Edward, Edward?
And whatten penance will ye drie for that?
    My deir son, now tell me O."
"I'le set my feit in yonder boat,
       Mither, mither,
I'le set my feit in yonder boat,
    And I'le fare ovir the sea O."

5. "And what wul ye doe wi your towirs and your ha,
        Edward, Edward?
And what wul ye doe wi your towirs and your ha,
    That were sae fair to see O?"
"I'le let thame stand tul they doun fa,
       Mither, mither,
I'le let thame stand tul they doun fa,
    For here nevir mair maun I bee O."

6. "And what wul ye leive to your bairns and your wife,
        Edward, Edward?
And what wul ye leive to your bairns and your wife,
    Whan ye gang ovir the sea O?"
"The warldis room, late them beg thrae life,
       Mither, mither,
The warldis room, late them beg thrae life,
    For thame nevir mair wul I see O."

7. "And what wul ye leive to your ain mither deir,
        Edward, Edward?
And what wul ye leive to your ain mither deir?
    My deir son, now tell me O."
"The curse of hell frae me sall ye beir,
       Mither, mither,
The curse of hell frae me sall ye beir,
    Sic counseils ye gave to me O."

C.

1. "What's that stain on your shirt sleeve?
    Son, please come tell me."
    "It is the blood of my little yellow dog
    That followed after me."

2. "It is too pale for your little yellow dog,
    Son, please come tell me."
    "It is the blood of my little yellow horse
    That I rode to town today."

3. "It is too pale for your little yellow horse,
    Son, please come tell me."
    "It is the blood of my own brother dear
    That rode by the side of me."

4. "Oh, what did you fall out about?
    Son, please come tell me."
    "We fell out about a sprout
    That might have made a tree."

5. "Oh, what will you do when your father comes home?
    Son, please come tell me."
    "I'll step on board of yondo ship
    And sail across the sea."

6. "Oh, what will you do with Katie dear?
    Son, please come tell me."
    "I'll take her on board of yondo ship
    To bear me company."

7. "Oh, when will you come back, my dear?
    Son, please come tell me."
    "When the sun rises never to set,
    And you know that'll never be."

BABYLON: OR, THE BONNIE BANKS
O FORDIE (14)

"Babylon" occurs as a pan-Germanic ballad. It is rather rare in America. The version printed here is unique to America.

Text A, Motherwell, p. 88; B, Vermont, from tradition, printed in *Bulletin,* 7:6.

A.

1. There were three laides lived in a bower,
    Eh vow bonnie

And they went out to pull a flower.
On the bonnie banks o Fordie.

2. They hadna pu'ed a flower but ane,
When up started to them a banisht man.

3. He's taen the first sister by her hand,
And he's turned her round and made her stand.

4. "It's whether will ye be a rank robber's wife,
Or will ye die by my wee pen-knife?"

5. "It's I'll not be a rank robber's wife,
But I'll rather die by your wee pen-knife."

6. He's killed this may, and he's laid her by,
For to bear the red rose company.

7. He's taken the second ane by the hand,
And he's turned her round and made her stand.

8. "It's whether will ye be a rank robber's wife,
Or will ye die by my wee pen-knife?"

9. "I'll not be a rank robber's wife,
But I'll rather die by your wee pen-knife."

10. He's killed this may, and he's laid her by,
For to bear the red rose company.

11. He's taken the youngest ane by the hand,
And he's turned her round and made her stand.

12. Says, "Will ye be a rank robber's wife,
Or will you die by my wee pen-knife?"

13. "I'll not be a rank robber's wife,
Nor will I die by your wee pen-knife.

14. "For I hae a brother in this wood,
And gin ye kill me, it's he'll kill thee."

15. "What's thy brother's name? come tell to me."
"My brother's name is Baby Lon."

16. "O sister, sister, what have I done!
O have I done this ill to thee!

17. "O since I've done this evil deed,
Good sall never be seen o me."

18. He's taken out his wee pen-knife,
And he's twyned himsel o his ain sweet life.

B.

1. There were three maids lived in a barn
      Heckey hi si bernio
    When up there rose a wicked man.
      On the bonny banks of Bernio.

2. He took the eldest by the hands,
    He whirled her round and made her stand.

3. "Heckry, lass, will you be young Robey's wife?
    Or rather would you die by my penknife?"

4. "Never will I be young Robey's wife;
    Rather would I die by your penknife."

5. So he took her life and laid it by
    To keep the greensward compan-eye.

6. He took the next one by the hand,
    He whirled her round and made her stand.

7. "Heckry, lass, will you be young Robey's wife?
    Or rather would you die by my penknife?"

8. "Never will I be young Robey's wife,
    Rather would I die by your penknife."

9. So he took her life and laid it by,
    To keep the greensward compan-eye.

10. He took the youngest by the hand,
    He whirled her round and made her stand.

11. "Heckry, lass, will you be young Robey's wife?
    Or rather would you die by my penknife?"

12. "Never will I be young Robey's wife.
    Neither will I die by your penknife."

13. So she took his life and laid it by,
    To keep her sisters compan-eye.

LEESOME BRAND (15)

This ballad, though very common on the Continent especially in Germanic countries, is rare in England and found not at all in America. The English version is not complete and it contains intrusive elements. The story as reconstructed from a consensus of the Germanic versions runs as follows: A girl is discovered by her mother (father) to be pregnant; alarmed at what is threatened, she warns her lover and the two flee on horseback. In the wood the girl's labor pains begin; she dismounts and lies on the ground, refusing all help from her lover, because a man must not see a woman in labor. The lover goes for water; at the spring a bird (two birds) warns him that the lady is dead. He returns, finds her and a child (children) who he thinks is dead. He digs a grave and buries them all, only to hear the cries of the child (children) from under the ground. He runs himself through with his sword. Cf. the Danish version here printed. The two different stanzaic forms in this ballad indicate blending of two different ballads on the same or a similar subject.

Text A, Buchan, i, 38; B, Danish, Prior, iii, 4.

Notes

28/1. white hynde: this reference is in no version of the story except the Scotch. It is obviously intrusive. The white hind is usually a bespelled woman or fairy lady whom the hero rescues or whom he kills only to discover his mistake. Child thinks that the last four stanzas are intrusive.

A.

1. My boy was scarcely ten years auld,
   Whan he went to an unco land,
   Where wind never blew, nor cocks ever crew,
   Ohon for my son, Leesome Brand!

2. Awa to that king's court he went,
   It was to serve for meat an fee;
   Gude red gowd it was his hire,
   And lang in that king's court stayd he.

3. He hadna been in that unco land
   But only twall months twa or three,
   Till by the glancing o his ee,
   He gaind the love o a gay ladye.

4. This ladye was scarce eleven years auld,
   When on her love she was right bauld;
   She was scarce up to my right knee,
   When oft in bed wi men I'm tauld.

5. But when nine months were come and gane,
   This ladye's face turnd pale and wane.

6. To Leesome Brand she then did say,
   "In this place I can nae mair stay.

7. "Ye do you to my father's stable,
   Where steeds do stand baith wight and able.

8.   "Strike ane o them upo the back,
     The swiftest will gie his head a wap.

9.   "Ye take him out upo the green,
     And get him saddled and bridled seen.

10. "Get ane for you, anither me,
     And lat us ride out ower the lee.

11. "Ye do you to my mother's coffer,
     And out of it ye'll take my tocher.

12. "Therein are sixty thousand pounds,
     Which all to me by right belongs."

13. He's done him to her father's stable,
     Where steeds stood baith wicht and able.

14. Then he strake ane upon the back,
     The swiftest gae his head a wap.

15. He's taen him out upo the green,
     And got him saddled and bridled seen.

16. Ane for him, and another for her,
     To carry them baith wi might and virr.

17. He's done him to her mother's coffer,
     And there he's taen his lover's tocher;

18. Wherein were sixty thousand pound,
     Which all to her by right belongd.

19. When they had ridden about six mile,
     His true love then began to fail.

20. "O wae's me," said that gay ladye,
     "I fear my back will gang in three.

21. "O gin I had but a gude midwife,
     Here this day to save my life,

22. "And ease me o my misery,
     O dear, how happy I woud be!"

23. "My love, we're far frae ony town,
     There is nae midwife to be foun.

24. "But if ye'll be content wi me,
     I'll do for you what man can dee."

25. "For no, for no, this maunna be,"
     Wi a sigh, replied this gay ladye.

26. "When I endure my grief and pain,
My companie ye maun refrain.

27. "Ye'll take your arrow and your bow,
And ye will hunt the deer and roe.

28. "Be sure ye touch not the white hynde,
For she is o the woman kind."

29. He took sic pleasure in deer and roe,
Till he forgot his gay ladye.

30. Till by it came that milk-white hynde,
And then he mind on his ladye syne.

31. He hasted him to yon greenwood tree,
For to relieve his gay ladye;

32. But found his ladye lying dead,
Likeways her young son at her head.

33. His mother lay ower her castle wa,
    And she beheld baith dale and down;
And she beheld young Leesome Brand,
    As he came riding to the town.

34. "Get minstrels for to play," she said,
    "And dancers to dance in my room;
For here comes my son, Leesome Brand,
    And he comes merrilie to the town."

35. "Seek nae minstrels to play, mother,
    Nor dancers to dance in your room;
But tho your son comes, Leesome Brand,
    Yet he comes sorry to the town.

36. "O I hae lost my gowden knife;
I rather had lost my ain sweet life.

37. "And I hae lost a better thing,
The gilded sheath that it was in."

38. "Are there nae gowdsmith here in Fife,
Can make to you anither knife?

39. "Are there nae sheath-makers in the land,
Can make a sheath to Leesome Brand?"

40. "There are nae gowdsmiths here in Fife,
Can make me sic a gowden knife;

41. "Nor nae sheath-makers in the land,
Can make to me a sheath again.

42.   "There ne'er was man in Scotland born,
          Ordaind to be so much forlorn.

43.   "I've lost my ladye I lovd sae dear,
          Likeways the son she did me bear."

44.   "Put in your hand at my bed head,
             There ye'll find a gude grey horn;
          In it three draps o' Saint Paul's ain blude,
             That hae been there sin he was born.

45.   "Drap twa o them o your ladye,
             And ane upo your little young son;
          Then as lively they will be
             As the first night ye brought them hame."

46.   He put his hand at her bed head,
             And there he found a gude grey horn,
          Wi three draps o' Saint Paul's ain blude,
             That had ben there sin he was born.

47.   Then he drappd twa on his ladye,
             And ane o them on his young son,
          And now they do as lively be,
             As the first day he brought them hame.

B.

MEDELWOLD AND SIDSELILLE

1.   All in their lofty bower so still
          Sat with her mother Sidselille.

2.   Gold web they wove, till on her gown
          The drops of milk ran trickling down.

3.   "Dear Sidselille, I'd gladly know,
          "How from thy bosom milk should flow?"

4.   "No milk, tho' so you seem to think,
          "But mead I had yestere'en to drink."

5.   "But those are things unlike indeed,
          "So white is milk, so brown the mead."

6.   "Then, since the truth I cannot hide,
          "I'm Medelwold's affianced bride."

7.   "And true is what thou hast even told?
          "The affianced thou of Medelwold?

8. "Then high on gallows hang shall he,
   "And blaze below the pile for thee."

9. Fair Sidselille in her mantle wrapt
   Sped to the chamber where he slept.

10. She waked him up with gentle knock,
    "Rise, Medelwold, the door unlock."

11. "Appointment I have none to keep,
    "Unlock to no one, while I sleep."

12. "O draw the bar, dear Medelwold,
    "My mother has the truth been told;

13. "And thou, she swears, shalt hang on high,
    "And burn on blazing faggots I."

14. "Nay, hang, that will I not for thee,
    "Nor burn below shalt thou for me.

15. "In casket store thy gold away,
    "While I go saddle me my grey."

16. He wrapp'd her well in purple weed,
    And laid her gently upon his steed.

17. But when they reach'd the grove of rose,
    She pray'd she might awhile repose.

18. "Of length of road dost thou complain?
    "Or does the saddle give thee pain?"

19. "Not of the road do I complain,
    "It is the saddle gives me pain."

20. His mantle blue he soon has spread,
    "Fair Sidselille, make that thy bed."

21. "O that my waiting maid were here!
    "Without some help my death is near."

22. "Thy maids are far away from thee,
    "Nor other servant here but me."

23. "I'd rather lay me down and die,
    "Than now let any man be nigh."

24. "Nay, bind thy kerchief round my head,
    "And I will serve in nurse's stead."

25. "O for a draught of water clear,
    "My sad and aching heart to cheer!"

26. Young Medelwold, so good and true,
     For water took her silver'd shoe;

27. And through the thicket broke his way,
     To where a distant streamlet lay.

28. Deep in the dale he reach'd the spring,
     And there two nightingales heard sing:

29. "With two small infants by her side
     "Your lady in the grove has died."

30. He heard, but heeded not their lay,
     And hasten'd back his weary way;

31. But when he found the grove again,
     Too true had been their doleful strain.

32. He dug a grave, was broad and deep,
     And laid all three therein to sleep;

33. But seem'd, while still he linger'd near,
     Beneath his foot their cries to hear.

34. So on a rock he stay'd his sword,
     And through his heart the weapon bored.

35. And there with her, his bride so true,
     Now buried lies her lover too.

HIND HORN (17)

This ballad is based on the story of King Horn as it occurs in the various romances on that subject. The Horn story had a continuous development in English and French from the 13th century through the 15th. The ballad characteristically selects the dramatic denouement of the story for its plot.

Text A, Scotland, Motherwell's MS. p. 106; B, Kinloch, p. 135, from tradition.

Notes

2/1. Jean: Rymenhild in the romance.

3. Not in romance tradition.

4. In romance she gives him a ring (no mention of diamonds) which will protect him so long as *he* is faithful. The giving of tokens and later recognition by means of them is a commonplace in folklore and romance. There are several stories and broadside ballads in which the lovers break a ring in half and each keeps one half. Later

the lovers are brought together by the matching of the halves. These ballads are the ancestors of the numerous broken-token songs in America.

9. beggar: palmer in the romance, but in the *Geste of King Horn* Horn gets into the castle disguised as a beggar.

17. This occurs at the wedding feast in the romance.

A.

1. In Scotland there was a babie born,
    Lill lal, etc.
And his name it was called young Hind Horn.
    With a fal lal, etc.

2. He sent a letter to our king
That he was in love with his daughter Jean.

3. He's gien to her a silver wand,
With seven living lavrocks sitting thereon.

4. She's gien to him a diamond ring,
With seven bright diamonds set therein.

5. "When this ring grows pale and wan,
You may know by it my love is gane."

6. One day as he looked his ring upon,
He saw the diamonds pale and wan.

7. He left the sea and came to land,
And the first that he met was an old beggar man.

8. "What news, what news?" said young Hind Horn;
"No news, no news," said the old beggar man.

9. "No news," said the beggar, "no news at a',
But there is a wedding in the king's ha.

10. "But there is a wedding in the king's ha,
That has halden these forty days and twa."

11. "Will ye lend me your begging coat?
And I'll lend you my scarlet cloak.

12. "Will you lend me your beggar's rung?
And I'll gie you my steed to ride upon.

13. "Will you lend me your wig o hair,
To cover mine, because it is fair?"

14. The auld beggar man was bound for the mill,
But young Hind Horn for the king's hall.

15.   The auld beggar man was bound for to ride,
      But young Hind Horn was bound for the bride.

16.   When he came to the king's gate,
      He sought a drink for Hind Horn's sake.

17.   The bride came down with a glass of wine,
      When he drank out the glass, and dropt in the ring.

18.   "O got ye this by sea or land?
      Or got ye it off a dead man's hand?"

19.   "I got not it by sea, I got it by land,
      And I got it, madam, out of your own hand."

20.   "O I'll cast off my gowns of brown,
      And beg wi you frae town to town.

21.   "O I'll cast off my gowns of red,
      And I'll beg wi you to win my bread."

22.   "Ye needna cast off your gowns of brown,
      For I'll make you lady o many a town.

23.   "Ye needna cast off your gowns of red,
      It's only a sham, the begging o my bread."

24.   The bridegroom he had wedded the bride,
      But young Hind Horn he took her to bed.

B.

1.   "Hynde Horn's bound love, and Hynde Horn's free,
      Whare was ye born, or in what countrie?"

2.   "In gude greenwud whare I was born,
      And all my friends left me forlorn.

3.   "I gave my love a silver wand,
      That was to rule oure all Scotland.

4.   "My love gave me a gay gowd ring,
      That was to rule abune a' thing."

5.   "As lang as that ring keeps new in hue,
      Ye may ken that your love loves you.

6.   "But whan that ring turns pale and wan,
      Ye may ken that your love loves anither man."

7.   He hoisted up his sails, and away sailed he,
      Till that he cam to a foreign countrie.

8. He looked at his ring; it was turnd pale and wan;
   He said, "I wish I war at hame again."

9. He hoisted up his sails, and hame sailed he,
   Until that he came to his ain countrie.

10. The first ane that he met wi
    Was wi a puir auld beggar man.

11. "What news, what news, my silly old man?
    What news hae ye got to tell to me?"

12. "Na news, na news," the puir man did say,
    "But this is our queen's wedding day."

13. "Ye'll lend me your begging weed,
    And I'll gie you my riding steed."

14. "My beggin weed is na for thee,
    Your riding steed is na for me."

15. But he has changed wi the beggar man,

    .   .   .   .

16. "Which is the gate that ye used to gae?
    And what are the words ye beg wi?"

17. "Whan ye come to yon high hill,
    Ye'll draw your bent bow nigh until.

18. "Whan ye come to yonder town,
    Ye'll let your bent bow low fall down.

19. "Ye'll seek meat for St. Peter, ask for St. Paul,
    And seek for the sake of Hynde Horn all.

20. "But tak ye frae nane of them a',
    Till ye get frae the bonnie bride hersel O."

21. Whan he cam to youn high hill,
    He drew his bent bow nigh until.

22. And whan he cam to yonder town,
    He lute his bent bow low fall down.

23. He saught meat for St. Peter, he askd for St. Paul,
    And he sought for the sake of Hynde Horn all.

24. But he would tak frae nan o them a',
    Till he got frae the bonnie bride hersel O.

25. The bride cam tripping doun the stair,
    Wi the scales o red gowd on her hair.

26.   Wi a glass of red win in her hand,
      To gie to the puir auld beggar man.

27.   It's out he drank the glass o wine,
      And into the glass he dropt the ring.

28.   "Got ye 't by sea, or got ye 't by land,
      Or got ye 't aff a drownd man's hand?"

29.   "I gat na 't by sea, I got na 't by land,
      Nor got I it aff a drownd man's hand.

30.   "But I got it at my wooing,
      And I'll gie it at your wedding."

31.   "I'll tak the scales o gowd frae my head,
      I'll follow you, and beg my bread.

32.   "I'll tak the scales of gowd frae my hair,
      I'll follow you for evermair."

33.   She has tane the scales o gowd frae her head,
      She has followed him to beg her bread.

34.   She has tane the scales o gowd frae her hair,
      And she has followed him for evermair.

35.   But atween the kitchen and the ha,
      There he lute his cloutie cloak fa.

36.   And the red gowd shined oure him a',
      And the bride frae the bridegroom was stown awa.

SIR LIONEL (18)

This ballad has much in common with the romance of *Sir Eglamour of Artois,* but the ballad story is badly garbled. The ballad story is vaguely this: A knight sees a lady in distress (in a tree) because a giant boar has just killed her lord. The boar returns, the knight kills it but is wounded. He is challenged by the giant who owned the boar, but is allowed a period of forty days to recover from his wounds, leaving his lady (the one who was sitting in the tree?) as hostage. At the appointed time he returns, slays the giant, and redeems the lady.

This ballad is common in America under the name of "Old Bangum." Here it has completely degenerated into a rollicking comic song with little story.

Text A, Percy, p. 32; B, from tradition in Missouri, printed in *JAF.,* 25:175.

A.

1. Sir Egrabell had sonnes three,
   Blow thy horne, good hunter
   Sir Lyonell was one of these,
   As I am a gentle hunter.

2. Sir Lyonell wold on hunting ryde,
   Vntill the forrest him beside.

3. And as he rode thorrow the wood,
   Where trees and harts and all were good,

4. And as he rode over the plaine,
   There he saw a knight lay slaine.

5. And as he rode still on the plaine,
   He saw a lady sitt in a graine.

6. "Say thou, lady, and tell thou me,
   What blood sheed heere has bee."

7. "Of this blood sheed we may all rew,
   Both wife and childe and man alsoe.

8. "For it is not past 3 days right
   Since Sir Broninge was mad a knight.

9. "Nor it is not more than 3 dayes agoe
   Since the wild bore did him sloe."

10. "Say thou, lady, and tell thou mee,
    How long thou wilt sitt in that tree."

11. She said, "I will sitt in this tree
    Till my friends doe feitch me."

12. "Tell me, lady, and doe not misse,
    Where that your friends dwellings is."

13. "Downe," shee said, "in yonder towne,
    There dwells my friends of great renowne.

14. Says, "Lady, I'le ryde into yonder towne
    And see wether your friends beene bowne.

15. "I my self wilbe the formost man
    That shall come, lady, to feitch you home."

16. But as he rode then by the way,
    He thought it shame to goe away;

17. And vmbethought him of a wile,
    How he might that wilde bore beguile.

18.   "Sir Egrabell," he said, "my father was;
      He neuer left lady in such a case.

19.   "Noe more will I" . . .

      .   .   .   .

20.   "And after that thou shalt doe mee
      Thy hawkes and thy lease alsoe.

21.   "Soe shalt thou doe at my command
      The litle fingar on thy right hand."

22.   "Ere I wold laue all this with thee,
      Vpoon this ground I rather dyee."

23.   The gyant gaue Sir Lyonell such a blow,
      The fyer out of his eyen did throw.

24.   He said then, "If I were saffe and sound,
      As within this hower I was in this ground,

25.   "It shold be in the next towne told
      How deare thy buffett it was sold;

26.   "And it shold haue beene in the next town said
      How well thy buffett it were paid."

27.   "Take 40 daies into spite,
      To heale thy wonds that beene soe wide.

28.   "When 40 dayes beene at an end,
      Heere meete thou me both safe and sound.

29.   "And till thou come to me againe,
      With me thoust leaue thy lady alone."

30.   When 40 dayes was at an end,
      Sir Lyonell of his wounds was healed sound.

31.   He tooke with him a litle page,
      He gaue to him good yeoman's wage.

32.   And as he rode by one hawthorne,
      Even there did hang his hunting horne.

33.   He sett his bugle to his mouth,
      And blew his bugle still full south.

34.   He blew his bugle lowde and shrill;
      The lady heard, and came him till.

35.   Sayes, "The gyant lyes vnder yond low,
      And well he heares your bugle blow.

36. "And bidds me of good cheere be,
    This night heele supp with you and me."

37. Hee sett that lady vppon a steede,
    And a litle boy before he yeede.

38. And said, "Lady, if you see that I must dye,
    As euer you loued me, from me flye.

39. "But, lady, if you see that I must liue,"
    .   .   .   .

B.

OLD BANGUM

There is a wild boar in these woods,
   Dillum down dillum
There is a wild boar in these woods,
   Dillum down
There is a wild boar in these woods
Who'll eat your flesh and drink your blood,
   Kibby ky cuddle down killy quo cum.

"Oh, how shall I this wild boar see?
I'll blow a blast and he'll come to me."

Old Bangum blew both loud and shrill;
The wild boar heard on Temple Hill.

The wild boar dashed with such a rash
He tore his way thru oak and ash.

Old Bangum drew his wooden knife
And swore he'd take the wild boar's life.

They fought four hours in a day;
At last the wild boar stole away.

They raced the wild boar to his den,
And found the bones of a thousand men.

THE CRUEL MOTHER (20)

Similar ballad stories are to be found in Germany. Most of the English-Scottish texts of this ballad are defective or they give only an
outline of the story. The American texts are much more coherent and
detailed.

Of the two texts from Scotland here printed, A is from manuscript sources, Scott, iii, 259; B, a much fuller one, is from oral tradition as collected by Greig and published in *Last Leaves,* etc., p. 21; C, traditional, from Maine, printed by Barry, p. 80.

A.

1. She sat down below a thorn,
    Fine flowers in the valley
    And there she has her sweet babe born.
    And the green leaves they grow rarely.

2. "Smile na sae sweet, my bonie babe,
    And ye smile sae sweet, ye'll smile me dead."

3. She's taen out her little pen-knife,
    And twinnd the sweet babe o its life.

4. She's howket a grave by the light o the moon,
    And there she's buried her sweet babe in.

5. As she was going to the church,
    She saw a sweet babe in the porch.

6. "O sweet babe, and thou were mine,
    I wad cleed thee in the silk so fine."

7. "O mother dear, when I was thine,
    You did no prove to me sae kind."

*   *   *   *   *   *   *

B.

1. There was king's daughter lived in the north
    Hey the rose an' the linsie, O
    An' she has courted her father's clerk,
    An' awa be the greenwood sidie, ().

2. She courted him a year an' a day,
    Till her appearance did her betray.

3. She leant her back untill a tree,
    Thinkin she would lighter be.

4. She leant her back untill a thorn,
    An' bonnie was the boys she has born.

5. She took out her little penknife,
    An' she put an end to their sweet life.

6. She's taen the napkin fae her neck,
    She made to them a linen sheet.

7. She laid them beneath a marble stone,
   Thinkin to win a maiden home.

8. She looked ower her father's castle wa,
   She saw twa bonnie boys playin at the ba.

9. "O bonnie boys, gin ye were mine,
   Ye sudna wear but the silk so fine;

10. "The sovilne an' the grass-green silk;
    Ye sudna drink but the farrow cow's milk."

11. "O cruel mother, when we were thine
    We saw neen o your silk so fine;

12. "Your sovilne an' your grass-green silk;
    And we drank neen o your farrow cow's milk."

13. "O bonnie boys, can ye tell me
    What kin' o a death I'll hae to dee?"

14. "Seven year a fish in the flood,
    Seven year a bird in the wood,

15. "Seven year a warnin bell,
    Seven year in deeps o hell."

16. "Welcome, welcome, fish in the flood,
    Welcome, welcome, bird in the wood,

17. "Welcome, welcome, warnin bell,
    But the God o Heaven keep me out o hell."

C.

1. There was a lady lived in York,
   It was all alone and alo-ne;
   She fell in love with her father's clerk,
   Down by the greenwood si-de.

2. She leaned her back against an oak,
   First it bent and then it broke,

3. She leaned her back against a thorn,
   And there those two pretty babes were born,

4. She took her penknife out of her pocket,
   And pierced those pretty babes to the heart,

5. She washed her penknife in the brook,
   The more she washed it the redder its look,

6.   She wiped her penknife on the clay,
     And there she wiped the stains away,

7.   She dug a grave both long and deep,
     She lay-ed those pretty babes in for to sleep,

8.   When she returned to her father's farm,
     She spied those pretty babes arm in arm,

9.   When she returned to her father's hall,
     She spied those pretty babes playing ball,

10. "Pretty babes! pretty babes, if thou art mine,"
         It was all alone and alo-ne;
     "I'll dress you up in satin so fine,"
         Al down by the greenwood si-de.

THE MAID AND THE PALMER (21)

This is the English version of a widely known continental ballad concerned with the Samaritan woman with an admixture of the legend of
Mary Magdalene. In these ballads the interlocutor is Christ. The fantastic penance of a series of transmigrations is found in different detail
as a regular part of this ballad. It also commonly occurs in some versions of the "Cruel Mother."
    Text, Percy, p. 461.

1.   The maid shee went to the well to washe,
         Lillumwham, lillumwham!
     The mayd she went to the well to washe,
         Whatt then? what then?
     The maid shee went to the well to washe,
     Dew ffell of her lilly white fleshe.
         Grandam boy, grandam boy, heye!
     Leg a derry, leg a merry, mett, mer, whoope, whir!
         Driuance, larumben, grandam boy, heye!

2.   While shee washte and while shee ronge,
     While shee hangd o the hazle wand.

3.   There came an old palmer by the way,
     Said, "God speed thee well, thou faire maid,

4.   "Hast either cupp or can,
     To giue an old palmer drinke therin."

5.   Sayes, "I have neither cupp nor cann,
     To giue an old palmer drinke therin."

6. "But an thy lemman came from Roome,
   Cupps and canns thou wold ffind soone."

7. Shee sware by God & good St. John,
   Lemman had shee neuer none.

8. Saies, "Peace, ffaire mayd, you are fforsworne!
   Nine children you haue borne.

9. "Three were buryed vnder thy bed's head,
   Other three vnder thy brewing leade.

10. "Other three on yon play greene;
    Count, maid, and there be 9."

11. "But I hope you are the good old man
    That all the world beleeues vpon.

12. "Old palmer, I pray thee,
    Pennaunce that thou wilt giue to me."

13. "Penance I can giue thee none,
    But 7 yeere to be a stepping-stone.

14. "Other seauen a clapper in a bell,
    Other 7 to lead an ape in hell.

15. "When thou hast thy penance done,
    Then thoust come a mayden home."

ST. STEPHEN AND HEROD (22)

This ballad is recovered from a 15th-century MS., the only known version in English, though there are close analogues in Germanic countries. The legend of the roasting cock crowing to confound a skeptic is common in Biblical story. Many such stories are told of Judas. The original story seems to concern the visit of the Wise Men to Herod at the time of Christ's birth. When Herod doubted that the Messiah was born and said that it was as impossible as the roast capon crowing, the cock arose from the dish, flapped its wings, and crowed *Cristus natus est.* This ballad, as do other Germanic versions, replaces the Wise Men with Stephen.

Text, Sloane MS. 2593 (B.M.).

Notes

7/1. gynnyst to brede: Kittredge would emend, gynnyst to wede, beginning to go mad:

1. Seynt Steuene was a clerk in kyng Herowdes halle,
   And seruyd him of bred and cloþ, as euery kyng befalle.

2. Steuyn out of kechone cam, wyth boris hed on honde;
    He saw a steere was fayr and bryȝt ouer bedlem stonde.

3. He kyst adound þe boris hed and went in to þe halle:
    "I forsak þe, kyng Herowdes, and þi werkes alle.

4. "I forsak þe, kyng Herowdes, and þi werkes alle;
    Þer is a chyld in Bedlem born is beter þan we alle."

5. "Quat eylyt þe, Steuene? quat is þe befalle?
    Lakkyt þe eyþer mete or drynk in kyng Herowdes halle?"

6. "Lakit me neyþer mete ne drynk in kyng Herowdes halle;
    Þer is a chyld in Bedlem born is beter þan we alle."

7. "Quat eylyt þe, Steuyn? Art þu wod, or þu gynnyst to brede?
    Lakkyt þe eyþer gold or fe, or ony ryche wede?"

8. "Lakyt me neyþer gold ne fe, ne non ryche wede;
    Þer is a chyld in Bedlem born xal helpyn vs at our nede."

9. "Þat is al so soþ, Steuyn, al so soþ, iwys,
    As þis capoun crowe xal þat lyþ here in myn dysh."

10. Þat word was not so sone seyd, þat word in þat halle,
    Þe capoun crew *cristus natus est!* among þe lordes alle.

11. "Rysyt vp, myn turmentowres, be to and al be on,
    And ledyt Steuyn out of þis town, and stonyt hym wyth ston!"

12. Tokyn he Steuene, and stonyd hym in the way,
    And þerfore is his euyn on Crystes owyn day.

JUDAS (23)

This is the oldest narrative in English composed in the ballad manner.
Whether it is a genuine ballad or not is open to argument. There is
no evidence that it had any growth in oral tradition, that it was ever
more than a literary piece; there is no evidence that it was sung. On
the other hand, it possesses the swift, condensed, dramatic way of telling a story that is uniquely ballad. "Judas" may well owe its ballad
quality to contemporary ballads of a more popular nature. At any
rate, it proves that the form and dramatic qualities that we think pe-
culiarly ballad were in existence before 1400. The story told here of
Judas and his sister seems to be unique among legends of Judas.

"Judas" is in the 13th-century MS. Trinity College, Cambridge,
B. 14. 39, from which the following text is taken.

1. Hit wes upon a Scere-þorsday þat ure loverd aros;
    Ful mild were þe words he spec to Judas.

2. "Judas, þou most of Jurselem, oure mete for to bugge;
   Þritti platen of selver þou bere upo þi rugge.

3. "Þou comest fer iþe brode stret, fer iþe brode strete;
   Summe of þine tunesmen þer þou meist imete."

4. . . with his . wicked woman .
   Imette wid is soster, the swikele wimon.

5. "Judas, þou were wrþe me stende þe wid ston,
   For þe false prophete þat þou bileuest upon."

6. "Be stille, leue soster, þin herte þe tobreke.
   Wiste min louerd Crist, ful wel he wolde be wreke."

7. "Judas, go þou on þe roc, heie upon þe ston;
   Lei þin heved i my barn, slep þou þe anon."

8. Sone so Judas of slepe was awake,
   Þritti platen of seluer from hym weren itake.

9. He drou hymselve bi þe cop, þat al it lauede ablode;
   Þe Jewes out of Jurselem awenden he were wode.

10. Foret hym com þe riched Jew that heiste Pilatus:
    "Wolte sulle þi lovered, þat hetter Jesus?"

11. "I nul sulle my loverd for nones cunnes eiste,
    Bote hit be for þe þritti platen that he me bitaiste."

12. "Solte sulle þi lord Crist for enes cunnes golde?"
    "Nay, bote hit be for þe platen þat he habben wolde."

13. In him com ur lord gon, as is postles seten at mete:
    "Wou sitte ye, postles, ant wi nule ye ete?

14. ["Wou sitte ye, postles, ant wi nule ye ete?]
    Ic am iboust ant isold today for oure mete."

15. Vp stod him Judas: "Lord, am I þat . . .?
    "I nas never þe stude þer me þe euel spec."

16. Vp him stod Peter, ant spec wid al is miste,
    Þau Pilatus him come wid ten hundred cnistes.

17. ["Þau Pilatus him come wid ten hundred cnistes,]
    Yet ic wolde, louerd, for þi love fiste."

18. "Still þou be, Peter, wel I þe icnowe;
    Þou wold fursake me þrien ar þe coc him crowe."

WILLIE'S LYKE-WAKE (25)

Stories abound among the Germanic people of a man or woman who feigns death to win a lover or to circumvent relatives, etc. *Lyke* is body; the *lyke-wake,* then, is the watch over the dead between the death and funeral. See Introduction, page 5, for the "Lyke Wake Dirge" as an example of the waking song sung on these occasions.

Text, Buchan, i, 185.

1. "O Willie my son, what makes you sae sad?"
   As the sun shines over the valley
   "I lye sarely sick for the love of a maid."
   Amang the blue flowers and the yellow.

2. "Were she an heiress or lady sae free,
   That she will take no pity on thee?

3. "O Willie, my son, I'll learn you a wile,
   How this fair maid ye may beguile.

4. "Ye'll gie the principal bellman a groat,
   And ye'll gar him cry your dead lyke-wake."

5. Then he gae the principal bellman a groat,
   He bade him cry his dead lyke-wake.

6. This maiden she stood till she heard it a',
   And down frae her cheeks the tears did fa.

7. She is hame to her father's ain bower:
   "I'll gang to yon lyke-wake ae single hour."

8. "Ye must take with you your ain brither John;
   It's not meet for maidens to ventur alone."

9. "I'll not take with me my brither, John,
   But I'll gang along, myself all alone."

10. When she came to young Willie's yate,
    His seven brithers were standing thereat.

11. Then they did conduct her into the ha,
    Amang the weepers and merry mourners a'.

12. When she lifted up the covering sae red,
    With melancholy countenance to look on the dead,

13. He's taen her in his arms, laid her gainst the wa,
    Says, "Lye ye here, fair maid, till day."

14. "O spare me, O spare me, but this single night,
    And let me gang hame a maiden sae bright."

15. "Tho all your kin were about your boer,
     Ye shall not be a maiden ae single hour.

16. "Fair maid, ye came here without a convoy,
     But ye shall return wi a horse and a boy.

17. "Ye came here a maiden sae mild
     But ye shall gae hame a wedded wife with child."

THE THREE RAVENS (26)
THE TWA CORBIES (26)

These are two of the most arresting ballads in English balladry. They
use the common folk belief in talking birds found so frequently in ballad. They illustrate splendidly how the ballad in its compact dramatic
form can make moving and powerful comment on the great matters
of life. "The Three Ravens" is simple, hopeful, inspiring, not sentimental.

Notes
   6/1. fallow doe: his lady from the land of the fairy in the form of
a doe?

"The Twa Corbies" is brittle and devastating and cynical, but aus-
tere and powerful. The last two lines are the supreme expression in
English of desolation, lonesomeness, and despair. They remind one of
the lines of Chaucer:
> "What is this world?
> What asketh men to have?
> Now with his love,
> Now in his colde grave
> Allone, withouten any compaignye."

Text A, Ritson, *Ancient Songs,* p. 155; B, Scott, iii, 239; C, from
tradition in Iowa, *MAF,* 29:2.

A.

1. There were three rauens sat on a tree,
        Downe a downe, hay down, hay downe
    There were three rauens sat on a tree,
        With a downe
    There were three rauens sat on a tree,
    They were as blacke as they might be.
        With a downe derrie, derrie, derrie, downe, downe

2. The one of them said to his mate,
    "Where shall we our breakfast take?"

3.   "Downe in yonder greene field,
     There lies a knight slain vnder his shield.

4.   "His hounds they lie downe at his feete,
     So well they can their master keepe.

5.   "His haukes they flie so eagerly,
     There's no fowle dare him come nie."

6.   Downe there comes a fallow doe,
     As great with yong as she might goe.

7.   She lift up his bloudy hed,
     And kist his wounds that were so red.

8.   She got him vp vpon her backe,
     And carried him to earthen lake.

9.   She buried him before the prime,
     She was dead herselfe e're euen-song time.

10. God send euery gentleman,
     Such haukes, such hounds, and such a leman.

B.

1.   As I was walking all alane,
     I heard twa corbies making a mane;
     The tane unto the t'other say,
     "Where sall we gang and dine to-day?"

2.   "In behint yon auld fail dyke,
     I wot there lies a new slain knight;
     And naebody kens that he lies there,
     But his hawk, his hound, and lady fair.

3.   "His hound is to the hunting gane,
     His hawk to fetch the wild-fowl hame,
     His lady's ta'en another mate,
     So we may mak our dinner sweet.

4.   "Ye'll sit on his white hause-bane,
     And I'll pike out his bonny blue een;
     Wi ae lock o his gowden hair
     We'll theek our nest when it grows bare.

5.   "Mony a one for him makes mane,
     But nane sall ken where he is gane;
     O'er his white banes, when they are bare,
     The wind sall blaw for evermair."

C.

1. There were three crows sat on a tree,
   Oh Billy Magee Magar!
   There were three crows sat on a tree,
   Oh Billy Magee Magar!
   There were three crows sat on a tree,
   And they were black as crows could be,
   And they all flapped their wings and cried
   Caw, caw, caw, Billy Magee Magar!
   And they all flapped their wings and cried
   Billy Magee Magar!

2. Said one old crow unto his mate,
   O Billy Magee Magar!
   Said one old crow unto his mate,
   O Billy Magee Magar!
   Said one old crow unto his mate,
   "What shall we do for grub to ate?"
   And they all flapped their wings and cried——
   Caw, caw, caw, Billy Magee Magar!
   And they all flapped their wings and cried
   Billy Magee Magar!

3. "There lies a horse on yonder plain,
   Who's by some cruel butcher slain,"
   And they all flapped their wings, etc.

4. "We'll perch ourselves on his backbone,
   And pick his eyes out one by one,"
   And they all flapped their wings, etc.

THE BOY AND THE MANTLE (29)

This ballad, like the several which follow it here, is rather more in the literary tradition than those which have preceded it. These are what Scott called Minstrel Ballads. The story is derived from a well-known French fabliau, "Cort Mantel," one of a group of such stories in which ladies at Arthur's court are tested by means of a mantle made in fairyland which will fit only a completely chaste woman. The analogous story of the testing of chastity by means of a drinking horn combined here with the mantle test is a separate story found in French, German, and other literatures of Europe; it seems to be older than the test-by-mantle story. A French version of the horn, the "Lai du Corn," is of the middle of the 12th century. The story is more vigorous, fresher. In the French "Cort Mantel" the ladies are absent when the boy appears with the mantle and therefore do not know the virtue of the mantle and what the results of trying it on may be; it is consequently more dramatic.

Text, Percy, p. 284.

1. In the third day of May
        to Carleile did come
    A curteous child,
        that cold much of wisdome.

2. A kirtle and a mantle
        this child had vppon,
    With brauches and ringes
        full richelye bedone.

3. He had a sute of silke,
        about his middle drawne;
    Without he cold of curtesye,
        he thought itt much shame.

4. "God speed thee, King Arthur,
        sitting att thy meate!
    And the goodly Queene Gueneuer!
        I cannot her fforgett.

5. "I tell you lords in this hall,
        I hett you all heede,
    Except you be the more surer,
        is you for to dread."

6. He plucked out of his potewer,
        and longer wold not dwell,
    He pulled forth a pretty mantle,
        betweene two nut-shells.

7. "Haue thou here, King Arthure,
        haue thou heere of mee;
    Giue itt to thy comely queene,
        shapen as itt is alreadye.

8. "Itt shall neuer become that wiffe
        that hath once done amisse;"
    Then euery knight in the king's court
        began to care for his.

9. Forth came dame Gueneuer,
        to the mantle shee her bed;
    The ladye shee was new-fangle,
        but yett shee was affrayd.

10. When shee had taken the mantle,
    shee stoode as she had beene madd;
    It was from the top to the toe
    as sheeres had itt shread.

11. One while was itt gaule,
    another while was itt greene;
    Another while was itt wadded;
    ill itt did her beseeme.

12. Another while was it blacke,
    and bore the worst hue;
    "By my troth," quoth King Arthur,
    "I thinke thou be not true."

13. Shee threw downe the mantle,
    that bright was of blee,
    Fast with a rudd redd
    to her chamber can shee flee.

14. Shee curst the weauer and the walker
    that clothe that had wrought,
    And bade a vengeance on his crowne
    that hither hath itt brought.

15. "I had rather be in a wood,
    vnder a greene tree,
    Then in King Arthur's court
    shamed for to bee."

16. Kay called forth his ladye,
    and bade her come neere;
    Saies, "Madam, and thou be guiltye,
    I pray thee hold thee there."

17. Forth came his ladye
    shortlye and anon,
    Boldlye to the mantle
    then is shee gone.

18. When she had tane the mantle,
    and cast it her about,
    Then was shee bare
    all aboue the buttocckes.

19. Then euery knight
    that was in the king's court
    Talked, laughed, and showted,
    full oft att that sport.

20. Shee threw downe the mantle.
        that bright was of blee,
  Ffast with a red rudd
        to her chamber can shee flee.

21. Forth came an old knight,
        pattering o're a creede,
  And he proferred to this little boy
        twenty markes to his meede,

22. And all the time of the Christmasse
        willinglye to ffeede;
  For why, this mantle might
        doe his wiffe some need.

23. When shee had tane the mantle,
        of cloth that was made,
  Shee had no more left on her
        but a tassell and a threed;
  Then euery knight in the king's court
        bade euill might shee speed.

24. Shee threw downe the mantle,
        that bright was of blee,
  And fast with a redd rudd
        to her chamber can shee flee.

25. Craddocke called forth his ladye,
        and bade her come in;
  Saith, "Winne this mantle, ladye,
        with a litle dinne.

26. "Winne this mantle, ladye,
        and it shalbe thine
  If thou neuer did amisse
        since thou wast mine."

27. Forth came Craddocke's ladye
        shortlye and anon,
  But boldlye to the mantle
        then is shee gone.

28. When shee had tane the mantle,
        and cast itt her about,
  Vpp att her great toe
        itt began to crinkle and crowt;
  Shee said, "Bowe downe, mantle,
        and shame me not for nought.

29. "Once I did amisse,
        I tell you certainlye,

When I kist Craddocke's mouth
vnder a greene tree,
When I kist Craddocke's mouth
before he marryed mee."

30. When she had her shreeuen,
and her sines shee had tolde,
The mantle stoode about her
right as shee wold;

31. Seemelye of coulour,
glittering like gold;
Then euery knight in Arthur's court
did her behold.

32. Then spake dame Gueneuer
to Arthur our king:
"She hath tane yonder mantle,
not with wright but with wronge!

33. "See you not yonder woman
that maketh her selfe soe clene?
I haue seene tane out of her bedd
of men fiueteene;

34. "Preists, clarkes, and wedded men,
from her by-deene;
Yett she taeth the mantle,
and maketh her-selfe cleane!"

35. Then spake the litle boy
that kept the mantle in hold;
Sayes, "King, chasten thy wiffe;
of her words shee is too bold.

36. "Shee is a bitch and a witch,
and a whore bold;
King, in thine owne hall
thou art a cuchold."

37. The litle boy stoode
looking ouer a dore;
He was ware of a wyld bore,
would haue werryed a man.

38. He pulld forth a wood kniffe,
fast thither than he ran;
He brought in the bore's head,
and quitted him like a man.

39. He brought in the bore's head,
and was wonderous bold;

He said there was neuer a cuchold's kniffe
    carue itt that cold.

40.   Some rubbed their kniues
        vppon a whetstone;
    Some threw them vnder the table,
        and said they had none.

41.   King Arthur and the child
        stood looking them vpon;
    All their kniue's edges
        turned backe againe.

42.   Craddoccke had a litle kniue
        of iron and of steele;
    He birtled the bore's head
        wonderous weele,
    That euery knight in the king's court
        had a morssell.

43.   The litle boy had a horne,
        of red gold that ronge;
    He said, "There was noe cuckolde
        shall drinke of my horne,
    But he shold itt sheede,
        wither behind or beforne."

44.   Some shedd on their shoulder,
        and some on their knee;
    He that cold not hitt his mouth
        put it in his eye;
    And he that was a cuckold,
        euery man might him see.

45.   Craddoccke wan the horne
        and the bore's head;
    His ladye wan the mantle
        vnto her meede;
    Euerye such a louely ladye,
        God send her well to speede!

THE MARRIAGE OF SIR GAWAIN (31)

This is the famous loathly lady story known widely in the Middle
Ages in tale and romance. The most important tellings are *The Wed-
ding of Sir Gawen and Dame Ragnell* and Chaucer's *Wife of Bath's
Tale*. The original story as it occurs in Arthurian tradition told of Ar-

thur being forced by a giant of a fellow with a great club either to
fight him or to return a year later with the answer to the question,
what women most desire in the world. Arthur is told the correct answer by an old hag but must promise her Gawain as a husband. Arthur meets the giant-baron, gives him the right answer, and so saves
his life. Gawain finally agrees to marry the hag, who turns out to be
a beautiful girl bewitched by a cruel stepmother. When she asks Gawain if he wishes her beautiful by day and hideous by night, he leaves
the decision to her. This breaks the spell, allows her to be beautiful
both day and night, and releases her bespelled brother the giant.

Text, Percy, p. 46.

1. Kinge Arthur liues in merry Carleile, and seemely is to see,
   And there he hath with him Queene Genever, that bride soe
   bright of blee.

2. And there he hath with him Queene Genever, that bride soe
   bright in bower,
   And all his barons about him stoode, that were both stiffe and
   stowre.

3. The king kept a royall Christmasse, of mirth and great honor,
   And when . . .

4. "And bring me word what thing it is that a woman will most
   desire;
   That shalbe thy ransome, Arthur," he sayes, "for I'le haue noe
   other hier."

5. King Arthur then held vp his hand, according thene as was the
   law;
   He tooke his leaue of the baron there, and homward can he
   draw.

6. And when he came to merry Carlile, to his chamber he is gone,
   And ther came to him his cozen Sir Gawaine, as he did make
   his mone.

7. And there came to him his cozen Sir Gawaine, that was a curte-
   ous knight;
   "Why sigh you soe sore, vnckle Arthur," he said, "or who hath
   done thee vnright?"

8. "O peace, O peace, thou gentle Gawaine, that faire may thee
   beffall!
   For if thou knew my sighing soe deepe, thou wold not meruaile
   att all.

9. "Ffor when I came to Tearne Wadling, a bold barron there I
   fand,
   With a great club vpon his backe, standing stiffe and strong.

10. "And he asked me wether I wold fight or from him I shold begone,
Or else I must him a ransome pay, and soe depart him from.

11. "To fight with him I saw noe cause; methought it was not meet;
For he was stiffe and strong with-all, his strokes were nothing
sweete.

12. "Therefor this is my ransome, Gawaine, I ought to him pay;
I must come againe, as I am sworne, Vpon the New Yeers day;

13. "And I must bring him word what thing it is . . .

.   .   .   .

* * * * * * *

14. Then king Arthur drest him for to ryde, in one soe rich array,
Toward the fore-said Tearne Wadling, that he might keepe his
day.

15. And as he rode over a more, hee see a lady where shee sate
Betwixt an oke and a greene hollen; she was cladd in red scarlett.

16. Then there as shold haue stood her mouth, then there was sett
her eye;
The other was in her forhead fast, the way that she might see.

17. Her nose was crooked and turnd outward, her mouth stood foule
a-wry;
A worse formed lady than shee was, neuer man saw with his eye.

18. To halch vpon him, King Arthur, this lady was full faine,
But King Arthur had forgott his lesson, what he shold say againe.

19. "What knight art thou," the lady sayd, "that will not speak
to me?
Of me be thou nothing dismayd, tho I be vgly to see.

20. "For I haue halched you curteouslye, and you will not me
againe;
Yett I may happen Sir Kinght," shee said, "to ease thee of thy
paine."

21. "Giue thou ease me, lady," he said, "or helpe me any thing,
Thou shalt have gentle Gawaine, my cozen, and marry him with
a ring."

22. "Why, if I help thee not, thou noble King Arthur, of thy owne
hearts desiringe,
Of gentle Gawaine . . .

* * * * * * *

23. And when he came to the Tearne Wadling, the baron there
    cold he finde,
    With a great weapon on his backe, standing stiffe and stronge.

24. And then he tooke King Arthur's letters in his hands, and away
    he cold them fling,
    And then he puld out a good browne sword, and cryd himselfe
    a king.

25. And he sayd, "I have thee and they land, Arthur, to doe as it
    pleaseth me,
    For this is not thy ransome sure, therefore yeeld thee to me."

26. And then bespoke him noble Arthur, and bad him hold his hand:
    "And giue me leaue to speake my mind in defence of all my
    land."

27. He said, "As I came over a more, I see a lady where shee sate
    Betweene an oke and a green hollen; she was clad in red scarlett.

28. "And she says a woman will haue her will, and this is all her
    cheef desire;
    Doe me right, as thou art a baron of sckill, this is thy ransome
    and all thy hyer."

29. He sayes, "An early vengeance light on her! She walkes on yon-
    der more;
    It was my sister that told thee this, and she is a misshappen hore.

30. "But heer I'le make maine avow to God to doe her an euill turne,
    For an euer I may thate fowle theefe get, in a fyer I will her
    burne."

                    *   *   *   *   *   *   *

31. Sir Lancelott and Sir Steven bold, they rode with them that day,
    And the formost of the company there rode the steward Kay.

32. Soe did Sir Banier and Sir Bore, Sir Garrett with them soe gay,
    Soe did Sir Tristeram that gentle knight, to the forrest fresh
    and gay.

33. And when he came to the greene forrest, vnderneath a greene
    holly tree,
    Their sate that lady in red scarlet that vnseemly was to see.

34. Sir Kay beheld this lady's face, and looked vppon her swire;
    "Whosoeuer kisses this lady," he saies, "of his kisse he stands in
    feare."

35. Sir Kay beheld the lady againe, and looked vpon her snout;
    "Whosoeuer kisses this lady," he saies, "of his kisse he stands in
    doubt."

36. "Peace, cozen Kay," then said Sir Gawaine, "amend thee of thy
    life;
    For there is a knight amongst vs all that must marry her to his
    wiffe."

37. "What! Wedd her to wiffe!" then said Sir Kay, "in the diuells
    name anon!
    Gett me a wiffe where-ere I may, for I had rather be slaine!"

38. Then some tooke vp their hawkes in hast, and some tooke vp
    their hounds,
    And some sware they wold not marry her for citty nor for
    towne.

39. And then be-spake him noble King Arthur, and sware there by
    this day,
    "For a litle foule sight and misliking . . .

                *   *   *   *   *   *   *

40. Then shee said, "Choose thee, gentle Gawaine, truth as I doe
    say,
    Whether thou wilt haue me in this liknesse in the night or else
    in the day."

41. And then bespake him gentle Gawaine, was one soe mild of
    moode,
    Sayes, "Well I know what I wold say, God grant it may be
    good!

42. "To haue thee fowle in the night when I with thee shold play;
    Yet I had rather, if I might haue thee fowle in the day."

43. "What! When lords goe with ther feires," shee said, "both to
    the ale and wine,
    Alas! Then I must hyde my selfe, I must not goe withinne."

44. And then bespake him gentle Gawaine, said, "Lady, that's but
    skill;
    And because thou art my owne lady, thou shalt haue all thy
    will."

45. Then she said, "Blessed be thou, gentle Gawain, this day that I
    thee see,
    For as thou seest me att this time, from hencforth I wilbe.

46. "My father was an old knight, and yett it chanced soe
    That he marryed a younge lady that brought me to this woe.

47. "Shee witched me, being a faire young lady, to the greene forrest
    to dwell,

And there I must walke in woman's liknesse, most like a feend of hell.

48. She witched my brother to a carlish b . . .
. . . .

* * * * * *

49. . . . .
"That looked soe foule, and that was wont on the wild more to goe."

50. "Come kisse her, brother Kay," then said Sir Gawaine, "and amend the of thy liffe;
I sweare this is the same lady that I marryed to my wiffe."

51. Sir Kay kissed that lady bright, standing vpon his ffeete;
He swore, as he was trew knight, the spice was neuer soe sweete.

52. "Well, cozen Gawaine," sayes Sir Kay, "thy chance is fallen arright,
For thou hast gotten one of the fairest maids I euer saw with my sight."

53. "It is my fortune," said Sir Gawaine, "for my vnckle Arthur's sake
I am glad as grasse wold be of raine, great joy that I may take."

54. Sir Gawaine tooke the lady by the one arme, Sir Kay tooke her by the tother,
They led her straight to King Arthur, as they were brother and brother.

55. King Arthur welcomed them there all, and soe did Lady Geneuer, his queene,
With all the knights of the Round Table, most seemly to be seene.

56. King Arthur beheld that lady faire that was soe faire and bright,
He thanked Christ in Trinity for Sir Gawaine that gentle knight.

57. Soe did the knights, both mor and lesse, rejoyced all that day
For the good chance that hapened was to Sir Gawaine and his lady gay.

KING HENRY (32)

This ballad preserves a cruder version of the loathly lady story and perhaps one closer to the original. The ballad is a close analogue to the *Hrolfr Kraki* saga and to the Gaelic story "The Daughter of King Under-waves," found in such collections as Campbell's *Popular Tales of the West Highlands*. The missing stanza after 17 probably told of his receiving her into his bed, turning away from her or putting a fold of blanket between them. Why this should be told of a King Henry and which King Henry is impossible to answer.

Text, Scott, ii, 132.

1. Lat never a man a wooing wend
    That lacketh thingis three;
    A routh o gold, an open heart,
    Ay fu o charity.

2. As this I speak of King Henry,
    For he lay burd-alone;
    And he's doen him to a jelly hunt's ha,
    Was seven miles frae a town.

3. He chas'd the deer now him before,
    An the roe down by the den,
    Till the fattest buck in a' the flock
    King Henry he has slain.

4. O he has doen him to his ha,
    To make him beerly cheer;
    An in it came a griesly ghost,
    Steed stappin i the fleer.

5. Her head hat the reef-tree o the house,
    Her middle ye mot wel span;
    He's thrown to her his gay mantle,
    Says, "Lady, hap your lingean."

6. Her teeth was a' like teather stakes,
    Her nose like club or mell;
    As I ken naething she 'peard to be,
    But the fiend that wons in hell.

7. "Some meat, some meat, ye King Henry,
    Some meat ye gie to me!"
    "An what meat's in this house, lady,
    An what hal I to gie?"
    "O ye do kill your berry-brown steed,
    An you bring him here to me."

8. O whan he slew his berry-brown steed,
    Wow but his heart was sair!
  Shee eat him up, skin an bane,
    Left naething but hide an hair.

9. "Mair meat, mair meat, ye King Henry,
    Mair meat ye gi to me!"
  "An what meat's in this house, lady,
    And what ha I to gi?"
  "O ye do kill your good gray-hounds,
    An ye bring them a' to me."

10. O whan he slew his good gray-hounds,
    Wow but his heart was sair!
  She eat them a' up, skin and bane,
    Left naething but hide an hair.

11. "Mair meat, mair meat, ye King Henry,
    Mair meat ye gi to me!"
  "An what meat's i this house, lady,
    An what ha I go gi?"
  "O ye do kill your gay gos-hawks,
    An ye bring them here to me."

12. O whan he slew his gay gos-hawks,
    Wow but his heart was sair!
  She eat them a' up, skin an bane,
    Left naething but feathers bare.

13. "Some drink, some drink, now, King Henry,
    Some drink ye bring to me!"
  "O what drink's i this house, lady,
    That you're nae welcome ti?"
  "O ye sew up your horse's hide,
    And bring in a drink to me."

14. And he's sewd up the bloody hide,
    A puncheon o wine put in;
  She drank it a' up at a waught,
    Left na ae drap ahin.

15. "A bed, a bed, now King Henry,
    A bed you mak to me!
  For ye maun pu the heather green,
    An mak a bed to me."

16. O pu'd has he the heather green,
    An made to her a bed,
  An up has he taen his gay mantle,
    An o'er it has he spread.

17. "Tak aff your claiths, now, King Henry,
        An lye down by my side!"
     "O God forbid," says King Henry,
        "That ever the like betide;
     That ever the fiend that wons in hell
        Shoud streak down by my side."

*   *   *   *   *   *   *

18. Whan night was gane, and day was come,
        An the sun shone throw the ha,
     The fairest lady that ever was seen
        Lay atween him an the wa.

19. "O well is me," says King Henry,
        "How lang'll this last wi me?"
     Then out it spake that fair lady,
        "Even till the day you dee.

20. "For I've met wi mony a gentle knight
        That's gien me sic a fill,
     But never before wi a courteous knight
        That ga me a' my will."

KEMP OWYNE (34)

This spirited and highly dramatic ballad is a reworking of the common unspelling story. Many such stories are found in Scandinavian folklore. Owyne (Owain) is a romance hero; he is nowhere else associated with such an adventure as this.

Text, Buchan, ii, 78.

Notes

2/4. Craigy's sea: another version of this ballad reads Eastmuir craigs.

1. Her mother died when she was young,
        Which gave her cause to make great moan;
     Her father married the warst woman
        That ever lived in Christendom.

2. She served her with foot and hand,
        In every thing that she could dee,
     Till once, in an unlucky time,
        She threw her in ower Craigy's sea.

3. Says, "Lie you there, dove Isabel,
        And all my sorrows lie with thee;
     Till Kemp Owyne come ower the sea,
        And borrow you with kisses three,

Let all the warld do what they will,
Oh borrowed shall you never be."

4. Her breath grew strang, her hair grew lang,
    And twisted thrice about the tree,
And all the people, far and near,
    Thought that a savage beast was she.

5. These news did come to Kemp Owyne,
    Where he lived, far beyond the sea;
He hasted him to Craigy's sea,
    And on the savage beast lookd he.

6. Her breath was strang, her hair was lang,
    And twisted was about the tree,
And with a swing she came about:
    "Come to Craigy's sea, and kiss with me.

7. "Here is a royal belt," she cried,
    "That I have found in the green sea;
And while your body it is one,
    Drawn shall your blood never be;
But if you touch me, tail or fin,
    I vow my belt your death shall be."

8. He stepped in, gave her a kiss,
    The royal belt he brought him wi;
Her breath was strang, her hair was lang,
    And twisted twice about the tree,
And with a swing she came about:
    "Come to Craigy's sea, and kiss with me.

9. "Here is a royal ring," she said,
    "That I have found in the green sea;
And while your finger it is on,
    Drawn shall your blood never be;
But if you touch me, tail or fin,
    I swear my ring your death shall be."

10. He stepped in, gave her a kiss,
    The royal ring he brought him wi;
Her breath was strang, her hair was lang,
    And twisted ance about the tree,
And with a swing she came about:
    "Come to Craigy's sea, and kiss with me.

11. "Here is a royal brand," she said,
    "That I have found in the green sea;
And while your body it is on,
    Drawn shall your blood never be;

But if you touch me, tail or fin,
  I swear my brand your death shall be."

12. He stepped in, gave her a kiss,
       The royal brand he brought him wi;
     Her breath was sweet, her hair grew short,
       And twisted nane about the tree,
     And smilingly she came about,
       As fair a woman as fair could be.

ALLISON GROSS (35)

Another transformation ballad which tells how a witch transforms a
person into an ugly worm and how he was unspelled by the queen of
fairyland. The use of the first person and the close analogy with Scandinavian ballads suggest that this is derived from some northern
source. Why the witch blows the horn is not clear, nor is the function
of sister Maisry. *Sir Magnus and the Elf-Maid,* Prior, iii, 344, is included here for comparison.

Text, Jamieson, ii, 187.

Notes

11/3. *her* must refer to the witch.

1. O Allison Gross, that lives in yon towr,
      The ugliest witch i the north country,
    Has trysted me ae day up till her bowr,
      An monny fair speech she made to me.

2. She stroaked n.y head, an she kembed my hair,
      An she set me down saftly on her knee;
    Says, "Gin ye will be my lemman so true,
      Sae monny braw things as I woud you gi."

3. She showd me a mantle o red scarlet,
      Wi gouden flowrs an fringes fine;
    Says, "Gin ye will be my lemman so true,
      This goodly gift it sal be thine."

4. "Awa, awa, ye ugly witch,
      Haud far awa, an lat me be;
    I never will be your lemman sae true,
      An I wish I were out o your company."

5. She neist brought a sark o the saftest silk,
      Well wrought wi pearles about the ban;
    Says, "Gin you will be my ain true love,
      This goodly gift you sal comman."

6. She showd me a cup of the good red gold,
     Well set wi jewls sae fair to see;
   Says, "Gin you will be my lemman sae true,
     This goodly gift I will you gi."

7. "Awa, awa, ye ugly witch,
     Had far awa, and lat me be;
   For I woudna ance kiss your ugly mouth
     For a' the gifts that you could gi."

8. She's turnd her right and round about,
     An thrice she blaw on a grass-green horn,
   An she sware by the meen and the stars abeen,
     That she'd gar me rue the day I was born.

9. Then out has she taen a silver wand,
     An she's turnd her three times roun an roun;
   She's mutterd sich words till my strength it faild,
     An I fell down senceless upon the groun.

10. She's turnd me into an ugly worm,
     And gard me toddle about the tree;
   And ay, on ilka Saturdays night,
     My sister Maisry came to me.

11. Wi silver bason an silver kemb,
     To kemb my heady upon her knee;
   But or I had kissd her ugly mouth,
     I'd rather a toddled about the tree.

12. But as it fell out on last Hallow-even,
     When the seely court was ridin by,
   The queen lighted down on a gowany bank,
     Nae far frae the tree where I wont to lye.

13. She took me up in her milk-white han,
     An she's stroakd me three times o'er her knee;
   She chang'd me again to my ain proper shape,
     An I ane mair maun toddle about the tree.

SIR MAGNUS AND THE ELF-MAID

1. The maiden wooes the handsome knight
     To plight to her his troth,
   Would give him gifts to sleep with her
     Of gold and silver both.
   "O Magnus plight thy troth to me,
     "So longingly I pray;
   "And thou canst answer 'nay' or 'no,'
     "Or 'yea and yea and yea.'"

2.   "I'll give thee a richly broider'd shirt,
          "As fine as e'er was bought,
      "And every seam, there is therein,
          "With silken thread is wrought.
      "O Magnus etc.

3.   "I'll give thee too a horse to ride
          "So stout of wind and bone,
      "He walks as well on billows blue
          "As on the hardest stone.
      "O Magnus etc.

4.   "I'll give thee a ship with gold belaid;
          "Will stem the roughest seas;
      "Its sails are all of scarlet cloth,
          "It flies with every breeze.
      "O Magnus etc.

5.   "I'll give thee a costly sword of gold,
          "The best thou couldest wield;
      "With it the victory shall be thine
          "On every battle field.
      "O Magnus etc.

6.   "And hark! I'll give thee a falcon blue,
          "No swifter sits on bough;
      "Such precious gifts would I not miss,
          "Were I a knight as thou."
      "O Magnus etc.

7.   "Thee would I gladly wed, wert thou
          "Like other woman-kind;
      "But thou'rt as foul a mountain elf,
          "As one on earth may find."
      "O Magnus etc.

8.   The Knight girt up his good grey steed,
          To Rendsborg he would ride,
      But seiz'd his skirt the elfin maid,
          "Nay here shalt thou abide."
      "O Magnus etc.

9.   The Knight he drew the costly blade,
          And at his side he wore,
      And chopp'd the maid to bits as fine
          As sand on ocean shore.
      "O Magnus etc.

10.   The maiden turn'd to a blazing fire,
          And rose in angry flake,

And made the mightiest forest trees
To tremble all and quake.
"O Magnus etc.

THOMAS RYMER (37)

Although we have no copy of this ballad earlier than about 1725, the
story of Thomas Rymer in romance form and probably also in ballad
form is much older. Thomas Rymer is Thomas of Erceldoune who
lived in Erceldoune, now Earlstoun, in Scotland in the 13th century.
Various prophetic poems and gnomic verses are attached to his name.
They account for his reputation only a little less than that of Merlin
as a necromancer and prophet. He is the author too of a "romance,"
the oldest form of which is lost, in which he tells of his visit to fairyland, of receiving the gift of prophecy from the queen. He induces her
to give him prophecies. The whole story is probably based on the romance of Ogier le Danois and Morgan the Fay. In this story Ogier is
taken to Avalon to live with Morgan for 200 years, at the end of
which time he is allowed to return to France to fight the foes of
Christendom. That task accomplished, he returns to Avalon to live
through eternity with Morgan.

Text A, Jamieson, ii, 7; B, Scott, ii, 251.

Notes

2. Conventional description of the fairy folk, for they generally
dressed in green, with little bells hanging from the braided mane of
the horses. 3/3. Ogier also mistakes Morgan for Queen of Heaven.
7. Elfland is often pictured as under the world and surrounded with
water or reached only by crossing a river. Here the river of blood
may be reminiscent of the Norse river of blood fed by the blood of all
the men who have died in battle. Cf. B, 16/3-4. 8/3. Eating of the
fruit (usually an apple) in fairyland would bind him to that place
forever. Stanzas 12-13 recount material that is not part of the fairy
tradition, but rather indicates Christian influence.

B.1. Huntlie bank: situated along the river Leader not far from
Erceldoun. Locally there is the belief that the fairies often gather
here. 18. There is a belief that the fairy must pay a tribute of living
creatures to hell and that they seduce away or abduct mortals for this
purpose. Cf. "Tam Lin."

A.

1. True Thomas lay o'er yond grassy bank,
    And he beheld a ladie gay,
    A ladie that was brisk and bold,
    Come riding oer the fernie brae.

2. Her skirt was of the grass-green silk,
    Her mantel of the velvet fine,
   At ilka tett of her horse's mane
    Hung fifty silver bells and nine.

3. True Thomas he took off his hat,
    And bowed him low down till his knee:
   "All hail, thou mighty Queen of Heaven,
    For your peer on earth I never did see."

4. "O no, O no, true Thomas," she says,
    "That name does not belong to me,
   I am but the queen of fair Elfland,
    And I'm come here for to visit thee.

* * * * * * *

5. "But ye maun go wi me now, Thomas,
    True Thomas, ye maun go wi me,
   For ye maun serve me seven years,
    Thro well or wae as may chance to be."

6. She turned about her milk-white steed,
    And took true Thomas up behind,
   And aye wheneer her bridle rang,
    The steed flew swifter than the wind.

7. For forty days and forty nights
    He wade thro red blude to the knee,
   And he saw neither sun nor moon,
    But heard the roaring of the sea.

8. O they rade on, and further on,
    Until they came to a garden green:
   "Light down, light down, ye ladie free,
    Some of that fruit let me pull to thee."

9. "O no, O no, True Thomas," she says,
    "That fruit maun not be touched by thee,
   For a' the plagues that are in hell
    Light on the fruit of this countrie.

10. "But I have a loaf here in my lap,
     Likewise a bottle of claret wine,
    And now ere we go farther on,
     We'll rest a while, and ye may dine."

11. When he had eaten and drunk his fill,
     "Lay down your head upon my knee,"
    The lady sayd, "ere we climb yon hill,
     And I will show you fairlies three.

12. "O see not ye yon narrow road,
    So thick beset wi thorns and briers?
  That is the path of righteousness,
    Tho after it but few enquires.

13. "And see not ye that braid braid road,
    That lies across yon lillie leven?
  That is the path of wickedness,
    Tho some call it the road to heaven.

14. "And see not ye that bonny road,
    Which winds about the fernie brae?
  That is the road to fair Elfland,
    Where you and I this night maun gae.

15. "But Thomas, ye maun hold your tongue,
    Whatever you may hear or see,
  For gin ae word you should chance to speak,
    You will ne'er get back to your ain countrie."

16. He has gotten a coat of the even cloth,
    And a pair of shoes of velvet green,
  And till seven years were past and gone
    True Thomas on earth was never seen.

B.

1. True Thomas lay on Huntlie bank,
    A ferlie he spied wi' his ee,
  And there he saw a lady bright,
    Come riding down by the Eildon Tree.

2. Her shirt was o the grass-green silk,
    Her mantle o the velvet fyne,
  At ilka tett of her horse's mane
    Hang fifty silver bells and nine.

3. True Thomas, he pulld aff his cap,
    And louted low down to his knee:
  "All hail, thou mighty Queen of Heaven,
    For thy peer on earth I never did see."

4. "O no, O no, Thomas," she said,
    "That name does not belang to me;
  I am but the queen of fair Elfland,
    That am hither come to visit thee.

5. "Harp and carp, Thomas," she said,
    "Harp and carp along wi me,

And if ye dare to kiss my lips,
  Sure of your bodie I will be."

6. "Betide me weal, betide me woe,
   That weird shall never daunton me."
  Syne he has kissed her rosy lips,
   All underneath the Eildon Tree.

7. "Now, ye maun go wi me," she said,
   "True Thomas, ye maun go wi me,
  And ye maun serve me seven years,
   Thro weal or woe, as may chance to be."

8. She mounted on her milk-white steed,
   She's taen True Thomas up behind,
  And aye wheneer her bridle rund,
   The steed flew swifter than the wind.

9. O they rade on, and farther on—
   The steed gaed swifter than the wind—
  Untill they reached a desart wide,
   And living land was left behind.

10. "Light down, light down, now, true Thomas,
    And lean your head upon my knee;
  Abide and rest a little speace,
    And I will shew you ferlies three.

11. "O see ye not yon narrow road,
    So thick beset with thorns and briers?
  That is the path of righteousness,
    Tho after it but few enquires.

12. "And see not ye that braid braid road,
    That lies across that lily leven?
  That is the path of wickedness,
    Tho some call it the road to heaven.

13. "And see not ye that bonny road,
    That winds about the fernie brae?
  That is the road to fair Elfland,
    Where thou and I this night maun gae.

14. "But, Thomas, ye maun hold your tongue,
    Whatever ye may hear or see,
  For, if you speak word in Elflyn land,
    Ye'll neer get back to your ain countrie."

15. O they rade on, and farther on,
    And they waded thro rivers aboon the knee,

And they saw neither sun nor moon,
But they heard the roaring of the sea.

16. It was mirk, mirk night, and there was nae stern light,
And they waded thro red blude to the knee;
For a' the blude that's shed on earth
Rins thro the springs o that countrie.

17. Syne they came on to a garden green,
And she pu'd an apple frae a tree:
"Take this for thy wages, true Thomas,
It will give the tongue that can never lie."

18. "My tongue is mine ain," true Thomas said;
"A gudely gift ye wad gie to me.
I neither dought to buy nor sell,
At fair or tryst where I may be.

19. "I dought neither speak to prince or peer,
Nor ask of grace from fair ladye."
"Now hold thy peace," the lady said,
"For as I say, so mist it be."

20. He has gotten a coat of the even cloth,
And a pair of shoes of velvet green,
And till seven years were gane and past
True Thomas on earth was never seen.

THE WEE WEE MAN (38)

The several versions of this lively Scotch fairy ballad tell very much
the same story. Traditionally the fairy is strong and traditionally the
fairy folk dance on the green and disappear in a twinkling. The fairy
palace, gorgeously splendid, which can also vanish instantly is generally
found, especially in romance.

Text, Herd, i, 95.

1. As I was wa'king all alone,
Between a water and a wa,
And there I spy'd a wee, wee man,
And he was the least that ere I saw.

2. His legs ere scarce a shathmont's length,
And thick and thimber was his thigh;
Between his brows there was a span,
And between his shoulders there was three.

3. He took up a meikle stane,

And he flang 't as far as I could see;
Though I had been a Wallace wight,
   I couldna liften 't to my knee.

4. "O wee, wee man, but thou be strang!
    O tell me where thy dwelling be?"
   "My dwelling's down at yon bonny bower;
    O will you go with me and see?"

5. On we lap, and awa we rade,
    Till we came to yon bonny green;
   We lighted down for to bait our horse,
    And out there came a lady fine.

6. Four and twenty at her back,
    And they were a' clad out in green;
   Though the King of Scotland had been there,
    The warst o them might hae been his queen.

7. On we lap, and awa we rade,
    Till we came to yon bonny ha,
   Whare the roof was o the beaten gould,
    And the floor was o the cristal a'.

8. When we came to the stair-foot,
    Ladies were dancing, jimp and sma,
   But in the twinkling of an eye,
    My wee, wee man was clean awa.

.

TAM LIN (39)

This finest of the fairy ballads is mentioned in 1549 as being old. It is unique in Scotland, where some dozen versions have been found. Though no ballad like "Tam Lin" exists, stories of the recovery of a loved one from the fairies or gods are very common and old.

   Text from Robert Burns and printed in Johnson's *Museum*, p. 423.

Notes

   1/3. Carterhaugh: According to the Glenriddell MS., in which one version of this ballad is found, Carterhaugh is a plain on the Yarrow near Selkirk and "on the plain they show two or three rings on the ground where, they say, the stands of milk and water stood and upon which grass never grows." 3. Note the interesting use of this six-line stanza as a kind of refrain to mark the changes of action. 5. The pulling of a rose, or a nut, or a sloe berry, etc., is a conventional method of summoning the lord of the fairy garden. 12. Note the dramatic nature of the dialogue and compare with 13. 16/3. Only fairy steeds would be so expensively and so inappropriately shod.

20. In other versions he warns her earlier not to pull the flower "that has these pimples grey; they would destroy the bonny babe." And in several versions it is her brother who sends her back to Carterhaugh to pull a certain plant that will rid her of her bairn. 26/4. Miles Cross: Probably a crossroad but might be a roadside shrine with a crucifix. Either place would give her protection against any supernatural creature.

After stanza 7 two or three stanzas have been omitted. They are here supplied from the version in Greig's *Last Leaves*.

> He's taen her by the milk-white han'
> Below the grass-green sleeve,
> An' he's laid her low at the foot of a wand
> An' never ance speired her leave.

> She turned her richt an' roon aboot
> To ask her true love's name;
> But she nothing heard, an' she nothing saw,
> But all the woods grew dim.

1. O I forbid you, maidens a',
     That wear gowd on your hair,
   To come or gae by Carterhaugh,
     For young Tam Lin is there.

2. There's nane that gaes by Carterhaugh
     But they leave him a wad,
   Either their rings, or green mantles,
     Or else their maidenhead.

3. Janet has kilted her green kirtle
     A little aboon her knee,
   And she has broded her yellow hair
     A little aboon her bree,
   And she's awa to Carterhaugh,
     As fast as she can hie.

4. When she came to Carterhaugh
     Tam Lin was at the well,
   And there she fand his steed standing,
     But away was himsel.

5. She had na pu'd a double rose,
     A rose but only twa,
   Till up then started young Tam Lin,
     Says, "Lady, thou's pu nae mae.

6. "Why pu's thou the rose, Janet,
     And why breaks thou the wand?
   Or why comes thou to Carterhaugh
     Withoutten my command?"

7. "Carterhaugh, it is my ain,
　　My daddie gave it me;
　I'll come and gang by Carterhaugh,
　　And ask nae leave at thee."

*　*　*　*　*　*　*

8. Janet has kilted her green kirtle
　　A little aboon her knee,
　And she has snooded her yellow hair
　　A little aboon her bree,
　And she is to her father's ha,
　　As fast as she can hie.

9. Four and twenty laides fair
　　Were playing at the ba,
　And out then cam the fair Janet,
　　Ance the flower amang them a'.

10. Four and twenty ladies fair
　　Were playing at the chess,
　And out then cam the fair Janet,
　　As green as onie glass.

11. Out then spak an auld grey knight,
　　Lay o'er the castle wa,
　And says, "Alas, fair Janet, for thee
　　But we'll be blamed a'."

12. "Haud your tongue, ye auld fac'd knight,
　　Some ill death may ye die!
　Father my bairn on whom I will,
　　I'll father nane on thee."

13. Out then spak her father dear,
　　And he spak meek and mild,
　"And ever alas, sweet Janet," he says,
　　"I think thou gaes wi child."

14. "If I gae wi child, father,
　　My sel maun bear the blame;
　There's neer a laird about your ha
　　Shall get the bairn's name.

15. "If my lover were an earthly knight,
　　As he's an elfin grey,
　I wad na gie my ain true-love
　　For nae lord that ye hae.

16. "The steed that my true-love rides on
　　Is lighter than the wind;

Wi siller he is shod before,
Wi burning gowd behind."

17. Janet has kilted her green kirtle
A little aboon her knee,
And she has snooded her yellow hair
A little aboon her bree,
And she's awa to Carterhaugh,
As fast as she can hie.

18. When she cam to Carterhaugh,
Tam Lin was at the well,
And there she fand his steed standing,
But away was himsel.

19. She had na pu'd a double rose,
A rose but only twa,
Till up then started young Tam Lin,
Says Lady, "Thou pu's nae mae.

20. "Why pu's thou the rose, Janet
Amang the groves sae green,
And a' to kill the bonie babe
That we gat us between?"

21. "O tell me, tell me, Tam Lin," she says,
"For's sake that died on tree,
If e'er ye was in holy chapel,
Or christendom did see?"

22. "Roxbrugh he was my grandfather,
Took me with him to bide,
And ance it fell upon a day
That wae did me betide.

23. "And ance it fell upon a day,
A cauld day and a snell,
When we were frae the hunting come,
That frae my horse I fell;
The Queen o Fairies she caught me,
In yon green hill to dwell.

24. "And pleasant is the fairy land,
But, an eerie tale to tell,
Ay at the end of seven years,
We pay a tiend to hell;
I am sae fair and fu o flesh,
I'm feard it be mysel.

25. "But the night is Halloween, lady,
The morn is hallowday;

Then win me, win me, an ye will,
  For weel I wat ye may.

26. "Just at the mirk and midnight hour
    The fairy folk will ride,
And they that wad their true-love win,
  At Miles Cross they maun bide."

27. "But how shall I thee ken, Tam Lin,
    Or how my true-love know,
Amang sae many unco knights
  The like I never saw?"

28. "O first let pass the black, lady,
    And syne let pass the brown,
But quickly run to the milk-white steed,
  Pu ye his rider down.

29. "For I'll ride on the milk-white steed,
    And ay nearest the town;
Because I was na earthly knight
  They gie me that renown.

30. "My right hand will be glovd, lady,
    My left hand will be bare,
Cockt up shall my bonnet be,
  And kaimd down shall my hair,
And thae's the takens I gie thee,
  Nae doubt I will be there.

31. "They'll turn me in your arms, lady,
    Into an esk and adder;
But hold me fast, and fear me not,
  I am your bairn's father.

32. "They'll turn me to a bear sae grim,
    And then a lion bold;
But hold me fast, and fear me not,
  As ye shall love your child.

33. "Again they'll turn me in your arms
    To a red het gaud of airn;
But hold me fast, and fear me not,
  I'll do to you nae harm.

34. "And last they'll turn me in your arms
    Into the burning gleed;
Then throw me into well water,
  O throw me in wi speed.

35. "And then I'll be your ain true-love,
    I'll turn a naked knight;

Then cover me wi your green mantle,
And cover me out o sight."

36. Gloomy, gloomy was the night,
And eerie was the way,
As fair Jenny in her green mantle
To Miles Cross she did gae.

37. About the middle o the night
She heard the bridles ring;
This lady was a glad at that
As any earthly thing.

38. First she let the black pass by,
And syne she let the brown;
But quickly she ran to the milk-white steed,
And pu'd the rider down.

39. Sae well she minded whae he did say,
And young Tam Lin did win;
Syne coverd him wi her green mantle,
As blythe's a bird in spring.

40. Out then spak the Queen of Fairies,
Out of a bush o broom:
"Them that has gotten young Tam Lin
Has gotten a stately groom."

41. Out then spak the Queen of Fairies,
And an angry woman was she:
"Shame betide her ill-far'd face,
And an ill death my she die,
For she's taen awa the boniest knight
In a' my companie.

42. "But had I kend, Tam Lin," she says,
"What now this night I see,
I wad hae taen out thy twa grey een,
And put in twa een o tree."

HIND ETIN (41)

This is a pan-Germanic ballad with many versions in every Germanic
language except English. In English only three texts are known and
they are all corrupt. The basic story tells of a girl who is seduced
away to the wood through the strange music of a dwarf or *etin* and
there she lives with him in a cave, bearing him seven children (or she

visits him periodically and the children are snatched away to the wood as they are born). In some versions she escapes, leaving her children; in others, she escapes, only to be taken back by the dwarf. Often the husband's home is in a cave, but sometimes it is under the sea and he is pictured as a merman. Printed here is such a story from the Danish.

Stanzas 15–16 and 48 to the end of Text A are probably supplied by the editor, Peter Buchan.

Text A, Buchan, i, 6; B, Prior, iii, 339.

A.

1. Lady Margaret sits in her bower door,
      Sewing at her silken seam;
    She heard a note in Elmond's wood,
      And wishd she there had been.

2. She loot the seam fa frae her side,
      And the needle to her tae,
    And she is on to Elmond's wood
      As fast as she could gae.

3. She hadna pu'd a nut, a nut,
      Nor broken a branch but ane,
    Till by it came a young hind chiel,
      Says, "Lady, lat alane.

4. "O why pu ye the nut, the nut,
      Or why brake ye the tree?
    For I am forester o this wood:
      Ye shoud spier leave at me."

5. "I'll ask leave at no living man,
      Nor yet will I at thee;
    My father is king o'er a' this realm,
      This wood belongs to me."

6. She hada pu'd a nut, a nut,
      Nor broken a branch but three,
    Till by it came him Young Akin,
      And gard her lat them be.

7. The highest tree in Elmond's wood,
      He's pu'd it by the reet,
    And he has built for her a bower,
      Near by a hallow seat.

8. He's built a bower, made it secure
      Wi carbuncle and stane;
    Tho travellers were never sae nigh,
      Appearance it had nane.

9. He's kept her there in Elmond's wood,
   For six lang years and one,
   Till six pretty sons to him she bear,
   And the seventh she's brought home.

10. It fell ance upon a day,
    This guid lord went from home,
    And he is to the hunting gane,
    Took wi him his eldest son.

11. And when they were on a guid way,
    Wi slowly pace did walk,
    The boy's heart being something wae,
    He thus began to talk:

12. "A question I woud ask, father,
    Gin ye woudna angry be."
    "Say on, say on, my bonny boy,
    "Ye 'se nae be quarrelld by me."

13. "I see my mither's cheeks aye weet,
    I never can see them dry;
    And I wonder what aileth my mither,
    To mourn continually."

14. "Your mither was a king's daughter,
    Sprung frae a high degree,
    And she might hae wed some worthy prince,
    Had she nae been stown by me.

15. "I was her father's cup-bearer,
    Just at that fatal time;
    I catchd her on a misty night,
    When summer was in prime.

16. "My luve to her was most sincere,
    Her luve was great for me,
    But when she hardships doth endure,
    Her folly she does see."

17. "I'll shoot the buntin o the bush,
    The linnet o the tree,
    And bring them to my dear mither,
    See if she'll merrier be."

18. It fell upo another day,
    This guid lord he thought lang,
    And he is to the hunting gane,
    Took wi him his dog and gun.

19. Wi bow and arrow by his side,
    He's aff, single, alane,

And left his seven children to stay
    Wi their mither at hame.

20.   "O I will tell to you, mither,
          Gin ye wadna angry be."
      "Speak on, speak on, my little wee boy,
          Ye'se nae be quarrelld by me."

21.   "As we came frae the hynd-hunting,
          We heard fine music ring."
      "My blessings on you, my bonny boy,
          I wish I'd been there my lane."

22.   He's taen his mither by the hand,
          His six brithers also,
      And they are on thro Elmond's wood,
          As fast as they coud go.

23.   They wistna weel where they were gaen,
          Wi the stratlins o their feet;
      They wistna weel where they were gaen,
          Till at her father's yate.

24.   "I hae nae money in my pocket,
          But royal rings hae three;
      I'll gie them you, my little young son,
          And ye'll walk there for me.

25.   "Ye'll gie the first to the proud porter,
          And he will lat you in;
      Ye'll gie the next to the butler-boy,
          And he will show you ben;

26.   "Ye'll gie the third to the minstrel
          That plays before the king;
      He'll play success to the bonny boy
          Came thro the wood him lane."

27.   He gae the first to the proud porter,
          And he opend an let him in;
      He gae the next to the butler-boy,
          And he has shown him ben;

28.   He gae the third to the minstrel
          That playd before the king;
      And he playd success to the bonny boy
          Came thro the wood him lane.

29.   Now when he came before the king,
          Fell low down on his knee;
      The king he turned round about,
          And the saut tear blinded his ee.

30. "Win up, win up, my bonny boy,
    Gang frae my companie;
    Ye look sae like my dear daughter,
    My heart will birst in three."

31. "If I look like your dear daughter,
    A wonder it is none;
    If I look like your dear daughter,
    I am her eldest son."

32. "Will ye tell me, ye little wee boy,
    Where may my Margaret be?"
    "She's just now standing at your yates,
    And my six brithers her wi."

33. "O where are all my porter-boys
    That I pay meat and fee,
    To open my yates baith wide and braid?
    Let her come in to me."

34. When she came in before the king,
    Fell low down on her knee.
    "Win up, win up, my daughter dear,
    This day ye'll dine wi me."

35. "Ae bit I canno eat, father,
    Nor ae drop can I drink,
    Till I see my mither and sister dear,
    For lang for them I think."

36. When she came before the queen,
    Fell low down on her knee;
    "Win up, win up, my daughter dear
    This day ye'se dine wi me."

37. "Ae bit I canno eat, mither,
    Nor ae drop can I drink,
    Until I see my dear sister,
    For lang for her I think."

38. When that these two sister met,
    She haild her courteouslie;
    "Come ben, come ben, my sister dear,
    This day ye 'se dine wi me."

39. "Ae bit I canno eat, sister,
    Nor ae drop can I drink,
    Until I see my dear husband,
    For lang for him I think."

40. "O where are all my rangers bold
  That I pay meat and fee,
To search the forest far an wide,
  And bring Akin to me?"

41. Out it speaks the little wee boy:
  Na, na, this maunna be;
Without ye grant a free pardon,
  I hope ye'll nae him see.

42. "O here I grant a free pardon,
  Well seald by my own han;
Ye may make search for Young Akin,
  As soon as ever you can."

43. They searched the country wide and braid,
  The forest far and near,
And found him into Elmond's wood,
  Tearing his yellow hair.

44. "Win up, win up now, Young Akin,
  Win up, and boun wi me;
We're messengers come from the court,
  The king wants you to see."

45. "O lat him take frae me my head,
  Or hang me on a tree;
For since I've lost my dear lady,
  Life's no pleasure to me."

46. "Your head will nae be touchd, Akin,
  Nor hangd upon a tree;
Your lady's in her father's court,
  And all he wants is thee."

47. When he came in before the king,
  Fell low down on his knee;
"Win up, win up now, Young Akin,
  This day ye 'se dine wi me."

48. But as they were at dinner set,
  The boy asked a boun:
"I wish we were in the good church,
  For to get christendoun.

49. "We hae lived in guid green wood
  This seven years and ane;
But a' this time, since e'er I mind,
  Was never a church within."

50. "Your asking's nae sae great, my boy,
    But granted it shall be;
    This day to guid church ye shall gang,
    And your mither shall gang you wi."

51. When unto the guid church she came,
    She at the door did stan;
    She was sae sair sunk down wi shame,
    She coudna come farer ben.

52. Then out it speaks the parish priest,
    And a sweet smile gae he;
    "Come ben, come ben, my lily flower,
    Present your babes to me.'

53. Charles, Vincent, Sam, and Dick,
    And likewise James and John;
    They calld the eldest Young Akin,
    Which was his father's name.

54. Then they staid in the royal court,
    And livd wi mirth and glee,
    And when her father was deceasd,
    Heir of the crown was she.

B.

THE LADY AND THE DWARF-KING

1. Fair Hermeline ask'd her father dear,
        The time drives on so slow
   "O might I to church a mass to hear?"
        So heavy the weight of woe.

2. "Yes surely, my daughter, I grant thy prayer,
   But be of the mountain dwarf beware."

3. In purple and gold the maid was dight,
   And all her fingers with gold were bright.

4. Fair Hermeline went by a small green lane,
   The Dwarf by the highroad across the plain.

5. Away to his cavern he drew the maid,
   And eight long years in the hill she stay'd.

6. She lived in his cave eight years or more,
   And there to the Dwarf seven sons she bore.

7. Fair Hermeline came and bent her knee;
   "O may I my father go and see?"

8. "Yes surely thou may'st to thy father go,
But say not a word of thy fate below."

9. "Nay that will I not; have thou no fear,
That anything reach my father's ear."

10. Fair Hermeline came to her home once more,
Her father was standing before his door.

11. "O Hermeline, answer child, and say,
Where hast thou been living so many a day?"

12. "I've dwelt so long in a mountain cave,
And borne to the Dwarf seven sons so brave."

13. "Go then to the table, my child and eat,
('Tis long thou has tasted no christian meat")

14. Fair Hermeline went to the board and ate,
The Dwarf knocked loud at her father's gate.

15. "What is it fair Hermeline talks of me?"
"'Tis nothing at all I have said of thee.

16. "I say that all honor to me he shows,
I say that his heart no malice knows."

17. The Dwarf on her lap gold apples threw
(That home to the cavern his lady drew.)

18. Fair Hermeline up from the table sprang,
The apples of gold they clashed and rang.

19. As Hermeline came to the mountain cave,
The Dwarf on her ear a buffet gave.

20. As came fair Hermeline under ground,
To welcome her stood her children round.

21. He whipp't her on with a birchen rod,
And sullen and vengeful in she trod.

22. Her first little boy, he brought a chair,
The second, he prayed her be seated there.

23. The third to his mother the water gave,
The fourth, he prayed her therin to lave.

24. The fifth with a napkin was near her side,
The sixth stood by, till her limbs were dried.

25. The seventh was her comfort, for he in time
Will surely avenge his father's crime.

CLERK COLVILLE (42)

This is an international ballad with excellent versions all over Europe. Again the English is corrupt and confused. The original story concerns a man who has loved a water sprite or a mermaid and has renounced her for a mortal love. He visits the mermaid afer he has been married and she contrives his death.
Text, Herd, i, 161.

Notes
2/4. His wife evidently knows about the water-sprite mistress; she does not in the European versions. There the young man is told by his mistress that he will die in three days if he deserts her. At stanza 6 a portion of the ballad has been lost; it probably told how she caused his sickness, for the European versions tell of her harming him by elf-knife wounds, a blow on the head, poison, etc. 8. She continues to work her destruction of him by getting him to bind a bit of her shirt around his head. Perhaps contact with her garment is enough to work the spell, but probably what is meant is that, once he has put the gore from her sark around his head, he cannot remove it and it magically gets tighter and tighter.

1. Clerk Colvill and his lusty dame
   Were walking in the garden green;
   The belt around her stately waist
   Cost Clerk Colvill of pounds fifteen.

2. "O promise me now, Clerk Colvill,
   Or it will cost ye muckle strife,
   Ride never by the wells of Slane,
   If ye wad live and brook your life."

3. "Now speak nae mair, my lusty dame,
   Now speak nae mair of that to me;
   Did I ne'er see a fair woman,
   But I wad sin with her body?"

4. He's taen leave o his gay lady,
   Nought minding what his lady said,
   And he's rode by the wells of Slane,
   Where washing was a bonny maid.

5. "Wash on, wash on, my bonny maid,
   That wash sae clean your sark of silk;"
   "And weel fa you, fair gentleman,
   Your body whiter than the milk."

6. Then loud, loud cry'd the Clerk Colvill,
   "O my head it pains me sair."

"Then take, then take," the maiden said,
"And frae my sark you'll cut a gare."

7. Then she's gied him a little bane-knife,
And frae her sark he cut a share;
She's ty'd it round his whey-white face,
But ay his head it aked mair.

8. Then louder cry'd the Clerk Colvill,
"O sairer, sairer akes my head."
"And sairer, sairer ever will,"
The maiden crys, "till you be dead."

9. Out then he drew his shining blade,
Thinking to stick her where she stood
But she was vanished to a fish,
And swam far off, a fair mermaid.

10. "O mother, mother, braid my hair;
My lusty lady, make my bed;
O brother, take my sword and spear,
For I have seen the false mermaid."

THE BROOMFIELD HILL (43)

This ballad may possibly be 15th or 16th century. It tells in ballad
form a merry anecdote that is told and retold in the literatures of
Europe. As would be expected, it is in such collections as the *Gesta
Romanorum* and the *Seven Wise Masters*.

Text, Scott, iii, 271.

Notes

5. Evidently the witch worked sleep magic on him at a distance.
6/3. To make him sleep the deeper in some versions; here it would
seem simply to tell him she was there. In some versions the girl makes
a wager that she can go to the young man and return maiden home.

1. There was a knight and a lady bright,
Had a true tryste at the broom;
The ane gaed early in the morning,
The other in the afternoon.

2. And ay she sat in her mother's bower door,
And ay she made her mane:
"O whether should I gang to the Broomfield Hill,
Or should I stay at hame?

3. "For if I gang to the Broomfield Hill,
My maidenhead is gone;

And if I chance to stay at hame,
My love will ca me mansworn."

4. Up then speake a witch-woman,
Ay from the room aboon:
"O ye may gang to the Broomfield Hill,
And yet come maiden hame.

5. "For when ye gang to the Broomfield Hill
Ye'll find your love asleep,
With a silver belt about his head,
And a broom-cow at his feet.

6. "Take ye the blossom of the broom,
The blossom it smells sweet,
And strew it at your true-love's head,
And likewise at his feet.

7. "Take ye the rings off your fingers,
Put them on his right hand,
To let him know, when he doth awake,
His love was at his command.

8. She pu'd the broom flower on Hive Hill,
And strewd on 's white hals-bane,
And that was to be wittering true
That maiden she had gane.

9. "O where were ye, my milk-white steed,
That I hae coft sae dear,
That wadna watch and waken me
When there was maiden here?"

10. "I stamped wi my foot, master,
And gard my bridle ring,
But na kin thing wald waken ye,
Till she was past and gane."

11. "And wae betide ye, my gay goss-hawk,
That I did love sae dear,
That wadna watch and waken me
When there was maiden here."

12. "I clapped wi my wings, master,
And aye my bells I rang,
And aye cry'd 'Waken, waken, master,'
Before the ladye gang."

13. "But haste and haste, my gude white steed,
To come the maiden till,
Or a' the birds of gude green wood
Of your flesh whall have their fill."

14.   "Ye need na burst your gude white steed
       Wi racing oer the howm;
Nae bird flies faster through the wood,
       Than she fled through the broom."

THE TWA MAGICIANS (44)

A very popular European ballad, found everywhere in a variety of details. This ballad story ultimately goes back to the type of folk tale in which the pursued turns itself into first one thing and then another to escape the pursuer, but the pursuer usually can cap any disguise assumed. The English ballad lacks the grace and sprightliness of most of the European versions.

Text, Buchan, i, 24.

1.   The lady stands in her bower door,
          As straight as willow wand;
      The blacksmith stood a little forebye,
          Wi hammer in his hand.

2.   "Weel may ye dress ye, lady fair,
          Into your robes o red,
      Before the morn at this same time,
          I'll gain your maidenhead."

3.   "Away, away, ye coal-black smith,
          Woud ye do me the wrang
      To think to gain my maidenhead,
          That I hae kept sae lang."

4.   Then she has hadden up her hand,
          And she sware by the mold,
      "I wudna be a blacksmith's wife
          For the full o a chest o gold.

5.   "I'd rather I were dead and gone,
          And my body laid in grave,
      Ere a rusty stock o coal-black smith
          My maidenhead shoud have."

6.   But he has hadden up his hand,
          And he sware by the mass,
      "I'll cause ye be my light leman
          For the hauf o that and less."

          O bide, lady, bide,
              And aye he bade her bide;
          The rusty smith your leman shall be,
              For a' your muckle pride.

7. Then she became a turtle dow,
   To fly up in the air,
   And he became another dow,
   And they flew pair and pair.

   O bide, lady, bide, &c.

8. She turnd hersell into an eel,
   To swim into youn burn,
   And he became a speckled trout,
   To gie the eel a turn.

   O bide, lady, bide, &c.

9. Then she became a duck, a duck,
   To puddle in a peel,
   And he became a rose-kaimd drake,
   To gie the duck a dreel.

   O bide, lady, bide, &c.

10. She turnd hersell into a hare,
    To rin upon yon hill,
    And he became a gude grey-hound,
    And boldly he did fill.

    O bide, lady, bide, &c.

11. Then she became a gay grey mare,
    And stood in yonder slack,
    And he became a gilt saddle,
    And sat upon her back.

    Was she wae, he hald her sae,
    And still he bade her bide;
    The rusty smith her leman was,
    For a' her muckle pride.

12. Then she became a het girdle,
    And he became a cake,
    And a' the ways she turnd hersell,
    The blacksmith was her make.

    Was she wae, &c.

13. She turnd hersell into a ship,
    To sail out ower the flood;
    He ca'ed a nail intill her tail,
    And syne the ship she stood.

    Was she wae, &c.

14. Then she became a silken plaid,
    And stretchd upon a bed,

And he became a green coverning,
And gaind her maidenhead.

Was she wae, &c.

KING JOHN AND THE BISHOP (45)

Riddle ballads are popular everywhere. The situation here seems to be oriental in origin. A story very like this is to be found in an Arabic historical work of the 9th century. Can the confusion be here between John and Henry II whose quarrel with the archbishop was notorious?
Text, Percy, p. 184.

1. Off an ancient story I'll tell you anon,
   Of a notable prince that was called King Iohn,
   In England was borne, with maine and with might;
   Hee did much wrong and mainteined litle right.

2. This noble prince was vexed in veretye,
   For he was angry with the Bishopp of Canterbury;
   Ffor his house-keeping and his good cheere,
   They rode post for him, as you shall heare.

3. They rode post for him verry hastilye;
   The king sayd the bishopp kept a better house then hee:
   A hundred men euen, as I (have heard) say,
   The bishopp kept in his house euerye day,
   And fifty gold chaines, without any doubt,
   In veluett coates waited the bishopp about.

4. The bishopp, he came to the court anon,
   Before his prince that was called King Iohn.
   As soone as the bishopp the king did see,
   "O," quoth the king, "the bishopp, thow art welcome to mee.
   There is noe man soe welcome to towne
   As thou that workes treason against my crowne."

5. "My leege," quoth the bishopp, "I wold it were knowne
   I spend, your grace, nothing but that that's my owne;
   I trust your grace will doe me noe deare
   For spending my owne trew gotten geere."

6. "Yes," quoth the king, "bishopp, thou must needs dye,
   Except thou can answere mee questions three;
   Thy head shalbe smitten quite from thy bodye,
   And all thy liuing remayne vnto mee."

7. "First," quoth the king, "tell me in this steade.
   With this crowne of gold heere vpon my head,

Amongst my nobilitye, with ioy and much mirth,
Lett me know within one pennye what I am worth.

8.   "Secondlye, tell me without any dowbt
How soone I may goe the whole world about;
And thirdly, tell me or euer I stinte,
What is the thing, bishopp, that I doe thinke.
Twenty dayes pardon thoust haue trulye,
And come againe and answere mee."

9.   The bishopp bade the king god night att a word;
He rode betwixt Cambridge and Oxenford,
But neuer a doctor there was soe wise
Cold shew him these questions or enterprise.

10. Wherein with bishopp was nothing gladd,
But in his hart was heauy and sadd,
And hyed him home to a house in the countrye,
To ease some part of his melanchollye.

11. His halfe-brother dwelt there, was feirce and fell,
Noe better but a shepard to the bishoppe himsell;
The shepard came to the bishopp anon,
Saying, My Lord, you are welcome home!

12. "What ayles you," quoth the shepard, "that you are soe sadd,
And had wonte to haue beene soe merry and gladd?"
"Nothing," quoth the bishopp, "I ayle att this time;
Will not thee availe to know, brother mine."

13. "Brother," quoth the shepard, "you haue heard itt,
That a ffoole may teach a wisemane witt;
Say me therfore whatsoeuer you will,
And if I doe you noe good, I'le doe you noe ill."

14. Quoth the bishop: "I haue beene att the court anon,
Before my prince is called King Iohn,
And there he hath charged mee
Against his crowne with traitorye.

15. "If I cannott answer his misterye,
Three questions hee hath propounded to mee,
He will haue my land soe faire and free,
And alsoe the head from my bodye.

16. "The first question was, to tell him in that stead,
With the crowne of gold vpon his head,
Amongst his nobilitye, with ioy and much mirth,
To lett him know within one penye what hee is worth.

17.   "And secondlye, to tell him with-out any doubt
How soone he may goe the whole world about;
And thirdlye, to tell him, or ere I stint,
What is the thinge that he does thinke."

18.   "Brother," quoth the shepard, "you are a man of learninge;
What neede you stand in doubt of soe small a thinge?
Lend me," quoth the shepard, "your minister's apparrell,
I'le ryde to the court and answere your quarrell.

19.   "Lend me your serving men, say me not nay,
With all your best horsses that ryd on the way;
I'le to the court, this matter to stay;
I'le speake with King John and heare what heele say."

20.   The bishopp with speed prepared then
To sett forth the shepard with horsse and man;
The shepard was liuely without any doubt;
I wott a royall companye came to the court.

21.   The shepard hee came to the court anon
Before his prince that was called King Iohn.
As soone as the king the shepard did see,
"O," quoth the king, "bishopp, thou art welcome to me."
The shepard was soe like the bishopp his brother,
The king cold not know the one from the other.

22.   Quoth the king, "Bishopp, thou art welcome to me
If thou can answer me my questions three."
Said the shepeard, "If it please your grace,
Show mee what the first question was."

23.   "First," quoth the king, "tell me in this stead,
With the crowne of gold vpon my head,
Amongst my nobilitye, with ioy and much mirth,
Within one pennye what I am worth."

24.   Quoth the shepard, "To make your grace noe offence,
I thinke you are worth nine and twenty pence;
For our Lord Iesus, that bought vs all,
For thirty pence was sold into thrall
Amongst the cursed Iewes, as I to you doe showe;
But I know Christ was one penye better then you."

25.   Then the king laught, and swore by St. Andrew
He was not thought to bee of such a small value.
"Secondlye, tell mee with-out any doubt
How soone I may goe the world round about."

26.   Saies the shepard, "It is noe time with your grace to scorne,
But rise betime with the sun in the morne,

And follow his course till his vprising,
And then you may know without any leasing."

27. "And this to your grace shall proue the same,
You are come to the same place from whence you came:
In twenty-four houres, with-out any doubt,
Your grace may the world goe round about;
The world round about, euen as I doe say,
If with the sun you can goe the next way."

28. "And thirdlye tell me or euer I stint,
What is the thing, bishoppe, that I doe thinke."
"That shall I doe," quoth the shepeard; "for veretye,
You thinke I am the bishopp of Canterburye."

29. "Why, art not thou? The truth tell to me;
For I doe thinke soe," quoth the king, "by St. Marye."
"Not soe," quoth the shepeard; "the truth shal be knowne,
I am his poore shepeard; my brother is att home."

30. "Why," quoth the king, "if itt soe bee,
I'le make thee bishopp here to mee."
"Noe, Sir," quoth the shepard, "I pray you be still,
For I'le not bee bishop but against my will;
For I am not fitt for any such deede,
For I can neither write nor reede."

31. "Why then," quoth the king, "I'le giue thee cleere
A pattent of three hundred pound a yeere;
That I will giue thee franke and free;
Take thee that, shepard, for coming to me.

32. "Free pardon I'le giue," the king's grace said,
"To saue the bishopp, his land and his head;
With him nor thee I'le be nothing wrath;
Here is the pardon for him and thee both."

33. Then the shepard he had noe more to say,
But tooke the pardon and rode his way:
When he came to the bishopp's place,
The bishopp asket anon how all things was.

34. "Brother," quoth the shepard, "I haue well sped,
For I haue saued both your land and your head;
The king with you is nothing wrath,
For heere is the pardon for you and mee both."

35. Then the bishope's hart was of a merry cheere:
"Brother, thy paines I'le quitt them cleere;
For I will giue thee a patent to thee and to thine
Of fifty pound a yeere, land good and fine."

36. .   .   .   .
      .   .   .   .
     "I will to thee noe longer croche nor creepe,
     Nor I'le serue thee noe more to keepe thy sheepe."

37. Whereeuer wist you shepard before,
     That had in his head witt such store
     To pleasure a bishopp in such a like case,
     To answer three questions to the kings grace?
     Whereuer wist you shepard gett cleare
     Three hundred and fifty pound a yeere?

38. I neuer hard of his fellow before.
     Nor I neuer shall. Now I need to say noe more.
     I neuer knew shepeard that goot such a liuinge
     But David, the shepeard, that was a king.

CAPTAIN WEDDERBURN'S COURTSHIP (46)

A converse of the ballad in which a girl wins a husband by answering riddles; here the Captain wins a wife by the same method. Riddles and riddling songs and stories are very old and especially popular in oriental literature and lore. The meter and stanzaic form of this ballad proclaim it as late and literary in spite of the fact that several versions from folk sources exist. The old element here is the riddle part. These riddles without a story are found in a 15th-century MS. A quotation from it will illustrate the song; it is printed by T. Wright, *Songs and Carols*, p. 33.

> "I have a ʒong suster fer beʒondyn the se
> Many be the drowryis that che sente me.
> Che sente me the cherye, withouten any ston,
> And so che dede the dowe, withouten any bon."

In America the ballad has been recovered from Nova Scotia and New England in forms close to the English versions. In addition a lyric made up of only the riddles is found in wider dispersion. So the material has come full circle.

Text A, Herd, 1, 161; B, Nova Scotia, from tradition, printed *JAF*, 23:377; C, Virginia, from tradition, as sung by Romey Pullen to M.E.L., 1947.

A.

1. The laird of Bristoll's daughter was in the woods walking,
    And by came Captain Wetherbourn, a servant to the king;
    And he said to his livery man, "Wer 't not against the law,
    I would tak her to mine ain bed, and lay her neist the wa."

2. "I'm into my father's woods, amongst my father's trees,
    O kind sir, let mee walk alane, O kind sir, if you please;
    The butler's bell it will be rung, and I'll be mist awa:
    I'll lye into mine ain bed, neither at stock nor wa."

3. "O my bonny lady, the bed it's not be mine,
    For I'll command my servants for to call it thine;
    The hangings are silk satine, the sheets are holland sma,
    And we's baith lye in ae bed, but you's lye neist the wa.

4. "And so, my bonny lady,—I do not know your name,—
    But my name's Captain Wetherburn, and I'm a man of fame;
    Tho your father and a' his men were here, I would na stand in
        awe
    To tak you to mine ain bed, and lay you neist the wa.

5. "Oh my bonny, bonny lady, if you'll gie me your hand,
    You shall hae drums and trumpets to sound at your command;
    Wi fifty men to guard you, sae weel their swords can dra,
    And wee's baith lye in ae bed, but you's lye neist the wa."

6. He's mounted her upon a steid, behind his gentleman,
    And he himself did walk afoot, to had his lady on,
    With his hand about her midle sae jimp, for fear that she should
        fa;
    She man lye in his bed, but she'll not lye neist the wa.

7. He's taen her into Edinburgh, his landlady cam ben:
    "And monny bonny ladys in Edinburgh hae I seen,
    But the like of this fine creature my eyes they never sa."
    "O dame bring ben a down-bed, for she's lye neist the wa."

8. "Hold your tongue, young man," she said, "and dinna trouble
        me,
    Unless you get to my supper, and that is dishes three;
    Dishes three to my supper, tho I eat nane at a',
    Before I lye in your bed, but I winna lye neist the wa.

9. "You maun get to my supper a cherry but a stane,
    And you man get to my supper a capon but a bane,
    And you man get a gentle bird that flies wanting the ga,
    Before I lye in your bed, but I'll not lye neist the wa."

10. "A cherry whan in blossom is a cherry but a stane;
    A capon when he's in the egg canna hae a bane;
    The dow it is a gentle bird that flies wanting the ga;
    And ye man lye in my bed, between me and the wa."

11. "Hold your tongue, young man," she said, "and dinna me per-
        plex,
    Unless you tell me questions, and that is questions six;

Tell me them as I shall aske the, and that is twa by twa,
Before I lye in your bed, but I'll not lye neist the wa.

12. "What is greener than the grass, what's higher than the tree?
What's war than a woman's wish, what's deeper than the sea?
What bird sings first, and whereupon the dew down first does
  fa?
Before I lye in your bed, but I'll not lye neist the wa."

13. "Virgus is greener than the grass, heaven's higher than a tree;
The deil's war than a woman's wish, hell's deeper than the sea;
The cock sings first, on the Sugar Loaf the dew down first does
  fa;
And ye man lye in my bed, betweest me and the wa."

14. "Hold your tongue, young man," she said, "I pray you give it
  o'er,
Unless you tell me questions, and that is questions four;
Tell me them as I shall ask them, and that is twa by twa,
Before I lye in your bed, but I winna lye neist the wa.

15. "You man get to me a plumb that does in winter grow;
And likewise a silk mantle that never waft gaed thro;
A sparrow's horn, a priest unborn, this night to join us twa.
Before I lye in your bed, but I winna lye neist the wa."

16. "There is a plumb in my father's yeard that does in winter
  grow;
Likewise he has a silk mantle that never waft gaed thro;
A sparrow's horn, it may be found, there's ane in every tae,
There's ane upo the mouth of him, perhaps there may be twa.

17. "The priest is standing at the door, just ready to come in;
Nae man could sae that he was born, to lie it is a sin;
For a wild boar bored his mother's side, he out of it did fa;
And you man lye in my bed, between me and the wa."

18. Little kent Grizey Sinclair, that morning when she raise,
'T was to be the hindermost of a' her single days;
For now she's Captain Wetherburn's wife, a man she never saw,
And she man lye in his bed, but she'll not lye neist the wa.

B.

SIX QUESTIONS

1. The Duke of Merchant's daughter walked out one summer's day.
She met a bold sea-captain by chance upon the way.
He says, "My pretty fair maid, if it was n't for the law,
I would have you in my bed this night by either stock or wa."

2. She sighed and said, "Young man, oh, do not me perplex.

   .   .   .   .

   You must answer me in questions six before that I gang awa',
   Or before that I lie in your bed by either stock or wa.—

3. "Oh, what is rounder than your ring? What's higher than the
      trees?
   Or what is worse than women's tongue? What's deeper than the
      seas?
   What bird sings first, what bird sings last? Or where does the
      dew first fall?—
   Before that I lie in your bed by either stock or wall."

4. "The globe is rounder than your ring. Sky's higher than the trees.
   The devil's worse than women's tongue. Hell's deeper than the
      seas.
   The roe sings first, the thirst sings last. On the earth the dew
      first falls,
   So you and I lie in one bed, and you lie next the wall."

5. "You must get for me some winter fruit which in December
      grew.
   You must get for me a silken cloak that ne'er a waft went
      through,
   A sparrow's thorn, a priest new-born, before that I gang awa',
   Before that I lie in your bed by either stock or wa'."

6. "My father's got some winter fruit which in December grew.
   My mother's got a silken cloak that ne'er a waft went through.
   Sparrow's thorns they 're easy found. There's one on every claw.
   So you and I lie in one bed, and you lie next the wa'."

7. "You must get for my wedding supper a chicken without a bone.
   You must get for my wedding supper a cherry without a stone.
   You must get for me a gentle bird, a bird without a gall,
   Before that I lie in your bed by either stock or wall."

8. "Oh, when the chicken 's in the egg, I'm sure it has no bone.
   And when the cherry 's in full bloom, I'm sure it has no stone.
   The dove it is a gentle bird. It flies without a gall,
   So you and I lie in one bed, and you lie next the wa'."

9. He took her by the lily-white hand and led her through the hall.
   He held her by the slender waist for fear that she would fall.
   He led her on his bed of down without a doubt at all,
   So he and she lies in one bed, and he lies next the wall.

C.

1. Bring me a cherry without a stone,
   Bring me a chicken without a bone,
   Bring me a ring without any end,
   Bring me a baby with no crying.

2. Where can I get a cherry without a stone?
   Where can I get a chicken without a bone?
   Where can I get a ring without any end?
   Where can I get a baby with no crying?

3. A cherry when it's booming has no stone,
   A chicken that's pipping has no bone,
   A ring has neither beginning nor end,
   A baby asleep has no crying.

PROUD LADY MARGARET (47)

Of the half dozen versions of this ballad, all but one contain the riddles. The exception recovered from oral tradition in the early 19th century makes the brother come back from the dead to teach his sister humility since her pride keeps him from resting quietly (a variation of the theme that excessive grief keeps the dead uncomfortable). One might think that the riddles here are intrusive since riddles tend to intrude, were it not for the fact that once in, riddles seldom if ever disappear; rather the remainder of the ballad is likely to go, leaving the riddle portion. For this reason, then, it would seem that originally this story told of a girl whose father was very wealthy and either he or she stipulated that her husband would be the one who could answer the riddles she put to him, with death as the penalty for failure (4/4 and 5/3 would confirm this view). Then a revenant (later her brother) appears, answers the riddles, and carries her away to the land of the dead or leaves her with the admonition against pride.

Text, Scott, iii, 275. Stanzas 6 and 9 were supplied by Scott from "another ballad" to complete the sense.

1. 'T was on a night, an evening bright,
     When the dew began to fa,
   Lady Margaret was walking up and down,
     Looking o'er her castle wa.

2. She looked east and she looked west,
     To see what she could spy,
   When a gallant knight came in her sight,
     And to the gate drew nigh.

3. "You seem to be no gentleman,
   You wear your boots so wide;
   But you seem to be some cunning hunter,
   You wear the horn so syde."

4. "I am no cunning hunter," he said,
   "Nor ne'er intend to be,
   But I am come to this castle
   To seek the love of thee.
   And if you do not grant me love,
   This night for thee I'll die."

5. "If you should die for me, sir knight,
   There's few for you will meane;
   For mony a better has died for me,
   Whose graves are growing green.

6. "But ye maun read my riddle," she said,
   "And answer my questions three;
   And but ye read them right," she said,
   "Gae stretch ye out and die.

7. "Now what is the flower, the ae first flower,
   Springs either on moor or dale?
   And what is the bird, the bonnie bonnie bird,
   Sings on the evening gale?"

8. "The primrose is the ae first flower
   Springs either on moor or dale,
   And the thristlecock is the bonniest bird
   Sings on the evening gale."

9. "But what's the little coin," she said,
   "Wald buy my castle bound?
   And what's the little boat," she said,
   "Can sail the world all round?"

10. "O hey, how mony small pennies
    Make thrice three thousand pound?
    Or hey, how mony salt fishes
    Swim a' the salt sea round?"

11. "I think you maun be my match," she said,
    "My match and something mair;
    You are the first e'er got the grant
    Of love frae my father's heir.

12. "My father was lord of nine castles,
    My mother lady of three;
    My father was lord of nine castles,
    And there's nane to heir but me.

13. "And round about a' thae castles
　　　You may baith plow and saw,
　　And on the fifteenth day of May
　　　The meadows they will maw."

14. "O hald your tongue, Lady Margaret," he said,
　　　"For loud I hear you lie;
　　Your father was lord of nine castles,
　　　Your mother was lady of three;
　　Your father was lord of nine castles,
　　　But ye fa heir to but three.

15. "And round about a' thae castles
　　　You may baith plow and saw,
　　But on the fifteenth day of May
　　　The meadows will not maw.

16. "I am your brother Willie," he said,
　　　"I trow ye ken na me;
　　I came to humble your haughty heart,
　　　Has gard sae mony die."

17. "If ye be my brother Willie," she said,
　　　"As I trow weel ye be,
　　This night I'll neither eat nor drink,
　　　But gae alang wi thee."

18. "O hold your tongue, Lady Margaret," he said,
　　　"Again I hear you lie;
　　For ye've unwashen hands and ye've unwashen feet,
　　　To gae to clay wi me.

19. "For the wee worms are my bedfellows,
　　　And cauld clay in my sheets,
　　And when the stormy winds do blow,
　　　My body lies and sleeps."

THE TWA BROTHERS (49)

This ballad is known only in Scotland and America. Much confusion exists among the various versions. The brothers are referred to as little; yet one, or possibly both, have a sweetheart. In some versions the stabbing is accidental, in others intentional; some have a legacy ending, some do not; in some the one brother gives the survivor various messages to give to his relatives that will mislead them as to what happened to him; others do not have this dialogue. The American texts change the details and hence the emphasis of the story constantly. Several editors have suggested that the ballad is originally an incest ballad of the general character of "Lizie Wan," and possibly of "Edward." Note that "Edward" stanzas are sometimes attached to this ballad.

Text A, Sharpe's *Ballad Book,* p. 56; B, from tradition in Missouri, *JAF,* 26:361.

A.

1. There were twa brethren in the north,
     They went to the school thegither.
   The one unto the other said,
     Will you try a warsle afore?

2. They warsled up, they warsled down,
     Till Sir John fell to the ground,
   And there was a knife in Sir Willie's pouch,
     Gied him a deadlie wound.

3. "Oh brither dear, take me on your back,
     Carry me to yon burn clear,
   And wash the blood from off my wound,
     And it will bleed nae mair."

4. He took him up upon his back,
     Carried him to yon burn clear,
   And washd the blood from off his wound,
     But aye it bled the mair.

5. "Oh brither dear, take me on your back,
     Carry me to yon kirk-yard,
   And dig a grave baith wide and deep,
     And lay my body there."

6. He's taen him up upon his back,
     Carried him to yon kirk-yard,
   And dug a grave baith deep and wide,
     And laid his body there.

7. "But what will I say to my father dear,
     Gin he chance to say, Willie, whar's John?"
   "Oh say that he's to England gone,
     To buy him a cask of wine."

8. "And what will I say to my mother dear,
     Gin she chance to say, Willie, whar's John?"
   "Oh say that he's to England gone,
     To buy her a new silk gown."

9. "And what will I say to my sister dear,
     Gin she chance to say, Willie, whar's John?"
   "Oh say that he's to England gone,
     To buy her a wedding ring."

10. "But what will I say to her you loe dear,
    Gin she cry, Why tarries my John?"
"Oh tell her I lie in Kirk-land fair,
    And home again will never come."

B.

TWO LITTLE BOYS

1. Two little boys going to school,
    Two little boys they be;
Two little boys going to school
    To learn their A B C.

2. "O, will you toss a ball with me,
    Or will you throw a stone?
Or will you wrestle along with me
    On the road as we go home?"

3. "I will not toss a ball with you,
    Nor will I throw a stone,
But I will wrestle along with you,
    On the road as we go home."

4. They wrestled up, they wrestled down,
    They wrestled around and around,
And a little penknife run through John's pocket,
    And he received a deadly wound.

5. "Take off, take off my fine cotton shirt,
    And tear it from gore to gore,
And bind it around that bloody bloody wound,
    That it may bleed no more."

6. So I took off his fine cotton shirt,
    And tore it from gore to gore,
And bound it around that bloody bloody wound,
    So it would bleed no more.

7. "O what shall I tell your mother, John,
    If she inquires for you?"
"O, tell her I've gone to the royal school
    My books to bring home."

8. "O what shall I tell your sister, John,
    If she inquires for you?"
"O, tell her I've gone down to the city,
    Some friends for to see."

9. "O, what shall I tell your true love, John,
   If she inquires for you?"
   "O, tell her I'm dead and lying in my grave,
   Way out in Idaho."

LIZIE WAN (51)

This seems most certainly to be an incest ballad, though not all versions make the girl name her brother as the father of her baby. Of course incest as a theme is likely to be modified with the passing of time. This ballad, too, often closes with "Edward" stanzas.

Text A, Herd, i, 91; B, traditional, from Vermont, printed in *Bulletin*, 7:6.

A.

1. Lizie Wan sits in her father's bower-door,
   Weeping and making a mane,
   And by there came her father dear:
   "What ails thee, Lizie Wan?"

2. "I ail, and I ail, dear father," she said,
   "And I'll tell you a reason for why;
   There is a child between my twa sides,
   Between my dear billy and I."

3. Now Lizie Wan sits at her father's bower-door,
   Sighing and making a mane,
   And by there came her brother dear:
   "What ails thee, Lizie Wan?"

4. "I ail, I ail, dear brither," she said,
   "And I'll tell you a reason for why;
   There is a child between my twa sides,
   Between you, dear billy, and I."

5. "And hast thou tald father and mother o that?
   And hast thou tald sae o me?"
   And he has drawn his gude braid sword,
   That hang down by his knee.

6. And he has cutted aff Lizie Wan's head,
   And her fair body in three,
   And he's awa to his mother's bower,
   And sair aghast was he.

7. "What ails thee, what ails thee, Geordy Wan?
   What ails thee sae fast to rin?
   For I see by thy ill colour
   Some fallow's deed thou hast done."

8. "Some fallow's deed I have done, mother,
        And I pray you pardon me;
    For I've cutted aff my greyhound's head;
        He wadna rin for me."

9. "Thy greyhound's bluid was never sae red,
        O my son Geordy Wan.
    For I see by thy ill colour
        Some fallow's deed thou hast done."

10. "Some fallow's deed I hae done, mother,
        And I pray you pardon me;
    For I hae cutted aff Lizie Wan's head
        And her fair body in three."

11. "O what wilt thou do when thy father comes hame,
        O my son Geordy Wan?"
    "I'll set my foot in a bottomless boat,
        And swim to the sea-ground."

12. "And when will thou come hame again,
        O my son Geordy Wan?"
    "The sun and the moon shall dance on the green
        That night when I come hame."

B.

1. Fair Lucy was sitting in her own cabin door,
        Making her laments alone;
    Who should come by but her own mother dear,
        Saying, "What makes Fair Lucy mourn?"

2. "I have a cause for to grieve," she said,
        "And a reason for to mourn;
    For the babe that lies in the cradle asleep,
        Dear mother, it is his own."

3. Fair Lucy was sitting in her own cabin door,
        Making her laments alone;
    Who should come by but her own brother dear,
        Saying, "What makes Fair Lucy mourn?"

4. "I have a cause for to grieve," she said,
        "And a reason for to mourn;
    For the babe that lies in the cradle asleep,
        Dear brother, it is your own."

5. He took her by the lily-white hand
        And he led her into the woods;
    What he did there, I never can declare,
        But he spilt Fair Lucy's blood.

6. "O, what is that upon your frock,
   My son, come tell to me."
   "It is one drop of Fair Lucy's blood,
   And that you plainly can see."

7. "What will your father say to you,
   When he returns to me?"
   "I shall step my foot on board a ship,
   And my face he never shall see."

8. "What will you do with your three little babes,
   My son, come tell to me?"
   "I shall leave them here at my father's command,
   For to keep him companee."

9. "What will you do with your pretty little wife,
   My son, come tell to me?"
   "She shall step her foot on board a ship,
   And sail the ocean with me."

10. "What will you do with your houses and lands,
    My son, come tell to me?"
    "I shall leave them here at my father's command,
    For to set my children free."

11. "When will you return again,
    My son, come tell to me?"
    "When the sun and the moon set on yonders green hill,
    And I'm sure that never can be."

YOUNG BEICHAN (53)

This famous fine ballad exists in many versions in England and America and it has close relatives among all Germanic countries and here and there in the south of Europe. Throughout, the story remains virtually unchanged. Beichan and Beecham are the usual names of the hero in Scotland and England; in America he is often Bateman, and the ballad is often *The Turkish Lady*. One is tempted to derive this ballad from the legend of Gilbert Becket, father of the Archbishop. A 1300 manuscript reprinted in the Percy Society publications contains the legend which is repeated constantly through the Middle Ages. According to this story, Gilbert Becket was captured by Saracens in the Holy Land. The Admiral's daughter fell in love with him. After Gilbert had escaped, the lady followed him to London and there in due time, after consultation with six bishops and the baptism of the lady, she and Gilbert were married. But the very next day Gilbert decided that he must make another pilgrimage to the Holy Land. He was gone for over three years during which time his wife had borne him a son, Thomas. The ballad is closer to the various stories in ballad form that are to be found on the Continent than it is to this legend. But certainly the ballad owes something to the legend in the way of general background.

Text A, Jamieson, ii, 127; B, traditional in Kentucky, printed in *JAF*, 20:251.

A.

1. Young Bekie was as brave a knight
    As ever saild the sea;
    An he's doen him to the court of France,
    To serve for meat and fee.

2. He had nae been i the court of France
    A twelvemonth nor sae long,
    Til he fell in love with the king's daughter,
    An was thrown in prison strong.

3. The king he had but ae daughter,
    Burd Isbel was her name;
    And she has to the prison-house gane,
    To hear the prisoner's mane.

4. "O gin a lady woud borrow me,
    At her stirrup-foot I woud rin;
    Or gin a widow wad borrow me,
    I woud swear to be her son.

5. "Or gin a virgin woud borrow me,
    I woud wed her wi a ring;
    I'd gi her ha's, I'd gie her bowers,
    The bonny towrs o Linne."

6. O barefoot, barefoot gaed she but,
    An barefoot came she ben;
    It was no for want o hose an shoone,
    Nor time to put them on.

7. But a' for fear that her father dear
    Had heard her making din.
    She's stown the keys o the prison-house dor
    An latten the prisoner gang.

8. O whan she saw him Young Bekie,
    Her heart was wondrous sair,
    For the mice but an the bold rottons
    Had eaten his yallow hair.

9. She's gien him a shaver for his beard,
    A comber till his hair,

Five hunder pound in his pocket,
To spen, an nae to spair.

10. She's gien him a steed was good in need,
An a saddle o royal bone,
A leash o hounds o ae litter,
An Hector called one.

11. Atween this twa a vow was made,
'T was made full solemnly,
That or three years was come an gane,
Well married they shoud be.

12. He had nae been in 's ain country
A twelvemonth till an end,
Till he's forcd to marry a duke's daughter,
Or than lose a' his land.

13. "Ohon, alas!" says Young Beckie,
"I know not what to dee;
For I canno win to Burd Isbel,
And she kensnae to come to me."

14. O it fell once upon a day
Burd Isbel fell asleep,
And up it starts the Belly Blin,
An stood at her bed-feet.

15. "O waken, waken, Burd Isbel,
How can you sleep so soun,
Whan this is Bekie's wedding day,
An the marriage gain on?

16. "Ye do ye to your mither's bowr,
Think neither sin nor shame;
And ye tak twa o your mither's marys,
To keep ye frae thinking lang.

17. "Ye dress yoursel in the red scarlet,
An your marys in dainty green,
An ye pit girdles about your middles
Woud buy an earldome.

18. "O ye gang down by yon sea-side,
An down by yon sea-stran;
Sae bonny will the Hollans boats
Come rowin till your han.

19. "Ye set your milk-white foot abord,
Cry, Hail ye, Domine!
An I shal be the steerer o 't,
To row you o'er the sea."

20. She's tane her till her mither's bowr,
        Thought neither sin nor shame,
     An she took twa o her mither's marys,
        To keep her frae thinking lang.

21. She dressd hersel i the red scarlet,
        Her marys i dainty green,
     And they pat girdles about their middles
        Woud buy an earldome.

22. An they gid down by yon sea-side,
        An down by yon sea-stran;
     Sae bonny did the Hollan boats
        Come rowin to their han.

23. She set her milk-white foot on board,
        Cried, Hail ye, Domine!
     An the Belly Blin was the steerer o 't,
        To row her o'er the sea.

24. Whan she came to Young Bekie's gate,
        She heard the music play;
     Sae well she kent frae a' she heard,
        It was his wedding day.

25. She's pitten her han in her pocket,
        Gin the porter guineas three;
     "Hae, tak ye that, ye proud porter,
        Bid the bride-groom speake to me."

26. O whan that he cam up the stair,
        He fell low down on his knee;
     He haild the king, and he haild the queen,
        And he haild him, Young Bekie.

27. "O I've been porter at your gates
        This thirty years an three;
     But there's three ladies at them now,
        Their like I never did see.

28. "There's ane o them dressd in red scarlet,
        And twa in dainty green,
     An they hae girdles about their middles
        Woud buy an earldome."

29. Then out it spake the bierly bride,
        Was a' goud to the chin;
     "'Gin she be braw without," she says,
        "We's be as braw within."

30. Then up it starts him, Young Bekie,

An the tears was in his ee:
"I'll lay my life it's Burd Isbel,
Come o'er the sea to me."

31. O quickly ran he down the stair,
An whan he saw 't was shee,
He kindly took her in his arms,
And kissd her tenderly.

32. "O hae ye forgotten, Young Bekie,
The vow ye made to me,
Whan I took you out o the prison strong,
Whan ye was condemnd to die?

33. "I gae you a steed was good in need,
An a saddle o royal bone,
A leash o hounds o ae litter,
An Hector called one."

34. It was well kent what the lady said,
That it wasnae a lee,
For at ilka word the lady spake,
The hound fell at her knee.

35. "Tak hame, tak hame your daughter dear,
A blessing gae her wi,
For I maun marry my Burd Isbel,
That's come oer the sea to me."

36. "Is this the custom o your house,
Or the fashion o your lan,
To marry a maid in a May mornin,
An send her back at even?"

B.

THE TURKISH LADY

1. There was a man who lived in England,
He was of some high degree;
He became uneasy, discontented,
Some fair land, some land to see.

2. He sailed east, he sailed west,
He sailed all over the Turkish shore,
Till he was caught and put in prison,
Never to be released any more.

3. The Turk he had but the one lone daughter,
She was of some high degree;

She stole the keys from her father's dwelling,
　　And declared Lord Batesman she'd set free.

4. She led him down to the lower cellar,
　　And drew him a drink of the strongest wine;
　"Every moment seems an hour;
　　Lord Batesman, if you were mine!

5. "Let's make a vow, let's make a promise,
　　Let's make a vow, let's make it stand:
　You vow you'll marry no other woman,
　　I will vow I'll marry no other man."

6. They made a vow, they made a promise,
　　They made a vow, they made it stand;
　He vowed he'd marry no other woman,
　　She vowed she'd marry no other man.

7. Seven long years has rolled around,
　　It seemed as if it was twenty-three;
　She bundled up her finest clothing,
　　Declared Lord Batesman she'd go see.

8. Seven long years has rolled around,
　　It seemed as if it were twenty-nine;
　She bundled up her finest clothing,
　　And declared Lord Batesman she'd go find.

9. She went till she came to the gate, she tingled;
　　It was so loud, but she wouldn't come in:
　"Is this your place," she cried, "Lord Batesman?
　　"Or is it that you've brought your new bride in?"

10. "Go remember him of a piece of bread;
　　Go remember him a glass of wine;
　Go remember him of the Turkish lady
　　Who freed him from the cold iron bonds."

11. He stamped his foot upon the floor;
　　He burst the table in pieces three,
　Saying, "I'll forsake both land and dwelling
　　For the Turkish lady that set me free."

12. She went till she came to the gate, she tingled;
　　It was so loud, but she wouldn't come in:
　"She's got more gold on her little finger
　　Than you, new bride and all your kin."

THE CHERRY-TREE CAROL (54)

This carol-ballad versifies the story found in the *Pseudo-Matthew Gospel,* where the fruit is a palm. There is no reference to Christ's birthday or to the discomfiture of Joseph. The ballad is found throughout Europe where the fruit varies from apple to berries to cherries. In America in several texts Joseph asks Jesus when his birthday will be. He usually answers, "The sixth day of January," but some texts have the fifth and some the seventh, suggesting to Sharp that these texts can be classified according to the period of calendar revision. Old Christmas was January 5 from 1752–1799; then a day was dropped, making it January 6, and finally another in 1900, making it January 7.

Text A, Sandys, *Christmas Carols,* p. 123; B, traditional, Kentucky, printed in *JAF,* 29:293.

A.

1. Joseph was an old man,
    and an old man was he,
   When he wedded Mary,
    in the land of Galilee.

2. Joseph and Mary walked
    through an orchard good,
   Where was cherries and berries,
    so red as any blood.

3. Joseph and Mary walked
    through an orchard green,
   Where was berries and cherries,
    as thick as might be seen.

4. O then bespoke Mary,
    so meek and so mild:
   "Pluck me one cherry, Joseph,
    for I am with child."

5. O then bespoke Joseph,
    with words most unkind:
   "Let him pluck thee a cherry
    that brought thee with child."

6. O then bespoke the babe,
    within his mother's womb:
   "Bow down then the tallest tree,
    for my mother to have some."

7. Then bowed down the highest tree
    unto his mother's hand;

Then she cried, "See Joseph,
    I have cherries at command."

8. O then bespake Joseph:
    "I have done Mary wrong;
But cheer up, my dearest,
    and be not cast down."

9. Then Mary plucked a cherry,
    as red as the blood,
Then Mary went home
    with her heavy load.

10. Then Mary took her babe,
    and sat him on her knee,
Saying, My dear son, tell me
    what this world will be.

11. "O I shall be as dead, mother,
    as the stones in the wall;
O the stones in the streets, mother,
    shall mourn for me all.

12. "Upon Easter-day, mother,
    my uprising shall be;
O the sun and the moon, mother,
    shall both rise with me."

B.

1. When Joseph was an old man,
    An old man was he,
He married Virgin Mary,
    The Queen of Galilee.

2. As Joseph and Mary
    Were walking one day:
"Here are apples, here are cherries
    Enough to behold."

3. Then Mary spoke to Joseph
    So meek and so mild:
"Joseph, gather me some cherries,
    For I am with child."

4. Then Joseph flew in anger,
    In anger flew he:
"Let the father of the baby
    Gather cherries for thee."

5. Then Jesus spoke a few words,
    A few words spoke he:

"Let my mother have some cherries;
  Bow low down, cherry-tree."

6. The cherry-tree bowed low down,
  Bowed low down to the ground,
  And Mary gathered cherries
  While Joseph stood around.

7. Then Joseph took Mary
  All on his right knee:
  "O, what have I done?
  Lord have mercy on me!"

8. Then Joseph took Mary all,
  All on his left knee:
  "O, tell me, little baby,
  When thy birthday will be."

9. "On the sixth day of January
  My birthday will be,
  When the stars in the elements
  Shall tremble with glee."

DIVES AND LAZARUS (56)

This is the Biblical story. In England as a ballad it dates from the
16th century. In America this ballad is rare, being found only in Virginia and that in a suspiciously literary version. Several songs on the
same general theme have been popular in America, such as "The
Tramp" and "The Little Family."

Text, 18th century broadside printed in Husk, *Songs of the Na-
tivity*, p. 94.

1. As it fell out upon a day,
  Rich Dives he made a feast,
  And he invited all his friends,
  And gentry of the best.

2. Then Lazarus laid him down and down,
  And down at Dives' door:
  "Some meat, some drink, brother Dives,
  Bestow upon the poor."

3. "Thou art none of my brother, Lazarus,
  That lies begging at my door;
  No meat nor drink will I give thee,
  Nor bestow upon the poor."

4. Then Lazarus laid him down and down,
  And down at Dives's wall:

"Some meat, some drink, brother Dives,
  Or with hunger starve I shall."

5. "Thou art none of my brother, Lazarus,
    That lies begging at my wall;
  No meat nor drink will I give thee,
    But with hunger starve you shall."

6. Then Lazarus laid him down and down,
    And down at Dives's gate:
  "Some meat, some drink, brother Dives,
    For Jesus Christ his sake."

7. "Thou art none of my brother, Lazarus,
    That lies begging at my gate;
  No meat nor drink will I give thee,
    For Jesus Christ his sake."

8. Then Dives sent out his merry men,
    To whip poor Lazarus away;
  They had no power to strike a stroke,
    But flung their whips away.

9. Then Dives sent out his hungry dogs,
    To bite him as he lay;
  They had no power to bite at all,
    But licked his sores away.

10. As it fell out upon a day,
    Poor Lazarus sickened and died;
  Then came two angels out of heaven
    His soul therein to guide.

11. "Rise up, rise up, brother Lazarus,
    And go along with me;
  For you've a place prepared in heaven,
    To sit on an angel's knee."

12. As it fell out upon a day,
    Rich Dives sickened and died;
  Then came two serpents out of hell,
    His soul therein to guide.

13. "Rise up, rise up, brother Dives,
    And go with us to see
  A dismal place, prepared in hell,
    From which thou canst not flee."

14. Then Dives looked up with his eyes,
    And saw poor Lazarus blest:
  "Give me one drop of water, brother Lazarus,
    To quench my flaming thirst.

15. "Oh had I as many years to abide
    As there are blades of grass,
    Then there would be an end, but now
    Hell's pains will ne'er be past.

16. "Oh was I now but alive again,
    The space of one half hour!
    Oh that I had my peace secure!
    Then the devil should have no power."

SIR PATRICK SPENS (58)

One of the finest, poetically and dramatically, of all the ballads. It occurs only in Scotland and England, with two texts recovered from America probably from printed versions. Two types of story are found. One tells of a voyage by Sir Patrick Spens and the shipwreck; the other is fuller, telling of Sir Patrick being sent either to take a princess (daughter of King of Norway or daughter of King of Scotland) to Norway or to fetch her home. This led Motherwell to suggest that the ballad recounts an actual event, the bringing home of Margaret of Norway in 1281 when many of the ships sent to fetch her foundered and their crews perished. Another legend tells of the death of the Maid of Norway, daughter of Margaret, in a storm as she was being taken to England from Norway to marry the son of Edward I. The name of Sir Patrick Spens appears in no Scottish or English records. No historical connection can be proved certainly, and, as Child remarks, none is necessary. It is interesting to study the three versions printed here. Most students will agree that the oldest text here, the Percy, is the finest in spite of the lack of detail. The compression and skillful evocation are the source of its great poetic appeal.

Text A, Percy Reliques, i, 71; B, Jamieson, i, 157; C, traditional in Scotland in the 18th century, Harris MS., Harvard.

Notes

7/1–2. These beautiful lines are consistently kept from version to version. 11/1. Aberdour: The ship was lost off the Scotch coast of Aberdeenshire.

A.

1. The king sits in Dumferling toune,
   Drinking the blude-reid wine:
   "O whar will I get guid sailor,
   To sail this schip of mine?"

2. Up and spak an eldern knicht,
   Sat at the kings richt kne:
   "Sir Patrick Spence is the best sailor
   That sails upon the se."

3. The king has written a braid letter,
     And signd it wi his hand,
   And sent it to Sir Patrick Spence,
     Was walking on the sand.

4. The first line that Sir Patrick red,
     A loud lauch lauched he;
   The next line that Sir Patrick red,
     The teir blinded his ee.

5. "O wha is this has don this deid,
     This ill deid don to me,
   To send me out this time o' the yeir,
     To sail upon the se!

6. "Mak hast, mak haste, my mirry men all,
     Our guid schip sails the morn."
   "O say na sae, my master deir,
     For I feir a deadlie storme.

7. "Late, late yestreen I saw the new moone,
     Wi the auld moone in hir arme,
   And I feir, I feir, my deir master,
     That we will cum to harme."

8. O our Scots nobles wer richt laith
     To weet their cork-heild schoone;
   Bot lang owre a' the play wer playd,
     Thair hats they swam aboone.

9. O lang, lang may their ladies sit,
     Wi thair fans into their hand,
   Or eir they se Sir Patrick Spence
     Cum sailing to the land.

10. O lang, lang may the ladies stand,
     Wi thair gold kems in their hair,
   Waiting for thair ain deir lords,
     For they'll se thame na mair.

11. Haf owre, haf owre to Aberdour,
     It's fiftie fadom deip,
   And thair lies guid Sir Patrick Spence,
     Wi the Scots lords at his feit.

B.

1. The king sits in Dunfermlin town,
     Sae merrily drinkin the wine:
   "Whare will I get a mariner,
     Will sail this ship o mine?"

2. Then up bespak a bonny boy,
     Sat just at the king's knee:
   "Sir Patrick Spence is the best seaman,
     That e'er set foot on sea."

3. The king has written a braid letter,
     Seald it wi his ain hand;
   He has sent word to Sir Patrick,
     To come at his command.

4. "O wha is this, or wha is that,
     Has tald the king o me?
   For I was never a good seaman,
     Nor ever intend to be."

5. They mounted sail on Munenday morn,
     Wi a' the haste they may,
   And they hae landed in Norraway,
     Upon the Wednesday.

6. They hadna been a month, a month
     In Norraway but three,
   Till lads o Norraway began to say,
     "Ye spend a' our white monie.

7. "Ye spend a' our good kingis goud,
     But and our queenis fee."
   "Ye lie, ye lie, ye liars loud,
     Sae weel's I hear you lie.

8. "For I brought as much white money
     As will gain my men and me;
   I brought half a fou o good red goud
     Out o'er the sea with me.

9. "Be't wind or weet, be't snaw or sleet,
     Our ships maun sail the morn."
   "O ever alack! my master dear,
     I fear a deadly storm.

10. "I saw the new moon late yestreen,
     Wi the auld moon in her arm;
   And if we gang to sea, master,
     I fear we'll suffer harm."

11. They hadna sailed a league on sea,
     A league but barely ane,
   Till anchors brak, and tap-masts lap;
     There came a deadly storm.

12. "Whare will I get a bonny boy
     Will tak thir sails in hand,

That will gang up to the tap-mast,
 See an he ken dry land?

13. Laith, laith were our good Scots lords
  To weet their leathern shoon;
 But or the morn at fair day-light,
  Their hats were wat aboon.

14. Mony was the feather bed,
  That flotterd on the faem,
 And mony was the good Scots lord
  Gaed awa that neer cam hame,
 And mony was the fatherless bairn
  That lay at hame greetin.

15. It's forty miles to Aberdeen,
  And fifty fathoms deep;
 And there lyes a' our good Scots lords,
  Wi Sir Patrick at their feet.

16. The ladies crackt their fingers white,
  The maidens tore their hair,
 A' for the sake o their true loves,
  For them they neer saw mair.

17. Lang, lang may our ladies stand,
  Wi their fans in their hand,
 Ere they see Sir Patrick and his men
  Come sailing to the land.

C.

1. Hie sits oor king in Dumfermline,
  Sits birlin at the wine;
 Says, "Whare will I get a bonnie boy
  That will sail the saut seas fine?
 That will hie owre to Norraway,
  To bring my dear dochter hame?"

2. Up it spak a bonnie boy,
  Sat by the king's ain knie:
 "Sir Patrick Spens is as gude a skipper
  As ever sailed the sea."

3. The king has wrote a broad letter,
  And signed it wi his hand,
 And sent it to Sir Patrick Spens,
  To read it gif he can.

4. The firsten line he luikit on,
  A licht lauchter gae he;

> But ere he read it to the end,
>> The tear blindit his ee.

5. "O wha is this, or wha is that,
>> Has tauld oor king o me?
> I wad hae gien him twice as muckle thank
>> To latten that abee!

6. "But eat an drink, my merrie young men,
>> Eat, an be weel forn;
> For blaw it wind, or blaw it weet,
>> Oor gude ship sails the morn."

7. Up it spak his youngest son,
>> Sat by Sir Patrick's knie:
> "I beg you bide at hame, father,
>> An I pray be ruled by me.

8. "For I saw the new mune late yestreen,
>> Wi the auld mune in her arms;
> An ever an alake, my father dear,
>> It's a token o diedly storms."

9. "It's eat an drink, my merrie young men,
>> Eat, an be weel forn;
> For blaw it wind, or blaw it weet,
>> Oor gude ship sails the morn."

10. They hadna sailed a league, a league,
>> A league but only three,
> When the whirlin wind an the ugly jaws
>> Cam drivin to their knie.

11. They hadna sailed a league, a league,
>> A league but only five,
> When the whirlin wind an the ugly jaws
>> Their gude ship began to rive.

12. They hadna sailed a league, a league,
>> A league but only nine,
> When the whirlin wind an the ugly jaws
>> Cam drivin to their chin.

13. "O whaur will I get a bonnie boy
>> Will tak the steer in hand,
> Till I mount up to oor tapmast,
>> To luik oot for dry land?"

14. "O here am I, a bonnie boy,
>> Will tak the steer in hand,

Till you mount up to oor tapmast,
To luik oot for dry land."

15.   He's gaen up to the tapmast,
To the tapmast sae hie;
He luikit around on every side,
But dry land he couldna see.

16.   He luikit on his youngest son,
An the tear blindit his ee;
Says, I wish you had been in your mother's bowr,
But there you'll never be.

17.   "Pray for yoursels, my merrie young men,
Pray for yoursels an me,
For the first landen that we will land
Will be in the boddam o the sea."

18.   Then up it raise the mermaiden,
Wi the comb an glass in her hand:
"Here's a health to you, my merrie young men,
For you never will see dry land."

19.   O laith, laith waur oor gude Scots lords
To weet their cork-heeled shoon;
But lang, lang ere the play was played,
Their yellow locks soomed aboun.

20.   There was Saturday, an Sabbath day,
An Monnonday at morn,
That feather-beds an silken sheets
Cam floatin to Kinghorn.

21.   It's och, och owre to Aberdour,
It's fifty faddoms deep;
An there lie a' oor gude Scots lords,
Wi Sir Patrick Spens at their feet.

22.   O lang, lang will his lady sit,
Wi the fan into her hand,
Until she see her ain dear lord
Come sailin to dry land.

23.   O lang, lang will his lady sit,
Wi the tear into her ee,
Afore she see her ain dear lord
Come hieing to Dundee.

24.   O lang, lang will his lady sit,
Wi the black shoon on her feet,
Afore she see Sir Patrick Spens
Come drivin up the street.

SIR ALDINGAR (59)

The general story told in this ballad of infidelity is common in chronicle, romance, exemplum, and ballad. Details vary much, but it is essentially the story of a queen accused by one of her husband's subjects whose attention she scorns, sending for someone to fight for her in judicial combat, of her savior appearing at the last moment before she is to be burned or executed, swearing to her innocence and then fighting for her a victorious fight. Presented here with the English ballad is a translation of a Danish analogue, "Ravengaard og Memering."

The Percy version printed here has been "touched up" a bit by the Bishop. He may have supplied the names of the king and queen, Elinor and Henry—certainly meant to be Henry II and Eleanor of Aquitaine. The only other version of the ballad does not name the two. There is no historical basis for such a story being associated with Queen Eleanor, other than her general reputation in the Middle Ages. The second version has more of a folk flavor. An illustration can be had by citing the stanzas when the king finds his lady with the leper "planted" in her bed.

"He looked on the leper man, Who lay on his queen's bed
He lifted up the snow-white sheets, And thus to him he said.
Plooky, plooky are your cheeks, And plooky is your chin,
And plooky are your armis twa, My bonny queen's layne in.
Since she has lain into your arms, She shall not lie in mine;
Since she has kissed your ugsome mouth, She never shall kiss mine."

Text A, Percy, p. 68; B, Prior, i, 151.

A.

1. Our king he kept a ffalse steward,
   Men called him Sir Aldingar,

   .   .   .   .   .   .

   .   .   .   .   .   .

2. He wold haue layen by our comely queene,
   Her deere worshipp to haue betraide;
   Our queene shee was a good woman,
   And euer more said him nay.

3. Aldingar was offended in his mind,
   With her hee was neuer content,
   But he sought what meanes he cold find out,
   In a fyer to haue her brent.

4. There came a lame lazer to the king's gates,
   A lazar was blind and lame;

He tooke the lazar vpon his backe,
   Vpon the queene's bed he did him lay.

5. He said, "Lye still, lazar, wheras thou lyest;
      Looke thou goe not away;
    I'le make thee a whole man and a sound
      In two howres of a day."

6. And then went forth Sir Aldingar,
      Our queene for to betray,
    And then he mett with our comlye king,
      Saies, "God you saue and see!

7. "If I had space, as I haue grace,
      A message I wold say to thee."
    "Say on, say on, Sir Aldingar,
      Say thou on and vnto me."

8. "I can let you now see one of the greiuosest sights
      That euer Christen king did see;
    Our queene hath chosen a new, new loue,
      She will haue none of thee.

9. "If shee had chosen a right good knight,
      The lesse had beene her shame;
    But she hath chosen a lazar man,
      Which is both blinde and lame."

10. "If this be true, thou Aldingar,
       That thou dost tell to me,
     Then will I make thee a rich knight
       Both of gold and fee.

11. "But if it be false, Sir Aldingar,
       That thou doest tell to me,
     Then looke for noe other death
       But to be hangd on a tree.
     Goe with me," saide our comly king,
       "This lazar for to see."

12. When the king he came into the queen's chamber,
       Standing her bed befor,
     "There is a lodly lome," says Harry King,
       "For our dame Queene Elinor!

13. "If thou were a man, as thou art none,
       Here thou sholdest be slaine;
     But a paire of new gallowes shall be built,
       Thoust hang on them soe hye.

14. "And a fayre fyer there shalbe bett,
       And brent our queene shal bee."

Fforth then walked our comlye king,
 And mett with our comly queene.

15. Saies, "God you saue, our queene, Madam,
  And Christ you saue and see!
 Heere you haue chosen a new, new loue,
  And you will haue none of mee.

16. "If you had chosen a right good knight,
  The lesse had beene your shame;
 But you haue chosen a lazar man,
  That is both blind and lame."

17. "Euer alacke!" said our comly queene,
  "Sir Aldingar is false to mee;
 But euer alacke!" said our comly queene,
  "Euer alas, and woe is mee!

18. "I had thought sweuens had neuer been true;
  I haue prooued them true at the last;
 I dreamed in my sweauen on Thursday at eueninge,
  In my bed wheras I lay.

19. "I dreamed a grype and a grimlie beast
  Had carryed my crowne away,
 My gorgett and my kirtle of golde,
  And all my faire heade-geere.

20. "How he wold haue worryed me with his tush,
  And borne me into his nest,
 Saving there came a little hawk,
  Flying out of the east.

21. "Saying there came a little hawke,
  Which men call a merlion;
 Vntill the ground he stroke him downe,
  That dead he did fall downe.

22. "Giffe I were a man, as I am none,
  A battell I would proue;
 I wold fight with that false traitor;
  Att him I cast my gloue!

23. "Seing I am able noe battell to make,
  You must grant me, my leege, a knight,
 To fight with that traitor, Sir Aldingar,
  To maintaine me in my right."

24. "I'le giue thee forty dayes," said our king,
  "To seeke thee a man therin;

If thou find not a man in forty dayes,
In a hott fyer thou shall brenn."

25.   Our queene sent forth a messenger;
He rode fast into the south;
He rode the countryes through and through,
Soe ffar vnto Portsmouth.

26.   .   .   .   .
.   .   .   .
He cold find never a man in the south country
That wold fight with the knight soe keene.

27.   The second messenger the queen forth sent
Rode far into the east;
But, blessed be God made sunn and moone!
He sped then all of the best.

28.   As he rode then by one riuer side,
There he mett with a little child;
He seemed noe more in a man's likenesse
Then a child of four yeeres old.

29.   He askt the queene's messenger how far he rode;
Loth he was him to tell;
The little one was offended att him,
Bid him adew, farwell.

30.   Said, "Turne thou againe, thou messenger,
Greete our queene well from me;
When bale is att hyest, boote is att next;
Helpe enough there may bee.

31.   "Bid our queene remember what she did dreame
In her bedd wheras shee lay;
Shee dreamed the grype and the grimly beast
Had carryed her crowne away;

32.   "Her gorgett and her kirtle of gold,
Alsoe her faire head-geere;
He wold haue werryed her with his tushe,
And borne her into his nest.

33.   "Saving there came a little hawke,
Men call him a merlyon;
Vntill the ground he did strike him downe,
That dead he did ffall downe.

34.   "Bidd the queene be merry att her hart,
Euermore light and glad;
When bale is att hyest, boote is at next,
Helpe enoughe there shalbe."

35. Then the queene's messenger rode backe,
    A gladed man then was hee;
    When he came before our queene,
    A gladd woman then was shee.

36. Shee gaue the messenger twenty pound,
    O lord, in gold and ffee;
    Saies, "Spend and spare not while this doth last,
    Then feitch thou more of me."

37. Our queene was put in a tunne to burne,
    She thought no thing but death;
    The were ware of the little one
    Came ryding forth of the east.

38. With a mu . . .
    A louelie child was hee;
    When he came to that fier,
    He light the queene full nigh.

39. Said, "Draw away these brands of fire
    Lie burning before our queene,
    And feitch me hither Sir Aldingar,
    That is a knight soe keene."

40. When Aldingar see that little one,
    Ffull litle of him hee thought;
    If there had beene halfe a hundred such,
    Of them he wold not haue wrought.

41. Hee sayd, "Come hither, Sir Aldingar;
    Thou seemust as bigge as a ffooder;
    I trust to God, ere I haue done with thee,
    God will send to vs [an] auger."

42. Saies, "The first stroke that's giuen, Sir Aldingar,
    I will giue vnto thee,
    And if the second giue thou may,
    Looke then thou spare not mee."

43. The litle one pulld forth a well good sword,
    I-wis itt was all of guilt;
    It cast light there over that feild,
    It shone soe all of guilt.

44. He stroke the first stroke att Aldingar,
    He stroke away his leggs by his knee;

    .   .   .   .

    .   .   .   .

45. Sayes, "Stand vp, stand vp, thou false traitor,
    And fight vpon thy feete;

For and thou thriue as thou begins,
   Of a height wee shalbe meete."

46. "A preist, a preist," sayes Aldingar,
   "Me for to houzle and shriue.
A preist, a preist," sayes Aldingar,
   "While I am a man liuing a-liue.

47. "I wold haue laine by our comlie queene;
   To it shee wold neuer consent;
I thought to haue betrayd her to our king,
   In a fyer to haue had her brent.

48. "There came a lame lazar to the king's gates,
   A lazar both blind and lame;
I tooke the lazar vpon my backe,
   In the Queene's bed I did him lay.

49. "I bad him, lie still, lazar, where he lay,
   Looke he went not away;
I wold make him a whole man and a sound
   In two houres of a day.

50.   .   .   .   .

      .   .   .   .   .   .

"Euer alacke!" sayes Sir Aldingar,
   "Falsing neuer doth well;

51. "Forgiue, forgiue me, queene, Madam.
   For Christ's loue forgiue me."
"God forgaue his death, Aldingar,
   And freely I forgiue thee."

52. "Now take thy wife, thou King Harry,
   And loue her as thou shold;
Thy wiffe shee is as true to thee
   As stone that lies on the castle wall."

53. The lazar vnder the gallow tree
   Was a pretty man and small;
The lazar vnder the gallow tree,
   Was made steward in King Henery's hall.

B.

RAVNGARD AND MEMERING

1. The Dame Gunild, she dwells in Spire,
   And her the great and rich admire,
         The Dame Gunild.

2. To woo her suitors come from South
In rich array and prime of youth,
          To Dame Gunild.

3. To woo her suitors come from West,
The wealthiest, bravest and the best,
          To Dame Gunild.

4. To woo her suitors come from North,
Men of well-earn'd renown and worth,
          To Dame Gunild.

5. To woo her suitors come from East,
For wealth and bravery not the least,
          To Dame Gunild.

6. To woo her too Duke Henry came,
And fate decreed them woe and shame.
          The Dame Gunild.

7. He woo'd and brought her home for wife;
Behind them followed storm and strife,
          The Dame Gunild.

8. The Duke to war must march away,
And her to guard bade Ravngard stay,
          The Dame Gunild.

9. "Of Brunswick, Sleswick, Spire take care,
But chiefly watch my consort dear,
          The Dame Gunild."

10. As steer'd the Duke his ship from land,
Rode Ravngard off along the strand,
          To Dame Gunild.

11. He round him wrapp'd his scarlet cloak,
And up to the lady went and spoke,
          To Dame Gunild.

12. "Hear now, I pray, my lord's last word,
And fetch me Adelring, his sword,
          My Dame Gunild."

13. "No such behest gave me the Duke,
When lately leave from me he took."
          Said Dame Gunild.

14. "Unless you give me Adelring,
A charge against you I shall bring,
          My Dame Gunild."

15 "Lie as thou wilt, on thee the shame,

For God will prove me free from blame."
Said Dame Gunild.

16.   The Duke from war march'd home again,
And Ravngard met the glittering train;
From Dame Gunild.

17.   "How has it fared with Spire this year?
And how is she, my wife so dear,
The Dame Gunild?"

18.   "Your land is in its wonted state,
But ill has lived your wife of late,
The Dame Gunild."

19.   "Ravngard, thy charge I deem untrue,
For faithlessness I never knew
In Dame Gunild."

20.   "'Tis what myself have seen with pain,
Gunild has with th' Archbishop lain,
The Dame Gunild."

21.   "I'll smite her down with heavy hand,
And none shall dare my wroth withstand,
Her, Dame Gunild."

22.   The Duke his scarlet mantle hent,
And up to his consort's chamber went,
To Dame Gunild.

23.   Gunild, as near her door he drew,
Rose up to show him honour due;
The Dame Gunild.

24.   "Welcome my noble Lord again!
How fared you in your late campaign?"
Said Dame Gunild.

25.   "Most lucky had I deem'd this year,
Such deeds of thee did I not hear,
My Dame Gunild."

26.   "My gracious lord, oh, say not so;
Of wrong or crime I nothing know."
Said Dame Gunild.

27.   "It little boots to plead or feign,
For with th' Archbishop thou hast lain,
My Dame Gunild."

28.   With ruthless hand he dealt the blows,

Nor one to help his lady rose,
   The Dame Gunild.

29. None but two courtly dames would dare
To pray the Duke her life to spare,
   The Dame Gunild's.

30. "My lord, be not this charge believ'd;
With lying tale you've been deceiv'd
   Of Dame Gunild."

31. "Let her then seek her out a knight,
Who does a joust with Ravngard fight,
   The Dame Gunild."

32. Bare, head and foot, her garments rent,
From out her door in sorrow went
   The Dame Gunild.

33. With tears she sought the banquet hall,
Where sat and drank the champions all,
   The Dame Gunild.

34. Those knights, as towards the door she drew,
Stood up to show her honour due,
   To Dame Gunild.

35. "Is here within a gallant knight,
Will for an injured lady fight,
   For Dame Gunild?"

36. Her cause would no one undertake,
Mute all, till Memering rose and spake,
   "O Dame Gunild!

37. "For fifteen years I serv'd your sire,
Fed at his board, and took his hire,
   My Dame Gunild;

38. "But saw you never in such a plight,
With thin and tatter'd raiment dight,
   My Dame Gunild;

39. "Never my master's child have seen
Walk barefoot o'er the castle green,
   My Dame Gunild.

40. "To some the merchant coin he told,
To some with cups he measur'd gold,
   My Dame Gunild;

41. "On Ravngard he the most bestow'd,

The one who first has treason show'd
My Dame Gunild:

42. "I've ever sat at table-end,
Whither good gifts are wont to wend,
My Dame Gunild;

43. "And now for you I'll take the field,
If Adelring to me you'll yield.
My Dame Gunild."

44. "If thou wilt take the field for me,
The sword I'll gladly fetch for thee."
Said Dame Gunild.

45. On the bare mould they drew a ring,
Where each his sword and shield should bring
For Dame Gunild.

46. "A solemn oath thou now shalt swear,
That Adelring thou dost not wear,
For Dame Gunild."

47. "So help me God! to me is known
Above the ground its hilt alone."
The Dame Gunild!

48. "And now an oath thou too shalt swear,
That thou sword Southwind doest not bear."
The Dame Gunild!

49. "So help me God from pain and woe!
That Southwind sword I do not know."
The Dame Gunild!

50. The first blow Ravngard on him laid,
In twain he sunder'd Memering's blade.
The Dame Gunild.

51. "Now," said the Duke, "may all men see,
How true is what is charg'd to thee:
My Dame Gunild."

52. "The charge, my lord, is still untrue,
Tho' broke my champion's sword in two."
Said Dame Gunild.

53. The first blow Memering on him laid,
In twain he sunder'd Ravngard's blade,
For Dame Gunild.

54. "Hold up now, Memering, stand aside,

And wait till I my shoe have tied,"
The Dame Gunild!

55. Down to the greensward Ravngard bent
And so his good sword Southwind hent.
The Dame Gunild!

56. "This villain perjury thou shalt mourn;
Thy guilty soul hast thou forsworn."
The Dame Gunild!

57. The first blow Ravngard on him laid,
In twain he sunder'd Memering's blade.
The Dame Gunild!

58. "Stay, Ravngard, now stand thou aside,
And wait till I my shoe have tied."
The Dame Gunild!

59. Down to the greensward Memering bent,
And Adelring his sword he hent.
For Dame Gunild!

60. "This perjury thou too hast to mourn,
Thy guilty soul hast thou forsworn,
For Dame Gunild."

61. "Nay, for I sware to me was known
Above the earth its hilt alone."
The Dame Gunild!

62. The first blow Memering on him laid,
In twain he sunder'd Ravngard's blade;
For Dame Gunild.

63. Memering heav'd yet one other blow,
And headless fell his guilty foe
'Fore Dame Gunild.

64. "See there, my lord, the champion's fate,
And now thy groundless wrath abate,"
Said Dame Gunild.

65. "For now, my lord, yourself my see,
That Ravngard basely lied on me,"
Said Dame Gunild.

66. Duke Henry tapp'd her cheek so fair,
"Forgive me, and be again as dear,
My Dame Gunild."

67. The gallant Memering homward sped,

With broken shins and bleeding head,
    To Dame Gunild.

68.   "Now, Lady, for thy father's soul
      My life long give me bread and bowl,
          My Dame Gunild."

69.   "Memering, my champion, stout and leal,
      Fear not, thy wounds myself will heal,"
          Said Dame Gunild.

70.   "And all thy days I'll give thee bread,
      And clothe thee too in scarlet red,"
          Said Dame Gunild.

FAIR ANNIE (62)

This ballad preserves an old story common to the Germanic countries
and to central Europe. Basically it is the story of a man who has
taken a woman by capture or purchase. After he has lived with her for
several years and she has borne him children, he decides to marry.
When he brings his bride home, the bride discovers (or her parents
who accompany her do) that the mistress is her lost sister. It ends
happily with the marriage of the man and the mistress. The finest literary version of this story is the 12th-century *Lai de Freisne* by Marie
de France. The European ballads are not earlier than the 15th century. Only the nub of the story is left in the few American texts
which have survived.

Text A, traditional in Scotland, printed in Scott, ii, 102; B, traditional in Virginia, printed in Sharp, i, 95.

Notes
4/2–4. Braided hair was a mark of virginity.

A.

1.   "It's narrow, narrow, make your bed,
          And learn to lie your lane;
      For I'm ga'n oer to the sea, Fair Annie,
          A braw bride to bring hame.
      Wi her I will get gowd and gear;
          Wi you I ne'er got nane.

2.   "But wha will bake my bridal bread,
          Or brew my bridal ale?
      And wha will welcome my brisk bride,
          That I bring o'er the dale?"

3.   "It's I will bake your bridal bread,

And brew your bridal ale,
And I will welcome your brisk bride,
That you bring oer the dale."

4. "But she that welcomes my brisk bride
        Maun gang like maiden fair;
    She maun lace on her robe sae jimp,
        And braid her yellow hair."

5. "But how can I gang maiden-like,
        When maiden I am nane?
    Have I not born seven sons to thee,
        And am with child again?"

6. She's taen her young son in her arms,
        Another in her hand,
    And she's up to the highest tower,
        To see him come to land.

7. "Come up, come up, my eldest son,
        And look oer yon sea-strand,
    And see your father's new-come bride,
        Before she come to land.

8. "Come down, come down, my mother dear,
        Come frae the castle wa.
    I fear, if langer ye stand there,
        Ye'll let yoursell down fa."

9. And she gaed down, and farther down,
        Her love's ship for to see,
    And the topmast and the mainmast
        Shone like the silver free.

10. And she's gane down, and farther down,
        The bride's ship to behold,
    And the topmast and the mainmast,
        They shone just like the gold.

11. She's taen her seven sons in her hand,
        I wot she didna fail;
    She met Lord Thomas and his bride,
        As they came o'er the dale.

12. "You're welcome to your house, Lord Thomas,
        You're welcome to your land;
    You're welcome with your fair ladye,
        That you lead by the hand.

13. "You're welcome to your ha's, ladye,
        Your welcome to your bowers;

You're welcome to your hame ladye,
  For a' that's here is yours."

14. "I thank thee, Annie; I thank thee, Annie,
    Sae dearly as I thank thee;
  You're the likest to my sister Annie,
    That ever I did see.

15. "There came a knight out o'er the sea,
    And steald my sister away;
  The shame scoup in his company,
    And land whereer he gae."

16. She hang ae napkin at the door,
    Another in the ha,
  And a' to wipe the trickling tears,
    Sae fast as they did fa.

17. And aye she served the lang tables,
    With white bread and with wine,
  And aye she drank the wan water,
    To had her colour fine.

18. And aye she served the lang tables,
    With white bread and with brown;
  And ay she turned her round about,
    Sae fast the tears fell down.

19. And he's taen down the silk napkin,
    Hung on a silver pin,
  And aye he wipes the tear trickling
    A' down her cheek and chin.

20. And aye he turn'd him round about,
    And smiled amang his men,
  Says, "Like ye best the old ladye,
    Or her that's new come hame?"

21. When bells were rung, and mass was sung,
    And a' men bound to bed,
  Lord Thomas and his new-come bride
    To their chamber they were gaed.

22. Annie made her bed a little forbye,
    To hear what they might say;
  "And ever alas!" Fair Annie cried,
    "That I should see this day!

23. "Gin my seven sons were seven young rats,
    Running on the castle wa,
  And I were a grey cat mysell,
    I soon would worry them a'.

24. "Gin my seven sons were seven young hares,
    Running o'er yon lilly lee,
    And I were a grew hound mysell,
    Soon worried they a' should be."

25. And wae and sad Fair Annie sat,
    And drearie was her sang,
    And ever, as she sobbd and grat,
    "Wae to the man that did the wrang."

26. "My gown is on," said the new-come bride,
    "My shoes are on my feet,
    And I will to Fair Annie's chamber,
    And see what gars her greet.

27. "What ails ye, what ails ye, Fair Annie,
    That ye make sic a moan?
    Has your wine barrels cast the girds,
    Or is your white bread gone?

28. "O wha was't was your father, Annie,
    Or wha was't was your mother?
    And had ye ony sister, Annie,
    Or had ye ony brother?"

29. "The Earl of Wemyss was my father,
    The Countess of Wemyss my mother;
    And a' the folk about the house
    To me were sister and brother."

30. "If the Earl of Wemyss was your father,
    I wot sae was he mine;
    And it shall not be for lack o gowd
    That ye your love sall tyne.

31. "For I have seven ships o mine ain,
    A' loaded to the brim,
    And I will gie them a' to thee,
    Wi four to thine eldest son:
    But thanks to a' the powers in heaven
    That I gae maiden hame!"

B.

1. Adieu, adieu, fair Annie, he did say,
   For twelve months and one day.
   It's twelve months be rolling round,
   Fair Annie thought the time being long.

2. She took her spy glass in her hands

And out of doors she went;
She looked to the East, West, both North and South,
And looked all under the sun.

3. She thought she saw Lord Thomas a-coming,
All bringing his new briden home.
She called her own seven sons:
I think I see your father a-coming
And bringing your step-mother home.

4. Come down, come down, dear mother they did say,
Some clothing to put on.
Saying: All of his merry, merry maids
Might as well to come as one.

5. Fair Annie she had a silken towel
Hanging on a silver pin,
And she wiped out her watery eyes
As she walked out and in.

6. The rest of them drunk ale, beer and wine,
But fair Annie she drunk cold well water
To keep her spirits alive.

7. There is a fair lady in our house,
Before tomorrow morning she'll be dead,
We will call to our waiting-maids
And have her taken out of town.
A word of two, Lord Thomas, she did say,
Before I go away.

8. I wish my sons was seven greyhounds
And I was a fox on the hill,
And they might have longer breath than I
That they might worry me down.

9. It's who is your father dear,
And who is your mother,
And who is your brother dear
And who is your sister?

10. It's King Henry he's my father dear,
Queen Chatry's my own mother
Prince Dudley your brother dear,
And Fair Annie she's my own sister.

11. If King Henry he's your own father dear,
Queen Chatry she's your own mother,
Prince Dudley your brother dear,
I'll ensure I'm your own sister.

12. We have seven ships all on the sea,

They're loaded to the brim,
And five of them I'll give to you
And two will carry me home,
And we'll have Lord Thomas burned.

CHILD WATERS (63)

Child's praise of this ballad as one "which has perhaps no superior in
English, and if not in English, perhaps nowhere" is extravagant,
though all would agree that it is a fine ballad. Its weakness lies in the
unmotivated ill treatment of the lady by Child Waters. A scrap of an
American version (Randolph, 1, 89) has the lady accompany him disguised as a page.
Text, Percy, p. 274.

1. Childe Watters in his stable stoode,
    And stroaket his milke-white steede;
    To him came a ffaire young ladye
    As ere did weare woman's weede.

2. Saies, "Christ you saue, good Chyld Waters."
    Sayes, "Christ you saue and see.
    My girdle of gold, which was too longe,
    Is now to short ffor mee.

3. "And all is with one chyld of yours,
    I ffeele sturre att my side;
    My gowne of greene, it is to strayght;
    Before it was to wide."

4. "If the child be mine, Faire Ellen," he sayd,
    "Be mine, as you tell mee,
    Take you Cheshire and Lancashire both,
    Take them your owne to bee.

5. "If the child be mine, Ffaire Ellen," he said,
    "Be mine, as you doe sweare,
    Take you Cheshire and Lancashire both,
    And make that child your heyre."

6. Shee saies, "I had rather haue one kisse,
    Child Waters, of thy mouth,
    Then I wold haue Cheshire and Lancashire both,
    That lyes by north and south.

7. "And I had rather haue a twinkling,
    Child Waters, of your eye,
    Then I wold haue Cheshire and Lancashire both,
    To take them mine oune to bee."

8.   "To-morrow, Ellen, I must forth ryde,
          Soe ffarr into the north countrye;
     The ffairest lady that I can ffind,
          Ellen, must goe with mee."
     "And euer I pray you, Child Watters,
          Your ffootpage let me bee!"

9.   "If you will my ffootpage be, Ellen,
          As you doe tell itt mee,
     Then you must cutt your gownne of greene
          An inche aboue your knee.

10. "Soe must you doe your yellow lockes,
          Another inch aboue your eye;
     You must tell noe man what is my name;
          My ffootpage then you shall bee."

11. All this long day Child Waters rode,
          Shee ran bare ffoote by his side;
     Yett was he neuer soe curteous a knight
          To say Ellen, will you ryde?

12. But all this day Child Waters rode,
          Shee ran barffoote thorow the broome;
     Yett he was neuer soe curteous a knight
          As to say, Put on your shoone.

13. "Ride softlye," shee said, "Child Watters;
          Why doe you ryde soe ffast?
     The child which is no mans but yours
          My bodye itt will burst."

14. He sayes, "Sees thou yonder water, Ellen,
          That fflowes from banke to brim?"
     "I trust to god, Child Waters," shee said,
          "You will neuer see mee swime."

15. But when shee came to the water's side,
          Shee sayled to the chinne:
     "Except the lord of heauen by my speed,
          Now must I learne to swime."

16. The salt waters bare vp Ellen's clothes,
          Our Ladye bare vpp her chinne,
     And Child Waters was a woe man, good Lord,
          To see Faire Ellen swime.

17. And when shee ouer the water was,
          Shee then came to his knee.
     He said, "Come hither, Ffaire Ellen,
          Loe yonder what I see!

18. "Seest thou not yonder hall, Ellen?
    Of redd gold shine the yates;
There's four and twenty ffayre ladyes,
    The ffairest is my wordlye make.

19. "Seest thou not yonder hall, Ellen?
    Of redd gold shineth the tower;
There is four and twenty ffaire ladyes,
    The fairest is my paramoure."

20. "I doe see the hall now, Child Waters,
    That of redd gold shineth the yates;
God giue good then of your selfe,
    And of your worldye make.

21. "I doe see the hall now, Child Waters,
    That of redd gold shineth the tower;
God giue good then of your selfe,
    And of your paramoure!"

22. There were four and twenty ladyes,
    Were playing att the ball,
And Ellen, was the ffairest ladye,
    Must bring his steed to the stall.

23. There were four and twenty faire ladyes
    Was playing att the chesse;
And Ellen, shee was the ffairest ladye,
    Must bring his horsse to grasse.

24. And then bespake Child Waters' sister,
    And these were the word said shee:
"You haue the prettyest ffootpage, brother,
    That euer I saw with mine eye;

25. "But that his belly it is soe bigg,
    His girdle goes wondrous hye;
And euer I pray you, Child Waters,
    Let him goe into the chamber with mee."

26. "It is more meete for a little ffootpage,
    That has run through mosse and mire,
To take his supper vpon his knee
    And sitt downe by the kitchen fyer,
Then to goe into the chamber with any ladye
    That weares soe rich attyre."

27. But when the had supped euery one,
    To bedd they took the way;
He sayd, "Come hither, my little footpage,
    Harken what I doe say.

28.   "And goe thee downe into yonder towne,
          And low into the street;
      The ffairest ladye that thou can find,
          Hyer her in mine armes to sleepe,
      And take her vp in thine armes two,
          For filinge of her ffeete."

29.   Ellen is gone into the towne,
          And low into the streete;
      The fairest ladye that shee cold find
          Shee hyred in his armes to sleepe,
      And tooke her in her armes two,
          For filing of her ffeete.

30.   "I pray you now, good Child Waters,
          That I may creepe in att your bedd's feete;
      For there is noe place about this house
          Where I may say a sleepe."

31.   This night and itt droue on affterward
          Till itt was neere the day:
      He sayd, "Rise vp, my litle ffoote-page,
          And giue my steed corne and hay;
      And soe doe thou the good blacke oates,
          That he may carry me the better away."

32.   And vp then rose Ffaire Ellen,
          And gaue his steed corne and hay,
      And soe shee did and the good blacke oates.
          That he might carry him the better away.

33.   Shee layned her backe to the manger side,
          And greiuouslye did groane;
      And that beheard his mother deere,
          And heard her make her moane.

34.   Shee said, "Rise vp, thou Child Waters,
          I thinke thou art a cursed man;
      For yonder is a ghost in thy stable,
          That greiuouslye doth groane,
      Or else some woman laboures of child,
          Shee is soe woe begone."

35.   But vp then rose Child Waters,
          And did on his shirt of silke;
      Then he put on his other clothes
          On his body as white as milke.

36.   And when he came to the stable-dore,
          Full still that hee did stand,

That hee might hear now Faire Ellen,
How shee made her monand.

37. Shee said, "Lullabye, my owne deere child.
Lullabye, deere child, deere.
I wold thy father were a king,
Thy mother layd on a beere!"

38. "Peace now," he said, "good Faire Ellen,
And be of good cheere, I thee pray,
And the bridall and the churching both,
They shall bee vpon one day."

FAIR JANET (64)

This is a pan-Germanic ballad, but the English is more restrained. In the continental versions the girl (daughter or sister) is accused before the king of having just given birth to an illegitimate child. The king devises the dancing and other such tests to determine the truth. Usually the girl is betrayed when milk runs from her breasts.

Text, traditional in Scotland, printed by Sharpe, *Ballad Book*, p. 1.

1. "Ye maun gang to your father, Janet,
Ye maun gang to him soon;
Ye maun gang to your father, Janet,
In case that his days are dune."

2. Janet's awa to her father,
As fast as she could hie:
"O what's your will wi me, father?
O what's your will wi me?"

3. "My will wi you, Fair Janet," he said,
"It is both bed and board;
Some say that ye loe Sweet Willie,
But ye maun wed a French lord."

4. "A French lord maun I wed, father?
A French lord maun I wed?
Then, by my sooth," quo Fair Janet,
"He's ne'er enter my bed."

5. Janet's awa to her chamber,
As fast as she could go;
Wha' the first ane that tapped there,
But Sweet Willie, her jo?

6. "O we maun part this love, Willie,
That has been lang between;

There's a French lord coming o'er the sea,
　　To wed me wi a ring;
There's a French lord coming o'er the sea,
　　To wed and tak me hame."

7. "If we maun part this love, Janet,
　　It causeth mickle woe;
If we maun part this love, Janet,
　　It makes me into mourning go."

8. "But ye maun gang to your three sisters,
　　Meg, Marion, and Jean;
Tell them to come to Fair Janet,
　　In case that her days are dune."

9. Willie's awa to his three sisters,
　　Meg, Marion, and Jean;
"O haste, and gang to Fair Janet,
　　I fear that her days are dune."

10. Some drew to them their silken hose,
　　Some drew to them their shoon,
Some drew to them their silk manteils,
　　Their coverings to put on,
And they're awa to Fair Janet,
　　By the hie light o the moon.

* * * * * * *

11. "O I have born this babe, Willie,
　　Wi mickle toil and pain;
Take hame, take hame, your babe, Willie,
　　For nurse I dare be nane."

12. He's tane his young son in his arms,
　　And kisst him cheek and chin,
And he's awa to his mother's bower,
　　By the hie light o the moon.

13. "O open, open, mother," he says,
　　"O open, and let me in;
The rain rains on my yellow hair,
　　And the dew drops o'er my chin,
And I hae my young son in my arms,
　　I fear that his days are dune."

14. With her fingers lang and sma
　　She lifted up the pin,
And with her arms lang and sma
　　Received the baby in.

15. "Gae back, gae back now, Sweet Willie,

And comfort your fair lady;
 For where ye had but ae nourice,
  Your young son shall hae three."

16. Willie he was scarce awa,
 And the lady put to bed,
  Whan in and came her father dear:
  " Make haste, and busk the bride."

17. "There's a sair pain in my head, father,
 There's a sair pain in my side;
  And ill, O ill, am I, father,
  This day for to be a bride."

18. "O ye maun busk this bonny bride,
 And put a gay mantle on;
  For she shall wed this auld French lord,
  Gin she should die the morn."

19. Some put on the gay green robes,
 And some put on the brown;
  But Janet put on the scarlet robes,
  To shine foremost throw the town.

20. And some they mounted the black steed,
 And some mounted the brown;
  But Janet mounted the milk-white steed,
  To ride foremost throw the town.

21. "O wha will guide your horse, Janet?
 O what will guide him best?"
  "O wha but Willie, my true-love?
  He kens I loe him best."

22. And when they cam to Marie's kirk,
 To tye the haly ban,
  Fair Janet's cheek looked pale and wan,
  And her colour gaed an cam.

23. When dinner it was past and done,
 And dancing to begin,
  "O we'll go take the bride's maidens,
  And we'll go fill the ring."

24. O ben than cam the auld French lord,
 Saying, "Bride, will ye dance with me?"
  "Awa, awa, ye auld French lord,
  Your face I downa see."

25. O ben than cam now Sweet Willie,
 He cam with ane advance:

"O I'll go tak the bride's maidens,
 And we'll go tak a dance."

26. "I've seen ither days wi you, Willie,
      And so has mony mae,
     Ye would hae danced wi me mysel,
      Let a' my maidens gae."

27. O ben than cam now Sweet Willie,
      Saying, "Bride, will ye dance wi me?"
     "Aye, by my sooth, and that I will,
      Gin my back should break in three."

28. She had nae turned her throw the dance,
      Throw the dance but thrice,
     Whan she fell doun at Willie's feet,
      And up did never rise.

29. Willie's taen the key of his coffer,
      And gien it to his man:
     "Gae hame, and tell my mother dear
      My horse he has me slain;
     Bid her be kind to my young son,
      For father he has nane."

30. The tane was buried in Marie's kirk,
      And the tither in Marie's quire;
     Out of the tane there grew a birk,
      And the tither a bonny brier.

LADY MAISRY (65)

This seems to be a local Scotch ballad. Burning, usually in a tun, was the penalty for unchastity. The American version here printed tones down the gruesomeness.

Text A, Jamieson, i, 73; B, traditional in Virginia, Sharp, i, 99.

A.

1. The young lords o the north country
      Have all a wooing gone,
     To win the love of Lady Maisry,
      But o them she woud hae none.

2. O they hae courted Lady Maisry
      Wi a' kin kind of things;
     An they hae sought her Lady Maisry
      Wi brotches an wi' rings.

3. An they ha sought her Lady Maisry

Frae father and frae mother;
An they ha sought her Lady Maisry
Frae sister an frae brother.

4. An they ha followd her Lady Maisry
      Thro chamber an thro ha;
    But a' that they coud say to her,
      Her answer still was Na.

5. "O had your tongues, young men," she says,
      "An think nae mair o me;
    For I've gien my love to an English lord,
      An think nae mair o me."

6. Her father's kitchy-boy heard that,
      An ill death may he dee!
    An he is on to her brother,
      As fast as gang coud he.

7. "O is my father an my mother well,
      But an my brothers three?
    Gin my sister Lady Maisry be well,
      There's naething can ail me."

8. "Your father and your mother is well,
      But an your brothers three;
    Your sister Lady Maisry's well,
      So big wi bairn gangs she."

9. "Gin this be true you tell to me,
      My mailison light on thee!
    But gin it be a lie you tell,
      You sal be hangit hie."

10. He's done him to his sister's bowr,
      Wi meikle doole an care;
    An there he saw her Lady Maisry,
      Kembing her yellow hair.

11. "O wha is aught that bairn," he says,
      "That ye sae big are wi?
    And gin ye winna own the truth,
      This moment ye sall dee."

12. She turnd her right an roun about,
      An the kem fell frae her han;
    A trembling seizd her fair body,
      An her rosy cheek grew wan.

13. "O pardon me, my brother dear,
      An the truth I'll tell to thee;

My bairn it is to Lord William,
　　An he is betrothed to me."

14. "O coud na ye gotten dukes, or lords,
　　Intill your ain country,
That ye draw up wi an English dog,
　　To bring this shame on me?

15. "But ye maun gi up the English lord,
　　Whan youre young babe is born;
For, gin you keep by him an hour langer,
　　Your life sall be forlorn."

16. "I will gi up this English blood,
　　Till my young babe be born;
But the never a day nor hour langer,
　　Tho my life should be forlorn."

17. "O whare is a' my merry young men,
　　Whom I gi meat and fee,
To pu the thistle and the thorn,
　　To burn this wile whore wi?"

18. "O whare will I get a bonny boy,
　　To help me in my need,
To rin wi hast to Lord William,
　　And bid him come wi speed?"

19. O out it spake a bonny boy,
　　Stood by her brother's side:
"O I would rin your errand, lady,
　　Oer a' the world wide.

20. "Aft I have run your errands, lady,
　　Whan blawn baith win and weet;
But now I'll rin your errand, lady,
　　Wi sat tears on my cheek."

21. O whan he came to broken briggs,
　　He bent his bow and swam,
And whan he came to the green grass growin,
　　He slackd his shoone and ran.

22. O whan he came to Lord William's gates,
　　He baed na to chap or ca,
But set his bent bow till his breast,
　　An lightly lap the wa;
An, or the porter was at the gate,
　　The boy was i the ha.

23. "O is my biggins broken, boy?
　　Or is my towers won?

Or is my lady lighter yet,
Of a dear daughter or son?"

24. "Your biggin is na broken, sir,
Nor is your towers won;
But the fairest lady in a' the lan
For you this day maun burn."

25. "O saddle me the black, the black,
Or saddle me the brown;
O saddle me the swiftest steed
That ever rade frae a town."

26. Or he was near a mile awa,
She heard his wild horse sneeze:
"Mend up the fire, my false brother,
It's na come to my knees."

27. O whan he lighted at the gate,
She heard his bridle ring:
"Mend up the fire, my false brother,
It's far yet frae my chin.

28. "Mend up the fire to me, brother,
Mend up the fire to me;
For I see him comin hard an fast
Will soon men't up to thee.

29. "O gin my hands had been loose, Willy,
Sae hard as they are boun,
I would have turnd me frae the gleed,
And castin out your young son."

30. "O I'll gar burn for you, Maisry,
Your father an your mother;
An I'll gar burn for you, Maisry,
Your sister an your brother.

31. "An I'll gar burn for you, Maisry,
The chief of a' your kin;
An the last bonfire that I come to,
Mysel I will cast in."

B.

1. Down stepped her old father dear,
He stepped over the floor.
It's how do you do, Lady Margrie, said he,
Since your became a whore?

2. O dear father, I am no whore,

Nor never expect to be;
But I have a child by an English lord,
And I hope he'll marry me.

3. Down stepped her old mother dear,
She stepped over the floor.
It's how do your do, Lady Margrie, said she,
Since your became a whore?

4. O dear mother, I am no whore,
Nor never expect to be;
But I have a child by an English lord,
And I hope he will marry me.

5. Down stepped her oldest brother dear,
He stepped over the floor.
It's how do you do, Lady Margrie, said he,
Since you became a whore?

6. Very bad, very bad, dear brother,
As you can plainly see,
For my father and mother is both gathering wood
To burn my poor body.

7. I wish I had some pretty little one,
One errand for to run.
I'd run to my young lord's house
And tell him I said to come,
And to come quickly,
For my father and mother are both gathering wood
To burn my poor body.

8. Down stepped her brother's eldest son,
And stepped down over the floor,
And says: Many a mile that I have run,
And one for you I'll go.

9. I wish him well, for ever well,
And here send him a ring,
In hopes that he may mourn after me
But come to my burying.

10. I wish him well, for ever well,
And here I send him a glove,
In hopes that he might mourn after me,
But seek him another true love.

11. He run and he run till he came to the broad water,
He pitched in and swum;
He swum to the other side
And took to his heels and run.

12. He run to the young lord's gate,
    And tingled on the bell;
    And no one was so ready to rise and let him in
    As the young lord himself.

13. What news, what news, my pretty little page,
    What news have you brought to me?

    .   .   .   .

    .   .   .   .

14. Go saddle unto me the make-speed horse,
    Go saddle unto me the brown,
    Go saddle unto me the fastest horse
    That ever run on ground.

15. .   .   .   .

    .   .   .   .

    He got his pistols and sword and bugle,
    And threw his bugle around his neck.

16. As he was going round them lone fields
    And a-going in full speed,
    The ring bursted off his finger
    And his nose broke out for to bleed.

17. O dear mother, I value you not one straw,
    For my young lord is coming,
    I hear his bugle blow.

    .   .   .   .   .

LORD INGRAM AND CHIEL WYET (66)

This dramatic story of the rivalry of two brothers (or nephew and uncle) is, like the preceding, less brutal than its Germanic analogues. It contains a number of ballad commonplaces and shows confusion with "Lady Maisry." The famous Danish ballad of "Ebbé Skammelson" which has many details in common with this ballad is given for comparison.

Text, traditional in Scotland, printed by Maidment, *North Country Garland*, p. 24.

Notes

10. The bonny boy who carries messages is common to many ballads and the description of his journey and reception is completely conventional. 14. Compare "Sir Patrick Spens."

    1. Lord Ingram and Chiel Wyet
       Was baith born in one bower;
       Laid baith their hearts on one lady,
       The less was their honour.

2. Chiel Wyet and Lord Ingram
    Was baith born in one hall;
    Laid baith their hearts on one lady,
    The worse did them befall.

3. Lord Ingram wood her Lady Maisery
    From father and from mother;
    Lord Ingram wood her Lady Maisery
    From sister and from brother.

4. Lord Ingram wood her Lady Maisery
    With leave of a' her kin;
    And every one gave full consent,
    But she said no to him.

5. Lord Ingram wood her Lady Maisery
    Into her father's ha;
    Chiel Wyet wood her Lady Maisery
    Amang the sheets so sma.

6. Now it fell out upon a day,
    She was dressing her head,
    That ben did come her father dear,
    Wearing the gold so red.

7. He said, "Get up now, Lady Maisery,
    Put on your wedding gown;
    For Lord Ingram he will be here,
    Your wedding must be done."

8. "I'd rather be Chiel Wyet's wife,
    The white fish for to sell,
    Before I were Lord Ingram's wife,
    To wear the silk so well.

9. "I'd rather be Chiel Wyet's wife,
    With him to beg my bread,
    Before I were Lord Ingram's wife,
    To wear the gold so red.

10. "Where will I get a bonny boy,
    Will win gold to his fee,
    And will run unto Chiel Wyet's,
    With this letter from me?"

11. "O here I am, the boy," says one,
    "Will win gold to my fee,
    And carry away any letter
    To Chiel Wyet from thee."

12. And when he found the bridges broke,
    He bent his bow and swam;

And when he found the grass growing,
    He hastened and he ran.

13. And when he came to Chiel Wyet's castle,
        He did not knock nor call,
    But set his bent bow to his breast,
        And lightly leaped the wall;
    And ere the porter opend the gate,
        The boy was in the hall.

14. The first line he looked on,
        A grieved man was he;
    The next line he looked on,
        A tear blinded his ee;
    Says, "I wonder what ails my one brother
        He'll not let my love be!

15. "But I'll send to my brother's bridal—
        The bacon shall be mine—
    Full four and twenty buck and roe,
        And ten tun of the wine;
    And bid my love be blythe and glad,
        And I will follow syne."

16. There was not a groom about that castle
        But got a gown of green,
    And all was blythe, and all was glad,
        But Lady Maisery she was neen.

17. There was no cook about that kitchen
        But got a gown of gray,
    And all was blythe, and all was glad,
        But Lady Maisery was wae.

18. Between Mary Kirk and that castle
        Was all spread ower with garl,
    To keep Lady Maisery and her maidens
        From tramping on the marl.

19. From Mary Kirk to that castle
        Was spread a cloth of gold,
    To keep Lady Maisery and her maidens
        From treading on the mold.

20. When mass was sung, and bells was rung,
        And all men bound for bed,
    Then Lord Ingram and Lady Maisery
        In one bed they were laid.

21. When they were laid into their bed—
        It was baith soft and warm—

He laid his hand over her side,
 Says, I think you are with bairn.

22. "I told you once, so did I twice,
 When ye came me to woo,
That Chiel Wyet, your only brother,
 One night lay in my bower.

23. "I told you twice, I told you thrice,
 Ere ye came me to wed,
That Chiel Wyet, your one brother,
 One night lay in my bed."

24. "O will you father your bairn on me,
 And on no other man?
And I'll give him to his dowry
 Full fifty ploughs of land."

25. "I will not father my bairn on you,
 Nor on no wrongeous man,
Though ye would give him to his dowry
 Five thousand ploughs of land."

26. Then up did start him Chiel Wyet,
 Shed by his yellow hair,
And gave Lord Ingram to the heart
 A deep wound and a sair.

27. Then up did start him Lord Ingram,
 Shed by his yellow hair,
And gave Chiel Wyet to the heart
 A deep wound and a sair.

28. There was no pity for that two lords,
 Where they were lying slain;
But all was for her Lady Maisery,
 In that bower she gaed brain.

29. There was no pity for that two lords,
 When they were lying dead;
But all was for her Lady Maisery,
 In that bower she went mad.

30. Said, "Get to me a cloak of cloth,
 A staff of good hard tree;
If I have been an evil woman,
 I shall beg till I dee.

31. "For a bit I'll beg for Chiel Wyet,
 For Lord Ingram I'll beg three;
All for the good and honorable marriage
 At Mary Kirk he gave me."

EBBÉ SKAMMELSON

1.   Northward in Thy Sir Skammel dwelt,
     For wealth and goodness known;
    Five sons had he, so courtly bred,
     And two to manhood grown.

2.   The one hight Ebbé Skammelson,
     And Peter one,—the young;
    A doleful story it is to hear,
     The fate that o'er them hung.

3.   Ebbé laid saddle upon his horse,
     And rode to an isle away,
    And there betroth'd fair Adelaide,
     A sweet and lovely may.

4.   He won the gentle Adelaide,
     A lily flower was she,
    And brought her home to his mother's house,
     And went himself to sea.

5.   But first in the ladies' lofty bower
     He wish'd his bride adieu;
    "While in the royal court I serve,
     Remain to your promise true.

6.   "Wait for me, gently Adelaide,
     Your honour keep in mind;
    Meanwhile I go to a distant land,
     A livelihood to find."

7.   But while young Ebbé serves at court,
     And rank and fame pursues,
    His brother Peter stays at home,
     And her, his trulove, woos.

8.   Ebbé he serves the king at court
     To earn him gold and fee;
    His brother Peter builds a ship
     And rigs it out for sea.

9.   His brother Peter builds a ship,
     And ploughs the salty tide,
    And steers across to North Jutland
     To court his brother's bride.

10.   And there young Peter Skammelson,
     In scarlet cloak array'd,

Mounts to the ladies' bower aloft,
    Where sits that lovely maid.

11. "My greeting, gentle Adelaide!
    Your troth if me you'll plight,
With love and honour all my days,
    Your favours I'll requite."

12. "How should I plight my love to you?
    Or share your house and land?
Your brother Ebbé, he it is,
    To whom I've pledged my hand.

13. "My vow to wait for eight whole years
    With all my kin I made;
I will not marry another man,
    And that the King too bade."

14. "But," answer'd Peter Skammelson
    In scarlet mantle dress'd;
"Ebbé is in the royal court,
    And makes your love his jest."

15. Then up his cruel mother spake,
    And evil rede she gave;
"Accept then Peter Skammelson,
    For Ebbé he is a knave.

16. "Ebbé is in the royal court,
    And glory wins and fame;
And there's in the Queen's bower the maid,
    Is Ebbé's latest flame.

17. "So take thou Peter, my younger son,
    With all his towers so red;
For Ebbé Skammelson, be sure,
    Another maid will wed."

18. "Nay hark thee, Peter Skammelson,
    Choose thee some other wife;
I give no other man my troth,
    So long as he has life."

19. "Hear then the truth," in earnest tone
    The mother so replied;
"Hear but the truth, fair Adelaide,
    Ebbé last autumn died."

20. Then rose the maiden Adelaide,
    As lily stalk so slim,
And Peter Skammelson betroth'd,
    And gave her hand to him.

21. They hasten'd for the marriage feast
       The luscious mead to brew,
     While Ebbé serv'd the king at court,
       And nothing of it knew.

22. Ebbé, when two months now were past,
       At dead of night awoke,
     And of the vivid dreams he had dream'd,
       He thus to his comrade spoke.

23. "It seem'd that through my room of stone
       A glowing fire did glide,
     And there my brother Peter burn,
       And burn my lovely bride."

24. "Then surely, Ebbé Skammelson,
       Some trouble is near at hand,
     For when one dreams of blazing fire,
       It bodes a naked brand.

25. "But that it was thy room of stone
       All in a blaze of fire;
     That bodes that Peter Skammelson
       Betrothes thy heart's desire."

26. Up started Ebbé Skammelson,
       And braced his sword to side,
     And sought the king, and furlough gain'd,
       Home to his friends to ride.

27. In eager haste he mounted horse,
       And he so swiftly flew,
     A seven day's journey home from court,
       The same he rode in two.

28. So well did Ebbé time his speed,
       As not to come too late,
     The day they held their wedding feast
       He reach'd his father's gate.

29. "Hark thee, and tell me, little page,
       What no I ask of thee;
     What means this joyous festival,
       And whence the company?"

30. "Here are the ladies met, who dwell
       Along the North-sea shore,
     And their's are all these gilded wains,
       That halt at Skammel's door.

31. "They've dress'd and deck'd thy brother's bride,
       And therefore are they gay;

Thy brother and gentle Adelaide
Keep here their wedding day."

32. Outside stood Ebbé's sisters two
With gold cups each in hand:
"O welcome, Ebbé, brother dear,
Back to your native land!"

33. Welcome so kind his sisters gave,
And rich rewards they won,
While e'en his parents stood aloof,
And welcome show'd him none.

34. Buckle or brooch he gave them each
Of gold all richly wrought;
Gifts he had bravely earn'd at court,
And home to his trulove brought.

35. The one begg'd him at home to stay;
The other forth to go;
"If but one night thou stayest here,
'Twill bring us bitter woe."

36. His parents pray'd him enter in
And take his seat at board;
But mute was Ebbé Skammelson,
And answer'd not a word.

37. He turn'd his horse to leave the yard,
And fain would ride away;
His mother caught and held the rein,
And begg'd him there to stay.

38. She brought him forth a cushion'd stool,
Would have him sit to dine,
"Nay," answer'd Ebbé Skammelson,
"Leave me to pour the wine."

39. With pearls and gold so gaily deck'd
There sat the lovely bride;
As oft as Ebbé upon her gazed,
With grief at heart he sigh'd.

40. When daylight waned, and o'er the field
Was shed the glistening dew,
Rising with grace the fair young bride
From banquet hall withdrew.

41. With joyous hearts to the bridal house
They led the gentle fair,
And Ebbé begg'd to head the train
The bridal torch to bear.

42. "And how!" said Ebbé, when they came
    Before the chamber door,
    "The troth you plighted me the first,
    Remember you no more?"

43. "I've since to your brother plighted troth,
    Given all I had to give,
    But will a mother be to you,
    As long as I may live."

44. "Not for a mother wooed I you,
    I wooed you for my wife:
    And therefore Peter Skammelson
    Has now to end his life.

45. "Consent, fair maiden Adelaide,
    With me to go away;
    And be my fate, e'en what it will,
    My brother I will slay."

46. "And though your brother you should kill,
    You would not gain my love,
    For I should grieve myself to death,
    As on her bough the dove."

47. To hear her Ebbé Skammelson
    With anger fiercely frown'd,
    And muttering vengeance on them both
    Stamp'd wildly on the ground.

48. With that into the bridal house
    They led the gentle bride,
    But Ebbé bare beneath his cloak
    A drawn sword at his side.

49. He enter'd in and slew the maid,
    Where near her bed she stood,
    And left her lofty crown of gold
    All swimming in her blood.

50. He took the gory dripping sword
    Slily beneath his cloak,
    And turning back to the banquet hall
    He thus to his brother spoke:

51. "Hark thee, young Peter Skammelson,
    'Tis time to leave the wine;
    Thy bride sits in her bridal bed,
    And seems for thee to pine."

52. Up rose young Peter Skammelson,
    But sad at heart was he;

For well his brother Ebbé's rage
Was in his face to see.

53.   "Now listen, Ebbé Skammelson,
And lay thy wrath aside,
Sleep thou with gentle Adelaide,
To thee I yield the bride."

54.   "Go, Peter, thou, nor longer leave
The maid to pine alone;
The bridal house and bridal bed
With roses are bestown."

55.   But as young Peter Skammelson
From banquet hall withdrew,
His brother cleft his head in twain,
And him so foully slew.

56.   Great was the grief in bridal house,
And great the hall's dismay,
For dead were bride and bridegroom both,
E'en on their wedding day.

57.   His father got a grievous wound,
His mother miss'd a hand;
And Ebbé Skammelson must forth
A vagrant from the land.

58.   His brother, murderously slain,
And gentle bride lay dead,
And far and wide must Ebbé rome,
And beg his daily bread.

59.   From such a wedding, Gracious God,
Hinder both young and old!
Sour is the wine, and harsh the mead,
Where such sad news is told.

GLASGERION (67)

Two versions are given here for comparison. The first is from the
Percy MS., the second a version based on the singing of an old woman
in Aberdeenshire and combined with additions from another piece and
so "improved" by Jamieson the editor. A list of celebrated harpers
would take us from Orpheus through the Middle Ages. A number of
ballads and folk songs tell of harpers harping fish out of the sea, birds
out of their nests, and milk from a maiden's breast.

This ballad as such is not found in America, but here as in England
are found a number of *songs of the night visit* which have a close af-

finity with "Glasgerion" (see Baskerville, *PMLA*, xxxv:565). Barry
points out that these stories end in three different ways: tragic—the
lady kills herself; the knight kills the interloper and then commits suicide; comic—the lady taunts the knight or the interloper and takes it
as a good joke. In the third type the lady jilts the knight in favor of
the interloper. Printed here as an analogue is "Jack the Jolly Tar"
as collected by Phillips Barry in Maine, *Bulletin*, iii:10.

A.

1. Glasgerion was a king's owne sonne,
    And a harper he was good;
   He harped in the king's chamber,
    Where cuppe and candle stoode,
   And soe did hee in the queen's chamber,
    Till ladies waxed wood.

2. And then bespake the king's daughter,
    And these words thus sayd shee:

   .   .   .   .

      .   .   .   .

3. Saide, "Strike on, strike on, Glasgerion,
    Of thy striking doe not blinne;
   There's neuer a stroke comes ouer thin harpe
    But it glads my hart within."

4. "Faire might you fall, lady!" quoth hee;
    "Who taught you now to speake?
   I haue loued you, lady, seuen yeere;
    My hart I durst neere breake."

5. "But come to my bower, my Glasgerryon,
    When all men are att rest;
   As I am a ladie true of my promise,
    Thou shalt bee a welcome guest."

6. But hom then came Glasgerryon,
    A glad man, Lord, was hee.
   "And come thou hither, Iacke, my boy,
    Come hither vnto mee.

7. "For the king's daughter of Normandye,
    Her loue is granted mee,
   And beffore the cocke haue crowen,
    Att her chamber must I bee."

8. "But come you hither master," quoth hee,
    "Lay your head downe on this stone;
   For I will waken you, master deere,
    Afore it be time to gone."

9. But vpp then rose that lither ladd,
        And did on hose and shoone;
    A coller he cast vpon his necke,
        Hee seemed a gentleman.

10. And when he came to that lady's chamber,
        He thrild vpon a pinn;
    The lady was true of her promise,
        Rose vp and lett him in.

11. He did not take the lady gay
        To boulster nor to bedd,
    But downe vpon her chamber-flore
        Full soone he hath her layd.

12. He did not kisse that lady gay
        When he came nor when he youd;
    And sore mistrusted that lady gay
        He was of some churlës blood.

13. But home then came that lither ladd,
        And did of his hose and shoone,
    And cast that coller from about his necke;
        He was but a churlës sonne:
    "Awaken," quoth hee, "my master deere,
        I hold it time to be gone.

14. "For I haue sadled your horsse, master,
        Well bridled I haue your steed;
    Haue not I serued a good breakfast,
        When time comes I haue need."

15. But vp then rose good Glasgerryon,
        And did on both hose and shoone;
    And cast a coller about his necke;
        He was a kingës sonne.

16. And when he came to that ladies chamber,
        He thrild vpon a pinn;
    The lady was more then true of promise,
        Rose vp and let him in.

17. Saies, "Whether haue you left with me
        Your braclett or your gloue?
    Or are you returned backe againe
        To know more of my loue?"

18. Glasgerryon swore a full great othe,
        By oake and ashe and thorne,
    "Lady, I was neuer in your chamber
        Sith the time that I was borne."

19.   "O then it was your litle foote-page
           Falsly hath beguiled me."
       And then shee pulld forth a litle pen-kniffe,
           That hanged by her knee,
       Says, "There shall neuer noe churlës blood
           Spring within my body."

20.   But home then went Glasgerryon,
           A woe man, good Lord, was hee;
       Sayes, "Come hither, thou Iacke, my boy,
           Come thou hither to me.

21.   "Ffor if I had killed a man to-night,
           Iacke, I wold tell it thee;
       But if I haue not killed a man to-night,
           Iacke, thou hast killed three!"

22.   And he puld out his bright browne sword,
           And dryed it on his sleeue,
       And he smote off that lither ladd's head,
           And asked noe man noe leaue.

23.   He sett the swords poynt till his brest,
           The pumill till a stone;
       Thorrow that falsenese of that lither ladd
           These three liues werne all gone.

B.

1.   Glenkindie was ance a harper gude,
          He harped to the king;
      And Glenkindie was ance the best harper
          That ever harpd on a string.

2.   He'd harpit a fish out o saut water,
          Or water out o a stane,
      Or milk out o a maiden's breast,
          That bairn had never nane.

3.   He's taen his harp intil his hand,
          He harpit and he sang,
      And ay as he harpit to the king,
          To haud him unthought lang.

4.   "I'll gie you a robe, Glenkindie,
          A robe o the royal pa,
      Gin ye will harp i the winter's night
          Afore my nobles a'."

            *   *   *   *   *   *   *

5. He's taen his harp intill his hand,
       He's harpit them a' asleep,
    Except it was the young countess,
       That love did waukin keep.

6. And first he has harpit a grave tune,
       And syne he has harpit a gay,
    And mony a sich atween hands
       I wat the lady gae.

7. Says, "Whan day is dawen, and cocks hae crawen,
       And wappit their wings sae wide,
    It's ye may come to my bower-door,
       And streek you by my side.

8. "But look that ye tell na Gib, your man,
       For naething that ye dee;
    For an ye tell him Gib, your man,
       He'll beguile baith you and me."

9. He's taen his harp intill his hand,
       He harpit and he sang,
    And he is hame to Gib, his man,
       As fast as he could gang.

10. "O mith I tell you, Gib, my man,
       Gin I a man had slain?"
    "O that ye micht, my gude master,
       Altho ye had slain ten."

11. "Then tak ye tent now, Gib, my man,
       My bidden for to dee;
    And but an ye wauken me in time,
       Ye sall be hangit hie.

12. "Whan day has dawen, and cocks hae crawen,
       And wappit their wings sae wide,
    I'm bidden gang till yon lady's bower,
       And streek me by her side."

13. "Gae hame to your bed, my good master;
       Ye've waukit, I fear, oer lang;
    For I'll wauken you in as good time
       As ony cock i the land."

14. He's taen his harp intill his hand,
       He harpit and he sang,
    Until he harpit his master asleep,
       Syne fast awa did gang.

15. And he is till that lady's bower,
       As fast as he could rin;

When he cam till that lady's bower,
    He chappit at the chin.

16. "O wha is this," says that lady,
    "That opens nae and comes in?"
  "It's I, Glenkindie, your ain true-love,
    O open and lat me in."

17. She kent he was nae gentle knicht
    That she had latten in,
  For neither when he gaed nor cam,
    Kist he her cheek or chin.

18. He neither kist her when he cam,
    Nor clappit her when he gaed,
  And in and at her bower window,
    The moon shone like the gleed.

19. "O ragged is your hose, Glenkindie,
    And riven is your sheen,
  And reaveld is your yellow hair,
    That I saw late yestreen."

20. "The stockings they are Gib, my man's,
    They came first to my hand,
  And this is Gib, my man's shoon,
    At my bed-feet they stand;
  I've reavelld a' my yellow hair
    Coming against the wind."

21. He's taen the harp intill his hand,
    He harpit and he sang,
  Until he cam to his master,
    As fast as he could gang.

22. "Won up, won up, my good master,
    I fear ye sleep o'er lang;
  There's nae a cock in a' the land
    But has wappit his wings and crawn."

23. Glenkindie's tane his harp in hand,
    He harpit and he sang,
  And he has reachd the lady's bower
    Afore that eer he blan.

24. When he cam to the lady's bower,
    He chappit at the chin:
  "O wha is that at my bower-door,
    That opens na and comes in?"
  "It's I, Glenkindie, your ain true-love,
    And in I canna win."

* * * * * * *

25.   "Forbid it, forbid it," says that lady,
          "That ever sic shame betide,
       That I should first be a wild loon's lass,
          And than a young knight's bride."

26.   He's taen his harp intill his hand,
          He harpit and he sang,
       And he is hame to Gib, his man,
          As fast as he could gang.

27.   "Come forth, come forth, now, Gib, my man,
          Till I pay you your fee;
       Come forth, come forth, now, Gib, my man,
          Weel pay it sall ye be."

28.   And he has taen him Gib, his man,
          And he has hangd him hie,
       And he's hangit him oer his ain yate,
          As high as high could be.

29.   There was nae pity for that lady,
          For she lay cald and dead,
       But a' was for him, Glenkindie,
          In bower he must go mad.

JACK THE JOLLY TAR

1.   As Jack walked out of London city, no one on Jack to take pity,
      As Jack walked out of London city, no one on Jack to take pity,
      Jack thought he heard the people say that in the streets he'd have
         to lay.
      A whang dang diddle-de-dang, fol-lo-day.

2.   There was a squire who lived quite handy, he courted the lawyer's
         daughter Nancy,
      He courted her both night and day, and agreed with her one night
         to lay.

3.   "I'll tie a string around my finger and hang it out of the chamber
         window,
      You come up and pull the string, and I'll come down and let
         you in."

4.   She tied a string around her finger and hung it out her chamber
         window,
      Jack came up and pulled the string, and she came down and let
         him in.

5.   She slipped the string from off her finger, but it dangled from her
         chamber window,

The squire came up and pulled the string; the string was pulled, but he couldn't get in.

6. To give the squire a friendly warning, she arose at daylight the next morning,
   There she saw Jack in a striped shirt, his face and hands all covered with dirt.

7. "How come you here, you saucy fellow? You've broke my household and robbed me of my treasure."
   "I came up and pulled the string, and you came down and let me in."

YOUNG HUNTING (68)

The basic story of this much confused ballad tells of Young Hunting telling his mistress that he has a new sweetheart. She beguiles him with drink and then kills him and weights his body and throws it in the river. When the king comes looking for his son the lady says she has not seen him, that he is probably drowned. The king's "duckers" dive for the body but find nothing. However, a little bird tells them that Hunting was murdered and thrown in the river. They use the floating candle to discover the body. The girl then accuses her maid, but the judicial fire won't burn the maid. They then put the mistress in and she burns fiercely.

In America this ballad becomes hopelessly corrupt. Usually the body is thrown in a well, with the consequent omission of the duckers and the floating candle; often the motive for the slaying is omitted; other ballads lend stanzas and lines.

Text A, traditional in Scotland, in Herd, ii, 67; B, traditional from Kentucky, printed in *JAF*, 20:252.

Notes

2/2. White skin is much desired by romance heroines too.

7/1. The talking bird or bird of truth is common in folklore, but here the bird is probably the dead lover who has taken this dramatic way to work his vengeance; the bird soul is a common motif in folk tale and folk song.

16/2, 17/2. Oaths by thorns, ash, corn, grass, etc., are remnants of vegetation oaths or they may be "conjuring" oaths, that is, oaths sworn on a plant that can work magic, like mandrake. Here it would seem she is swearing by the earth and the sky.

22/4. Lighted candles were stuck in loaves of bread and then set afloat on the river. Where they gleamed brightest marked the resting place of the drowned man.

25/4. Here the fire serves as a judicial test.

A.

1. O Lady, rock never your young son young
       One hour longer for me,
   For I have a sweetheart in Garlick's Wells
       I love thrice better than thee.

2. "The very sols of my love's feet
       Is whiter then thy face."
   "But nevertheless na, Young Hunting,
       Ye'll stay wi me all night.'"

3. She has birld in him Young Hunting
       The good ale and the beer,
   Till he was as fou drunken
       As any wild-wood steer.

4. She has birld in him Young Hunting
       The good ale and the wine,
   Till he was as fou drunken
       As any wild-wood swine.

5. Up she has tain him Young Hunting,
       And she has had him to her bed,

   .   .   .   .

       .   .   .   .   .   .

6. And she has minded her on a little penknife,
       That hangs low down by her gare,
   And she has gin him Young Hunting
       A deep wound and a sare.

7. Out an spake the bonny bird,
       That flew abon her head:
   "Lady, keep well thy green clothing
       Fra that good lord's blood."

8. "O better I'll keep my green clothing
       Fra that good lord's blood
   Nor thou can keep thy flattering toung,
       That flatters in thy head.

9. "Light down, light down, my bonny bird,
       Light down upon my hand,

   .   .   .   .

       .   .   .   .   .   .

10. "O siller, O siller shall be thy hire,
       An goud shall be thy fee,
   An every month into the year
       Thy cage shall changed be."

11. "I winna light down, I shanna light down,
  I winna light on thy hand;
For soon, soon wad ye do to me
  As ye done to Young Hunting."

12. She has booted an spird him Young Hunting
  As he had been gan to ride,
A hunting-horn about his neck,
  An the sharp sourd by his side.

13. And she has had him to yon wan water,
  For a' man calls it Clyde,
. . . .
. . . . . .

14. The deepest pot intill it all
  She has puten Young Hunting in;
A green truff upon his breast,
  To hold that good lord down.

15. It fell once upon a day
  The king was going to ride,
And he sent for him Young Hunting,
  To ride on his right side.

16. She has turnd her right and round about,
  She sware now by the corn,
"I saw na thy son, Young Hunting,
  Sen yesterday at morn."

17. She has turnd her right and round about,
  She swear now by the moon,
"I saw na thy son, Young Hunting,
  Sen yesterday at noon.

18. "It fears me sair in Clyde Water
  That he is drownd therein."
O thay ha sent for the king's duckers,
  To duck for Young Hunting.

19. They ducked in at the tae water-bank,
  Thay ducked out at the tither:
"We'll duck no more for Young Hunting,
  All tho he wear our brother."

20. Out an spake the bonny bird,
  That flew abon their heads,
. . . .
. . . . . .

21. "O he's na drownd in Clyde Water,

He is slain and put therein;
The lady that lives in yon castil
Slew him and put him in.

22. "Leave aff your ducking on the day,
And duck upon the night;
Whear ever that sakeless knight lys slain,
The candles will shine bright."

23. Thay left off their ducking o the day,
And ducked upon the night,
The candles shone full bright.
And where that sakeless knight lay slain,

24. The deepest pot intill it a'
Thay got Young Hunting in;
A green turff upon his brest,
To hold that good lord down.

25. O thay ha sent aff men to the wood
To hew down baith thorn an fern,
That they might get a great bonefire
To burn that lady in.
"Put na the wyte on me," she says,
"It was her, May Catheren."

26. Whan thay had tane her, May Catheren,
In the bonefire set her in;
It wad na take upon her cheeks,
Nor take upon her chin,
Nor yet upon her yellow hair,
To healle the deadly sin.

27. Out they hae tain her, May Catheren,
And they hay put that lady in;
O it took upon her cheek, her cheek,
An it took upon her chin,
An it took on her fair body,
She burnt like hoky-gren.

B.

LOVING HENRY

1. "Get down, get down, loving Henry," she said,
"And stay all night with me;
But there's another girl in the Urgent land,
That you love better than me."

2. "I could get down if I would get down,
    And stay all night with you,
But there is a girl in the Urgent land
    That I love better than you."

3. As he leaned over his saddle skirts,
    To kiss her rosy cheeks,
All in her right hand she held a sharp knife,
    And in him she plunged it deep.

4. "I could have got down if I would got down,
    And stayed all night with you,
For there is no other girl in this wide world
    That I love better than you."

5. "Must I ride east? Must I ride west?
    Or anywhere under the sun,
To get the doctor so kind and good,
    To cure this wounded one?"

6. "You needn't to ride east, nor you needn't to ride west,
    Nor anywhere under the sun,
For there is no other but God alone
    Can cure this wounded one."

7. She took him by his lily-white hand,
    And led him across the yard;
She pitched him in that doomful well,
    Where the water is cold and deep.

8. "Lie there, lie there, loving Henry," she said,
    "Till the meat drops off your bone,
For there's a little girl in the Urgent land
    That will mourn for your return."

9. As she was on her way back home,
    Little birdie was sitting on a limb;
"Go home, go home, you cruel little girl,
    And there lament for him."

10. "Fly down, fly down, little birdie," she called,
    And sit on my right knee,
For the costly cords that's around my waist
    Will be supplied to thee."

11. "I could fly down if I would fly down,
    And sit on your right knee;
But the way you murdered your own true love,
    Surely you would murder me."

12. "I wish I had my cedar bow,
    My arrow and my string;

      I would shoot a diamond through your heart,
        And you'd no longer sing."

13.   "Although you have no cedar bow,
        No arrow nor no string,
     So I'll fly to the tops of some tall tree
        And there I'll sit and sing."

CLERK SAUNDERS (69)

Probably the original of this ballad contained a conversation between
the sister and the seven brothers (one English version preserves that
and most European versions do) in which they ask her such questions
as: Whose horse was before the door? Her answer, No horse but a
hind. Finally, "Who is that, May Margaret, You and the wa' between?" "O it is my bower-maiden," she says, "As sick as sick can be.
. . ." They reply, "We hae been east, and we've been west, And low
beneath the moon; But all the bower-women e'er we saw Hadna goud
buckles in their shoon." A set of questions and answers that remind
of "Our Goodman."

    Text, traditional in Scotland, Herd, ii, 419.

1.   Clark Sanders and May Margret
       Walkt ower yon graveld green,
    And sad and heavy was the love,
       I wat, it fell this twa between.

2.   "A bed, a bed," Clark Sanders said,
       "A bed, a bed for you and I."
    "Fye no, fye no," the lady said,
       "Until the day we married be.

3.   "For in it will come my seven brothers,
       An a' their torches burning bright;
    They'll say, We hae but ae sister,
       And here her lying wi a knight."

4.   "Ye'l take the sourde fray my scabbord,
       And lowly, lowly lift the gin,
    And you may say, your oth to save,
       You never let Clark Sanders in.

5.   "Yele take a napken in your hand,
       And ye'l ty up baith your een,
    An ye may say, your oth to save,
       That ye saw na Sandy sen late yestreen.

6.   "Yele take me in your armes twa,
       Yele carrey me ben into your bed,

And ye may say, your oth to save,
    In your bower-floor I never tread."

7. She has taen the sourde fray his scabbord,
        And lowly, lowly lifted the gin;
    She was to swear, her oth to save,
        She never let Clerk Sanders in.

8. She has tain a napkin in her hand,
        And she ty'd up baith her eeen;
    She was to swear, her oth to save,
        She saw na him sene late yestreen.

9. She has taen him in her armes twa,
        And carried him ben into her bed;
    She was to swear, her oth to save,
        He never in her bower-floor tread.

10. In and came her seven brothers,
        And all their torches burning bright;
    Says thay, We hae but ae sister,
        And see there her lying wi a knight.

11. Out and speaks the first of them,
        "A wat they hay been lovers dear."
    Out and speaks the next of them,
        "They hay been in love this many a year."

12. Out an speaks the third of them,
        "It wear great sin this twa to twain."
    Out an speaks the fourth of them,
        "It wear a sin to kill a sleeping man."

13. Out an speaks the fifth of them,
        "A wat they'll near be twaind by me."
    Out an speaks the sixt of them,
        "We'l tak our leave an gae our way."

14. Out an speaks the seventh of them,
        "Altho there wear no a man but me,

        .   .   .   .   .   .

    I bear the brand, I'le gar him die."

15. Out he has taen a bright long brand,
        And he has striped it throw the straw,
    And throw and throw Clarke Sanders' body
        A wat he has gard cold iron gae.

16. Sanders he started, an Margret she lapt,
        Intill his arms whare she lay,

And well and wellsom was the night,
    A wat it was between these twa.

17. And they lay still, and sleeped sound,
        Untill the day began to daw;
    And kindly till him she did say
        "It's time, trew-love, ye wear awa."

18. They lay still, and sleeped sound,
        Untill the sun began to shine;
    She lookt between her and the wa,
        And dull and heavy was his eeen.

19. She thought it had been a loathsome sweat,
        A wat it had fallen this twa between;
    But it was the blood of his fair body,
        A wat his life days wair na lang.

20. "O Sanders, I'le do for your sake
        What other ladys would na thoule;
    When seven years is come and gone,
        There's near a shoe go on my sole.

21. "O Sanders, I'le do for your sake
        What other ladies would think mare;
    When seven years is come an gone,
        Ther's nere a comb go in my hair.

22. "O Sanders, I'le do for your sake
        What other ladies would think lack;
    When seven years is come an gone,
        I'le wear nought but dowy black."

23. The bells gaed clinking throw the towne,
        To carry the dead corps to the clay,
    An sighing says her May Margret,
        "A wat I bide a doulfou day."

24. In an come her father dear,
        Stout steping on the floor;

    .   .   .   .   .   .

        .   .   .   .   .   .

25. "Hold your toung, my doughter dear,
        Let all your mourning a bee;
    I'le carry the dead corps to the clay,
        An I'le come back an comfort thee."

26. "Comfort well your seven sons,
        For comforted will I never bee;
    For it was neither lord nor loune
        That was in bower last night wi mee."

THE CLERK'S TWA SONS O OWSENFORD (72)

European ballads presenting this general situation are fairly common. Text, traditional in Scotland, 17th century. Kinloch, v, 403.

1. O I will sing to you a sang,
   But oh my heart is sair!
   The clerk's twa sons in Owsenford
   Has to learn some unco lair.

2. They hadna been in fair Parish
   A twelvemonth an a day,
   Till the clerk's twa sons o Owsenford
   Wi the mayor's twa daughters lay.

3. O word's gaen to the mighty mayor,
   As he saild on the sea,
   That the clerk's twa sons o Owsenford
   Wi his twa daughters lay.

4. "If they hae lain wi my twa daughters,
   Meg and Marjorie,
   The morn, or I taste meat or drink,
   They shall be hangit hie."

5. O word's gaen to the clerk himself,
   As he sat drinkin wine,
   That his twa sons in fair Parish
   Were bound in prison strong.

6. Then up and spak the clerk's ladye,
   And she spak powrfully:
   "O tak with ye a purse of gold,
   Or take with ye three,
   And if ye canna get William,
   Bring Andrew hame to me."

   *   *   *   *   *   *   *

7. "O lye ye here for owsen, dear sons,
   Or lie ye here for kye?
   Or what is it that ye lie for,
   Sae sair bound as ye lie?"

8. "We lie not here for owsen, dear father,
   Nor yet lie here for kye,
   But it's for a little o dear bought love
   Sae sair bound as we lie."

9. O he's gane to the mighty mayor,
    And he spoke powerfully:
"Will ye grant me my twa sons' lives,
    Either for gold or fee?
Or will ye be sae gude a man
    As grant them baith to me?"

10. "I'll no grant ye yere twa sons' lives,
    Neither for gold or fee,
Nor will I be sae gude a man
    As gie them back to thee;
Before the morn at twelve o'clock
    Ye'll see them hangit hie."

11. Up an spak his twa daughters,
    An they spak powrfully:
"Will ye grant us our twa loves' lives,
    Either for gold or fee?
Or will ye be sae gude a man
    As grant them baith to me."

12. "I'll no grant ye yere twa loves' lives,
    Neither for gold or fee,
Nor will I be sae gude a man
    As grant their lives to thee;
Before the morn at twelve o'clock
    Ye'll see them hangit hie."

13. O he's taen out these proper youths,
    And hangd them on a tree,
And he's bidden the clerk o Owsenford
    Gang hame to his ladie.

14. His lady sits on yon castle-wa,
    Beholding dale an doun,
An there she saw her ain gude lord
    Come walkin to the toun.

15. "Ye're welcome, welcome, my ain gude lord,
    Ye're welcome hame to me;
But where away are my twa sons?
    Ye should hae brought them wi ye."

16. "It's I've putten them to a deeper lair,
    An to a higher schule;
Yere ain twa sons ill no be here
    Till the hallow days o Yule."

17. "O sorrow, sorrow come mak my bed,
    An dool come lay me doun!
For I'll neither eat nor drink,
    Nor set a fit on ground."

LORD THOMAS AND FAIR ANNET (73)

This and the two ballads which follow have been very popular not only abroad but in America. They have similarities of story and probably for that reason have borrowed back and forth incident, stanza, and line. The Lord Thomas and Fair Annet type ends as here, or it ends with Annet killing her lover and often the other girl. Stanzas 16, 17, 18 sound as if they had come from a fairy ballad. For the rose and brier ending see the Introduction. In America this ballad is widely found under a variety of names, "Fair Eleanor," "The Brown Bride," "Three Lovers," etc. "Sir Peter's Leman," an analogous Danish ballad, is included here for comparison.

Text A, Percy Reliques, ii, 259; B, Pepy's *Ballads,* iii, 316; C, traditional in Kentucky, printed *JAF,* 20:254; D, Olrick, *A Book of Danish Ballads* (tr. Smith-Dampier), p. 229.

A.

1. Lord Thomas and Fair Annet
    Sate a' day on a hill;
   Whan night was cum, and sun was sett,
    They had not talkt their fill.

2. Lord Thomas said a word in jest,
    Fair Annet took it ill:
   "A, I will nevir wed a wife
    Against my ain friends' will."

3. "Gif ye wull nevir wed a wife,
    A wife wull neir wed yee."
   Sae he is hame to tell his mither,
    And knelt upon his knee.

4. "O rede, O rede, mither," he says,
    "A gude rede gie to mee;
   O sall I tak the nut-browne bride,
    And let Faire Annet bee?"

5. "The nut-browne bride haes gowd and gear,
    Fair Annet she has gat nane;
   And the little beauty Fair Annet haes
    O it wull soon be gane."

6. And he has till his brother gane:
    "Now brother, rede ye mee;
   A, sall I marrie the nut-browne bride,
    And let Fair Annet bee?"

7. "The nut-browne bride has oxen, brother,
    The nut-browne bride has kye;

I wad hae ye marrie the nut-browne bride,
 And cast Fair Annet bye.

8. "Her oxen may dye i the house, billie,
  And her kye into the byre,
 And I sall hae nothing to mysell
  Bot a fat fadge by the fyre."

9. And he has till his sister gane:
  "Now, sister, rede ye mee;
 O sall I marrie the nut-browne bride,
  And set Fair Annet free?"

10. "I'se rede ye tak Fair Annet, Thomas,
  And let the browne bride alane;
 Lest ye sould sigh, and say, Alace,
  What is this we brought hame!"

11. "No, I will tak my mither's counsel,
  And marrie me owt o hand;
 And I will tak the nut-browne bride,
  Fair Annet may leive the land."

12. Up then rose Fair Annet's father,
  Twa hours or it wer day,
 And he is gane into the bower
  Wherein Fair Annet lay.

13. "Rise up, rise up, Fair Annet," he says,
  "Put on your silken sheene;
 Let us gae to St. Marie's kirke,
  And see that rich weddeen."

14. "My maides, gae to my dressing-roome,
  And dress to me my hair;
 Whaireir yee laid a plait before,
  See yee lay ten times mair.

15. "My maids, gae to my dressing-room,
  And dress to me my smock;
 The one half is o the holland fine,
  The other o needle-work."

16. The horse Fair Annet rade upon,
  He amblit like the wind;
 Wi siller he was shod before,
  Wi burning gowd behind.

17. Four and twenty siller bells
  Wer a' tyed till his mane,
 And yae tift o the norland wind,
  They tinkled ane by ane.

18.   Four and twenty gay gude knichts
      Rade by Fair Annet's side,
  And four and twenty fair ladies,
      As gin she had bin a bride.

19.   And whan she cam to Marie's kirk,
      She sat on Marie's stean;
  The cleading that Fair Annet had on
      It skinkled in their een.

20.   And whan she cam into the kirk,
      She shimmerd like the sun;
  The belt that was about her waist
      Was a' wi pearles bedone.

21.   She sat her by the nut-browne bride,
      And her een they wer sae clear,
  Lord Thomas he clean forgat the bride,
      Whan Fair Annet drew near.

22.   He had a rose into his hand,
      He gae it kisses three,
  And reaching by the nut-browne bride,
      Laid it on Fair Annet's knee.

23.   Up than spak the nut-browne bride,
      She spak wi meikle spite:
  "And whair gat ye that rose-water,
      That does mak yee sae white?"

24.   "O I did get the rose-water
      Whair ye wull neir get nane,
  For I did get that very rose-water
      Into my mither's wame."

25.   The bride she drew a long bodkin
      Frae out her gay head-gear,
  And strake Fair Annet unto the heart,
      That word spak nevir mair.

26.   Lord Thomas he saw Fair Annet wex pale,
      And marvelit what mote bee;
  But whan he saw her dear heart's blude,
      A' wood-wroth wexed hee.

27.   He drew his dagger, that was sae sharp,
      That was sae sharp and meet,
  And drave it into the nut-browne bride,
      That fell deid at his feit.

28.   "Now stay for me, dear Annet," he sed,
      "Now stay, my dear," he cry'd;

Then strake the dagger untill his heart,
And fell deid by her side.

29. Lord Thomas was buried without kirk-wa,
Fair Annet within the quiere,
And o the tane thair grew a birk,
The other a bonny briere.

30. And ay they grew, and ay they threw,
As they wad faine be neare;
And by this ye may ken right weil
They were twa luvers deare.

B.

1. Lord Thomas he was a bold forrester,
And a chaser of the king's deer;
Faire Ellinor was a fair woman,
And Lord Thomas he loved her dear.

2. "Come riddle my riddle, dear mother," he said,
"And riddle us both as one,
Whether I shall marry Fair Ellinor,
And let the brown girl alone."

3. "The brown girl she has got houses and lands,
And Fair Ellinor she has got none;
Therefore I charge you on my blessing
To bring me the brown girl home."

4. And as it befell on a high holidaye,
As many did more beside,
Lord Thomas he went to Fair Ellinor,
That should have been his bride.

5. But when he came to Fair Ellinor's bower,
He knocked there at the ring;
But who was so ready as fair Ellinor
For to let Lord Thomas in.

6. "What news, what news, Lord Thomas," she said,
"What news, hast thou brought unto me?"
"I am come to bid thee to my wedding,
And that is bad news to thee."

7. "Oh God forbid, Lord Thomas," she said,
"That such a thing should be done;
I thought to have been thy bride my own self,
And you to have been the brid's-groom.

8. "Come riddle my riddle, dear mother," she sayd,
"And riddle it all in one;
Whether I shall go to Lord Thomas's wedding,
Or whether I shall tarry at home."

9. "There's many that are your friends, daughter,
And many that are your fo;
Therefore I charge you on my blessing,
To Lord Thomas's wedding don't go."

10. "There's many that are my friends, mother,
If a thousand more were my foe,
Betide my life, betide my death,
To Lord Thomas's wedding I'le go."

11. She cloathed herself in gallant attyre,
And her merry men all in green,
And as they rid thorough everye town,
They took her to have been a queene.

12. But when she came to Lord Thomas's gate,
She knocked there at the ring;
But who was so ready as Lord Thomas
To lett Fair Ellinor in.

13. "Is this your bride?" Fair Ellin she sayd,
"Methinks she looks so wondrous browne;
Thou mightest have had as fair a woman
As ever trod on the ground."

14. "Despise her not, Fair Ellin," he sayd,
"Despise her not now unto mee;
For better I love thy little finger
Than all her whole body."

15. This browne bride had a little penknife,
That was both long and sharp,
And betwixt the short ribs and the long
Prickd Fair Ellinor to the heart.

16. "Oh Christ now save thee," Lord Thomas he said,
"Methinks thou lookst wondrous wan;
Thou wast usd for to look with as fresh a colour
As ever the sun shin'd on."

17. "Oh art thou blind, Lord Thomas?" she sayd,
"Or canst thou not very well see?
Oh dost thou not see my own heart's blood
Runs trickling down my knee?"

18. Lord Thomas he had a sword by his side,
As he walked about the hall;

He cut off his bride's head from her shoulders,
And he threw it against the wall.

19. He set the hilte against the ground,
And the point against his heart;
There was never three lovers that ever met
More sooner they did depart.

C.

THE BROWN GIRL

1. "Mother, O mother, go riddle my sport;
Go riddle it all as one:
Must I go marry fair Alender,
Or bring the brown girl home?"

2. "The Brown girl she has house and land,
Fair Alender has none;
Therefore I warn you as a blessing,
Go bring the brown girl home."

3. "Go saddle up my milk-white steed,
Go saddle him up for me;
I'll go invite fair Alender
All to my wedding meal."

4. He rode, he rode till he came to the hall;
He tingled on the ring;
Nobody so ready as Fair Alender
To rise and let him in.

5. "What news? what news?" Fair Alender cried,
"What news have you brought to me?"
"I've come to invite you to my wedding,
Is that good news to thee?"

6. "Bad news, bad news," Fair Alender cried,
"Bad news you have brought to me;
I once did think I would be your bride,
And you my bridegroom be.

7. "Mother, O mother, go riddle my sport;
Go riddle it all as one;
Must I go to Lord Thomas's wedding,
Or tarry with thee at home?"

8. She dressed herself in scarlet red,
Her maidens they dressed in green,

And every town that they rode through,
    They took her to be some queen.

9. She rode, she rode, till she came to the hall;
    She tingled on the ring;
Nobody so ready as Lord Thomas himself,
    To rise and let her in.

10. He took her by the lily-white hand,
    And led her across the hall;
And led her up to the head of the table,
    Amongst the fair maids all.

11. Is this your bride," Fair Alender cried,
    "That looks so wonderful brown?
You once could of got as fair a lady
    As ever the sun shone on."

12. The brown girl had a little penknife,
    It was both keen and sharp;
Between the long ribs and the short,
    She entered Fair Alender's heart.

13. "What's the matter? What's the matter?" Lord Thomas he
    cried.
    "O don't you plainly see?
O don't you see my own heart's blood
    A-trickling down by me?"

14. He took the brown girl by the hand,
    He led her across the hall;
He drew (his) bright sword, he cut her head off,
    And threw it against the wall.

15. He put the butt against the ground,
    The point against his breast;
Here three young lovers all died to-day,
    God send them all to rest!

D.

SIR PETER'S LEMAN

1. Sir Peter and Kirsteen sat over the board,
    (While summer doth blow)
    They spake so many a jesting word.
    But day is dawning all in the East.

2. "Now tell me, Sir Peter, and do not fail,
    When shall we drink thy blithe bridale?"

3. "Oh, so far hence is my bridal gay
   No lady thither can find the way."

4. "And were it two hundred miles or more,
   Yet would I ride to that castle door!"

5. "And wilt thou to the bridal come,
   Then leave my golden gifts at home."

6. "And may I not bear them and fear no blame?
   Thou didst not bestow them for my shame!"

7. She wrapped herself in the scarlet fine,
   She went to the high-loft and poured the wine.

8. Up spake the bride to her serving-maid:
   "What lady now poureth the wine so red?"

9. The serving-maid up and spake so free:
   "Sir Peter's light-o'-love is she."

10. "And is she his love, that gay ladye,
    Why rideth he hither to wed with me?"

11. They feasted till far the night was sped,
    And the bride must go to the bridal bed.

12. To bridal bed the bride must fare,
    And the bridal torch did young Kirsteen bear.

13. The sheets of silk o'er the bed she drew:
    "There lies the swaim I loved so true!"

14. Young Kirsteen locked the door with speed
    And the fire she set to roof and reed.

15. The fire she set and did not stay,
    And most o'er the place where Sir Peter lay.

16. Sir Peter waked not in bridal bed
    Till the flames in his young bride's hair shone red.

17. "Kirsteen, Kirsteen, spare thou me!
    In time to come I'll be good to thee."

18. Loud she laughed then, little Kirsteen:
    "Right well wilt thou keep thy word, I ween!"

19. Greater than all was his hurt and harm,
    That the bride must burn in the bridegroom's arm.

20. All must die in that woeful hour—
    Fifteen maidens that lay in the bower.

21. And in that hour so sore
    Died thirty knights and more.

FAIR MARGARET AND SWEET WILLIAM (74)

This ballad tells the same story as the preceding, with the added details of the rejected girl committing suicide at home and then appearing as a ghost to her lover, causing him to go to her house, find her dead, and then die himself. Two fragments of this ballad are sung in Beaumont and Fletcher's *The Knight of the Burning Pestle,* c. 1611. No extant versions are older than the 18th century. The ballad was very popular in America probably because, like 73 and 75, it was in the early song books. Many variations in the story occur in America where the dropping of the ghostly visitation is characteristic.

Text A, English tradition, Percy Papers; B, tradition, Kentucky, printed in *JAF,* 23:381.

A.

1.   Sweet William would a wooing ride,
        His steed was lovely brown;
     A fairer creature than Lady Margaret
        Sweet William could find none.

2.   Sweet William came to Lady Margaret's bower,
        And knocked at the ring,
     And who so ready as Lady Margaret
        To rise and to let him in.

3.   Down then came her father dear,
        Clothed all in blue:
     "I pray, Sweet William, tell to me
        What love's between my daughter and you?"

4.   "I know none by her," he said,
        "And she knows none by me;
     Before tomorrow at this time
        Another bride you shall see."

5.   Lady Margaret at her bower-window,
        Combing of her hair,
     She saw Sweet William and his brown bride
        Unto the church repair.

6.   Down she cast her iv'ry comb,
        And up she tossd her hair,
     She went out from her bowr alive,
        But never so more came there.

7.   When day was gone, and night was come,
        All people were asleep,
     In glided Margaret's grimly ghost,
        And stood at William's feet.

8. "How d'ye like your bed, Sweet William?
　　How d'ye like your sheet?
　And how d'ye like that brown lady,
　　That lies in your arms asleep?"

9. "Well I like my bed, Lady Margaret,
　　And well I like my sheet;
　But better I like that fair lady
　　That stands at my bed's feet."

10. When night was gone, and day was come,
　　All people were awake,
　The lady waket out of her sleep,
　　And thus to her lord she spake.

11. "I dreamd a dream, my wedded lord,
　　That seldom comes to good;
　I dreamd that our bowr was lin'd with white swine,
　　And our brid-chamber full of blood."

12. He called up his merry men all,
　　By one, by two, by three,
　"We will go to Lady Margaret's bower,
　　With the leave of my wedded lady."

13. When he came to Lady Margaret's bower,
　　He knocked at the ring,
　And who were so ready as her brethren
　　To rise and let him in.

14. "Oh is she in the parlor," he said,
　　"Or is she in the hall?
　Or is she in the long chamber,
　　Amongst her merry maids all?"

15. "She's not in the parlor," they said,
　　"Nor is she in the hall;
　But she is in the long chamber,
　　Laid out against the wall."

16. "Open the winding sheet," he cry'd,
　　"That I may kiss the dead;
　That I may kiss her pale and wan
　　Whose lips used to look so red."

17. Lady Margaret died on the over night,
　　Sweet William died on the morrow;
　Lady Margaret died for pure, pure love,
　　Sweet William died for sorrow.

18. On Margaret's grave there grew a rose,
　　On Sweet William's grew a briar;

They grew till they joind in a true lover's knot,
And then they died both together.

B.

SWEET WILLIAM

1. Sweet William he arose on last May morning,
    He dressed himself in blue;
  "Come and tell unto me that long, long love
    Between Lydia Margaret and you."

2. "I know no harm of Lydia Margaret, my love,
    And I hope she knows none of me.
  By eight o'clock to-morrow morning
    Lydia Margaret my new bride shall see."

3. Lydia Margaret was standing in her boughing-door,
    A-combing back her hair.
  Who you reckon she spy but Sweet William and his bride?
    To the stone wall she drew nigh.

4. Lydia Margaret threw down her ivory comb,
    And quickly she wrapped up her hair;
  She went away to her own bedroom,
    And there she sang so clear.

5. The day being past and the night a-coming on,
    When they all were lying asleep,
  Lydia Margaret she arose with her tears in her eyes
    And stood at Sweet William's bed-feet.

6. "How do you like your blanket, sir?
    'T is how do you like your sheet?
  How do you like that fair lady
    Lies in your arms asleep?"

7. "Very well I like my blanket;
    Very well I like my sheet:
  Much better I like the fair lady
    A-talking at my bed-feet."

8. The night a-bein' past and the day a-comin' on,
    When they all were lying awake,
  Sweet William arose with trouble in his breast
    With the dreams that he dreamt last night.

9. "Such dreams, such dreams, such dreams," said he,
    "Such dreams, I fear, ain't good:
  I dreamed last night of young science in my room;
    My new bride's bed was blood."

10. Sweet William he called on his merry maids all,
        By one, by two, by three;
     Among them all he asked his bride
        Lydia Margaret he might go see.

11. "Is Margaret in her boughing-door,
        Or is she in her hall,
     Or is she in the kitchen-room
        Among the merry maids all?"

12. "She's neither in her boughing-door;
        She's neither in her hall;
     Tho' she is dead, in her own bed's made,
        Made up 'gainst yonders wall."

13. First he kissed her red rosy cheeks,
        And then he kissed her chin,
     And then he kissed her snowy-white breast,
        But the breath always stayed in.

14. Lydia Margaret she died like it might a-been to-day;
        Sweet William he dies to-morrow;
     Lydia Margaret she died for pure love's sake;
        Sweet William he died for sorrow.

15. Lydia Margaret was buried in the east of the church,
        Sweet William was buried in the west;
     And out of Lydia Margaret's grave grows a red, red rose,
        Spread over Sweet William's breast.

LORD LOVEL (75)

Except perhaps for "Barbara Allen," this is the most widely known ballad today. American versions are very close to the second version of the English printed here, a 19th-century broadside. "Lord Lovel" circulated widely in broadsides and in early song books.

Text A, English tradition, Percy Papers; B, 19th-century American broadside.

A.

1. "And I fare you well, Lady Ouncebell,
        For I must needs be gone,
     And this time two year I'll meet you again,
        To finish the loves we begun."

2. "That is a long time, Lord Lovill," said she,
        "To live in fair Scotland."
     "And so it is, Lady Ouncebell,
        To leave a fair lady alone."

3.   He had not been in fair Scotland
     Not half above half a year,
  But a longin mind came into his head,
     Lady Ouncebell he woud go see her.

4.   He called up his stable-groom,
     To sadle his milk-white stead;
  Dey down, dey down, dey down dery down,
     I wish Lord Lovill good speed.

5.   He had not been in fair London
     Not half above half a day,
  But he heard the bells of the high chapel ring,
     They rang with a ceserera.

6.   He asked of a gentleman,
     That set there all alone,
  What made the bells of the high chapel ring,
     The ladys make all their moan.

7.   "One of the king's daughters are dead," said he,
     "Lady Ouncebell was her name;
  She died for love of a courteous young night,
     Lord Lovill he was the same."

8.   He caused her corps to be set down,
     And her winding sheet undone,
  And he made a vow before them all
     He'd never kiss woman again.

9.   Lady Ouncebell died on the yesterday,
     Lord Lovill on the morrow;
  Lady Ouncebell died for pure true love,
     Lord Lovill died for sorrow.

10.   Lady Ouncebell was buried in the high chancel,
     Lord Lovill in the choir;
  Lady Ouncebell's breast sprung out a sweet rose,
     Lord Lovill's a bunch of sweet brier.

11.   They grew till they grew to the top of the church,
     And then they could grow no higher;
  They grew till they grew to a true-lover's not,
     And then they tyed both together.

12.   An old woman coming by that way,
     And a blessing she did crave,
  To cut off a bunch of that true-lover's not,
     And buried them both in one grave.

B.

1. Lord Lovel he stood at his castle-gate,
    Combing his milk-white steed,
  When up came Lady Nancy Belle,
    To wish her lover good speed, speed,
      To wish her lover good speed.

2. "Where are you going, Lord Lovel?" she said,
    "Oh where are you going?" said she;
  "I'm going, my Lady Nancy Belle,
    Strange countries for to see."

3. "When will you be back, Lord Lovel?" she said,
    "Oh when will you come back?" said she;
  "In a year or two, or three, at the most,
    I'll return to my fair Nancy."

4. But he had not been gone a year and a day,
    Strange countries for to see,
  When languishing thoughts came into his head,
    Lady Nancy Belle he would go see.

5. So he rode, and he rode, on his milk-white steed,
    Till he came to London town,
  And there he heard St Pancras bells,
    And the people all mourning round.

6. "Oh what is the matter?" Lord Lovel he said,
    "Oh what is the matter?" said he;
  "A lord's lady is dead," a woman replied,
    "And some call her Lady Nancy."

7. So he ordered the grave to be opened wide,
    And the shroud he turned down,
  And there he kissed her clay-cold lips,
    Till the tears came trickling down.

8. Lady Nancy she died, as it might be, today,
    Lord Lovel he died as tomorrow;
  Lady Nancy she died out of pure, pure grief,
    Lord Lovel he died out of sorrow.

9. Lady Nancy was laid in St. Pancras church,
    Lord Lovel was laid in the choir;
  And out of her bosom there grew a red rose,
    And out of her lover's a briar.

10. They grew, and they grew, to the church-steeple too,
    And then they could grow no higher;
  So there they entwined in a true-lover's knot,
    For all lovers true to admire.

THE LASS OF ROCH ROYAL (76)

This ballad is rather rare in spite of the fact that it is a moving and tragic story. No continental version exists, and only a few in America. However, the *Who will shoe my bonny feet?* stanzas (18–21) are very widely known. They are sung alone in America as lyric, are combined with other songs at will. Whether these stanzas are original with this ballad or not is hard to determine. Most versions begin with them as a kind of motivation for her setting out.

Text A, Elizabeth Cochrane's Song Book, c. 1790.

Notes
11. His mother is impersonating him.

1. Fair Isabell of Rochroyall,
      She dreamed where she lay,
    She dreamd a dream of her love Gregory,
      A little before the day.

2. O huly, huly rose she up,
      And huly she put on,
    And huly, huly she put on
      The silks of crimsion.

3. "Gar sadle me the black," she sayes,
      "Gar sadle me the broun;
    Gar sadle me the swiftest steed
      That ever rode the toun.

4. "Gar shoe him with the beat silver,
      And grind him with the gold;
    Gar put two bells on very side,
      Till I come to some hold."

5. She had not rode a mile, a mile,
      A mile but barely three,
    Till that she spyed a companie
      Come rakeing oere the lee.

6. "O whether is this the first young may,
      That lighted and gaed in;
    Or is this the second young may,
      That neer the sun shined on?
    Or is this Fair Isabell of Roch Royall,
      Banisht from kyth and kin."

7. "O I am not the first young may,
      That lighted and gaed in;
    Nor neither am I the second young may,
      That neer the sun shone on;

8. "But I'm Fair Isabell of Roch Royall
　　Banisht from kyth and kin;
　I'm seeking my true-love Gregory,
　　And I woud I had him in."

9. "O go your way to yon castle,
　　And ride it round about,
　And there you'll find Love Gregory;
　　He's within, without any doubt."

10. O she's away to yon castle,
　　She's tirled at the pin:
　"O open, open, Love Gregory,
　　And let your true-love in."

11. "If you be the lass of the Rochroyall,
　　As I trow not you be,
　You will tell me some of our love-tokens,
　　That was betwixt you and me."

12. "Have you not mind, Love Gregory,
　　Since we sat at the wine;
　When we changed the rings off our fingers,
　　And ay the worst fell mine?

13. "Mine was of the massy gold,
　　And thine was of the tin;
　Mine was true and trusty both,
　　And thine was false within."

14. "If you be the lass of the Roch Royall,
　　As I trow not you be,
　You will tell me some other love-token
　　That was betwixt you and me."

15. "Have you not mind, Love Gregory,
　　Since we sat at the wine,
　We changed the smocks off our two backs,
　　And ay the worst fell mine?

16. "Mine was of the holland fine,
　　And thine was course and thin;
　So many blocks have we two made,
　　And ay the worst was mine."

17. "Love Gregory, he is not at home,
　　But he is to the sea;
　If you have any word to him,
　　I pray you you leav't with me."

* * * * * * *

18. "O who will shoe my bony foot?
     Or who will glove my hand?
     Or who will bind my midle jimp
     With the broad lilly band?

19. "Or who will comb my bony head
     With the red river comb;
     Or who will be my bairn's father
     Ere Gregory he come home?"

20. "O I's gar shoe thy bony foot,
     And I's gar glove thy hand,
     And I's gar bind thy midle jimp
     With the broad lilly band.

21. "And I's gar comb thy bony head
     With the red river comb?
     But there is none to be thy bairn's father
     Till Love Gregory he come home."

22. "I'll set my foot on the ship-board,
     God send me wind and more!
     For there's never a woman shall bear a son
     Shall make my heart so sore."

23. "I dreamed a dream now since yestreen,
     That I never dreamed before;
     I dreamd that the lass of the Rochroyall
     Was knocking at the door."

24. "Ly still, ly still, my é dear son,
     Ly still, and take a sleep;
     For it's neither ane hour, nor yet a half,
     Since she went from the gate."

25. "O wo be to you, ill woman,
     And ane ill death mott you die!
     For you might have come to my bed-side,
     And then have wakened me.

26. "Gar sadle me the black," he sayes,
     "Gar sadle me the broun;
     Gar sadle me the swiftest steed
     That ever rode the toun.

27. "Gar shoe him with the beat silver,
     Gar grind him with the gold;
     Cause put two bells on every side,
     Till I come to some hold."

28. They sadled him the black, the black,

So did they him the broun;
So did they him the swiftest steed
  That ever rode to toun.

29. They shoed him with the beat silver,
       They grind him with the gold;
     They put two bells on every side,
       Till he came to some hold.

30. He had not rode a mile, a mile,
       A mile but barely three,
     Till that he spyed her comely corps
       Come raking oere the lee.

31. "Set doun, set doun these comely corps,
       Let me look on the dead;"
     And out he's ta'en his little pen-knife,
       And slitted her winding sheet.

32. And first he kist her cheek, her cheek,
       And then he kist her chin;
     And then he kist her rosy lips,
       But there was no breath within.

33. "Gar deall, gar deall for my love sake
       The spiced bread and the wine;
     For ere the morn at this time
       So shall you deal for mine.

34. "Gar deall, gar deall for my love sake
       The pennys that are so small;
     For ere the morn at this time,
       So shall you deall for all."

35. The one was buried in Mary kirk,
       The other in Mary quire;
     Out of the one there sprung a birk,
       Out of the other a bryar;
     So thus you may well know by that
       They were two lovers dear.

SWEET WILLIAM'S GHOST (77)

This is one of the most dramatic of the revenant ballads. The Danish analogue is printed here for comparison.

Text A, Ramsay, *Tea Table Miscellany*, p. 324; B, Prior, iii, 76.

Notes

4/3. The idea is that he cannot make his settled abode in the land of the dead because he still has this earthly tie. Another version reads:

"But gie me my faith and troth, Margrat/An let me pass on my way." 6. Almost all ballads concerned with revenants have this stanza. 14. The conventional signal for the dead to return. References abound in classical literature, in early Germanic myth and legend, in old English and throughout the ballads. The proper order is white or gray, red, black. By the time the black cock has crowed, all must be safe in their graves. 15–16. Betray the nice literary hand of the 18th-century poet. A Newfoundland version contains an interesting detail. When Margaret asks him to allow her to share his coffin, he replies that his parents are at his head and feet, three hell-hounds at his side—the hounds stand for drunkenness, pride, and deluding a maid.

A.

1. There came a ghost to Margret's door,
    With many a grievous groan,
  And ay he tirled at the pin,
    But answer made she none.

2. "Is that my father Philip,
    Or is't my brother John?
  Or is't my true-love, Willy,
    From Scotland new come home?"

3. "'T is not thy father Philip,
    Nor yet thy brother John;
  But 't is thy true-love, Willy,
    From Scotland new come home.

4. "O Sweet Margaret, O dear Margret,
    I pray thee speak to me;
  Give me my faith and troth, Margret,
    As I gave it to thee."

5. "Thy faith and troth thou's never get,
    Nor yet will I thee lend,
  Till that thou come within my bower,
    And kiss my cheek and chin."

6. "If I shoud come within thy bower,
    I am no earthly man;
  And shoud I kiss thy rosy lips,
    Thy days will not be lang.

7. "O sweet Margret, O dear Margret,
    I pray thee speak to me;
  Give me my faith and troth, Margret,
    As I gave it to thee."

8. "Thy faith and troth thou's never get,
    Nor yet will I thee lend,

Till you take me to yon kirk,
And wed me with a ring."

9.   "My bones are buried in yon kirk-yard,
Afar beyond the sea,
And it is but my spirit, Margret,
That's now speaking to thee."

10.   She stretched out her lilly-white hand,
And, for to do her best,
"Hae, there's your faith and troth, Willy,
God send your soul good rest."

11.   Now she has kilted her robes of green
A piece below her knee,
And a' the live-lang winter night
The dead corp followed she.

12.   "Is there any room at your head, Willy?
Or any room at your feet?
Or any room at your side, Willy,
Wherein that I may creep?"

13.   "There's no room at my head, Margret,
There's no room at my feet;
There's no room at my side, Margret,
My coffin's made so meet."

14.   Then up and crew the red, red cock,
And up then crew the gray:
"'Tis time, tis time, my dear Margret,
That you were going away."

15.   No more the ghost to Margret said,
But, with a grievous groan,
Evanishd in a cloud of mist,
And left her all alone.

16.   "O stay, my only true-love, stay,"
The constant Margret cry'd;
Wan grew her cheeks, she closd her een,
Stretched her soft limbs, and dy'd.

B.

SIR OGEY AND LADY ELSEY

1.   Three maidens in their chamber,
The two were weaving gold,
And wept the third her bridegroom,
Lay buried in the mould.

2. It was the rich Sir Ogey,
    He rode to an isle away,
  He wooed the Lady Elsey,
    And won that lovely may.

3. He won the Lady Elsey,
    Betroth'd his gentle bride,
  And on his very wedding night
    Before her eyes he died.

4. So sorely wept the lady
    And wrung her hands for woe,
  The knight Sir Ogey heard it
    Down in his grave below.

5. So sorely wept the lady,
    So sorely beat her breast,
  The knight Sir Ogey heard it,
    No longer could he rest.

6. He rose, the knight Sir Ogey,
    With coffin on his back,
  And stagger'd towards her chamber
    A dismal weary track.

7. He tapped her door with coffin,
    He wore no robe of skin;
  "Wake up, my gentle Elsey,
    And let thy bridegroom in."

8. Some while lay Lady Elsey,
    And much in doubt was she;
  "But can it be Sir Ogey
    Is hither come to me?"

9. Up spake the Lady Elsey,
    And tears were on her cheek;
  "Come, if the name of Jesus
    Thou still dost dare to speak."

10. "Rise then, dear Lady Elsey,
    And open me the door,
  For name I can Lord Jesus,
    As I could do before."

11. Up rose the Lady Elsey
    And bitter tears she shed,
  And let him in to her chamber,
    The cold buried dead:

12. She took her comb, fair Elsey,
    She comb'd his tangled hair,

And every lock she straighten'd,
    She dropp'd on it a tear.

13. "Now hear me, dear Sir Ogey,
    The truth I pray thee tell,
How under ground thou farest
    Down in thy cell."

14. "'Tis so down in that earth house,
    Where I must tarry now,
'Tis as the joys of heaven,
    If happy thou."

15. "Then hear me, knight Sir Ogey,
    And grant the boon I crave,
To go with thee, my dearest,
    And share thy grave."

16. "'Tis so down in that earth-house,
    My narrow lonely cell,
'Tis like to hellish torture,
    O cross thyself well!

17. "So oft as thou art weeping,
    And grievest thee so sore,
Is brimming full my coffin
    With blood and gore.

18. "Above my head is growing
    The grass so sweet,
But lothely snakes are twining
    About my feet.

19. "Yet when I hear thee singing,
    And thou art glad,
Then is my grave's small chamber
    With roses clad.

20. "The white cock now is crowing,
    And down must I below;
To earth wend all my fellows,
    And with them I must go.

21. "The red cock now is crowing,
    And down must I below;
To earth must wend all dead men,
    And I too must go.

22. "And now the black cock's crowing
    Home I must go below;

Unlock'd are all the portals,
    And I too must go."

23. Uprose the knight Sir Ogey,
    Took coffin on his back,
And stagger'd towards the churchyard
    A dismal weary track.

24. And what did Lady Elsey
    So sorrowful of mood?
She walk'd beside her bridegroom
    Across the murky wood.

25. But when she reach'd the churchyard,
    She saw his golden hair,
How pale it grew and paler,
    That once had been so fair.

26. And when she had cross'd the churchyard
    Up to the church's door,
Grew pale Sir Ogey's cheek too,
    As roses red before.

27. At hand and foot Sir Ogey
    Was fading away,
Fading his cheerful rosy cheeks
    To clods of clay.

28. "Now hear me, Lady Elsey,
    Hear me, my bride so dear,
No longer mourn thy husband,
    Nor drop for him a tear.

29. "But wend thee home, dear Elsey,
    In peace to sleep;
No longer mourn thy bridegroom,
    No longer weep.

30. "See yon small stars above thee,
    How wanes their light;
And see how fast is fleeting
    The hour of night."

31. She turn'd her towards the heavens,
    The stars, she saw them wane,
But slipp'd to his grave the deadman,
    She saw him not again.

32. He slipp'd away, the deadman,
    And down he went below,
And full of grief his lady
    Must homeward go.

33.   Sorely she wept, fair Elsey,
          And daily did she pray,
       That live she might no longer
          Than year and day.

34.   So sick she grew for sorrow,
          She laid her on her bed,
       And, ere that month was ended,
          Was on her bier, and dead.

THE UNQUIET GRAVE (78)

This is a fragment, but it is an exquisitely beautiful ballad as it is.
The first two lines set the mood of beauty and sadness. The evocative
power of the whole is remarkable. The ballad is concerned with the
world-wide belief that excess grief disturbs the dead. Excess tears wet
the winding sheet, or they fill the coffin with blood, or the tears scald
the dead through the shroud. Others believe that excess tears form
a wide river over which the dead must pass, or fill pitchers that dead
children must carry.

Text, English tradition, printed in *Folklore Record,* i, 60.

Notes
2/4. The conventional period of grieving.   3/3. The lines that
follow will remind one of Hardy's poem: *Ah, are you digging on my
grave?*

1.   "The wind doth blow today, my love,
          And a few small drops of rain;
       I never had but one true-love,
          In cold grave she was lain.

2.   "I'll do as much for my true-love
          As any young man may;
       I'll sit and mourn all at her grave
          For a twelvemonth and a day."

3.   The twelvemonth and a day being up,
          The dead began to speak:
       "Oh who sits weeping on my grave,
          And will not let me sleep?"

4.   "'T is I, my love, sits on your grave,
          And will not let you sleep;
       For I crave one kiss of your clay-cold lips,
          And that is all I seek."

5.   "You crave one kiss of my clay-cold lips;
          But my breath smells earthy strong;

    If you have one kiss of my clay-cold lips,
      Your time will not be long.

6. "'T is down in yonder garden green,
    Love, where we used to walk,
    The finest flower that ere was seen
      Is withered to a stalk.

7. "The stalk is withered dry, my love,
    So will our hearts decay;
    So make yourself content, my love,
      Till God calls you away."

THE WIFE OF USHER'S WELL (79)

This ballad is not complete in any version except in versions that have been "remade" in America. The oldest English text contains no motivation for the return of the sons, nor an account of their actions at home. In spite of this, it is still a highly dramatic and affecting ballad. Note the expressiveness of stanzas 11 and 12. In America this ballad is widely found remade into a coherent story. The three boys become children sent to the north country to learn their *grammarye;* often the motivation for their return is, as in "The Unquiet Grave," to warn their mother against excess weeping; often the children seem to return in answer to the mother's prayer.

    Text A, Scott, ii, 111; B, tradition, from Georgia, printed in *JAF,* 44:63.

A.

1. There lived a wife at Usher's Well,
    And a wealthy wife was she;
    She had three stout and stalwart sons,
      And sent them o'er the sea.

2. They hadna been a week from her,
    A week but barely ane,
    Whan word came to the carline wife
      That her three sons were gane.

3. They hadna been a week from her,
    A week but barely three,
    Whan word came to the carlin wife
      That her sons she'd never see.

4. "I wish the wind may never cease,
    Nor fashes in the flood,
    Till my three sons come hame to me,
      In earthly flesh and blood."

5. It fell about the Martinmass,
      When nights are lang and mirk,
    The carlin wife's three sons came hame,
      And their hats were o the birk.

6. It neither grew in syke nor ditch,
      Nor yet in ony sheugh;
    But at the gates o Paradise,
      That birk grew fair eneugh.

          *   *   *   *   *   *   *

7. "Blow up the fire, my maidens,
      Bring water from the well;
    For a' my house shall feast this night,
      Since my three sons are well."

8. And she has made to them a bed,
      She's made it large and wide,
    And she's taen her mantle her about,
      Sat down at the bed-side.

          *   *   *   *   *   *

9. Up then crew the red, red cock,
      And up and crew the gray;
    The eldest to the youngest said,
      "'T is time we were away."

10. The cock he hadna crawd but once,
      And clapped his wings at a',
    When the youngest to the eldest said,
      "Brother, we must awa.

11. "The cock doth craw, the day doth daw,
      The channerin worm doth chide;
    Gin we be mist out o our place,
      A sair pain we maun bide.

12. "Fare ye weel, my mother dear.
      Farewell to barn and byre.
    And fare ye weel, the bonny lass
      That kindles my mother's fire."

B.

1. There was a woman lived in Ardell,
      And babies, she had three;
    She sent them away to the North country
      To learn their granerlee.

2. They had not been gone two week—
   I am sure it was not three—
   Till old grim Death come knocking at the door,
   And tuck these babies away.

3. When their mother heard of that,
   She wrung her hands full sore;
   "Alas! alas!" their mother said,
   "I will see my babes no more."

4. "There is a King in Heaven, I know,
   Who I know wears a crown.
   "Oh, pray, Lord, do send my babies down."

5. Christmas time was drawing near;
   The night drew long and cold;
   These three babies come running down the hill,
   Into their mother's hall.

6. The table was spread with bread and wine;
   "Come, eat and drink, my sweet little babies,
   Come, eat and drink, it is mine."

7. "I do not want your bread, dear mare,
   Or neither want your wine,
   For yander stands our Saviour dear,
   And to Him we now must go."

8. She put them in the back room to sleep,
   Spread over with clean sheet,
   And over the top spread a golden sheet,
   To make them venture sleep.

9. "Wake up, wake up," said the oldest one,
   "The chickens will soon crow for day,
   And yander stands our Saviour dear,
   And to Him we now must go.

10. "Farewell, dear father, farewell, dear mother,
    Farewell to Aunt Kate and Kane,
    For yander stands our Saviour dear,
    And to Him we now must remain."

LITTLE MUSGRAVE AND
LADY BARNARD (81)

This ballad is at least as old as the Elizabethan age, for it is quoted in
several plays of that period. It seems to be wholly English. In America it has developed in oral tradition into several interesting variants.

Phillips Barry, *British Ballads from Maine,* uses this ballad to illustrate a discussion of how folk songs develop.

Text A, *Wit Restored in Several Select Poems Not Formerly Publisht,* 1658; B, tradition from Kentucky, printed in *Bulletin,* 4:12; C, tradition from New Hampshire, printed in *Bulletin,* 3:3.

A.

1. As it fell one holy-day,
        Hay downe
      As many be in the yeare,
   When young men and maids together did goe,
        Their mattins and masse to heare.

2. Little Musgrave came to the church-dore;
        The preist was at private masse;
   But he had more minde of the faire women
        Than he had of our lady's grace.

3. The one of them was clad in green,
        Another was clad in pall,
   And then came in my lord Bernard's wife,
        The fairest amònst them all.

4. She cast an eye on Little Musgrave,
        As bright as the summer sun;
   And then bethought this Little Musgrave,
        This lady's heart have I woonn.

5. Quoth she, "I have loved thee, Little Musgrave,
        Full long and many a day."
   "So have I loved you, fair lady,
        Yet never word durst I say."

6. "I have a bower at Buckelsfordbery,
        Full daintyly it is deight;
   If thou wilt wend thither, thou Little Musgrave,
        Thou's lig in mine arms all night."

7. Quoth he, "I thank yee, faire lady,
        This kindnes thou showest to me;
   But whether it be to my weal or woe,
        This night I will lig with thee."

8. With that he heard, a little tyne page,
        By his ladye's coach as he ran:
   All though I am my ladye's foot-page,
        Yet I am Lord Barnard's man.

9. My lord Barnard shall knowe of this,
        Whether I sink or swim;

And ever where the bridges were broake
He laid him downe to swimme.

10. "A sleepe or wake, thou Lord Barnard,
    As thou art a man of life,
For Little Musgrave is a Bucklesfordbery,
    A bed with thy own wedded wife."

11. "If this be true, thou little tinny page,
    This thing thou tellest to me,
Then all the land in Bucklesfordbery
    I freely will give to thee.

12. "But if it be a ly, thou little tinny page,
    This thing thou tellest to me,
On the hyest tree in Bucklesfordbery
    Then hanged shalt thou be."

13. He called up his merry men all:
    "Come saddle me my steed;
This night must I to Buckellsfordbery,
    For I never had greater need."

14. And some of them whistld, and some of them sung,
    And some these words did say,
And ever when my lord Barnard's horn blew,
    "Away, Musgrave, away!"

15. "Methinks I hear the thresel-cock,
    Methinks I hear the jaye;
Methinks I hear my lord Barnard,
    And I would I were away."

16. "Lye still, lye still, thou Little Musgrave,
    And huggell me from the cold;
'T is nothing but a shephard's boy,
    A driving his sheep to the fold.

17. "Is not thy hawke upon a perch?
    Thy steed eats oats and hay;
And thou a fair lady in thine armes,
    And wouldst thou bee away?"

18. With that my lord Barnard came to the dore,
    And lit a stone upon;
He plucked out three silver keys,
    And he opend the dores each one.

19. He lifted up the coverlett,
    He lifted up the sheet:
"How now, how now, thou Littell Musgrave,
    Doest thou find my lady sweet?"

20. "I find her sweet," quoth Little Musgrave,
        "The more 't is to my paine;
    I would gladly give three hundred pounds
        That I were on yonder plaine."

21. "Arise, arise, thou Littell Musgrave,
        And put thy clothës on;
    It shall n'ere be said in my country
        I have killed a naked man.

22. "I have two swords in one scabberd,
        Full deere they cost my purse;
    And thou shalt have the best of them,
        And I will have the worse."

23. The first stroke that Little Musgrave stroke,
        He hurt Lord Barnard sore;
    The next stroke that Lord Barnard stroke
        Little Musgrave nere struck more.

24. With that bespake this faire lady,
        In bed whereas she lay:
    "Although thou'rt dead, thou Little Musgrave,
        Yet I for thee will pray.

25. "And wish well to thy soule will I,
        So long as I have life;
    So will I not for thee, Barnard,
        Although I am thy wedded wife."

26. He cut her paps from off her brest;
        Great pitty it was to see
    That some drops of this ladie's heart's blood
        Ran trickling downe her knee.

27. "Woe worth you, woe worth, my mery men all
        You were n'ere borne for my good;
    Why did you not offer to stay my hand,
        When you see me wax so wood?

28. "For I have slaine the bravest sir knight
        That ever rode on steed;
    So have I done the fairest lady
        That ever did woman's deed.

29. "A grave, a grave," Lord Barnard cryd,
        "To put these lovers in;
    But lay my lady on the upper hand,
        For she came of the better kin."

B.

LITTLE MATHIE GROVE

1. Holiday, holiday, on the very first day of the year, year,
    On the very first day of the year,
    Little Mathie Grove went to the church
    The Holy Word for to hear, hear,
    The Holy Word for to hear.

2. The first came in was Lily-white,
    The next came in was a girl,
    The next came in was Lord Daniel's wife,
    The fairest one in the world, world,
    The fairest one in the world.

3. She placed her eye on little Mathie Grove,
    And said, "Go home with me this night;
    Go home with me this night for to lie,
    Go home with me this night."

4. "I can't go home with you this night,
    For fear I do lost my life,
    For the rings that's on your fingers says
    You are Lord Daniel's wife, wife,
    Says you are Lord Daniel's wife."

5. "But what if I am Lord Daniel's wife,
    Lord Daniel's gone from home;
    He has gone to the high King's house
    To see his fences, sir, sir,
    To see his fences, sir."

6. There stood that Little Foot-page,
    Hearing every word that they did say,
    He says, "Lord Daniel shall hear this
    Before the break of day, day,
    Before the break of day."

7. It was fourteen miles to the King's House,
    And seven of them he run;
    He run till he came to the broad river side,
    He bowed to his breast and swum, swum,
    He bowed to his breast and swum.

8. He swum till he came to the other side,
    He buckled up his shoes and run, run,
    He buckled up his shoes and run.
    He run till he came to the high King's gate,
    He rattled his bell and rung, rung,
    He rattled his bell and rung.

9. The first came out was Lord Daniel,
      Said, "What news have you to tell?
   Is your old scafel a-burning down,
      Or is your tavern won, won,
      Or is your tavern won?"

10. "My old scafel is not burnt down,
      But neither is my tavern won,
   But your wife is at home, in the bed,
      With Little Mathie Grove alone, lone,
      With Little Mathie Grove alone."

11. He had a trumpet and it would blow,
      And every time it would sound,
   It seemed for to say,
      "Rise up and go, go,"
      It says, "Rise up and go."

12. She says, "No, no, lie still with me,
      And keep me from the cold,
   It is nothing but them shepherd boys
      A-driving their sheep to the fold, fold.
      Driving their sheep to the fold."

13. They turned then, to hugging and kissing,
      Till they returned to sleep,
   And when they wakened the next morning,
      Lord Daniel was at their bed-feet, feet,
      Lord Daniel was at their bed-feet.

14. Says, "How do you like your blanket, Sir,
      And how do you like your sheet?
   Or how do you like this fair young miss
      That lies in your arms so sweet, sweet,
      That lies in your arms so sweet?"

15. "Very well do I like my blanket, Sir,
      Very well do I like my sheet,
   Much better do I like this fair young miss
      That lies in my arms asleep, sleep,
      That lies in my arms asleep."

16. "Get up, get up, put on your clothes,
      And fight me like a man,
   I can't have it said in the fairest land,
      That I slew a naked man, man,
      That I slew a naked man."

17. "How can I get up, put on my clothes,
      And fight you for my life,
   For I see you have two very bright swords,
      And me not as much as a knife, knife,
      And me not as much as a knife."

18. "Sir, I have two very bright swords
    Which cost me deep in purse,
    And you can have the very best one,
      And I will take the worst, worst,
      And I will take the worst."

19. The very first lick little Mathie stroke,
    He wounded him deep and sore,
    But the very first lick Lord Daniel stroke,
      Little Mathie couldn't fight no more, more
      Little Mathie couldn't fight no more.

20. He took this lady by the hand,
    And placed her on his knee;
    Says, "Which do you love the best,
      Little Mathie Grove or me, me,
      Little Mathie Grove or me?"

21. "Very well do I like your red rosy cheeks,
    Much better do I like your chin,
    Much better do I like Little Mathie Grove
      Than you or any of your kin, kin,
      Than you or any of your kin."

22. He took this lady by the lily-white hand,
    He led her out in the lane;
    He drew his sword from his side,
      He split her head into twin, twin,
      He split her head into twin.

23. "O don't you hear them larkins say,
    Don't you hear them sparrows cry,
    To-day I have slain the two fairest ones,
      And to-morrow I will have to die, die,
      And to-morrow I will have to die.

C.
LORD BANNER

1. Four and twenty laides fair, all being at a ball,
    Lord Banner's wife, she being there, the fairest of them all.
    And Young Lagrue from Scotland as fair as the rising sun,
    She looked at him and he looked at her, and the like it was never
    known.

2. Says she, "Oh, will you take a ride, oh, will you take a ride?
    You shall have servants to wait on you and a fair lady by your
    side."

"Oh, no, oh, no, I dare not do it, I'll not, for all of my life,
For by the ring on your forefinger you are Lord Banner's wife."

3. "What if I am Lord Banner's wife? Lord Banner is not at
   home;
   He has gone over to Convention to take Young Henry's throne."
   But one of his pages being there, which heard and see all that
   was done,
   He swore that his master should hear of this before the next
   rising sun.

4. He ran till he came to the river's side and he ploughed to his
   breast and swam;
   He swam till he came to the other side and he took to his heels
   and run.
   He ran till he came to the castle there; so loud he rapped at the
   door;
   And who was there so ready as Lord Banner to let him in.

5. "Oh, is there any of my towers down nor any of my towers
   three,
   Or has there anything happened unto my fair lady?"
   "Oh, no, there's none of your towers down, and there's none of
   your towers three,
   But young Lagrue from Scotland is in bed with your fair lady."

6. "If this be a lie you tell to me, which I suppose it to be,
   I will rig a gallows and hanged you shall be."
   "If this be a lie I tell of you, which you suppose it to be,
   You need not rig a gallows, but hang me on a tree!"

7. And he called by one of his merry, merry men, by one, by two,
   by three,
   Saying, "We will ride over to old Scotland this fair couple for
   to see."
   "What's this I hear so loud in my ear that sounds so loud and
   drear?"
   "It is Lord Banner's bugle, and he will soone be here!"

8. "Lie still, lie still and keep me warm and keep me from the
   cold,—
   It's only Lord Banner's shepherd boy a-driving sheep to the
   fold."
   They huddled and they cuddled; they both fell fast asleep,
   And when they awoke in the morning, Lord Banner, he stood
   at their feet.

9. "How do you like my blankets fine, and how do you like my
   sheets?

And how do you like that fair maid that lies in your arms
    asleep?"
"Quite well I like your blankets fine, quite well I like your
    sheets,
But I like this fair maid better that lies in my arms asleep."

10.   "Rise up, rise up, put on your clothes as quick as ever you can,
I'll never have it said in old Scotland that I fought with a naked
    man."
"Oh, no, oh, no, I dare not do it, oh, not for all of my life,
For by your side you have two broadswords while I have nary
    a knife."

11.   "What if I have the two broadswords—they cost me deep in
    purse!
You shall have the very best one, and I will take the worst,
And you may strike the very first blow and strike it like a man,
And I will strike the second blow and I'll kill you if I can."

12.   Young Lagrue he struck the very first blow, that wounded Lord
    Banner sore;
Lord Banner struck the second blow and laid him in his gore.
Then he took his fair lady by the lily-white hand and he gave
    her kisses three,
Saying, "Which of the two do you love best; this Young Lagrue
    or me?"

13.   "Quite well I like your rosy cheeks, quite well I like your chin,
But I'd ten times rather have Young Lagrue than you or all of
    your kin!"
He grabbed her by the hair of the head and he split her head
    in two;
She sank upon her bended knees by the side of Young Lagrue.

14.   Then he put the heel of the sword to the floor and the point unto
    his breast,
Saying, "Was there ever three lovers more easily laid at rest?
Go dig my grave, go dig my grave, go dig it both wide and deep,
And place my fair lady by my side and Young Lagrue at my
    feet."

CHILD MAURICE (83)

This ballad tells a modified Sohrab and Rustum story. It was in print
in Scotland as early as 1750 and after that it was often reprinted so
that the several versions probably stem from print rather than oral
tradition.

    Text, Percy, p. 346.

1. Childe Maurice hunted ithe siluer wood,
        He hunted itt round about,
    And noebodye that he ffound therin,
        Nor none there was with-out.

2.   .   .   .   .

          .   .   .   .
      And he tooke his siluer combe in his hand,
          To kembe his yellow lockes.

3. He sayes, "Come hither, thou little ffoot-page,
        That runneth lowlye by my knee,
    Ffor thou shalt goe to Iohn Steward's wiffe
        And pray her speake with mee.

4.   .   .   .   .

          .   .   .   .   .
      I, and greete thou doe that ladye well,
          Euer soe well ffroe mee.

5. "And, as itt ffalls, as many times
        As knotts beene knitt on a kell,
    Or marchant men gone to leeue London,
        Either to buy ware or sell.

6. "And, as itt ffalles, as many times
        As any hart can thinke,
    Or schoole-masters are in any schoole-house,
        Writting with pen and inke;
    Ffor if I might, as well as shee may,
        This night I wold with her speake.

7. "And heere I send her a mantle of greene,
        As greene as any grasse,
    And bidd her come to the siluer wood,
        To hunt with Child Maurice.

8. "And there I send her a ring of gold,
        A ring of precyous stone,
    And bidd her come to the siluer wood,
        Let ffor no kind of man."

9. One while this litle boy he yode,
        Another while he ran,
    Vntill he came to Iohn Steward's Hall,
        I-wis he neuer blan.

10. And of nurture the child had good,
        Hee ran vp hall and bower ffree,
    And when he came to this lady ffaire,
        Sayes, "God you saue and see.

11. "I am come ffrom Child Maurice,
      A message vnto thee;
    And Child Maurice, he greetes you well,
      And euer soe well ffrom mee.

12. "And, as itt ffalls, as oftentimes
      As knotts beene knitt on a kell,
    Or marchant-men gone to leeue London,
      Either ffor to buy ware or sell.

13. "And as oftentimes he greetes you well
      As any hart can thinke,
    Or schoolemasters are in any schoole,
      Wryting with pen and inke.

14. "And heere he sends a mantle of greene,
      As greene as any grasse,
    And he bidds you come to the siluer wood,
      To hunt with Child Maurice.

15. "And heere he sends you a ring of gold
      A ring of the precyous stone;
    He prayes you to come to the siluer wood,
      Let ffor no kind of man."

16. "Now peace, now peace, thou litle ffoot-page,
      Ffor Christes sake, I pray thee,
    Ffor if my lord heare one of these words,
      Thou must be hanged hye!"

17. Iohn Steward stood vnder the castle-wall,
      And he wrote the words euerye one,

      .   .   .   .

          .   .   .   .

18. And he called vnto his hors-keeper,
      "Make readye you my steede."
    I, and soe hee did to his chamberlaine,
      "Make readye thou my weede."

19. And he cast a lease vpon his backe,
      And he rode to the siluer wood,
    And there he sought all about,
      About the siluer wood.

20. And there he ffound him Child Maurice
      Sitting vpon a blocke,
    With a siluer combe in his hand,
      Kembing his yellow locke.

                *   *   *   *   *   *   *

21.   But then stood vp him Child Maurice,
           And sayd these words trulye:
       "I doe not know your ladye," he said,
           "If that I doe her see."

22.   He sayes, "How now, how now, Child Maurice?
           Alacke, how may this bee?
       Ffor thou hast sent her loue-tokens,
           More now then two or three.

23.   "Ffor thou hast sent her a mantle of greene,
           As greene as any grasse,
       And bade her come to the siluer woode,
           To hunt with Child Maurice.

24.   "And thou hast sent her a ring of gold,
           A ring of precyous stone
       And bade her come to the siluer wood,
           Let ffor noe kind of man.

25.   "And by my ffaith, now, Child Maurice,
           The tone of vs shall dye!"
       "Now be my troth," sayd Child Maurice,
           "And that shall not be I."

26.   But hee pulled forth a bright browne sword,
           And dryed itt on the grasse,
       And soe ffast he smote att Iohn Steward,
           I-wisse he neuer did rest.

27.   Then hee pulled fforth his bright browne sword,
           And dryed itt on his sleeue,
       And the ffirst good stroke Iohn Stewart stroke,
           Child Maurice head he did cleeue.

28.   And he pricked itt on his sword's poynt,
           Went singing there beside,
       And he rode till he came to that ladye ffaire,
           Wheras this ladye lyed.

29.   And sayes, "Dost thou know Child Maurice head,
           If that thou dost itt see?
       And lapp itt soft, and kisse itt offt,
           Ffor thou louedst him better than mee."

30.   But when shee looked on Child Maurice head,
           She neuer spake words but three:
       "I neuer beare no child but one,
           And you haue slaine him trulye."

31.   Sayes, "Wicked be my merrymen all,
          I gaue meate, drinke, and clothe!
       But cold they not haue holden me
          When I was in all that wrath!

32.   "Ffor I haue slaine one of the curteousest knights
          That euer bestrode a steed,
       Soe haue I done one of the fairest ladyes
          That euer ware womans weede!"

BONNY BARBARA ALLEN (84)

Traditionally most comments on this famous ballad begin with the
quotation from Pepys: "In perfect pleasure I was to hear her [Mrs.
Knipp, the actress] sing, and especially her little Scotch song of Barbary Allen," and the one from Goldsmith: "The music of the finest
singer is dissonance to what I felt when our old dairy-maid sung me
to tears with 'Johny Armstrong's Last Goodnight,' or 'The cruelty of
Barbara Allen.'" The source of the ballad is unknown; the John
Graeme in Ramsay's version cannot be identified. The ballad has no
continental analogues. In America, however, it has had the widest
geographical spread of any ballad and it has thrown off more texts
and tunes than any other. The basic story has been kept, but details
of all sorts have been added: John Graeme gives Barbara gifts as he
dies; Barbara blames her parents for her action; her mother dies with
her; Barbara curses her lover; he curses her; the lover is repentant;
a Negro version makes Barbara a man. No version tries to do much
with the basic weakness of the story, the lack of sufficient motivation
for Barbara's action toward the young man. Can it be that Barbara
Allen is a ballad of the type of "Lord Thomas and Fair Annet," and
that the original story told of Sir John jilting Barbara for another
girl, repenting of his action when he was dying, and sending for her?
    Text A, Allan Ramsay, *Tea-Table Miscellany*, iv, 46; B, tradi-
tional, from Virginia, printed in *JAF*, 29:161; C, traditional in Mississippi, *JAF*, 28:146.

A.

1.   It was in and about the Martinmas time,
         When the green leaves were a falling,
      That Sir John Graeme, in the West Country,
         Fell in love with Barbara Allan.

2.   He sent his men down through the town,
         To the place where she was dwelling:
      "O haste and come to my master dear,
         Gin ye be Barbara Allan."

3. O hooly, hooly rose she up,
        To the place where he was lying,
    And when she drew the curtain by,
        "Young man, I think you're dying."

4. "O it's I'm sick, and very, very sick,
        And 't is a' for Barbara Allan."
    "O the better for me ye's never be,
        Tho your heart's blood were a spilling.

5. "O dinna ye mind, young man," said she,
        "When ye was in the tavern a drinking,
    That ye made the healths gae round and round,
        And slighted Barbara Allan?"

6. He turned his face unto the wall,
        And death was with him dealing:
    "Adieu, adieu, my dear friends all,
        And be kind to Barbara Allan."

7. And slowly, slowly raise she up,
        And slowly, slowly left him,
    And sighing said, she coud not stay,
        Since death of life had reft him.

8. She had not gane a mile but twa,
        When she heard the dead-bell ringing,
    And every jow that the dead-bell geid,
        It cry'd, Woe to Barbara Allan!

9. "O mother, mother, make my bed.
        O make it saft and narrow.
    Since my love died for me to-day,
        I'll die for him to-morrow."

B.

1. "In Scotland was I bred and born;
        In Yorkshire was my dwelling;
    And there I fell in love with a pretty fair maid,
        And her name was Barbara Ellen.

2. "I sent a boy down to her house,
        To the house that she did dwell in;
    I sent him to her father's house.
        Her name was Barbara Ellen."

3. "Look up, look up at my bed-head,
        You'll see a napkin hanging;

In that you'll find a gold watch and chain,
  And that's for Barbara Ellen.

4. "Look down, look down at my bed-foot,
    You'll see a trunk a-standing;
  It's full of gold and jewelry,
    And that's for Barbara Ellen.

5. "Look down, look down at my bed-side,
    You'll see a bowl o'erflowing;
  And in that bowl there's my heart's blood,
    That's shed for Barbara Ellen."

6. So slowly she put on her clothes;
    So slowly she went walking;
  So slowly, as she crossed the field,
    She met the corpse a-coming.

7. "Oh, lay him down, oh, lay him down,
    That I may gaze upon him."
  The more she gazed, and still she gazed,
    She could not keep from smiling.

8. The young men cried out, "Oh fie! for shame
    Hard-hearted Barbara Ellen!
  There's many a wealthy squire died
    For cruel Barbara Ellen."

9. She went down into yonder vale;
    She could hear the dead-bell's knelling,
  And every toll it seemed to say,
    "Hard-hearted Barbara Ellen!"

10. "Oh, father, father! dig my grave,
    And dig it deep and narrow;
  For a young man died for me to-day,
    I'll die for him to-morrow."

11. On the one was buried a red rose bud,
    On the other, a sweet brier;
  And they grew and they grew to the church-steeple top,
    Till they could grow no higher.
  There they twined in a true-lover's knot,
    For all true lovers to admire.

C.

1. It was in the month of May
    When all the sweet was dwelling;
  A young girl on her death bed lay,
    For the love of Barbry Allen.

2. She sent her servant into town
   Where Barbry was dwelling:
   "Your truelove said for you to go there,
   If your name be Barbry Allen."

3. Slowly, slowly, he got up,
   So slowly, slowly he did go;
   And when he got there he said, "Dear girl,
   I'm sure you must be dying."

4. "Oh, yes, I'm sick, and very sick,
   And all the doctors can't cure me;
   I am not any better, nor never will be,
   If I can't get Barbry Allen."

5. "Oh, yes, you're sick, and very sick,
   And all the doctors can't cure you;
   You are not any better, nor never will be,
   For you can't get Barbry Allen."

6. She turned her pale face to the wall;
   He turned his back upon her;
   And before he got away from town
   He heard her death bell ringing.

7. And every knock it seemed to say,
   "Cruel, cruel, is your name,
   And wicked is your nature,
   For you could have saved this poor girl's life,
   If you had done your duty."

8. "Yes; cruel, cruel, is my name,
   And wicked is my nature,
   For I could have saved this poor girl's life
   If I had done my duty."

9. His true lover died on Saturday night,
   And Barbry died on Sunday;
   His mother died for the love of both;
   They were buried on Easter Monday.

YOUNG BENJIE (86)

Here is printed Scott's version from the Border *Minstrelsy*. Scott
may have supplied certain stanzas, for this version, unlike most,
tells a complete story. The custom of watching a corpse and laying
charms on it so that it could be induced to speak and reveal its slayer

was common in Scotland. One way to induce the corpse to speak was to leave the door ajar. The scene of the brothers sitting around the body of their dead sister, the door ajar, the candles burning low, as they waited for their dead sister to speak is typical ballad drama.

Text, traditional in Scotland, printed in Scott, iii, 251.

1. Of a' the maids o fair Scotland
   The fairest was Marjorie,
   And Young Benjie was her ae true-love,
   And a dear true-love was he.

2. And wow! but they were lovers dear,
   And they loved fu constantlie;
   But ay the mair, when they fell out,
   The sairer was their plea.

3. And they hae quarrelled on a day,
   Till Marjorie's heart grew wae,
   And she said she'd chuse another luve,
   And let Young Benjie gae.

4. And he was stout, and proud-hearted,
   And thought o't bitterlie,
   And he's gaen by the wan moon-light
   To meet his Marjorie.

5. "O open, open, my true-love,
   O open, and let me in."
   "I dare na open, Young Benjie,
   My three brothers are within."

6. "Ye lied, ye lied, ye bonny burd,
   Sae loud's I hear ye lie;
   As I came by the Lowden banks,
   They bade gude een to me.

7. "But fare ye weel, my ae fause love,
   That I hae loved sae lang.
   It sets ye chuse another love,
   And let Young Benjie gang."

8. Then Marjorie turned her round about,
   The tear blinding her ee:
   "I darena, darena let thee in
   But I'll come down to thee."

9. Then saft she smiled, and said to him,
   "O what ill hae I done?"
   He took her in his armis twa,
   And threw her oer the linn.

10. The stream was strang, the maid was stout,
    And laith, laith to be dang,
But ere she wan the Lowden banks
    Her fair colour was wan.

11. Then up bespak her eldest brother,
    "O see na ye what I see?"
And out then spak her second brother,
    "It's our sister Marjorie."

12. Out then spak her eldest brother,
    "O how shall we her ken?"
And out then spak her youngest brother,
    "There's a honey-mark on her chin."

13. Then they've taen up the comely corpse,
    And laid it on the grund:
"O wha has killed our ae sister,
    And how can he be found?

14. "The night it is her low lykewake,
    The morn her burial day,
And we maun watch at mirk midnight,
    And hear what she will say."

15. Wi doors ajar, and candle-light,
    And torches burning clear,
The streikit corpse, till still midnight,
    They waked, but naething hear.

16. About the middle o the night
    The cocks began to craw,
And at the dead hour o the night
    The corpse began to thraw.

17. "O wha has done the wrang, sister,
    Or dared the deadly sin?
Wha wae sae stout, and feared nae dout,
    As thraw ye oer the linn?"

18. "Young Benjie was the first ae man
    I laid my love upon;
He was sae stout and proud-hearted,
    He threw me oer the linn."

19. "Sall we Young Benjie head, sister?
    Sall we Young Benjie hang?
Or sall we pike out his twa gray een,
    And punish him ere he gang?"

20. "Ye mauna Benjie head, brother,
    Ye mauna Benjie hang,

But ye maun pike out his twa gray een,
 And punish him ere he gang.

21. "Tie a green gravat round his neck,
  And lead him out and in,
 And the best ae servant about your house
  To wait Young Benjie on.

22. "And ay, at every seven year's end,
  Ye'll tak him to the linn;
 For that's the penance he maun drie,
  To scug his deadly sin."

YOUNG JOHNSTONE (88)

Motherwell's reciter explained the lack of motivation in this ballad by saying that the Young Johnstone started from his sleep and unwittingly stabbed his lady, thinking she was one of his pursuers.

Text, Herd, p. 305.

1. The knight stands in the stable-door,
  As he was for to ryde,
 When out then came his fair lady,
  Desiring him to byde.

2. "How can I byde? How dare I byde?
  How can I byde with thee?
 Have I not killd thy ae brother?
  Thou hadst nae mair but he."

3. "If you have killd my ae brother,
  Alas, and woe is me!
 But if I save your fair body,
  The better you'll like me."

4. She's tane him to her secret bower,
  Pinnd with a siller pin,
 And she's up to her highest tower,
  To watch that none come in.

5. She had na well gane up the stair,
  And entered in her tower,
 When four and twenty armed knights
  Came riding to the door.

6. "Now God you save, my fair lady,
  I pray you tell to me,
 Saw you not a wounded knight
  Come riding by this way?"

7. "Yes, bloody, bloody was his sword,
        And bloody were his hands;
    But if the steed he rides be good,
        He's past fair Scotland's strands.

8. "Light down, light down then, gentlemen,
        And take some bread and wine;
    The better you will him pursue
        When you shall lightly dine."

9. "We thank you for your bread, lady,
        We thank you for your wine;
    I would gie thrice three thousand pounds
        Your fair body was mine."

10. Then she's gane to her secret bower,
        Her husband dear to meet;
    But he drew out his bloody sword,
        And wounded her sae deep.

11. "What aileth thee now, good my lord?
        What aileth thee at me?
    Have you not got my father's gold,
        But and my mother's fee?"

12. "Now live, now live, my fair lady,
        O live but half an hour,
    There's ne'er a leech in fair Scotland
        But shall be at thy bower."

13. "How can I live? How shall I live?
        How can I live for thee?
    See you not where my red heart's blood
        Runs trickling down my knee?"

JELLON GRAME (90)

This ballad was first printed in Scott, ii, 20. Other versions exist, with much story variation.

1. O Jellon Grame sat in Silver Wood,
        He whistled and he sang,
    And he has calld his little foot-page,
        His errand for to gang.

2. "Win up, my bonny boy," he says,
        "As quick as e'er you may,
    For ye maun gang for Lillie Flower,
        Before the break of day."

3. The boy he's buckled his belt about,
   And thro the green-wood ran,
   And he came to the ladies bower-door,
   Before the day did dawn.

4. "O sleep ye, or wake ye, Lillie Flower?
   The red run's i the rain."
   'I sleep not aft, I wake right aft;
   Wha's that that kens my name?"

5. "Ye are bidden come to Silver Wood,
   But I fear you'll never win hame;
   Ye are bidden come to Silver Wood,
   And speak wi Jellon Grame."

6. "O I will gang to Silver Wood,
   Though I shoud never win hame,
   For the thing I most desire on earth
   Is to speak wi Jellon Grame."

7. She had no ridden a mile, a mile,
   A mile but barely three,
   Ere she came to a new made grave,
   Beneath a green oak tree.

8. O then up started Jellon Grame,
   Out of a bush hard bye:
   "Light down, light down now, Lillie Flower,
   For it's here that ye maun ly."

9. She lighted aff her milk-white steed,
   And knelt upon her knee:
   "O mercy, mercy, Jellon Grame,
   For I'm nae prepar'd to die.

10. "Your bairn, that stirs between my sides,
    Maun shortly see the light;
    But to see it weltring in my blude
    Woud be a piteous sight."

11. "O shoud I spare your life," he says,
    "Until that bairn be born,
    I ken fu well your stern father
    Woud hang me on the morn."

12. "O spare my life now, Jellon Grame,
    My father ye neer need dread;
    I'll keep my bairn i the good green wood,
    Or wi it I'll beg my bread."

13. He took nae pity on that ladie,

Tho she for life did pray;
But pierced her thro the fair body,
As at his feet she lay.

14. He felt nae pity for that ladie,
  Tho she was lying dead;
But he felt some for the bonny boy,
  Lay weltring in her blude.

15. Up has he taen that bonny boy,
  Gien him to nurices nine,
Three to wake, and three to sleep,
  And three to go between.

16. And he's brought up that bonny boy,
  Calld him his sister's son;
He thought nae man would eer find out
  The deed that he had done.

17. But it sae fell out upon a time,
  As a hunting they did gay,
That they rested them in Silver Wood,
  Upon a summer-day.

18. Then out it spake that bonny boy,
  While the tear stood in his eye,
"O tell me this now, Jellon Grame,
  And I pray you dinna lie.

19. "The reason that my mother dear
  Does never take me hame?
To keep me still in banishment
  Is baith a sin and shame."

20. "You wonder that your mother dear
  Does never send for thee;
Lo, there's the place I slew thy mother,
  Beneath that green oak tree."

21. Wi that the boy has bent his bow,
  It was baith stout and lang,
And through and thro him Jellon Grame
  He's gard an arrow gang.

22. Says, "Lye you thare now, Jellon Grame,
  My mellison you wi;
The place my mother lies buried in
  Is far too good for thee."

BONNY BEE HOM (92)

The talisman that makes a man invulnerable or that tells of his love's death by the color of a stone is a ballad commonplace, as is the lady's vow in stanza 4.

Text, Jamieson, i, 185.

1. By Arthur's Dale as late I went
   I heard a heavy moan;
   I heard a ladie lammenting sair,
   And ay she cried Ohone!

2. "Ohon, alas! what shall I do,
   Tormented night and day.
   I never loved a love but ane,
   And now he's gone away.

3. "But I will do for my true-love
   What ladies woud think sair,
   For seven years shall come and go
   Ere a kaim gang in my hair.

4. "There shall neither a shoe gang on my foot,
   Nor a kaim gang in my hair,
   Nor eer a coal nor candle-light
   Shine in my bower nae mair."

5. She thought her love had been on the sea,
   Fast sailling to Bee Hom;
   But he was in a quiet chamer,
   Hearing his ladies moan.

6. "Be husht, be husht, my ladie dear,
   I pray thee mourn not so;
   For I am deep sworn on a book
   To Bee Hom for to go."

7. She has gien him a chain of the beaten gowd,
   And a ring with a ruby stone:
   "As lang as this chain your body binds,
   Your blude can never be drawn.

8. "But gin this ring shoud fade or fail,
   Or the stone shoud change its hue,
   Be sure your love is dead and gone,
   Or she has proved untrue."

9. He had no been at Bonny Bee Hom
   A twelve month and a day,

Till, looking on his gay gowd ring,
The stone grew dark and gray.

10. "O ye take my riches to Bee Hom,
And deal them presentlie,
To the young that canna, the auld that maunna,
And the blind that does not see."

11. Now death has come into his bower,
And split his heart in twain;
So their twa souls flew up to heaven,
And there shall ever remain.

LAMKIN (93)

Numerous versions of this harsh story are found in Scotland, England, and America; the basic plot, however, varies little. This ballad needs detailed study. The numerous versions would suggest that it has long been in tradition; the unmotivated action of Lamkin in his brutal killings would suggest that the basic story has been lost. Why would Lamkin kill the lady and her baby just to avenge the wrong of the lord's not paying him, when he realizes that he would be hanged for the deed? The Devil was sometimes referred to as Wearie. Could it be that the original story was a fairy (later Devil) capture story, and that Lamkin is killing *his* wife for running away with a fairy lover? Barry advanced the suggestion that Lamkin was originally a leper and killed the baby to secure blood to wash himself and so effect a cure. Lamkin is called Linfinn in a ballad from Maine (reprinted here) which Barry collected and Fannie Eckstorm annotated (*JAF*, 52:70). Barry suggested that Linfinn means white man who lived by a *linn*, stream, and that white man would mean leper. Hence his killing the baby to procure blood. Later the leper became a mason because masons were said in Ireland to mix blood with their cement. But this is rather wide speculation.

Text, A, Jamieson, i, 176; B, traditional, from Maine, printed in *JAF*, 52:72; C, traditional, from Indiana, printed in *JAF*, 48:317; D, traditional, from Ohio, printed in *JAF*, 29:163.

A.

1. It's Lamkin was a mason good
as ever built wi stane;
He built Lord Wearie's castle,
but payment got he nane.

2. "O pay me, Lord Wearie,
come, pay me my fee."
"I canna pay you, Lamkin,
for I maun gang oer the sea."

3. "O pay me now, Lord Wearie,
        come, pay me out o hand."
    "I canna pay you, Lamkin,
        unless I sell my land."

4. "O gin ye winna pay me,
        I here sall mak a vow,
    Before that ye come hame again,
        ye sall hae cause to rue."

5. Lord Wearie got a bonny ship,
        to sail the saut sea faem;
    Bade his lady weel the castle keep,
        ay till he should come hame.

6. But the nourice was a fause limmer
        as e'er hung on a tree;
    She laid a plot wi Lamkin,
        whan her lord was o'er the sea.

7. She laid a plot wi Lamkin,
        when the servants were awa,
    Loot him in at a little shot-window,
        and brought him to the ha.

8. "O whare's a' the men o this house,
        that ca me Lamkin?"
    "They're at the barn-well thrashing;
        't will be lang ere they come in."

9. "And whare's the women o this house,
        that ca me Lamkin?"
    "They're at the far well washing;
        't will be lang ere they come in."

10. "And whare's the bairns o this house,
        that ca me Lamkin?"
    "They're at the school reading;
        't will be night or they come hame."

11. "O whare's the lady o this house,
        that ca's me Lamkin?"
    "She's up in her bower sewing,
        but we soon can bring her down."

12. Then Lamkin's tane a sharp knife,
        that hang down by his gaire,
    And he has gien the bonny babe
        a deep wound and a sair.

13. Then Lamkin he rocked,
        and the fause nourice sang,

Till frae ilkae bore o the cradle
    the red blood out sprang.

14. Then out it spak the lady
    as she stood on the stair:
  "What ails my bairn, nourice,
    that he's greeting sae sair?

15. "O still my bairn, nourice,
    O still him wi the pap."
  "He winna still, lady,
    for this nor for that."

16. "O still my bairn, nourice,
    O still him wi the wand."
  "He winna still, lady,
    for a' his father's land."

17. "O still my bairn, nourice,
    O still him wi the bell."
  "He winna still, lady,
    till ye come down yoursel."

18. O the firsten step she steppit,
    she steppit on a stane;
  But the neisten step she steppit,
    she met him Lamkin.

19. "O mercy, mercy, Lamkin,
    hae mercy upon me!
  Though you've taen my young son's life,
    ye may let mysel be."

20. "O sall I kill her, nourice,
    or sall I let her be?"
  "O kill her, kill her, Lamkin,
    for she ne'er was good to me."

21. "O scour the bason, nourice,
    and mak it fair and clean,
  For to keep this lady's heart's blood,
    for she's come o noble kin."

22. "There need nae bason, Lamkin,
    lat it run through the floor;
  What better is the heart's blood
    o the rich than o the poor?"

23. But ere three months were at an end,
    Lord Wearie came again;

But dowie, dowie was his heart
    when first he came hame.

24.   "O wha's blood is this," he says,
    "That lies in the chamer?"
    "It is your lady's heart's blood;
      't is as clear as the lamer."

25.   "And wha's blood is this," he says,
    "that lies in my ha?"
    "It is your young son's heart's blood;
      't is the clearest ava."

26.   O sweetly sang the black-bird
    that sat upon the tree;
    But sairer grat Lamkin,
      when he was condemnd to die.

27.   And bonny sang the mavis,
    out o the thorny brake;
    But sairer grat the nourice,
      when she was tied to the stake.

B.

FALSE LINFINN

1. Said the lord to his lady as he went away from home,
    "Beware of the Linfinn, for he'll do you much harm."

2. "I care not for Linfinn nor none of his kin,
    I keep my doors bolted and my windows pinned in."

3. "How shall I get her down?" . . .
    .   .   .   .

4. They pricked it and they pricked it and they pricked it full sore
    Till the blood ran from the cradle in streams on the floor.

5. "I've rocked it and fed it on breast milk and pap,
    Why can't you come down and rock it on your lap?"

6. "How can I come down so late in the night
    Without any fire or bright candlelight?"

7. "There are fifteen bright candles burning and one as bright as
    the sun;
    You can come down here by the light of one of them!"

8. She started to come down, not thinking any harm,
    And the Linfinn stood ready to catch her in his arms.

9. "O spare me, Mr. Linfinn, till one o'clock at night,

And you shall have as much money as you can carry in your
cart."

10. "If I had as much money as I could haul in my cart,
I'd rather see a sword run through your red heart."

11. "O spare me, O spare me, O spare me," she cries,
"And you shall have my daughter Betsy, she's the pride of all
flowers."

12. "Bring down your daughter Betsy, she may do some good
For to hold the silver basin for to catch your heart's blood."

13. "O Betsy, dearest Betsy, stay right where you be,
Until your noble father comes a-riding home from sea."

14. As Betsy was a-sittin' in her chamber most high,
She saw her noble father come a-riding close by.

15. Says, "Father, dearest father, pray do not blame me,
For the Linfinn and the wet nurse has murdered Ma-mee."

16. The wet nurse was hung on the gallows so high,
And the Linfinn was burned to a stake standing by.

17. "Farewell to old England, old Ireland," says he,
And the landlord went a-mourning for his fair ladye.

C.

Oh, Lamkin was a mason
    And he built well with stone;
He built my lord's castle,
    But payment he got none.

"O pay me, O pay me;
    Come pay me my fee."
"I cannot pay you, Lamkin,
    Until I sail o'er the sea."

Then his young son in the castle
    Was murdered one day
By Falseness and Lamkin
    While the servants were away.

Then out spoke my lady:
    "Have mercy on me;
Though you've taken my young son's life,
    O have mercy on me."

Lady Betty was lying
    In her chamber so high,

When she heard her dear daddy
   Come riding hard by.

"O Daddy, O Daddy,
   You need not blame me,
For Falseness and Lamkin
   Have killed your lady."

Then Lamkin was hanged
   On yon gallows so high,
And Falseness was burned
   In a fire hard by.

Then sweetly sang the wild birds
   As they soared upon high,
For Falseness and Lamkin
   Deserved well to die.

D.

1.   False Lambkin was a mason,
     As good as ever laid stone;
   He built Lord Arnold's castle,
     And the Lord paid him none.

2.   False Lambkin he swore
     That revenged he would be
   On Lord Arnold's castle,
     Or on his family.

3.   Said the Lord to his Lady,
     "I'm going from home;
   And what would you do,
     If False Lambkin should come?"

4.   "Oh, I fear not False Lambkin,
     Nor more of his kind;
   For I'll keep my doors fastened,
     And my windows pinned in."

5.   So she kept her doors fastened,
     And her windows pinned in,
   All except one kitchen window,
     Where Lambkin came in.

6.   "Oh, where is Lord Arnold?
     Is he not at home?"
   "No; he's gone to old Ireland
     To see his dear son."

7.   "Oh, where is his Lady?

Has she gone along?"
"No; she's in her chamber,
    Where no man can get in."

8. "Oh, what shall I do,
    That I may get in?"
"You must pierce this little babe's heart
    With your silver bodkin."

9. So he pierced the little babe's heart,
    Till the blood did spin
Out into the cradle.
    So falsely she did sing:

10. "Oh, hushy-by baby.
    Oh, what aileth thee?
Come down, loving mistress;
    Oh, come down and see."

11. "Oh, how can I come down
    So late in the night,
When there is no moon a-shining,
    Nor stars to give light?"

12. "Oh, your (you've?) seven bright lanterns,
    As bright as the sun.
Come down, loving mistress;
    Oh, come down by one."

13. She had not advanced
    But steps two or three,
Till she spied False Lambkin
    A-standing close by.

14. "Oh, spare me, False Lambkin;
    And I will go back,
And get you all the money
    You can carry in your sack."

15. "I want none of your money,
    Nor nothing that I know,
That will spare this bright sword
    From your neck white as snow."

16. "Oh, spare me, False Lambkin;
    Oh, spare me one hour;
And I'll call down daughter Betsey,
    The queen of the bower."

17. "Go, call down daughter Betsey,
    So neat and so clean

> To hold the silver basin
> To catch your blood in."

18. "Daughter Betsey, stay up
    In your chamber so high,
    Till you see your dear father
    In a ship sailing nigh."

19. Daughter Betsey staid up
    In her chamber so high,
    Till she saw her dear father
    In a ship sailing nigh."

20. When Lord Arnold came to the castle
    And opened the door,
    He saw his companion
    Lying dead on the floor.

21. False Lambkin was hung
    On a gallows so high;
    And the false nurse was burnt
    To a stake standing by.

THE MAID FREED FROM THE GALLOWS (95)

This ballad is known all over Europe from Sicily to Scandinavia and from Russia to Ireland. In Scotland, England, and America it has pretty much lost the story and reduced the dialogue to a formalized and conventional cliché. The original story probably told of a girl (wife or sweetheart) captured by pirates or sailors; they allow her to take them to her father. She asks the father to ransom her; he refuses. Then she goes with them successively to mother, sister, and brother and asks the same question of each. All refuse her. Then at last she goes to her husband, who replies, "Better lose all the gold than you." Three days later the father dies. She says, "Let him die; I'll dress in red." And so for mother, though now she dresses in yellow. And the brother (green mourning) and the sister (white). But should the dear husband die, the mourning, she says, will be black. For detailed studies of this ballad, see *Folklore Fellows Communications*, cv:1–265; Sager, *Modern Philology*, 27:129. In America the ballad has had extraordinary development as ballad, song, children's game, drama, *cante-fable*, folk tale. For an account of its ramifications, see Reed Smith, *South Carolina Ballads*, chap. 8; Parsons, *Folktales of Andros Island*, pp. 152 ff.; Scarborough, *On the Trail of Negro Folksongs*, pp. 35 ff.

Text A, traditional in England, Percy Papers; B, traditional in Maine, Barry, p. 208; C, traditional in Jamaica, printed in *PMLA*,

29:455; D, traditional in Maine, Barry, p. 389 is a secondary ballad from "The Maid Freed from the Gallows."

A.

1. "O Good Lord Judge, and sweet Lord Judge,
        Peace for a little while!
    Methinks I see my own father,
        Come riding by the stile.

2. "Oh father, oh father, a little of your gold,
        And likewise of your fee
    To keep my body from yonder grave
        And my neck from the gallows-tree."

3. "None of my gold now you shall have,
        Nor likewise of my fee;
    For I am come to see you hangd,
        And hanged you shall be."

4. "Oh good Lord Judge, and sweet Lord Judge,
        Peace for a little while
    Methinks I see my own mother
        Come riding by the stile.

5. "Oh mother, oh mother, a little of your gold,
        And likewise of your fee
    To keep my body from yonder grave,
        And my neck from the gallows-tree."

6. "None of my gold now shall you have,
        Nor likewise of my fee;
    For I am come to see you hangd
        And hanged you shall be."

7. "Oh good Lord Judge, and sweet Lord Judge,
        Peace for a little while,
    Methinks I see my own brother
        Come riding by the stile.

8. "Oh brother, oh brother, a little of your gold,
        And likewise of your fee
    To keep my body from yonder grave,
        And my neck from the gallows-tree."

9. "None of my gold now shall you have,
        Nor likewise of my fee;
    For I am come to see you hangd,
        And hanged you shall be."

10. "Oh good Lord Judge, and sweet Lord Judge,
        Peace for a little while,

Methinks I see my own sister,
Come riding by the stile.

11. "Oh sister, oh sister, a little of your gold,
And likewise of your fee
To keep my body from yonder grave,
And my neck from the gallows-tree."

12. "None of my gold now shall you have,
Nor likewise of my fee,
For I am come to see you hangd,
And hanged you shall be."

13. "Oh good Lord Judge, and sweet Lord Judge,
Peace for a little while,
Methinks I see my own true-love
Come riding by the stile."

14. "Oh true-love, oh true-love, a little of your gold,
And likewise of your fee
To save my body from yonder grave,
And my neck from the gallows-tree."

15. "Some of my gold now you shall have,
And likewise of my fee,
For I am come to see you saved,
And saved you shall be."

B.

THE GOLDEN BALL

1. She lookèd over the hills for many a day
And saw her father coming.

She said: "O father,
Have you found my golden ball?
Or have you come to set me free?
Or have you come to see me hanged
Upon the Linden Tree?"

"I haven't found your golden ball,
I haven't come to set you free;
But I have come to see you hanged
Upon the Linden Tree."

2. She lookèd over the hills for many a day
And saw her mother coming.

She said: "O mother,
Have you found my golden ball?

Or have you come to set me free?
Or have you come to see me hanged
Upon the Linden Tree?"

"I haven't found your golden ball,
I haven't come to set you free,
But I have come to see you hanged
Upon the Linden Tree."

[The stanzas for the brother and sister
are similar.]

3.   She lookèd over the hills for many a day
And saw her grandmother coming.

She said: "O grandmother,
Have you found my golden ball?
Or have you come to set me free?
Or have you come to see me hanged
Upon the Linden Tree?"

"Yes, I have found your golden ball,
So I have come to set you free;
I have not come to see you hanged
Upon the Linden Tree."

C.

Deh was a princess propose to be married. During de time she was
going on to de day of marriage, she do somet'ing against de rule and
regulation of her royalty dat cause her to be brought up in trial, found
guilty, an' sentenced to be hung. What she did was against de family
rule, so none of dem prepare any help to escape her from de gallows.

De day come fo' her execution. De hour is at hand. She said to de
hang-man, "My time is at han'; save me five an' twenty minutes mo'!"
She look off an' see her fader was coming.

Ay! ay! deh come me only fader
Who trabbel so many mile!
Do you bring me gold an' silver
To save me body from de eart'?

Fader say,

No, no, Sarey!
I came to see you hung,
An' now you mus' be hung, girl,
You' body is boun' to de eart'.

An' she say, "Still, gentlemen, save me five an' twenty minute more!"
Mudder is coming.

Mudder! mudder!

Coming trabbling so many mile,
Do you bring me gold an' silver
To save me body from de eart'?
Mudder replied same as de fader,
No, no Sarey!
I came to see you hung,
An' hung you mus' be hung,
You' body is boun' to de eart'.

Ah say, "Gentlemen, save me five an' twenty minute more!" An' she look far away off yonder, an' saw a bright light, sparkling light, brillian' light. So ev'rybody dat was waiting to see her hung get frightened, t'ink dey was doing wrong to her. So all moving off to de way whe' de brightness is coming direct to de gallows. So all move an' leave de princess alone on de gallows stage.

So she mek her escape, pull de rope as how it was fixed to her an' move herself to a safe place beyon' de light dat is coming. An' she sing,

Ye do come, me only husban',
Trabbel so many mile!
Do you bring me gold an' silver
To save me body from de eart'?

No answer. Repeat twice. An' de power of de chariot an' de great light come up to de gallows, cut it down, mash it up. Great heap, mountain of gold and silver and all great pieces of precious stones, diamonds an' rubies an' all precious t'ing! Der was no end of it. And tek her up. She was help in by her husban' an' save!

Dat's why when people marry, dey drive so rapidly home, horse jump an' mek big! An' pour out money like mountains. Dat's why de king an' princess so rich now.

D.

THE GALLOWS TREE
(Cf. Child 95)

1. My love he was as fine a fellow
   As ever nature formed or the sun shone on,
   And how to gain him I do not know,
   For I hear his sentence is to be hung.

2. As I was walking the streets of Derry,
   His charming features I chanced to espy;
   He looked more like some commanding officer
   Than any young man condemned to die.

3. When he got to the first step of the gallows,
   His own father he chanced to see.

"Step up, step up, my beloved father,
I have one word to exchange with thee.

4. "Where is my love, oh, where is my jewel,
That she don't come and visit me?
Or does she think it a shame or a scandal
To see me die on the gallows tree?"

5. When he got to the second step of the gallows,
His own dear sister by chance he did see.
"Step up, step up, my beloved sister,
I have one word to exchange with thee."

6. He took a gold ring off from his finger,
And wrapped it in her silk so fine;
"Take this, take this, my beloved sister,
And keep your brother close in your mind."

7. And when he got to the top of the gallows
His own dear sweetheart by chance did see,
Riding in a coach that was lined with linen,
So swift she rode and swift rode she.

8. "Come down, come down, from that dreary gallows,
I have your pardon from George our King,
And in spite of them all I'll make you my husband
And crown your name in the bloom of spring."

THE GAY GOSHAWK (96)

There are many stories and songs in which a girl feigns death or takes a sleeping potion to simulate death so that she can come to her lover. There is no close analogue, though, for this ballad. The use of the bird as messenger is common enough in ballad; as ballads become more rational, the nightingales and goshawks are supplanted by parrots.

Text, Jamieson-Brown MS. No. 6.

1. "O well's me o my gay goss-hawk,
That he can speak and flee;
He'll carry a letter to my love,
Bring back another to me."

2. "O how can I your true-love ken,
Or how can I her know?
Whan frae her mouth I never heard couth,
Nor wi my eyes her saw."

3. "O well sal ye my true-love ken,

As soon as you her see;
For, of a' the flowrs in fair Englan,
The fairest flowr is she.

4. "At even at my love's bowr-door
    There grows a bowing birk,
An sit ye down and sing thereon,
    As she gangs to the kirk.

5. "An four and twenty ladies fair
    Will wash and go to kirk,
But well shall ye my true-love ken,
    For she wears goud on her skirt.

6. "An four and twenty gay ladies
    Will to the mass repair,
But well sal ye my true-love ken,
    For she wears goud on her hair."

7. O even at that lady's bowr-door
    There grows a bowin birk,
An she set down and sang thereon,
    As she ged to the kirk.

8. "O eet and drink, my marys a',
    The wine flows you among,
Till I gang to my shot-window,
    An hear yon bonny bird's song.

9. "Sing on, sing on, my bonny bird,
    The song ye sang the streen,
For I ken by your sweet singin
    You're frae my true-love sen."

10. O first he sang a merry song,
    An then he sang a grave,
An then he peckd his feathers gray,
    To her the letter gave.

11. "Ha, there's a letter frae your love,
    He says he sent you three;
He canna wait your love langer,
    But for your sake he'll die.

12. "He bids you write a letter to him;
    He says he's sent you five
He canno wait your love langer,
    Tho you're the fairest woman alive."

13. "Ye bid him bake his bridal-bread,
    And brew his bridal-ale,

An I'll meet him in fair Scotlan
 Lang, lang or it be stale."

14. She's doen her to her father dear,
  Fa'n low down on her knee:
 "A boon, a boon, my father dear,
  I pray you, grant it me."

15. "Ask on, ask on, my daughter,
  An granted it sal be;
 Except ae squire in fair Scotlan,
  An him you sall never see."

16. "The only boon, my father dear,
  That I do crave of the,
 Is, gin I die in southin lands,
  In Scotland to bury me.

17. "An the firstin kirk that ye come till,
  Ye gar the bells be rung,
 An the nextin kirk that ye come till,
  Ye gar the mess be sung.

18. "An the thirdin kirk that ye come till,
  Ye deal gold for my sake,
 An the fourthin kirk that ye come till,
  Ye tarry there till night."

19. She is doen her to her bigly bowr,
  As fast as she coud fare,
 An she has tane a sleepy draught,
  That she had mixed wi care.

20. She's laid her down upon her bed,
  An soon she's fa'n asleep,
 And soon oer every tender limb
  Cauld death began to creep.

21. Whan night was flown, an day was come,
  Nae ane that did her see
 But thought she was as surely dead
  As ony lady coud be.

22. Her father an her brothers dear
  Gard make to her a bier;
 The tae half was o guide red gold,
  The tither o silver clear.

23. Her mither an her sisters fair
  Gard work for her a sark;
 The tae half was o cambrick fine,
  The tither o needle work.

24. The firstin kirk that they came till,
    They gard the bells be rung,
    An the nextin kirk that they came till,
    They gard the mess be sung.

25. The thirdin kirk that they came till,
    They dealt gold for her sake,
    An the fourthin kirk that they came till,
    Lo, there they met her make.

26. "Lay down, lay down the bigly bier,
    Lat me the dead look on."
    Wi cherry cheeks and ruby lips
    She lay an smil'd on him.

27. "O ae sheave o your bread, true-love,
    An ae glass o your wine,
    For I hae fasted for your sake
    These fully days is nine.

28. "Gang hame, gang hame, my seven bold brothers,
    Gang hame and sound your horns;
    An ye may boast in southin lans
    Your sister's playd you scorn."

JOHNIE SCOT (99)

This story may be based on an actual event that occurred during the reign of Charles II.

Text A, Jamieson-Brown MS. No. 5; B, traditional in Tennessee, printed in *JAF*, 42:273.

A.

1. O Johney was as brave a knight
   As ever saild the sea,
   An he's done him to the English court,
   To serve for meat and fee.

2. He had na been in fair England
   But yet a little while,
   Untill the kingis ae daughter
   To Johney proves wi chil.

3. O word's come to the king himsel,
   In his chair where he sat,
   That his ae daughter was wi bairn
   To Jack, the Little Scott.

4. "Gin this be true that I do hear,

As I trust well it be,
Ye pit her into prison strong,
    An starve her till she die."

5. O Johney's on to fair Scotland,
    A wot he went wi speed,
An he has left the kingis court,
    A wot good was his need.

6. O it fell upon a day
    That Johney he thought lang,
An he's gane to the good green wood,
    As fast as he coud gang.

7. "O whare will I get a bonny boy,
    To rin my errand soon,
That will rin into fair England,
    And haste him back again?"

8. O up it starts a bonny boy,
    Gold yallow was his hair,
I wish his mither meickle joy,
    His bonny love mieckle mair.

9. "O here am I, a bonny boy,
    Will rin your errand soon;
I will gang into fair England,
    And come right soon again."

10. O whan he came to broken briggs,
    He bent his bow and swam;
An whan he came to the green grass growan,
    He slaikid his shoone an ran.

11. Whan he came to yon high castel,
    He ran it roun about,
An there he saw the king's daughter,
    At the window looking out.

12. "O here's a sark o silk, lady,
    Your ain han sewd the sleeve;
You'r bidden come to fair Scotlan,
    Speer nane o your parents leave.

13. "Ha, take this sark o silk, lady,
    Your ain han sewd the gare;
You'r bidden come to good green wood,
    Love Johney waits you there."

14. She's turned her right and roun about,
    The tear was in her ee:

"How can I come to my true-love,
 Except I had wings to flee?

15. "Here am I kept wi bars and bolts,
  Most grievous to behold;
 My breat-plate's o the sturdy steel,
  Instead of the beaten gold.

16. "But tak this purse, my bonny boy,
  Ye well deserve a fee,
 An bear this letter to my love,
  An tell him what you see."

17. Then quickly ran the bonny boy
  Again to Scotlan fair,
 An soon he reached Pitnachton's towrs,
  An soon found Johney there.

18. He pat the letter in his han
  An taul him what he sa,
 But eer he half the letter read,
  He loote the tears doun fa.

19. "O I will gae back to fair Englan,
  Tho death shoud me betide,
 An I will relieve the damesel
  That lay last by my side."

20. Then out it spake his father dear,
  "My son, you are to blame;
 An gin you'r catchd on English groun,
  I fear you'll neer win hame."

21. Then out it spake a valiant knight,
  Johny's best friend was he;
 "I can commaun five hunder men,
  An I'll his surety be."

22. The firstin town that they came till,
  They gard the bells be rung;
 An the nextin town that they came till,
  They gard the mess be sung.

23. The thirdin town that they came till,
  They gard the drums beat roun;
 The king but an his nobles a'
  Was startld at the soun.

24. Whan they came to the king's palace
  They rade it roun about,
 And there they saw the king himsel,
  At the window looking out.

25. "Is this the Duke o Albany,
     Or James, the Scottish king?
    Or are ye some great foreign lord,
     That's come a visiting?"

26. "I'm nae the Duke of Albany,
     Nor James, the Scottish king;
    But I'm a valiant Scottish knight,
     Pitnachton is my name."

27. "O if Pitnachton be your name,
     As I trust well it be,
    The morn, or I tast meat or drink,
     You shall be hanged hi."

28. Then out it spake the valiant knight
     That came brave Johney wi;
    "Behold five hunder bowmen bold,
     Will die to set him free."

29. Then out it spake the king again,
     An a scornfu laugh laugh he;
    "I have an Italian i my house
     Will fight you three by three."

30. "O grant me a boon," brave Johney cried;
     "Bring your Italian here;
    Then if he fall beneath my sword,
     I've won your daughter dear."

31. Then out it came that Italian,
     An a gurious ghost was he;
    Upo the point o Johney's sword
     This Italian did die.

32. Out has he drawn his lang, lang bran,
     Struck it across the plain:
    "Is there any more o your English dogs
     That you want to be slain?"

33. "A clark, a clark," the king then cried,
     "To write her tocher free."
    "A priest, a priest," says Love Johney,
     "To marry my love and me.

34. "I'm seeking nane o your gold," he says,
     "Nor of your silver clear;
    I only seek your daughter fair,
     Whose love has cost her dear."

B.

JOHNNY SCOT

1. Johnny Scot, a handsome right—
   Old England is so wide—
   The fairest lady in old England
   By Johnny Scot's with child.

2. King Ed'ard wrote young Johnny a letter
   And sealed it with his hand.
   He sent it away to young Johnny Scot
   As fast as a letter could go.

3. The very first lines, young Johnny, he read,
   It caused him for to smile.
   And the very next line he read
   The tears run down for a while—

4. Saying, "Away to old England I must go,
   King Ed'ard has sent for me."
   "Away to old England if you do go,
   I doubt you coming back.
   Five hundred of our best life-guards,
   Shall bear you company."

5. He dressed his servants all in green;
   His self he dressed in white.
   And every town that he rode through,
   They tuk him to be some knight.

6. He rode till he come to King Ed'ard's gate.
   He dingled there at the ring,
   And no one was so ready as Ed'ard himself
   To rise and let him come in.

7. "Is this young Johnny Scot?" he said,
   "Or old Johnny Scotling's son,
   Or is it the young bastard-getter
   From Scotland has come in?"

8. "It is not young Johnny Scot,
   Nor old Johnny Scotling's son;
   This is the very grand Scot Lord,
   And Johnny Scot is my name."

9. This young lady come peeping down stairs.
   "Come down, come down," said he.
   "Oh, no, I have to wear the studdiest steel
   Instead of the beating gold."

10.   "If it's mine," young Johnny he said,
      "And mine I expect it to be,
      I will make it the heir of all my land,
      And you my gaily dee."

11.   "No, no," King Ed'ard he said,
      "Oh, no, that never can't be.
      We have an Italian in our town,
      That has killed more lords than three,
      And before sunrise tomorrow morning,
      A dead man you shall be."

12.   The Italian flew over young Johnny's head
      As swift as any bird.
      He pierced the Italian through the heart
      With the point of his broad sword.
      And he whipped King Ed'ard and all of his men;
      And the king, he like to a-hung.

13.   "Hold your arm," King Ed'ard he said,
      "And pray do spare me;
      You can make it the heir of all your land
      And she your gaily dee."

WILLIE O WINSBURY (100)

Here is the same situation as in the preceding, but with an extraordinary ending for a ballad. The American versions differ little from this.

Text, Campbell MS. ii, 38.

1.   The king he hath been a prisoner,
        A prisoner lang in Spain, O
     And Willie o the Winsbury
        Has lain lang wi his daughter at hame, O.

2.   "What aileth thee, my daughter Janet,
        Ye look so pale and wan?
     Have ye had any sore sickness,
        Or have ye been lying wi a man?
     Or is it for me, your father dear,
        And biding sae lang in Spain?"

3.   "I have not had nay sore sickness,
        Nor yet been lying wi a man;
     But it is for you, my father dear,
        In biding sae lang in Spain."

4.   "Cast ye off your berry-brown gown,

Stand straight upon the stone,
That I may ken ye by yere shape,
    Whether ye be a maiden or none."

5. She's coosten off her berry-brown gown,
    Stooden straight upo yon stone;
Her apron was short, and her haunches were round,
    Her face it was pale and wan.

6. "Is it a man o might, Janet?
    Or is it to a man of fame?
Or is it to any of the rank robbers
    That's lately come out o Spain?"

7. "It is not to a man of might," she said,
    "Nor is it to a man of fame;
But it is to William of Winburry;
    I could lye nae langer my lane."

8. The king's called on his merry men all,
    By thirty and by three:
"Go fetch me William of Winburry,
    For hanged he shall be."

9. But when he cam the king before,
    He was clad o the red silk;
His hair was like to threeds o gold,
    And his skin was as white as milk.

10. "It is nae wonder," said the king,
    "That my daughter's love ye did win;
Had I been a woman, as I am a man,
    My bedfellow ye should hae been.

11. "Will ye marry my daughter Janet,
    By the truth of thy right hand?
I'll gie ye gold, I'll gie ye money,
    And I'll gie ye an earldom o land."

12. "Yes, I'll marry yere daughter Janet,
    By the truth of my right hand;
But I'll hae nane o yer gold, I'll hae nane o yer money,
    Nor I winna hae an earldom o land.

13. "For I hae eighteen corn-mills,
    Runs all in water clear,
And there's as much corn in each o them
    As they can grind in a year."

WILLIE O DOUGLAS DALE (101)

The situation in this ballad is conventional enough though the working out is unique. Note the episodic type of action rather than the usual dramatic action.

Text, Jamieson-Brown MS. fol. 8.

Notes

19/1. roddins: mountain ash was believed to help bring about successful childbirth. 24. In the ballads at least, no man was permitted to attend a woman in travail.

1. O Willy was a brave a lord
    As ever saild the sea,
    And he has gane to the English court,
    To serve for meat and fee.

2. He had nae been at the kingis court
    A twelvemonth and a day,
    Till he longd for a sight o the king's daughter,
    But ane he coud never see.

3. O it fell ance upon a day
    To the green wood she has gane,
    An Willy he has followed her,
    With the clear light o the moon.

4. He looted him low, by her did go,
    Wi his hat intill his hand;
    "O what's your will wi me, Sir Knight?
    I pray keep your hat on."

5. "O I am not a knight, Madam
    Nor never thinks to be;
    For I am Willy o Douglassdale,
    An I serve for meat and fee."

6. "O I'll gang to my bowr," she says,
    "An sigh baith even an morn
    That ever I saw your face, Willy,
    Or that ever ye was born.

7. "O I'll gang to my bowr," she says,
    "An I'll pray baith night and day,
    To keep frae your tempting looks,
    An frae your great beauty."

8. O in a little after that
    He keepit Dame Oliphant's bowr,
    An the love that passd between this twa,
    It was like paramour.

9. "O narrow, narrow's my gown, Willy,
        That wont to be sae wide;
   An short, short is my coats, Willy,
        That wont to be sae side;
   An gane is a' my fair colour,
        An low laid is my pride.

10. "But an my father get word of this,
        He'll never drink again;
    An gin my mother get word of this,
        In her ain bowr she'll go brain;
    An gin my bold brothers get word o this,
        I fear Willy, you'll be slain."

11. "O will you leave your father's court,
        An go along wi me?
    I'll carry you unto fair Scotland,
        And mak you a lady free."

12. She pat her han in her pocket
        An gae him five hunder poun:
    "An take you that now, Squire Willy,
        Till awa that we do won."

13. Whan day was gane, and night was come,
        She lap the castle-wa;
    But Willy kepit his gay lady,
        He was laith to let her fa.

14. Whan night was gane, an day come in,
        An lions gaed to their dens,
    An ay the lady followd him,
        An the tears came hailing down.

15. "O want ye ribbons to your hair?
        Or roses to your shoone?
    Or want ye as meickle dear bought love
        As your ain heart can contain?"

16. "I want nae ribbons to my hair,
        Nor roses till my shoone;
    An Ohone, alas, for dear bought love
        I have mair nor I can contain."

17. O he's pu'd the oak in good green wood,
        An he's made to her a fire;
    He coverd it o'er wi withred leaves,
        An gard it burn thro ire.

18. He made a bed i the good green wood,
        An he's laid his lady down,

An he's coverd her o'er wi fig-tree leaves,
    But an his ain night-gown.

19. "O had I a bunch o yon red roddins,
    That grows in yonder wood,
But an a drink o water clear,
    I think it woud do me good."

20. He's pu'd her a bunch o yon red roddins,
    That grew beside yon thorn,
But an a drink o water clear,
    Intill his hunting-horn.

21. He's bent his bow, and shot the deer,
    An thro the green wood gane,
An ere that he came back again
    His lady took travailing.

22. "O up ye tak that horn," she says,
    "An ye blaw a blast for me;
Gin my father be in good green wood,
    Sae seen's he'll come me ti."

23. "O gin there be a man on earth
    That ye loo better nor me,
Ye blaw the horn yoursel," he says,
    "For it's never be blawn by me."

24. O he's bent his bow, an shot the deer,
    An thro the green wood has he gane,
An lang or he came back again
    His lady bare him a son.

25. O up has he tane his bonny young son,
    An washn him wi the milk,
An up has he tane his gay lady,
    An rowd her i the silk.

26. He's bent his bow, and shot the deer,
    An thro the green wood has he gane,
Till he met wi a well-fard may,
    Her father's flock feeding.

27. "Ye leave your father's flock feeding,
    An go along wi me;
I'll carry you to a lady fair,
    Will gi you both meat and fee."

28. O whan she came the lady before,
    She's fa'n down on her knee:
"O what's your will wi me, my dame?
    An a dame you seem to be."

29. "O I'm Dame Oliphant, the king's daughter,
    Nae doubt but ye've heard o me;
  Will you leave your father's flock feeding,
    An go to Scotlan wi me?

30. "An ye sal get a nouriship
    Intill an earldome,
  An I will gar provide for the
    To marry some brave Scotsman."

31. The may she keepit the bonny boy,
    An Willy led his lady,
  Until they took their fair shippin,
    Then quikly hame came they.

32. The win was fair, an the sea was clear,
    An they a' wan safe to lan;
  He's haild her lady of Douglassdale,
    Himsel the lord within.

THE BAILIFF'S DAUGHTER OF
ISLINGTON (105)

This ballad has counterparts in Latin countries. It is found in America in virtually the same form as the English. It has either begotten or influenced several songs in which a girl and a soldier or sailor, separated for a long time, meet in something of this situation. "The Love Token," "Pretty Fair Miss" are common titles. An example of such a ballad is *B* from tradition in Georgia, and printed in *JAF*, 29:201.

Text A, English broadside, Roxburghe *Ballads*, ii, 457.

A.

1. There was a youth, and a well belovd youth,
    And he was a esquire's son,
  He loved the bayliff's daughter dear,
    That lived in Islington.

2. She was coy, and she would not believe
    That he did love her so,
  No, nor at any time she would
    Any countenance to him show.

3. But when his friends did understand
    His fond and foolish mind,
  They sent him up to fair London,
    An apprentice for to bind.

4. And when he had been seven long years,
       And his love he had not seen,
   "Many a tear have I shed for her sake
       When she little thought of me."

5. All the maids of Islington
       Went forth to sport and play—
   All but the bayliff's daughter dear—
       She secretly stole away.

6. She put off her gown of gray,
       And put on her puggish attire
   She's up to fair London gone,
       Her true-love to require.

7. As she went along the road,
       The weather being hot and dry,
   There was she aware of her true-love,
       At length came riding by.

8. She stept to him, as red as any rose,
       And took him by the bridle-ring:
   "I pray you, kind sir, give me one penny,
       To ease my weary limb."

9. "I prithee, sweetheart, canst thou tell me
       Where that thou wast born?"
   "At Islington, kind sir," said she,
       "Where I have had many a scorn."

10. "I prithee, sweetheart, canst thou tell me
       Whether thou dost know
    The bailiff's daughter of Islington?"
       "She's dead, sir, long ago."

11. "Then will I sell my goodly steed,
       My saddle and my bow;
    I will into some far countrey,
       Where no man doth me know."

12. "O stay, O stay, thou goodly youth;
       She's alive, she is not dead;
    Here she standeth by thy side,
       And ready to be thy bride."

13. "O farewel grief, and welcome joy,
       Ten thousand times and more.
    For now I have seen my own true-love,
       That I thought I should have seen no more."

B.
THE LOVE TOKEN

A pretty fair miss all in the garden,
A journeyole soldier passing by.
He did stop and kindly address her
By saying, "Kind miss, will you marry me?"

"No, kind sir, a man of honor,
A man of honor you may be.
Would you impose upon a lady
Whose bride to you is not to be?"

"I have a sweetheart cross the ocean,
He has been gone for seven long year,
And if he's dead, I hope he is happy,
Or in some battle being slain.

"And if he is to some fair girl married,
I love the girl that married him."
He run his hands all in his pockets
And pulled out rings that she had gave him.

Straight down before him she did fall:
He picked her up all in his arms,
Giving kisses by one, two, three,
Saying, "If I had staid there seven years longer,
No girl but you could have married me."

THE KNIGHT AND SHEPHERD'S DAUGHTER (110)

This ballad originated in Scotland. It belongs to the general pattern of a man who is forced to marry a woman beneath him socially or one physically unattractive, to have her turn out very desirable in the end. This ballad borrows freely from others. The indebtedness to "Child Waters" in the beginning is close.

Text A, traditional in Scotland, Kinloch, v, 255; B, traditional in Maine, printed in *Bulletin*, 9 : 7.

A.

1. There was a shepherd's dochter
    Kept sheep upon yon hill,
    And by cam a gay braw gentleman,
    And wad hae had his will.

2. He took her by the milk-white hand,
    And laid her on the ground,

And whan he got his will o her
   He lift her up again.

3. "O syne ye've got your will o me,
   Your will o me ye've taen,
'T is all I ask o you, kind sir,
   Is to tell to me your name."

4. "Sometimes they call me Jack," he said,
   "Sometimes they call me John,
But whan I am in the king's court,
   My name is Wilfu Will."

5. Then he loup on his milk-white steed,
   And straught away he rade,
And she did kilt her petticoats,
   And after him she gaed.

6. He never was sae kind as say,
   O lassie will ye ride?
Nor ever had she the courage to say,
   O laddie will ye bide.

7. Until they cam to a wan water,
   Which was called Clyde,
And then turned about his horse,
   Said, "Lassie will ye ride?"

8. "I learned it in my father's hall,
   I learned it for my weel,
That whan I come to deep water,
   I can swim as it were an eel.

9. "I learned it in my mother's bower,
   I learned it for my better,
That whan I come to broad water,
   I can swim like ony otter."

10. He plunged his steed into the ford,
   And straught way thro he rade,
And she set in her lilly feet,
   And thro the water wade.

11. And whan she cam to the king's court,
   She tirled on the pin,
And wha sae ready's the king himsel
   To let the fair maid in?

12. "What is your will wi me, fair maid?
   What is your will wi me?"
"There is a man into your court
   This day has robbed me."

13. "O has he taen your gold," he said,
       "Or has he taen your fee?
    Or has he stown your maidenhead,
       The flower of your bodye?"

14. "He has na taen my gold, kind sir,
       Nor as little has he taen my fee,
    But he has taen my maidenhead,
       The flower of my bodye."

15. "O gif he be a married man,
       High hangit shall he be,
    But gif he be a bachelor,
       His body I'll grant thee."

16. "Sometimes they call him Jack," she said,
       "Sometimes they call him John,
    But whan he's in the king's court,
       His name is Sweet William."

17. "There's not a William in a' my court,
       Never a one but three,
    And one of them is the Queen's brother;
       I wad laugh gif it war he."

18. The king called on his merry men,
       By thirty and by three;
    Sweet Willie, wha used to be foremost man,
       Was the hindmost a' but three.

19. O he cam cripple, and he cam blind,
       Cam twa-fald oer a tree:
    "O be he cripple, or be he blind,
       This very same man is he."

20. "O whether will ye marry the bonny may,
       Or hang on the gallows-tree?"
    "O I will rather marry the bonny may,
       Afore that I do die."

21. But he took out a purse of gold,
       Weel locked in a glove:
    "O tak ye that, my bonny may,
       And seek anither love."

22. "O I will hae none o your gold," she says,
       "Nor as little ony of your fee,
    But I will hae your ain body,
       The king has granted me."

23. O he took out a purse of gold,

A purse of gold and store;
"O tak ye that, fair may," he said,
"Frae me ye'll neer get mair."

24. "O haud your tongue, young man," she says,
"And I pray you let me be;
For I will hae your ain body,
The king has granted me."

25. He mounted her on a bonny bay horse,
Himsel on the silver grey;
He drew his bonnet out oer his een,
He whipt and rade away.

26. O whan they cam to yon nettle bush,
The nettles they war spread:
"O an my mither war but here," she says,
"These nettles she wad sned."

27. "O an I had drank the wan water
Whan I did drink the wine,
That eer a shepherd's dochter
Should hae been a love o mine!"

28. "O may be I'm a shepherd's dochter,
And may be I am nane;
But you might hae ridden on your ways,
And hae let me alane."

29. O whan they cam unto yon mill,
She heard the mill clap:

.   .   .   .

.   .   .   .

30. "Clap on, clap on, thou bonny mill,
Weel may thou, I say,
For mony a time thou's filled my pock
Wi baith oat-meal and grey."

31. "O an I had drank the wan water
Whan I did drink the wine,
That eer a shepherd's dochter
Should hae been a love o mine!"

32. "O may be I'm a shepherd's dochter,
And may be I am nane;
But you might hae ridden on your ways,
And hae let me alane.

33. "But yet I think a fitter match
Could scarcely gang thegither

Than the King of France's auld dochter
And the Queen of Scotland's brither."

B.

1. A shepherd's daughter watching sheep—
   Knight William riding by;
   "O what will I give that pretty fair maid,
   One night with me to lie!"
         Ri fol diddle O day.

2. He took her by the slender waist,
   And laid her on the green;
   He took her by the lily-white hand,
   And lifted her up again.

3. He mounted on his milk-white steed,
   And swiftly he did ride;
   She, being young and nimble foot,
   She followed him side by side.

4. And when she came to the King's castle,
   She knocked so loud did ring;
   O who was so ready as the King himself,
   To rise and let her in.

5. "What news, what news, my pretty fair maid,
   What news have you brought to me?
   Has any of my goods been stole this night,
   Or any of my castles won?"
   "But I've been robbed of my body,
   Which grieves me worse than all."

6. "If he be a married man,
   Hanged he shall be;
   But if he be a single man,
   His body I'll give to thee."

7. The King called up his merry men all,
   By one, by two, by three;
   Knight William used to be the first—
   The last of all came he.

8. Knight William brought five hundred pounds,
   And laid it on the aisle;
   Says he, "Take this, you wanton girl,
   And go maintain your child!"

9. "I don't want your gold," she said,
   "Nor I don't want your fee;

But I will have your fair body,
Which the King has given to me!"

10. After the wedding it was o'er,
      And all was through and done;
    She proved to be the King's daughter,
      And he but a blacksmith's son.

THE BAFFLED KNIGHT (112)

Stories on this theme in European folklore and literature are legion.
Text, Ritson, *Ancient Songs*, p. 159.

1. Yonder comes a courteous knight,
      Lustely raking ouer the lay;
    He was well ware of a bonny lasse,
      As she came wandring ouer the way.
    Then she sang downe a downe, hey downe derry (bis)

2. "Ioue you speed, fayre lady," he said,
      "Among the leaues that be so greene;
    If I were a king, and wore a crowne,
      Full soone, fair lady, shouldst thou be a queen.

3. "Also Ioue saue you, faire lady,
      Among the roses that be so red;
    If I haue not my will of you,
      Full soone, faire lady, shall I be dead."

4. Then he lookt east, then hee lookt west,
      Hee lookt north, so did he south;
    He could not finde a privy place,
      For all lay in the diuel's mouth.

5. "If you will carry me, gentle sir,
      A mayde vnto my father's hall,
    Then you shall haue your will of me,
      Vnder purple and vnder paule."

6. He set her vp vpon a steed,
      And him selfe vpon another,
    And all the day he rode her by,
      As though they had been sister and brother.

7. When she came to her father's hall,
      It was well walled round about;
    She yode in at the wicket-gate,
      And shut the foure-eard foole without.

8. "You had me," quoth she, "abroad in the field,

Among the corne, amidst the hay,
Where you might had your will of mee,
For, in good faith, sir, I neuer said nay.

9. "Ye had me also amid the field,
Among the rushes that were so browne,
Where you might had your will of me,
But you had not the face to lay me downe."

10. He pulled out his nut-browne sword,
And wipt the rust off with his sleeue,
And said, Ioue's curse come to his heart
That any woman would beleeue!

11. When you haue your owne true-loue
A mile or twaine out of the towne,
Spare not for her gay clothing,
But lay her body flat on the ground.

THE GREAT SILKIE OF SULE SKERRY (113)

Silkie is seal and Sule Skerry is a small island off the northern coast of Scotland. All northern peoples believed that a race of people lived under the water in the north and that under water they had the appearance of seals, but that by doffing their "seal skins" they could become human beings of conventional appearance. Like the swan maidens, in their human manifestation they had to put their skins on again to return to their seal state. Stories are told of these seal women consorting with human men, their husbands hiding the seal garment so that they cannot return to the under-water state. This is the story of a woman who has had a child by one of these seal men. As the ballad opens, she is singing a lullaby to the child. The father returns, begging for the child to carry it under the sea, and predicting that the woman will marry a gunner who will kill them both. Version A was not known by Child. It tells a much longer and coherent story. After stanza 13, a stanza or two has been omitted evidently telling of the mother marrying a human being and his shooting the seals, father and son.

Text A, Menzies, *Orcadian Musings,* p. 140; B, traditional in Scotland, *Proc. Soc. Antiquaries of Scotland,* i, 86.

A.

1. In Norway lands there lived a maid,
"Hush, ba, loo lillie," this maid began;
"I know not where my baby's father is,
Whether by land or sea does he travel in."

2. It happened on a certain day,
   When this fair lady fell fast asleep,
  That in cam' a good grey selchie,
   And set him doon at her bed feet,

3. Saying, "Awak, awak, my pretty fair maid,
   For oh! how sound as thou dost sleep.
  An' I'll tell thee where thy baby's father is;
   He's sittin' close at they bed feet."

4. "I pray, come tell to me thy name,
   Oh! tell me where does thy dwelling be?"
  "My name it is good Hein Mailer,
   An' I earn my livin' oot o' the sea.

5. "I am a man upon the land;
   I am a selchie in the sea;
  An whin I'm far frae every strand,
   My dwellin' is in Shool Skerrie."

6. "Alas! alas! this woeful fate;
   This weary fate that's been laid for me!
  That a man should come frae the wast o'hoy,
   To the Norway lands to have a bairn wi' me."

7. "My dear, I'll wed thee with a ring,
   With a ring, my dear, I'll wed wi' thee."
  "Thoo may go wed thee weddens wi' whom thoo wilt;
   For I'm sure thoo'll never wed none wi' me."

8. "Thoo will nurse my little wee son
   For seven long years upo' thy knee,
  An' at the end o' seven long years
   I'll come back an' pay the norish fee."

9. She's nursed her little wee son
   For seven long years upo' her knee,
  An' at the end o' seven long years
   He cam' back wi' gold an' white monie.

10. She says, "My dear, I'll wed thee wi' a ring,
   With a ring, my dear, I'll wed wi' thee."
  "Thoo may go wed thee weddens wi' whom thee will;
   For I'm sure thoo'll never wed none wi' me.

11. "But I'll put a gold chain around his neck,
   An' a gey good gold chain it'll be,
  That if ever he comes to the Norway lands,
   Thoo may hae a gey good guess on hi'.

12. "An thoo will get a gunner good,
   An' a gey good gunner it will be,

An' he'll gae oot on a May mornin'
An' shoot the son an' the grey selchie."

13. Oh! sha has got a gunner good,
An' a gey good gunner it was he,
An' he gaed oot on a May mornin'
An' he shot the son and the grey selchie.

14. "Alas! alas! this woeful fate!
This weary fate that's been laid for me!"
An' ance or twice she sobbed and sighed,
An' her tender heart did brak in three.

B.

1. An eartly nourris sits and sings,
And aye she sings, Ba, lily wean!
Little ken I my bairnis father,
Far less the land that he staps in.

2. Then ane arose at her bed-fit,
An a grumly guest I'm sure was he:
"Here am I, thy bairnis father,
Although that I be not comelie.

3. "I am a man, upo the lan,
An I am a silkie in the sea;
And when I'm far and far frae lan,
My dwelling is in Sule Skerrie."

4. "It was na weel," quo the maiden fair,
"It was na weel, inded," quo she,
"That the Great Silkie of Sule Skerrie
Suld hae come and aught a bairn to me."

5. Now he has taen a purse of goud,
And he has pat it upo her knee,
Saying, "Gie to me my little young son,
An tak thee up thy nourris-fee.

6. "An it sall come to pass on a simmer's day,
When the sin shines het on evera stane,
That I will tak my little young son,
An teach him for to swim the faem.

7. "An thu sall marry a proud gunner,
An a proud gunner I'm sure he'll be,
An the very first schot that ere he schoots,
He'll schoot baith my young son and me."

JOHNIE COCK (114)

This fine ballad is not found in written form before the 18th century, but it must be considerably older than that. Percy suggests that the mention of a wolf as present in Scotland would give the ballad "great antiquity," but as a matter of fact wolves were known in Scotland in the 17th century. Only one version has been found in America and that in Virginia.

Text A, traditional in England, Percy, No. 5; B, John Fry, *Pieces of Ancient Poetry*, etc., p. 51; C, Scott, i, 59; D, traditional in Virginia, Davis, *Traditional Ballads of Virginia*, p. 386.

Notes

1/4. iron bands: Many passages in this ballad are difficult to explain. This may mean that the dogs are bespelled. The mother, realizing that, takes to her bed. This may account for the fact that the dogs give no warning of the coming of the seven foresters.

3/4. fords of hell: Hell in tradition is often reached by crossing a river, often of blood.

4/3. scarlett . . . Lincoln green: He has put off the garb of the king's man and put on that of the outlaw.

6/1. Baridhouplee, etc. The proper names cannot be surely identified though they certainly belong to the north; Percy notes that Pickeram Side is in Northumbria.

8/1. little pen knife . . . three quarters long: illustrates the conventionality of the ballad phrasing; three quarters is three quarters of a yard.

8/4. Liver was thought by many people to be the seat of life and was consequently removed at once and eaten to transfer the virtue of the dead to the living. The folk tales commonly tell of the slayer removing the tongue of a slain animal, but usually for purposes of identification. Drinking blood is common in early societies, again often with the idea of transferring virtue from the slain to the living.

13/3. American leather strikes an incongruous modern note. The reference is not clear; American hides were imported into England from early colonial times. Morocco leather was made from American hides as early as 1798.

15/3. sister's son: evidently one of the foresters; version F confirms this. Almost always the romances indicate an uncle-nephew (sister's son) relation between the important protagonists of a story.

17. This is a general folk belief of Scotland; it is also told of the bear.

18–19. The address to the weapons and the fighting on stubs of legs is fairly common in epic tradition.

20. boy: usually bird. The bird as messenger is common in folk tradition.

A.

1. Johny he has risen up i the morn,
   Calls for water to wash his hands;
   But little knew he that his bloody hounds
   Were bound in iron bands.
   Were bound in iron bands.

2. Johny's mother has gotten word o that,
   And care-bed she has taen:
   "O Johny, for my benison,
   I beg you'l stay at hame;
   For the wine so red, and the well baken bread,
   My Johny shall want nane.

3. "There are seven forsters at Pickeram Side,
   At Pickeram where they dwell,
   And for a drop of thy heart's bluid
   They wad ride the fords of hell."

4. Johny he's gotten word of that,
   And he's turnd wondrous keen;
   He's put off the red scarlett,
   And he's put on the Lincoln green.

5. With a sheaf of arrows by his side,
   And a bent bow in his hand,
   He's mounted on a prancing steed,
   And he has ridden fast oer the strand.

6. He's up i Braidhouplee, and down i Bradyslee,
   And under a buss o broom,
   And there he found a good dun deer,
   Feeding in a buss of ling.

7. Johny shot, and the dun deer lap,
   And she lap wondrous wide,
   Until they came to the wan water,
   And he stemd her of her pride.

8. He 'as taen out the little pen-knife,
   'T was full three quarters long,
   And he has taen out of that dun deer
   The liver bot and the tongue.

9. They eat of the flesh, and they drank of the blood,
   And the blood it was so sweet,
   Which caused Johny and his bloody hounds
   To fall in a deep sleep.

10. By then came an old palmer,
    And an ill death may he die!

For he's away to Pickram Side,
    As fast as he can drie.

11. "What news, what news?" says the Seven Forsters,
    "What news have ye brought to me?"
"I have noe news," the palmer said,
    "But what I saw with my eye.

12. "High up i Bradyslee, low down i Bradisslee,
    And under a buss of scroggs,
O there I spied a well-wight man,
    Sleeping among his dogs.

13. "His coat it was of light Lincoln,
    And his breeches of the same,
His shoes of the American leather,
    And gold buckles tying them."

14. Up bespake the Seven Forsters,
    Up bespake they ane and a':
"O that is Johny o Cockleys Well,
    And near him we will draw."

15. O the first y stroke that they gae him,
    They struck him off by the knee;
Then up bespake his sister's son:
    "O the next 'll gar him die."

16. "O some they count ye well-wight men,
    But I do count ye nane;
For you might well ha wakend me,
    And askd gin I wad be taen.

17. "The wildest wolf in aw this wood
    Wad not ha done so by me;
She'd ha wet her foot ith wan water,
    And sprinkled it oer my brae,
And if that wad not ha wakend me,
    She wad ha gone and let me be.

18. "O bows of yew, if ye be true.
    In London, where ye were bought,
Fingers five, get up belive,
    Manhuid shall fail me nought."

19. He has killd the Seven Forsters,
    He has killd tham all but ane,
And that wan scarce to Pickeram Side,
    To carry the bode-words hame.

20. "Is there never a boy in a' this wood
    That will tell what I can say;

That will go to Cockley's Well,
    Tell my mither to fetch me away?"

21.   There was a boy into that wood,
      That carried the tidings away,
    And many ae was the well-wight man
      At the fetching o Johny away.

B.

1.   Johnny Cock, in a May morning,
      Sought water to wash his hands,
    And he is awa to louse his dogs
      That's tied wi iron bans.
      That's tied wi iron bans.

2.   His coat it is of the light Lincum green,
      And his breiks are of the same;
    His shoes are of the American leather,
      Silver buckles tying them.

3.   He hunted up, and so did he down,
      Till he came to yon bush of scrogs,
    And then to yon wan water,
      Where he slept among his dogs.

*   *   *   *   *   *   *

4.   Johnny Cock out-shot a' the foresters,
      And out-shot a the three;
    Out shot a' the foresters,
      Wounded Johnny aboun the bree.

5.   "Woe be to you, foresters,
      And an ill death may you die!
    For there would not a wolf in a' the wood
      Have done the like to me.

6.   "For 't would ha' put its foot in the coll water
      And ha strinkled it on my bree,
    And gin that would not have done,
      Would have gane and lett me be.

7.   "I often took to my mother
      The dandoo and the roe,
    But now I'l take to my mother
      Much sorrow and woe.

8.   "I often took to my mother
      The dandoo and the hare,

But now I'l take to my mother
Much sorrow and much care."

C.

1. Johnie rose up in a May morning,
     Called for water to wash his hands:
   "Gar loose to me the gude graie dogs,
     That are bound wi iron bands."

2. When Johnie's mother gat word o that,
     Her hands for dule she wrang:
   "O Johnie, for my bennison,
     To the grenewood dinna gang."

3. "Eneugh ye hae o the gude wheat-bread,
     And eneugh o the blude-red wine,
   And therefore for nae vennison, Johnie,
     I pray ye, stir frae hame."

4. But Johnie's buskt up his gude bend bow,
     His arrows, ane by ane,
   And he has gane to Durrisdeer,
     To hunt the dun deer down.

5. As he came down by Merriemass,
     And in by the benty line,
   There has he espied a deer lying,
     Aneath a bush of ling.

6. Johnie he shot, and the dun deer lap,
     And he wounded her on the side,
   But atween the water and the brae,
     His hounds they laid her pride.

7. And Johnie has bryttled the deer sae weel
     That he's had out her liver and lungs,
   And wi these he has feasted his bludey hounds
     As if they had been erl's sons.

8. They eat sae much o the vennison,
     And drank sae much o the blude,
   That Johnie and a' his bludey hounds
     Fell asleep as they had been dead.

9. And by there came a silly auld carle,
     An ill death mote he die!
   For he's awa to Hislinton,
     Where the Seven Foresters did lie.

10. "What news, what news, ye gray-headed carle?

What news bring ye to me?"
"I bring nae news," said the gray-headed carle,
"Save what these eyes did see.

11. "As I came down by Merriemass,
    And down amang the scroggs,
The bonniest childe that ever I saw
    Lay sleeping amang his dogs.

12. "The shirt that was upon his back
    Was o the holland fine;
The doublet which was over that
    Was o the Lincome twine.

13. "The buttons that were on his sleeve
    Were o the gowd sae gude;
The gude graie hounds he lay amang,
    Their mouths were dyed wi blude."

14. Then out and spak the first forester,
    The heid man ower them a':
"If this be Johnie o Breadislee,
    Nae nearer will we draw."

15. But up and spak the sixth forester,
    His sister's son was he:
"If this be Johnie o Breadislee,
    We soon shall gar him die."

16. The first flight of arrows the foresters shot
    They wounded him on the knee;
And out and spak the seventh forester,
    "The next will gar him die."

17. Johnie's set his back against an aik,
    His fute against a stane,
And he has slain the Seven Foresters,
    He has slain them a' but ane.

18. He has broke three ribs in that ane's side,
    But and his collar bane;
He's laid him twa-fald ower his steed,
    Bade him carry the tidings hame.

19. "O is there na a bonnie bird
    Can sing as I can say,
Could flee away to me mother's bower,
    And tell to fetch Johnie away?"

20. The starling flew to his mother's windowstane,
    It whistled and it sang,

And aye the ower-word o the tune
    Was, Johnie tarries lang!

21.   They made a rod o the hazel-bush,
       Another o the slae-thorn tree,
    And mony, mony were the men
       At fetching our Johnie.

22.   Then out and spake his auld mother,
       And fast her teirs did fa;
    Ye wad nae be warnd, my son Johnie,
       Frae the hunting to bide awa.

23.   "Aft hae I brought to Breadlislee
       The less gear and the mair,
    But I neer brought to Breadislee
       What grieved my heart sae sair.

24.   "But wae betyde that silly auld carle,
       An ill death shall he die;
    For the highest tree on Merriemass
       Shall be his morning's fee."

25.   Now Johnie's gude ben bow is broke,
       And his gude graie dogs are slain,
    And his bodie lies dead in Durrisdeer,
       And his hunting it is done.

D.

1.   "Come, Buck, come, Bouncer, my three bloodhounds,
       For tomorrow we must go
    Away to the Broadway Low
       To hunt the buck and doe."

2.   Johnny's mother heard him say so

       .   .   .   .

    "My blessings on you Johnny," she said,
       "Take counsel and stay at home.

3.   "There are the seven foresters
       In the Broadway Low,
    And for three drops of thy heart's blood
       Would dare three sobs to hell."

4.   Johnny heard his mother say so,
       Made him wondrous keen;
    He threw off his robes of red
       And put on a light Lincoln green.

5.   Johnny saddled his steed

And his three bloodhounds at his command,
And a sheaf of arrows at his side
    As he rode along the strand.

6.   Johnny shot and the dun deer left

    .   .   .   .   .

Till he came to the waters wide;
    There he laid himself down to sleep.

7.   First he drew out his fine bugle horn
    And blew a blast of pride,
Which awoke six of the seven foresters
    That lay by the hawthorn side.

8.   Up jumped the seventh forester
    And said, "That is a blast well blown.
Are there a man among you all
    Can blow such as him?"

9.   They rode over hills and vales

    .   .   .   .

Till they came to a silly old man,
    By an ill death may he die.

10.   "What news have you, old man, for me?

    .   .   .   .

Or else by the sword that hangs by my side,
    By the point you shall die."

11.   ".   .   .   .   .   .

    No news have I for thee;
Only yonder lies the widow's fairest son
    That ever my eyes could see."

12.   They rode over hills
    And mountains high
Till they came to the very spot
    Where Johnny Cock did lie.

13.   They bent three bows
    And broad arrows did they let fly;
They wounded poor Johnny Cock
    A little above the eye.

14.   "Woe be to you, seven foresters,
    That would do such a deed to I.
Is there a wolf in the Broadway Low
    That would do such a deed to me?"

15.   Johnny bent a bow
    Bent of an ivory bone,

       And shot among the seven foresters
         And killed them all but one.

16.   Besides he wounded the seventh forester
         And broke his collar bone,
       And threw him across his saddle
         To carry the tidings home.

17.   "Is there any pretty bird in the Broadway Low
         That can whistle what I say,
       That will go to fair Eleanor's window
         And take fair Johnny away?"

ROBYN AND GANDELEYN (115)

This ballad is found in the Sloan MS. 2593, c. 1450. The dialect is
northern. Robin here is not Robin Hood, though there may be some
influence from the Robin Hood tradition. Gandeleyn suggests Gamelyn of the romance by that name, and again there seems to be no connection.

Notes
  1/5. This line is the refrain.

1.   I herde a carpyng of a clerk,
         Al at ȝone wodes ende,
       Of gode Robyn and Gandeleyn;
         Was þer non oþer þynge.
       Robynn lyth in grene wode bowndyn

2.   Stronge theuys wern þo chylderin non,
         But bowmen gode and hende;
       He wentyn to wode to getyn hem fleych,
         If God wold it hem sende.

3.   Al day wentyn þo chylderin too,
         And fleych fowndyn he non,
       Til it were a-geyn euyn;
         Þe chylderin wold gon hom.

4.   Half an honderid of fat falyf der
         He comyn a-ȝon,
       And alle he wern fayr and fat i-now,
         But markyd was þer non:
       "Be dere God," seyde gode Robyn,
         "Here of we xul haue on."

5.   Robyn bent his joly bowe,
         Þer in he set a flo;

    Þe fattest der of alle
      Þe herte he clef a to.

6. He hadde not þe der i-flawe,
     Ne half out of þe hyde,
    There cam a schrewde arwe out of þe west,
     Þat felde Robertes pryde.

7. Gandeleyn lokyd hym est and west,
     Be euery syde:
    "Hoo hat myn mayster slayin?
     Ho hat don þis dede?
    Xal I neuer out of grene wode go
     Til I se (his) sydis blede."

8. Gandeleyn lokyd hym est and lokyd west,
     And sowt vnder þe sunne;
    He saw a lytil boy
     He clepyn Wrennok of Donne.

9. A good bowe in his hond,
     A brod arwe þer ine,
    And fowre and twenti goode arwys,
     Trusyd in a þrumme:
    "Be war þe, war þe, Gandeleyn,
     Her-of þu xalt han summe.

10. "Be war þe, war þe Gandeleyn,
     Her of þu gyst plente."
    "Euer on for an oþer," seyde Gandeleyn;
     "Mysaunter haue he xal fle.

11. "Qwer-at xal our marke be?"
     Seyde Gandeleyn.
    "Eueryche at oþeris herte,"
     Seyde Wrennok ageyn.

12. "Ho xal ȝeue þe ferste schote?"
     Seyde Gandeleyn.
    "And I xul ȝeue þes on be-forn,"
     Seyde Wrennok ageyn.

13. Wrennok schette a ful good schote,
     And he schet not to hye;
    Þrow þe sanchoþis of his bryk;
     It towchyd neyþer thye.

14. "Now hast þu ȝouyn me on be-forn,"
     Al þus to Wrennok seyde he,
    "And þrow þe myȝt of our lady
     A bettere I xal ȝeue þe."

15. Gandeleyn bent his goode bowe,
  And set þer in a flo;
 He schet þrow his grene certyl,
  His herte he clef on too.

16. "Now xalt þu neuer ȝelpe, Wrennok,
  At ale ne at wyn,
 Þat þu hast slawe goode Robyn,
  And his knaue Gandeleyn.

17. "Now xalt þu neuer ȝelpe, Wrennok,
  At wyn ne at ale,
 Þat þu hast slawe goode Robyn,
  And Gandeleyn his knaue."

 Robin lyȝth in grene wode bowndyn.

ROBIN HOOD AND GUY OF GISBORNE (118)

This story is a bit incoherent at the beginning because of lost stanzas;
and later the confusion resulting from lack of motivation of Robin
Hood's action in going to seek Little John when, as far as one can as-
certain, he could not know that Little John was in trouble suggests
that we do not have the best version of what was an excellent and
spirited ballad. A fragment of a drama based on this ballad exists in
a MS. of the 15th century now at Trinity College, Cambridge.
 Text, Percy, p. 262.

1. When shawes beene sheene, and shradds full fayre,
  And leeues both large and longe,
 Itt is merry, walking in the fayre fforrest,
  To heare the small birds songe.

2. The woodweele sang, and wold not cease,
  Amongst the leaues a lyne:
 And it is by two wight yemen,
  By deare God, that I meane.

   * * * * * *

3. "Me thought they did mee beate and binde,
  And tooke my bow mee froe;
 If I bee Robin a-liue in this lande,
  I'le be wrocken on both them towe."

4. "Sweauens are swift, master," quoth Iohn,
  "As the wind that blows ore a hill;
 Ffor if itt be neuer soe lowde this night,
  To-morrow it may be still."

5. "Buske yee, bowne, yee, my merry men all,
        Ffor Iohn shall goe with mee;
   For I'le goe seeke yond wight yeomen
        In greenwood where the bee."

6. The cast on their gowne of greene,
        A shooting gone are they,
   Vntill they came to the merry greenwood,
        Where they had gladdest bee."
   There were the ware of a wight yeoman,
        His body leaned to a tree.

7. A sword and a dagger he wore by his side,
        Had beene many a man's bane,
   And he was cladd in his capull-hyde,
        Topp, and tayle, and mayne.

8. "Stand you still, master," quoth Litle Iohn,
        "Vnder this trusty tree,
   And I will goe to yond wight yeoman,
        To know his meaning trulye."

9. "A, Iohn, by me thou setts noe store,
        And that's a ffarley thinge;
   How offt send I my men beffore,
        And tarry my-selfe behinde?

10. "It is noe cunning a knaue to ken,
        And a man but heare him speake;
    And itt were not for bursting of my bowe,
        Iohn, I wold thy head breake."

11. But often words they breeden bale,
        That parted Robin and Iohn;
    Iohn is gone to Barnesdale,
        The gates he knowes eche one.

12. And when hee came to Barnesdale,
        Great heauinesse there hee hadd;
    He ffound two of his fellowes
        Were slaine both in a slade,

13. And Scarlett a ffoote flyinge was,
        Ouer stockes and stone,
    For the sheriffe with seuen score men
        Fast after him is gone.

14. "Yett one shoote I'le shoote," says Litle Iohn,
        "With Crist his might and mayne;
    I'le make yond fellow that flyes soe fast
        To be both glad and ffaine."

15. Iohn bent vp a good veiwe bow,
    And ffetteled him to shoote;
    The bow was made of a tender boughe,
    And fell downe to his foote.

16. "Woe worth thee, wicked wood," sayd Litle Iohn,
    "That ere thou grew on a tree.
    Ffor this day thou art my bale,
    My boote when thou shold bee!"

17. This shoote it was but loosely shott,
    The arrowe flew in vaine,
    And it mett one of the sheriffes men;
    Good William a Trent was slaine.

18. It had beene better for William a Trent
    To hange vpon a gallowe
    Then for to lye in the greenwoode,
    There slaine with an arrowe.

19. And it is sayd, when men be mett,
    Six can doe more then three:
    And they haue tane Litle Iohn,
    And bound him ffast to a tree.

20. "Thou shalt be drawen by dale and downe," quoth the sheriffe,
    "And hanged hye on a hill."
    "But thou may ffayle," quoth Litle Iohn,
    "If itt be Christs owne will."

21. Let vs leaue talking of Litle Iohn,
    For hee is bound fast to a tree,
    And talke of Guy and Robin Hood,
    In the green woode where they bee.

22. How these two yeomen together they mett,
    Vnder the leaues of lyne,
    To see what marchandise they made
    Euen at that same time.

23. "Good morrow, good fellow," quoth Sir Guy;
    "Good morrow, good ffellow," quoth hee;
    "Methinkes by this bow thou beares in thy hand,
    A good archer thou seems to bee."

24. "I am wilfull of my way," quoth Sir Guye,
    "And of my morning tyde."
    "I'le lead thee through the wood," quoth Robin,
    "Good ffellow, I'le be thy guide."

25. "I seeke an outlaw," quoth Sir Guye,

"Men call him Robin Hood;
I had rather meet with him vpon a day
Then forty pound of golde."

26. "If you tow mett, itt wold be seene whether were better
Afore yee did part awaye;
Let vs some other pastime find,
Good ffellow, I thee pray.

27. "Let vs some other masteryes make,
And wee will walke in the woods euen;
Wee may chance meet with Robin Hoode
At some vnsett steven."

28. They cutt them downe the summer shroggs
Which grew both vnder a bryar,
And sett them three score rood in twinn,
To shoote the prickes full neare.

29. "Leade on, good ffellow," sayd Sir Guye,
"Leade on, I doe bidd thee."
"Nay, by my faith," quoth Robin Hood,
"The leader thou shalt bee."

30. The first good shoot that Robin ledd
Did not shoote an inch that pricke ffroe;
Guy was an archer good enoughe,
But he cold neere shoote soe.

31. The second shoote Sir Guy shott,
He shott within the garlande;
But Robin Hoode shott it better then hee,
For he cloue the good pricke-wande.

32. "Gods blessing on thy heart!" sayes Guye,
"Goode ffellow, thy shooting is goode;
For an thy hart be as good as thy hands,
Thou were better then Robin Hood.

33. "Tell me thy name, good ffellow," quoth Guy,
"Vnder the leaues of lyne."
"Nay, by my faith," quoth good Robin,
"Till thou haue told me thine."

34. "I dwell by dale and downe," quoth Guye,
"And I haue done many a curst turne;
And he that calles me by my right name
Calles me Guye of good Gysborne."

35. "My dwelling is in the wood," sayes Robin;
"By thee I set right nought;

My name is Robin Hood of Barnesdale,
　　A ffellow thou hast long sought."

36.　He that had neither beene a kithe nor kin
　　　Might haue seene a full fayre sight,
　　To see how together these yeomen went,
　　　With blades both browne and bright.

37.　To haue seene how these yeomen together fought,
　　　Two howers of a summers day;
　　Itt was neither Guy nor Robin Hood
　　　That ffettled them to flye away.

38.　Robin was reacheles on a roote,
　　　And stumbled at that tyde,
　　And Guy was quicke and nimble with-all,
　　　And hitt him ore the left side.

39.　"Ah, deere Lady!" sayd Robin Hoode,
　　　"Thou art both mother and may.
　　I thinke it was neuer man's destinye
　　　To dye before his day."

40.　Robin thought on Our Lady deere,
　　　And soone leapt vp againe,
　　And thus he came with an awkwarde stroke;
　　　Good Sir Guy hee has slayne.

41.　He tooke Sir Guy's head by the hayre,
　　　And sticked itt on his bowes end;
　　"Thou hast beene traytor all thy liffe,
　　　Which thing must haue an ende."

42.　Robin pulled forth an Irish kniffe,
　　　And nicked Sir Guy in the fface,
　　That hee was neuer on a woman borne
　　　Cold tell who Sir Guye was.

43.　Saies, "Lye there, lye there, good Sir Guy,
　　　And with me be not wrothe;
　　If thou haue had the worse stroakes at my hand,
　　　Thou shalt haue the better cloathe."

44.　Robin did off his gowne of greene,
　　　Sir Guye hee did it throwe;
　　And hee put on that capull-hyde,
　　　That cladd him topp to toe.

45.　"The boew, the arrowes, and litle horne,
　　　And with me now I'le beare;

Ffor now I will goe to Barnesdale,
  To see how my men doe ffare."

46. Robin sett Guyes horne to his mouth,
    · A lowd blast in it he did blow;
  That beheard the sheriffe of Nottingham,
    As he leaned vnder a lowe.

47. "Hearken! hearken!" sayd the sheriffe,
    "I heard noe tydings but good;
  For yonder I heare Sir Guyes horne blowe,
    For he hath slaine Robin Hoode.

48. "For yonder I heare Sir Guyes horne blowe,
    Itt blowes soe well in tyde,
  For yonder comes that wighty yeoman,
    Cladd in his capull-hyde.

49. "Come higher, thou good Sir Guy,
    Aske of mee what thou wilt haue."
  "I'le none of thy gold," sayes Robin Hood,
    "Nor I'le none of itt haue.

50. "But now I haue slaine the master," he sayd,
    "Let me goe strike the knaue;
  That is all the reward I aske,
    Nor noe other will I haue."

51. "Thou art a madman," said the shiriffe,
    "Thou sholdest haue had a knight's ffee;
  Seeing thy asking beene soe badd,
    Well granted it shall be."

52. But Litle Iohn heard his master speake,
    Well he knew that was his steuen;
  "Now shall I be loset," quoth Litle Iohn,
    "With Christs might in heauen."

53. But Robin hee hyed him towards Litle Iohn,
    Hee thought hee wold loose him beliue;
  The sheriffe and all his companye
    Fast after him didn driue.

54. "Stand abacke! stand abacke!" sayd Robin;
    Why draw you mee soe neere?
  Itt was neuer the vse in our contrye
    One's shift another shold heere."

55. But Robin pulled forth an Irysh kniffe,
    And losed Iohn hand and ffoote,
  And gaue him Sir Guyes bow in his hand,
    And bade it be his boote.

56. But Iohn tooke Guyes bow in his hand—
        His arrowes were rawstye by the roote—
     The sheriffe saw Litle Iohn draw a bow
        And ffettle him to shoote.

57. Towards his house in Nottingam
        He ffled full fast away,
     And soe did all his companye,
        Not one behind did stay.

58. But he cold neither soe fast goe,
        Nor away soe fast runn,
     But Litle Iohn, with an arrow broade
        Did cleaue his heart in twinn.

ROBIN HOOD AND THE MONK (119)

This ballad is from a 15th-century manuscript, F.f. 5.48, in the Cambridge University Library. It is an excellent ballad in the best tradition of Robin Hood. Unfortunately a break occurs at stanza (30/3) so that we cannot know how Robin Hood's men became aware of his plight. Note the lyric quality of the beginning; ballads usually plunge immediately into the action without any such setting of mood. In the early Robin Hood ballads, Robin is always represented as being very religious and a special devotee of the Virgin.

1. In somer, when þe shawes be sheyne,
        And leves be large and long,
    Hit is full mery in feyre foreste
        To here þe foulys song:

2. To se þe dere draw to þe dale,
        And leve þe hilles hee,
    And shadow hem in þe levës grene,
        Vnder the grene-wode tre.

3. Hit befel on Whitsontide,
        Erly in a May mornyng,
    The son vp feyre can shyne,
        And the briddis mery can syng.

4. "This is a mery mornyng," seid Litull John,
        "Be hym þat dyed on tre;
    A more mery man þen I am one
        Lyves not in Cristiantë.

5. "Pluk vp þi hert, my dere mayster,"
        Litull John can sey,

"And thynk hit is a full fayre tyme
In a mornyng of May."

6. "ʒe, on thyng greves me," seid Robyn,
   "And does my hert mych woo,
Þat I may not no solem day
   To mas nor matyns goo.

7. "Hit is a fourtnet and more," seid he,
   "Syn I my sauyour see;
To day wil I to Notyngham," seid Robyn,
   "With þe myght of mylde Marye."

8. Than spake Moche, þe mylner sun,
   Euer more wel hym betyde!
"Take twelue of þi wyght ʒemen,
   Well weppynd, be þi side.
Such on wolde þi selfe slon,
   Þat twelue dar not abyde."

9. "Of all my mery men," seid Robyn,
   "Be my feith I wil non haue,
But Litull John shall beyre my bow,
   Till þat me list to drawe."

10. "Þou shall beyre þin own," seid Litull Jon,
    "Maister, and I wyl beyre myne,
And we well shete a peny," seid Litull Jon,
    "Vnder þe grene-wode lyne."

11. "I wil not shete a peny," seyd Robyn Hode,
    "In feith, Litull John, with the,
But euer for on as þou shetis," seide Robyn,
    "In feith I holde þe thre."

12. Thus shet þei forth, þese ʒemen too,
    Bothe at buske and brome,
Til Litull John wan of his maister
    Fiue shillings to hose and shone.

13. A ferly strife fel þem betwene,
    As they went bi the wey;
Litull John seid he had won fiue shillings,
    And Robyn Hode seid schortly nay.

14. With þat Robyn Hode lyed Litul Jon,
    And smote hym with his hande;
Litul Jon waxed wroth þerwith,
    And pulled out his bright bronde.

15. "Were þou not my maister," seid Litull John,
    "Þou shuldis by hit ful sore;

   Get þe a man wher þou wilt,
    For þou getis me no more."

16. Þen Robyn goes to Notyngham,
    Hym selfe mornyng allone,
   And Litull John to mery Scherwode,
    The pathes he knew ilkone.

17. Whan Robyn came to Notyngham,
    Sertenly withouten layn,
   He prayed to God and myld Mary
    To bryng hym out saue agayn.

18. He gos in to Seynt Mary chirch,
    And kneled down before the rode;
   Alle þat euer were þe church within
    Beheld wel Robyn Hode.

19. Beside hym stod a gret-hedid munke,
    I pray to God woo he be;
   Fful sone he knew gode Robyn,
    As sone as he hym se.

20. Out at þe durre he ran,
    Fful sone and anon;
   Alle þe ʒatis of Notyngham
    He made to be sparred euerychon.

21. "Rise vp," he seid, "þou prowde schereff,
    Buske þe and make þe bowne;
   I haue spyed þe kynggis felon,
    Ffor sothe he is in þis town.

22. "I haue spyed þe false felon,
    As he stondis at his masse;
   Hit is long of þe," seide þe munke,
    "And euer he fro vs passe.

23. "Þis traytur name is Robyn Hode,
    Vnder þe grene-wode lynde;
   He robbyt me onys of a hundred pound,
    Hit shalle neuer out of my mynde."

24. Vp þen rose þis prowde shereff,
    And radly made hym ʒare;
   Many was þe moder son
    To þe kyrk with hym can fare.

25. In at þe durres þei throly thrast,
    With staves ful gode wone;
   "Alas, alas!" seid Robyn Hode,
    "Now mysse I Litull John."

26. But Robyn toke out a too-hond sworde,
    Þat hangit down be his kne;
  Þer as þe schereff and his men stode thyckust,
    The þurwarde wolde he.

27. Thryes thorowout þem he ran þen,
    For soþe as I yow sey,
  And woundyt mony a moder son,
    And twelue he slew þat day.

28. His sworde vpon þe schireff hed
    Sertanly he brake in too;
  "Þe smyth þat þe made," seid Robyn,
    "I pray to God wyrke hym woo!

29. "Ffor now as I weppynlesse," seid Robyn,
    "Alasse! agayn my wylle;
  But if I may fle þese traytors fro,
    I wot þei wil me kyll."

30. Robyn in to the churchë ran,
    Throout hem euerilkon,

*   *   *   *   *   *

31. Sum fel in swonyng as þei were dede,
    And lay stil as any stone;
  Non of theym were in her mynde
    But only Litull Jon.

32. "Let be your rule," seid Litull Jon,
    "Ffor his luf þat dyed on tre,
  ȝe þat shulde be duȝty men;
    Het is gret shame to se.

33. "Oure maister has bene hard bystode
    And ȝet scapyd away;
  Pluk vp your hertis, and leve þis mone,
    And harkyn what I shal say.

34. "He has seruyd Oure Lady many a day,
    And ȝet wil, securly;
  Þerfor I trust in hir specialy
    No wyckud deth shal he dye.

35. "Þerfor be glad," seid Litul John,
    "And let þis mournyng be;
  And I shal þe munkis gyde,
    With þe myght of mylde Mary.

36. .   .   .   .
    "We will go but we too;
  And I mete hym," seid Litul John.

37.   "Loke þat ȝe kepe wel owre tristil-tre,
           Vnder þe levys smale,
       And spare non of this venyson,
           Þat gose in thys vale."

38.   Fforþe þen went these ȝemen too,
           Litul John and Moche on fere,
       And lokid on Moche emys hows,
           Þe hye way lay fyll nere.

39.   Litul John stode at a wyndow in þe mornyng,
           And lokid forþ at a stage;
       He was war where þe munke came ridyng,
           And with hym a litul page.

40.   "Be my feith," seid Litul John to Moch,
           "I can þe tel tithyngous gode;
       I se wher þe munke cumys rydyng,
           I know hym be his wyde hode."

41.   They went in to the way, þese ȝemen boþe,
           As curtes men and hende;
       Þei spyrred tithyngus at þe munke,
           As they hade bene his frende.

42.   "Ffro whens come ȝe?" seid Litull Jon,
           "Tel vs tithyngus, I you pray,
       Off a false owtlay, callid Robyn Hode,
           Was takyn, ȝisterday.

43.   "He robbyt me and my felowes boþe
           Of twenti marke in serten;
       If þat false owtlay be takyn,
           Ffor soþe we wolde be fayn."

44.   "So did he me," seid þe munke,
           "Of a hundred pound and more;
       I layde furst hande hym apon,
           ȝe may thonke me þerfore."

45.   "I pray God thanke you," seid Litull John,
           "And we wil when we may;
       We wil go with you, with your leve,
           And bryng yow on your way.

46.   "Ffor Robyn Hode hase many a wilde felow,
           I tell you in certen;
       If þei wist ȝe rode þis way,
           In feith ȝe shulde be slayn."

47.   As þei went talking be þe way
           The munke and Litull John,

John toke þe munkis horse be þe hede,
Fful sone and anon.

48. Johne toke þe munkis horse be þe hed,
Ffor soþe as I yow say;
So did Much þe litull page,
Ffor he shulde not scape away.

49. Be þe golett of þe hode
John pulled þe munke down;
John was nothyng of hym agast,
He lete hym falle on his crown.

50. Litull John was sore agrevyd,
And drew owt his swerde in hye;
This munke saw he shulde be ded,
Lowd mercy can he crye.

51. "He was my maister," seid Litull John,
"Þat þou hase browȝt in bale;
Shalle þou neuer cum at our kyng,
Ffor to telle hym tale."

52. John smote of þe munkis hed,
No longer wolde he dwell;
So did Moch þe litull page,
Ffor ferd lest he wolde tell.

53. Þer þei beryed hem boþe
In nouþer mosse nor lyng,
And Litull John and Much infere
Bare þe letturs to oure kyng.

54. .   .   .   .   .   .
He knelid down vpon his kne:
"God ȝow saue, my lege lorde,
Ihesus yow saue amd se!

55. "God yow saue, my lege kyng!"
To speke John was full bolde;
He gaf hym þe letturs in his hond,
The kyng did hit vnfold.

56. Þe kyng red þe letturs anon,
And seid, "So mot I the,
Þer was neuer ȝoman in mery Inglond
I longut so sore to se.

57. "Wher is þe munke þat þese shuld haue brouȝt?"
Oure kyng can say.
"Be my trouth," seid Litull John,
He dyed after þe way."

58. Þe kyng gaf Moch and Litul Jon
  Twenti pound in sertan,
And made þeim ȝemen of þe crown,
  And bade þeim go agayn.

59. He gaf John þe seel in hand,
  The sheref for to bere,
To bryng Robyn hym to,
  And no man do hym dere.

60. John toke his leve at oure kyng,
  Þe sothe as I yow say;
Þe next way to Notyngham
  To take, he ȝede þe way.

61. Whan John came to Notyngham
  The ȝatis were sparred ychon;
John callid vp þe porter,
  He answerid sone anon.

62. "What is þe cause," seid Litul Jon,
  "Þou sparris þe ȝates so fast?"
"Because of Robyn Hode," seid þe porter,
  "In depe prison is cast.

63. "John and Moch and Wyll Scathlok,
  Ffor sothe as I yow say,
Þei slew oure men vpon our wallis,
  And sawten vs euery day."

64. Litull John spyrred after þe schereff,
  And sone he hym fonde;
He oppyned þe kyngus priue seell,
  And gaf hym in his honde.

65. Whan þe scheref saw þe kyngus seell,
  He did of his hode anon:
"Wher is þe munke þat bare þe letturs?"
  He seid to Litull John.

66. "He is so fayn of hym," seid Litul John,
  "Ffor soþe as I yow say,
He has made hym abot of Westmynster,
  A lorde of þat abbay."

67. The scheref made John gode chere,
  And gaf hym wyne of the best;
At nyȝt þei went to her bedde,
  And euery man to his rest.

68. When þe scheref was on slepe,
  Dronken of wyne and ale,

Litul John and Moch for soþe
Toke þe way vnto þe jale.

69. Litul John callid vp þe jayler,
       And bade hym rise anon;
     He seyd Robyn Hode had brokyn prison,
       And out of hit was gon.

70. The porter rose anon sertan,
       As sone as he herd John calle;
     Litul John was redy with a swerd,
       And bare hym to þe walle.

71. "Now wil I be porter," seid Litul John,
       "And take þe keyes in honde."
     He toke þe way to Robyn Hode,
       And sone he hym vnbonde.

72. He gaf hym a gode swerd in his hond,
       His hed with for to kepe,
     And there as þe walle was lowyst
       Anon down can þei lepe.

73. Be þat þe cok began to crow,
       The day began to spryng;
     The scheref fond þe jaylier ded,
       The comyn bell made he ryng.

74. He made a crye thoroout al þe town,
       Wheder he be ȝoman or knave,
     Þat cowþe bryng hym Robyn Hode,
       His warison he shuld haue.

75. "Ffor I dar neuer," seid þe scheref,
       "Cum before oure kyng;
     Ffor if I do, I wot serten
       Ffor soþe he wil me heng."

76. The scheref made to seke Notyngham,
       Bothe be strete and stye,
     And Robyn was in mery Scherwode,
       As liȝt as lef on lynde.

77. Then bespake gode Litull John,
       To Robyn Hode can he say,
     "I haue done þe a gode turne for nay euyll,
       Quyte þe whan þou may.

78. "I haue done þe a gode turne," seid Litull John,
       "Ffor sothe as I yow say;

I haue brouȝt þe under grene-wode lyne;
Ffare wel, and haue gode day."

79. "Nay, be my trouth," seid Robyn Hode,
"So shall hit neuer be;
I make þe maister," seid Robyn Hode,
"Off alle my men and me."

80. "Nay, be my trouth," seid Litull John,
"So shalle hit neuer be;
But lat me be a felow," seid Litull John,
"No noder kepe I be."

81. Thus John gate Robyn Hod out of prison,
Sertan withoutyn layn;
Whan his men saw hym hol and sounde,
Ffor sothe they were full fayne.

82. They filled in wyne, and made hem glad,
Vnder þe levys smale,
And ȝete pastes of venyson,
Þat gode was with ale.

83. Than worde came to our kyng
How Robyn Hode was gone,
And how þe scheref of Notyngham
Durst neuer like hym vpon.

84. Then bespake oure cumly kyng,
In an angur hye:
Litull John hase begyled þe schereff,
In faith so hase he me.

85. Litul John has begyled vs bothe,
And þat full wel I se;
Or ellis þe schereff of Notyngham
Hye hongut shulde he be.

86. "I made hem ȝemen of þe crowne,
And gaf hem fee with my hond;
I gaf hem grith," seid oure kyng,
"Thorowout all mery Inglond.

87. "I gaf theym grith," þen seid oure kyng;
"I say, so mot I the,
Ffor sothe soch a ȝeman as he is on
In all Inglond ar not thre.

88. "He is trew to his maister," seid our kyng;
"I sey, be swete Seynt John,
He louys better Robyn Hode
Then he dose vs ychon.

89. "Robyn Hode is euer bond to hym,
    Bothe in strete and stalle;
  Speke no more of this mater," seid oure kyng,
    "But John has begyled vs alle."

90. Thus endys the talkyng of the munke
    And Robyn Hode i-wysse;
  God, þat is euer a crowned kyng,
    Bryng vs all to his blisse!

ROBIN HOOD'S DEATH (120)

This is the conventional account of Robin Hood's death as found in the later broadside ballads and in the Geste. Here and there this version is incomplete; it is from the Percy MS., pages of which were torn out and used by the maids to light the fires in Humphry Pitt's house where the MS. was found.

The later accounts of Robin Hood's death as found in the Garland ballads tell of his going to Kirkless where his cousin prioress bleeds him and leaves him a locked room to bleed to death. Robin Hood calls Little John with three weak blasts from his horn. Little John wants to burn the hall, but Robin Hood will not permit it since he never harmed a woman. He shoots his arrow and asks that his grave be dug where the arrow falls. A version of this is found in Virginia.

Notes

8. Her reply is lost, but must have been a kind of dramatic forewarning of what is to come. Why an old woman should curse Robin, friend of the old and poor, is hard to guess. 9/3. other women? weeping because of the treachery they sense. 18. Child suggests that Little John is outside, calling through a window. 19. The lost stanzas must tell of the argument between Robin Hood and Red Roger, who is evidently the instigator of the treachery.

1. "I will neuer eate nor drinke," Robin Hood said,
    "Nor meate will doo me noe good,
  Till I haue beene att merry Churchlees,
    My vaines for to let blood."

2. "That I reade not," said Will Scarllett,
    "Master, by the assente of me,
  Without halfe a hundred of your best bowmen
    You take to goe with yee.

3. "For there a good yeoman doth abide
    Will be sure to quarrell with thee,
  And if thou haue need of vs, master,
    In faith we will not flee."

4. "And thou be feard, thou William Scarlett,
        Att home I read thee bee,"
    "And you be wrothe, my deare master,
        You shall neuer heare more of mee."

5. "For there shall noe man wi me goe,
        Nor man with mee ryde,
    And Litle Iohn shall be my man,
        And beare my benbow by my side."

6. "You'st beare your bowe, master, your selfe,
        And shoote for a peny with mee."
    "To that I doe assent," Robin Hood sayd,
        "And soe, Iohn, lett it bee."

7. They two bolde children shotten together,
        All day theire selfe in ranke,
    Vntill they came to blacke water,
        And over it laid a planke.

8. Vpon it there kneeled an old woman,
        Was banning Robin Hood.
    "Why dost thou bann Robin Hoode?" said Robin,

        .   .   .   .   .   .

        *   *   *   *   *   *   *

[About half a page is missing from the MS.]

9.   .   .   .   .   .   .
        "To giue to Robin Hoode;
    Wee weepen for his deare body,
        That this day must be lett bloode."

10. "The dame prior is my aunt's daughter,
        And nie vnto my kinne;
    I know shee wold me noe harme this day,
        For all the world to winne."

11. Forth then shotten these children two,
        And they did neuer lin,
    Vntill they came to merry Churchlees,
        To merry Churchlee with-in.

12. And when they came to merry Churchlees,
        They knoced vpon a pin;
    Vpp then rose dame prioresse,
        And lett good Robin in.

13. Then Robin gaue to dame prioresse
        Twenty pound in gold,

> And bad her spend while that wold last,
>   And shee shold haue more when shee wold.

14. And downe then came dame prioresse,
        Downe she came in that ilke,
    With a pair off blood-irons in her hands,
        Were wrapped all in silke.

15. "Sett a chaffing-dish to the fyer," said dame prioresse,
        "And stripp thou vp thy sleeue."
    I hold him but an vnwise man
        That will noe warning leeue.

16. Shee laid the blood-irons to Robin Hood's vaine,
        Alacke, the more pitye!
    And pearct the vaine, and let out the bloode,
        That full red was to see.

17. And first it bled, the thicke, thicke bloode,
        And afterwards the thinne,
    And well then wist good Robin Hoode
        Treason there was within.

18. "What cheere my master?" said Litle Iohn;
        "In faith, Iohn, litle goode;"

    .   .   .   .   .   .

    .   .   .   .   .   .

                *   *   *   *   *   *

[A page is missing here.]

19. "I haue upon a gown of greene,
        Is cut short by my knee,
    And in my hand a bright browne brand
        That will well bite of thee."

20. But forth then of a shot -windowe
        Good Robin Hood he could glide;
    Red Roger, with a grounden glaue,
        Thrust him through the milke-white side.

21. But Robin was light and nimble of foote,
        And thought to abate his pride,
    Ffor betwixt his head and his shoulders
        He made a wound full wide.

22. Says, Ly there, ly there, Red Roger,
        The doggs they must thee eate.
    "For I may haue my houzle," he said,
        "For I may both goe and speake.

23.　"Now giue me mood," Robin said to Litle Iohn,
　　　"Giue me mood with thy hand;
　　I trust to God in heauen soe hye
　　　My houzle will be bestand."

24.　"Now giue me leaue, giue me leaue, master," he said,
　　　"For Christs loue giue leaue to me,
　　To set a fier within this hall,
　　　And to burne vp al Churchlee."

25.　"That I reade not," said Robin Hoode then,
　　　"Litle Iohn, for it may not be;
　　If I shold doe any widow hurt, at my latter end,
　　　God," he said, "wold blame me;

26.　"But take me vpon thy backe, Litle Iohn,
　　　And beare me to yonder streete,
　　And there make me a full fayre graue,
　　　Of grauell and of greete.

27.　"And sett my bright sword at my head,
　　　Mine arrowes at my feete,
　　And lay my vew-bow by my side,
　　　My met-yard wi　　．　　．　　．

[Last half page is missing.]

ROBIN HOOD AND THE POTTER (121)

This ballad is found in a manuscript of the late 15th century (Cambridge E.e.4.35). It is one of an increasing number of ballads in which Robin Hood is worsted in a fight, but often makes friends with his adversary. The protagonists are butchers, tinkers, pindars, shepherds, beggars. The later ballads of this type tend more and more to depict Robin Hood in contemptible roles and to make his various adversaries the heroes. Can it be that these ballads were made to flatter such groups or that they were composed by representatives of such groups? A play was composed about 1500 based on this ballad. The ballad of "Robin Hood and the Butcher" is a close analogue of this. Stories relating the adventures of a hero in disguise are common in folklore and literature; Robin Hood is completely in the tradition of Wallace, Hereward, Eustace the Monk, Fulk Fitz-Warine. Note that the beginning of this ballad is distinctly literary (cf. "Robin Hood and the Monk").

1.　In schomer, when the leves spryng,
　　　The bloschoms on euery bowe,

So merey doyt the berdys syng
Yn wodys merely now.

2. Herkens, god yemen,
   Comley, corteys, and god
On of the best þat yeuer bare bowe,
   Hes name was Roben Hode.

3. Roben Hood was the yeman's name,
   That was boyt corteys and ffre;
Ffor the loffe of owre ladey,
   All wemen werschepyd he.

4. Bot as the god yeman stod on a day,
   Among hes mery maney,
He was ware of a prowd potter,
   Cam dryfyng ower the ley.

5. "Yonder comet a prod potter," seyde Roben,
   "That long hayt hantyd þis wey;
He was neuer so corteys a man
   On peney of pawage to pay."

6. "Y met hem bot at Went-breg," seyde Lytyll John,
   "And therefore yeffell mot he the!
Seche thre strokes he me gafe,
   Yet by my seydys cleffe þey.

7. "Y ley forty shillings," seyde Lytyll John,
   "To pay het thes same day,
Ther ys nat a man among hus all
   A wed schall make hem ley."

8. "Here ys forty shillings," seyde Roben,
   "More, and thow dar say,
Þat y schall make þat prowde potter,
   A wed to me schall he ley."

9. There thes money they leyde,
   They toke het a yeman to kepe;
Roben beffore the potter he breyde,
   And bad hem stond stell.

10. Handys apon hes hors he leyde,
    And bad the potter stonde foll stell;
The potter schorteley to hem seyde,
   "Ffelow, what ys they well?"

11. "All thes thre yer, and more, potter," he seyde,
    "Thow hast hantyd thes wey,
Yet were tow neuer so cortys a man
   On peney of pauage to pay."

12. "What ys they name," seyde þe potter,
    "Ffor pauage thow aske of me?"
"Roben Hod ys mey name,
    A wed schall thow leffe me."

13. "Wed well y non leffe," seyde þe potter,
    "Nor pavag well y non pay;
Awey they honde ffro mey hors!
    Y well the tene eyls, be mey ffay."

14. The potter to hes cart he went,
    He was not to seke;
A god to-hande staffe þerowt he hent,
    Beffore Roben he leppyd.

15. Roben howt with a swerd bent,
    A bokeler en hes hond;
The potter to Roben he went,
    And seyde, Ffelow let mey hors go.

16. Togeder then went these to yemen,
    Het was a god seyt to se;
Thereof low Robyn hes men,
    There they stod onder a tre.

17. Leytell John to hes ffelowhes seyde,
    "Yend potter well steffeley stonde,"
The potter, with a acward stroke,
    Smot the bokeler owt of hes honde.

18. And are Roben meyt get het agan
    Hes bokeler at hes ffette,
The potter yn the neke hem toke,
    To the gronde sone he yede.

19. That saw Roben hes men,
    As thay stod onder a bow.
"Let vs helpe owre master," seyde Lytell John,
    "Yonder potter," seyde he, "els well hem slo."

20. Thes yemen went with a breyde,
    To ther mast(er) they cam.
Leytell John to hes mast(er) seyde,
    Ho haet the wager won?

21. "Schall y haffe yowre forty shillings," seyde Lytl John.
    "Or ye, master, schall haffe myne?"
"Yeff they were a hundred," seyde Roben,
    "Y ffeythe, they ben all theyne."

22. "Het ys fol leytell cortesey," seyde þe potter,
    "As y haffe harde weyse men saye,

Yeffe a pore yeman com drywyng on the wey,
    To let hem of hes gorney."

23. "Be mey trowet, thow seys soyt," seyde Roben,
        "Thow seys god yemenrey;
    And thow dreyffe fforthe yeuery day.
        Thow schalt neuer be let ffor me.

24. "Y well prey the, god potter,
        A ffelischepe well thow haffe?
    Geffe me they clothyng, and þow schalt hafe myne;
        Y well go to Notyggam."

25. "Y gra(n)t thereto," seyde the potter,
        "Thow schalt ffeynde me a ffelow gode;
    Bot thow can sell mey pottys well,
        Com ayen as thow yode."

26. "Nay, be mey trowt," seyde Roben,
        "And then y bescro mey hede,
    Yeffe y bryng eny pottys ayen,
        And eney weyffe well hem chepe."

27. Than spake Leytell John,
        And all hes ffelowhes heynd,
    "Master, be well ware of the screffe of Notynggam,
        Ffor he ys leytell howr ffrende."

28. "Heyt war howte!" seyde Roben,
        "Ffelowhes, let me a lone;
    Thorow the helpe of Howr Ladey,
        To Notynggam well y gon."

29. Robyn went to Notynggam,
        Thes pottys ffor to sell,
    The potter abode with Roben's men,
        There he ffered not eylle.

30. Tho Roben droffe on hes wey,
        So merey ower the londe:
    Her es more, and affter ys to saye,
        The best ys beheynde.

31. When Roben cam to Notynggam,
        The soyt yef y scholde saye,
    He set op hes hors anon,
        And gaffe hem hotys and haye.

32. Yn the medys of the towne,
        There he schowed hes ware;
    "Pottys! pottys!" he gan crey foll sone,
        "Haffe hansell ffor the mare!"

33. Ffoll effen agenest the screffey's gate
     Schowed he hes chaffare;
   Weyffes and wedowes abowt hem drow,
     And chepyd ffast of hes ware.

34. Yet, "Pottys, gret chepe!" creyed Robyn,
     "Y loffe yeffell thes to stonde."
   And all that say hem sell
     Seyde he had be no potter long.

35. The pottys that were werthe pens ffeyffe,
     He solde tham ffor pens thre;
   Preveley seyde man and weyffe,
     "Ywnder potter schall neuer the."

36. Thos Roben solde ffoll ffast,
     Tell he had pottys bot ffeyffe,
   Op he hem toke of hes care,
     And sende hem to the screffey's weyffe.

37. Thereof sche was ffoll ffayne,
     "Gereamarsey, ser," than seyde sche;
   "When ye com to thes contre ayen,
     Y schall bey of they pottys, so mot y the."

38. "Ye schall haffe of the best," seyde Roben,
     And sware be the Treneytë;
   Ffoll corteysley sche gan hem call,
     "Com deyne with the screfe and me."

39. "God amarsey," seyde Roben,
     "Yowre bedyng schall be doyn."
   A mayden yn the pottys gan bere,
     Roben and þe screffe weffe ffolowed anon.

40. Whan Roben yn to the hall cam,
     The screffë sone he met;
   The potter cowed of corteysey,
     And sone the screffe he gret.

41. "Lo, ser, what thes potter hayt geffe yow and me;
     Ffeyffe pottys smalle and grete!"
   "He ys ffoll wellcom," seyd the screffe;
     "Let os was, and go to mete."

42. As they sat at her methe,
     With a nobell chere,
   To of the screffes men gan speke
     Off a gret wager;

43. Off a schotyng, was god and ffeyne,
     Was made the thother daye,

Off forty shillings, the soyt to saye,
　　Who scholde thes wager wen.

44. Styll than sat thes prowde potter,
　　　Thos than thowt he;
　　An y am a trow cerstyn man,
　　　Thes schotyng well y se.

45. Whan they had ffared of the best,
　　　With bred and ale and weyne,
　　To the bottys the made them prest,
　　　With bowes and boltys ffoll ffeyne.

46. The screffes men schot ffoll ffast,
　　　As archares þat weren godde;
　　There cam non ner ney the marke
　　　Bey halffe a god archares bowe.

47. Stell then stod the prowde potter,
　　　Thos than seyde he;
　　And y had a bow, be the rode,
　　　On schot scholde yow se.

48. "Thow schall haffe a bow," seyde the screffe,
　　　"The best þat thow well cheys of thre;
　　Thou semyst a stalward and a stronge,
　　　Asay schall thow be."

49. The screffe commandyd a yeman þat stod hem bey
　　　Affter bowhes to weynde;
　　The best bow þat the yeman browthe
　　　Roben set on a stryng.

50. "Now schall y wet and thow be god,
　　　And polle het op to they nere."
　　"So god me helpe," seyde the prowde potter,
　　　"Þys ys bot ryȝt weke gere."

51. To a quequer Roben went,
　　　A god bolt owthe he toke;
　　So ney on to the marke he went,
　　　He ffayled not a fothe.

52. All they schot abowthe agen,
　　　The screffes men and he;
　　Off the marke he welde not ffayle,
　　　He cleffed the preke on thre.

53. The screffes men thowt gret schame
　　　The potter the mastry wan;

The screffë lowe and made god game,
    And seyde, "Potter, thow art a man.

54. .   .   .   .   .   .

      .   .   .   .   .
  "Thow art worthey to bere a bowe
    Yn what plas that þow goe."

55. "Yn mey cart y haffe a bowe,
    Ffor soyt," he seyde, "and that a godde;
  Yn mey cart ys the bow
    That gaffe me Robyn Hode."

56. "Knowest thow Robyn Hode?" seyde the screffe,
    "Potter, y prey the tell thow me."
  "A hundred torne y haffe schot with hem,
    Vnder hes tortyll-tre."

57. "Y had leuer nar a hundred ponde," seyde þe screffe,
    "And sware be the Trenitë,

    .   .   .   .
    Þat the ffals outelawe stod be me."

58. "And ye well do afftyr mey red," seyde þe potter,
    "And boldeley go with me,
  And to morow, or we het bred,
    Roben Hode well we se."

59. "Y wel queyt the," kod the screffe,
    "Y swere be God of meythe."
  Schetyng thay left, and hom þey went,
    Her soper was reddy deythe.

60. Vpon the morow, when het was day,
    He boskyd hem fforthe to reyde;
  The potter hes cart fforthe gan ray,
    And wolde not leffe beheynde.

61. He toke leffe of the screffys wyffe,
    And thankyd her of all thyng;
  "Dam, ffor mey loffe and ye well þys were,
    Y geffe yow here a golde ryng."

62. "Gramarsey," seyde the weyffe,
    "Ser, god eylde het the."
  The screffes hart was neuer so leythe,
    The ffeyre fforeyst to se.

63. And when he cam yn to the fforeyst,
    Yonder the leffes grene,
  Berdys there sange on bowhes prest,
    Het was gret goy to se.

64. "Here het ys merey to be," seyde Roben,
    "Ffor a man that had hawt to spende;
Be mey horne I schall awet
    Yeff Roben Hode be here."

65. Roben set hes horne to hes mowthe,
    And blow a blast þat was ffoll god;
Þat herde hes men þat þere stode,
    Ffer downe yn the wodde.

66. "I her mey master blow," seyde Leytell John,
    .   .   .   .
    .   .   .   .   .   .
    They ran as thay were wode.

67. Whan thay to that master cam,
    Leytell John wold not spare;
"Master, how haffe yow ffare yn Notynggam?
    How haffe you solde yowre ware?"

68. "Ye, be mey trowthe, Leytyll John,
    Loke thow take no care;
Y haffe browt the screffe of Notynggam,
    Ffor all howre chaffare."

69. "He ys ffoll wellcom," seyde Lytyll John,
    "Thes tydyng ys ffoll godde;
The screffe had leuer nar a hundred ponde
    He had neuer sene Roben Hode."

70. "Had I west þat befforen,
    At Notynggam when we were,
Thow scholde not com yn ffeyre fforest
    Of all thes thowsend eyre."

71. "That wot y well," seyde Roben,
    "Y thanke God that ye be here;
Thereffore schall ye leffe yowre hors with hos,
    And all yowre hother gere."

72. "That ffend I Godys fforbod," kod the screffe,
    "So to lese mey godde;
    .   .   .   .
    .   .   .   .

73. "Hether ye cam on hors ffoll hey,
    And hom schall ye go on ffote;
And gret well they weyffe at home,
    The woman ys ffoll godde.

74. "Y schall her sende a wheyt palffrey,

Het ambellet be mey ffey,

.   .   .   .   .

.   .   .   .   .   .

75. "Y schall her send a wheyt palffrey,
        Het hambellet as the weynde;
     Nere ffor the loffe of yowre weyffe,
        Off more sorow scholde yow seyng."

76. Thes parted Robyn Hode and the screffe;
        To Notynggam he toke the waye;
     Hes weyffe ffeyre welcomed hem hom,
        And to hem gan sche saye:

77. "Seyr, how haffe yow ffared yn grene fforeyst?
        Haffe ye browt Roben hom?"
     "Dam, the deyell spede hem, bothe bodey and bon;
        Y haffe hade a ffoll gret skorne.

78. "Of all the god that y haffe lade to grene wod,
        He hayt take het ffro me;
     All bot thes ffeyre palffrey,
        That he hayt sende to the."

79. With þat sche toke op a lowde lawhyng,
        And swhare be hem þat deyed on tre,
     'Now haffe yow payed ffor all þe pottys
        That Roben gaffe to me.

80. "Now ye be com hom to Notynggam,
        Ye schall haffe god ynowe."
     Now speke we of Roben Hode,
        And of the pottyr ondyr the grene bowhe.

81. "Potter, what was they pottys worthe
        To Notynggam þat y ledde with me?"
     "They wer worthe to nobellys," seyde he,
        "So mot y treyffe or the;
     "So cowde y had ffor tham,
        And y had there be."

82. "Thow schalt hafe ten ponds," seyde Roben,
        "Of money ffeyre and ffre;
     And yeuer whan thow comest to grene wod,
        Wellcom, potter, to me."

83. Thes partyd Robyn, the screffe, and the potter,
        Ondernethe the grene-wod tre;
     God haffe mersey on Roben Hodys solle,
        And saffe all god yemanrey!

ROBIN HOOD AND THE
CURTAL FRIAR (123)

The version printed here is 17th century; an earlier one exists in an incomplete form in the Percy MS. Both stem from an older and more traditional form. Here the friar and his fifty ban dogs definitely suggest a folktale. The summoning of help by blowing a horn or whistling is commonplace and is found constantly in literature and legend from the time of the Song of Roland. Curtal is probably Lat. *curtilarius,* keeper of the monastery garden, though there is the possibility that it might mean short-frocked, after the manner of the Franciscans. Fountains Abbey was a monastery in Yorkshire. This ballad too was reworked into a play.

Text, Pepys, i, 78.

1. In summer time, when leaves grow green,
       And flowers are fresh and gay,
   Robin Hood and his merry men
       Were disposed to play.

2. Then some would leap, and some would run,
       And some would use artillery:
   "Which of you can a good bow draw,
       A good archer to be?

3. "Which of you can kill a buck?
       Or who can kill a do?
   Or who can kill a hart of greece,
       Five hundred foot him fro?"

4. Will Scadlock he killd a buck,
       And Midge he killd a do,
   And Little John killd a hart of greece,
       Five hundred foot him fro.

5. "God's blessing on thy heart," said Robin Hood,
       "That hat shot such a shot for me;
   I would ride my horse an hundred miles,
       To finde one could match with thee."

6. That caused Will Scadlock to laugh,
       He laughed full haertily:
   "There lives a curtal frier in Fountains Abby
       Will beat both him and thee.

7. "That curtal frier in Fountains Abby
       Well can a strong bow draw;

He will beat you and your yeomen,
　　Set them all on a row."

8.　Robin Hood took a solemn oath,
　　　It was by Mary free,
　　That he would neither eat nor drink
　　　Till the frier he did see.

9.　Robin Hood put on his harness good,
　　　And on his head a cap of steel,
　　Broad sword and buckler by his side,
　　　And they became him weel.

10.　He took his bow into his hand,
　　　It was made of a trusty tree,
　　With a sheaf of arrows at his belt,
　　　To the Fountains Dale went he.

11.　And comming unto Fountains Dale,
　　　No further would he ride;
　　There was he aware of a curtal frier,
　　　Walking by the water-side.

12.　The fryer had on a harniss good,
　　　And on his head a cap of steel,
　　Broad sword and bucler by his side,
　　　And they became him weel.

13.　Robin Hood lighted of his horse,
　　　And tied him to a thorn:
　　"Carry me over the water, thou curtal frier,
　　　Or else's thy life's forlorn."

14.　The frier took Robin Hood on his back,
　　　Deep water he did bestride,
　　And spake neither good word nor bad,
　　　Till he came at the other side.

15.　Lightly leapt Robin Hood off the frier's back;
　　　The frier said to him again
　　Carry me over this water, fine fellow,
　　　Or it shall breed thy pain.

16.　Robin Hood took the frier on's back,
　　　Deep water he did bestride,
　　And spake neither good word or bad,
　　　Till he came at the other side.

17.　Lightly leapt the fryer off Robin Hood's back;
　　　Robin Hood said to him again,
　　Carry me over this water, thou curtal frier,
　　　Or it shall breed thy pain.

18. The frier took Robin Hood on's back again,
  And stept up to the knee;
  Till he came at the middle stream,
   Neither good nor bad spake he.

19. And coming to the middle stream,
  There he threw Robin in:
  "And chuse thee, chuse thee, fine fellow,
   Whether thou wilt sink or swim."

20. Robin Hood swam to a bush of broom,
  The frier to a wicker wand;
  Bold Robin Hood is gone to shore,
   And took his bow in hand.

21. One of his best arrows under his belt
  To the frier he let flye;
  The curtal frier, with his steel buckler,
   He put that arrow by.

22. "Shoot on, shoot on, thou fine fellow,
  Shoot on as thou hast begun;
  If thou shoot here a summer's day,
   Thy mark I will not shun."

23. Robin Hood shot passing well,
  Till his arrows all were gone;
  They took their swords and steel bucklers,
   And fought with might and maine;

24. From ten oth' clock that day,
  Till four ith' afternoon;
  Then Robin Hood came to his knees,
   Of the frier to beg a boon.

25. "A boon, a boon, thou curtal frier,
  I beg it on my knee;
  Give me leave to set my horn to my mouth,
   And to blow blasts three."

26. "That will I do," said the curtal frier,
  "Of thy blasts I have no doubt;
  I hope thou'lt blow so passing well
   Till both thy eyes fall out."

27. Robin Hood set his horn to his mouth,
  He blew but blasts three;
  Half a hundred yeomen, with bows bent,
   Came raking over the lee.

28. "Whose men are these," said the frier,
  "That come so hastily?"

    "These men are mine," said Robin Hood;
      "Frier, what is that to thee?"

29. "A boon, a boon," said the curtal frier,
      "The like I gave to thee;
    Give me leave to set my fist to my mouth,
      And to whute whutes three."

30. "That will I do," said Robin Hood,
      "Or else I were to blame;
    Three whutes in a frier's fist
      Would make me glad and fain."

31. The frier he set his fist to his mouth,
      And whuted whutes three;
    Half a hundred good ban-dogs
      Came running the frier unto.

32. "Here's for every man of thine a dog,
      And I my self for thee."
    "Nay, by my faith," quoth Robin Hood,
      "Frier, that may not be."

33. Two dogs at once to Robin Hood did go,
      The one behind, the other before;
    Robin Hood's mantle of Lincoln green
      Off his back they tore.

34. And whether his men shot east or west,
      Or they shot north or south,
    The curtal dogs, so taught they were,
      They kept their arrows in their mouth.

35. "Take up thy dogs," said Little John,
      "Frier, at my bidding be."
    "Whose man art thou," said the curtal frier,
      "Comes here to prate with me?"

36. "I am Little John, Robin Hood's man,
      Frier, I will not lie;
    If thou take not up thy dogs doon,
      I'le take up them and three."

37. Little John had a bow in his hand,
      He shot with might and main;
    Soon half a score of the frier's dogs
      Lay dead upon the plain.

38. "Hold thy hand, good fellow," said the curtal frier,
      "Thy master and I will agree;
    And we will have new orders taken,
      With all the haste that may be."

39. "If thou wilt forsake fair Fountains Dale,
    And Fountains Abby free,
  Every Sunday throughout the year,
    A noble shall be thy fee.

40. "And every holy day throughout the year,
    Changed shall thy garment be,
  If thou wilt go to fair Nottingham,
    And there remain with me."

41. This curtal frier had kept Fountains Dale
    Seven long years or more;
  There was neither knight, lord, nor earl
    Could make him yield before.

THE JOLLY PINDER OF WAKEFIELD (124)

This is another in the series of ballads on the theme of the besting of
Robin Hood in fight and Robin's persuading his antagonist to join the
band in the Green Wood. Many of these ballads show verbal similarities. Wakefield is in York.

Text, Pepys, ii, 100.

1. In Wakefield there lives a jolly pinder,
    In Wakefield, all on a green. (bis)

2. "There is neither knight not squire," said the pinder,
    "Nor baron that is so bold, (bis)
  Dare make a trespasse to the town of Wakefield,
    But his pledge goes to the pinfold." (bis)

3. All this beheard three witty young men,
    'T was Robin Hood, Scarlet, and John;
  With that they spyed the jolly pinder,
    As he sate under a thorn.

4. "Now turn again, turn again," said the pinder,
    "For a wrong way have you gone;
  For you have forsaken the king his highway,
    And made a path over the corn."

5. "O that were great shame," said jolly Robin,
    "We being three, and thou but one."
  The pinder leapt back then thirty good foot,
    'T was thirty good foot and one.

6. He leaned his back fast unto a thorn,
    And his foot unto a stone,
  And there he fought a long summer's day,

A summer's day so long,
Till that their swords, on their broad bucklers,
Were broken fast unto their hands.

* * * * * * *

7. "Hold thy hand, hold thy hand," said Robin Hood,
"And my merry men euery one;
For this is one of the best pinders
That ever I try'd with sword.

8. "And wilt thou forsake thy pinder his craft,
And live in the green wood with me?

. . . .

. . . .

9. "At Michaelmas next my covant comes out,
When every man gathers his fee;
I'le take my blew blade all in my hand,
And plod to the green wood with thee."

10. "Hast thou either meat or drink," said Robin Hood,
"For my merry men and me?"

. . . .

. . . .

11. "I have both bread and beef," said the pinder,
"And good ale of the best."
"And that is meat good enough," said Robin Hood,
"For such unbidden guest.

12. "O wilt thou forsake the pinder his craft,
And go to the green wood with me?
Thou shalt have a livery twice in the year,
The one green, the other brown shall be."

13. "If Michaelmas day were once come and gone
And my master had paid me my fee,
Then would I set as little by him
As my master doth set by me."

ROBIN HOOD AND LITTLE JOHN (125)

This ballad is probably 16th century. It belongs to a group of Robin Hood ballads related by the fact that they employ middle rime in the third line of the stanza and were sung to the same tunes.

Text A, *A Collection of Old Ballads,* i, 75; B, traditional, of Virginia, *JAF,* 23:432.

A.

1. When Robin Hood was about twenty years old,
   With a hey down down and a down
   He happened to meet Little John,
   A jolly brisk blade, right fit for the trade,
   For he was a lusty young man.

2. Tho he was calld Little, his limbs they were large,
   And his stature was seven foot high;
   Where-ever he came, they quak'd at his name,
   For soon he would make them to fly.

3. How came they acquainted, I'll tell you in brief,
   If you will but listen a while;
   For this very jest, amongst all the rest,
   I think it may cause you to smile.

4. Bold Robin Hood said to his jolly bowmen,
   Pray tarry you here in this grove;
   And see that you all observe well my call,
   While through the forest I rove.

5. We have had no sport for these fourteen long days,
   Therefore now abroad will I go;
   Now should I be beat, and cannot retreat,
   My horn I will presently blow.

6. Then did he shake hands with his merry men all,
   And bid them at present good b'w'ye;
   Then, as near a brook his journey he took,
   A stranger he chancd to espy.

7. They happened to meet on a long narrow bridge,
   And neither of them would give way;
   Quoth bold Robin Hood, and sturdily stood,
   "I'll show you right Nottingham play."

8. With that from his quiver an arrow he drew,
   A broad arrow with a goose-wing.
   The stranger reply'd, "I'll liquor thy hide,
   If thou offerst to touch the string."

9. Quoth bold Robin Hood, "Thou dost prate like an ass,
   For were I to bend but my bow,
   I could send a dart quite thro thy proud heart,
   Before thou couldst strike me one blow."

10. "Thou talkst like a coward," the stranger reply'd;
    "Well armd with a long bow you stand,
    To shoot at my breast, while I, I protest,
    Have nought but a staff in my hand."

11. "The name of a coward," quoth Robin, "I scorn,
    Wherefore my long bow I'll lay by;
  And now, for thy sake, a staff will I take;
    The truth of thy manhood to try."

12. Then Robin Hood stept to a thicket of trees,
    And chose him a staff of ground-oak;
  Now this being done, away he did run
    To the stranger, and merrily spoke:

13. "Lo! see my staff, it is lusty and tough,
    And here on the bridge we will play;
  Whoever falls in, the other shall win
    The battel, and so we'll away."

14. "With all my whole heart," the stranger reply'd;
    "I scorn in the least to give out."
  This said, they fell to't without more dispute,
    And their staffs they did flourish about.

15. And first Robin he gave the stranger a bang,
    So hard that it made his bones ring;
  The stranger he said, "This must be repaid,
    I'll give you as good as you bring.

16. "So long as I'm able to handle my staff,
    To die in your debt, friend, I scorn."
  Then to it each goes, and followed their blows,
    As if they had been threshing of corn.

17. The stranger gave Robin a crack on the crown,
    Which caused the blood to appear;
  Then Robin, enrag'd, more fiercely engag'd,
    And followed his blows more severe.

18. So thick and so fast did he lay it on him,
    With a passionate fury and ire,
  At every stroke, he made him to smoke,
    As if he had been all on fire.

19. O then into fury the stranger he grew,
    And gave him a damnable look,
  And with it a blow that laid him full low,
    And tumbld him into the brook.

20. "I prithee, good fellow, O where art thou now?"
    The stranger, in laughter, he cry'd.
  Quoth bold Robin Hood, "Good faith, in the flood,
    And floating along with the tide.

21. "I needs must acknowledge thou art a brave soul;
    With thee I'll no longer contend;

For needs must I say, thou hast got the day,
Our battel shall be at an end."

22. Then unto the bank he did presently wade,
And pulld himself out by a thorn;
Which done, at the last, he blowd a loud blast
Straitway on his fine bugle-horn.

23. The eccho of which through the vallies did fly,
At which his stout bowmen appeard,
All cloathed in green, most gay to be seen;
So up to their master they steerd.

24. "O what's the matter?" quoth William Stutely;
"Good master, you are wet to the skin."
"No matter," quoth he; "The lad which you see,
In fighting, hath tumbld me in."

25. "He shall not go scot-free," the others reply'd;
So strait they were seizing him there,
To duck him like wise, but Robin Hood cries,
He is a stout fellow, forbear.

26. "There's no one shall wrong thee, friend, be not afraid;
These bowmen upon me do wait;
There's threescore and nine; if thou wilt be mine,
Thou shalt have my livery strait.

27. "And other accoutrements fit for a man;
Speak up, jolly blade, never fear;
I'll teach you also the use of the bow,
To shoot at the fat fallow-deer."

28. "O here is my hand," the stranger reply'd,
"I'll serve you with all my whole heart;
My name is John Little, a man of good mettle;
Nere doubt me, for I'll play my part."

29. "His name shall be alterd," quoth William Stutely,
"And I will his godfather be;
Prepare then a feast, and none of the least,
For we will be merry," quoth he.

30. They presently fetchd in a brace of fat does,
With humming strong liquor likewise;
They loved what was good; so, in the greenwood,
This pretty sweet babe they baptize.

31. He was, I must tell you, but seven foot high,
And, may be, an ell in the waste;
A pretty sweet lad; much feasting they had;
Bold Robin the christning grac'd.

32.   With all his bowmen, which stood in a ring,
        And were of the Nottingham breed;
      Brave Stutely comes then, with seven yeomen,
        And did in this manner proceed.

33.   "This infant was called John Little," quoth he.
        "Which name shall be changed anon;
      The words we'll transpose, so where-ever he goes,
        His name shall be calld Little John."

34.   They all with a shout made the elements ring,
        So soon as the office was ore;
      To feasting they went, with true merriment,
        And tippld strong liquor gillore.

35.   Then Robin he took the pretty sweet babe,
        And cloathed him from top to the toe
      In garments of green, most gay to be seen,
        And gave him a curious long bow.

36.   "Thou shalt be an archer as well as the best,
        And range in the greenwood with us;
      Where we'll not want gold nor silver, behold,
        While bishops have ought in their purse.

37.   "We live here like squires, or lords of renown,
        Without ere a foot of free land;
      We feast on good cheer, with wine, ale, and beer,
        And everything at our command."

38.   Then musick and dancing did finish the day;
        At length, when the sun waxed low,
      Then all the whole train the grove did refrain,
        And unto their caves they did go.

39.   And so ever after, as long as he livd,
        Altho he was proper and tall,
      Yet nevertheless, the truth to express,
        Still Little John they did him call.

B.

1.   Scarce sixteen years old was bold Robin Hood,
       When first he met Little John,
     A steady young blade well fit for his trade,
       And he was a handsome young man.

2.   Although he was little, his limbs they were large,
       His height about seven feet high;

And wherever he came he straight cut his name,
    And quickly he made them all fly.

3. "I have not been sporting for fourteen long days,
    So now abroad I will go,
And if I get beat, and I can't retreat,
    My horn I will suddenly blow."

4. Thus took he the leave of his merry men all,
    And bid them a pleasant good-by,
And down to the brook a journey he took,
    And a stranger he chanced for to spy.

5. There these two fellows met on a long narrow bridge,
    And neither of them would give way;
The stranger he said, "I will lather your hide;
    I will show you fine Nottingham play."

6. "You speak as a fool," bold Robin replied.
    "If I should bend my long bow,
I would shoot a dart then quite through your heart,
    Before you could give me one blow."

7. "You speak as a coward," the stranger replied,
    "To bend your long bow as I stand,
To shoot at my breast, as I do protest,
    And I but a staff in my hand."

8. "The name of a coward I do disdain;
    Therefore my long bow I'll lay by;
And now for your sake a staff I will take,
    And the strength of your manhood I'll try."

9. Robin stepped down in a thicket of wood,
    And chose him a staff of brown oak,
And that being done, he straight back did come,
    To the stranger he merrily spoke:

10. "Oh, here is my staff both steady and stout;
    Therefore on this bridge let us play.
Whichever falls in, the other shall win,
    And after all that we'll away."

11. Robin struck the stranger a crack on the crown,
    Which caused the red blood to appear.
The stranger enraged, then closely engaged,
    And laid on his blows most severe.

12. "As long as I'm able my staff for to handle,
    To die in your debt I would scorn."

And so thick and so fast they laid on each other,
  As though they were threshing out corn.

13.   The stranger struck Robin a crack on the crown,
        That caused him a terrible flow,
      And with the same blow he laid him quite low,
        And tumbled him into the brook.

14.   "Oh, where are you now, my gay fellow?" he said;
        And with a loud laugh he replied,
      "It's I, by my faith," bold Robin Hood said,
        "I am floating away with the tide."

15.   Robin floated down all into the deep,
        And drew himself out by a thorn,
      And with his last gasp he blew a loud blast,
        A blast on his own bugle-horn,

16.   Which caused all the hills and the valleys to ring,
        And all his gay men to appear.
      There were threescore and ten, all clothed in green,
        That straightway to the master did steer.

17.   "Oh, what is the matter?" said William Stellee,
        "Methinks you are wet to the skin."
      "No matter," said he, "the lad that you see
        By fair fighting has tumbled me in."

18.   "He shall not go free," said William Stellee,
        While still stood the poor stranger there;
      "We will duck him likewise." Bold Robin replies,
        "He is a stout fellow, forbear."

19.   "His name is John Little, he is made of good metal,
        No doubt he will play his own part."
      "He shall not go free," said William Stellee,
        "Therefore his godfather I'll be."

20.   They called him a babe; he was none of the least;
        They had rum and all liquors likewise,
      And there in the woods these bold fellows stood,
        While this little babe was baptized.

ROBIN HOOD AND THE TANNER (126)

See the remarks under "Robin Hood and the Potter." A version very
like this is in Davis, *Traditional Ballads of Virginia*, p. 393.
    Text, Pepys, ii, 111.

  1.   In Nottingham there lives a jolly tanner,

With a hey down down a down down
His name is Arthur a Bland;
There is nere a squire in Nottinghamshire
Dare bid bold Arthur stand.

2. With a long pike-staff upon his shoulder,
    So well he can clear his way;
By two and by three he makes them to flee,
    For he hath no list to stay.

3. And as he went forth, in a summer's morning,
    Into the forrest of merry Sherwood,
To view the red deer, that range here and there,
    There met he with bold Robin Hood.

4. As soon as bold Robin Hood did him espy,
    He thought some sport he would make;
Therefore out of hand he bid him to stand,
    And thus to him he spake:

5. "Why, what art thou, thou bold fellow,
    That ranges so boldly here?
In sooth, to be brief, thou lookst like a thief,
    That comes to steal our king's deer.

6. "For I am a keeper in this forrest;
    The king puts me in trust
To look to his deer, that range here and there,
    Therefore stay thee I must."

7. "If thou beest a keeper in this forrest,
    And hast such a great command,
Yet thou must have more partakers in store,
    Before thou make me to stand."

8. "Nay, I have no more partakers in store,
    Or any that I do need;
But I have a staff of another oke graff,
    I know it will do the deed."

9. "For thy sword and thy bow I care not a straw,
    Nor all thine arrows to boot;
If I get a knop upon thy bare scop,
    Thou canst as well shite as shoote."

10. "Speak cleanly, good fellow," said jolly Robin,
    "And give better terms to me,
Else I'le thee correct for thy neglect,
    And make thee more mannerly."

11. "Marry gep with a wenion!" quoth Arthur a Bland,
    "Art thou such a goodly man?

I care not a fig for thy looking so big;
    Mend thou thyself where thou can."

12.   Then Robin Hood he unbuckled his belt;
    He laid down his bow so long;
    He took up a staff of another oke graff,
      That was both stiff and strong.

13.   "I'le yield to thy weapon," said jolly Robin,
    "Since thou wilt not yield to mine;
    For I have a staff of another oke graff,
      Not half a foot longer then thine.

14.   "But let me measure," said jolly Robin,
    "Before we begin our fray;
    For I'le not have mine to be longer then thine,
      For that will be called foul play."

15.   "I pass not for length," bold Arthur reply'd,
    "My staff is of oke so free;
    Eight foot and a half, it will knock down a calf,
      And I hope it will knock down thee."

16.   Then Robin Hood could no longer forbear;
    He gave him such a knock,
    Quickly and soon the blood came down,
      Before it was ten a clock.

17.   Then Arthur he soon recovered himself,
    And gave him such a knock on the crown,
    That on every hair of bold Robin Hood's head,
      The blood came trickling down.

18.   Then Robin Hood raged like a wild bore,
    As soon as he saw his own blood;
    Then Bland was in hast, he laid on so fast,
      As though he had been staking of wood.

19.   And about, and about, and about they went,
    Like two wild bores in a chase,
    Striving to aim each other to maim,
      Leg, arm, or any other place.

20.   And knock for knock they lustily dealt,
    Which held for two hours and more,
    That all the wood rang at every bang,
      They ply'd their work so sore.

21.   "Hold thy hand, hold thy hand," said Robin Hood,
    "And let our quarrel fall;
    For here we may thresh our bones into mesh,
      And get no coyn at all.

22. "And in the forrest of merry Sherwood
  Hereafter thou shalt be free."
 "God-a-mercy for naught, my freedom I bought,
  I may thank my good staff, and not thee."

23. "What tradesman art thou?" said jolly Robin,
  "Good fellow, I prethee me show;
 And also me tell in what place thou dost dwell,
  For both these fain would I know."

24. "I am a tanner," bold Arthur reply'd,
  "In Nottingham long have I wrought;
 And if thou'lt come there, I vow and do swear
  I will tan thy hide for naught."

25. "God a mercy, good fellow," said jolly Robin,
  "Since thou art so kind to me;
 And if thou wilt tan my hide for naught,
  I will do as much for thee.

26. "But if thou'lt forsake thy tanner's trade,
  And live in green wood with me,
 My name's Robin Hood, I swear by the rood
  I will give thee both gold and fee."

27. "If thou be Robin Hood," bold Arthur reply'd,
  "As I think well thou art,
 Then here's my hand, my name's Arthur a Bland,
  We two will never depart.

28. "But tell me, O tell me, where is Little John?
  Of him fain would I hear;
 For we are alide by the mothers' side,
  And he is my kinsman near."

29. Then Robin Hood blew on the beaugle horn,
  He blew full lowd and shrill,
 But quickly anon appear'd Little John,
  Come tripping down a green hill.

30. "O what is the matter," then said Little John,
  "Master, I pray you tell.
 Why do you stand with your staff in your hand?
  I fear all is not well."

31. "O man, I do stand, and he makes me to stand,
  The tanner that stands thee beside;
 He is a bonny blade, and master of his trade,
  For soundly he hath tand my hide.

32. "He is to be commended," then said Little John,
  "If such a feat he can do;

If he be so stout, we will have a bout,
    And he shall tan my hide too."

33. "Hold thy hand, hold thy hand," said Robin Hood,
    "For as I do understand,
He's a yeoman good, and of thine own blood,
    For his name is Arthur a Bland."

34. Then Little John threw his staff away,
    As far as he could it fling,
And ran out of hand to Arthur a Bland,
    And about his neck did cling.

35. With loving respect, there was no neglect,
    They were neither nice nor coy,
Each other did face, with a lovely grace,
    And both did weep for joy.

36. Then Robin Hood took them both by the hand,
    And danc'd round about the oke tree;
"For three merry men, and three merry men,
    And three merry men we be.

37. "And ever hereafter, as long as I live,
    We three will be all one;
The wood shall ring, and the old wife sing,
    Of Robin Hood, Arthur, and John."

ROBIN HOOD AND THE TINKER (127)

Text, Pepys, ii, 107.

1. In summer time, when leaves grow green,
    Down a down a down
And birds sing on every tree,
    Hey down a down a down

Robin Hood went to Nottingham,
    Down a down a down
As fast as hee could dree.
    Hey down a down a down

2. And as hee came to Nottingham
    A Tinker he did meet,
And seeing him a lustly blade,
    He did him kindly greet.

3. "Where dost thou live?" quoth Robin Hood,
    "I pray thee now mee tell;

        Sad news I hear there is abroad,
           I fear all is not well."

4.   "What is that news?" the Tinker said;
        "Tell mee without delay;
     I am a tinker by my trade,
        And do live at Banbura."

5.   "As for the news," quoth Robin Hood,
        "It is but as I hear;
     Two tinkers they were set ith' stocks,
        For drinking ale and bear."

6.   "If that be all," the Tinker said,
        "As I may say to you,
     Your news it is not worth a fart,
        Since that they all bee true.

7.   "For drinking of good ale and bear,
        You wil not lose your part."
     "No, by my faith," quoth Robin Hood,
        "I love it with all my heart.

8.   "What news abroad?" quoth Robin Hood;
        "Tell mee what thou dost hear;
     Being thou goest from town to town,
        Some news thou need not fear."

9.   "All the news," the Tinker said,
        "I hear, it is for good;
     It is to seek a bold outlaw,
        Which they call Robin Hood.

10. "I have a warrant from the king,
        To take him where I can;
     If you can tell me where hee is,
        I will make you a man.

11. "The king will give a hundred pound
        That hee could but him see;
     And if wee can but now him get,
        It will serve you and mee."

12. "Let me see that warrant," said Robin Hood;
        "I'le see if it bee right;
     And I will do the best I can
        For to take him this night."

13. "That will I not," the Tinker said;
        "None with it I will trust;
     And where hee is if you'll not tell,
        Take him by force I must."

14. But Robin Hood perceiving well
    How then the game would go,
"If you will go to Nottingham,
    Wee shall find him I know."

15. The Tinker had a crab-tree staff,
    Which was both good and strong;
Robin hee had a good strong blade,
    So they went both along.

16. And when they came to Nottingham,
    There they both tooke one inn;
And they calld for ale and wine,
    To drink it was no sin.

17. But ale and wine they drank so fast
    That the Tinker hee forgot
What thing he was about to do;
    It fell so to his lot

18. That while the Tinker fell asleep,
    Hee made then haste away,
And left the Tinker in the lurch,
    For the great shot to pay.

19. But when the Tinker wakened,
    And saw that he was gone,
He calld then even for his host,
    And thus hee made his moan.

20. "I had a warrant from the king,
    Which might have done me good,
That is to take a bold outlaw,
    Some call him Robin Hood.

21. "But now my warrant and mony's gone,
    Nothing I have to pay;
And he that promisd to oe my friend,
    He is gone and fled away."

22. "That friend you tell on," said the host,
    "They call him Robin Hood;
And when that first hee met with you,
    He ment you little good."

23. "Had I known it had been hee,
    When that I had him here,
Th' one of us should have tri'd our strength
    Which should have paid full dear.

24. "In the mean time I must away;

No longer here I'le bide;
But I will go and seek him out,
   What ever do me betide.

25. "But one thing I would gladly know,
        What here I have to pay."
     "Ten shillings just," then said the host;
        "I'le pay without delay.

26. "Or elce take here my working-bag,
        And my good hammer too;
     And if that I light but on the knave,
        I will then soon pay you."

27. "The onely way," then said the host,
        "And not to stand in fear,
     Is to seek him among the parks,
        Killing of the king's deer."

28. The Tinker hee then went with speed,
        And made then no delay,
     Till he had found then Robin Hood,
        That they might have a fray.

29. At last hee spy'd him in a park,
        Hunting then of the deer.
     "What knave is that," quoth Robin Hood,
        "That doth come mee so near?"

30. "No knave, no knave," the Tinker said,
        "And that you soon shall know,
     Whether of us hath done most wrong,
        My crab-tree staff shall show."

31. Then Robin drew his gallant blade,
        Made then of trusty steel;
     But the Tinker laid on him so fast
        That he made Robin reel.

32. Then Robin's anger did arise;
        He fought full manfully,
     Vntill hee had made the Tinker
        Almost then fit to fly.

33. With that they had a bout again,
        They ply'd their weapons fast;
     The Tinker threshed his bones so sore
        He made him yeeld at last.

34. "A boon, a boon," Robin hee cryes,
        "If thou wilt grant it mee."

"Before I do it," the Tinker said,
   "I'le hang thee on this tree."

35. But the Tinker looking him about,
   Robin his horn did blow;
Then came unto him Little John,
   And William Scadlock too.

36. "What is the matter," quoth Little John,
   "You sit in th' highway side?"
"Here is a Tinker that stands by,
   That hath paid well my hide."

37. "That Tinker," then said Little John,
   "Fain that blade I would see,
And I would try what I could do,
   If hee'l do as much for mee."

38. But Robin hee then wishd them both
   They should the quarrel cease,
"That henceforth wee may bee as one,
   And ever live in peace.

39. "And for the jovial Tinker's part,
   A hundred pound I'le give,
In th' year to maintain him on,
   As long as he doth live.

40. "In manhood hee is a mettle man,
   And a mettle man by trade;
I never thought that any man
   Should have made me so fraid.

41. "And if hee will bee one of us,
   Wee will take all one fare,
And whatsoever wee do get,
   He shall have his full share."

42. So the Tinker was content
   With them to go along,
And with them a part to take,
   And so I end my song.

ROBIN HOOD NEWLY REVIVED (128)

This ballad explains how Will Scarlet came to join Robin Hood's band. It certainly owes much to the old romance of *Gamelyn* in which a similar situation occurs.

Text, Pepys, ii, 101.

1. Come listen a while, you gentlemen all,
       With a hey down down a down down
   That are in this bower within,
       For a story of gallant bold Robin Hood
   I purpose to begin.

2. "What time of the day?" quoth Robin Hood then;
       Quoth Little John, "'T is in the prime."
   "Why then we will to the green wood gang,
       For we have no vittles to dine."

3. As Robin Hood walkt the forrest along—
       It was in the mid of the day—
   There was he met of a deft young man
       As ever walkt on the way.

4. His doublet it was of silk, he said,
       His stockings like scarlet shone,
   And he walkt on along the way,
       To Robin Hood then unknown.

5. A herd of deer was in the bend,
       All feeding before his face:
   "Now the best of ye I'le have to my dinner,
       And that in a little space."

6. Now the stranger he made no mickle adoe,
       But he bends and a right good bow,
   And the best buck in the herd he slew,
       Forty good yards him full froe.

7. "Well shot, well shot," quoth Robin Hood then,
       "That shot it was shot in time;
   And if thou wilt accept of the place,
       Thou shalt be a bold yeoman of mine."

8. "Go, play the chiven," the stranger said,
       "Make haste and quickly go;
   Or with my fist, be sure of this,
       I'le give thee buffets store."

9. "Thou hadst not best buffet me," quoth Robin Hood,
       "For though I seem forlorn,
   Yet I can have those that will take my part,
       If I but blow my horn."

10. "Thou wast not best wind thy horn," the stranger said,
       "Beest thou never so much in hast,
    For I can draw out a good broad sword,
        And quickly cut the blast."

11.   Then Robin Hood bent a very good bow,
        To shoot, and that he would fain;
    The stranger he bent a very good bow,
        To shoot at bold Robin again.

12.   "O hold thy hand, hold thy hand," quoth Robin Hood,
        "To shoot it would be in vain,
    For if we would shoot the one at the other,
        The one of us may be slain.

13.   "But let's take our swords and our broad bucklers,
        And gang under yonder tree."
    "As I hope to be sav'd," the stranger said,
        "One foot I will not flee."

14.   Then Robin Hood lent the stranger a blow
        Most scar'd him out of his wit.
    "Thou never felt blow," the stranger he said,
        "That shall be better quit."

15.   The stranger he drew out a good broad sword,
        And hit Robin on the crown,
    That from every haire of bold Robin's head
        The blood ran trickling down.

16.   "God a mercy, good fellow," quoth Robin Hood then,
        "And for this that thou hast done;
    Tell me, good fellow, what thou art,
        Tell me where thou doest woon."

17.   The stranger then answered bold Robin Hood,
        "I'le tell thee where I did dwell;
    In Maxfield was I bred and born,
        My name is Young Gamwell.

18.   "For killing of my own father's steward,
        I am forc'd to this English wood,
    And for to seek an vncle of mine;
        Some call him Robin Hood."

19.   "But thou art a cousin of Robin Hood's then?
        The sonner we should have done."
    "As I hope to be sav'd," the stranger then said,
        "I am his own sister's son."

20.   But, lord! What kissing and courting was there,
        When these two cousins did greet!
    And they went all that summers day,
        And Little John did meet.

21.   But when they met with Little John,
        He there unto him did say,

"O master, where have you been,
  You have tarried so long away?"

22. "I met with a stranger," quoth Robin Hood then,
  "Full sore he hath beaten me."
  "Then I'le have a bout with him," quoth Little John,
  "And try if he can beat me."

23. "Oh no, oh no," quoth Robin Hood then,
  "Little John, it may not be so,
  For he's my own dear sister's son,
  And cousins I have no mo.

24. "But he shall be a bold yeoman of mine,
  My chief man next to thee;
  And I Robin Hood, and thou Little John,
  And Scarlet he shall be.

25. "And wee 'l be three of the bravest outlaws
  That is in the North Country."
  If you will have any more of bold Robin Hood,
  In his second part it will be.

THE BOLD PEDLAR AND ROBIN HOOD (132)

This version comes straight out of oral tradition in Surrey. It is still
found in Nova Scotia and New England, usually in abbreviated form.
  Text, Dixon, p. 71.

1. There chanced to be a pedlar bold,
  A pedlar bold he chanced to be;
  He rolled his pack all on his back,
  And he came tripping oer the lee.
    Down a down a down a down,
    Down a down a down

2. By chance he met two troublesome blades,
  Two troublesome blades they chanced to be;
  The one of them was bold Robin Hood,
  And the other was Little John so free.

3. "O pedlar, pedlar, what is in thy pack?
  Come speedilie and tell to me."
  "I've several suits of the gay green silks,
  And silken bow-strings two or three."

4. "If you have several suits of the gay green silk,
  And silken bow-strings two or three,

Then it's by my body," cries Little John,
    "One half of your pack shall belong to me."

5. "O nay, o nay," says the pedlar bold,
    "O nay, o nay, that never can be;
  For there's never a man from fair Nottingham
    Can take one half my pack from me."

6. Then the pedlar he pulled off his pack,
    And put it a little below his knee,
  Saying, If you do move me one perch from this,
    My pack and all shall gang with thee."

7. Then Little John he drew his sword,
    The pedlar by his pack did stand;
  They fought until they both did sweat,
    Till he cried, "Pedlar, pray hold your hand!"

8. Then Robin Hood he was standing by,
    And he did laugh most heartilie;
  Saying, "I could find a man, of a smaller scale,
    Could thrash the pedlar and also thee."

9. "Go you try, master," says Little John,
    "Go you try, master, most speedilie,
  Or by my body," says Little John,
    "I am sure this night you will not know me."

10. Then Robin Hood he drew his sword,
    And the pedlar by his pack did stand;
  They fought till the blood in streams did flow,
    Till he cried, "Pedlar, pray hold your hand!"

11. "Pedlar, pedlar, what is thy name?
    Come speedilie and tell to me."
  "My name, my name I neer will tell,
    Till both your names you have told to me."

12. "The one of us is bold Robin Hood,
    And the other Little John so free."
  "Now," says the pedlar, "it lays to my good will,
    Whether my name I chuse to tell to thee.

13. "I am Gamble Gold of the gay green woods,
    And travelled far beyond the sea;
  For killing a man in my father's land
    From my country I was forced to flee."

14. "If you are Gamble Gold of the gay green woods,
    And travelled far beyond the sea,
  You are my mother's own sister's son;
    What nearer cousins then can we be?"

15. They sheathed their swords with friendly words,
         So merrilie they did agree;
     They went to a tavern, and there they dined,
         And bottles cracked most merrilie.

ROBIN HOOD AND THE BEGGAR, I (133)

The usual story of a besting of Robin Hood. This ballad belongs to
the group riming the middle of line 3 of each stanza. As a story it
lacks motivation, perhaps supplied in the original of which this may be
a variant. Why does Robin Hood change clothes with the beggar? He
did not know that the disguise would come in handy when he got to
Nottingham.

Text, Pepys, ii, 116.

1. Come light and listen, you gentlemen all,
         Hey down, down, and a down
         That mirth do love for to hear,
     And a story true I'le tell unto you,
         If that you will but draw near.

2. In elder times, when merriment was,
         And archery was holden good,
     There was an outlaw, as many did know,
         Which men called Robin Hood.

3. Vpon a time it chanced so
         Bold Robin was merry disposed,
     His time to spend he did intend,
         Either with friends or foes.

4. Then he got vp on a gallant brave steed,
         The which was worth angels ten;
     With a mantle of green, most brave to be seen,
         He left all his merry men.

5. And riding towards fair Nottingham,
         Some pastime for to spy,
     There was he aware of a jolly beggar
         As ere he beheld with his eye.

6. An old patcht coat the beggar had on,
         Which he daily did vse for to wear;
     And many a bag about him did wag,
         Which made Robin Hood to him repair.

7. "God speed, God speed," said Robin Hood,
     "What countryman? tell to me."

"I am Yorkeshire, sir; but e're you go far,
 Some charity give vnto me."

8. "Why, what wouldst thou have?" said Robin Hood,
 "I pray thee tell vnto me."
 "No lands nor livings," the beggar he said,
 "But a penny for charitie."

9. "I have no money," said Robin Hood then,
 "But, a ranger within the wood,
 I am an outlaw, as many do know,
 My name it is Robin Hood.

10. "But yet I must tell thee, bonny beggar,
 That a bout with thee I must try;
 Thy coat of gray lay down I say,
 And my mantle of green shall lye by."

11. "Content, content," the beggar he cry'd,
 "Thy part it will be the worse;
 For I hope this bout to give thee the rout,
 And then have at thy purse."

12. The beggar he had a mickle long staffe,
 And Robin had a nut-brown sword;
 So the beggar drew nigh, and at Robin let fly,
 But gave him never a word.

13. "Fight on, fight on," said Robin Hood then.
 "This game well pleaseth me."
 For every blow that Robin did give,
 The beggar gave buffets three.

14. And fighting there full hard and sore,
 Not far from Nottingham town,
 They never fled, till from Robin's head
 The blood came trickling down.

15. "O hold thy hand," said Robin Hood then,
 "And thou and I will agree."
 "If that be true," the beggar he said,
 "Thy mantle come give vnto me."

16. "Nay a change, a change," cri'd Robin Hood;
 "Thy bags and coat give to me,
 And this mantle of mine I'le to thee resign,
 My horse and my braverie."

17. When Robin Hood had got the beggar's clothes,
 He looked round about,

"Methinks," said he, "I seem to be
   A beggar brave and stout.

18. "For now I have a bag for my bread,
      So have I another for corn;
   I have one for salt, and another malt,
      And one for my little horn.

19. "And now I will a begging goe,
      Some charitie for to find."
   And if any more of Robin you'l know,
      In this second part it's behind.

20. Now Robin he is to Nottingham bound,
      With his bags hanging down to his knee,
   His staff, and his coat, scarce worth a groat,
      Yet merrilie passed he.

21. As Robin he passed the streets along,
      He heard a pittiful cry;
   Three brethren deer, as he did hear,
      Condemned were to dye.

22. Then Robin he highed to the sheriffs house,
      Some reliefe for to seek;
   He skipt, and leapt, and capored full high,
      As he went along the street.

23. But when to the sheriff's doore he came,
      There was a gentleman fine and brave,
   "Thou beggar," said he, "Come tell vnto me
      What is that thou wouldest have?"

24. "No meat, nor drink," said Robin Hood then,
      "That I come here to crave,
   But to beg the lives of yeomen three,
      And that I fain would have."

25. "That cannot be, thou bold beggar,
      Their fact it is so cleer;
   I tell to thee, hangd they must be,
      For stealing of our king's deer."

26. But when to the gallows they did come,
      There was many a weeping eye:
   "O hold your peace," said Robin then,
      "For certainly they shall not dye."

27. Then Robin he set his horn to his mouth,
      And he blew but blastes three,
   Till a hundred bold archers brave
      Came kneeling down to his knee.

28.   "What is your will, master?" they said,
      "We are here at your command."
   "Shoot east, shoot west," said Robin Hood then,
      "And look that you spare no man."

29.   Then they shot east, and they shot west;
      Their arrows were so keen
   The sheriffe he, and his companie,
      No longer must be seen.

30.   Then he stept to these brethren three,
      And away he had them tane;
   But the sheriff was crost, and many a man lost,
      That dead lay on the plain.

31.   And away they went into the merry greenwood,
      And sung with a merry glee,
   And Robin took these brethren good
      To be of his yeomandrie.

ROBIN HOOD AND THE BEGGAR, II (134)

This ballad has nothing but general tradition in common with the preceding. Even though Robin Hood is depicted here as a weak and revengeful person and his men as deceitful and mercenary, this is a good, swiftly moving, humorous ballad with a great deal of life. The trick by which the beggar conquers those who attack him in such a cowardly manner makes the story interesting and dramatic.

Text MS., Douce H.H. 88, Bodleian.

1.   Lyth and listen, gentlemen,
      That's come of high born blood;
   I'll tell you of a brave booting
      That befel Robin Hood.

2.   Robin Hood upon a day,
      He went forth him alone,
   And as he came from Barnesdale
      Into a fair evening,

3.   He met a beggar on the way,
      That sturdily could gang;
   He had a pike-staff in his hand,
      That was baith stark and strang.

4.   A clouted cloak about him was,
      That held him from the cold;

> The thinnest bit of it, I guess,
>   Was more than twenty fold.

5. His meal-pock hang about his neck,
      Into a leathern fang,
    Well fastened with a broad buckle,
      That was both stark and strang.

6. He had three hats upon his head,
      Together sticked fast;
    He cared neither for wind nor weet,
      In lands wherever he past.

7. Good Robin coost him in his way,
      To see what he might be;
    If any beggar had money,
      He thought some part had he.

8. "Tarry, tarry," good Robin says,
      "Tarry, and speak with me."
    He heard him as he heard him not,
      And fast his way can hie.

9. "It be's not so," says good Robin,
      "Nay, thou must tarry still."
    "By my troth," says the bold beggar,
      "Of that I have no will.

10. "It is far to my lodging-house,
      And it is growing late;
    If they have supt ere I come in,
      I will look wondrous blate."

11. "Now, by my troth," says good Robin,
      "I see well by thy fare,
    If thou chear well to thy supper,
      Of mine thou takes no care;

12. "Who wants my dinner all the day,
      And wots not where to lie,
    And should I to the tavern go,
      I want money to buy.

13. "Sir, thou must lend me some money,
      Till we two meet again."
    The beggar answered cankerdly,
      "I have no money to lend.

14. "Thou art as young man as I,
      And seems to be as sweer;
    If thou fast till thou get from me,
      Thou shalt eat none this year."

15. "Now, by my troth," says good Robin,
     "Since we are sembled so,
   If thou have but a small farthing,
     I'll have it ere thou go.

16. "Therefore, lay down thy clouted cloak,
     And do no longer stand,
   And loose the strings of all thy pocks;
     I'll ripe them with my hand.

17. "And now to thee I make a vow,
     If thou make any din,
   I shall see if a broad arrow
     Can pierce a beggar's skin."

18. The beggar smil'd, and answer made:
     "Far better let me be;
   Think not that I will be afraid
     For thy nip crooked tree.

19. "Or that I fear thee any whit
     For thy curn nips of sticks;
   I know no use for them so meet
     As to be pudding-pricks.

20. "Here I defy thee to do me ill,
     For all thy boistrous fare;
   Thou's get nothing from me but ill,
     Would thou seek it evermair."

21. Good Robin bent his noble bow—
     He was an angry man—
   And in it set a broad arrow;
     Yet er 't was drawn a span,

22. The beggar, with his noble tree,
     Reacht him so round a rout
   That his bow and his broad arrow
     In flinders flew about.

23. Good Robin bound him to his brand,
     But that provd likewise vain;
   The beggar lighted on his hand
     With his pike-staff again.

24. I wot he might not draw a sword
     For forty days and more;
   Good Robin could not speak a word,
     His heart was never so sore.

25. He could not fight, he could not flee,
     He wist not what to do;

    The beggar, with his noble tree,
      Laid lusty flaps him to.

26. He paid good Robin back and side,
      And beft him up and down,
    And with his pike-staff still on laid
      Till he fell in a swoon.

27. "Fy! stand up, man," the beggar said,
      "'T is a shame to go to rest;
    Stay still till thou get thy mony told,
      I think it were the best.

28. "And syne go to the tavern-house,
      And buy both wine and ale;
    Hereat thy friends will crack full crouse,
      Thou has been at a dale."

29. Good Robin answerd never a word,
      But lay still as a stane;
    His cheeks were white as any clay,
      And closed were his eyne.

30. The beggar thought him dead but fail,
      And boldly bownd away;
    I would you had been at the dale,
      And gotten part of the play.

31. Now three of Robin's men, by chance,
      Came walking on the way,
    And found their master in a trance,
      On ground where he did lie.

32. Up have they taken good Robin,
      Making a piteous bier,
    Yet saw they no man there at whom
      They might the matter spear.

33. They looked him all round about,
      But wounds on him saw none,
    Yet at his mouth came bocking out
      The blood of a good vein.

34. Cold water they have taken syne,
      And cast into his face;
    Then he began to lift his eyne,
      And spake within short space.

35. "Tell us, dear master," says his men,
      "How with you stands the case?"

Good Robin sighd ere he began
  To tell of his disgrace.

36. "I have been watchman in this wood
    Near hand this forty year,
  Yet I was never so hard bestead
    As you have found me here.

37. "A beggar with a clouted cloak,
    In whom I feard no ill,
  Hath with a pike-staff clawd my back;
    I fear 't shall never be well.

38. "See, where he goes out oer yon hill,
    With hat upon his head;
  If ever you loved your master well,
    Go now revenge this deed.

39. "And bring him back again to me,
    If it lie in your might,
  That I may see, before I die,
    Him punisht in my sight.

40. "And if you may not bring him back,
    Let him not go loose on;
  For to us all it were great shame
    If he escapt again."

41. "One of us shall with you remain,
    Because you're ill at ease;
  The other two shall bring him back,
    To use him as you please."

42. "Now, by my troth," says good Robin,
    "I trow there's enough said;
  If he get scouth to weild his tree,
    I fear you'll both be paid."

43. "Be ye not feard, our good master,
    That we two can be dung
  With any blutter base beggar,
    That hath nought but a rung.

44. "His staff shall stand him in no stead;
    That you shall shortly see;
  But back again he shall be led,
    And fast bound shall he be,
  To see if you will have him slain,
    Or hanged on a tree."

45. "But cast you slily in his way,
    Before he be aware,

And on his pike-staff first lay hands;
    You'll speed the better far."

46. Now leave we Robin with his man,
        Again to play the child,
    And learn himself to stand and gang
        By haulds, for all his eild.

47. Now pass we to the bold beggar,
        That raked oer the hill,
    Who never mended his pace no more
        For he had done no ill.

48. The young men knew the country well,
        So soon where he would be,
    And they have taken another way,
        Was nearer by miles three.

49. They rudely ran with all their might,
        Spar'd neither dub nor mire,
    They stirred neither at laigh nor hight,
        No travel made them tire,

50. Till they before the beggar wan,
        And coost them in his way;
    A little wood lay in a glen,
        And there they both did stay.

51. They stood up closely by a tree,
        In ilk side of the gate,
    Until the beggar came them to,
        That thought not of such fate.

52. And as he was betwixt them past,
        They leapt upon him baith;
    The one his pike-staff gripped fast,
        They feared for its scaith.

53. The other he held in his sight
        A drawn dirk to his breast,
    And said, "False carl, quit thy staff,
        Or I shall be thy priest."

54. His pike-staff they have taken him frae,
        And stuck it in the green;
    He was full leath to let it gae,
        It better might have been.

55. The beggar was the feardest man
        Of one that ever might be;

To win away no way he can,
Nor help him with his tree.

56. He wist not wherefore he was tane,
      Nor how many was there;
   He thought his life-days had been gone,
      And grew into despair.

57. "Grant me my life," the beggar said,
      For him that died on tree,
   And take away that ugly knife,
      Or then for fear I'll die.

58. "I grievd you never in all my life,
      By late nor yet by ayre;
   Ye have great sin, if ye should slay
      A silly poor beggar."

59. "Thou lies, false lown," they say again,
      "By all that may be sworn;
   Thou hast near slain the gentlest man
      That ever yet was born.

60. "And back again thou shalt be led,
      And fast bound shalt thou be,
   To see if he will have thee slain,
      Or hanged on a tree."

61. The beggar then thought all was wrong;
      They were set for his wrack;
   He saw nothing appearing then
      But ill upon worse back.

62. Were he out of their hands, he thought,
      And had again his tree,
   He should not be had back for nought,
      With such as he did see.

63. Then he bethought him on a wile,
      If it could take effect,
   How he the young men might beguile,
      And give them a begeck.

64. Thus for to do them shame or ill
      His beastly breast was bent;
   He found the wind grew something shril,
      To further his intent.

65. He said, "Brave gentlemen, be good,
      And let the poor man be;

When ye have taken a beggar's blood,
    It helps you not a flee.

66. "It was but in my own defence,
    If he hath gotten skaith;
  But I will make a recompence,
    Much better for you baith.

67. "If ye will set me safe and free,
    And do me no danger,
  An hundred pounds I will you give,
    And much more good silver.

68. "That I have gathered these many years,
    Under this clouted cloak,
  And hid up wonder privately,
    In bottom of my pock."

69. The young men to a council yeed,
    And let the beggar gae;
  They wist how well he had no speed
    From them to run away.

70. They thought they would the money take,
    Come after what so may,
  And then they would not bring him back,
    But in that part him slay.

71. By that good Robin would not know
    That they had gotten coin;
  It would content him for to show
    That there they had him slain.

72. They said, "False carl, soon have done
    And tell forth that money;
  For the ill turn thou hast done
    'T is but a simple fee.

73. "And yet we will not have thee back,
    Come after what so may,
  If thou will do that which thou spake,
    And make us present pay."

74. O then he loosd his clouted cloak,
    And spread it on the ground,
  And thereon laid he many a pock,
    Betwixt them and the wind.

75. He took a great bag from his hase;
    It was near full of meal;

          Two pecks in it at least there was,
            And more, I wot full well.

76.   Upon his cloak he laid it down,
            The mouth he opend wide,
        To turn the same he made him bown,
            The young men ready spy'd.

77.   In every hand he took a nook
            Of that great leathern meal,
        And with a fling that meal he shook
            Into their faces hail.

78.   Wherein he blinded them so close
            A stime they could not see;
        And then in heart he did rejoice,
            And clapt his lusty tree.

79.   He thought if he had done them wrong
            In mealing of their cloaths,
        For to strike off the meal again
            With his pike-staff he goes.

80.   Or any one of them could red their eyne,
            Or yet a glimmering could see,
        Ilk ane of them a dozen had,
            Well laid on with the tree.

81.   The young men were right swift of foot,
            And boldly ran away;
        The beggar could them no more hit,
            For all the haste he may.

82.   "What ails this haste?" the beggar said,
            "May ye not tarry still,
        Until your money be receiv'd?
            I'll pay you with good will.

83.   "The shaking of my pocks, I fear,
            Hath blown into your eyne;
        But I have a good pike-staff here
            Will ripe them out full clean."

84.   The young men answerd neer a word,
            They were dumb as a stane;
        In the thick wood the beggar fled,
            Eer they riped their eyne.

85.   And syne the night became so late,
            To seek him was but vain:
        But judge ye, if they looked blate
            When they came home again.

86.   Good Robin speard how they had sped;
          They answerd him, "Full ill."
      "That cannot be," good Robin says,
          "Ye have been at the mill.

87.   "The mill it is a meatrif place,
          They may lick what they please;
      Most like ye have been at that art,
          Who would look to your cloaths."

88.   They hanged their heads, and droped down,
          A word they could not speak.
      Robin said, "Because I fell a-swoon,
          I think you'll do the like.

89.   "Tell on the matter, less and more,
          And tell me what and how
      Ye have done with the bold beggar
          I sent you for right now."

90.   And then they told him to an end,
          As I have said before,
      How that the beggar did them blind,
          What misters process more.

91.   And how he lin'd their shoulders broad
          With his great trenchen tree,
      And how in the thick wood he fled,
          Eer they a stime could see.

92.   And how they scarcely could win home,
          Their bones were beft so sore:
      Good Robin cry'd, "Fy! Out, for shame!
          We're sham'd for evermore."

93.   Altho good Robin would full fain
          Of his wrong revenged be,
      He smil'd to see his merry young men
          Had gotten a taste of the tree.

ROBIN HOOD AND ALLEN A DALE (138)

A 17th-century ballad with a longer folk tradition behind it. It has the type of good drama and humor associated with the best of the Robin Hood ballads.

Text, Pepys, ii, 110.

1.   Come listen to me, you gallants so free,
         All you that loves mirth for to hear,

And I will you tell of a bold outlaw,
    That lived in Nottinghamshire. (bis)

2. As Robin Hood in the forest stood,
        All under the green-wood tree,
    There was he ware of a brave young man,
        As fine as fine might be.

3. The youngster was clothed in scarlet red,
        In scarlet fine and gay,
    And he did frisk it over the plain,
        And chanted a roundelay.

4. As Robin Hood next morning stood,
        Amongst the leaves so gay,
    There did he espy the same young man
        Come drooping along the way.

5. The scarlet he wore the day before,
        It was clean cast away;
    And every step he fetcht a sigh,
        "Alack and a well a day!"

6. Then stepped forth brave Little John,
        And Nick the miller's son,
    Which made the young man bend his bow,
        When as he see them come.

7. "Stand off, stand off," the young man said,
        "What is your will with me?"
    "You must come before our master straight,
        Vnder yon green-wood tree."

8. And when he came bold Robin before,
        Robin askt him courteously,
    "O hast thou any money to spare
        For my merry men and me?"

9. "I have no money," the young man said,
        "But five shillings and a ring;
    And that I have kept this seven long years,
        To have it at my wedding.

10. "Yesterday I should have married a maid,
        But she is now from me tane,
    And chosen to be an old knight's delight,
        Whereby my poor heart is slain."

11. "What is thy name?" then said Robin Hood,
        "Come tell me, without any fail."
    "By the faith of my body," then said the young man,
        "My name it is Allin a Dale."

12. "What will thou give me," said Robin Hood,
    "In ready gold or fee,
To help thee to thy true-love again,
    And deliver her unto thee?"

13. "I have no money," then quoth the young man,
    "No ready gold nor fee,
But I will swear upon a book
    Thy true servant for to be."

14. "How many miles is it to thy true-love?
    Come tell me without any guile."
"By the faith of my body," then said the young man,
    "It is but five little mile."

15. Then Robin he hasted over the plain,
    He did neither stint nor lin,
Vntil he came unto the church
    Where Allin should keep his wedding.

16. "What dost thou do here?" the bishop he said,
    "I prethee now tell to me."
"I am a bold harper," quoth Robin Hood,
    "And the best in the north countrey."

17. "O welcome, O welcome," the bishop he said,
    "That musick best pleaseth me."
"You shall have no musick," quoth Robin Hood,
    "Till the bride and the bridegroom I see."

18. With that came in a wealthy knight,
    Which was both grave and old,
And after him a finikin lass,
    Did shine like glistering gold.

19. "This is no fit match," quoth bold Robin Hood,
    "That you do seem to make here;
For since we are come unto the church,
    The bride she shall chuse her own dear."

20. Then Robin Hood put his horn to his mouth,
    And blew blasts two or three;
When four and twenty bowmen bold
    Came leaping over the lee.

21. And when they came into the church-yard,
    Marching all on a row,
The first man was Allin a Dale,
    To give bold Robin his bow.

22. "This is thy true-love," Robin he said,

"Young Allin, as I hear say;
And you shall be married at this same time,
    Before we depart away."

23. "That shall not be," the bishop he said,
        "For thy word shall not stand;
    They shall be three times askt in the church,
        As the law is of our land."

24. Robin Hood pulld off the bishop's coat,
        And put it on Little John;
    "By the faith of my body," then Robin said,
        "This cloath doth make thee a man."

25. When Little John went into the quire,
        The people began for to laugh;
    He askt them seven times in the church,
        Least three times should not be enough.

26. "Who gives me this maid," then said Little John,
        Quoth Robin, "That do I,
    And he that doth take her from Allin a Dale
        Full dearly he shall her buy."

27. And thus having ended this merry wedding,
        The bride lookt as fresh as a queen,
    And so they returned to the merry green wood,
        Amongst the leaves so green.

ROBIN HOOD'S PROGRESS TO
NOTTINGHAM (139)

This is an extravagantly heroic account of Robin Hood's exploits
against fifteen foresters when he was only fifteen years old. The story
is told with more restraint in the "Life of Robin Hood," in a manuscript of the 16th century and printed in William J. Thoms, *Early
English Prose Romances,* ii, 65–149 (1858). A fragment of this ballad is found in Nova Scotia.
    Text, Pepys, ii, 104.

1. Robin Hood hee was and a tall young man,
            Derry derry down
        And fifteen winters old,
    And Robin Hood he was a proper young man,
        Of courage stout and bold.
            Hey down derry derry down

2. Robin Hood he would and to fair Nottingham,
        With the general for to dine;

There was he ware of fifteen forresters,
    And a drinking bear, ale and wine.

3. "What news? What news?" said bold Robin Hood;
    "What news, fain wouldst thou know?
Our king hath provided a shooting-match.
    And I'm ready with my bow."

4. "We hold it in scorn," then said the forresters,
    "That ever a boy so young
Should bear a bow before our king,
    That's not able to draw one string."

5. "I'le hold you twenty marks," said bold Robin Hood,
    "By the leave of Our Lady,
That I'le hit a mark a hundred rod,
    And I'le cause a hart to dye."

6. "We'l hold you twenty mark," then said the forresters,
    "By the leave of Our Lady,
Thou hitst not the marke a hundred rod,
    Nor causest a hart to dye."

7. Robin Hood he bent up a noble bow,
    And a broad arrow he let flye,
He hit the mark a hundred rod,
    And he caused a hart to dy.

8. Some said hee brake ribs one or two,
    And some said hee brake three;
The arrow within the hart would not abide,
    But it glanced in two or three.

9. The hart did skip, and the hart did leap,
    And the hart lay on the ground;
"The wager is mine," said bold Robin Hood,
    "If 't was for a thousand pound."

10. "The wager's none of thine," then said the forresters,
    "Although thou beest in haste;
Take up thy bow, and get thee hence,
    Lest wee thy sides do baste."

11. Robin Hood hee took up his noble bow,
    And his broad arrows all amain,
And Robin Hood he laught, and begun to smile,
    As hee went over the plain.

12. Then Robin Hood hee bent his noble bow,
    And his broad arrows he let flye,
Till fourteen of these fifteen forresters
    Vpon the ground did lye.

13.   He that did this quarrel first begin
          Went tripping over the plain;
      But Robin Hood he bent his noble bow,
          And he fetcht him back again.

14.   "You said I was no archer," said Robin Hood,
          "But say so now again."
      With that he sent another arrow
          That split his head in twain.

15.   "You have found mee an archer," said Robin Hood,
          "Which will make your wives for to wring,
      And wish that you had never spoke the word,
          That I could not draw one string."

16.   The people that lived in fair Nottingham
          Came running out amain,
      Supposing to have taken bold Robin Hood,
          With the forresters that were slain.

17.   Some lost legs, and some lost arms,
          And some did lose their blood,
      But Robin Hood hee took up his noble bow,
          And is gone to the merry green wood.

18.   They carryed these forresters into fair Nottingham,
          As many there did know;
      They digd them graves in their church-yard,
          And they buried them all a row.

ROBIN HOOD RESCUING WILL STUTLY (141)

This ballad is a late broadside composed rather to be read than to be sung. It is largely imitative and literary. It is included here so that a comparison may be made between the type it represents and the traditional ballad. It is found in Virginia in a somewhat abbreviated form and also from print.

Text, Pepys, ii, 106.

1.   When Robin Hood in the green-wood livd,
          Derry derry down
          Vnder the green-wood tree,
      Tidings there came to him with speed,
          Tidings for certainty,
              Hey down derry derry down.

2.   That Will Stutly surprized was,
          And eke in prison lay;

Three varlets that the sheriff had hired
    Did likely him betray.

3. I, and to-morrow hanged must be,
    To-morrow as soon as it is day;
  But before they could this victory get,
    Two of them did Stutly slay.

4. When Robin Hood he heard this news,
    Lord! he was grieved sore,
  I, and unto his merry men said,
    Who altogether swore,

5. That Will Stutly should rescued be,
    And be brought safe again;
  Or else should many a gallant wight
    For his sake there be slain.

6. He cloathed himself in scarlet then,
    His men were all in green;
  A finer show, throughout the world,
    In no place could be seen.

7. Good lord! it was a gallant sight
    To see them all on a row;
  With every man a good broad sword,
    And eke a good yew bow.

8. Forth of the green wood are they gone,
    Yea, all couragiously,
  Resolving to bring Stutly home,
    Or every man to die.

9. And when they came the castle neer
    Whereas Will Stutly lay,
  "I hold it good," saith Robin Hood,
    "Wee here in ambush stay,

10. "And send one forth some news to hear,
    To yonder palmer fair,
  That stands under the castle-wall,
    Some news he may declare."

11. With that steps forth a brave young man,
    Which was of courage bold;
  Thus hee did say to the old man:
    "I pray thee, palmer old,

12. "Tell me, if that thou rightly ken,
    When must Will Stutly die,
  Who is one of bold Robin's men,
    And here doth prisoner lie?"

13.   "Alack, alass," the palmer said,
        "And for ever wo is me!
      Will Stutly hanged must be this day,
        On yonder gallows-tree.

14.   "O had his noble master known,
        Hee would some succour send;
      A few of his bold yeomandree
        Full soon would fetch him hence."

15.   "I, that is true," the young man said;
        "I, that is true," said hee;
      "Or, if they were neer to this place,
        They soon would set him free.

16.   "But fare thou well, thou good old man,
        Farewell, and thanks to thee;
      If Stutly hanged be this day,
        Revengd his death will be."

17.   He was no sooner from the palmer gone,
        But the gates was opened wide,
      And out of the castle Will Stutly came,
        Guarded on every side.

18.   When hee was forth from the castle come,
        And saw no help was nigh,
      Thus he did say unto the sheriff,
        Thus he said gallantly:

19.   "Now seeing that I needs must die,
        Grant me one boon," says he;
      "For my noble master nere had man
        That yet was hangd on the tree.

20.   "Give me a sword all in my hand,
        And let mee be unbound,
      And with thee and thy men I'le fight,
        Vntill I lie dead on the ground."

21.   But his desire he would not grant,
        His wishes were in vain;
      For the sheriff had sworn he hanged should be,
        And not by the sword be slain.

22.   "Do but unbind my hands," he saies,
        "I will no weapons crave,
      And if I hanged be this day,
        Damnation let me have."

23.   "O no, O no," the sheriff he said,
        "Thou shalt on the gallows die,

I, and so shall thy master too,
 If ever in me it lie."

24. "O dastard coward!" Stutly cries,
  "Thou faint-heart peasant slave!
 If ever my master do thee meet,
  Thou shalt thy paiment have.

25. "My noble master thee doth scorn,
  And all thy cowardly crew;
 Such silly imps unable are
  Bold Robin to subdue."

26. But when he was to the gallows come,
  And ready to bid adiew,
 Out of a bush leaps Little John,
  And steps Will Stutly to.

27. "I pray thee, Will, before thou die,
  Of thy dear friends take leave;
 I needs must borrow him a while,
  How say you, master sheriff?"

28. "Now, as I live," the sheriff he said,
  "That varlet will I know;
 Some sturdy rebell is that same,
  Therefore let him not go."

29. With that Little John so hastily
  Away cut Stutly's bands,
 And from one of the sheriff his men,
  A sword twicht from his hands.

30. "Here, Will, here, take thou this same,
  Thou canst it better sway;
 And here defend thy self a while,
  For aid will come straight way."

31. And there they turned them back to back,
  In the middle of them that day,
 Till Robin Hood approached neer,
  With many an archer gay.

32. With that an arrow by them flew,
  I wist from Robin Hood;
 "Make haste, make haste," the sheriff he said,
  "Make haste, for it is good."

33. The sheriff is gone; his doughty men
  Thought it no boot to stay,

But, as their master had them taught,
  They run full fast away.

34. "O stay, O stay," Will Stutly said,
  "Take leave ere you depart;
You nere will catch bold Robin Hood
  Vnless you dare him meet."

35. "O ill betide you," quoth Robin Hood,
  "That you so soon are gone;
My sword may in the scabbord rest,
  For here our work is done."

36. "I little thought when I came here,
  When I came to this place,
For to have met with Little John,
  Or seen my masters face."

37. Thus Stutly was at liberty set,
  And safe brought from his foe.
"O thanks, O thanks to my master,
  Since here it was not so."

38. "And once again, my fellows,
  We shall in the green woods meet,
Where we will make our bow-strings twang,
  Musick for us most sweet."

LITTLE JOHN A BEGGING (142)

A 17th-century ballad with a background in tradition.
Text, Pepys, ii, 119.

1. All you that delight to spend some time
    With a hey down down a down down
  A merry song for to sing,
Vnto me draw neer, and you shall hear
  How Little John went a begging.

2. As Robin Hood walked the forrest along,
  And all his yeomandree,
Sayes Robin, "Some of you must a begging go,
  And, Little John, it must be thee."

3. Sayes John, "If I must a begging go,
  I will have a palmer's weed,
With a staff and a coat, and bags of all sorts,
  The better then I shall speed.

4. "Come, give me now a bag for my bread,
    And another for my cheese.
And one for a peny, when as I get any,
    That nothing I may leese."

5. Now Little John he is a begging gone,
    Seeking for some relief;
But of all the beggars he met on the way,
    Little John he was the chief.

6. But as he was walking himself alone,
    Four beggars he chanced to spy,
Some deaf, and some blind, and some came behind;
    Says John, Here's brave company!

7. "Good-morrow," said John, "my brethren dear,
    Good fortune I had you to see;
Which way do you go? pray let me know,
    For I want some company.

8. "O what is here to do?" then said Little John,
    "Why rings all these bells?" said he;
"What dog is a hanging? come, let us be ganging,
    That we the truth may see."

9. "Here is no dog a hanging," then one of them said,
    "Good fellow, we tell unto thee;
But here is one dead wil give us cheese and bred,
    And it may be one single peny."

10. "We have brethren in London," another he said,
    "So have we in Coventry,
In Barwick and Dover, and all the world over,
    But nere a crookt carril like thee.

11. "Therefore stand thee back, thou crooked carel,
    And take that knock on the crown."
"Nay," said Little John, "I'le not yet be gone,
    For a bout will I have with you round.

12. "Now have at you all," then said Little John,
    "If you be so full of your blows;
Fight on, all four, and nere give ore,
    Whether you be friends or foes."

13. John nipped the dumb, and made him to rore,
    And the blind that could not see,
And he that a cripple had been seven years,
    He made him run faster then he.

14. And flinging them all against the wall,
    With many a sturdie bang,

It made John sing, to hear the gold ring,
    Which against the walls cryed twang.

15.   Then he got out of the begger's cloak
       Three hundred pound in gold;
    "Good fortune had I," then said Little John,
       "Such a good sight to behold."

16.   But what found he in a begger's bag,
       But three hundred pound and three?
    "If I drink water while this doth last,
       Then an ill death may I dye.

17.   "And my begging-trade I will now give ore,
       My fortune hath bin so good;
    Therefore I'le not stay, but I will away
       To the forrest of merry Sherwood."

18.   And when to the forrest of Sherwood he came,
       He quickly there did see
    His master good, bold Robin Hood,
       And all his company.

19.   "What news? What news?" then said Robin Hood,
       "Come, Little John, tell unto me;
    How hast thou sped with thy begger's trade?
       For that I fain would see."

20.   "No news but good," then said Little John,
       "With begging ful wel I have sped;
    Six hundred and three I have here for thee,
       In silver and gold so red."

21.   Then Robin took Little John by the hand,
       And danced about the oak-tree:
    "If we drink water while this doth last,
       Then an il death may we die!"

22.   So to conclude my merry new song,
       All you that delight it to sing,
    'Tis of Robin Hood, that archer good,
       And how Little John went a begging.

ROBIN HOOD AND THE BISHOP (143)

Robin Hood and his men have numerous adventures of this sort with the clergy. Such adventures are part of the outlaw tradition in general as are the disguise as a woman and the forced mass. Compare the two ballads which follow.

Text, Pepys, ii, 109.

1. Come gentlemen all, and listen a while,
     Hey down down an a down
     And a story I'le to you unfold;
   I'le tell you how Robin Hood served the Bishop,
     When he robbed him of his gold.

2. As it fell out on a sun-shining day,
     When Phebus was in his prime,
   Then Robin Hood, that archer good,
     In mirth would spend some time.

3. And as he walkd the forrest along,
     Some pastime for to spy,
   There was he aware of a proud bishop,
     And all his company.

4. "O what shall I do?" said Robin Hood then,
     "If the Bishop he doth take me,
   No mercy he'l show unto me, I know,
     But hanged I shall be."

5. Then Robin was stout, and turned him about,
     And a little house there he did spy;
   And to an old wife, for to save his life,
     He loud began for to cry.

6. "Why, who art thou?" said the old woman,
     "Come tell it to me for good."
   "I am an out-law, as many do know,
     My name it is Robin Hood.

7. "And yonder's the Bishop and all his men,
     And if that I taken be,
   Then day and night he'l work me spight,
     And hanged I shall be."

8. "If thou be Robin Hood," said the old wife,
     "As thou dost seem to be,
   I'le for thee provide, and thee I will hide
     From the Bishop and his company.

9. "For I well remember, one Saturday night
     Thou bought me both shoes and hose;
   Therefore I'le provide thy person to hide,
     And keep thee from thy foes."

10. "Then give me soon thy coat of gray,
      And take thou my mantle of green;

Thy spindle and twine unto me resign,
   And take thou my arrows so keen."

11. And when that Robin Hood was so araid,
        He went straight to his company;
     With his spindle and twine, he oft lookt behind
        For the Bishop and his company.

12. "O who is yonder," quoth Little John,
        "That now comes over the lee?
     An arrow I will at her let flie,
        So like an old witch looks she."

13. "O hold thy hand, hold thy hand," said Robin then,
        "And shoot not thy arrows so keen;
     I am Robin Hood, thy master good,
        And quickly it shall be seen."

14. The Bishop he came to the old woman's house,
        And he called with furious mood,
     "Come let me soon see, and bring unto me,
        That traitor Robin Hood."

15. The old woman he set on a milk-white steed,
        Himselfe on a dapple-gray,
     And for joy he had got Robin Hood,
        He went laughing all the way.

16. But as they were riding the forrest along,
        The Bishop he chanc'd for to see
     A hundred brave bow-men bold
        Stand under the green-wood tree.

17. "O who is yonder," the Bishop then said,
        "That's ranging within yonder wood?"
     "Marry," says the old woman, "I think it to be
        A man calld Robin Hood."

18. "Why, who art thou," the Bishop he said,
        "Which I have here with me?"
     "Why, I am an old woman, thou cuckoldy bishop;
        Lift up my leg and see."

19. "Then woe is me," the Bishop he said,
        "That ever I saw this day!"
     He turnd him about, but Robin so stout
        Calld him, and bid him stay.

20. Then Robin took hold of the Bishop's horse,
        And ty'd him fast to a tree;
     Then Little John smil'd his master upon,
        For joy of that company.

21. Robin Hood took his mantle from's back,
         And spread it upon the ground,
     And out of the Bishop's portmantle he
         Soon told five hundred pound.

22. "So now let him go," said Robin Hood.
         Said Little John, "That may not be;
     For I vow and protest he shall sing us a mass
         Before that he goe from me."

23. Then Robin Hood took the Bishop by the hand,
         And bound him fast to a tree,
     And made him sing a mass, God wot,
         To him and his yeomandree.

24. And then they brought him through the wood,
         And set him on his dapple-gray,
     And gave the tail within his hand,
         And bade him for Robin Hood pray.

ROBIN HOOD AND THE BISHOP
OF HEREFORD (144)

Text, Elizabeth Cochrane's *Song-Book*, p. 149.

1. Some they will talk of bold Robin Hood,
        And some of barons bold,
    But I'll tell you how he servd the Bishop of Hereford,
        When he robbed him of his gold.

2. As it befel in merry Barnsdale,
        And under the green-wood tree,
    The Bishop of Hereford was to come by,
        With all his company.

3. "Come, kill a venson," said bold Robin Hood,
        "Come kill me a good fat deer;
    The Bishop of Hereford is to dine with me to-day,
        And he shall pay well for his cheer.

4. "We'll kill a fat venson," said bold Robin Hood,
        "And dress it by the highway-side;
    And we will watch the Bishop narrowly,
        Lest some other way he should ride."

5. Robin Hood dressed himself in shepherd's attire,
        With six of his men also;
    And, when the Bishop of Hereford came by,
        They about the fire did go.

6. "O what is the matter?" then said the Bishop,
    "Or for whom do you make this a-do?
    Or why do you kill the king's venson,
    When your company is so few?"

7. "We are shepherds," said bold Robin Hood,
    "And we keep sheep all the year,
    And we are disposed to be merry this day,
    And to kill of the king's fat deer."

8. "You are brave fellows!" said the Bishop,
    "And the king of your doings shall know;
    Therefore make hast and come along with me,
    For before the king you shall go."

9. "O pardon, O pardon," said bold Robin Hood,
    "O pardon, I thee pray!
    For it becomes not your lordship's coat
    To take so many lives away."

10. "No pardon, no pardon," says the Bishop,
    "No pardon I thee owe;
    Therefore make haste, and come along with me,
    For before the king you shall go."

11. Then Robin set his back against a tree,
    And his foot against a thorn,
    And from underneath his shepherd's coat
    He pulld out a bugle-horn.

12. He put the little end to his mouth,
    And a loud blast did he blow,
    Till threescore and ten of bold Robin's men
    Came running all on a row;

13. All making obeysance to bold Robin Hood;
    'T was a comely sight for to see:
    "What is the matter, master," said Little John,
    "That you blow so hastily?"

14. "O here is the Bishop of Hereford,
    And no pardon we shall have."
    "Cut off his head, master," said Little John,
    "And throw him into his grave."

15. "O pardon, O pardon," said the Bishop,
    "O pardon, I thee pray!
    For if I had known it had been you,
    I'd have gone some other way."

16. "No pardon, no pardon," said Robin Hood,
    "No pardon I thee owe;

Therefore make haste and come along with me,
For to merry Barnsdale you shall go."

17. Then Robin he took the Bishop by the hand,
And led him to merry Barnsdale;
He makd him to stay and sup with him that night,
And to drink wine, beer, and ale.

18. "Call in the reckoning," said the Bishop,
"For methinks it grows wondrous high."
"Lend me your purse, Bishop," said Little John,
"And I'll tell you bye and bye."

19. Then Little John took the bishop's cloak,
And spread it upon the ground,
And out of the bishop's portmantua
He told three hundred pound.

20. "Here's money enough, master," said Little John,
"And a comely sight 't is to see;
It makes me in charity with the Bishop,
Tho he heartily loveth not me."

21. Robin Hood took the Bishop by the hand,
And he caused the music to play,
And he made the Bishop to dance in his boots,
And glad he could get so away.

ROBIN HOOD AND QUEEN KATHERINE (145)

It is difficult to decide which of the Queen Katherines was meant here, though probably it was Catherine of Aragon or Catherine Howard. Sir Richard Lee is one of the characters in the "Geste of Robin Hood." Robin Hood according to the older tradition was born at Locksly in Yorkshire. Finsbury was a green outside of London laid out for the practice of archery.

Text, Pepys, ii, 103.

1. Gold tane from the king's harbengers,
Down a down a down
As seldome hath been seen,
Down a down a down
And carried by bold Robin Hood
For a present to the queen.
Down a down a down.

2. "If that I live a year to an end,"
Thus gan Queen Katherin say,

"Bold Robin Hood, I will be thy friend,
　And all thy yeomen gay."

3.　The queen is to her chamber gone,
　　As fast as she can wen;
　She cals unto her her lovely page,
　　His name was Richard Patringten.

4.　"Come hither to mee, thou lovely page,
　　Come thou hither to mee;
　For thou must post to Notingham,
　　As fast as thou canst dree.

5.　"And as thou goest to Notingham,
　　Search all those English wood;
　Enquire of one good yeoman or another
　　That can tell thee of Robin Hood."

6.　Sometimes he went, sometimes hee ran,
　　As fast as he could win;
　And when hee came to Notingham,
　　There he took up his inne.

7.　And when he came to Notingham,
　　And had took up his inne,
　He calls for a pottle of Renish wine,
　　And drank a health to his queen.

8.　There sat a yeoman by his side;
　　"Tell mee, sweet page," said hee,
　"What is thy business or the cause,
　　So far in the North Country?"

9.　"This is my business and the cause,
　　Sir, I'le tell it to you for good,
　To inquire of one good yeoman or another
　　To tell mee of Robin Hood."

10.　"I'le get my horse betime in the morn,
　　By it be break of day,
　And I will shew thee bold Robin Hood,
　　And all his yeomen gay."

11.　When that he came at Robin Hood's place,
　　Hee fell down on his knee;
　"Queen Katherine she doth greet you well,
　　She greets you well by mee.

12.　"She bids you post to fair London court,
　　Not fearing any thing;
　For there shall be a little sport,
　　And she hath sent you her ring."

13. Robin took his mantle from his back—
   It was of the Lincoln green—
And sent it by this lovely page,
   For a present unto the queen.

14. In summer time, when leaves grow green,
   It is a seemly sight to see
How Robin Hood himself had drest,
   And all his yeomandry.

15. He cloathed his men in Lincoln green,
   And himself in scarlet red,
Black hats, white feathers, all alike;
   Now bold Robin Hood is rid.

16. And when he came at London's court,
   Hee fell downe on his knee:
"Thou art welcome, Locksly," said the queen,
   "And all thy good yeomendree."

17. The king is into Finsbury field,
   Marching in battel ray,
And after follows bold Robin Hood,
   And all his yeomen gay.

18. "Come hither, Tepus," said the king,
   "Bow-bearer after mee,
Come measure mee out with this line
   How long our mark shall be."

19. "What is the wager?" said the queen,
   "That must I now know here."
"Three hundred tun of Renish wine,
   Three hundred tun of beer.

20. "Three hundred of the fattest harts
   That run on Dallom lee;
That's a princely wager," said the king,
   "That needs must I tell thee."

21. With that bespake one Clifton then,
   Full quickly and full soon;
"Measure no mark for us, most sovereign leige,
   Wee'l shoot at sun and moon."

22. "Ful fifteen score your mark shall be,
   Ful fifteen score shall stand."
"I'le lay my bow," said Clifton then,
   "I'le cleave the willow wand."

23. With that the king's archers led about,
    While it was three and none;
  With that the ladies began to shout,
    "Madam, your game is gone!"

24. "A boon, a boon," Queen Katherine cries,
    "I crave on my bare knee;
  Is there any knight of your privy counsel
    Of Queen Katherine's part will be?

25. "Come hither to mee, Sir Richard Lee,
    Thou art a knight full good;
  For I do know by thy pedigree
    Thou springst from Goweres blood.

26. "Come hither to me, thou Bishop of Herefordshire"—
    For a noble priest was he—
  "By my silver miter," said the bishop then,
    "I'le not bet one peny.

27. "The king hath archers of his own,
    Full ready and full light,
  And these be strangers every one,
    No man knows what they height."

28. "What wilt thou bet," said Robin Hood,
    "Thou seest our game the worse?"
  "By my silver miter," said the bishop then,
    "All the mony within my purse."

29. "What is in thy purse?" said Robin Hood,
    "Throw it down on the ground."
  "Fifteen score nobles," said the bishop then,
    "It's neer an hundred pound."

30. Robin Hood took his bagge from his side,
    And threw it down on the green;
  William Scadlocke went smiling away,
    "I know who this mony must win."

31. With that the queen's archers led about,
    While it was three and three;
  With that the ladies gave a shout,
    "Woodcock, beware thyn ee!"

32. "It is three and three, now," said the king,
    "The next three pays for all."
  Robin Hood went and whispered to the queen,
    "The kings part shall be but small."

33. Robin Hood he led about,
      He shot it under hand,
   And Clifton with a bearing arrow,
      He clave the willow wand.

34. And little Midge, the Miller's son,
      Hee shot not much the worse;
   He shot within a finger of the prick;
      "Now, bishop, beware thy purse!"

35. "A boon, a boon," Queen Katherine cries,
      "I crave on my bare knee,—
   That you will angry be with none
      That is of my party."

36. "They shall have forty days to come,
      And forty days to go,
   And three times forty to sport and play;
      Then welcome friend or fo."

37. "Then thou art welcome, Robin Hood," said the queen,
      "And so is Little John,
   So is Midge, the Miller's son;
      Thrice welcome every one."

38. "Is this Robin Hood?" the king now said;
      "For it was told to mee
   That he was slain in the pallace-gate,
      So far in the North Country."

39. "Is this Robin Hood," said the bishop then,
      "As I see well to be?
   Had I knowne that had been that bold outlaw,
      I would not have bet one peny.

40. "Hee took me late one Saturday at night,
      And bound mee fast to a tree.
   And made mee sing a mass, God wot,
      To him and his yeomendree."

41. "What and if I did?" says Robin Hood,
      "Of that mass I was full fain;
   For recompense to thee," he says,
      "Here's half thy gold again."

42. "Now nay, now nay," saies Little John,
      "Master, that shall not be;
   We must give gifts to the king's officers;
      That gold will serve thee and mee."

ROBIN HOOD'S CHASE (146)

This 17th-century ballad is a continuation of the preceding.
Text, Pepys, ii, 104.

1. Come you gallants all, to you I do call,
        With a hey down down a down down
        That now is within this place,
    For a song I will sing of Henry the king,
        How he did Robin Hood chase.

2. Queen Katherine she a match then did make,
        As plainly doth appear,
    For three hundred tun of good red wine,
        And three hundred tun of beer.

3. But yet her archers she had to seek,
        With their bows and arrows so good;
    But her mind it was bent, with a good intent,
        To send for bold Robin Hood.

4. But when bold Robin Hood he came there,
        Queen Katherine she did say,
    "Thou art welcome, Locksley," said the queen,
        "And all thy yeomen gay.

5. "For a match at shooting I have made,
        And thou my part must be."
    "If I miss the mark, be it light or dark,
        Then hanged I will be."

6. But when the game came to be playd,
        Bold Robin he then drew nigh;
    With his mantle of green, most brave to be seen,
        He let his arrows fly.

7. And when the game it ended was,
        Bold Robin wan it with a grace,
    But after, the king was angry with him,
        And vowed he would him chase.

8. What though his pardon granted was
        While he with them did stay,
    But yet the king was vexed at him
        When as he was gone his way.

9. Soon after the king from the court did hie,
        In a furious angry mood,

And often enquire, both far and near,
  After bold Robin Hood.

10. But when the king to Nottingham came,
      Bold Robin was then in the wood.
    "O come now," said he, "and let me see
      Who can find me bold Robin Hood."

11. But when that Robin Hood he did hear
      The king had him in chase,
    Then said Little John, "'T is time to be gone,
      And go to some other place."

12. Then away they went from merry Sherwood,
      And into Yorkshire he did hie,
    And the king did follow, with a hoop and a hallow,
      But could not come him nigh.

13. Yet jolly Robin he passed along,
      He went straight to Newcastle town,
    And there stayed he hours two or three,
      And then he for Berwick was gone.

14. When the king he did see how Robin did flee,
      He was vexed wondrous sore;
    With a hoop and a hallow he vowed to follow,
      And take him, or never give ore.

15. "Come now, let's away," then cries Little John,
      "Let any man follow that dare;
    To Carlile wee'l hie with our company,
      And so then to Lancaster."

16. From Lancaster then to Chester they went,
      And so did king Henery;
    But Robin away, for he durst not stay,
      For fear of some treachery.

17. Saies Robin, "Come, let us to London go,
      To see our noble queen's face;
    It may be she wants our company
      Which makes the king so us chase."

18. When Robin he came Queen Katherine before,
      He fell upon his knee.
    "If it please your Grace, I am come to this place,
      To speak with king Henery."

19. Queen Katherine she answered bold Robin again,
      "The king is gone to merry Sherwood;
    And when he went he to me did say
      He would go seek Robin Hood."

20.   "Then fare you well, my gracious queen,
          For to Sherwood I will hie apace;
      For fain would I see what he would with me,
          If I could but meet with his Grace."

21.   But when King Henery he came home,
          Full weary, and vexed in mind,
      When he did hear Robin had been there,
          He blamed Dame Fortune unkind.

22.   "You are welcome home," Queen Katherine cried,
          "Henry, my sovereign liege;
      Bold Robin Hood, that archer good,
          Your person hath been to seek."

23.   But when King Henry he did hear
          That Robin had been there him to seek,
      This answer he gave, "He's a cunning knave,
          For I have sought him this whole three weeks."

24.   "A boon! a boon!" Queen Katherine cried,
          "I beg it here on your Grace,
      To pardon his life, and seek no more strife."
          And so endeth Robin Hood's chase.

ROBIN HOOD'S GOLDEN PRIZE (147)

Stories like this have wide circulation in the Middle Ages. See the
Gesta Romanorum.
    Text, Pepys, ii, 114.

1.   I have heard talk of bold Robin Hood,
              Derry derry down
          And of brave Little John,
      Of Fryer Tuck, and Will Scarlet,
          Loxley, and Maid Marion.
              Hey down derry derry down

2.   But such a tale as this before
          I think there was never none;
      For Robin Hood disguised himself,
          And to the wood is gone.

3.   Like to a fryer, bold Robin Hood
          Was accoutered in his array;
      With hood, gown, beads, and crucifix,
          He past upon the way.

4.   He had not gone past miles two or three,
          But it was his chance to spy

Two lusty priests, clad all in black,
    Come riding gallantly.

5. "Benedicete," then said Robin Hood,
        "Some pitty on me take;
    Cross you my hand with a silver groat,
        For Our dear Ladies sake.

6. "For I have been wandring all this day,
        And nothing could I get;
    Not so much as one poor cup of drink,
        Nor bit of bread to eat."

7. "Now, by my holydame," the priests repli'd,
        "We never a peny have;
    For this morning have been robd,
        And could no mony save."

8. "I am much afraid," said bold Robin Hood,
        "That you both do tell a lye;
    And now before that you go hence,
        I am resolvd to try."

9. When as the priests heard him say so,
        Then they rode away amain;
    But Robin Hood betook him to his heels,
        And soon overtook them again.

10. Then Robin Hood laid hold of them both,
        And pulld them down from their horse:
    "O spare us, fryer!" the priests cry'd out,
        "On us have some remorse!"

11. "You said you had no mony," quoth he,
        "Wherefore, without delay,
    We three will fall down on our knees,
        And for mony we will pray."

12. The priests they could not him gainsay,
        But down they kneeled with speed;
    "Send us, O send us," then quoth they,
        "Some mony to serve our need."

13. The priests did pray with mournful chear,
        Sometimes their hands did wring,
    Sometimes they wept and cried aloud,
        Whilst Robin did merrily sing.

14. When they had been praying an hour's space,
        The priests did still lament;
    Then quoth bold Robin, "Now let's see
        What mony heaven hath us sent.

15. "We will be sharers now all alike
        Of the mony that we have;
     And there is never a one of us
        That his fellows shall deceive."

16. The priests their hands in their pockets put,
        But mony would find none:
     "We'll search our selves," said Robin Hood,
        "Each other, one by one."

17. Then Robin Hood took pains to search them both,
        And he found good store of gold;
     Five hundred peeces presently
        Vpon the grass was told.

18. "Here is a brave show," said Robin Hood,
        "Such store of gold to see,
     And you shall each one have a part,
        Cause you prayed so heartily."

19. He gave them fifty pound a-peece,
        And the rest for himself did keep;
     The priests durst not speak one word,
        But they sighed wondrous deep.

20. With that the priests rose up from their knees,
        Thinking to have parted so;
     "Nay, stay," said Robin Hood, "one thing more
        I have to say ere you go.

21. "You shall be sworn," said bold Robin Hood,
        "Vpon this holy grass,
     That you will never tell lies again,
        Which way soever you pass.

22. "The second oath that you here must take,
        All the days of your lives
     You never shall tempt maids to sin,
        Nor lye with other men's wives.

23. "The last oath you shall take, it is this,
        Be charitable to the poor;
     Say you have met with a holy fryer,
        And I desire no more."

24. He set them upon their horses again,
        And away then they did ride;
     And hee returnd to the merry green-wood,
        With great joy, mirth and pride.

ROBIN HOOD AND MAID MARIAN (150)

Maid Marian originally had nothing to do with Robin Hood or the
Robin Hood tradition. She drifted into England by way of the May
Games and folk plays. In the plays and chapbooks of the Elizabethan
period in which Robin Hood is made aristocratic and given an earl-
dom before being banished to the green wood, Maid Marion is arbi-
trarily made his lady. This is the only ballad which represents that
development of the story. It is included here for that reason, for it is
a poor thing.

Text, Ritson, *Robin Hood,* ii, 157.

1. A bonny fine maid of a noble degree,
         With a hey down down a down down
        Maid Marian calld by name,
    Did live in the North, of excellent worth,
        For she was a gallant dame.

2. For favour and face, and beauty most rare,
        Queen Hellen shee did excell;
    For Marian then was praisd of all men
        That did in the country dwell.

3. 'T was neither Rosamond nor Jane Shore,
        Whose beauty was clear and bright,
    That could surpass this country lass,
        Beloved of lord and knight.

4. The Earl of Hintington, nobly born,
        That came of noble blood,
    To Marian went, with a good intent,
        By the name of Robin Hood.

5. With kisses sweet their red lips meet,
        For shee and the earl did agree;
    In every place, they kindly imbrace,
        With love and sweet unity.

6. But fortune bearing these lovers a spight,
        That soon they were forced to part,
    To the merry green wood then went Robin Hood,
        With a sad and sorrowfull heart.

7. And Marian, poor soul, was troubled in mind,
        For the absence of her friend;
    With finger in eye, shee often did cry,
        And her person did much comend.

8. Perplexed and vexed, and troubled in mind,
   Shee drest her self like a page,
And ranged the wood to find Robin Hood,
   The bravest of men in that age.

9. With quiver and bow, sword, buckler, and all,
   Thus armed was Marian most bold,
Still wandering about to find Robin out,
   Whose person was better then gold.

10. But Robin Hood, hee himself had disguised,
   And Marian was strangly attir'd,
That they provd foes, and so fell to blowes,
   Whose vallour bold Robin admir'd.

11. They drew out their sword, and to cutting they went,
   At least an hour or more,
That the blood ran apace from bold Robin's face,
   And Marian was wonded sore.

12. "O hold thy hand, hold thy hand," said Robin Hood,
   "And thou shalt be one of my string,
To range the wood with bold Robin Hood,
   To hear the sweet nightingall sing."

13. When Marian did hear the voice of her love,
   Her self shee did quickly discover,
And with kisses sweet she did him greet,
   Like to a most loyall lover.

14. When bold Robin Hood his Marian did see,
   Good lord, what clipping was there!
With kind imbraces, and jobbing of faces,
   Providing of gallant cheer.

15. For Little John took his bow in his hand,
   And wandring in the wood,
To kill the deer, and make good chear,
   For Marian and Robin Hood.

16. A stately banquet they had full soon,
   All in a shaded bower,
Where venison sweet they had to eat,
   And were merry that present hour.

17. Great flaggons of wine were set on the board,
   And merrily they drunk round
Their boules of sack, to strengthen the back,
   Whilst their knees did touch the ground.

18. First Robin Hood began a health
   To Marian his onely dear,

And his yeomen all, both comely and tall,
    Did quickly bring up the rear.

19.   For in a brave veine they tost off their bouls,
        Whilst thus they did remain,
    And every cup, as they drunk up,
        They filled with speed again.

20.   At last they ended their merryment,
        And went to walk in the wood,
    Where Little John and Maid Marian
        Attended on bold Robin Hood.

21.   In sollid content together they livd,
        With all their yeomen gay;
    They livd by their hands, without any lands,
        And so they did many a day.

22.   But now to conclude, an end I will make
        In time, as I think it good,
    For the people that dwell in the North can tell
        Of Marian and bold Robin Hood.

SIR HUGH, OR, THE JEW'S DAUGHTER (155)

Many versions of this ballad exist in England and America. Although there is no documentary evidence of the ballad before the 17th century, the story in chronicle goes back to the 13th century. It is first related in the *Annals of the Monastery of Waverley* under the year 1255. Other chronicles of the 13th century tell the story with added details. Chaucer's *Prioress's Tale* is an analogue.

The chronicle account may be condensed as follows: Hugh and his school fellows were playing near the house where many Jews from all over England were congregated. Hugh was kidnaped by the Jews, tortured and crucified. They threw his body into a stream, but the water rejected it; then they buried the body, but the next day it was above ground. Then they threw it into a well, but at once a bright light shone from the well and a sweet odor rose from it. The miracle drew people to the spot, and they discovered the body marked as Christ had been. The Jews were caught and eighteen hanged. Other chronicles tell of the finding of the body by the boy's mother. The legend belongs to the great mass of such legends found all over Europe—stories born of superstition, covetousness, prejudice, and ignorance, and kept alive and added to by the same forces.

Text A, Jamieson, i, 151; B, traditional in England, Percy Papers; C, traditional in Indiana, printed in *JAF*, 29:165; D, traditional in Connecticut, printed in *JAF*, 29:166.

A.

1. Four and twenty bonny boys
      Were playing at the ba,
   And by it came him sweet Sir Hugh,
      And he playd o'er them a'.

2. He kickd the ba with his right foot,
      And catchd it wi his knee,
   And throuch-and-thro the Jew's window
      He gard the bonny ba flee.

3. He's doen him to the Jew's castell,
      And walkd it round about;
   And there he saw the Jew's daughter,
      At the window looking out.

4. "Throw down the ba, ye Jew's daughter,
      Throw down the ba to me!"
   "Never a bit," says the Jew's daughter,
      "Till up to me come ye."

5. "How will I come up? How can I come up?
      How can I come to thee?
   For as ye did to my auld father,
      The same ye'll do to me."

6. She's gane till her father's garden,
      And pu'd an apple red and green;
   'T was a' to wyle him sweet Sir Hugh,
      And to entice him in.

7. She's led him in through ae dark door,
      And sae has she thro nine;
   She's laid him on a dressing-table,
      And stickit him like a swine.

8. And first came out the thick, thick blood,
      And syne came out the thin,
   And syne came out the bonny heart's blood;
      There was nae mair within.

9. She's rowd him in a cake o lead,
      Bade him lie still and sleep;
   She's thrown him in Our Lady's draw-well,
      Was fifty fathom deep.

10. When bells were rung, and mass was sung,
      And a' the bairns came hame,
   When every lady gat hame her son,
      The Lady Maisry gat nane.

11.   She's taen her mantle her about,
      Her coffer by the hand,
    And she's gane out to seek her son,
      And wanderd o'er the land.

12.   She's doen her to the Jew's castell,
      Where a' were fast asleep:
    "Gin ye be there, my sweet Sir Hugh,
      I pray you to me speak."

13.   She's doen her to the Jew's garden,
      Thought he had been gathering fruit:
    "Gin ye be there, my sweet Sir Hugh,
      I pray you to me speak."

14.   She neard Our Lady's deep draw-well,
      Was fifty fathom deep:
    "Whareer ye be, my sweet Sir Hugh,
      I pray you to me speak."

15.   "Gae hame, gae hame, my mither dear,
      Prepare my winding sheet,
    And at the back o merry Lincoln
      The morn I will you meet."

16.   Now Lady Maisry is gane hame,
      Made him a winding sheet,
    And at the back o merry Lincoln
      The dead corpse did her meet.

17.   And a' the bells o merry Lincoln
      Without men's hands were rung,
    And a' the books o merry Lincoln
      Were read without man's tongue,
    And neer was such a burial
      Sin Adam's days begun.

B.

1.   Four and twenty bonny boys
      War playing at the ba;
    Then up and started sweet Sir Hew,
      The flower amang them a'.

2.   He hit the ba a kick wi's fit,
      And kept it wi his knee,
    That up into the Jew's window
      He gart the bonny ba flee.

3.   "Cast down the ba to me, fair maid,
      Cast doun the ba to me."

"O ne'er a bit o the ba ye get
    Till ye cum up to me.

4. "Cum up, sweet Hew, cum up, dear Hew,
    Cum up and get the ba."
  "I canna cum, I da na cum,
    Without my play-feres twa."

5. "Cum up, sweet Hew, cum up, dear Hew,
    Cum up and play wi me."
  "I cann cum, I darna cum,
    Without my play-feres three."

6. She's gane into the Jew's garden,
    Where the grass grew lang and green;
  She powd an apple red and white,
    To wyle the young thing in.

7. She wyl'd him into ae chamber,
    She wyl'd him into twa,
  She wyl'd him to her ain chamber,
    The fairest o them a'

8. She laid him on a dressing-board,
    Where she did sometimes dine;
  She put a penknife in his heart,
    And dressed him like a swine.

9. Then out and cam the thick, thick blude,
    Then out and cam the thin;
  Then out and cam the bonny heart's blude,
    Where a' the life lay in.

10. She rowd him in a cake of lead,
    Bad him lie still and sleep;
  She cast him in the Jew's draw-well,
    Was fifty fadom deep.

11. She's tane her mantle about her head,
    Her pike-staff in her hand,
  And prayed Heaven to be her guide
    Unto some uncouth land.

12. His mither she cam to the Jew's castle,
    And there ran thryse about:
  "O sweet Sir Hew, gif ye be here,
    I pray ye to me speak."

13. She cam into the Jew's garden,
    And there ran thryse about:
  "O sweet Sir Hew, gif ye be here,
    I pray ye to me speak."

14.   She cam unto the Jew's draw-well,
      And there ran thryse about:
    "O sweet Sir Hew, gif ye be here,
      I pray ye to me speak."

15.   "How can I speak, how dare I speak,
      How can I speak to thee?
    The Jew's penknife sticks in my heart,
      I canna speak to thee.

16.   "Gang hame, gang hame, O mither dear,
      And shape my winding sheet,
    And at the birks of Mirryland town
      There you and I shall meet."

17.   Whan bells war rung, and mass was sung,
      And a' men bound for bed,
    Every mither had her son,
      But sweet Sir Hew was dead.

C.

THE JEWISH LADY

1.   It rained a mist, it rained a mist,
      It rained all over the land;
    Till all the boys throughout the town
      Went out to toss their ball, ball, ball,
      Went out to toss their ball.

2.   At first they tossed their ball too high,
      And then again too low,
    Till over in the Jewish garden it fell,
      Where no one was darst to go, go, go,
      Where no one was darst to go.

3.   Out came a Jewish lady,
      All dressed so gay and fine.
    "Come in, my pretty little boy," she said,
      "And you shall have your ball, ball, ball,
      And you shall have your ball."

4.   At first she showed him a yellow dish apple,
      And a gay gold ring,
    And then a cherry as red as blood,
      To entice this little boy in, in, in,
      To entice this little boy in.

5.   She took him by his little white hand,
      And led him through the hall,

And then unto a cellar so deep,
　　Where no one could hear him lament, lament,
　　Where no one could hear him lament.

6.　"If any my playmates should call for me,
　　　You may tell them that I'm asleep ;
　　But if my mother should call for me,
　　　You may tell her that I am dead,
　　Aud buried with a prayer-book at my feet,
　　　And a bible at my head, head, head,
　　　And a bible at my head."

D.

1.　There was a little boy,
　　　Who tossed his ball so high ;
　　There was a little boy,
　　　Who tossed his ball so low ;

2.　He tossed his ball so low,
　　　He tossed his ball so high,
　　He tossed it into a merry Jew's garden,
　　　Where all the Jews do lie.

3.　Then out came a merry Jew's maiden,
　　　All dressed up in green ;
　　"Come here, come here, my little boy,
　　　And fetch your ball again."

4.　She enticed him with an apple,
　　　She enticed him with a pear,
　　She enticed him with a cherry red,
　　　And so she enticed him there.

5.　She led him through the garden,
　　　She led him through the hall,
　　She led him through the kitchen,
　　　Amid the servants all.

6.　She sat him on a chair of gold
　　　And gave him sugar sweet ;
　　She laid him on the dresser
　　　And killed him like a sheep.

7.　She took him to the bedroom
　　　And laid him on the bed ;
　　She put a bible at his feet
　　　And a prayer-book at his head.

8. She put a prayer-book at his head
        And a bible at his feet;
    And all the people that passed by
        Thought the little boy was asleep.

QUEEN ELEANOR'S CONFESSION (156)

This ballad is first found in broadsides of the 17th century. It is also to be found in several of the standard collections of the 18th and 19th centuries, such as Percy's *Reliques* (1765), Motherwell's *Minstrelsy,* Kinloch's *Ancient Ballads of Scotland.*

Eleanor was the wife first of Louis VII of France and then of Henry II of England. No evidence exists in history to support the story told here, or the insinuations. The situation in which a wife confesses to her husband disguised as a priest occurs widely in medieval fabliau literature; Peele uses it in his play *Edward I,* where it is told of Eleanor of Castile. In the fabliaux the wife usually penetrates the disguise and so is able to turn the confession to her advantage, a twist that makes the story more dramatic.

Text, *A Collection of Old Ballads,* i, 18.

Notes

6/2. Whitehall: royal residence in 16th and 17th centuries; it was burned in 1698. 14/3. Fair Rosamond: Rosamond Clifford, mistress of Henry II. She lived in the laybrinth of Woodstock, where, according to a legend evidently concocted after Eleanor's death, Eleanor sought her out and made her drink poison.

1. Queen Elenor was a sick woman,
        And afraid that she should dye;
    Then she sent for two fryars of France,
        For to speak with them speedily.

2. The King calld down his nobles all,
        By one, by two, and by three,
    And sent away for Earl Martial,
        For to speak with him speedily.

3. When that he came before the King,
        He fell on his bended knee;
    "A boon, a boon! our gracious king,
        That you sent so hastily."

4. "I'll pawn my living and my lands,
        My septer and my crown,
    That whatever Queen Elenor says,
        I will not write it down.

5. "Do you put on one fryar's coat,
    And I'll put on another,
    And we will to Queen Elenor go,
    One fryar like another."

6. Thus both attired then they go;
    When they came to Whitehall,
    The bells they did ring, and the quirister's sing,
    And the torches did light them all.

7. When that they came before the Queen,
    They fell on their bended knee:
    "A boon, a boon! our gracious queen,
    That you sent so hastily."

8. "Are you two fryars of France?" she said,
    "Which I suppose you be;
    But if you are two English fryars,
    Then hanged shall you be."

9. "We are two fryars of France," they said,
    "As you suppose we be;
    We have not been at any mass
    Since we came from the sea."

10. "The first vile thing that ere I did
    I will to you unfold;
    Earl Martial had my maidenhead,
    Underneath this cloath of gold."

11. "That is a vile sin," then said the king,
    "God may forgive it thee!"
    "Amen! Amen!" quoth Earl Martial,
    With a heavy heart then spoke he.

12. "The next vile thing that ere I did
    To you I'll not deny;
    I made a box of poyson strong,
    To poyson King Henery."

13. "That is a vile sin," then said the King,
    "God may forgive it thee!"
    "Amen! Amen!" quoth Earl Martial,
    "And I wish it so may be."

14. "The next vile thing that ere I did
    To you I will discover;
    I poysoned Fair Rosamond,
    All in fair Woodstock bower."

15. "That is a vile sin," then said the King,
    "God may forgive it thee!"

"Amen! Amen!" quoth Earl Martial,
    "And I wish it so may be."

16. "Do you see yonders little boy,
    A tossing of that ball?
  That is Earl Martial eldest son,
    And I love him the best of all.

17. "Do you see yonders little boy,
    A catching of the ball?
  That is King Henry's sone," she said,
    "And I love him the worst of all.

18. "His head is like unto a bull,
    His nose is like a boar."
  "No matter for that," King Henry said,
    "I love him the better therefore."

19. The King pulld of his fryar's coat,
    And appeard all in red;
  She shrieked and she cry'd, she wrong her hands,
    And said she was betrayd.

20. The King looked over his left shoulder,
    And a grim look looked he,
  And said, "Earl Martial, but for my oath,
    Then hanged shouldst thou be."

GUDE WALLACE (157)

Eight variants of this ballad exist from the 18th and 19th centuries, though it is probably somewhat older in oral tradition. It is based on Blind Harry's *Wallace* (c. 1465), the metrical life of Sir William Wallace, national hero of Scotland (1270–1305). All variants develop an incident related in *Wallace*, 5th book, lines 1080–1119; two of the versions preface this incident with an account also derived from *Wallace*, 4th book, lines 704–787. This tells of Wallace coming to the home of his lady and discovering that she has sold him to the English but that now she is repentant; she helps Wallace clothe himself in her garments and so escape the ambush (Alexander Laing, *Thistle of Scotland*, p. 100).

Text, Maidment, *Scottish Ballads and Songs*, p. 83.

1. "Had we a king," said Wallace then,
    "That our kind Scots might live by their own!
  But betwixt me and the English blood
    I think there is an ill seed sown."

2. Wallace him over a river lap,
       He lookd low down to a linn;
    He was war of gay lady
       Was even at the well washing.

3. "Well mot ye fare, fair maiden," he said,
       "And ay well mot ye fare and see!
    Have ye any tidings me to tell,
       I pray you'll show them unto me."

4. "I have no tidings you to tell,
       Nor yet no tidings you to ken;
    But into that hostler's house
       There's fifteen of your Englishmen.

5. "And they are seeking Wallace there,
       For they've ordained him to be slain."
    "O God forbid!" said Wallace then,
       For he's o'er good a kind Scotsman.

6. "But had I money me upon,
       And evn this day, as I have none,
    Then would I to that hostler's house,
       And evn as fast as I could gang."

7. She put her hand in her pocket,
       She told him twenty shillings o'er her knee;
    Then he took off both hat and hood,
       And thankd the lady most reverently.

8. "If e'er I come this way again,
       Well paid your money it shall be."
    Then he took off both hat and hood,
       And thankd the lady most reverently.

9. He leand him twofold o'er a staff,
       So did he threefold o'er a tree,
    And he's away to the hostler's house,
       Even as fast as he might dree.

10. When he came to the hostler's house,
       He said, "Good-ben be here!" quoth he.
    And English captain, being deep load,
       He asked him right cankerdly,

11. "Where was you born, thou crooked carle,
       And in what place, and what country?"
    "'Tis I was born in fair Scotland,
       A crooked carle although I be."

12. The English captain swore by th' rood,
       "We are Scotsmen as well as thee,

And we are seeking Wallace; then
  To have him merry we should be."

13. "The man," said Wallace, "Ye're looking for,
  I seed him within these days three;
And he has slain an English captain,
  And ay the fearder the rest may be."

14. "I'd give twenty shillings," said the captain,
  "To such a crooked carle as thee,
If you would take me to the place
  Where that I might proud Wallace see."

15. "Hold out your hand," said Wallace then,
  "And show your money and be free,
For tho you'd bid an hundred pound,
  I never bade a better bode," said he.

16. He struck the captain oer the chafts,
  Till that he never chewed more;
He stickd the rest about the board,
  And left them all a sprawling there.

17. "Rise up, goodwife," said Wallace then,
  "And give me something for to eat;
For it's near two days to an end
  Since I tasted one bit of meat."

18. His board was scarce well covered,
  Nor yet his dine well scantly dight,
Till fifteen other Englishmen
  Down all about the door did light.

19. "Come out, come out," said they, "Wallace!" Then,
  "For the day is come that ye must die."
And they thought so little of his might,
  But ay the fearder they might be.

20. The wife ran but, the gudeman ran ben,
  It put them all into a fever;
Then five he sticked where they stood,
  And five he trampled in the gutter.

21. And five he chased to yon green wood,
  He hanged them all out-oer a grain;
And gainst the morn at twelve o'clock,
  He dined with his kind Scottish men.

THE BATTLE OF OTTERBURN (161)

This ballad celebrates the Battle of Otterburne, fought in 1388 near Otterburne in Northumberland between a raiding host of Scots under James, Earl of Douglas, and the English led by Henry Percy. It was a bitter fight, but the Scots won, though Douglas was killed. Read the spirited account in Froissart's *Chronicles* (Ch. xxxviii of the Thomas Johnes translation).

Manuscript copies of the 16th century survive; but probably ballads concerned with this battle existed from the time of the event. The six versions vary in details but agree in substance.

Text A, Cotton MS. Cleopatra C.iv (c. 1550); B, Scott, i, 345.

Notes

1/1. Lamasse: The festival of the wheat harvest, held August 12, at which a loaf of new wheat bread was offered to the church. The battle took place on August 19. 2/1. yerlle of Fyffe . . . Sulway: The earl of Fyfe was one of the leaders of the Scotch western army that moved to attack Carlisle on the Solway; the eastern army drove toward Durham and Newcastle. 3. All place names in Northumberland. 8/1. Percy: Hotspur, 1364–1403. See Shakespeare's *Richard II* and *1 Henry IV*. He was captured by the Scotch at Otterburn, was killed in the Battle of Shrewsbury. 35/2. cronykle: The deference to source is common among the romance writers; here it certainly suggests a conscious working of the ballad from written sources. 38. May be founded on the fact that Percy rushed into the battle without waiting for the men arriving with the Bishop of Durham. 49. Not accurate. The fighting was hand to hand; the archers had no part. 50. Again not accurate. Douglas and Percy did not fight against one another. Douglas was wounded but ordered his banner be kept flying so that his men would not know. Other versions of the ballad say that one of his own men killed him. 62. The Scots' losses are grossly exaggerated.

A.

1. Yt fell abowght the Lamasse tyde,
      Whan husbondes wynnes ther haye,
    The dowghtye Dowglasse bowynd hym to ryde,
      In Ynglond to take a praye.

2. The yerlle of Fyffe, wythowghten stryffe,
      He bowynd hym over Sulway;
    The grete wolde ever to-gether ryde;
      That raysse they may rewe for aye.

3. Over Hoppertope hyll they cam in,
    And so down by Rodclyffe crage;
   Vpon Grene Lynton they lyghted dowyn,
    Styrande many a stage.

4. And boldely brente Northomberlond,
    And haryed many a townyn;
   They dyd owr Ynglyssh men grete wrange,
    To batell that were not bowyn.

5. Than spake a berne vpon the bent,
    Of comforte that was not colde,
   And sayd, "We haue brente Northomberlond,
    We haue all welth in holde.

6. "Now we haue haryed all Bamborowe schyre,
    All the welth in the worlde haue wee,
   I rede we ryde to New Castell,
    So styll and stalworthlye."

7. Vpon the morrowe, when it was day,
    The standerds schone full bryght;
   To the Newe Castell the toke the waye,
    And thether they cam full ryght.

8. Syr Henry Perssy laye at the New Castell,
    I tell yow wythowtten drede;
   He had byn a march-man all hys dayes,
    And kepte Barwyke vpon Twede.

9. To the Newe Castell when they cam,
    The Skottes they cryde on hyght,
   "Syr Hary Perssy, and thou byste within,
    Com to the fylde, and fyght.

10. "For we haue brente Northomberlonde,
    Thy erytage good and ryght,
   And syne my logeyng I haue take
    Wyth my brande dubbyd many a knyght."

11. Syr Harry Perssy cam to the walles,
    The Skottyssch oste for to se;
   And sayd, "And thou hast brente Northomberlond,
    Full sore it rewyth me.

12. "Yf thou hast haryed all Bamborowe schyre,
    Thow hast done me grete envye;
   For the trespasse thow hast me done,
    The tone of vs schall dye."

13. "Where schall I byde the?" sayd the Dowglas,
    "Or where wylte thow com to me?"

"At Otterbourne, in the hygh way,
　　Ther mast thow well logeed be.

14.　"The roo full rekeles ther sche rinnes,
　　　To make the game and glee;
　　The fawken and the fesaunt both,
　　　Among the holtes on hye.

15.　"Ther mast thow haue thy welth at wyll,
　　　Well looged ther mast be;
　　Yt schall not be long or I com the tyll,"
　　　Sayd Syr Harry Perssye.

16.　"Ther schall I byde the," sayd the Dowglas,
　　　"By the fayth of my bodye."
　　"Thether schall I com," sayd Syr Harry Perssy,
　　　"My trowth I plyght to the."

17.　A pype of wyne he gaue them over the walles,
　　　For soth as I yow saye;
　　Ther he mayd the Dowglasse drynke,
　　　And all hys ost that daye.

18.　The Dowglas turnyd hym homewarde agayne,
　　　For soth withowghten naye;
　　He toke hys logeyng at Oterborne,
　　　Vpon a Wedynsday.

19.　And ther he pyght hys standerd dowyn,
　　　Hys gettyng more and lesse,
　　And syne he warned hys men to goo
　　　To chose ther geldynges gresse.

20.　A Skottysshe knyght hoved vpon the bent,
　　　A wache I dare well saye;
　　So was he ware on the noble Perssy,
　　　In the dawnyng of the daye.

21.　He prycked to hys pavyleon-dore,
　　　As faste as he myght ronne;
　　"Awaken, Dowglas," cryed the knyght,
　　　"For hys love that syttes in trone.

22.　"Awaken, Dowglas," cryed the knyght,
　　　"For thow maste waken wyth wynne;
　　Yender haue I spyed the prowde Perssye,
　　　And seven stondardes wyth hym."

23.　"Nay by my trowth," the Dowglas sayed,
　　　"It ys but a fayned taylle;
　　He durst not loke on my brede banner
　　　For all Ynglonde so haylle.

24. "Was I not yesterdaye at the Newe Castell,
    That stondes so fayre on Tyne?
For all the men the Perssy had,
    He coude not garre me ones to dyne."

25. He stepped owt at his pavelyon-dore,
    To loke and it were lesse:
"Araye yow, lordynges, one and all,
    For here bygynnes no peysse.

26. "The yerle of Mentaye, thow arte my eme,
    The forwarde I gyve to the.
The yerlle of Huntlay, cawte and kene,
    He schall be wyth the.

27. "The lorde of Bowghan, in armure bryght,
    On the other hand he schall be;
Lord Jhonstoune and Lorde Maxwell,
    They to schall be wyth me.

28. "Swynton, fayre fylde vpon your pryde!
    To batell make yow bowen
Syr Davy Skotte, Syr Walter Stewarde,
    Syr Jhon of Agurstone!"

29. The Perssy cam byfore hys oste,
    Wych was ever a gentyll knyght;
Vpon the Dowglas lowde can he crye,
    "I wyll holde that I haue hyght.

30. "For thou hast brente Northomberlonde,
    And done me grete envye;
For thys trespasse thou hast me done,
    The tone of vs schall dye."

31. The Dowglas answerde hym agayne,
    Wyth grett wurdes vpon hye,
And sayd, "I haue twenty agaynst thy one,
    Byholde, and thou maste see."

32. Wyth that the Perssy was grevyd sore,
    For soth as I yow saye;
He lyghted down vpon his foote,
    And schoote hys horsse clene awaye.

33. Euery man sawe that he dyd soo,
    That ryall was euer in rowght;
Euery man schoote hys horsse hym froo,
    And lyght hym rowynde abowght.

34. Thus Syr Hary Perssye toke the fylde,
    For soth as I yow saye;

Jhesu Cryste in hevyn on hyght
   Dyd helpe hym well that daye.

35. But nyne thowzand, ther was no moo,
     The cronykle wyll not layne;
   Forty thowsande of Skottes and fowre
     That day fowght them agayne.

36. But when the batell byganne to ioyne.
     In hast ther cam knyght;
   The letters fayre furth hath he tayne,
     And thus he sayd full ryght;

37. "My lorde your father he gretes yow well,
     Wyth many a noble knyght;
   He desyres yow to byde
     That he may see thys fyght.

38. "The Baron of Grastoke ys com out of the west,
     Wyth hym a noble companye;
   All they loge at your fathers thys nyght,
     And the batell fayne wolde they see."

39. "For Jhesus love," sayd Syr Harye Perssy,
     "That dyed for yow and me,
   Wende to my lorde my father agayne,
     And saye thow sawe me not wyth yee.

40. "My trowth ys plyght of yonne Skottysh knyght,
     It nedes me not to layne,
   That I schulde byde hym vpon thys bent,
     And I haue hys trowth agayne.

41. "And if that I weynde of thys growende,
     For soth, onfowghten awaye,
   He wolde me call but a kowarde knyght
     In hys londe another daye.

42. "Yet had I lever to be rynde and rente,
     By Mary, that mykkel maye,
   Then ever my manhood schulde be reprovyd
     Wyth a Skotte another day.

43. "Wherfore schote, archars, for my sake,
     And let scharpe arowes flee;
   Mynstrells, playe vp for your waryson,
     And well quyt it schall bee.

44. "Euery man thynke on hys trewe-love,
     And marke hym to the Trenite;
   For to God I make myne avowe
     Thys day wyll I not flee."

45. The blodye harte in the Dowglas armes,
    Hys standerde stoode on hye,
  That euery man myght full well knowe;
    By syde stode starrës thre.

46. The whyte lyon on the Ynglyssh perte,
    For soth as I yow sayne,
  The lucettes and the cressawntes both
    The Skottes favght them agayne.

47. Vpon Sent Androwe lowde can they crye,
    And thrysse they schowte on hyght,
  And syne merked them one owr Ynglysshe men,
    As I haue tolde yow ryght.

48. Sent George the bryght, owr ladyes knyght,
    To name they were full fayne;
  Owr Ynglyssh men they cryde on hyght,
    And thrysse the schowtte agayne.

49. Wyth that scharpe arowes bygan to flee,
    I tell yow in sertayne;
  Men of armes byganne to joyne,
    Many a dowghty man was ther slayne.

50. The Perssy and the Dowglas mette,
    That ether of other was fayne;
  They swapped together whyll that the swette,
    Wyth swordes of fyne collayne.

51. Tyll the bloode from ther bassonnettes ranne,
    As the roke doth in the rayne;
  "Yelde the to me," sayd the Dowglas,
    "Or elles thow schalt be slayne.

52. "For I see by thy bryght bassonet,
    Thow arte sum man of myght;
  And so I do by thy burnysshed brande;
    Thow arte an yerle, or elles a knyght."

53. "By my good faythe," sayd the noble Perssye,
    "Now haste thow rede full ryght;
  Yet wyll I never yelde me to the,
    Whyll I may stonde and fyght."

54. They swapped together whyll that they swette,
    Wyth swordës scharpe and long;
  Ych on the other so faste thee beette,
    Tyll ther helmes cam in peyses dowyn.

55. The Perssy was a man of strenghth,
    I tell yow in thys stounde;

He smote the Dowglas at the swordës length
 That he felle to the growynde.

56. The sworde was scharpe, and sore can byte,
  I tell yow in sertayne;
 To the harte he cowde hym smyte,
  Thus was the Dowglas slayne.

57. The stonderdes stode styll on eke a syde,
  Wyth many a grevous grone;
 Ther the fowght the day, and all the nyght,
  And many a dowghty man was slayne.

58. Ther was no freke that ther wolde flye,
  But styffely in stowre can stond,
 Ychone hewyng on other whyll they myght drye,
  Wyth many a bayllefull bronde.

59. Ther was slayne vpon the Skottës syde,
  For soth and sertenly,
 Syr James a Dowglas ther was slayne,
  That day that he cowde dye.

60. The yerlle of Mentaye he was slayne,
  Grysely groned vpon the growynd;
 Syr Davy Skotte, Syr Walter Stewarde,
  Syr Jhon of Agurstoune.

61. Syr Charllës Morrey in that place,
  That never a fote wold flee;
 Syr Hewe Maxwell, a lorde he was,
  Wyth the Dowglas dyd he dye.

62. Ther was slayne vpon the Skottës syde,
  For soth as I yow saye,
 Of fowre and forty thowsande Scottes
  Went but eyghtene awaye.

63. Ther was slayne vpon the Ynglysshe syde,
  For soth and sertenlye,
 A gentell knyght, Syr Jhon Fechewe,
  Yt was the more pety.

64. Syr James Hardbotell ther was slayne,
  For hym ther hartes were sore;
 The gentyll Lovell ther was slayne,
  That the Perssys standerd bore.

65. Ther was slayne vpon the Ynglyssh perte,
  For soth as I yow saye,
 Of nyne thowsand Ynglyssh men
  Fyve hondert cam away.

66. The other were slayne in the fylde;
    Cryste kepe ther sowlles from wo!
    Seyng ther was so fewe fryndes
    Agaynst so many a foo.

67. Then on the morne they mayde them beerys
    Of byrch and haysell graye;
    Many a wydowe, wyth wepyng teyres,
    Ther makes they fette awaye.

68. Thys fraye bygan at Otterborn,
    Bytwene the nyght and the day;
    Ther the Dowglas lost hys lyffe,
    And the Perssy was lede awaye.

69. Then was ther a Scottysh prisoner tayne,
    Syr Hewe Mongomery was hys name;
    For soth as I yow saye,
    He borowed the Perssy home agayne.

70. Now let vs all for the Perssy praye
    To Jhesu most of myght,
    To bryng hys sowlle to the blysse of heven,
    For he was a gentyll knyght.

B.

1. It fell about the Lammas tide,
   When the muir-men win their hay,
   The doughty Douglas bound him to ride
   Into England, to drive a prey.

2. He chose the Gordons and the Graemes,
   With them the Lindesays, light and gay;
   But the Jardines wald not with him ride,
   And they rue it to this day.

3. And he has burnd the dales of Tyne,
   And part of Bambrough shire,
   And three good towers on Reidswire fells,
   He left them all on fire.

4. And he marchd up to Newcastle,
   And rode it round about:
   "O wha's the lord of this castle?
   Or wha's the lady o 't?"

5. But up spake proud Lord Percy then,
   And O but he spake hie.
   "I am the lord of this castle,
   My wife's the lady gay."

6. "If thou 'rt the lord of this castle,
      Sae weel it pleases me,
   For ere I cross the Border fells,
      The tane of us shall die."

7. He took a lang spear in his hand,
      Shod with the metal free,
   And for to meet the Douglas there
      He rode right furiouslie.

8. But O how pale his lady lookd,
      Frae aff the castle-wa,
   When down before the Scottish spear
      She saw proud Percy fa.

9. "Had we twa been upon the green,
      And never an eye to see,
   I wad hae had you, flesh and fell,
      But your sword sall gae wi me."

10. "But gae ye up to Otterbourne,
      And, wait there dayis three,
   And, if I come not ere three dayis end,
      A fause knight ca ye me."

11. "The Otterbourne's a bonnie burn;
      'T is pleasant there to be;
   But there is nought at Otterbourne
      To feed my men and me.

12. "The deer rins wild on hill and dale,
      The birds fly wild from tree to tree;
   But there is neither bread nor kale
      To feed my men and me.

13. "Yet I will stay at Otterbourne,
      Where you shall welcome be;
   And, if ye come not at three dayis end,
      A fause lord I'll ca thee."

14. "Thither will I come," proud Percy said,
      "By the might of Our Ladye."
   "There will I bide thee," said the Douglas,
      "My troth I plight to thee."

15. They lighted high on Otterbourne,
      Upon the bent sae brown;
   They lighted high on Otterbourne,
      And threw their pallions down.

16. And he that had a bonnie boy,
      Sent out his horse to grass;

And he that had not a bonnie boy,
    His ain servant he was.

17. But up then spake a little page,
    Before the peep of dawn:
  "O waken ye, waken ye, my good lord,
    For Percy's hard at hand."

18. "Ye lie, ye lie, ye liar loud!
    Sae loud I hear ye lie:
  For Percy had not men yestreen
    To fight my men and me.

19. "But I have dreamd a dreary dream;
    Beyond the Isle of Sky,
  I saw a dead man win a fight,
    And I think that man was I."

20. He belted on his guid braid sword,
    And to the field he ran,
  But he forgot the helmet good,
    That should have kept his brain.

21. When Percy wi the Douglas met,
    I wat he was fu fain;
  They swakked their swords, till sair they swat,
    And the blood ran down like rain.

22. But Percy with his good broad sword,
    That could so sharply wound,
  Has wounded Douglas on the brow,
    Till he fell to the ground.

23. Then he calld on his little foot-page,
    And said, "Rune speedilie,
  And fetch my ain dear sister's son,
    Sir Hugh Montgomery."

24. "My nephew good," the Douglas said,
    "What recks the death of ane!
  Last night I dreamd a dreary dream,
    And I ken the day's thy ain.

25. "My wound is deep; I fain would sleep;
    Take thou the vanguard of the three,
  And hide me by the braken-bush,
    That grows on yonder lilye lee.

26. "O bury me by the braken-bush,
    Beneath the blooming brier;
  Let never living mortal ken
    That a kindly Scot lies here."

27.   He lifted up that noble lord,
         Wi the sault tear in his ee;
      He hid him in the braken-bush,
         That his merrie men might not see.

28.   The moon was clear, the day drew near,
         The spears in flinders flew,
      But mony a gallant Englishman
         Ere day the Scotsmen slew.

29.   The Gordons good, in English blood
         They steepd their hose and shoon;
      The Lindsays flew like fire about,
         Till all the fray was done.

30.   The Percy and Montgomery met,
         That either of other were fain;
      They swapped swords, and they twa swat,
         And aye the blood ran down between.

31.   "Now yield thee, yield thee, Percy," he said,
         "Or else I vow I'll lay thee low!"
      "To whom must I yield," quoth Earl Percy,
         "Now that I see it must be so?"

32.   "Thou shalt not yield to lord nor loun,
         Nor yet shalt thou yield to me;
      But yield thee to the braken-bush,
         That grows upon yon lilye lee."

33.   "I will not yield to a braken-bush,
         Nor yet will I yield to a brier;
      But I would yield to Earl Douglas,
         Or Sir Hugh the Montgomery, if he were here."

34.   As soon as he knew it was Montgomery,
         He struck his sword's point in the gronde;
      The Montgomery was a courteous knight,
         And quickly took him by the honde.

35.   This deed was done at the Otterbourne,
         About the breaking of the day;
      Earl Douglas was buried at the braken-bush,
         And the Percy led captive away.

THE HUNTING OF THE CHEVIOT (162)

This is one of the most famous of all ballads, because it is innately a beautiful and stirring dramatic poem and because of the praise it has had from Sidney, Addison, and others. Sidney's words might apply to the preceding ballad, but the fact that this one was known to be popular in his time suggests that he had this one in mind: "Certainly I must confess my own barbarousness. I never heard the olde song of Percy and Douglas that I found not my heart moved more then with a trumpet and yet it is sung but by some blinde crouder, with no rougher voyce then rude stil: which being so evill apparelled in the dust and cobwebbes of that uncivill age, what would it worke trymmed in the gorgeous eloquence of Pindar." Sidney is probably referring to a version very like that preserved in MS. Ashmole 48, Bodleian, c. 1550. The version generally known from the 17th century down is the broadside version of which many copies survive. This is the version Addison praised in the *Spectator*, Nos. 70 and 74, and probably the one Johnson meant when he said that he had rather been the author of Chevy Chase than all his works. Since it is the one so generally known and since the language is simpler, it has been included here with the earlier and more traditional version. A comparison of the two versions is interesting as showing the difference between a traditional ballad and one worked over for broadside publication.

"Chevy Chase" is probably concerned with the same conflict as the preceding ballad, but it takes much more liberty—perhaps consciously —with history.

Text A, MS. Ashmole, 48, Bodleian, c. 1550; B, Percy MS., p. 188; C, traditional in Maine, Barry, p. 242.

Notes

1. Note that Percy is the aggressor as he raids into Scotland, and that it is a poaching raid more in keeping with knighthood than a cattle raiding. Chevy is a shortened form of Cheviot, the hills between England and Scotland.

63. This stanza illustrates the confusion of history in the ballad (not that it matters); the Battle of Homildon was fought fourteen years later between English and Scots, and Percy, said to be killed at "Chevy Chase," was in command of the English.

A.

1. The Persë owt off Northombarlonde,
        and avowe to God mayd he
   That he wold hunte in the mowntayns
        off Chyviat within days thre,
   In the magger of doughtë Dogles,
        and all that euer with him be.

2. The fattiste hartes in all Cheviat
        He sayd he wold kyll, and cary them away.
   "By my feth," sayd the dougheti Doglas agayn,
        "I wyll let that honytyng yf that I may."

3. Then the Persë owt off Banborowe cam,
    with him a myghtee meany,
   With fiftene hondrith archares bold off blood and bone;
    the wear chosen owt of shyars thre.

4. This begane on a Monday at morn,
    in Cheviat the hillys so he;
   The chylde may rue that ys vn-born,
    it wos the mor pittë.

5. The dryvars thorowe the woodës went
    for to reas the dear;
   Bomen byckarte vppone the bent
    with ther browd aros cleare.

6. Then the wyld thorowe the woodës went,
    on euery syde shear;
   Greahondes thorowe the grevis glent,
    for to kyll thear dear.

7. This begane in Chyviat the hyls abone,
    yerly on a Monnyn-day;
   Be that it drewe to the oware off none,
    a hondrith fat hartës ded ther lay.

8. The blewe a mort vppone the bent,
    the semblyde on sydis shear;
   To the quyrry then the Persë went,
    to see the bryttlynge off the deare.

9. He sayd, "It was the Duglas promys
    this day to met me hear;
   But I wyste he wolde faylle, verament;
    a great oth the Persë swear."

10. At the laste a squyar off Northomberlonde
    lokyde at his hand full ny;
    He was war a the doughetie Doglas commynge
    with him a myghttë meany.

11. Both with spear, bylle, and brande,
    yt was a myghtti sight to se;
    Hardyar men, both off hart nor hande,
    wear not in Cristiantë.

12. The wear twenti hondrith spear-men good,
    without any feale;
    The wear borne along be the watter a Twyde,
    yth bowndës of Tividale.

13. "Leave of the brytlyng of the dear," he sayd,
    "and to your boys lock ye tayk good hede;

For neuer sithe ye wear on your mothar's borne
    had ye neuer so mickle nede."

14. The dougheti Dogglas on a stede,
      he rode alle his men beforne;
    His armor glytteryde as dyd a glede;
      a boldar barne was never born.

15. "Tell me whos men ye ar," he says,
      "or whos men that ye be.
    Who gave youe leave to hunte in this Chyviat chays
      in the spyt of myn and of me."

16. The first mane that ever him an answear mayd,
      yt was the good lord Persë:
    "We wyll not tell the whoys men we ar," he says,
      "nor whos men that we be;
    But we wyll hounte hear in this chays,
      in the spyt of thyne and of the.

17. "The fattiste hartës in all Chyviat
      we haue kyld, and cast to carry them away."
    "Be my troth," sayd the doughetë Dogglas agayn,
      "therfor the ton of vs shall de this day."

18. Then sayd the doughtë Doglas
      unto the lord Persë:
    "To kyll alle thes giltles men,
      alas, it wear great pittë!

19. "But, Persë, thowe art a lord of lande,
      I am a yerle callyd within my contrë;
    Let all our men vppon a parti stande,
      and do the battell off the and of me."

20. "Nowe Cristes cors on his crowne," sayd the Lorde Persë,
      "who-so-euer ther-to says nay!
    Be my troth, doughttë Doglas," he says,
      "thow shalt neuer se that day.

21. "Nethar in Ynglonde, Skottlonde, nar France,
      nor for no man of a woman born,
    But, and fortune be my chance,
      I dar met him on man for on."

22. Then bespayke a squyar off Northombarlonde,
      Richard Wytharyngton was his nam;
    "It shall neuer be told in Sothe-Ynglonde," he says,
      "to Kyng Herry the Fourth for sham.

23. "I wat youe byn great lordës twaw,
      I am a poor squyar of lande;

I wylle neuer se my captayne fyght on a fylde,
   and stande my selffe and loocke on,
But whylle I may my weppone welde,
   I wylle not fayle both hart and hande."

24. That day, that day, that dredfull day!
     that first fit here I fynde;
   And youe wyll here any more a the hountynge a the Chyviat,
     yet ys ther mor behynde.

25. The Yngglyshe men hade ther bowys yebent,
     ther hartes were good yenoughe;
   The first off arros that the shote off,
     seven skore spear-men the sloughe.

26. Yet byddys the yerle Doglas vppon the bent,
     a captayne good yenoughe,
   And that was sene verament,
     for he wrought hom both woo and wouche.

27. The Dogglas partyd his ost in thre,
     lyk a cheffe cheften off pryde;
   With suar spears off myghttë tre,
     the cum in on euery syde;

28. Thrughe our Yngglyshe archery
     gave many a wounde fulle wyde;
   Many a doughtetë the garde to dy,
     which ganyde them no pryde.

29. The Ynglyshe men let ther boys be,
     and puled owt brandes that wer brighte;
   It was a hevy syght to se
     bryght swordes on basnites lyght.

30. Thorowe ryche male and myneyeple,
     many sterne the strocke done streght;
   Many a freyke that was fulle fre,
     ther vndar foot dyd lyght.

31. At last the Duglas and the Persë met,
     lyk to captayns of myght and of mayne;
   The swapte togethar tylle the both swat,
     with swordes that wear of fyn myllan.

32. Thes worthë freckys for to fyght,
     ther-to the wear fulle fayne,
   Tylle the bloode owte off thear basnetes sprente,
     as euer dyd heal or rayn.

33. "Yelde the, Persë," sayde the Doglas,
     "and i feth I shalle the brynge

Wher thowe shalte haue a yerls wagis
    of Jamy our Skottish kynge.

34. "Thoue shalte haue thy ransom fre,
      I hight the hear this thinge;
    For the manfullyste man yet art thowe
      that euer I conqueryd in filde fighttynge."

35. "Nay," sayd the lord Persë,
      "I tolde it the beforne,
    That I wolde neuer yeldyde be
      to no man of a woman born."

36. With that ther cam an arrowe hastely,
      forthe off a myghttë wane;
    Hit hathe strekene the yerle Duglas
      in at the brest-bane.

37. Thorowe lyvar and longës bathe
      the sharpe arrowe ys gane,
    That neuer after in all his lyffe-days
      he spayke mo wordës but ane,
    That was, "Fyghte ye, my myrry men, whyllys ye may,
      for my lyff-days ben gan."

38. The Persë leanyde on his brande,
      and sawe the Duglas de;
    He tooke the dede mane by the hande,
      and sayd, "Wo ys me for the!

39. "To haue savyde thy lyffe, I wolde haue partyde with
      my landes for years thre,
    For a better man, of hart nare of hande,
      was nat in all the north contrë."

40. Off all that se a Skottishe knyght,
      was callyd Ser Hewe the Monggombyrry;
    He sawe the Duglas to the deth was dyght,
      he spendyd a spear, a trusti tre.

41. He rod vppone a corsiare
      throughe a hondrith archery;
    He neuer stynttyde, nar neuer blane,
      tylle he cam to the good lord Persë.

42. He set vppone the lorde Persë
      a dynte that was full soare;
    With a suar spear of a myghtte tre
      clean thorow the body he the Persë ber,

43. A the tothar syde that a man myght se
      a large cloth-yard and mare;

Towe bettar captayns wear nat in Cristiantë
than that day slan wear ther.

44. An archar off Northomberlonde
say slean was the lord Persë;
He bar a bende bowe in his hand,
was made off trusti tre.

45. An arow that a cloth-yarde was lang
to the harde stele halyde he;
A dynt that was both sad and soar
he sat on Ser Hewe the Monggombyrry.

46. The dynt yt was both sad and sar
that he of Monggomberry sete;
The swane-fethars that his arrowe bar
with his hart-blood the wear wete.

47. Ther was neuer a freake wone foot wolde fle,
but still in stour dyd stand,
Heawyng on yche othar, whylle the myghte dre,
with many a balfull brande.

48. This battell begane in Chyviat
an owar befor the none,
And when even-songe bell was rang,
the battell was nat half done.

49. The tocke—on ethar hande
be the lyght off the mone;
Many hade no strenght for to stande,
in Chyviat the hillys abon.

50. Of fifteen hondrith archars of Ynglonde
went away but seuenti and thre;
Of twenti hondrith spear-men of Skotlonde,
but even five and fifti.

51. But all wear slayne Cheviat within;
the hade no strengthe to stand on hy;
the chylde may rue that ys unborne,
it was the mor pittë.

52. Thear was slayne, withe the lord Persë,
Ser Johan of Agerstone,
Ser Rogar, the hinde Hartly,
Ser Wyllyam, the bolde Hearone.

53. Ser Jorg, the worthë Loumle,
a knyghte of great renowen,
Ser Raff, the ryche Rugbe,
with dyntes wear beaten dowene.

54. For Wetharryngton my harte was wo,
    that euer he slayne shulde be;
  For when both his leggis wear hewyne in to,
    yet he knyled and fought on hys kny.

55. Ther was slayne, with the dougheti Duglas,
    Ser Hewe the Monggombyrry,
  Ser Dauy Lwdale, that worthë was,
    his sistars son was he.

56. Ser Charls a Murrë in that place,
    that neuer a foot wolde fle;
  Ser Hewe Maxwelle, a lorde he was,
    with the Doglas dyd he dey.

57. So on the morrowe the mayde them byears
    off birch and hasell so gray;
  Many wedous, with wepyng tears,
    cam to fache ther makys away.

58. Tivydale may carpe off care,
    Northombarlond may mayk great mon,
  For towe such captayns as slayne wear thear
    on the March-parti shall neuer be non.

59. Word ys commen to Eddenburrowe,
    to Jamy the Skottishe kynge,
  That dougheti Duglas, lyff-tenant of the Marches,
    he lay slean Chyviot within.

60. His handdës dyd he weal and wryng,
    he sayd, alas, and woe ys me!
  Such an othar captayn Skotland within,
    he sayd, ye-feth shuld neuer be.

61. Word ys commyn to lovy Londone,
    till the fourth Harry our kynge,
  That lord Persë, leyff-tenante of the Marchis,
    he lay slayne Chyviat within.

62. "God haue merci on his solle," sayde Kyng Harry,
    "good lord, yf they will it be!
  I haue a hondrith captayns in Ynglonde," he sayd,
    "as good as euer was he:
  But, Persë, and I brook my lyffe,
    thy deth well quyte shall be."

63. As our noble kynge mayd his avowe,
    lyke a noble prince of renowen,
  For the deth of the lord Persë
    he dyde the battell of Hombyll-down;

64. Wher syx and thrittë Skottishe knyghtes
       on a day wear beaten down;
    Glendale glytteryde on ther armor bryght,
       over castille, towar, and town.

65. This was the hontynge off the Cheviat,
       that tear begane this spurn;
    Old men that knowen the grownede well yenoughe
       call it the battell of Otterburn.

66. At Otterburn begane this spurne,
       vppone a Monnynday;
    Ther was the doughtë Doglas slean,
       the Persë neuer went away.

67. Ther was neuer a tym on the Marche-partës
       sen the Doglas and the Persë met,
    But yt ys mervele and the rede blude ronne not,
       as the reane doys in the stret.

68. Ihesue Crist our balys bete,
       and to the blys vs brynge!
    Thus was the hountynge of the Chivyat:
       God send vs alle good endyng!

B.

1. God prosper long our noble king,
       our liffes and saftyes all!
    A woefull hunting once there did
       in Cheuy Chase befall.

2. To driue the deere with hound and horne
       Erle Pearcy took the way;
    The child may rue that is vnborne
       the huntin of that day!

3. The stout Erle of Northumberland
       a vow to God did make
    His pleasure in the Scottish woods
       three sommers days to take,

4. The cheefest harts in Cheuy Chase
       to kill and beare away:
    These tydings to Erle Douglas came
       in Scottland, where he lay.

5. Who sent Erle Pearcy present word
       he wold prevent his sport;
    The English erle, not fearing that,
       did to the woods resort,

6. With fifteen hundred bowmen bold,
       all chosen men of might,
   Who knew ffull well in time of neede
       to ayme their shafts arright.

7. The gallant greyhounds swiftly ran
       to chase the fallow deere;
   On Munday they began to hunt,
       ere daylight did appeare.

8. And long before high noone the had
       a hundred fat buckes slaine;
   Then hauing dined, the drouyers went
       to rouze the deare againe.

9. The bowmen mustered on the hills,
       well able to endure;
   Theire backsids all with speciall care
       that day were guarded sure.

10. The hounds ran swiftly through the woods
        the nimble deere to take,
    That with their cryes the hills and dales
        an eccho shrill did make.

11. Lord Pearcy to the querry went
        to view the tender deere;
    Quoth he, "Erle Douglas promised once
        this day to meete me heere;

12. "But if I thought he wold not come
        noe longer wold I stay."
    With that a braue younge gentlman
        thus to the erle did say:

13. "Loe, yonder doth Erle Douglas come,
        hys men in armour bright;
    Full twenty hundred Scottish speres
        all marching in our sight.

14. "All men of pleasant Tinydale,
        fast by the riuer Tweede."
    "O cease your sportts!" Erle Pearcy said,
        "and take your bowes with speede.

15. "And now with me, my countrymen,
        your courage forth advance!
    For there was neuer champion yett,
        In Scotland nor in Ffrance,

16. "That euer did on horsebacke come,
        but, and if my hap it were,

I durst encounter man for man,
 with him to breake a spere."

17. Erle Douglas on his milke-white steede,
  most like a baron bold,
 Rode formost of his company,
  whose armor shone like gold.

18. "Shew me," sayd hee, "whose men you bee
  that hunt soe boldly heere,
 That without my consent doe chase
  and kill my fallow deere."

19. The first man that did answer make
  was noble Pearcy hee,
 Who sayd, "Wee list not to declare
  nor shew whose men wee bee;

20. "Yett wee will spend our deerest blood
  thy cheefest harts to slay."
 Then Douglas swore a solemone oathe,
  and thus in rage did say:

21. "Ere thus I will outbraued bee,
  one of vs tow shall dye;
 I know thee well, an erle thou art;
  Lord Pearcy, soe am I.

22. "But trust me, Pearcye, pittye it were,
  and great offence, to kill
 Then any of these our guiltlesse men,
  for they haue done none ill.

23. "Let thou and I the battell trye,
  and set our men aside."
 "Accurst bee he" Erle Pearcye sayd,
  "by whome it is denyed."

24. Then stept a gallant squire forth—
  Witherington was his name—
 Who said, "I wold not haue it told
  to Henery our king, for shame,

25. "That e're my captaine fought on foote,
  and I stand looking on.
 You bee two erles," quoth Witheringhton,
  "And I am squier alone;

26. "I'le doe the best that doe I may,
  while I haue power to stand;
 While I haue power to weeld my sword,
  I'le fight with hart and hand."

27. Our English archers bent their bowes;
    their harts were good and trew;
  Att the first flight of arrowes sent,
    full foure score Scotts the slew.

28. To driue the deere with hound and horne,
    Dauglas bade on the bent;
  Two captaines moued with mickle might,
    their speres to shiuers went.

29. They closed full fast on euerye side,
    noe slacknes there was dound,
  But many a gallant gentleman
    lay gasping on the ground.

30. O Christ! it was great greeue to see
    how eche man chose his spere,
  And how the blood out of their brests
    did gush like water cleare.

31. At last these two stout erles did meet,
    like captaines of great might;
  like lyons woode they layd on lode;
    that made a cruell fight.

32. The fought vntill they both did sweat,
    with swords of tempered steele,
  Till blood downe their cheekes like raine
    the trickling downe did feele.

33. "O yeeld thee, Pearcye!" Douglas sayd,
    "and in faith I will thee bringe
  Where thou shall high advanced bee
    by Iames our Scottish king.

34. "Thy ransome I will freely giue,
    and this report of thee,
  Thou art the most couragious knight
    that ever I did see."

35. "Noe, Douglas!" quoth Erle Percy then,
    "thy profer I doe scorne;
  I will not yeelde to any Scott
    that euer yett was borne!"

36. With that there came an arrow keene,
    out of an English bow,
  Which stroke Erle Douglas on the brest
    a deepe and deadlye blow.

37. Who neuer sayd more words then these:
    "Fight on, my merry men all!

For why, my life is att an end,
    Lord Pearcy sees my fall."

38.   Then leauing liffe, Erle Pearcy tooke
      the dead man by the hand;
    Who said, "Erle Dowglas, for thy life,
      wold I had lost my land!

39.   "O Christ! my verry hart doth bleed
      for sorrow for thy sake,
    For sure, a more redoubted knight
      mischance cold neuer take."

40.   A knight amongst the Scotts there was
      which saw Erle Douglas dye,
    Who streight in hart did vow revenge
      vpon the Lord Pearcye.

41.   Sir Hugh Mountgomerye was he called,
      who, with a spere full bright,
    Well mounted on a gallant steed,
      ran feircly through the fight,

42.   And past the English archers all,
      without all dread or feare,
    And through Erle Percyes body then
      he thrust his hatfull spere.

43.   With such a vehement force and might
      his body he did gore,
    The staff ran through the other side
      a large cloth-yard and more.

44.   Thus did both those nobles dye,
      whose courage none cold staine;
    An English archer then perceiued
      the noble erle was slaine.

45.   He had a good bow in his hand,
      made of a trusty tree;
    An arrow of a cloth-yard long
      to the hard head haled hee.

46.   Against Sir Hugh Mountgomerye
      his shaft full right he sett;
    The grey-goose-winge that was there-on
      in his harts bloode was wett.

47.   This fight from breake of day did last
      till setting of the sun,
    For when the rung the euening-bell
      the battele scarse was done.

48. With stout Erle Percy there was slaine
    Sir Iohn of Egerton,
  Sir Robert Harcliffe and Sir William,
    Sir Iames, that bold barron.

49. And with Sir George and Sir Iames,
    both knights of good account,
  Good Sir Raphe Rbbye there was slaine,
    whose prowesse did surmount.

50. For Witherington needs must I wayle
    as one in dolefull dumpes,
  For when his leggs were smitten of,
    he fought vpon his stumpes.

51. And with Erle Dowglas there was slaine
    Sir Hugh Mountgomerye,
  And Sir Charles Morrell, that from feelde
    one foote wold neuer flee;

52. Sir Roger Heuer of Harcliffe tow;
    his sisters sonne was hee;
  Sir David Lambwell, well esteemed,
    but saved he cold not bee.

53. And the Lord Maxwell, in like case,
    with Douglas he did dye;
  Of twenty hundred Scottish speeres,
    scarce fifty-fiue did flye.

54. Of fifteen hundred Englismen
    went home but fifty-three;
  The rest in Cheuy Chase were slaine,
    vnder the greenwoode tree.

55. Next day did many widdows come
    their husbands to bewayle;
  They washt their wounds in brinish teares,
    but all wold not prevayle.

56. Theyr bodyes, bathed in purple blood
    the bore with them away;
  They kist them dead a thousand times
    ere the were cladd in clay.

57. The newes was brought to Eddenborrow
    where Scottlands king did rayne,
  That braue Erle Douglas soddainlye
    was with an arrow slaine.

58. "O heauy newes!" King Iames can say;
    "Scotland may wittenesse bee

I haue not any captaine more
of such account as hee."

59. Like tydings to King Henery came,
within as short a space,
That Pearcy of Northumberland
was slaine in Cheuy Chase.

60. "Now God be with him!" said our king,
"sith it will noe better bee;
I trust I haue within my realme
fiue hundred as good as hee.

61. "Yett shall not Scotts nor Scottland say
but I will vengeance take,
And be revenged on them all
for braue Erle Percyes sake."

62. This vow the king did well performe
after on Humble-downe;
In one day fifty knights were slayne,
with lords of great renowne.

63. And of the rest, of small account,
did many hundreds dye:
Thus endeth the hunting in Cheuy Chase,
made by the Erle Pearcye.

64. God saue our king, and blesse this land
with plentye, ioy, and peace,
And grant henceforth that foule debate
twixt noble men may ceaze!

C.

1. God prosper long our noble king,
Our lives and safety all;
A woeful hunting once there did
At Shiver Chase befall.

2. To drive the deers with hound and horn
Earl Percy went his way.
The child may rue that is unborn
The hunting of that day.

3. The gird Lord of Northumberland
A vow to God did make
His pleasure in the Scottish woods
Three summer days to take,

4. The chiefest harts at Shiver Chase
To kill and bear away.

These tidings to Earl Douglas sped
    In Scotland where he lay.

5. He sent Earl Percy of his word—
    He would prevent that sport.
But England's earl, no fear of that,
    Did to those woods resort.

6. His fifteen hundred bowmen bold,
    All chosen men of might,
Who knew full well in time of need
    To aim their shafts aright.

7. His gallant grayhounds swiftly ran
    To chase the fallow deer.
On Monday they began to hunt
    Ere daylight did appear.

8. Yea, long before high noon they had
    A hundred fat bucks slain.
Then having dined, the drove-yers went
    To rouse the deers again.

[Stanzas 9, 10, 11, 12 are missing.]

13. Lo! yonder doth Lord Douglas come,
    With men in armor bright;
Full twenty hundred Scottish spears
    A-marching into sight.

14. Oh, cease your sports, Earl Percy said,
    And take your bows with speed;
Ye men of pleasant Tivetdale,
    Fast by the river Tweed.

15. And now with me, my countrymen,
    With courage, never fear;
I durst encounter any man
    With him to break a spear.

[Stanza 16 is consolidated with 15.]

17. Earl Douglas on his milk-white steed
    Wast like a baron bold;
Rode foremost of his companee
    Whose armor shawn like gold.

18. Show me, he said, whose men ye be
    That hunt so boldly here;
That without my consent do chase
    And slay my fallow deer.

19.   The first man that did answer make
          Was noble Percy he,
       Who said, We list not to declare
          Nor tell what men we be.

20.   Yet will we spend our dearest blood
          Thy chiefest harts to slay.
       Then Douglas swore a mighty oath
          And thus in rage did say:

21.   Ere thus will I out-braved be,
          One of us twain shall die;
       I know thee well, thou art an earl,
          Lord Percy. So am I.

[Stanza 22 is missing.]

23.   Let thou and I the battle try,
          And save our men aside.
       Cursed be he, Earl Percy said,
          By whom this is denied.

24.   Then stepped a gal-yant squire a-forth,
          Withrington was his name,
       Who said, I would not have it told
          To our King Henry's shame,

25.   That e'er my captain fought on foot
          And I stood looking on.
       You be two earls, said Withrington,
          And I a squire alone,

26.   But I'll do all that do I may,
          While I have strength to stand,
       While I keep power to wield my sword,
          I'll fight with heart and hand.

[Stanzas 27 and 28 are missing.]

29.   The fight did last from high noonday
          Till setting of the sun;
       For when they rung the evening bell
          The battle scarce was done.

30.   Oh! God! it was a grief to see,
          And likewise for to hear,
       The cries of men fast in their gore
          And scattered there and here.

31.   With stout Earl Percy there was slain
          Sir John of Edgerton,

Sir Robert Ratscliff, and Sir John,
 Sir James the bold baron.

32. Likewise Sir George and stout Sir James,
 Both knights of good account;
And Sir Ralph Rabby there was slain
 Whose courage none surmount.

33. For Withrington all hearts were sad
 And lost in doleful dumps,
Yet when both legs were smitten off
 He fought upon the stumps.

34. Of fifteen hundred Englishmen
 Went home but fifty-three,
The rest were dead at Shiver Chase
 Beneath the greenwood tree.

35. Next day did many widows come
 Their husbands to bewail;
To wash the wounds and shed salt tears,
 But all without avail.

36. The bodies stiff in purple gore
 They bare with them away;
They kissed them dead a thousand times
 Ere they were wrapped in clay.

37. God save our king and bless our land
 With plenty, joy and peace;
And grant that henceforth fool debate
 'Twixt noble lords may cease.

KING HENRY FIFTH'S CONQUEST
OF FRANCE (164)

This ballad is from broadside sources, all late 18th century. Agincourt was widely celebrated in song and story from the 15th century; it may be that this ballad rests on a more traditional one. The story of the tennis balls is found here and there in the 15th century even in some of the English chronicles (though not the French); it may have been picked up from the romance of Alexander. There seems to be no basis for it in fact. Similar stories have been told about other conquerors from Alexander to Miles Standish. Henry V was 27 and the Dauphin of France 19 at the time of Agincourt.

 This ballad is found rarely in America (Tennessee, Vermont). The American texts, except for minor verbal differences, are identical with the English. See H. H. Flanders, *The New Green Mountain Songster*, pp. 192–195.

Text A, Percy MS., ii, 597; B, traditional in Vermont, *Bulletin,*
4:10.

A.

1. As our king lay musing on his bed,
       He bethought himself upon a time
   Of a tribute that was due from France,
       Had not been paid for so long a time.
           Fal, lal, etc.

2. He called for his lovely page,
       His lovely page then called he,
   Saying, "You must go to the king of France,
       To the king of France, sir, ride speedily."

3. O then went away this lovely page,
       This lovely page then away went he;
   And when he came to the king of France,
       Low he fell down on his bended knee.

4. "My master greets you, worthy sir;
       Ten ton of gold that is due to he,
   That you will send him his tribute home,
       Or in French land you soon will him see."

5. "Your master's young and of tender years,
       Not fit to come into my degree,
   And I will send him three tennis-balls,
       That with them he may learn to play."

6. O then returned this lovely page,
       This lovely page then returned he,
   And when he came to our gracious king,
       Low he fell down on his bended knee.

7. "What news, what news, my trusty page?
       What is the news you have brought to me?"
   "I have brought such news from the king of France
       That you and he will never agree.

8. "He says you're young and of tender years,
       Not fit to come into his degree,
   And he will send you three tennis-balls
       That with them you may learn to play."

9. "Recruit me Cheshire and Lancashire,
       And Derby Hills that are so free;
   No marryd man nor no widow's son;
       For no widow's curse shall go with me."

10. They recruited Cheshire and Lancashire,

  And Derby Hills that are so free;
   No marryd man nor no widow's son;
    Yet there was a jovial bold company.

11. O then we marchd into the French land,
   With drums and trumpets so merrily;
  And then bespoke the king of France,
   "Lo, yonder comes proud King Henry."

12. The first shot that the Frenchmen gave,
   They killd our Englishmen so free;
  We killd ten thousand of the French,
   And the rest of them they ran away.

13. And then we marched to Paris gates,
   With drums and trumpets so merrily.
  O then bespoke the king of France,
   "The Lord have mercy on my men and me!"

14. "O I will send him his tribute home,
   Ten ton of gold that is due to he,
  And the finest flower that is in all France
   To the Rose of England I will give free."

B.

1. A king was sitting on his throne,
  And on his throne was sitting he;
  He bethought himself of a tribute due,
  Been due in France so many years.

2. Then he called up his little page,
  His little page then called he;
  Saying, "You must go to the king of France,
  And demand that tribute due to me."

3. Away, away went that little page,
  Away, away and away went he,
  Until he came to the king of France,
  Then he fell down on his bended knee.

4. "My master's great as well as you,
  My master's great as well as you;
  He demands that tribute, tribute due,
  Or in French land you will him see."

5. "Your master's young, of tender age,
  Not fit to come to my degree;
  To him I send five tennis balls,
  That in French land he dare not be."

6. Away, away went the little page,
   Away, away and away went he,
   Until he came to his master dear,
   Then he fell down on his bended knee.

7. "What news, what news, my little page?
   What news, what news do you bring to me?"
   "Such news, such news, my master dear,
   The king and you will not agree."

8. "He says you're young, of tender age,
   Not fit to come to his degree;
   To you he sends five tennis balls,
   That in French land you dare not be."

9. The king he numbered up his men,
   One by two and two by three,
   Until he got thirty thousand men,
   A noble jolly bold company.

10. "No married men, no widow's son,
    No married men can follow me;
    No married men, no widow's son,
    A widow's son can't follow me."

11. Now he's marched off to the king of France,
    With drums and trumpets so merrily;
    And the first that spoke was the king of France,
    Saying "Yonder comes proud King Henry!"

12. The first broadside those Frenchmen gave,
    They slew our men so bitterly;
    And the next broadside our English gave,
    They killed five thousand and thirty three;
    And the next that spoke was the King of France,
    Saying: "Lord, have mercy on my men and me!"

13. "Now if you'll march back from whence you came,
    With drums and trumpets so merrily,
    The finest flower in all French land,
    Five tons of gold shall be your fee."

14. Now he's marched back from whence he came,
    With drums and trumpets so merrily,
    And the finest flower in all French land,
    Five tons of gold now is his fee.

SIR ANDREW BARTON (167)

From almost contemporary accounts we learn that the rich ship of John Barton, a Scotchman, was captured by the Portuguese in 1474 and that the King of Scotland gave Barton's sons letters of reprisal against the Portuguese. These letters were renewed as late as 1506. The three sons took to the sea against the Portuguese but evidently interpreted their letters of marque very liberally, for they were soon preying on ships of other nations including the English. Most of the accounts center on the exploits of Andrew Barton, evidently the most daring of the three. The English finally sent Sir Thomas and Sir Edward Howard against him. He was defeated and killed in the battle that followed; Henry VIII defended the English to the King of Scotland by claiming that Barton was a pirate.

This ballad is rather generally found in America, though it is frequently mixed with "Henry Martyn" (250). Two versions are general; one follows the English telling of the chase and defeat and death of Barton. The American version is more frank; the three brothers deliberately choose a career of piracy to support their families. In the second important American version Barton wins the fight and continues his career.

Text, Percy MS., p. 490.

Notes

8/1. Charles Howard in the ballad displaces Thomas and Edward; Charles was Lord Admiral of the Fleet. His being mentioned as Earl of Nottingham in Stanza 78 suggests that the ballad is early 17th century, for he was made Earl of Nottingham in 1596. 52/4. In the rigging, the topcastle, Barton carried heavy beams which could be dropped on the deck of a vessel coming alongside in a boarding position and so cause much damage.

1. As itt beffell in midsumer-time,
       When burds singe sweetlye on euery tree,
   Our noble king, King Henery the Eighth,
       Ouer the riuer of Thames past hee.

2. Hee was no sooner ouer the riuer,
       Downe in a fforrest to take the ayre,
   But eighty merchants of London Cittye
       Came kneeling before King Henery there.

3. "O yee are welcome, rich merchants,
       Good saylers, welcome unto me!"
   They swore by the rood the were saylers good,
       But rich merchants they cold not bee.

4. "To Ffrance nor Fflanders dare we nott passe,
   Nor Burdeaux voyage wee dare not ffare,
   And all ffor a ffalse robber that lyes on the seas,
   And robbs vs of our merchants-ware."

5. King Henery was stout, and he turned him about,
   And swore by the Lord that was mickle of might,
   "I thought he had not beene in the world throughout
   That durst haue wrought England such vnright."

6. But euer they sighed, and said, alas!
   Vnto King Harry this answere againe:
   "He is a proud Scott that will robb vs all
   If wee were twenty shipps and hee but one."

7. The king looket ouer his left shoulder,
   Amongst his lord and barrons soe ffree:
   "Haue I neuer lords in all my realme
   Will ffeitch yond traitor vnto mee?"

8. "Yes, that dare I!" sayes my lord Chareles Howard,
   Neere to the king wheras hee did stand;
   "If that Your Grace will giue me leaue,
   My selfe wilbe the only man."

9. "Thou shalt haue six hundred men," saith our king,
   "And chuse them out of my realme soe ffree;
   Besids marriners and boyes,
   To guide the great shipp on the sea."

10. "I'le goe speake with Sir Andrew," sais Charles, my lord Haw-
    ard;
    "Vpon the sea, if hee be there;
    I will bring him and his shipp to shore,
    Or before my prince I will neuer come neere."

11. The ffirst of all my lord did call,
    A noble gunner hee was one;
    This man was three score yeeres and ten,
    And Peeter Simon was his name.

12. "Peeter," said hee, "I must sayle to the sea,
    To seeke out an enemye God be my speed!
    Before all others I haue chosen thee;
    Of a hundred guners thoust be my head."

13. "My lord," sais hee, "if you haue chosen mee
    Off a hundred gunners to be the head,
    Hange me att your maine-mast tree
    If I misse my marke past three pence bread."

14. The next of all my lord he did call,
     A noble bowman hee was one;
   In Yorekeshire was this gentleman borne,
     And William Horsley was his name.

15. "Horsley," sayes hee, "I must sayle to the sea,
     To seeke out an enemye; God be my speede!
   Before all others I haue chosen thee;
     Of a hundred bowemen thoust be my head."

16. "My lord," sais hee, "if you haue chosen mee
     Of a hundred bowemen to be the head,
   Hang me att your mainemast-tree
     If I misse my marke past twelue pence bread."

17. With pikes, and gunnes, and bowemen bold,
     This noble Howard is gone to the sea
   On the day before midsummer-euen,
     And out att Thames mouth sayled they.

18. They had not sayled dayes three
     Vpon their iourney they tooke in hand,
   But there they mett with a noble shipp,
     And stoutely made itt both stay and stand.

19. "Thou must tell me thy name," sais Charles, my lord Haward,
     "Or who thou art, or ffrom whence thou came,
   Yea, and where thy dwelling is,
     To whom and where thy shipp does belong."

20. "My name," sayes hee, "is Henery Hunt,
     With a pure hart and a penitent mind;
   I and my shipp they doe belong
     Vnto the New-castle that stands vpon Tine."

21. "Now thou must tell me, Harry Hunt,
     As thou hast sayled by day and by night,
   Hast thou not heard of a stout robber?
     Men calls him Sir Andrew Bartton, knight."

22. But euer he sighed, and sayd, "Alas!
     Ffull well, my lord, I know that wight;
   He robd me of my merchant's ware,
     And I was his prisoner but yesternight.

23. "As I was sayling vppon the sea,
     And a Burdeaux voyage as I did ffare,
   He clasped me to his archborde,
     And robd me of all my merchants-ware.

24. "And I am a man both poore and bare,
     And euery man will haue hos owne of me,

And I am bound towards London to ffare,
    To complaine to my prince Henerye."

25. "That shall not need," sais my lord Haward;
    "If thou canst lett me this robber see,
Ffor euery peny he hath taken thee ffroe,
    Thou shalt be rewarded a shilling," quoth hee.

26. "Now God fforefend," saies Henery Hunt,
    "My lord, you shold worke soe ffarr amisse!
God keepe you out of that traitors hands!
    For you wott ffull litle what a man hee is.

27. "Hee is brasse within, and steele without,
    And beames hee beares in his topcastle stronge;
His shipp hath ordinance cleane round about;
    Besids, my lord, hee is verry well mand.

28. "He hath a pinnace, is deerlye dight,
    Saint Andrews crosse, that is his guide;
His pinnace beares nine score men and more,
    Besids fifteen cannons on euery side.

29. "If you were twenty shippes, and he but one,
    Either in archbord or in hall,
He would ouercome you euerye one,
    And if his beames they doe downe ffall."

30. "This is cold comfort," sais my lord Haware,
    "To wellcome a stranger thus to the sea;
I'le bring him and his shipp to shore,
    Or else into Scottland hee shall carrye mee."

31. "Then you must gett a noble gunner, my lord,
    That can sett well with his eye,
And sink his pinnace into the sea,
    And soone then ouer come will hee bee.

32. "And when that you haue done this,
    If you chance Sir Andrew for to bord,
Lett no man to his topcastle goe;
    And I will giue you a glasse, my lord,

33. "And then you need to ffeare no Scott,
    Whether you sayle by day or by night;
And to-morrow; by seuen of the clocke,
    You shall meete with Sir Andrew Bartton, knight.

34. "I was his prisoner but yester night,
    And he hath taken mee sworne," quoth hee;
"I trust my Lord God will me fforguie
    And if that oath then broken bee.

35. "You must lend me sixe peces, my lord," quoth hee,
    "Into my shipp, to sayle the sea,
And to-morrow, by nine of the clocke,
    Your Honour againe then will I see."

* * * * * * *

36. And the hache-bord where Sir Andrew lay
    Is hached with gold deerlye dight.
"Now by my ffaith," sais Charles, my lord Haward,
    "Then yonder Scott is a worthye wight!

37. "Take in your ancyents and your standards,
    Yea that no man shall them see,
And put me fforth a white willow wand,
    As merchants vse to sayle the sea."

38. But they stirred neither top nor mast,
    But Sir Andrew they passed by:
"Whatt English are yonder," said Sir Andrew,
    "That can so litle curtesye?

39. "I haue beene admirall ouer the sea
    More then these yeeres three;
There is neuer an English dog, nor Portingall,
    Can passe this way without leaue of mee.

40. "But now yonder pedlers, they are past,
    Which is no litle greffe to me:
Ffeich them backe," sayes Sir Andrew Bartton,
    "They shall all hang att my maine-mast tree."

41. With that the pinnace itt shott of,
    That my lord Haward might itt well ken;
Itt stroke downe my lords fforemast,
    And killed fourteen of my lord his men.

42. "Come hither, Simon!" sayes my lord Haward,
    "Looke that thy words be true thou sayd,
I'le hang thee att my maine-mast tree
    If thou misse thy marke past twelue pence bread."

43. Simon was old, but his hart itt was bold;
    Hee tooke downe a peece, and layd itt ffull lowe;
Hee put in chaine yeards nine,
    Besids other great shott lesse and more.

44. With that hee lett his gun-shott goe;
    Soe well hee settled itt with his eye,
The ffirst sight that Sir Andrew sawe,
    Hee see his pinnace sunke in the sea.

45.   When hee saw his pinace sunke,
          Lord! in his hart hee was not well.
      "Cutt my ropes! Itt is time to be gone!
          I'le goe ffeitch yond pedlers backe my selfe!"

46.   When my lord Haward saw Sir Andrew loose,
          Lord! in his hart that he was ffaine:
      "Strike on your drummes! Spread out your ancyents!
          Sound out your trumpetts! Sound out amaine!"

47.   "Ffight on, my men," sais Sir Andrew Bartton;
          "Weate howsoeuer this geere will sway,
      Itt is my lord Admirall of England
          Is come to seeke mee on the sea."

48.   Simon had a sonne; with shott of a gunn—
          Well Sir Andrew might itt ken—
      He shott itt in att a priuye place,
          And killed sixty more of Sir Andrew's men.

49.   Harry Hunt came in att the other syede,
          And att Sir Andrew hee shott then;
      He droue downe his fformast tree,
          And killed eighty more of Sir Andriwes men.

50.   "I haue done a good turne," sayes Harry Hunt;
          "Sir Andrew is not our king's ffreind;
      He hoped to haue vndone me yesternight,
          But I hope I haue quitt him well in the end."

51.   "Euer alas!" sayd Sir Andrew Barton,
          "What shold a man either thinke or say?
      Yonder ffalse theeffe is my strongest enemye,
          Who was my prisoner but yesterday.

52.   "Come hither to me, thou Gourden good,
          And be thou readye att my call,
      And I will giue thee three hundred pound
          If thou wilt lett my beames downe ffall."

53.   With that hee swarued the maine-mast tree,
          Soe did he itt with might and maine;
      Horseley, with a bearing arrow,
          Stroke the Gourden through the braine.

54.   And he ffell into the haches againe,
          And sore of this wound that he did bleed;
      Then word went throug Sir Andrew's men,
          That the Gourden hee was dead.

55.   "Come hither to me, Iames Hambliton,
          Thou art my sister's sonne, I haue no more;

I will giue thee six hundred pound
    If thou will lett my beames downe ffall."

56. With that he swarued the maine-mast tree,
      Soe did hee itt with maight and maine;
    Horseley, with another broad arrow,
      Strake the yeaman through the braine.

57. That hee ffell downe to the haches againe;
      Sore of his wound that hee did bleed;
    Couetousness getts no gaine,
      Itt is verry true, as the Welchman sayd.

58. But when hee saw his sister's sonne slaine,
      Lord! in his heart hee was not well.
    "Goe ffeitch me downe my armour of proue,
      Ffor I will to the topcastle my-selfe.

59. "Goe ffeitch me downe my armour of prooffe,
      For itt is guilded with gold soe cleere;
    God be with my brother, Iohn of Bartton!
      Amongst the Portingalls hee did itt weare."

60. But when hee had his armour of prooffe,
      And on his body hee had itt on,
    Euery man that looked att him
      Sayd, "Gunn nor arrow hee neede feare none."

61. "Come hither, Horsley!" says my lord Haward,
      "And looke your shaft that itt goe right;
    Shoot a good shoote in the time of need,
      And ffor thy shooting thoust be made a knight."

62. "I'le doe my best," sayes Hoslay then,
      "Your Honor shall see beffore I goe;
    If I shold be hanged att your mainemast,
      I haue in my shipp but arrowes tow."

63. But att Sir Andrew hee shott then;
      Hee made sure to hitt his marke;
    Vnder the spole of his right arme
      Hee smote Sir Andrew quite throw the hart.

64. Yett ffrom the tree hee wold not start,
      But hee clinged to itt with might and maine;
    Vnder the coller then of his iacke,
      He stroke Sir Andrew thorrow the braine.

65. "Ffight on my men," sayes Sir Andrew Bartton,
      "I am hurt, but I am not slaine;
    I'le lay mee downe and bleed a-while,
      And then I'le rise and ffight againe.

66. "Ffight on my men," sayes Sir Andrew Bartton,
     "These English doggs they bite soe lowe;
    Ffight on ffor Scottland and Saint Andrew
     Till you heare my whistle blowe!"

67. But when the cold not heare his whistle blow,
     Sayes Harry Hunt, "I'le lay my head
    You may bord yonder noble shipp, my lord,
     For I know Sir Andrew hee is dead."

68. With that they borded this noble shipp,
     Soe did they itt with might and maine;
    The ffound eighteen score Scotts aliue,
     Besids the rest were maimed and slaine.

69. My lord Haward tooke a sword in his hand,
     And smote of Sir Andrew's head;
    The Scotts stood by did weepe and mourne,
     But neuer a word durst speake or say.

70. He caused his body to be taken downe,
     And ouer the hatch-bord cast into the sea,
    And about his middle three hundred crownes:
     "Whersoever thou lands, itt will bury thee."

71. With his head they sayled into England againe,
     With right good will, and fforce and main,
    And the day beffore Newyeeres euen
     Into Thames mouth they came againe.

72. My lord Haward wrote to King Heneryes grace,
     With all the newes hee cold him bring:
    "Such a Newyeeres gifft I haue brought to your Grace
     As neuer did subiect to any king.

73. "Ffor merchandyes and manhood,
     The like is nott to be ffound;
    The sight of these wold doe you good,
     Ffor you haue not the like in your English ground."

74. But when hee heard tell that they were come,
     Full royally hee welcomed them home;
    Sir Andrew's shipp was the king's Newyeeres guifft;
     A brauer shipp you neuer saw none.

75. Now hath our king Sir Andrew's shipp,
     Besett with pearles and precyous stones;
    Now hath England two shipps of warr,
     Two shipps of warr, before but one.

76. "Who holpe to this?" sayes King Henerye,
     "That I may reward him ffor his paine."

"Harry Hunt, and Peeter Simon,
   William Horseleay, and I the same."

77. "Harry Hunt shall haue his whistle and chaine,
   And all his iewells, whatsoeuer they bee,
  And other rich giffts that I will not name,
   For his good service he hath done mee.

78. "Horslay, right thoust be a knight,
   Lands and liuings thou shalt haue store;
  Howard shall be erle of Nottingham,
   And soe was neuer Haward before.

79. "Now, Peeter Simon, thou art old;
   I will maintaine thee and thy sonne;
  Thou shalt haue fiue hundred pound all in gold
   Ffor the good service that thou hast done."

80. Then King Henerye shiffted his roome;
   In came the Queene and ladyes bright;
  Other arrands they had none
   But to see Sir Andrew Bartton, knight.

81. But when they see his deadly fface,
   His eyes were hollow in his head;
  "I wold giue a hundred pound," sais King Henerye,
   "The man were aliue as hee is dead!

82. "Yett, ffor the manfull part that hee hath playd,
   Both heere and beyond the sea,
  His men shall haue halfe a crowne a day
   To bring them to my brother, King Iamye."

JOHNIE ARMSTRONG (169)

This grand old ballad is one of the best of the Border songs and one of the best of the outlaw ballads. Johnie and the Armstrongs would, however, insist that they were no outlaws, but free men, not to be curbed by either the English king or the Scottish and free to raid on both sides of The Debatable Land. John Armstrong of the ballad was one of the leaders of the strong Armstrong clan in the first quarter of the 16th century; with three thousand horsemen at his back, he was virtually lord of the Border. In 1530 James V took an army to the Border to bring it into submission. The chronicles bear out the account in the ballad of how Johnie was enticed into the presence of the king by promise of safe conduct and then taken and executed. The ballad exists in two versions, the one picturing Johnie as spirited and defiant, and the other, printed by Alan Ramsay in *The Ever Green* (ii, 190) "copied from a gentleman's mouth of the name of Armstrong, who is the sixth generation from this John," showing him in a less favorable light, trying in vain to bargain with the king for his life. Goldsmith left testimony of his fondness for this ballad: "The music of the finest singer is dissonance to what I felt when our old dairy-maid sung me to tears with Johnny Armstrong's Last Good Night, or the Cruelty of Barbara Allen."

Text, *Wit Restored,* etc., p. 301.

Notes

15/3. The hero in epic, romance, and ballad seldom falls in fair fight, but treacherously. Cf. "Chevy Chase."

17. The babe vowing vengeance on its father's murderers is common in Scandinavian heroic story. It is likely to occur in the stories of peoples that practice personal blood revenge.

1. There dwelt a man in faire Westmerland,
   Ionnë Armestrong men did him call,
   He had nither lands nor rents coming in,
   Yet he kept eight score men in his hall.

2. He had horse and harness for them all,
   Goodly steeds were all milke-white;
   O the golden bands an about their necks,
   And their weapons, they were all alike.

3. Newes then was brought unto the king
   That there was sicke a won as hee,
   That livëd lyke a bold out-law,
   And robbëd all the north country.

4. The king he writt an a letter then,
   A letter which was large and long;
   He signed it with his owne hand,
   And he promised to doe him no wrong.

5. When this letter came Ionnë untill,
   His heart it was as blythe as birds on the tree.
   "Never was I sent for before any king,
   My father, my grandfather, nor none but mee.

6. "And if wee goe the king before,
   I would we went most orderly;
   Every man of you shall have his scarlet cloak,
   Laced with silver laces three.

7. "Every won of you shall have his velvett coat,
   Laced with sillver lace so white;
   O the golden bands an about your necks,
   Black hatts, white feathers, all alyke."

8. By the morrow morninge at ten of the clock,
    Towards Edenburough gon was hee,
  And with him all his eight score men ;
    Good lord, it was a goodly sight for to see!

9. When Ionnë came befower the king,
    He fell downe on his knee,
  "O pardon, my soveraine leighe," he said,
    "O pardon my eight score men and me!"

10. "Thou shalt have no pardon, thou traytor strong,
    For thy eight score men nor thee ;
  For to-morrow morning by ten of the clock,
    Both thou and them shall hang on the gallow-tree."

11. But Ionnë look'd over his left shoulder,
    Good Lord, what a grevious look looked hee !
  Saying, "Asking grace of a graceles face—
    Why there is none for you nor me."

12. But Ionnë had a bright sword by his side,
    And it was made of the mettle so free,
  That had not the king stept his foot aside,
    He had smitten his head from his faire boddë.

13. Saying, "Fight on, my merry men all,
    And see that none of you be taine ;
  For rather then men shall say we were hanged,
    Let them report how we were slaine."

14. Then, God wott, faire Eddenburrough rose,
    And so besett poore Ionnë rounde,
  That fowerscore and tenn of Ionnës best men
    Lay gasping all upon the ground.

15. Then like a mad man Ionnë laide about,
    And like a mad man then fought hee,
  Untill a falce Scot came Ionnë behinde,
    And runn him through the faire boddee.

16. Saying, "Fight on, my merry men all,
    And see that none of you be taine ;
  For I will stand by and bleed but awhile,
    And then will I come and fight againe."

17. Newes then was brought to young Ionne Armestrong,
    As he stood by his nurse's knee,
  Who vowed if ere he liv'd for to be a man,
    O the treacherous Scots revengd he'd be.

THE DEATH OF QUEEN JANE (170)

This was a very popular ballad especially in Scotland; it was just the kind of story the makers and printers of broadsides liked to get hold of. There seems to be no historical foundation for the account of the Queen's death as related in the ballad. The birth of the prince was a natural one, but the Queen died twelve days later.

The American texts that follow show the history of this ballad in America and illustrate in general the sort of changes a folk song can undergo. In America are found versions like the English. Then there is a second type in which Queen Jane becomes a "neighbor" and the whole ballad is democritized. ("In labor" in the original may have been heard as *neighbor*.) The third type results from a mixture with "The Brown Girl" and so the action becomes the punishment of a jilted lover. Queen Jane has become Sally here. Finally the narrative element has disappeared and we have a lyric built on a climax of relations and the refrain line: "The Rose of England shall flourish no more."

Text A, Percy Papers; B, traditional in Scotland, Macmath MS., p. 68; C, Ireland via Kentucky, *Bulletin,* 2:6; D, traditional in Virginia, Sharp, i, 231.

A.

1. Queen Jane was in labour full six weeks and more,
    And the women were weary, and fain would give oer:
   "O women, O women, as women ye be,
    Rip open my two sides, and save my baby!"

2. "O royal Queen Jane, that thing may not be;
    We'll send for King Henry to come unto thee."
   King Henry came to her, and sate on her bed:
    "What ails my dear lady, her eyes look so red?"

3. "O royal King Henry, do one thing for me:
    Rip open my two sides, and save my baby!"
   "O royal Queen Jane, that thing will not do;
    If I lose your fair body, I'll lose your baby too."

4. She wept and she waild, and she wrung her hands sore;
    O the flour of England must flurish no more!
   She wept and she waild till she fell in a swoond,
    They opend her two sides, and the baby was found.

5. The baby was christened with joy and much mirth,
    Whilst poor Queen Jane's body lay cold under earth;
   There was ringing and singing and mourning all day,
    The princess Elizabeth went weeping away.

6. The trumpets in mourning so sadly did sound,
And the pikes and the muskets did trail on the ground.

.   .   .   .

.   .   .   .

B.

1. "Ye midwives and women-kind, do one thing for me;
Send for my mother, to come and see me."

2. Her mother was sent for, who came speedilie:
"O Jeanie, Queen Jeanie, are you gaun to dee?"

3. "O mother, dear mother, do one thing for me;
O send for King Henry, to come and see me."

4. King Henry was sent for, who came speedilie:
"O Jeanie, Queen Jeanie, are ye gaun to dee?"

5. "King Henry, King Henry, do one thing for me;
O send for a doctor, to come and see me."

6. The doctor was sent for, who came speedilie:
"O Jeanie, Queen Jeanie, are ye gaun to dee?"

7. "O doctor, oh doctor, do one thing for me;
Open my left side, and let my babe free."

8. He opened her left side, and then all was o'er,
And the best flower in England will flourish no more.

C.

JANE WAS A NEIGHBOR

1. Oh, Jane was a neighbor for six months or more,
Till the neighbors grew weary and left her alone.

2. "Oh neighbor, oh neighbor, oh neighbor," said she,
"Won't you send for my father to come and see me?"

3. Her father was sent for, and immejitly came;
Settin' down by the bedside,—"What's the matter of Jane?"

4. Then she cried and she murmured till she wept her heart sore,
Saying: "The red rose of England shall flourish no more!"

5. "Oh father, oh father, oh father," said she,
"Won't you send for my mother to come and see me?"

6. Her mother was sent for, and immejitly came;
Settin' down by the bedside, "What's the matter of Jane?"

7. Then she cried and she murmured till she wept her heart sore,
    Saying: "The red rose of England shall flourish no more!"

8. "Oh mother, oh mother, oh mother," said she,
    "Won't you send for King Henry to come and see me?"

9. King Henry was sent for and immejitly came;
    Settin' down by the bedside,—"What's the matter of Jane?"

10. Then she cried and she murmured till she wept her heart sore,
    Saying: "The red rose of England shall flourish no more!"

D.

1. King Henry was sent for
    All in the time of her need;
    King Henry he came
    In the time of her need.

2. King Henry he stooped
    And kissed her on the lips.
    "What's the matter with my flower,
    Makes her eyes look so red?"

3. "King Henry, King Henry,
    Will you take me to be,
    To pierce my side open
    And save my baby?"

4. "O no, Queen Jane,
    Such thing never shall be,
    To lose my sweet flower
    For to save my baby."

5. Queen Jane she turned over
    And fell in a swound;
    Her side were pierced
    And her baby was found.

6. How bright was the mourning,
    How yellow were the bed,
    How costly was the shroud
    Queen Jane were wrapped in.

7. There's six followed after
    And six carried her along;
    King Henry he followed
    With his black mourning on.

8. King Henry he wept
    And wrung his hands till they're sore.
    The flower of England
    Shall never be no more.

MARY HAMILTON (173)

This ballad first appears in print in Scott's *Minstrelsy of the Scottish Border,* 1802. Scott had it in eight different versions from tradition. Twenty-eight versions are printed in Child; and since then many more versions have been recovered, mostly from print. The origin of the story has puzzled ballad collectors from the time of Scott to the present. The Queen referred to is certainly Mary Stuart. She had as her constant companions from childhood four girls, the four Marys: Mary Seaton, Mary Beaton, Mary Livingston, and Mary Fleming. They went with Mary to France in 1548 and returned with her in 1561. Eventually all except Mary Seaton married and left the Queen's service; Mary Seaton became a nun. Most versions of the ballad include Seaton and Beaton, but omit Fleming and Livingston; for one they substitute Carmichael and for the other Hamilton. There is, however, no evidence that persons of those names were ever associated with Mary Stuart. As Child says, it is impossible to weave all the versions into "an intelligible and harmonious story"; yet there is a core of common story: Mary Hamilton has a baby "to the highest Stuart," i.e., Lord Darnley, Mary's husband. She destroys it and is herself executed by order of the Queen. No record of such a happening exists and no gossip, not even in the writings of John Knox.

Andrew Lang and others have believed that the ballad may be a confusion of the Queen's Marys with an event that happened at the court of Czar Peter of Russia. A Mary Hambleton, a Scotch girl, lady-in-waiting to Queen Catherine, loved Ivan Orlof, an aide-de-camp of the Czar. When a dead baby was found, Mary was accused of having had an illegitimate child and killing it. She was found guilty and executed on March 14, 1719. Orloff was banished to Siberia. (See Andrew Lang, "Blackwood's Magazine," September, 1895; Tolman, *PMLA,* 42:422; Child, iii, 382.)

This theory is tempting. Stanza 13 suggests that the unfortunate girl was over the sea from home. Note also the implication of Stanzas 14–16. Against this is the suggestion, now rather more generally accepted, that the ballad is based on an affair at the Scotch court involving a French waiting maid and the Queen's apothecary. The girl was executed in December, 1565, for killing her newborn baby. A stanza in a version given to Scott in 1804 by a man who had had it from his aged mother makes reference to an apothecary as the lady's lover:

> My love he was a pottinger,
> Mony drink he gae me,
> And a to put back that bonnie babe,
> But alas, it wad na do.

At first the ballad may have told the story of the French lady, and then Darnley and Hamilton may have been substituted for them. There is the possibility that the two stories—the Scotch and the Russian—may have intermingled. Whatever the origin, this ballad is one of the most dramatic and moving in the annals of balladry. In America as in England it is now rare in tradition, and over the years the tendency has been to generalize and gloss over the story element and keep the lyrical stanzas like the moving last stanza.

Text, Sharp's *Ballad Book,* p. 18.

1. Word's gane to the kitchen,
    And word's gane to the ha,
  That Marie Hamilton gangs wi bairn
    To the hichest Stewart of a'.

2. He's courted her in the kitchen,
    He's courted her in the ha,
  He's courted her in the laight cellar,
    And that was warst of a'.

3. She's tyed it in her apron
    And she's thrown it in the sea;
  Says, "Sink ye, swim ye, bonny wee babe!
    "You'l neer get mair o me."

4. Down then cam the auld queen,
    Goud tassels tying her hair:
  "O Marie, where's the bonny wee babe
    That I heard greet sae sair?"

5. "There never was a babe intill my room,
    As little designs to be;
  It was but a touch o my sair side,
    Come oer my fair bodie."

6. "O Marie, put on your robes o black,
    Or else your robes o brown,
  For ye maun gang wi me the night,
    To see fair Edinbro town."

7. "I winna put on my robes o black,
    Nor yet my robes o brown;
  But I'll put on my robes o white,
    To shine through Edinbro town."

8. When she gaed up the Cannogate,
    She laughd loud laughters three;
  But whan she cam down the Cannogate
    The tear blinded her ee.

9. When she gaed up the Parliament stair,
     The heel cam off her shee;
   And lang or she cam down again
     She was condemnd to dee.

10. When she cam down the Cannogate,
     The Cannogate sae free,
   Many a ladie lookd oer her window,
     Weeping for this ladie.

11. "Ye need nae weep for me," she says,
     "Ye need nae weep for me;
   For had I not slain mine own sweet babe,
     This death I wadna dee.

12. "Bring me a bottle of wine," she says,
     "The best that eer ye hae,
   That I may drink to my well-wishers,
     And they may drink to me.

13. "Here's a health to the jolly sailors,
     That sail upon the main;
   Let them never let on to my father and mother
     But what I'm coming hame.

14. "Here's a health to the jolly sailors,
     That sail upon the sea;
   Let them never let on to my father and mother
     That I cam here to dee.

15. "Oh little did my mother think,
     The day she cradled me,
   What lands I was to travel through,
     What death I was to dee.

16. "Oh little did my father think,
     The day he held up me,
   What lands I was to travel through,
     What death I was to dee.

17. "Last night I washed the queen's feet,
     And gently laid her down;
   And a' the thanks I've gotten the nicht
     To be hangd in Edinbro town!

18. "Last nicht there was four Maries,
     The nicht ther'l be but three;
   There was Marie Seton, and Marie Beton,
     And Marie Carmichael, and me."

THE RISING IN THE NORTH (175)

This is a typical minstrel ballad and for that reason included. It exists in only one version—Percy MS.; it is doubtful that the folk had much to do with it. In this same category too are "Northumberland Betrayed by Douglas" (176) and "The Earl of Westmorland" (177). "The Rising in the North" gives an account of the northern rebellion of 1569 by the Earls of Northumberland and Westmoreland against the queen. It is accurate only in general outline. For a discussion of the historical background, see Child, iii, 401.

1. Listen, liuely lordings all,
       And all that beene this place within:
    If you'le giue eare vnto my songe,
       I will tell you how this geere did begin.

2. It was the good Erle of Westmorlande,
       A noble erle was callëd hee,
    And he wrought treason against the crowne;
       Alas, itt was the more pittye.

3. And soe itt was the Erle of Northumberland,
       Another good noble erle was hee;
    They tooken both vopon one part,
       Against the crowne they wolden bee.

4. Earle Pearcy is in his garden gone,
       And after walkes his awne ladye:
    "I heare a bird sing in my eare
       That I must either ffight or fflee."

5. "God fforbidd," shee sayd, "good my lord,
       That euer soe that it shalbee!
    But goe to London to the court,
       And faire ffall truth and honestye!"

6. "But nay, now nay, my ladye gay,
       That euer it shold soe bee;
    My treason is knowen well enoughe;
       Att court I must not bee."

7. "But goe to the court yet, good my lord,
       Take men enowe with thee;
    If any man will doe you wrong,
       You warrant they may bee."

8. "But nay, now nay, my lady gay,
       For soe itt must not bee;

If I goe to the court, ladye,
    Death will strike me, and I must dye."

9. "But goe to the court yett, good my lord,
    I my-selfe will ryde with thee;
If any man will doe you wronge,
    Your borrow I shalbee."

10. "But nay, now nay, my lady gay,
    For soe it must not bee;
For if I goe to the court, ladye,
    Thou must me neuer see.

11. "But come hither, thou little foot-page,
    Come thou hither vnto mee,
For thou shalt goe a message to Master Norton,
    In all the hast that euer may bee.

12. "Comend me to that gentleman;
    Bring him here this letter from mee,
And say, I pray him earnestlye
    That hee will ryde in my companye."

13. But one while the foot-page went,
    Another while he rann;
Vntill he came to Master Norton,
    The ffoot-page neuer blanne.

14. And when he came to Master Nortton,
    He kneeled on his knee,
And tooke the letter betwixt his hands,
    And lett the gentleman it see.

15. And when the letter itt was reade,
    Affore all his companye,
I-wis, if you wold know the truth,
    There was many a weeping eye.

16. He said, "Come hither, Kester Nortton,
    A ffine ffellow thou seemes to bee;
Some good councell, Kester Nortton,
    This day doe thou giue to me."

17. "Marry, I'le giue you councell, ffather.
    If you'le take councell att me,
That if you haue spoken the word, father
    That backe againe you doe not flee."

18. "God a mercy! Christopher Nortton,
    I say, God a mercye!
If I doe liue and scape with liffe,
    Well advanced shalt thou bee.

19. "But come you hither, my nine good sonnes,
    In men's estate I thinke you bee;
    How many of you, my children deare,
    On my part that wilbe?"

20. But eight of them did answer soone,
    And spake ffull hastilye,
    Sayes, "We wilbe on your part, ffather,
    Till the day that we doe dye."

21. "But God a mercy!" my children deare,
    And euer I say God a mercy!
    And yett my blessing you shall haue,
    Whether-soeuer I liue or dye.

22. "But what sayst thou, thou Ffrancis Nortton,
    Mine eldest sonne and mine heyre trulye?
    Some good councell, Ffrancis Nortton,
    This day thou giue to me."

23. "But I will giue you councell, ffather,
    If you will take councell att mee;
    For if you wold take my councell, father,
    Against the crowne you shold not bee."

24. "But ffye vpon thee, Ffrancis Nortton!
    I say ffye vpon thee!
    When thou was younge and tender of age
    I made ffull much of thee."

25. "But your head is white, ffather," he sayes,
    "And your beard is wonderous gray;
    Itt were a shame ffor your countrye
    If you shold rise and fflee away."

26. "But ffye vpon thee, thou coward Ffrancis!
    Thou neuer tookest that of mee!
    When thou was younge and tender of age
    I made too much of thee!"

27. "But I will goe with you, father," quoth hee;
    "Like a naked man will I bee;
    He that strikes the first stroake against the crowne,
    An ill death may hee dye!"

28. But then rose vpp Master Nortton, that esquier,
    With him a ffull great companye;
    And then the erles they comen downe
    To ryde in his companye.

29. Att Whethersbye the mustered their men,
    Vpon a ffull fayre day;

Thirteen thousand there were seene
  To stand in battel ray.

30. The Erle of Westmoreland, he had in his ancyent
    The dunn bull in sight most hey,
  And three doggs with golden collers
    Were sett out royallye.

31. The Erle of Northumberland, he had in his ancyent
    The halfe moone in sight soe hye,
  As the Lord was crucifyed on the crosse,
    And set forthe pleasantlye.

32. And after them did rise good Sir George Bowes,
    After them a spoyle to make;
  The erles returned backe againe,
    Thought euer that knight to take.

33. This barron did take a castle then,
    Was made of lime and stone;
  The vttermost walls were ese to be woon;
    The erles haue woon them anon.

34. But tho they woone the vttermost walls,
    Quickly and anon,
  The innermost walles the cold not winn;
    The were made of a rocke of stone.

35. But newes itt came to leeue London,
    In all the speede that euer might bee;
  And word it came to our royall queene
    Of all the rebells in the north countrye.

36. Shee turned her grace then once about,
    And like a royall queene shee sware;
  Sayes, "I will ordaine them such a breake-fast
    As was not in the north this thousand yeere!"

37. Shee caused thirty thousand men to be made,
    With horsse and harneis all quicklye;
  And shee caused thirty thousand men to be made,
    To take the rebells in the north countrye.

38. They tooke with them the false Erle of Wardwicke,
    Soe did they many another man;
  Vntill they came to Yorke castle,
    I-wis they neuer stinted nor blan.

* * * * * * *

39. .   .   .   .
    .   .   .   .

"Spread thy ancyent, Erle of Westmoreland!
 The halfe-moone ffaine wold wee see!"

40.   But the halfe-moone is fled and gone,
        And the dun bull vanished awaye;
      And Ffrancis Nortton and his eight sonnes
        Are ffled away most cowardly.

41.   Ladds with mony are counted men,
        Men without mony are counted none;
      But hold your tounge! why say you soe?
        Men wilbe men when mony is gone.

CAPTAIN CAR, OR, EDOM O GORDON (178)

This violent and bitter story belongs to the troubled times of Queen
Mary. The chronicles are contradictory as to details, but it seems that
Adam Gordon either sent Captain Car or went himself to raid the
Forbes' holdings (Gordons were the Queen's party; Forbeses of the
Reformed faith). In the course of the raid they came to the castle of
Towie defended only by the wife of the owner, John Forbes. She re-
fused to give up the house; the attackers fired it and all inside—some
twenty-seven members of the family and the servants—perished. The
ballad was widely known in tradition and as a result the name Captain Carr came to be a by-word for cruelty and ruthlessness.

Text, Cotton MS. Vespasian, 4, xxv, 67, 16th century.

1.   It befell at Marynmas,
        When wether waxed colde,
      Captaine Care said to his men,
        We must go take a holde.

            Syck, sike, and to-towe sike,
              And sike and like to die;
            The sikest nighte that euer I abode,
              God lord haue mercy on me!

2.   "Haille, master, and wether you will,
        And wether ye like it best."
      "To the castle of Crecrynbroghe,
        And there we will take our reste."

3.   "I know wher is a gay castle,
        Is builded of lyme and stone;
      Within their is a gay ladie,
        Her lord is riden and gone.

4.   The ladie she lend on her castle-walle,
        She loked vpp and downe;

There was she ware of an host of men,
Come riding to the towne.

5. "Se yow, my meri men all,
And se yow what I see?
Yonder I see an host of men,
I muse who they bee."

6. She thought he had ben her wed lord,
As he comd riding home;
Then was it traitur Captaine Care
The lord of Ester-towne.

7. They wer no soner at supper sett,
Then after said the grace,
Or Captaine Care and all his men
Wer lighte aboute the place.

8. "Gyue ouer thi howsse, thou lady gay,
And I will make the a bande;
To-nighte thou shall ly within my armes,
To-morrow thou shall ere my lande."

9. Then bespacke the eldest sonne,
That was both whitt and redde:
"O mother dere, geue ouer your howsse,
Or elles we shalbe deade."

10. "I will not geue ouer my hous," she saithe,
"Not for feare of my lyffe;
It shalbe talked throughout the land,
The slaughter of a wyffe.

11. "Fetch me my pestilett,
And charge me my gonne,
That I may shott at yonder bloddy butcher,
The lord of Easter-towne."

12. Styfly vpon her wall she stode,
And lett the pellettes flee;
But then she myst the blody bucher,
And she slew other three.

13. "I will not geue ouer my hous," she saithe,
"Neitheir for lord nor lowne;
Nor yet for traitour Captaine Care,
The lord of Easter-towne.

14. "I desire of Captine Care,
And all his bloddye band,

That he would saue my eldest sonne,
The care of all my lande."

15. "Lap him in a shete," he sayth,
"And let him downe to me,
And I shall take him in my armes,
His waran shall I be."

16. The captayne sayd unto him selfe:
Wyth sped, before the rest,
He cut his tonge out of his head,
His hart out of his brest.

17. He lapt them in a handkerchef,
And knet it of notes three,
And cast them ouer the castell-wall,
At that gay ladye.

18. "Fye vpon the, Captayne Care,
And all thy bloddy band!
For thou hast slayne my eldest sonne,
The ayre of all my land."

19. Then bespake the youngest sonne,
That sat on the nurse's knee,
Sayth, "Mother gay, geue ouer your house;
It smoldereth me."

20. "I wold geue my gold," she saith,
"And so I wolde my ffee,
For a blaste of the westryn wind,
To dryue the smoke from thee.

21. "Fy vpon the, John Hamleton,
That euer I paid the hyre!
For thou hast broken my castle-wall,
And kyndled in the ffyre."

22. The lady gate to her close parler,
The fire fell aboute her head;
She toke vp her children thre,
Seth, Babes we are all dead.

23. Then bespake the hye steward,
That is of hye degree;
Saith, "Ladie gay, you are in close,
Wether ye fight or flee."

24. Lord Hamleton dremd in his dream,
In Carluall where he laye,

His halle were all of fyre,
 His ladie slayne or daye.

25. "Busk and bowne, my merry men all,
 Even and go ye with me;
For I dremd that my haal was on fyre,
 My lady slayne or day."

26. He buskt him and bownd hym,
 And like a worthi knighte;
And when he saw his hall burning,
 His hart was no dele lighte.

27. He sett a trumpett till his mouth,
 He blew as it plead his grace;
Twenty score of Hamlentons
 Was light about the place.

28. "Had I knowne as much yesternighte
 As I do to-daye,
Captaine Care and all his men
 Should not haue gone so quite.

29. "Fye vpon the, Captaine Care,
 And all thy blody bande!
Thou haste slayne my lady gay,
 More wurth then all thy lande.

30. "If thou had ought eny ill will," he saith,
 "Thou shoulde haue taken my lyffe,
And haue saved my children thre,
 All and my louesome wyffe."

THE BONNY EARL OF MURRAY (181)

Was there at one time a fully developed narrative ballad that told the dramatic story of the conflict between James Stewart, Earl of Murray, and the Earl of Huntly? If there was, it is lost and all that remains are two songs, more lyric than narrative, recalling the event. The story is dramatic enough to call for a full account. Huntly procured a commission from the king to bring Murray to trial and then proceeded to Donibristle, where Murray was staying with his mother. Murray refused to surrender, Huntly fired the house, all inside were forced out. Murray, waiting until the last moment, slipped out unnoticed and was making good his escape when someone noticed him because the top of his helmet was on fire. He was caught and killed. Although Huntly had no part in the actual killing, his men forced him to stab the corpse, so that later he would not be able to disclaim responsibility. Though the body of Murray was kept lying in state in the church for months to remind all that his murderers were unpunished, Huntly went free. One wonders why all the dramatic story was passed by, by the ballad maker.

In America the ballad has been found very rarely. The version given here illustrates Child's B text.

Text A, Ramsay, *Tea Table Miscellany,* p. 356; B, traditional in Wisconsin, *JAF,* 20:156.

A.

1.   Ye Highlands, and ye Lawlands,
         Oh where have you been?
     They have slain the Earl of Murray,
         And they layd him on the green.

2.   "Now wae be to thee, Huntly!
         And wherefore did you sae?
     I bade you bring him wi you,
         But forbade you him to slay."

3.   He was a braw gallant,
         And he rid at the ring;
     And the bonny Earl of Murray,
         Oh he might have been a king!

4.   He was a braw gallant,
         And he playd at the ba;
     And the bonny Earl of Murray
         Was the flower amang them a'.

5.   He was a braw gallant,
         And he playd at the glove;
     And the bonny Earl of Murray,
         Oh he was the Queen's love!

6.   Oh lang will his lady,
         Look o'er the castle Down,
     Eer she see the Earl of Murray
         Come sounding thro the town!
     Eer she, etc.

B.

Oh mourn, oh mourn, ye Lowlands,
    Oh mourn, ye Highlands a',
They have slain the Earl o' Murray,
    On the greensward ha' he fa'.

Oh shame be to ye Huntly,
    To treat your brother sae,

To meet him wi' your claymore,
   An' in his bed to slay.

Oh, your lady will be sorrowfu'
   Whe ye to hame have sped,
An' she learns the Earl o' Murray
   You have murdered in his bed.

An' your corn will often ripen,
   An' your meadow grass grow green
Ere you in Dinnybristle town
   Will daurna to be seen.

THE LAIRD OF LOGIE (182)

This spirited and romantic ballad was generally popular in Scotland and England. Wemyss of Logie was apprehended for his part in the raid on Holyrood House in 1591 with Bothwell and was condemned to death. But he escaped "by the policy of one of the Dutch [should be Danish] maids, with whom he entertained a secret love. The gentlewoman, named Mistress Margaret Twinslace, coming one night, whilst the king and queen were in bed, to his keepers, shewed that the king called for the prisoner, to ask of him some question. The keepers, suspecting nothing, for they knew her to be the principal maid of the chamber, conveyed him to the door of the Bed-chamber, and making a stay without, as they were commanded, the gentlewoman did let him down at a window, by a cord that she had prepared. . . . This, with the manner of his escape, ministered great occasion of laughter; and not many days after, the king being pacified by the queen's means, he was pardoned, and took to wife the gentlewoman who had in this sort hazarded her credit for his safety." (Spottiswood, *History of the Church of Scotland,* p. 389.) Most versions follow these events more or less faithfully; one version, however, makes Logie's offense stealing a kiss from the lady. He is saved by the queen's forging a release for him in the king's hand.

Text, Scott, p. 128.

1.   I will sing, if ye will hearken,
     If ye will hearken unto me;
   The king has taen a poor prisoner,
     The wanton laird o Young Logie.

2.   Young Logie's laid in Edinburgh chapel,
     Carmichael's the keeper o the key;
   And May Margaret's lamenting sair,
     A' for the love of Young Logie.

3. "Lament, lament na, May Margaret,
   And of your weeping let me be;
   For ye maun to the king himsell,
   To seek the life of Young Logie."

4. May Margaret has kilted her green cleiding,
   And she has curld back her yellow hair.
   "If I canna get Young Logie's life,
   Farewell to Scotland for evermair!"

5. When she came before the king,
   She knelit lowly on her knee.
   "O what's the matter, May Margaret?
   And what needs a' this courtesie?"

6. "A boon, a boon, my noble liege,
   A boon, a boon I beg of thee,
   And the first boon that I come to crave
   Is to grant me the life of Young Logie."

7. "O na, O na, May Margaret,
   Forsooth, and so it mauna be;
   For a' the gowd o fair Scotland
   Shall not save the life of Young Logie."

8. But she has stown the king's redding-kaim,
   Likewise the queen her wedding knife,
   And sent the tokens to Carmichael,
   To cause Young Logie get his life.

9. She sent him a purse o the red gowed,
   Another of the white monie;
   She sent him a pistol for each hand,
   And bade him shoot when he gat free.

10. When he came to the Tolbooth stair,
    There he let his volley flee;
    It made the king in his chamber start,
    Een in the bed where he might be.

11. "Gae out, gae out, my merrymen a',
    And bid Carmichael come speak to me;
    For I'll lay my life the pledge o that
    That yon's the shot o Young Logie."

12. When Carmichael came before the king,
    He fell low down upon his knee;
    The very first word that the king spake
    Was, "Where's the laird of Young Logie?"

13. Carmichael turnd him round about,
    I wot the tear blinded his ee:

"There came a token frae your Grace
  Has taen away the laird frae me."

14. "Hast thou playd me that, Carmichael?
      And hast thou playd me that?" quoth he;
    "The morn that Justice Court's to stand,
      And Logie's place ye maun supplie."

15. Carmichael's awa to Margaret's bower,
      Even as fast as he may dree:
    "O if Young Logie be within,
      Tell him come and speak with me."

16. May Margaret turnd her round about,
      I wot a loud laugh laughed she:
    "The egg is chippd, the bird is flown,
      Ye'll see nae mair of Young Logie."

17. The tane is shipped at the pier of Leith,
      The tother at the Queen's Ferrie,
    And she's gotten a father to her bairn,
      The wanton laird of Young Logie.

THE LADS OF WAMPHRAY (184)

This ballad from the early 17th century is a good example of the clan
feud ballad. It recounts an incident from the feud history of the
Johnstones and the Chichtons. William Johnstone of Wamphray,
nicknamed The Galliard (a galliard is a spirited dance, hence a gay,
happy-go-lucky fellow), raids Sim Chichton's stable but gets a blind
horse by mistake. Though he tries to hide behind a bush, they capture
him and hang him. His nephew comes with a band of Johnstones and
destroys many Chictons and drives them out of Wamphray.

Text, Glenriddell MSS., xi, 34 (1791).

1. Twixt the Girthhead and Langwood-end
   Lived the Galiard and Galiard's men.

2. It is the lads of Lethenha
   The greatest rogues among them a'.

3. It is the lads of Leverhay
   That drove the Crichtons' gier away.

4. It is the lads of the Kirkhill,
   The gay Galiard and Will o Kirkhill,

5. But and the lads o Stefenbiggin,
   They broke the house in at the riggin.

6. The lads o Fingland and Hellbackhill,
   They were neer for good, but aye for ill.

7. Twixt the Staywood Bass and Langside Hill,
   They stelld the broked cow and branded bull.

8. It is the lads o the Girthhead,
   The diel's in them for pride and greed.

* * * * * *

9. The Galiard is to the stable gane;
   Instead of the Dun, the Blind he's taen.

10. "Come out now, Simmy o the Side,
    Come out and see a Johnston ride!

11. "Here's the boniest horse in a' Nithside,
    And a gentle Johnston aboon his hide."

12. Simmy Crichton's mounted then,
    And Crichtons has raised mony a ane.

13. The Galiard thought his horse had been fleet,
    But they did outstrop him quite out o sight.

14. As soon as the Galiard the Crichton he saw,
    Beyond the saugh-bush he did draw.

15. The Crichtons there the Galiard hae taen,
    And nane wi him but Willy alane.

16. "O Simmy, Simmy, now let me be,
    And I vow I'll neer do a Crichton wrang!

17. "O Simmy, Simmy, now let me be,
    And a peck o goud I'll gie to thee!

18. "O Simmy, Simmy let me gang,
    And my wife shall heap it wi her hand!"

19. But the Crichtons wadna let Willy bee,
    But they hanged him high upon a tree.

20. O think then Will he was right wae,
    And he saw his uncle guided sae.

21. "But if ever I live Wamphray to see,
    My uncle's death revenged shall be!"

22. Back to Wamphray Willy's gane,
    And riders has raised mony a ane.

23. Saying, My lads, if ye'll be true,
    Ye's a' be clad in the noble blue.

24. Back to Nidsdale they are gane,
And away the Crichtons' nout they hae taen.

25. As they came out at the Wallpath-head,
The Crichtons bad them light and lead.

26. And when they came to the Biddess-burn,
The Crichtons bad them stand and turn.

27. And when they came to the Biddess-strand,
The Crichtons they were hard at hand.

28. But when they cam to the Biddess-law,
The Johnstons bad them to stand and draw.

29. Out then spake then Willy Kirkhill:
"Of fighting, lads, ye's hae your fill."

30. Then off his horse Willy he lap,
And a burnished brand in his hand he took.

31. And through the Crichtons Willy he ran,
And dang them down both horse and man.

32. O but these lads were wondrous rude,
When the Biddess-burn ran three days blood!

33. "I think, my lads, we've done a noble deed;
We have revenged the Galiard's blood.

34. "For every finger o the Galiard's hand,
I vow this day I've killed a man."

35. And hame for Wamphray they are gane,
And away the Crichtons' nout they've taen.

36. "Sin we've done na hurt, nor we'll take na wrang,
But back to Wamphray we will gang."

37. As they came in at Evan head,
At Reaklaw-holm they spred abroad.

38. "Drive on, my lads, it will be late;
We'll have a pint at Wamphray Gate.

39. "For where eer I gang, or eer I ride,
The lads o Wamphray's on my side.

40. "For of a' the lads that I do ken,
The lads o Wamphray's king o men."

DICK O THE COW (185)

Another Border raid ballad. This time the fool gets the better of the Scotch raiders. The cow in Dick's name has nothing to do with cattle; it may refer to a place.

Text, Percy Papers, 1775.

Notes

    25/2. key to the stable.   26/3. St. Mary knot: hamstrung them?

1.   Now Liddisdale has lain long in,
        Fa la
    There is no rideing ther a ta;
        Fa la
    Their horse is growing so lidder and fatt
        That are lazie in the sta.
        Fa la la didle

2.   Then Johnë Armstrang to Willie can say,
        Billie, a rideing then will we;
    England and us has been long at a feed;
        Perhaps we may hitt of some bottie.

3.   Then they'r comd on to Hutton Hall,
        They rade that proper place about;
    But the laird he was the wiser man,
        For he had left nae gear without.

4.   Then he had left nae gear to steal,
        Except six sheep upon a lee;
    Says Johnie, I'de rather in England die
        Before their six sheep good to Liddisdale with me.

5.   "But how cald they the man we last with mett,
        Billie, as we came over the know?"
    "That same he is an innocent fool,
        And some men calls him Dick o the Cow."

6.   "That fool has three as good kyne of his own
        As is in a' Cumberland, billie," quoth he;
    "Betide my life, betide my death,
        These three kyne shal go to Liddisdaile with me."

7.   Then they'r comd on to the poor fool's house,
        And they have broken his wals so wide;
    They have loosd out Dick o the Cow's kyne three,
        And tane three coerlets off his wife's bed.

8.   Then on the morn, when the day grew light,
        The shouts and crys rose loud and high:

"Hold thy tongue, my wife," he says,
"And of thy crying let me bee.

9. "Hald thy tongue, my wife," he says,
"And of thy crying let me bee,
And ay that where thou wants a kow,
Good sooth that I shal bring the three."

10. Then Dick's comd on to lord and master,
And I wate a drerie fool was he.
"Hald thy tongue, my fool," he says,
"For I may not stand to jest with thee."

11. "Shame speed a your jesting, my lord," quo Dickie,
"For nae such jesting grees with me;
Liddesdaile has been in my house this last night,
And they have tane my three kyne from me.

12. "But I may nae langer in Cumberland dwel,
To be your poor fool and your leel,
Unless ye give me leave, my lord,
To go to Liddisdale and steal."

13. "To give thee leave, my fool," he says,
"Thou speaks against mine honour and me;
Unless thou give me thy trouth and thy right hand
Thou'l steal frae nane but them that sta from thee."

14. "There is my thought and my right hand;
My head shal hing on Hairibie,
I'le never crose Carlele sands again,
If I steal frae a man but them that sta frae me."

15. Dickie has tane leave at lord and master,
And I wate a merrie fool was he;
He has bought a bridle and a pair of new spurs,
And has packed them up in his breek-thigh.

16. Then Dickie's come on for Puddinburn,
Even as fast as he may drie;
Dickie's come on for Puddinburn,
Where there was thirty Armstrongs and three.

17. "What's this comd on me!" quo Dickë,
"What meakle wae's this happend on me,
"Where here is but ae innocent fool,
And there is thirty Armstrongs and three!"

18. Yet he's comd up to the hall among them all;
So wel he became his courtisie:

"Well may ye be, my good Laird's Jock!
 But the deil bless all your companie.

19. "I'm come to plain of your man Fair Johnie Armstrong,
 And syne his billie Willie," quo he.
"How they have been in my house this last night,
 And they have tane my three ky frae me."

20. Quo Johnie Armstrong, "We'll him hang;"
 "Nay," thain quo Willie, "we'll him slae;"
But up bespake another young man, "We'll nit him in a four-
 nooked sheet,
 Give him his burden of batts, and lett him gae."

21. Then up bespake the good Laird's Jock,
 The best falla in the companie.
"Sitt thy way down a little while, Dickë,
 And a peice of thine own cow's hough I'le give to thee."

22. But Dicki's heart it grew so great
 That hever a bitt of it he dought to eat;
But Dickie was warr of ane auld peat-house,
 Where there al the night he thought for to sleep.

23. Then Dickie was warr of that auld peat-house,
 Where there al the night he thought for to ly;
And a' the prayers the poor fool prayd was,
 "I wish I had a mense for my own three kye!"

24. Then it was the use of Puddinburn,
 And the house of Mangertoun, all haile!
These that came not at the first call
 They gott no more meat till the next meall.

25. The lads, that hungry and aevery was,
 Above the door-head they flang the key;
Dickie took good notice to that;
 Says, there's a bootie younder for me.

26. Then Dickie's gane into the stable,
 Where there stood thirty horse and three;
He has ty'd them a' with St Mary knot,
 All these horse but barely three.

27. He has ty'd them a' with St Mary knott,
 All these horse but barely three;
He has loupen on one, taken another in his hand,
 And out at the door and gane is Dickie.

28. Then on the morn, when the day grew light,
 The shouts and cryes rose loud and high;

    "What's that theife?" quo the good Laird's Jock;
      "Tel me the truth and the verity.

29. "What's that theife?" quo the good Laird's Jock.
      "See unto me ye do not lie."
    "Dick o the Cow has been in the stable this last night,
      And has my brother's horse and mine frae me."

30. "Ye wad never be teld it," quo the Laird's Jock;
      "Have ye not found my tales fu leel?
    Ye wade never out of England bide,
      Till crooked and blind and a' wad steal."

31. "But will thou lend me thy bay?" Fair Johnë Armstrong can
      say,
      "There's nae nae horse loose in the stable but he;
    And I'le either bring ye Dick of the Kow again,
      Or the day is come that he must die."

32. "To lend thee my bay," the Laird's Jock can say,
      "He's both worth gold and good monie;
    Dick o the Kow has away twa horse,
      I wish no thou should no make him three."

33. He has tane the Laird's Jack on his back
      The twa-handed sword that hang lieugh by his thigh;
    He has tane the steel cap on his head,
      And on is he to follow Dickie.

34. Then Dickie was not a mile off the town,
      I wate a mile but barely three,
    Till John Armstrong has o'ertane Dick o the Kow,
      Hand for hand on Cannobei lee.

35. "Abide the, bide now, Dickie than,
      The day is come that thow must die;"
    Dickie looked oer his left shoulder;
      "Johnnie, has thow any mo in thy company?

36. "There is a preacher in owr chapell,
      And a' the lee-lang day teaches he;
    When day is gane, and night is come,
      There's never a word I mark but three.

37. "The first and second's Faith and Conscience;
      The third, is Johnie, Take head of thee;
    But what faith and conscience had thow, traitor,
      When thou took my three kye frae me?

38. "And when thou had tane my three kye,
      Thou thought in thy heart thou was no wel sped;

But thou sent thi billie Willie oer the know,
    And he took three coerlets of my wife's bed."

39.   Then Johne lett a spear fa leaugh by his thigh,
    Thought well to run the innocent through;
But the powers above was more than his,
    He ran but the poor fool's jerkin through.

40.   Together they ran or ever they blan—
    This was Dickie, the fool, and hee—
Dickie could not win to him with the blade of the sword,
    But he feld him with the plummet under the eye.

41.   Now Dickie has feld Fair Johnë Armstrong,
    The prettiest man in the south countrey;
"Gramercie," then can Dickie say,
    "I had twa horses, thou hast made me three."

42.   He has tane the laird's jack off his back
    The twa-handed sword that hang leiugh by his thigh;
He has tane the steel cape off his head:
    "Johnie, I'le tel my master I met with thee."

43.   When Johnë wakend out of his dream,
    I wate a dreiry man was he:
"Is thou gane now, Dickie, than?
    The shame gae in thy company!

44.   "Is thou gane now, Dickie, than?
    The shame go in thy companie!
For if I should live this hundred year,
    I shal never fight with a fool after the."

45.   Then Dickie comed home to lord and master,
    Even as fast as he may driee:
"Now Dickie, I shal neither eat meat nor drink
    Till high hanged that thou shall be!"

46.   "The shame speed the liars, my lord!" quo Dickie,
    "That was no the promise ye made to me;
For I'd never gane to Liddesdale to steal
    Till that I sought my leave at thee."

47.   "But what gart thow steal the Laird's-Jock's horse?
    And, kimmer, what gart thou steal him?"
"For lang might thow in Cumberland dwelt
    Or the Laird's Jock had stolen ought frae thee."

48.   "Indeed I wate ye leed, my lord,
    And even so loud as I hear ye lie;
I wan him frae his man, Fair Johnë Armstrong,
    Hand for hand on Cannonbie lee.

49. "There's the jack was on his back,
    The twa-handed sword that hung lewgh by his thigh;
    There's the steel cap was on his head;
    I have a' these takens to lett you see."

50. "If that be true thou to me tels—
    I trow thou dare not tel a lie—
    I'le give thee twenty pound for the good horse,
    Wel teld in thy cloke-lap shall be.

51. "And I'le give thee one of my best milk-kye,
    To maintain thy wife and children three;
    And that may be as good, I think,
    As ony twa o thine might be."

52. "The shame speed the liars, my lord!" quo Dicke,
    "Trow ye ay to make a fool of me?
    I'le either have thirty pound for the good horse,
    Or els he's gae to Mattan fair wi me."

53. Then he has given him thirty pound for the good horse,
    All in gold and good monie;
    He has given him one of his best milk-kye,
    To maintain his wife and children three.

54. Then Dickie's come down through Carlile town,
    Even as fast as he may drie:
    The first of men that he with mett
    Was my lord' brother, Bailife Glazenberrie.

55. "Well may ye be, my good Ralph Scrupe!"
    "Welcome, my brother's fool!" quo he;
    "Where did thou gett Fair Johnie Armstrong's horse?"
    "Where did I get him but steall him," quo he.

56. "But will thou sell me Fair Johnie Armstrong's horse?
    And, billie, will thou sel him to me?" quo he.
    "Ay, and tel me the monie on my cloke-lap,
    For there's not one fathing I'le trust thee."

57. "I'le give thee fifteen pound for the good horse,
    Wel teld on thy cloke-lap shal be;
    And I'le give thee one of my best milk-kye,
    To maintain thy wife and thy children three."

58. "The shame speed the liars, my lord!" quo Dickë,
    "Trow ye ay to make a fool of me?" quo he;
    "I'le either have thirty pound for the good horse,
    Or else he's to Mattan Fair with me."

59. He has given him thirty pound for the good horse,
    All in gold and good monie;

He has given him one of his best milk-kye,
To maintain his wife and children three.

60. Then Dickie lap a loup on high,
And I wate a loud laughter leugh he:
"I wish the neck of the third horse were browken,
For I have a better of my own, and onie better can be."

61. Then Dickie comd hame to his wife again;
Judge ye how the poor fool he sped;
He has given her three score of English pounds
For the three auld coerlets was tane of her bed.

62. "Hae, take thee there twa as good kye,
I trow, as al thy three might be;
And yet here is a white-footed naigg;
I think he'le carry booth thee and me.

63. "But I may no langer in Cumberland dwell;
The Armstrongs the'le hang me high."
But Dickie has tane leave at lord and master,
And Burgh under Stanemiur there dwels Dickie.

KINMONT WILLIE (186)

Kinmont Willie (William Armstrong, Will of Kinmouth) was captured by the English though he was a member of a Scotch party operating under a truce. The English refused to give him up because he
was such a notorious raider. The Scotch then under Sir Walter
Scott of Branxholm, lord of Buccleuch, made a surprise attack on the
castle at Carlisle, effected a breach in the wall, and succeeded in rescuing the prisoner and escaping with him back to Scotland on April
13, 1596. Sir Walter Scott says he got this ballad from tradition, but
that it was "much mangled by reciters" and as a consequence he
emended it to make it intelligible.

Text, Scott, i, 111.

Notes

1. Sakelde: Mr. Sakelde was deputy of Lord Scroop, who was
warden of the west marshes of England. Haribee is the place of execution near Carlisle, where Kinmont Willie was imprisoned. 4/1.
Liddel-rack: the ford in the Liddle River between England and Scotland. 16. Spotiswood, *History of the Church of Scotland*, says the
Scots had 2000 horses; the English account says 500. 19/4. Woodhouselee: the last house on the Scottish Border before they entered
The Debatable Land, the no man's land between England and Scotland.

1. O have ye na heard o the fause Sakelde?
       O have ye na heard o the keen Lord Scroop?
   How they hae taen bauld Kinmont Willie,
       On Haribee to hang him up?

2. Had Willie had but twenty men,
       But twenty men as stout as he,
   Fause Sakelde had never the Kinmont taen,
       We eight score in his companie.

3. They band his legs beneath the steed,
       They tied his hands behind his back;
   They guarded him, fivesome on each side,
       And they brought him ower the Liddel-rack.

4. They led him thro the Liddel-rack,
       And also thro the Carlisle sands;
   They brought him to Carlisle castell,
       To be at my Lord Scroop's commands.

5. "My hands are tied, but my tongue is free,
       And whae will dare this deed avow?
   Or answer by the border law?
       Or answer to the bauld Buccleuch?"

6. "Now haud thy tongue, thou rank reiver!
       There's never a Scot shall set ye free;
   Before ye cross my castle-yate,
       I trow ye shall take farewell o me."

7. "Fear na ye that, my lord," quo Willie;
       "By the faith o my bodie, Lord Scroop," he said,
   "I never yet lodged in a hostelrie
       But I paid my lawing before I gaed."

8. Now word is gane to the bauld Keeper,
       In Branksome Ha where that he lay,
   That Lord Scroope has taen the Kinmont Willie,
       Between the hours of night and day.

9. He has taen the table wi his hand,
       He garrd the red wine spring on hie;
   "Now Christ's curse on my head," he said,
       "But avenged of Lord Scroop I'll be!

10. "O is my basnet a widow's curch?
        Or my lance a wand of the willow-tree?
    Or my arm a ladye's lilye hand?
        That an English lord should lightly me.

11. "And have they taen him Kinmont Willie,
        Against the truce of Border tide,

And forgotten that the bauld Bacleuch
   Is keeper here on the Scottish side?

12.   "And have they een taen him Kinmont Willie,
         Withouten either dread or fear,
      And forgotten that the bauld Bacleuch
         Can back a steed, or shake a spear?"

13.   "O were there war between the lands,
         As well I wot that there is none,
      I would slight Carlisle castell high,
         Tho it were builded of marble-stone.

14.   "I would set that castell in a low,
         And sloken it with English blood;
      There's nevir a man in Cumberland
         Should ken where Carlisle castell stood.

15.   "But since nae war's between the lands,
         And there is peace, and peace should be,
      I'll neither harm English lad or lass,
         And yet the Kinmont freed shall be!"

16.   He has calld him forty marchmen bauld,
         I trow they were of his ain name,
      Except Sir Gilbert Elliot, calld
         The Laird of Stobs, I mean the same.

17.   He has calld him forty marchmen bauld,
         Were kinsmen to the bauld Buccleuch,
      With spur on heel, and splent on spauld,
         And gleuves of green, and feathers blue.

18.   There were five and five before them a',
         Wi hunting-horns and bugles bright;
      And five and five came wi Buccleuch,
         Like Warden's men, arrayed for fight.

19.   And five and five like a mason-gang,
         That carried the ladders lang and hie;
      And five and five like broken men;
         And so they reached the Woodhouselee.

20.   And as we crossd the Bateable Land,
         When to the English side we held,
      The first o men that we met wi,
         Whae sould it be but fause Sakelde!

21.   "Where be ye gaun, ye hunters keen?"
         Quo fause Sakelde, "come tell to me."
      "We go to hunt an English stag,
         Has trespassed on the Scots' countrie."

22. "Where be ye gaun, ye marshal-men?"
    Quo fause Sakelde, "come tell me true!"
    "We go to catch a rank reiver,
    Has broken faith wi the bauld Buccleuch."

23. "Where are ye gaun, ye mason-lads,
    Wi a' your ladders lang and hie?"
    "We gang to herry a corbie's nest,
    That wons not far frae Woodhouselee."

24. "Where be ye gaun, ye broken men?"
    Quo fause Sakelde, "come tell to me,"
    Now Dickie of Dryhope led that band,
    And the nevir a word o lear had he.

25. "Why trespass ye on the English side?
    Row-footed outlaws, stand!" quo he;
    The ne'er a word had Dickie to say,
    Sae he thrust the lance thro his fause bodie.

26. Then on we held for Carlisle toun,
    And at Staneshaw-bank the Eden we crossd;
    The water was great, and meikle of spait,
    But the nevir a horse nor a man we lost.

27. And when we reachd the Staneshaw-bank,
    The wind was rising loud and hie;
    And there the laird garrd leave our steeds,
    For fear that they should stamp and nie.

28. And when we left the Staneshaw-bank,
    The wind began full loud to blaw;
    But 'twas wind and weet, and fire and sleet,
    When we came beneath the castel-wa.

29. We crept on knees, and held our breath,
    Till we placed the ladders against the wa;
    And sae ready was Buccleuch himsell
    To mount the first before us a'.

30. He has taen the watchman by the throat,
    He flung him down upon the lead:
    "Had there not been peace between our lands,
    Upon the other side thou hadst gaed."

31. "Now sound out, trumpets!" quo Buccleuch;
    "Let's waken Lord Scroope right merrillie."
    Then loud the Warden's trumpets blew
    "O whae dare meddle wi me?"

32. Then speedilie to wark we gaed,
    And raised the slogan ane and a',

And cut a hole thro a sheet of lead,
   And so we wan to the castel-ha.

33.   They thought King James and a' his men,
      Had won the house wi bow and speir;
   It was but twenty Scots and ten
      That put a thousand in sic a stear!

34.   Wi coulters and wi forehammers,
      We garrd the bars bang merrilie,
   Untill we came to the inner prison,
      Where Willie o Kinmont he did lie.

35.   And when we cam to the lower prison,
      Where Willie o Kinmont he did lie,
   "O sleep ye, wake ye, Kinmont Willie,
      Upon the morn that thou's to die?"

36.   "O I sleep saft, and I wake aft,
      It's lang since sleeping was fleyd frae me;
   Gie my service back to my wyfe and bairns,
      And a' gude fellows that speer for me."

37.   Then Red Rowan has hente him up,
      The starkest men in Teviotdale:
   "Abide, abide now, Red Rowan,
      Till of my Lord Scroope I take farewell.

38.   "Farewell, farewell, my gude Lord Scroope!
      My gude Lord Scroope, farewell!" he cried;
   "I'll pay you for my lodging-maill
      When first we meet on the border-side."

39.   Then shoulder high, with shout and cry,
      We bore him down the ladder lang;
   At every stride Red Rowan made,
      I wot the Kinmont's airns playd clang.

40.   "O mony a time," quo Kinmont Willie,
      "I have ridden horse baith wild and wood;
   But a rougher beast that Red Rowan
      I ween my legs have neer bestrode.

41.   "And mony a time," quo Kinmont Willie,
      "I've pricked a horse out oure the furs;
   But since the day I backed a steed
      I nevir wore sic cumbrous spurs."

42.   We scarce had won the Staneshaw-bank,
      When a' the Carlisle bells were rung,
   And a thousand men, in horse and foot,
      Cam wi the keen Lord Scroope along.

43. Buccleuch has turned Eden Water,
    Even where it flowd frae bank to brim,
And he has plunged in wi a' his band,
    And safely swam them thro the stream.

44. He turned him on the other side,
    And at Lord Scroope his glove flung he:
"If ye like na my visit in merry England,
    In fair Scotland come visit me!"

45. All sore astonished stood Lord Scroope,
    He stood as still as rock of stane;
He scarcely dared to trew his eyes
    When thro the water they had gane.

46. "He is either himsell a devil frae hell,
    Or else his mother a witch maun be,
I wad na have ridden that wan water
    For a' the gowd in Christentie."

ARCHIE O CAWFIELD (188)

Another rescue ballad very like 186 and 187. A Scottish and an American version are given here so that the process of transformation of a specific story to a general one can be noticed. This ballad has been found in New England but not elsewhere in America.

Text A, Percy Papers; B, traditional in Massachusetts, Child, iii, 494.

Notes

A 4/1. Ha: Hall. Child thinks that this ballad was originally told about Armstrongs and later the Halls were substituted.

A.

1. Late in an evening forth as I went,
    'T was on the dawning of the day;
I heard two brothers make their moan,
    I listend well what they did say.

2. "   .   .   .   .   .   .
    .   .   .   .
We were three born brethren,
    There's one of us condemnd to die."

3. Then up bespake Jock the laird:
    "If I had but a hundred men,
A hundred o th best i Christenty,

I wad go on to fair Dumfries,
   I wad loose my brother and set him free."

4. So up bespake then Dicky Ha,
      He was the wisest o the three,
    "A hundred men we'll never get,
      Neither for gold nor fee,
    But some of them will us betray;
      They'l neither fight for gold nor fee.

5. "Had I but ten well-wight men,
      Ten o the best i Christenty,
    I wad gae on to fair Dumfries,
      I wad loose my brother and set him free.

6. "Jocky Ha, our cousin, 's be the first man"
      For leugh o Liddesdale cracked he;
    "An ever we come till a pinch,
      He'll be as good as only three."

7. They mounted ten well-wight men,
      The o the best i Christenty;

                  .   .   .   .   .   .

          .   .   .   .   .

8. There was horsing and horsing of haste,
      And cracking o whips out o'er the lee,
    Till they came to fair Barngliss,
      And they ca'd the smith right quietly.

9. He has shod them a' their horse,
      He's shod them siccer and honestly,
    And he as turnd the cawkers backwards oer,
      Where foremost they were wont to be.

10. And there was horsing, horsing of haste,
      And cracking of whips out oer the lee,
    Until they came to Bonshaw wood,
      Where they held their council privately.

11. Some says, We'll gang the Annan road,
      It is the better road, said they;
    Up bespak then Dicky Ha,
      The wisest of that company.

12. "Annan road's a publick road,
      It's no the road that makes for me;
    But we will through at Hoddam ford,
      It is the better road," said he.

13. And there was horsing, horsing o haste,
      And cracking of whips out oer the lea,

Until they came to fair Dumfries,
 And it was newly strucken three.

14. Up bespake the Jocky Ha,
 For leugh o Liddesdale cracked he:
"I have a mare, they ca her Meg,
 She is the best i Christenty;
An ever we come till a pinch,
 She'll bring awa both thee and me."

15. "But five we'll leave to had our horse,
 And five will watch, guard for to be;
Who is the man," said Dicky then,
 "To the prison-door will go with me?"

16. Up bespak then Jocky Ha,
 For leugh o Liddesdale cracked he:
"I am the man," said Jocky than,
 "To the prison-door I'll go with thee."

17. They are up the jail-stair,
 They stepped it right soberly,
Until they came to the jail-door;
 They ca'd the prisoner quietly.

18. "O sleeps thou, wakes thou, Archie, my billy?
 O sleeps thou, wakes thou, dear billy?"
"Sometimes I sleep, sometimes I wake;
 But who's that knows my name so well?" said he.
"I am thy brother Dicky," he says;
 "This night I'm come to borrow thee."

19. But up bespake the prisoner then,
 And O but he spak woefully!
"Today has been a justice-court,

 . . . . .

And a' Liddesdale were here the night,
 The morn's the day at I'se to die."

20. "What is thy crime, Archie, my billy?
 What is the crime they lad to thee?"
"I brake a spear i the warden's breast,
 For saving my master's land," said he.

21. "If that be a' the crime they lay to thee, Archie, my billy,
 If that be the crime they lay to thee,
Work thou within, and me without,
 And thro good strength I'll borrow thee."

22. "I cannot work, billy," he says,
 "I cannot work, billy, with thee,

For fifteen stone of Spanish iron
    Lyes fast to me with lock and key."

23.   When Dicky he heard that,
        "Away, thou crabby chiel!" cried he;
    He's taen the door aye with his foot,
        And fast he followd it with his knee.
    Till a' the bolts the door hung on,
        O th' prison-floor he made them flee.

24.   "Thou's welcome, welcome, Archy, my billy,
        Thou's aye right dear welcome to me;
    There shall be straiks this day," he said,
        "This day or thou be taen from me."

25.   He's got the prisoner on o his back,
        He's gotten him irons and aw,

    .   .   .   .

        .   .   .   .   .   .

26.   Up bespak then Jocky Ha,
        "Let some o th' prisoner lean on me."
    "The diel o there," quo Dicky than,
        "He's no the wightdom of a flea."

27.   They are on o that gray mare,
        And they are on o her aw three,
    And they linked the irons about her neck,
        And galloped the street right wantonly.

28.   "To horse, to horse," then, "all," he says,
        "Horse ye with all the might ye may,
    For the jailor he will waken next;
        And the prisoners had a' wan away."

29.   There was horsing, horsing of haste,
        And cracking o whips out oer the lea,
    Until they came to the Bonshaw Shield;
        There they held their council privately.

30.   Some says, "We'll gang the Annan road;
        It is the better road," said they;
    But up bespak than Dicky Ha,
        The wisest of that company:

31.   "Annan road's a publick road,
        It's not the road that makes for me;
    But we will through at Annan Holme,
        It is the better road," said he;
    "An we were in at Wamfrey Gate,
        The Johnstones they will a' help me."

32. But Dicky looked oer his left shoulder,
  I wait a wiley look gave he;
He spied the lieutenant coming,
  And a hundred men of his company.

33. "So horse ye, horseye, lads!" he said,
  "O horse ye, sure and siccerly!
For yonder is the lieutenant,
  With a hundred men of his company."

34. There was horsing, horsing of haste,
  And cracking o whips out oer the lea,
Until they came to Annan Holme,
  And it was running like a sea.

35. But up bespak the lieutenant,
  Until a bonny lad said he,
"Who is the man," said the lieutenant,
  "Rides foremost of yon company?"

36. Then up bespak the bonny lad,
  Until the lieutenant said he,
"Some men do ca him Dicky Ha,
  Rides foremost of yon company."

37. "O haste ye, haste ye!" said the lieutenant,
  "Pursue with a' the might ye may!
For the man had needs to be well saint
  That comes thro the hands o Dicky Ha."

38. But up bespak Jock the laird,
  "This has been a dearsome night to me;
I've a colt of four years old,
  I wait he wannelld like the wind;
If ever he come to the deep,
  He will plump down, leave me behind."

39. "Wae light o thee and thy horse baith, Jock,
  And even so thy horse and thee!
Take thou mine, and I'll take thine,
  Foul fa the warst horse i th' company!
I'll cast the prisoner me behind;
  There'll no man die but him that's fee."

40. There they've a' taen the flood,
  And they have taen it hastily;
Dicky was the hindmost took the flood,
  And foremost on the land stood he.

41. Dicky's turnd his horse about,
  And he has turnd it hastilly:

"Come through, come thro, my lieutenant,
    Come thro this day, and drink wi me,
And thy dinner's be dressed in Annan Holme,
    It sall not cost thee one penny."

42. "I think some witch has bore the, Dicky,
        Or some devil in hell been thy daddy;
    I would not swum that wan water doublehorsed,
        For a' the gold in Christenty.

43. "But throw me thro my irons, Dicky,
        I wait they cost me full dear."
    "O devil be there," quo Jocky Hall,
        "They'l be good shoon to my gray mare."

44. O up bespoke then Jock the laird,
        "This night has been a dearsome night to me;
    For yesternight the Cawfield was my ain,
        Landsman again I neer sall be."

45. "Now wae light o thee and thy lands baith, Jock,
        And even so baith the land and thee!
    For gear will come and gear will gang,
        But three brother again we never were to be."

B.

1. As I walked out one morning in May,
        Just before the break of day,
    I heard two brothers a making their moan,
        And I listened a while to what they did say.
            I heard, etc.

2. "We have a brother in prison," said they,
        "Oh in prison lieth he!
    If we had but ten men just like ourselves,
        The prisoner we would soon set free."

3. "Oh no, no, no!" bold Dickie said he,
        "Oh no, no, no, that never can be!
    For forty men is full little enough
        And I for to ride in their companie.

4. "Ten to hold the horses in,
        Ten to guard the city about,
    Ten for to stand at the prison-door,
        And ten to fetch poor Archer out."

5. They mounted their horses, and so rode they.
        Who but they so merrilie!

They rode till they came to a broad river's side,
    And there they alighted so manfullie.

6. They mounted their horses, and so swam they,
    Who but they so merrilie!
They swam till they came to the other side,
    And there they alighted so manfullie.

7. They mounted their horses, and so rode they,
    Who but they so merrilie!
They rode till they came to that prison-door,
    And then they alighted so manfullie.

8. .   .   .   .
    .   .   .   .
"For I have forty men in my companie,
    And I have come to set you free."

9. "Oh no, no, no!" poor Archer says he,
    "Oh no, no, no, that never can be!
For I have forty pounds of good Spanish iron
    Betwixt my ankle and my knee."

10. Bold Dickie broke lock, Bold Dickie broke key,
    Bold Dickie broke everything that he could see;
He took poor Archer under one arm,
    And carried him out so manfullie.

11. They mounted their horses, and so rode they,
    Who but they so merrilie!
They rode till they came to that broad river's side,
    And there they alighted so manfullie.

12. "Bold Dickie, Bold Dickie," poor Archer says he,
    "Take my love horse to my wife and children three;
For my horse grows lame, he cannot swim,
    And here I see that I must die."

13. They shifted their horse, and so swam they,
    Who but they so merrilie!
They swam till they came to the other side,
    And there they alighted so manfullie.

14. "Bold Dickie, Bold Dickie," poor Archer says he,
    "Look you yonder there and see;
For the high-sheriff he is a coming,
    With an hundred men in his companie."

15. "Bold Dickie, Bold Dickie," High-sheriff said he,
    "You're the damndest rascal that ever I see!
Go bring me back the iron you've stole,
    And I will set the prisoner free."

16.   "Oh no, no, no!" Bold Dickie said he,
        "Oh no, no, no, that never can be!
      For the iron 't will do to shoe the horses,
        The blacksmith rides in our companie."

17.   "Bold Dickie, Bold Dickie," High-sheriff says he,
        "You're the damndest rascal that ever I see!"
      "I thank ye for nothing," Bold Dickie says he,
        "And you're a damned fool for following me."

HOBIE NOBLE (189)

This is another heroic ballad in which Hobie Noble is treacherously
betrayed to the English; but rather than confess to stealing the lord's
horse, he submits to the punishment the English are glad to give him.
The source of the ballad is not known.

  Text, Scott, i, 164.

1.   Foul fa the breast first treason bred in!
       That Liddisdale may safely say,
     For in it there was baith meat and drink,
       And corn unto our geldings gay.
           Fala la diddle, etc.

2.   We were stout-hearted men and true,
       As England it did often say;
     But now we may turn our backs and fly,
       Since brave Noble is seld away.

3.   Now Hobie he was an English man,
       And born into Bewcastle dale,
     But his misdeeds they were sae great,
       They banishd him to Liddisdale.

4.   At Kershope-foot the tryst was set,
       Kershope of the lily lee;
     And there was traitour Sim o the Mains,
       With him a private companie.

5.   Then Hobie has graithed his body weel,
       I wat it was wi baith good iron and steel;
     And he has pulld out his fringed grey,
       And there, brave Noble, he rade him weel.

6.   Then Hobie is down the water gane,
       Een as fast as he may drie;
     Tho they shoud a' brusten and broken their hearts,
       Frae that tryst Noble he would not be.

7.   "Weel may ye be, my feiries five,
        And aye, what is your wills wi me?"
     Then they cryd a' wi ae consent,
        "Thou'rt welcome here, brave Noble, to me.

8.   "Wilt thou with us in England ride,
        And thy safe-warrand we will be,
     If we get a horse worth a hundred punds,
        Upon his back that thou shalt be.

9.   "I dare not with you into England ride,
        The land-sergeant has me at feid;
     I know not what evil may betide
        For Peter of Whitfield his brother's dead.

10. "And Anton Shiel, he loves not me,
        For I gat twa drifts of his sheep;
     The great Earl of Whitfield loves me not,
        For nae gear frae me he eer coud keep.

11. "But will ye stay till the day gae down,
        Until the night come oer the grund,
     And I'll be a guide worth only twa
        That may in Liddisdale be fund.

12. "Tho dark the night as pick and tar,
        I'll guide ye o'er yon hills fu hie,
     And bring ye a' in safety back,
        If you'll be true and follow me.

13. He's guided them oer moss and muir,
        Oer hill and houp, and mony ae down,
     Til they came to the Foulbogshiel,
        And there brave Noble he lighted down.

14. Then word is gane to the land-sergeant,
        In Askirton where that he lay:
     "The deer that ye hae hunted lang
        Is seen into the Waste this day."

15. "Then Hobie Noble is that deer;
        I wat he carries the style fu hie!
     Aft has he beat your slough-hounds back,
        And set yourselves at little eie.

16. "Gar warn the bows of Hartlie-burn,
        See they shaft their arrows on the wa!
     Warn Willeva and Spear Edom,
        And see the morn they meet me a'.

17. "Gar meet me on the Rodrie-haugh,
        And see it be by break o day;

And we will on to Conscowthart Green,
    For ther, I think, w'll get our prey."

18.   Then Hobie Noble has dreamd a dream,
    In the Foulbogshiel where that he lay;
He thought his horse was neath him shot,
    And he himself got hard away.

19.   The cocks could crow, and the day could dawn,
    And I wat so even down fell the rain;
If Hobie had no wakend at that time,
    In the Foulbogshiel he had been tane or slain.

20.   "Get up, get up, my feiries five—
    For I wat here makes a fu ill day—
And the warst clock of this companie
    I hope shall cross the Waste this day."

21.   Now Hobie thought the gates were clear,
    But, ever alas! it was not sae;
They were beset wi cruel men and keen,
    That away brave Noble could not gae.

22.   "Yet follow me, my feiries five,
    And see of me ye keep good ray,
And the worst clock of this companie
    I hope shall cross the Waste this day."

23.   There was heaps of men now Hobie before,
    And other heaps was him behind,
That had he been as wight as Wallace was
    Away brave Noble he could not win.

24.   Then Hobie he had but a laddies sword,
    But he did more than a laddies deed;
In the midst of Conscouthart Green,
    He brake it oer Jers a Wigham's head.

25.   Now they have tane brave Hobie Noble,
    Wi his ain bowstring they band him sae;
And I wat his heart was neer sae sair
    As when his ain five band him on the brae.

26.   They have tane him on for West Carlisle;
    They asked him if he knew the way;
Whateer he thought, yet little he said;
    He knew the way as well as they.

27.   They hae tane him up the Ricker-gate;
    The wives they cast their windows wide;
And ilka wife to anither can say,
    That's the man loosd Jock o the Side!

28. "Fy on ye, women! why ca ye me man?
       For it's nae man that I'm usd like;
     I'm but like a forfoughen hound,
       Has been fighting in a dirty syke."

29. Then they hae tane him up thro Carlisle town,
       And set him by the chimney-fire;
     They gave brave Noble a wheat loaf to eat,
       And that was little his desire.

30. Then they gave him a wheat loaf to eat
       And after that a can o beer;
     Then they cried a', wi ae consent,
       "Eat, brave Noble, and make good cheer!

31. "Confess my lord's horse, Hobie," they say,
       "And the morn in Carlile thou'st no die."
     "How shall I confess them?" Hobie says,
       "For I never saw them with mine eye."

32. Then Hobie has sworn a fu great aith,
       By the day that he was gotten or born,
     He never had onything o my lord's
       That either eat him grass or corn.

33. "Now fare thee weel, sweet Mangerton!
       For I think again I'll neer thee see;
     I wad betray nae lad alive,
       For a' the goud in Christentie.

34. "And fare thee well now, Liddisdale,
       Baith the hie land and the law.
     Keep ye weel frae traitor Mains!
       For goud and gear he'll sell ye a'.

35. "I'd rather be ca'd Hobie Noble,
       In Carlisle, where he suffer for his faut,
     Before I were ca'd traitor Mains!
       That eats and drinks of meal and maut."

THE LOCHMABEN HARPER (192)

Several versions of this ballad depict an ingenious trick by which
the blind harper stole the king's horse without being suspected.

Text, Dixon, *Scottish Traditional Versions of Ancient Ballads,*
p. 37.

Notes

7/1. Reflects the welcome always extended to harpers in the Middle
Ages and Elizabethan times.

1. There was a jolly harper-man,
        That harped aye frae toun to toun;
    A wager he made, with two knights he laid
        To steal King Henry's Wanton Brown.

2. Sir Roger, he wagered five ploughs o land,
        Sir Charles wagered five thousand pound,
    And John he's taen the deed in hand,
        To steal King Henry's Wanton Brown.

3. He's taen his harp into his hand,
        And he gaed harping thro the toun,
    And as the king in his palace sat,
        His ear was touched wi the soun.

4. "Come in, come in, ye harper-man,
        Some o your harping let me hear."
    "Indeed, my liege, and by your grace,
        I'd rather hae stabling to my mare."

5. "Ye'll gang to yon outer court,
        That stands a little below the toun;
    Ye'll find a stable snug and neat,
        Where stands my stately Wanton Brown."

6. He's down him to the outer court,
        That stood a little below the toun;
    There found a stable snug and neat,
        For stately stood the Wanton Brown.

7. Then he has fixd a good strong cord
        Unto his grey mare's bridle-rein,
    And tied it unto that steed's tail,
        Syne shut the stable-door behin.

8. Then he harped on, an he carped on,
        Till all were fast asleep;
    Then down thro bower and ha he's gone,
        Even on his hands and feet.

9. He's to yon stable snug and neat,
        That lay a little below the toun;
    For there he placed his ain grey mare,
        Alang wi Henry's Wanton Brown.

10. "Ye'll do you down thro mire an moss,
        Thro mony bog an lairy hole;
    But never miss your Wanton slack;
        Ye'll gang to Mayblane, to your foal."

11. As soon's the door he had unshut,
        The mare gaed prancing frae the town,

An at her bridle-rein was tied
Henry's stately Wanton Brown.

12. Then she did rin thro mire an moss,
Thro mony bog an miery hole;
But never missed her Wanton slack
Till she reached Mayblane, to her foal.

13. When the king awaked from sleep
He to the harper-man did say,
"O waken ye, waken ye, jolly John,
We've fairly slept till it is day.

14. "Win up, win up, ye harper-man,
Some mair o harping ye'll gie me."
He said, "My liege, wi a' my heart,
But first my gude grey mare maun see."

15. Then forth he ran, and in he came,
Dropping mony a feigned tear:
"Some rogues hae broke the outer court,
An stown awa my gude grey mare."

16. "Then by my sooth," the king replied,
"If there's been rogues into the toun,
I fear, as well as your grey mare,
Awa is my stately Wanton Brown."

17. "My loss is great," the harper said,
"My loss is twice as great, I fear;
In Scotland I lost a gude grey steed,
An here I've lost a gude grey mare."

18. "Come on, come on, ye harper-man,
Some o your music lat me hear;
Well paid ye'se be, John, for the same,
An likewise for your gude grey mare."

19. When that John his money received,
Then he went harping frae the toun,
But little did King Henry ken
He'd stown awa his Wanton Brown.

20. The knights then lay ower castle-wa,
An they beheld baith dale an down,
An saw the jolly harper-man
Come harping on to Striveling toun.

21. Then, "By my sooth," Sir Roger said,
"Are ye returned back to toun?
I doubt my lad ye hae ill sped
Of stealing o the Wanton Brown."

22. "I hae been into fair England,
        An even into Lunan toun,
     An in King Henry's outer court,
        An stown awa the Wanton Brown."

23. "Ye lie, ye lie," Sir Charles he said,
        "An aye sae loud's I hear ye lie;
     Twall armed men, in armour bright,
        They guard the stable night and day."

24. "But I did harp them all asleep,
        An managed my business cunninglie;
     If ye make light o what I say,
        Come to my stable an ye'll see.

25. "My music pleasd the king sae well
        Mair o my harping he wishd to hear;
     An for the same he paid me well,
        And also for my gude grey mare."

26. Then he drew out a gude lang purse,
        Well stored wi gowd and white monie,
     An in a short time after this
        The Wanton Brown he lat them see.

27. Sir Roger produced his ploughs o land,
        Sir Charles produced his thousand pounds,
     Then back to Henry, the English king,
        Restored the stately Wanton Brown.

THE DEATH OF PARCY REED (193)

There seems to be no evidence that the events here related actually
occurred, yet they are true to the spirit of the troubled times on both
sides of the Border in the 15th and 16th centuries. Here is a ballad of
vengeance and betrayal.

Text A, Robert White's Papers, annotated Child, iv. 25; B, Dixon,
p. 99.

A.

1. The Liddesdale Crosiers hae ridden a race,
        And they had far better staid at hame,
     For they have lost a gallant gay,
        Young Whinton Crosier it was his name.

2. For Parcy Reed he has him taen,
        And he's delivered him to law,
     But auld Crosier has made answer
        That he'll gar the house of the Troughend fa.

3. So as it happened on a day
   That Parcy Reed is a hunting gane,
   And the false Halls of Girsonsfield
   They all along with him are gane.

4. They hunted up and they hunted down,
   They hunted all Reedwater round,
   Till weariness has on him seized;
   At the Batinghope he's fallen asleep.

5. O some they stole his powder-horn,
   And some put water in his lang gun:
   "O waken, waken, Parcy Reed!
   For we do doubt thou sleeps too sound.

6. "O waken, O waken, Parcy Reed!
   For we do doubt thou sleeps too long;
   For yonder's the five Crosiers coming,
   They're coming by the Hingin Stane.

7. "If they be five men, we are four,
   If ye will all stand true to me;
   Now every one of you may take one,
   And two of them ye may leave to me."

8. "We will not stay, nor we dare not stay,
   O Parcy Reed, for to fight with thee;
   For thou wilt find, O Parcy Reed,
   That they will slay both us and thee."

9. "O stay, O stay, O Tommy Hall,
   O stay, O man, and fight with me!
   If we see the Troughend again,
   My good black mare I will give thee."

10. "I will not stay, nor I dare not stay,
    O Parcy Reed, to fight for thee;
    For thou wilt find, O Parcy Reed,
    That they will slay both me and thee."

11. "O stay, O stay, O Johnnie Hall,
    O stay, O man, and fight for me!
    If I see the Troughend again,
    Five yoke of oxen I will give thee."

12. "I will not stay, nor I dare not stay,
    O Parcy Reed, for to fight with thee;
    For thou wilt find, O Parcy Reed,
    That they will slay both me and thee."

13. "O stay, O stay, O Willie Hall,
    O stay, O man, and fight for me!
  If we see the Troughend again,
    The half of my land I will give thee."

14. "I will not stay, nor I dare not stay,
    O Parcy Reed, for to fight with thee;
  For thou wilt find, O Parcy Reed,
    That they will slay both me and thee."

15. "Now foul fa ye, ye traitors all,
    That ever ye should in England won.
  You have left me in a fair field standin.
    And in my hand an uncharged gun.

16. "O fare thee well, my wedded wife,
    O fare you well, my children five.
  And fare thee well, my daughter Jane,
    That I love best that's born alive!

17. "O fare thee well, my brother Tom.
    And fare you well his children five.
  If you had been with me this day,
    I surely had been man alive.

18. "Farewell all friends! as for my foes,
    To distant lands may they be tane,
  And the three false Halls of Girsonsfield,
    They'll never be trusted nor trowed again."

B.

1. God send the land deliverance
    Frae every reaving, riding Scot;
  We'll sune hae neither cow nor ewe,
    We'll sune hae neither staig nor stot.

2. The outlaws come frae Liddesdale,
    They herry Redesdale far and near;
  The rich man's gelding it maun gang,
    They canna pass the puir man's mear.

3. Sure it were weel, had ilka thief
    Around his neck a halter strang;
  And curses heavy may they light
    On traitors vile oursels amang.

4. Now Parcy Reed has Crosier taen,
    He has delivered him to the law;
  But Crosier says he'll do waur than that,
    He'll make the tower o Troughend fa.

5. And Crosier says he will do waur,
   He will do waur if waur can be;
   He'll make the bairns a' fatherless,
   And then, the land it may lie lee.

6. "To the hunting, ho!" cried Parcy Reed,
   "The morning sun is on the dew;
   The cauler breeze frae off the fells
   Will lead the dogs to the quarry true.

7. "To the hunting, ho!" cried Parcy Reed,
   And to the hunting he has gane;
   And the three fause Ha's o Girsonsfield
   Alang wi him he has them taen.

8. They hunted high, they hunted low,
   By heathery hill and birken shaw;
   They raised a buck on Rooken Edge,
   And blew the mort at fair Ealylawe.

9. They hunted high, they hunted low,
   They made the echoes ring amain;
   With music sweet o horn and hound,
   They merry made fair Redesdale glen.

10. They hunted high, they hunted low,
    They hunted up, they hunted down,
    Until the day was past the prime,
    And it grew late in the afternoon.

11. They hunted high in Batinghope,
    When as the sun was sinking low;
    Says Parcy then, Ca off the dogs,
    We'll bait our steeds and homeward go.

12. They lighted high in Batinghope,
    Atween the brown and benty ground;
    They had but rested a little while
    Till Parcy Reed was sleeping sound.

13. There's nane may lean on a rotten staff,
    But him that risks to get a fa;
    There's nane may in a traitor trust,
    And traitors black were every Ha.

14. They've stown the bridle off his steed,
    And they've put water in his lang gun;
    They've fixed his sword within the sheath
    That out again it winna come.

15.   "Awaken ye, waken ye, Parcy Reed,
          Or by your enemies be taen;
      For yonder are the five Crosiers
          A-coming owre the Hingin-stane."

16.   "If they be five, and we be four,
          Sae that ye stand alang wi me,
      Then every man ye will take one,
          And only leave but two to me:
      We will them meet as brave men ought,
          And make them either fight or flee."

17.   "We mayna stand, we canna stand,
          We daurna stand alang wi thee;
      The Crosiers haud thee at a feud,
          And they wad kill baith thee and we."

18.   "O turn thee, turn thee, Johnie Ha,
          O turn thee, man, and fight wi me;
      When ye come to Troughend again,
          My gude black naig I will gie thee;
      He cost full twenty pound o gowd,
          Atween my brother John and me!"

19.   "I mayna turn, I canna turn,
          I daurna turn and fight wi thee;
      The Crosiers haud thee at a feud,
          And they wad kill baith thee and me."

20.   "O turn thee, turn thee, Willie Ha,
          O turn thee, man, and fight wi me;
      When ye come to Troughend again,
          A yoke o owsen I'll gie thee."

21.   "I mayna turn, I canna turn,
          I daurna turn and fight wi thee;
      The Crosiers haud thee at a feud,
          And they wad kill baith thee and me."

22.   "O turn thee, turn thee, Tommy Ha,
          O turn now, man, and fight wi me;
      If ever we come to troughend again,
          My daughter Jean I'll gie to thee."

23.   "I mayna turn, I canna turn,
          I daurna turn and fight wi thee;
      The Crosiers haud thee at a feud,
          And they wad kill baith thee and me."

24.   "O shame upon ye, traitors a'!
          I wish your hames ye may never see;

Ye've stown the bridle off my naig,
  And I can neither fight nor flee.

25. "Ye've stown the bridle off my naig,
  And ye've put water i my lang gun;
Ye've fixed my sword within the sheath
  That out again it winna come."

26. He had but time to cross himsel,
  A prayer he hadna time to say,
Till round him came the Crosiers keen,
  All riding graithed and in array.

27. "Weel met, weel met, now, Parcy Reed,
  Thou art the very man we sought;
Owre lang hae we been in your debt,
  Now will we pay you as we ought.

28. "We'll pay thee at the nearest tree,
  Where we shall hang thee like a hound."
Brave Parcy raisd his fankit sword,
  And felld the foremost to the ground.

29. Alake, and wae for Parcy Reed,
  Alake, he was an unarmed man;
Four weapons pierced him all at once,
  As they assailed him there and than.

30. They fell upon him all at once,
  They mangled him most cruellie;
The slightest wound might have caused his deid,
  And they hae gien him thirty-three;
They hacket off his hands and feet,
  And left him lying on the lee.

31. "Now, Parcy Reed, we've paid our debt,
  Ye canna weel dispute the tale,"
The Crosiers said, and off they rade;
  The rade the airt o Liddesdale.

32. It was the hour o gloaming gray,
  When herds come in frae fauld and pen;
A herd he saw a huntsman lie,
  Says he, "Can this be Laird Troughen?"

33. "There's some will ca me Parcy Reed,
  And some will ca me Laird Troughen;
It's little matter what they ca me,
  My faes hae made me ill to ken.

34. "There's some will ca me Parcy Reed,
  And speak my praise in tower and town;

It's little matter what they do now,
　　My life-blood rudds the heather brown.

35.　"There's some will ca me Parcy Reed,
　　　And a' my virtues say and sing;
　　I would much rather have just now
　　　A draught o water frae the spring."

36.　The herd flung aff his clouted shoon
　　　And to the nearest fountain ran;
　　He made his bonnet serve a cup,
　　　And wan the blessing o the dying man.

37.　"Now, honest herd, ye maun do mair,
　　　Ye maun do mair, as I you tell;
　　Ye maun bear tidings to Troughend,
　　　And bear likewise my last farewell.

38.　"A farewell to my wedded wife,
　　　A farewell to my brother John,
　　Wha sits into the Troughend tower
　　　Wi heart as black as any stone.

39.　"A farewell to my daughter Jean,
　　　A farewell to my young sons five;
　　Had they been at their father's hand,
　　　I had this night been man alive.

40.　"A farewell to my followers a',
　　　And a' my neighbours gude at need;
　　Bid them think how the treacherous Ha's
　　　Betrayed the life o Parcy Reed.

41.　"The laird o Clennel bears my bow,
　　　The laird o Brandon bears my brand;
　　Wheneer they ride i the Border-side,
　　　They'll mind the fate o the laird Troughend."

THE LAIRD OF WARISTON (194)

This ballad gives the student an excellent opportunity to study a ballad in relation to the events it depicts. In 1600 Jean Livingston Kincaid with the help of her nurse, Janet Murdo, and Robert Weir, a former servant, killed her husband, John Kincaid of Wariston. The details of the affair can be had from the records of the trial of Weir (summarized by Child).

Text A, Jamieson, i, 109; B, Buchan, i, 56.

Notes

1. According to one account Jean was 19; another makes her 21.
3. The records bring out the fact that they were married against their wishes and that "they were constantly quarreling." 4/3. Weir said Kincaid bit her arm; the version in the Kinloch MSS. says the "laird strake her on the mouth." 5/4. Here and also in the Kinloch version the suggestion is that the lady was prompted by the devil; Weir is not mentioned in either version. But compare the second version here printed from Buchan's Ballads. 7. The actual murder was done by Weir; he clubbed the laird to death. 9. She was beheaded; the nurse was burned. Four years later Weir was captured and executed.

A.

1. Down by yon garden green
        Sae merrily as she gaes;
    She has twa weel-made feet,
        And she trips upon her taes.

2. She has twa weel-made feet,
        Far better is her hand;
    She's as jimp in the middle
        As ony willow-wand.

3. "Gif ye will do my bidding,
        At my bidding for to be,
    It's I will make you lady
        Of a' the lands you see."

       *   *   *   *   *   *   *

4. He spak a word in jest;
        Her answer wasna good;
    He threw a plate at her face,
        Made it a' gush out o blood.

5. She wasna frae her chamber
        A step but barely three,
    When up and at her richt hand
        There stood Man's Enemy.

6. "Gif ye will do my bidding,
        At my bidding for to be,
    I'll learn you a wile
        Avenged for to be."

7. The Foul Thief knotted the tether,
        She lifted his head on hie,
    The nourice drew the knot
        That gard lord Waristoun die.

8. Then word is gane to Leith,
 Also to Edinburgh town,
That the lady had killd the laird,
 The laird o Waristoun.

* * * * * * *

9. "Tak aff, tak aff my hood,
 But lat my petticoat be;
Put my mantle o'er my head,
 For the fire I downa see.

10. "Now, a' ye gentle maids,
 Tak warning now by me,
And never marry ane
 But wha pleases your ee.

11. "For he married me for love,
 But I married him for fee;
And sae brak out the feud
 That gard my dearie die."

B.

1. "My mother was an ill woman,
 In fifteen years she married me;
I hadna wit to guide a man
 Alas! ill counsel guided me.

2. "O Warriston, O Warriston,
 I wish that ye may sink for sin!
I was but bare fifteen years auld,
 Whan first I enterd your yates within.

3. "I hadna been a month married,
 Till my gude lord went to the sea;
I bare a bairn ere he came hame,
 And set it on the nourice knee.

4. "But it fell ance upon a day,
 That my gude lord returnd from sea;
Then I did dress in the best array,
 As blythe as ony bird on tree.

5. "I took my young son in my arms,
 Likewise my nourice me forebye,
And I went down to yon shore-side,
 My gude lord's vessel I might spy.

6. "My lord he stood upon the deck,
        I wyte he haild me courteouslie."
   "Ye are thrice welcome, my lady gay,
        Whae's aught that bairn on your knee?"

7. She turnd her right and round about,
        Says, "Why take ye sic dreads o me?
   Alas! I was too young married,
        To love another man but thee."

8. "Now hold your tongue, my lady gay,
        Nae mair falsehoods ye'll tell to me;
   This bonny bairn is not mine,
        You've loved another while I was on sea."

9. In discontent then hame she went,
        And aye the tear did blin her ee;
   Says, "Of this wretch I'll be revenged
        For these harsh words he's said to me."

10. She's counselld wi her father's steward
         What way she coud revenged be;
    Bad was the counsel then he gave,
         It was to gar her gude lord dee.

11. The nourice took the deed in hand,
         I wat she was well paid her fee;
    She kiest the knot, and the loop she ran,
         Which soon did gar this young lord dee.

12. His brother lay in a room hard by,
         Alas! that night he slept too soun;
    But then he wakend wi a cry,
         "I fear my brother's putten down.

13. "O get me coal and candle light,
         And get me some gude companie."
    But before the light was brought,
         Warriston he was gart dee.

14. They've taen the lady and fause nourice,
         In prison strong they hae them boun;
    The nourice she was hard o heart,
         But the bonny lady fell in swoon.

15. In it came her brother dear,
         And aye a sorry man was he:
    "I woud gie a' the lands I heir,
         O bonny Jean, to borrow thee."

16. "O borrow me, brother, borrow me?
       O borrowd shall I never be;
    For I gart kill my ain gude lord,
       And life is nae pleasure to me."

17. In it came her mother dear,
       I wyte a sorry woman was she:
    "I woud gie my white monie and gowd,
       O bonny Jean, to borrow thee."

18. "Borrow me, mother, borrow me?
       O borrowd shall I never be;
    For I gart kill my ain gude lord,
       And life's now nae pleasure to me."

19. Then in it came her father dear,
       I wyte a sorry man was he;
    Says, "Ohon, alas! my bonny Jean,
       If I had you at hame wi me!

20. "Seven daughters I hae left at hame,
       As fair women as fair can be;
    But I would gie them ane by ane,
       O bonny Jean, to borrow thee."

21. "O borrow me, father, borrow me?
       O borrowd shall I never be;
    I that is worthy o the death,
       It is but right that I shoud dee."

22. Then out it speaks the king himsell,
       And aye as he steps in the fleer;
    Says, "I grant you your life, lady,
       Because you are of tender year."

23. "A boon, a boon, my liege the king,
       The boon I ask, ye'll grant to me."
    "Ask on, ask on, my bonny Jean,
       Whateer ye ask it's granted be."

24. "Cause take me out at night, at night,
       Lat not the sun upon me shine,
    And take me to yon heading-hill,
       Strike aff this dowie head o mine.

25. "Ye'll take me out at night, at night,
       When there are nane to gaze and see,
    And hae me to yon heading-hill,
       And ye'll gar head me speedilie."

26. They've taen her out at nine at night,
       Loot not the sun upon her shine,

And had her to yon heading-hill,
    And headéd her baith neat and fine.

27. Then out it speaks the king himsell,
    I wyte a sorry man was he:
  "I've travelld east, I've travelld west,
    And sailed far beyond the sea,
  But I never saw a woman's face
    I was sae sorry to see dee.

28. "But Warriston was sair to blame,
    For slighting o his lady so;
  He had the wyte o his ain death,
    And bonny lady's overthrow."

LORD MAXWELL'S LAST GOODNIGHT (195)

This is a tangled story of a long feud between the Maxwells and the Johnstones in the early part of the 17th century. This ballad was inspired by the execution of John, ninth Lord Maxwell, who had killed Sir James Johnstone. It is included here largely because Byron said that the good-night in the first canto of *Childe Harold* was suggested by this ballad. A *good-night* became almost a genre of poetry in the 16th and 17th centuries; it was a sort of farewell to the world. Cf. Essex' Last Goodnight.

Text, traditional in Scotland, Percy Papers.

1. "Good lord of the land, will you stay thane
    About my faither's house,
  And walk into these gardines green,
    In my arms I'll the embraice.

2. "Ten thousand times I'll kiss thy face;
    Make sport, and let's be mery."
  "I thank you, lady fore your kindness;
    Trust me, I may not stay with the.

3. "For I have kil'd the laird Johnston;
    I vallow not the feed;
  My wiked heart did still incline;
    He was my faither's dead.

4. "Both night and day I did proced,
    And a' on him revainged to be;
  But now have I gotten what I long sowght,
    Trust me, I may not stay with the.

5. "Adue, Dumfriese, that proper place,
    Fair well, Carlaurike faire,

Adue the castle of the Trive,
　　And all my buldings there!

6.　"Adue, Lochmaben gaits so faire,
　　　And the Langhm shank, where birks bobs bony,
　　Adue, my leady and only joy,
　　　Trust me, I may not stay with the.

7.　"Adue, fair Eskdale, up and doun,
　　　Wher my poor frends do duell;
　　The bangisters will beat them doun,
　　　And will them sore compell.

8.　"I'll reveinge the cause mysell,
　　　Again when I come over the sea;
　　Adue, my leady and only joy!
　　　Fore, trust me, I may not stay with the.

9.　"Adue, Dumlanark! fals was ay,
　　　And Closburn, in a band;
　　The laird of the Lag from my faither fled
　　　When the Jhohnstones struck of his hand.

10.　"They wer three brethren in a band;
　　　I pray they may never be merry;
　　Adue, my leady and only joy!
　　　Trust me, I may not stay with the.

11.　"Adue, madam my mother dear,
　　　But and my sisters two.
　　Fair well, Robin in the Orchet,
　　　Fore the my heart is wo.

12.　"Adue, the lillie, and fair well, rose,
　　　And the primros spreads fair and bony,
　　Adue, my leady and only joy,
　　　Fore, trust me, I may not stay with the."

13.　He took out a good gold ring,
　　　Where at hang sygnets three:
　　"Take thou that, my own kind thing,
　　　And ay have mind of me.

14.　"Do not mary another lord
　　　Agan or I come over the sea;
　　Adue, my leady and only joy!
　　　For, trust me, I may not stay with the."

15.　The wind was fair, and the ship was clare,
　　　And the good lord went away;
　　The most part of his frends was there,
　　　Giving him a fair convoy.

16. They drank the wine, they did not spare,
     Presenting in that good lord's sight;
  Now he is over the floods so gray;
     Lord Maxwell has te'n his last good-night.

BONNY JOHN SETON (198)

This ballad recounts a minor skirmish between the troops of the king
and those of the Covenanters for the defense of Aberdeen. It is interesting to see that the ballad concentrates the whole affair on the activity and death of one of the king's men, John Seton, who was killed
by a lucky cannon shot.

Text, Maidment, *North Countrie Garland,* p. 15.

1. Upon the eighteenth day of June,
     A dreary day to see,
  The southern lords did pitch their camp
     Just at the bridge of Dee.

2. Bonny John Seton of Pitmeddin,
     A bold baron was he,
  He made his testament ere he went out,
     The wiser man was he.

3. He left his land to his young son,
     His lady her dowry,
  A thousand crowns to his daughter Jean,
     Yet on the nurse's knee.

4. Then out came his lady fair,
     A tear into her ee;
  Says, stay at home, my own good lord,
     O stay at home with me."

5. He looked over his left shoulder,
     Cried, Souldiers, follow me.
  O then she looked in his face,
     An angry woman was she:
  "God send me back my steed again,
     But neer let me see thee."

6. His name was Major Middleton
     That manned the bridge of Dee,
  His name was Colonel Henderson
     That let the cannons flee.

7. His name was Major Middleton
   That manned the bridge of Dee,
   And his name was Colonel Henderson
   That dung Pitmeddin in three.

8. Some rode on the black and grey,
   And some rode on the brown,
   But the bonny John Seton
   Lay gasping on the ground.

9. Then bye there comes a false Forbes,
   Was riding from Driminere,
   Says, "Here there lies a proud Seton;
   This day they ride the rear."

10. Cragievar said to his men,
    "You may play on your shield;
    For the proudest Seton in all the lan
    This day lies on the field."

11. "O spoil him! spoil him!" cried Cragievar,
    "Him spoiled let me see;
    For on my word," said Cragievar,
    "He had no good will at me."

12. They took from him his armour clear,
    His sword, likewise his shield;
    Yea, they have left him naked there,
    Upon the open field.

13. The Highland men, they're clever men
    At handling sword and shield,
    But yet they are too naked men
    To stay in battle field.

14. The Highland men are clever men
    At handling sword or gun,
    But yet they are too naked men
    To bear the cannon's rung.

15. For a cannon's roar in a summer night
    Is like thunder in the air;
    There's not a man in Highland dress
    Can face the cannon's fire.

THE BONNIE HOUSE OF AIRLIE (199)

In 1640 followers of Charles began to be punished by the destruction of their property. This ballad tells of the burning of the castle of Airlie by the Duke of Argyle while the lord of the castle was away with the king. The defiance and scorn of the lady are invention of the ballad; she was not present when the castle was destroyed.

The ballad survives in America in a version very like the English type printed here, and also in a more generalized version in which the background is made that of the War of the Roses.

Text A, Sharpe's *Ballad Book,* p. 59; B, traditional in Maine, Barry, p. 268.

A.

1. It fell on a day, and a bonny simmer day,
      When green grew aits and barley,
   That there fell out a great dispute
      Between Argyll and Airlie.

2. Argyll has raised an hunder men,
      An hunder harnessd rarely,
   And he's awa by the back of Dunkell,
      To plunder the castle of Airlie.

3. Lady Ogilvie looks o'er her bower-window.
      And oh, but she looks weary,
   And there she spy'd the great Argyll,
      Come to plunder the bonny house of Airlie.

4. "Come down, come down, my Lady Ogilvie,
      Come down, and kiss me fairly."
   "O I winna kiss the fause Argyll,
      If he should na leave a standing stane in Airlie."

5. He hath taken her by the left shoulder,
      Says, "Dame where lies thy dowry?"
   "O it's east and west yon wan water side,
      And it's down by the banks of the Airlie."

6. They hae sought it up, they hae sought it down,
      They hae sought it maist severly,
   Till they fand it in the fair plumb-tree
      That shines on the bowling-green of Airlie.

7. He hath taken her by the middle sae small,
      And O but she grat sairly!
   And laid her down by the bonny burn-side,
      Till they plundered the castle of Airlie.

8.   "Gif my gude lord war here this night,
         As he is with King Charlie,
      Neither you, nor ony ither Scottish lord,
         Durst avow to the plundering of Airlie.

9.   "Gif my gude lord war now at hame,
         As he is with his king,
      There durst nae a Campbell in a' Argyll
         Set fit on Airlie green.

10.   "Ten bonny sons I have born unto him,
         The eleventh neer saw his daddy;
      But though I had an hundred mair,
         I'd gie them a' to King Charlie."

B.

1.   It was in the Wars of the Roses white and red,
         And in the days of Prince Charley;
      Argyle drew up with his ten thousand strong
         Before the courts of Arley.

2.   A maiden fair from a window high
         Looked down to him quite surley,
      She wished for her Knight with his soldiers strong
         To defend the courts of Arley.

3.   "Come down to me, my fair young maid,
         Come down and kiss me fairly,
      As I vow and I swear by the broad sword I wear
         I will not leave a standing stone in Arley."

4.   "I will not come down, young man," said she,
         "I will not come down to you from Arley,
      I will not come down, young man," said she,
         "And I will not kiss you squarely."

5.   "But there's one thing I would ask of you,
         And I hope you will grant it fairly,
      It is, take me down to the low green valley low,
         That I may not see the plundering of Arley."

6.   He took me by my left shoulder,
         He turned me round quite squarely,
      He carried me up to the highest mountain top,
         Saying, "Look well upon the plundering of Arley."

7.   "If my brave Knight had been at home,
         Instead of in the wars with Prince Charley,
      Then you with all your ten thousand strong
         Would never had the plundering of Arley."

THE GYPSY LADDIE (200)

This ballad was very popular and continues to be so. No version has been found earlier than the latter half of the 18th century, but as a ballad it is probably a good bit older. In the latter part of the 15th century and the early part of the 16th there was much resentment against the "Egyptians" and they were repeatedly ordered from the country. The name Johnny Faa frequently appears, several times sentenced to be hanged for not leaving the country. There is no evidence in history or tradition that the story here told is factual. Later the ballad is associated with the family of the Earl of Cassilis (Cassilis may come by corruption of Earl of the Castle), but wholly without justification.

The American versions vary considerably. In general they work away from the narrative to a pure lyric with much contamination from other ballads and songs. In many American versions the lady tries to return to her husband, but often he has taken another wife, or refuses to have her; in some versions the Gypsy tires of her and casts her off.

Text A, Allan Ramsay, *Tea-Table Miscellany,* p. 427; B, *The Edinburgh Magazine and Literary Miscellany,* November 1817, p. 309; C, traditional in Nova Scotia, *JAF,* 18:191; D, traditional in Kentucky, *JAF,* 48:385.

A.

1.　The gypsies came to our good lord's gate,
　　　And wow but they sang sweetly!
　　They sang sae sweet and sae very compleat
　　　That down came the fair lady.

2.　And she came tripping down the stair,
　　　And a' her maids before her;
　　As soon as they saw her well-far'd face,
　　　They coost the glamer o'er her.

3.　"Gae tak frae me this gay mantile,
　　　And bring to me a plaidie;
　　For if kith and kin and a' had sworn,
　　　I'll follow the gypsie laddie.

4.　"Yestreen I lay in a well-made bed,
　　　And my good lord beside me;
　　This night I'll ly in a tenant's barn,
　　　Whatever shall betide me."

5.　"Come to your bed," says Johny Faa,
　　　"Oh come to your bed, my deary;

For I vow and I swear, by the hilt of my sword,
 That your lord shall nae mair come near ye."

6. "I'll go to bed to my Johny Faa,
 I'll go to bed to my deary;
For I vow and I swear, by what past yestreen,
 That my lord shall nae mair come near me.

7. "I'll mak a hap to my Johnny Faa,
 And I'll mak a hap to my deary;
And he's get a' the coat gaes round,
 And my lord shall nae mair come near me."

8. And when our lord came hame at een,
 And speir'd for his fair lady,
The tane she cry'd, and the other reply'd,
 "She's away with the gypsie laddie."

9. "Gae saddle to me the black, black steed,
 Gae saddle and make him ready;
Before that I either eat or sleep,
 I'll gae seek my fair lady."

10. And we were fifteen well-made men,
 Altho we were nae bonny;
And we were a' put down for ane,
 A fair young wanton lady.

B.

1. The gypsies they came to my lord Cassilis' yett,
 And O but they sang bonnie.
They sang sae sweet and sae complete
 That down came our fair ladie.

2. She came tripping down the stairs,
 And all her maids before her;
As soon as they saw her weel-far'd face,
 They coost their glamourie owre her.

3. She gave to them the good wheat bread,
 And they gave her the ginger;
But she gave them a far better thing,
 The gold rings off her fingers.

4. "Will ye go with me, my hinny and my heart?
 Will ye go with me, my dearie?
And I will swear, by the staff of my spear,
 That your lord shall nae mair come near thee."

5. "Gae take from me my silk mantel,
    And bring to me a plaidie,
   For I will travel the world owre
      Along with the gypsie laddie.

6. "I could sail the seas with my Jockie Faa,
    I could sail the seas with my dearie;
   I could sail the seas with my Jockie Faa,
      And with pleasure could drown with my dearie."

7. They wandred high, they wandred low,
    They wandred late and early,
   Untill they came to an old tenant's-barn,
      And by this time she was weary.

8. "Last night I lay in a weel-made bed,
    And my noble lord beside me,
   And now I must ly in an old tenant's barn,
      And the black crew glowring owre me."

9. "O hold your tongue, my hinny and my heart,
    O hold your tongue, my dearie,
   For I will swear, by the moon and the stars,
      That thy lord shall nae mair come near thee!"

10. They wandred high, they wandred low,
     They wandred late and early,
    Untill they came to that wan water,
       And by this time she was wearie.

11. "Aften have I rode that wan water,
     And my lord Cassilis beside me,
    And now I must set in my white feet and wade,
       And carry the gypsie laddie."

12. By and by came home this noble lord,
     And asking for his ladie,
    The one did cry, the other did reply,
       "She is gone with the gypsie laddie."

13. "Go saddle to me the black," he says,
     "The brown rides never so speedie,
    And I will neither eat nor drink
       Till I bring home my ladie."

14. He wandred high, he wandred low,
     He wandred late and early,
    Untill he came to that wan water,
       And there he spied his ladie.

15. "O wilt thou go home, my hinny and my heart,
     O wilt thou go home, my dearie?

And I'll close thee in a close room,
 Where no man shall come near thee."

16. "I will not go home, my hinny and my heart,
 I will not go home, my dearie;
If I have brewn good beer, I will drink of the same,
 And my lord shall nae mair come near me.

17. "But I will swear, by the moon and the stars,
 And the sun that shines so clearly,
That I am as free of the gypsie gang
 As the hour my mother did bear me."

18. They were fifteen valiant men,
 Black, but very bonny,
And they lost all their lives for one,
 The Earl of Cassillis' ladie.

C.

1. The Gypsy Daisy came riding o'er the plain,
 He sang so loud and clearly,
He sang till he made the green woods ring,
 And charmed the heart of a Lady.

Refrain

Red Lady dingo, dingo day,
 Red Lady dingo, dingo Daisy;
Red Lady dingo, dingo day,
 She's away with the Gypsy Daisy.

2. "Come saddle me my old brown hack,
 The gray one is not so speedy,
I'll ride all day, and I'll ride all night,
 Till I overtake my Lady."

3. He rode till he came to the riverside,
 The waters flowed so freely,
The tears down his cheeks did flow,
 And then he saw his Lady.

4. "Could you forsake your house and home,
 Could you forsake your baby,
Could you forsake your own wedded Lord,
 And go with the Gypsy Daisy?"

5. "Yes, I'll forsake my house and home,
 Yes, I'll forsake my baby,
Yes I'll forsake my own wedded Lord,
 And go with the Gypsy Daisy.

6. "Last night I lay on a bed of down,
    The Land Lord lay by me;
   To-night I'll lay on the damp cold ground,
    Along with the Gypsy Daisy."

D.

BLACK JACK DAVIE

1. Black Jack Davie came riding thru the plain;
   He sang so loud and clearly
   He made the green woods around him ring
   To charm the heart of a lady,
   To charm the heart of a lady.

2. "How old are you, my pretty little Miss?
   How old are you, my honey?"
   She made him an answer, with a hug and a kiss,
   "I'll be sixteen next Sunday,
   I'll be sixteen next Sunday."

3. "Will you go with me, my pretty little Miss?
   Will you go with me, my honey?
   I'll swear by the sword that hangs by my side
   You never shall want for money,
   You never shall want for money."

4. She took off her high-heeled shoes,
   All made of Spanish leather.
   She put on her low-heeled shoes,
   And they rode off together,
   And they rode off together.

5. The landlord he came home at night
   Inquiring for his lady.
   The chambermaid made this reply,
   "She's gone with Black Jack Davie,
   She's gone with Black Jack Davie."

6. "Go bridle and saddle my little yellow mare;
   The grey one's not so speedy.
   I've rode all day, and I'll ride all night
   So that I'll overtake my lady,
   So that I'll overtake my lady."

7. He rode till he came to the dark blue sea;
   It looked so dark and dreary,
   And there he spied his own, dear bride
   By the side of Black Jack Davie,
   By the side of Black Jack Davie.

8. "Will you forsake your house and home?
Will you forsake your baby?
Will you forsake your own married love,
And go with Black Jack Davie?
And go with Black Jack Davie?"

9. She took off her blue gloves,
All made of Spanish leather.
She bade him farewell with her lily white hand,
She said farewell forever,
She said farewell forever.

THE BARON OF BRACKLEY (203)

This ballad had best be read as a general story of bravery, of treachery, of Border heroics rather than as a historical ballad following
closely on the events. It is perhaps based on a feud between John Gordon of Brackley and John Farquharson of Inverey over a matter of
cattle Gordon had stolen from Farquharson.

Text, Buchan's *Gleanings,* p. 68.

Notes
41. Cf. Johnie Armstrong.

1. Inverey cam doun Deeside, whistlin and playin,
He was at brave Braikley's yett ere it was dawin.

2. He rappit fu loudly an wi a great roar,
Cried, "Cum doun, cum doun, Braikley, and open the door.

3. "Are ye sleepin, Baronne, or are ye wakin?
Ther's sharpe swords at your yett, will gar your blood spin.

4. "Open the yett, Braikley, and lat us within,
Till we on the green turf gar your bluid rin."

5. Out spak the brave baronne, owre the castell-wa:
"Are ye cum to spulyie and plunder mi ha?

6. "But gin ye be gentlemen, licht and cum in.
Gin ye drink o my wine, ye'll nae gar my bluid spin.

7. "Gin ye be hir'd widifus, ye may gang by,
Ye may gang to the lawlands and steal their fat ky.

8. "Ther spulyie like rievers o wyld kettrin clan,
Who plunder unsparing baith houses and lan.

9. "Gin ye be gentlemen, licht an cum in,
Ther's meat an drink i my ha for every man.

10. "Gin ye be hir'd widifus, ye may gang by,
    Gang doun to the lawlands, and steal horse and ky."

11. Up spak his ladie, at his bak where she lay,
    "Get up, get up, Braikley, and be not afraid;
    The'r but young hir'd widifus wi belted plaids."

12. "Cum kiss me, mi Peggy, I'le nae langer stay,
    For I will go out and meet Inverey.

13. "But haud your tongue, Peggy, and mak nae sic din,
    For yon same hir'd widifus will prove themselves men."

14. She called on her marys, they cam to her hand;
    Cries, "Bring me your rocks, lassies, we will them command.

15. "Get up, get up, Braikley, and turn bak your ky,
    Or me an mi women will them defy.

16. "Cum forth then, mi maidens, and show them some play;
    We'll ficht them, and shortly the cowards will fly.

17. "Gin I had a husband, whereas I hae nane,
    He woud nae ly i his bed and see his ky taen.

18. "Ther's four-and-twenty milk-whit calves, twal of them ky,
    In the woods o Glentanner, it's ther thei a'ly.

19. "Ther's goat i the Etnach, and sheep o the brae,
    An a' will be plundered by young Inverey."

20. "Now haud your tongue, Peggy, and gie me a gun,
    Ye'll see me gae furth, but I'll never cum in.

21. "Call mi brother William, mi unkl also,
    Mi cousin James Gordon; we'll mount and we'll go."

22. When Braikley was ready and stood i the closs,
    He was the bravest baronne that eer mounted horse.

23. Whan all wer assembld o the castell green,
    No man like brave Braikley was ther to be seen.

24. .   .   .   .
    "Turn bak, brother William, ye are a bridegroom;

25. "Wi bonnie Jean Gordon, the maid o the mill;
    O sichin and sobbin she'll soon get her fill."

26. "I'm no coward, brother, 'tis kend I'm a man;
    I'll ficht i your quarrel as lang's I can stand.

27. "I'll ficht, my dear brother, wi heart and gude will,
    And so will young Harry that lives at the mill.

28.   "But turn, mi dear brother, and nae langer stay:
      What'll cum o your ladie, gin Braikley thei slay?

29.   "What'll cum o your ladie and bonnie young son?
      O what'll cum o them when Braikley is gone?"

30.   "I never will turn. Do you think I will fly?
      But here I will ficht, and here I will die."

31.   "Strik dogs," crys Inverey, "and ficht till ye're slayn,
      For we are four hundered, ye are but four men.

32.   "Strik, strik, ye proud boaster, your honour is gone,
      Your lands we will plunder, your castell we'll burn."

33.   At the head o the Etnach the battel began,
      At Little Auchoilzie thei killd the first man.

34.   First thei killd ane, and soon they killd twa,
      Thei killd gallant Braikley, the flour o them a'.

35.   Thei killd William Gordon, and James o the Knox,
      And brave Alexander, the flour o Glenmuick.

36.   What sichin and moaning was heard i the glen,
      For the Baronne o Braikley, who basely was slayn!

37.   "Cam ye bi the castell, and was ye in there?
      Saw ye pretty Peggy tearing her hair?"

38.   "Yes, I cam by Braikley, and I gaed in there,
      And there saw his ladie braiding her hair.

39.   "She was rantin, and dancin, and singin for joy,
      And vowin that nicht she woud feest Inverey.

40.   "She eat wi him, drank wi him, welcomd him in,
      Was kind to the man that had slayn her baronne."

41.   Up spake the son on the nourice's knee,
      "Gin I live to be a man, revenged I'll be."

42.   Ther's dool i the kitchin, and mirth i the ha,
      The Baronne o Braikley is dead and awa.

JAMIE DOUGLAS (204)

Lady Barbara Erskine was married in 1670 to James, Marquis of Douglas. They were separated by mutual consent by act of the Privy Council in 1681. Tradition (and gossip) had it that the Lady was maligned by Blackwood, her husband's factor, who accused her of entertaining a lover (Lockwood in A) in her husband's absence.

Printed herewith is an old song, "Waly, Waly, Gin Love Be Bony," which was first printed in Ramsay's *Tea-Table Miscellany* (c. 1727) some fifty years before any known copy of the ballad. Stanzas from this song have drifted not only into versions of this ballad but into other ballads and songs. A later printing of the song contains the following stanza which is frequently found in lyrics:

> When cockle-shells turn siller bells,
> And mussles grow on evry tree,
> When frost and snaw shall warm us a'
> Then shall my love prove true to me.

One would guess that this song may be the remnant of a ballad from which most of the narrative has been lost. At any rate it is an interesting example of drift.

Text A, Kinloch MSS., i, 93, 16th century; B, traditional in Scotland, Motherwell, p. 299; "Waly, etc.," from Ramsay, *Tea-Table Miscellany* (ed. 1729), p. 176.

Notes

B. 8. Lady Barbara's father was dead when she left her husband. B. 10/2. She had but one child.

A.

1. I was a lady of high renown
       As lived in the north countrie;
   I was a lady of high renown
       Whan Earl Douglas loved me.

2. Whan we came through Glasgow toun,
       We war a comely sight to see;
   My gude lord in velvet green,
       And mysel in cramasie.

3. Whan we cam to Douglas toun,
       We war a fine sight to behold;
   My gude lord in cramasie,
       And I myself in shining gold.

4. Whan that my auld son was born,
       And set upon the nurse's knee,
   I was as happy a woman as eer was born,
       And my gude lord he loved me.

5. But oh, an my young son was born,
       And set upon the nurse's knee,
   And I mysel war dead and gane,
       For a maid again I'll never be.

6. There cam a man into this house,
　　And Jamie Lockhart was his name,
　And it was told to my gude lord
　　That I was in the bed wi him.

7. There cam anither to this house,
　　And a bad friend he was to me;
　He put Jamie's shoon below my bed-stock,
　　And bade my gude lord come and see.

8. O wae be unto thee, Blackwood,
　　And ae an ill death may ye dee!
　For ye was the first and the foremost man
　　That parted my gude lord and me.

9. Whan my gude lord cam in my room,
　　This grit falsehood for to see,
　He turnd about, and, wi a gloom,
　　He straucht did tak farewell o me.

10. "O fare thee well, my once lovely maid!
　　O fare thee well, once dear to me!
　O fare thee well, my once lovely maid!
　　For wi me again ye sall never be."

11. "Sit doun, sit doun, Jamie Douglas,
　　Sit thee doun and dine wi me,
　And I'll set thee on a chair of gold,
　　And a silver towel on thy knee."

12. "Whan cockle-shells turn silver bells,
　　And mussels they bud on a tree,
　Whan frost and snaw turns fire to burn,
　　Then I'll sit down and dine wi thee."

13. O wae be unto thee, Blackwood,
　　And ae an ill death may ye dee!
　Ye war the first and foremost man
　　That parted my gude lord and me.

14. Whan my father he heard word
　　That my gude lord had forsaken me,
　He sent fifty o his brisk dragoons
　　To fesh me hame to my ain countrie.

15. That morning before I did go,
　　My bonny palace for to leave,
　I went into my gude lord's room,
　　But alas, he wad na speak to me.

16. "Fare thee well, Jamie Douglas,
　　Fare thee well, my ever dear to me,

Fare thee well, Jamie Douglas,
    Be kind to the three babes I've born to thee."

B.

1. O waly, waly up yon bank,
    And waly, waly doun yon brae,
And waly, waly by yon burn-side,
    Where me and my luve used to gae.

2. Oh Johnie, Johnie, but love is bonnie
    A little while, when it is new;
But when loves grows aulder, it grows mair caulder,
    And it fades awa like the mornin dew.

3. I leaned my back against an aik,
    I thocht it was a trusty tree;
But first it bowed, and syne it brak,
    And sae did my fause luve to me.

4. Once I lay sick, and very sick,
    And a friend of mine cam to visit me,
But the small bird whispered in my love's ears.
    That he was ower lang in the room wi me.

5. "It's come down stairs, my Jamie Douglas,
    Come down stairs, luve, and dine wi me;
I'll set you on a chair of gold,
    And court ye kindly on my knee."

6. "When cockle-shells grow silver bells,
    And gold it grows on every tree,
When frost and snaw turns fiery balls,
    Then, love, I'll come down and dine wi thee."

7. If I had known what I know now,
    That love it was sae ill to win,
I should neer hae wet my cherry cheek
    For onie man or woman's son.

8. When my father he cam to know
    That my first luve had sae slighted me,
He sent four score of his soldiers bright
    To guard me home to my own countrie.

9. Slowly, slowly rose I up,
    And slowly, slowly I came down,
And when he saw me sit in my coach,
    He made his drums and trumpets sound.

10.   It's fare ye weel, my pretty palace,
        And fare ye weel, my children three,
      And I hope your father will get mair grace,
        And love you better than he's done to me.

11.   When we came near to bonnie Edinburgh toun,
        My father cam for to meet me;
      He made his drums and trumpets sound,
        But they were no comfort at all to me.

12.   "It's hold your tongue, my daughter dear,
        And of your weeping pray let be;
      For a bill of divorcement I'll send to him,
        And a better husband I'll you supply."

13.   "O hold your tongue, my father dear,
        And of your folly pray now let be;
      For there's neer a lord shall enter my bower,
        Since my first love has so slighted me."

WALY, WALY, GIN LOVE BE BONNY
(Cf. Jamie Douglas 204.)

1.   O waly, waly up the bank,
        And waly, waly, down the brae,
      And waly, waly yon burn-side,
        Where I and my love wont to gae!

2.   I lean'd my back unto an aik,
        I thought it was a trusty tree;
      But first it bow'd, and syne it brak,
        Sae my true-love did lightly me.

3.   O waly, waly, but love be bonny
        A little time, while it is new;
      But when it is auld, it waxeth cauld,
        And fades away like morning dew.

4.   O wherefore shoud I busk my head?
        Or wherefore shoud I kame my hair?
      For my true-love has me forsook,
        And says he'll never love me mair.

5.   Now Arthur-Seat shall be my bed,
        The sheets shall ne'er be fyl'd by me;
      Saint Anton's well shall be my drink,
        Since my true-love has forsaken me.

6.   Martinmas wind, when wilt thou blaw,
        And shake the green leaves off the tree?

O gentle death, when wilt thou come?
    For of my life I am weary.

7.   'Tis not the frost that freezes fell,
      Nor blawing snaw's inclemency;
    'Tis not sic cauld that makes me cry,
      But my love's heart grown cauld to me.

8.   When we came in by Glasgow town,
      We were a comely sight to see;
    My love was cled in the black velvet,
      And I mysell in cramasie.

9.   But had I wist, before I kiss'd,
      That love had been sae ill to win,
    I'd lock'd my heart in a case of gold,
      And pin'd it with a silver pin.

10.   Oh, oh, if my young babe were born,
      And set upon the nurse's knee,
    And I mysell were dead and gane!
      For a maid again I'll never be.

BOTHWELL BRIDGE (206)

On June 22, 1679, the royal army under the command of the Duke of Monmouth moved against the Covenanters at Bothwell Bridge on the Clyde. The Covenanters after a stubborn fight on the bridge were routed by cannon fire, whereupon the King's forces crossed and soon dispersed the main body.

    Text, Scott, iii, 209.

Notes

    2/1. Earlston: William Gordon of Earlston, a staunch Covenanter. 12/3. Claverhouse: John Graham of Claverhouse, Viscount Dundee. Scott introduces him in *Old Mortality*. He was a staunch foe of the Covenanters. His cornet, his nephew, had been killed in the fight at Drumclog.

1.   "O Billie, billie, bonny billie,
      Will ye go to the wood wi me?
    We'll ca our horse hame masterless,
      An gar them trow slain men are we."

2.   "O no, O no," says Earlstoun,
      "For that's the thing that mauna be;
    For I am sworn to Bothwell Hill,
      Where I maun either gae or die."

3.   So Earlstoun rose in the morning,
        An mounted by the break o day,
    An he has joind our Scottish lads,
        As they were marching out the way,

4.   "Now, farewell, father, and farewell, mother,
        An fare ye weel, my sisters three,
    An fare ye well, my Earlstoun,
        For thee again I'll never see."

5.   So they're awa to Bothwell Hill,
        An waly, they rode bonnily!
    When the Duke o Monmouth saw them comin,
        He went to view their company.

6.   "Ye're welcome, lads," then Monmouth said,
        "Ye're welcome, brave Scots lads, to me;
    And sae are you, brave Earlstoun,
        The foremost o your company.

7.   "But yield your weapons ane an a',
        O yield your weapons, lads, to me;
    For, gin ye'll yield your weapons up,
        Ye'se a' gae hame to your country."

8.   Out then spak a Lennox lad,
        And waly, but he spoke bonnily,
    "I winna yield my weapons up,
        To you nor nae man that I see."

9.   Then he set up the flag o red,
        A' set about wi bonny blue.
    "Since ye'll no cease, and be at peace,
        See that ye stand by ither true."

10.   They stelld their cannons on the height,
        And showrd their shot down in the how,
    An beat our Scots lads even down;
        Thick they lay slain on every know.

11.   As e'er you saw the rain down fa,
        Or yet the arrow frae the bow,
    Sae our Scottish lads fell even down,
        As they lay slain on every know.

12.   "O hold your hand," then Monmouth cry'd,
        "Gie quarters to your men for me;"
    But wicked Claverhouse swore an oath
        His cornet's death revengd sud be.

13.   "O hold your hand," then Monmouth cry'd.
        "If ony thing you'll do for me;

Hold up your hand, you cursed Graeme,
 Else a rebel to our king ye'll be."

14. Then wicked Claverhouse turnd about—
 I wot an angry man was he—
And he has lifted up his hat,
 And cry'd, God bless his Majesty!

15. Than he's awa to London town,
 Ay een as fast as he can dree;
Fause witnesses he has wi him taen,
 An taen Monmouth's head frae his body.

16. Alang the brae beyond the brig,
 Mony brave man lies cauld and still;
But lang we'll mind, and sair we'll rue,
 The bloody battle of Bothwell Hill.

LORD DERWENTWATER (208)

James Ratcliffe, Earl of Derwentwater, was captured in the battle of
Preston in November, 1715, and conveyed to London and lodged in
the Tower. He pled guilty of treason to the King (he was supporting
the Pretender) and was executed on February 24, 1716.

 Text, Motherwell, p. 349.

Notes

 1 and 3. Suggest "Sir Patrick Spens." 8/2. horse stumbling was a
sign of bad luck; in some versions his nose bleeds, also foretelling bad
fortune.

1. Our king has wrote a lang letter,
 And sealed it owre with gold;
He sent it to my lord Dunwaters,
 To read it if he could.

2. He has not sent it with a boy, with a boy,
 Nor with anie Scotch lord;
But he's sent it with the noblest knight
 Eer Scotland could afford.

3. The very first line that my lord did read,
 He gave a smirking smile;
Before he had the half o't read,
 The tears from his eyes did fall.

4. "Come saddle to me my horse," he said,
 "Come saddle to me with speed;

For I must away to fair London town,
　　For me was neer more need."

5.　Out and spoke his lady gay,
　　　In child-bed where she lay:
　　"I would have you make your will, my lord Dunwaters,
　　　Before you go away."

6.　"I leave to you, my eldest son,
　　　My houses and my land;
　　I leave to you, my second son,
　　　Ten thousand pounds in hand.

7.　"I leave to you, my lady gay—
　　　You are my wedded wife—
　　I leave to you, the third of my estate;
　　　That'll keep you in a lady's life."

8.　They had not rode a mile but one,
　　　Till his horse fell owre a stane:
　　"It's warning gude eneuch," my lord Dunwaters said,
　　　"Alive I'll neer come hame."

9.　When they came into fair London town,
　　　Into the courtiers' hall,
　　The lords and knichts in fair London town
　　　Did him a traitor call.

10.　"A traitor! a traitor!" says my lord,
　　　A traitor! how can that be,
　　An it was na for the keeping of five thousand men
　　　To fight for King Jamie?

11.　"O all you lords and knichts in fair London town,
　　　Come out and see me die;
　　O all you lords and knichts into fair London town,
　　　Be kind to my ladie.

12.　"There's fifty pounds in my right pocket,
　　　Divide it to the poor;
　　There's other fifty pounds in my left pocket,
　　　Divide it from door to door."

GEORDIE (209)

Early commentators on this ballad have supposed that Geordie is
George Gordon, fourth earl of Huntly. He was imprisoned on a political charge and ransomed, though not by his wife. The many versions of this ballad are corrupted by association with other songs and
ballads; in America there is wide variation in the text.

Text A, Johnson's *Musical Museum*, p. 357; B, traditional in Scotland, Buchan, ii, 143; C, traditional in Virginia, *JAF*, 32:504.

A.

1. There was a battle in the north,
   And nobles there was many,
   And they hae killd Sir Charlie Hay,
   And they laid the wyte on Geordie.

2. O he has written a lang letter,
   He sent it to his lady:
   "Ye maun cum up to Enbrugh town,
   To see what word's o Geordie."

3. When first she lookd the letter on,
   She was baith red and rosy;
   But she had na read a word but twa
   Till she wallowt like a lily.

4. "Gar get to me my gude grey steed,
   My menyie a' gae wi me,
   For I shall neither eat nor drink
   Till Enbrugh town shall see me."

5. And she has mountit her gude grey steed,
   Her menyie a' gaed wi her,
   And she did neither eat nor drink
   Till Enbrugh town did see her.

6. And first appeard the fatal block,
   And syne the aix to head him,
   And Geordie cumin down the stair,
   And bands o airn upon him.

7. But tho he was chaind in fetters strang,
   O airn and steel sae heavy,
   There was na ane in a' the court
   Sae bra a man as Geordie.

8. O she's down on her bended knee,
   I wat she's pale and weary:
   "O pardon, pardon, noble king,
   And gie me back my dearie."

9. "I hae born seven sons to my Geordie dear,
   The seventh neer saw his daddie;
   O pardon, pardon, noble king,
   Pity a waefu lady."

10. "Gar bid the headin-man mak haste,"
    Our king reply'd fu lordly.

"O noble king, tak a' that's mine,
    But gie me back my Geordie."

11. The Gordons cam, and the Gordons ran,
        And they were stark and steady,
    And ay the word amang them a'
        Was, Gordons, keep you ready!

12. An aged lord at the king's right hand
        Says, "Noble king, but hear me;
    Gar her tell down five thousand pound,
        And gie her back her dearie."

13. Some gae her marks, some gae her crowns,
        Some gae her dollars many,
    And she's telld down five thousand pound,
        And she's gotten again her dearie.

14. She blinkit blythe in her Geordie's face,
        Says, "Dear I've bought thee, Geordie;
    But there sud been bluidy bouks on the green
        Or I had tint my laddie."

15. He claspit her by the middle sma,
        And he kist her lips sae rosy:
    "The fairest flower o woman-kind
        Is my sweet, bonie lady!"

B.

1. "I choosed my love at the bonny yates of Gight,
        Where the birks an the flowers spring bony,
    But pleasures I had never one,
        But crosses very mony.

2. "First I was mistress of Pitfan
        And madam of Kincraigie,
    And now my name is bonny Lady Anne,
        And I am Gight's own lady.

3. "He does not use me as his wife,
        Nor cherish me as his lady,
    But day by day he saddles the grey,
        And rides off to Bignet's lady."

4. Bignet he got word of this,
        That Gight lay wi his lady,
    He swore a vow, and kept it true,
        To be revengd on's body.

5. Where will I get a bonny boy
    Will run my errand shortly,
That woud run on to the bonny yates o Gight
    Wi a letter to my lady?"

6. Gight has written a broad letter,
    And seald it soon and ready,
And sent it on to Gight's own yates,
    For to acquaint his lady.

7. The first of it she looked on,
    O dear! she smiled bonny;
But as she read it till an end
    The tears were thick an mony.

8. "Come saddle to me the black," she says,
    "Come saddle him soon and shortly,
Ere I ride down to Edinburgh town,
    Wi a lang side sark to Geordy."

9. When she came to the boat of Leith,
    I wad she did na tarry;
She gave the boatman a guinea o gold
    To boat her oer the ferry.

10. As she gaed oer the pier of Leith,
    Among the peerls many,
She dealt the crowns and dukedoons,
    Bade them a' pray for Geordy.

11. As she gaed up the tolbooth-stair,
    Among the nobles many,
Every one sat hat on head,
    But hat in hand stood Geordy.

12. "Has he brunt? or has he slain?
    Or has he robbëd any?
Or has he done any other crime,
    That gars you head my Geordy."

13. "He hasna brunt, he hasna slain,
    He hasna robbëd any;
But he has done another crime,
    For which he will pay dearly."

14. In it comes him First Lord Judge,
    Says, "George, I'm sorry for you;
You must prepare yourself for death,
    For there'll be nae mercy for you."

15. In it comes him Second Lord Judge,
    Says, "George I'm sorry for you;

You must prepare yourself for death,
    For there'll be nae mercy for you."

16. Out it speaks Gight's lady herself,
    And vow, but she spake wordy!
    "Is there not a lord among you all
      Can plead a word for Geordy?"

17. Out it speaks the first Lord Judge:
    "What lady's that amang you
    That speaks to us so boldly here,
      And bids us plead for Geordy?"

18. Out then spake a friend, her own,
    And says, "It's Gight's own lady,
    Who is to come to plead her own lord's cause,
      To which she's true and steady.

19. The queen, looking oer her shott-window,
    Says, "Ann, I'm sorry for you;
    If ye'll tell down ten thousand crowns,
      Ye shall get home your Geordy."

20. She's taen the hat out of his hand,
    And dear! it set her bonny;
    She's beggd the red gold them among,
      And a' to borrow Geordy.

21. She turnd her right and round about
    Among the nobles many;
    Some gave her dollars, some her crowns,
      And some gave guineas many.

22. She spread her mantle on the floor,
    O dear! she spread it bonny,
    And she told down that noble sum;
      Says, Put on your hat, my Geordy.

23. But out it speaks him gleid Argyle,
    Says, "Woe be to your body!
    I wish that Gight had lost his head,
      I should enjoyd his lady."

24. She looked oer her left shoulder,
    A proud look and a saucy;
    Says, "Woe be to you, gleid Argyle!
      Ye'll neer be like my Geordy."

25. "You'll hae me to some writer's house,
    And that baith seen and shortly,
    That I may write down Gight's lament,
      And how I borrowed Geordy."

26. When she was in her saddle set,
    And aye behind her Geordy,
Birds neer sang blyther in the bush
    Than she behind her Geordy.

27. "O bonny George, but I love thee well,
    And O sae dear as I love thee.
The sun and moon and firmament above
    Bear witness how I love thee."

28. "O bonny Ann, but I love thee well,
    And O sae dear as I love thee.
The birds in the air, that fly together pair and pair,
    Bear witness, Ann, that I love thee."

C.

1. Go saddle up my milk-white steed,
    Go saddle it full gayly,
Until I write to the earthen sires(?)
    To plead for the life of Georgie.

2. She rid till she come to the earthen sires' office
    So early in the morning;
She tumbled down on her bended knees,
    Saying, "Spare me the life of Georgie!"

3. There were an old man stepped up to her,
    He looked as if he was pleasing;
"O pretty miss! if it lays in my power,
    I'll spare you the life of Georgie."

4. The judge looked over his left shoulder,
    He looked as if he was angry;
Says, "Now, pretty miss, you've come too late,
    For Georgie he's condemned already!"

5. "Did Georgie ever trample on the king's highway,
    Or did he murder any?"—
"He stole sixteen of the milk-white steeds,
    And conveyed them away to the army."

6. Georgie he was hung in a white silk robe,
    Such robes there was not many,
Because he was of that royal blood,
    And was loved by a virtuous lady.

BONNIE JAMES CAMPBELL (210)

This is only a fragment—a lyrical remnant of a ballad probably telling the story, all-too-common among the Campbells, of the untimely death of one of the clan. The subject of the ballad has not surely been identified; he may be the James Campbell who died in the battle of Genlivet in 1594.

Text A, Herd's MSS., i, 40; B, Finlay, *Scottish Ballads*, I, xxxiii.

A.

1. O it's up in the Highlands, and along the sweet Tay,
    Did bonie James Campbell ride monie a day.

2. Sadled and bridled, and bonie rode he;
    Hame came horse, hame came sadle, but ne'er hame cam he.

3. And doun cam his sweet sisters, greeting sae sair,
    And down cam his bonie wife, tearing her hair.

4. "My house is unbigged, my barn's unbeen,
    My corn's unshorn, my meadow grows green."

B.

1. Hie upon Hielands, and laigh upon Tay,
    Bonnie George Campbell rode out on a day.

2. He saddled, he bridled, and gallant rode he,
    And hame cam his guid horse, but never cam he.

3. Out cam his mother dear, greeting fu sair,
    And out cam his bonnie bryde, riving her hair.

4. "The meadow lies green, the corn is unshorn,
    But bonnie George Campbell will never return."

5. Saddled and bridled and booted rode he,
    A plume in his helmet, a sword at his knee.

6. But toom cam his saddle, all bloody to see,
    Oh, hame cam his guid horse, but never cam he!

BEWICK AND GRAHAM (211)

Only late texts of this ballad survive, but they show evidence of being based on much older material. The identity of the Bewick and the Graham who figure here is not determined, nor the circumstances behind the story. Sir Walter Scott points out that this is one of the latest allusions to blood-brotherhood, or sworn-brotherhood in literature, a relation that was common in the literature of the Middle Ages and in the life of the Heroic Age. Blood-brothers were legally brothers in fact, with all the responsibilities and privileges of real brotherhood.

Text, Broadside, Percy Papers.

1. Old Grahame he is to Carlisle gone,
   Where Sir Robert Bewick there met he;
   In arms to the wine they are gone,
   And drank till they were both merry.

2. Old Grahame he took up the cup,
   And said, "Brother Bewick, here's to thee;
   And here's to our two sons at home,
   For they live best in our country."

3. "Nay, were thy son as good as mine,
   And of some books he could but read,
   With sword and buckler by his side,
   To see how he could save his head,

4. "They might have been calld two bold brethren
   Where ever they did go or ride;
   They might have been calld two bold brethren,
   They might have crackd the Border-side.

5. "Thy son is bad, and is but a lad,
   And bully to my son cannot be;
   For my son Bewick can both write and read,
   And sure I am that cannot he."

6. "I put him to school, but he would not learn,
   I bought him books, but he would not read;
   But my blessing he's never have
   Till I see how his hand can save his head."

7. Old Grahame called for an account,
   And he askd what was for to pay;
   There he paid a crown, so it went round,
   Which was all for good wine and hay.

8. Old Grahame is into the stable gone,
   Where stood thirty good steed and three;
   He's taken his own steed by the head,
   And home rode he right wantonly.

9. When he came home, there did he espy,
   A loving sight to spy or see,
   There did he espy his own three sons,
   Young Christy Grahame, the foremost was he.

10. There did he espy his own three sons,
        Young Christy Grahame, the foremost was he.
     "Where have you been all day, father,
        That no counsel you would take by me?"

11. "Nay, I have been in Carlisle town,
        Where Sir Robert Bewick there met me;
     He said thou was bad, and calld thee a lad,
        And a baffled man by thou I be.

12. "He said thou was bad, and calld thee a lad,
        And bully to his son cannot be;
     For his son Bewick can both write and read,
        And sure I am that cannot thee.

13. "I put thee to school, but thou would not learn,
        I bought thee books, but thou would not read;
     But my blessing thou's never have
        Till I see with Bewick thou can save thy head."

14. "Oh, pray forbear, my father dear;
        That ever such a thing should be!
     Shall I venture my body in field to fight
        With a man that's faith and troth to me?"

15. "What's that thou sayst, thou limmer loon?
        Or how dare thou stand to speak to me?
     If thou do not end this quarrel soon,
        Here is my glove thou shalt fight me."

16. Christy stoopd low unto the ground,
        Unto the ground, as you'll understand.
     "O father, put on your glove again,
        The wind hath blown it from your hand."

17. "What's that thou sayst, thou limmer loon?
        Or how dare thou stand to speak to me?
     If thou do not end this quarrel soon,
        Here is my hand thou shalt fight me."

18. Christy Grahame is to his chamber gone,
        And for to study, as well might be,
     Whether to fight with his father dear,
        Or with his bully Bewick he.

19. "If it be my fortune my bully to kill,
        As you shall boldly understand,
     In every town that I ride through,
        They'll say, There rides a brotherless man!

20. "Nay, for to kill my bully dear,
        I think it will be a deadly sin;

And for to kill my father dear,
  The blessing of heaven I neer shall win.

21. "O give me your blessing, father," he said,
  "And pray well for me for to thrive;
If it be my fortune my bully to kill,
  I swear I'll neer come home alive."

22. He put on his back a good plate-jack,
  And on his head a cap of steel,
With sword and buckler by his side;
  O gin he did not become them well.

23. "O fare thee well, my father dear,
  And fare thee well, thou Carlisle town.
If it be my fortune my bully to kill,
  I swear I'll neer eat bread again."

24. Now we'll leave talking of Christy Grahame,
  And talk of him again belive;
But we will talk of bonny Bewick,
  Where he was teaching his scholars five.

25. Now when he had learnd them well to fence,
  To handle their swords without any doubt,
He's taken his own sword under his arm,
  And walkd his father's close about.

26. He lookd between him and the sun,
  To see what farleys he coud see;
There he spy'd a man with armour on,
  As he came riding over the lee.

27. "I wonder much what man yon be
  That so boldly this way does come;
I think it is my nighest friend,
  I think it is my bully Grahame.

28. "O welcome, O welcome, bully Grahame.
  O man, thou art my dear, welcome.
O man, thou art my dear, welcome.
  For I love thee best in Christendom."

29. "Away, away, O bully Bewick,
  And of thy bullyship let me be.
The day is come I never thought on;
  Bully, I'm come here to fight with thee."

30. "O no! not so, O bully Grahame!
  That eer such a word should spoken be.
I was thy master, thou was my scholar:
  So well as I have learnèd thee."

31.   "My father he was in Carlisle town,
  Where thy father Bewick there met he;
He said I was bad, and he calld me a lad,
  And a baffled man by thou I be."

32.   "Away, away, O bully Grahame,
  And of all that talk, man, let us be!
We'll take three men of either side
  To see if we can our fathers agree.

33.   "Away, away, O bully Bewick,
  And of thy bullyship let me be!
But if thou be a man, as I trow thou art,
  Come over this ditch and fight with me."

34.   "O no! not so, my bully Grahame.
  That eer such a word should spoken be!
Shall I venture my body in field to fight
  With a man that's faith and troth to me?"

35.   "Away, away, O bully Bewick,
  And of all that care, man, let us be!
If thou be a man, as I trow thou art,
  Come over this ditch and fight with me."

36.   "Now, if it be my fortune thee, Grahame, to kill,
  As God's will's, man, it all must be;
But if it be my fortune thee, Grahame, to kill,
  'T is home again I'll never gae."

37.   "Thou art of my mind then, bully Bewick,
  And sworn-brethren will we be;
If thou be a man, as I trow thou art,
  Come over this ditch and fight with me."

38.   He flang his cloak from off his shoulders,
  His psalm-book out of his hand flang he,
He clapd his hand upon the hedge,
  And oer lap he right wantonly.

39.   When Grahame did see his bully come,
  The salt tear stood long in his eye.
"Now needs must I say that thou art a man,
  That dare venture thy body to fight with me.

40.   "Now I have a harness on my body;
  I know that thou hath none on thine;
But as little as thou hath on thy back,
  Sure as little shall there be on mine."

41.   He flang his jack from off his back,
  His steel cap from his head flang he;

He's taken his sword into his hand,
    He's tyed his horse unto a tree.

42. Now they fell to it with two broad swords,
    For two long hours fought Bewick and he;
Much sweat was to be seen on them both,
    But never a drop of blood to see.

43. Now Grahame gave Bewick an ackward stroke,
    An ackward stroke surely struck he;
He struck him now under the left breast,
    Then down to the ground as dead fell he.

44. "Arise, arise, O bully Bewick,
    Arise and speak three words to me!
Whether this be thy deadly wound,
    Or God and good surgeons will mend thee."

45. "O horse, O horse, O bully Grahame,
    And pray do get thee far from me.
Thy sword is sharp, it hath wounded my heart,
    And so no further can I gae.

46. "O horse, O horse, O bully Grahame,
    And get thee far from me with speed!
And get thee out of this country quite.
    That none may know who's done the deed."

47. "O if this be true, my bully dear,
    The words that thou dost tell to me,
The vow I made, and the vow I'll keep;
    I swear I'll be the first that die.

48. Then he stuck his sword in a moody-hill,
    Where he lap thirty good foot and three;
First he bequeathed his soul to God,
    And upon his own sword-point lap he.

49. Now Grahame he was the first that died,
    And then came Robin Bewick to see;
"Arise, arise, O son," he said,
    "For I see thou's won the victory.

50. "Arise, arise, O son," he said,
    "For I see thou's won the victory."
"Father could ye not drunk your wine at home,
    And letten me and my brother be?

51. "Nay, dig a grave both low and wide,
    And in it us two pray bury;
But bury my bully Grahame on the sun-side,
    For I'm sure he's won the victory."

52. Now we'll leave talking of these two brethren,
  In Carlisle town where they lie slain,
And talk of these two good old men,
  Where they were making a pitiful moan.

53. With that bespoke now Robin Bewick:
  "O man, was I not much to blame?
I have lost one of the liveliest lads
  That ever was bred unto my name."

54. With that bespoke my good lord Grahame,
  "O man, I have lost the better block;
I have lost my comfort and my joy,
  I have lost my key, I have lost my lock.

55. "Had I gone through all Ladderdale,
  And forty horse had set on me,
Had Christy Grahame been at my back,
  So well as he woud guarded me."

56. I have no more of my song to sing,
  But two or thee words to you I'll name;
But't will be talk'd in Carlisle town
  That these two old men were all the blame.

THE DUKE OF ATHOLE'S NURSE (212)

We have no definite information about the source of this ballad. It was very popular in the north, where it still exists in tradition. The Duke of Athole's Nurse longs for a sight of her sweetheart, discovers she is talking to him, but also that he now loves another. She sends him to a tavern with the promise to meet him there, but instead sends her brothers to slay him. The landlady dresses him in maid's clothes and so he escapes detection.

Text, Buchan, ii, 23.

1. As I gaed in yon greenwood-side,
  I heard a fair maid singing;
Her voice was sweet, she sang sae complete
  That all the woods were ringing.

2. "O I'm the Duke o Athole's nurse,
  My post is well becoming;
But I woud gie a' my half-year's fee
  For ae sight o my leman."

3. "Ye say ye're the Duke o Athole's nurse,
  Your post is well becoming;

      Keep well, keep well your half-year's fee,
        Ye'se hae twa sights o your leman."

4.   He leand him ower his saddle-bow
      And cannilie kissd his dearie.
    "Ohon and alake! anither has my heart,
      And I darena mair come near thee."

5.   "Ohon and alake! if anither hae your heart,
      These words hae fairly undone me;
    But let us set a time, tryst to meet again,
      Then in gude friends you will twine me.

6.   "Ye will do you down to yon tavern-house
      And drink till the day be dawing,
    And, as sure as I ance had a love for you,
      I'll come there and clear your lawing.

7.   "Ye'll spare not the wine, altho it be fine,
      Nae Malago, tho it be rarely,
    But ye'll aye drink the bonnie lassie's health
      That's to clear your lawing fairly."

8.   Then he's done him down to yon tavern-house
      And drank till day was dawing,
    And aye he drank the bonny lassie's health
      That was coming to clear his lawing.

9.   And aye as he birled, and aye as he drank,
      The gude beer and the brandy,
    He spar'd not the wine, altho it was fine,
      The sack nor the sugar candy.

10.   "It's a wonder to me," the knight he did say,
      "My bonnie lassie's sae delaying;
    She promisd, as sure as she loved me ance,
      She woud be here by the dawing."

11.   He's done him to a shott-window,
      A little before the dawing,
    And there he spied her nine brothers bauld,
      Were coming to betray him.

12.   "Where shall I rin? where shall I gang?
      Or where shall I gang hide me?
    She that was to meet me in friendship this day
      Has sent nine men to slay me."

13.   He's gane to the landlady o the house,
      Says, "O can you supply me?
    For she that was to meet me in friendship this day
      Has sent nine men to slay me."

14. She gae him a suit o her ain female claise
     And set him to the baking;
   The bird never sang mair sweet on the bush
     Nor the knight sung at the baking.

15. As they came in at the ha-door,
     Sae loudly as they rappit!
   And when they came upon the floor,
     Sae loudly as they chappit!

16. "O had ye a stranger here last night,
     Who drank till the day was dawing?
   Come show the chamber where he lyes in,
     We'll shortly clear his lawing."

17. "I had nae stranger here last night
     That drank till the day was dawing;
   But ane that took a pint, and paid it ere he went,
     And there's naething to clear o his lawing."

18. A lad amang the rest, being o a merry mood,
     To the young knight fell a-talking;
   The wife took her foot and gae him a kick,
     Says, "Be busy, ye jilt, at your baking."

19. They stabbed the house baith but and ben,
     The curtains they spared nae riving,
   And for a' that they did search and ca,
     For a kiss o the knight they were striving.

THE BRAES O YARROW (214)

This beautiful ballad has many touches of old story: the warning
dream, blood revenge for wrong to family, drinking the blood of the
slain lover, strangling herself with her hair, drawing the dead man
home by wrapping her hair about his waist. There is great poetry too
in the refrain which is a poignant commentary on the tragic action.
No source of this in tradition has been found. The many versions attest to the popularity of this ballad.

A close analogue of this ballad is found in Scandinavia. A version
from Prior, iii, 371, is given here for comparison.

The American versions of this ballad are confused, being contami-
nated with later poems on the subject and with the ballad "Rare Willie Drowned in Yarrow." They follow more closely the versions that
have the refrain "Yn the dowie banks of yarrow." See Child, iv, 522.

Text, Scott, iii, 72.

1. Late at een, drinkin the wine,
     Or early in a mornin,

The set a combat them between,
    To fight it in the dawnin.

2. "O stay at hame, my noble lord,
    O stay at hame, my marrow,
  My cruel brother will you betray,
    On the dowy houms o Yarrow."

3. "O fare ye weel, my lady gaye,
    O fare ye weel, my Sarah,
  For I maun gae, tho I neer return
    Frae the dowy banks o Yarrow."

4. She kissed his cheek, she kaimd his hair,
    As she had done before, O;
  She belted on his noble brand,
    An he's awa to Yarrow.

5. O he's gane up yon high, high hill—
    I wat he gaed wi sorrow—
  An in a den spied nine armd men,
    I the dowy houms o Yarrow.

6. "O ir ye come to drink the wine,
    As ye hae doon before, O?
  Or ir ye come to wield the brand,
    On the dowy banks o Yarrow."

7. "I im no come to drink the wine,
    As I hae don before, O,
  But I im come to wield the brand,
    On the dowy houms o Yarrow."

8. Four he hurt, an five he slew,
    On the dowy houms o Yarrow,
  Till that stubborn knight came him behind,
    An ran his body thorrow.

9. "Gae hame, gae hame, good-brother John,
    An tell your sister Sarah
  To come an lift her noble lord,
    Who's sleepin sound on Yarrow."

10. "Yestreen I dreamd a dolefu dream;
    I kend there wad be sorrow;
  I dreamd I pu'd the heather green,
    On the dowy banks o Yarrow."

11. She gaed up yon high, high hill—
    I wat she gaed wi sorrow—

An in a den spy'd nine deadmen,
    On the dowy houms o Yarrow."

12. She kissd his cheek, she kaimd his hair,
    As oft she did before, O;
She drank the red blood frae him ran,
    On the dowy houms o Yarrow.

13. "O haud your tongue, my douchter dear,
    For what needs a' this sorrow?
I'll wed you on a better lord
    Than him you lost on Yarrow."

14. "O haud your tongue, my father dear,
    An dinna grieve your Sarah;
A better lord was never born
    Than him I lost on Yarrow.

15. "Tak hame your ousen, tak hame your kye,
    For they hae bred our sorrow;
I wiss that they had a' gane mad
    When they cam first to Yarrow."

SIR HELMER BLAA AND HIS BRIDE'S BROTHERS

1. Sir Helmer Blaa with hawk and hound
Was riding through the forest ground.
        So well he sits in saddle.

2. He saw just under a mountain side
His lady-fair's seven brothers ride.

3. Sir Helmer ask'd his squire so true,
"What thinkest thou were best to do?"

4. "'Twere best, the truth if I may say,
To spur our steeds and ride away."

5. "That to my bride shall ne'er be said,
That I before her brothers fled."

6. No coward he, Sir Helmer Blaa,
He boldly rode and met his foe.

7. "Sir Helmer, meet we thee again?
Our honourd uncle thou hast slain:

8. "Thou, thou, it was, our uncle slew,
And never paid what fine was due.

9. "And now thou hast made our sister thine,
Our leave unask'd, unpaid the fine."

10. "Safe in my treasure chest I hold,
    To pay the death, ten marks of gold."

11. "We'll take of thee but one amend,
    Thy left foot and thy dexter hand."

12. "Ere ye shall get my hands or feet,
    Some other fate yourselves may meet."

13. Sir Helmer Blaa his sabre drew,
    And at a stroke Sir Ebbe slew.

14. When Lang and Ove slaughter'd lay,
    His sword had just come into play.

15. He then kill'd Wolf and Edgar White,
    And so were four in equal plight.

16. Torkild and Thor the next he sped,
    So lay in all six brothers dead.

17. Then rose as red as blood Sir Paul,
    A courteous man belov'd by all.

18. "Sir Helmer, lay this feud aside,
    My sister I'll give thee for bride."

19. His terms with joy Sir Helmer heard,
    And in the greensward stuck his sword.

20. "Thanks, good Sir Paul! and I agree;
    Henceforth a brother see in me."

21. Like loving brethren home they rode,
    Such courtesy each the other show'd;

22. And when Sir Helmer reach'd his hall,
    His sister too he gave Sir Paul.

23. Gaily they drank their wedding feast,
    Nor has their friendship ever ceas'd.

RARE WILLIE DROWNED IN YARROW (215)
OR
THE WATER O GAMRIE

The original story of this ballad probably told of a girl who dreamed
that her absent true-love was pulling heather on the banks of Yarrow
and who went to seek him, only to find him drowned. It is much confused in both England and America with the preceding.

Text, Gibb MS., p. 370.

1. "Willie's fair, an Willie's rare,
        An Willie's wondrous bonny,
    An Willie's promised to marry me,
        If eer he marry ony."

2. "O sister dear, I've dreamed a dream,
        I'm afraid it's unco sorrow;
    I dreamed I was pu'in the heather green,
        In the dowie dens o Yarrow."

3. "O sister dear, I'll read your dream,
        I'm afraid it will be sorrow;
    Ye'll get a letter ere it's een
        Your lover's drowned in Yarrow."

4. She socht him up, she socht him doun,
        In mickle dule an sorrow;
    She found him neath a buss o brume,
        In the dowie dens o Yarrow.

5. Her hair it was three quarters lang,
        Its colour it was yallow;
    She tied it to his middle sma,
        And pu'ed him oot o Yarrow.

6. "My bed it was made wide yestreen,
        The nicht it sall be narrow;
    There's neer a man lie by my side
        Since Willie's drowned in Yarrow."

THE MOTHER'S MALISON, OR, CLYDE'S WATER (216)

Text, Buchan, i, 140.

1. Willie stands in his stable-door,
        And clapping at his steed,
    And looking oer his white fingers
        His nose began to bleed.

2. "Gie corn to my horse, mother,
        And meat to my young man,
    And I'll awa to Maggie's bower;
        I'll win ere she lie down."

3. "O bide this night wi me, Willie,
        O bide this night wi me;
    The best an cock o a' the reest
        At your supper shall be."

4. "A' your cocks, and a' your reests,
  I value not a prin,
 For I'll awa to Meggie's bower;
  I'll win ere she lie down."

5. "Stay this night wi me, Willie,
  O stay this night wi me;
 The best an sheep in a' the flock
  At your supper shall be."

6. "A' your sheep, and a' your flocks,
  I value not a prin,
 For I'll awa' to Meggie's bower;
  I'll win ere she lie down."

7. "O an ye gang to Meggie's bower,
  Saw sair against my will,
 The deepest pot in Clyde's water,
  My malison ye's feel."

8. "The guid steed that I ride upon
  Cost me thrice thretty pound;
 And I'll put trust in his swift feet
  To hae me safe to land."

9. As he rade ower yon high, high hill,
  And down yon dowie den,
 The noise that was in Clyde's water
  Woud feard five huner men.

10. "O roaring Clyde, ye roar ower loud,
  Your streams seem wondrous strang;
 Make me your wreck as I come back,
  But spare me as I gang."

11. Then he is on to Maggie's bower,
  And tirled at the pin;
 "O sleep ye, wake ye, Meggie," he said,
  "Ye'll open, lat me come in."

12. "O wha is this at my bower-door,
  That calls me by my name?"
 "It is your first love, sweet Willie,
  This night newly come hame."

13. "I hae few lovers thereout, thereout,
  As few hae I therein;
 The best an love that ever I had
  Was here just late yestreen."

14. "The warstan stable in a' your stables,
  For my puir steed to stand!

The warstan bower in a' your bowers,
   For me to lie therein!
My boots are fu o Clyde's water,
   I'm shivering at the chin."

15.   "My barns are fu o corn, Willie,
     My stables are fu o hay;
My bowers are fu o gentlemen,
     They'll nae remove till day."

16.   "O fare ye well, my fause Meggie,
     O farewell, and adieu.
I've gotten my mither's malison
     This night coming to you."

17.   As he rode ower yon high, high hill,
     And down yon dowie den,
The rushing that was in Clyde's water
     Took Willie's cane frae him.

18.   He leand him ower his saddle-bow,
     To catch his cane again;
The rushing that was in Clyde's water
     Took Willie's hat frae him.

19.   He leand him ower his saddle-bow,
     To catch his hat thro force;
The rushing that was in Clyde's water
     Took Willie frae his horse.

20.   His brither stood upo the bank,
     Says, "Fye, man, will ye drown?
Ye'll turn ye to your high horse head
     And learn how to swom."

21.   "How can I turn to my horse head
     And learn how to swom?
I've gotten my mither's malison,
     It's here that I maun drown."

22.   The very hour this young man sank
     Into the pot sae deep,
Up it wakend his love Meggie
     Out o her drowsy sleep.

23.   "Come here, come here, my mither dear,
     And read this dreary dream;
I dreamd my love was at our gates,
     And nane wad let him in."

24.   "Lye still, lye still now, my Meggie,
     Lye still and tak your rest;

> Sin your true-love was at your yates,
>> It's but twa quarters past."

25.   Nimbly, nimbly raise she up,
>> And nimbly pat she on,
> And the higher that the lady cried,
>> The louder blew the win.

26.   The first an step that she steppd in,
>> She stepped to the queet;
> "Ohon, alas!" said that lady,
>> "This water's wondrous deep."

27.   The next an step that she wade in,
>> She wadit to the knee;
> Says she, "I coud wide farther in,
>> If I my love coud see."

28.   The next an step that she wade in,
>> She wadit to the chin;
> The deepest pot in Clyde's water
>> She got sweet Willie in.

29.   "You've had a cruel mither, Willie,
>> And I have had anither;
> But we shall sleep in Clyde's water
>> Like sister an like brither."

THE FALSE LOVER WON BACK (218)

Text, Buchan's MSS., i, 144.

1.   A fair maid sat in her bower-door,
>> Wringing her lily hands,
> And by it came a sprightly youth,
>> Fast tripping o'er the strands.

2.   "Where gang ye, young John," she says,
>> "Sae early in the day?
> It gars me think, by your fast trip,
>> Your journey's far away."

3.   He turnd about wi surly look,
>> And said, "What's that to thee?
> I'm gaen to see a lovely maid,
>> Mair fairer far than ye."

4.   "Now hae ye playd me this, fause love,
>> In simmer, mid the flowers?

I shall repay ye back again,
   In winter, mid the showers,

5.   "But again, dear love, and again, dear love,
      Will ye not turn again?
   For as ye look to other women,
      I shall to other men."

6.   "Make your choice of whom you please,
      For I my choice will have;
   I've chosen a maid more fair than thee,
      I never will deceive."

7.   But she's kilt up her claithing fine,
      And after him gaed she;
   But aye he said, "Ye'll turn again,
      Nae farder gae wi me."

8.   "But again, dear love, and again, dear love,
      Will ye never love me again?
   Alas for loving you sae well,
      And you nae me again."

9.   The first an town that they came till,
      He bought her brooch and ring;
   And aye he bade her turn again,
      And gang nae farder wi him.

10.   "But again, dear love, and again, dear love,
      Will ye never love me again?
   Alas for loving you sae well,
      And you nae me again."

11.   The next an town that they came till,
      He bought her muff and gloves;
   But aye he bade her turn again,
      And choose some other loves.

12.   "But again, dear love, and again, dear love,
      Will ye never love me again?
   Alas for loving you sae well,
      And you nae me again."

13.   The next an town that they came till,
      His heart it grew mair fain,
   And he was as deep in love wi her
      As she was ower again.

14.   The next an town that they came till,
      He bought her wedding gown,
   And made her lady of ha's and bowers,
      Into sweet Berwick town.

THE GARDENER (219)

This ballad is included to show that the ballad can be light, airy, inconsequential.

Text, Kinloch, p. 74.

1. The gardener stands in his bower-door,
    With a primrose in his hand,
   And by there came a leal maiden,
    As jimp 's a willow wand.
   And by, etc.

2. "O lady, can you fancy me,
    For to be my bride,
   You'll get a' the flowers in my garden,
    To be to you a weed.

3. "The lily white shall be your smock;
    Becomes your body neat;
   And your head shall de deckd with jelly-flower,
    And the primrose in your breast.

4. "Your gown shall be o the sweet-william,
    Your coat o camovine,
   And your apron o the salads neat,
    That taste baith sweet and fine.

5. "Your stockings shall be o the broad kail-blade,
    That is baith broad and lang;
   And narrow, narrow at the coot,
    And broad, broad at the brawn.

6. "Your gloves shall be the marygold,
    All glittering to your hand,
   Well spread oer wi the blue blaewort,
    That grows in corn-land."

7. "O fare you well, young man," she says,
    "Farewell, and I bid adieu;
   Since you've provided a weed for me,
    Among the summer flowers,
   Then I'll provide another for you,
    Among the winter showers.

8. "The new-fallen snow to be your smock;
    Becomes your body neat;
   And your head shall be deckd with the eastern wind,
    And the cold rain on your breast."

KATHARINE JAFFRAY (221)

This fine ballad exists in two types. In one a Scots girl agrees to marry a Scots lord, but an English lord comes courting and succeeds in winning the consent of the girl's parents to his suit. On the wedding day the Scots lord carries the bride away. In the second version the rivalry is between two Scotsmen, that is, there is no Border rivalry; this version often names one of the suitors as Lochinvar and one version begins with the line: Lochnagar (Lochinvar) came fae the west. Scott's *Lochinvar* was modeled on this ballad.

Text, Herd's MSS., i, 61; ii, 56.

1. There lived a lass in yonder dale,
      And doun in yonder glen, O
    And Kathrine Jaffray was her name,
      Well known by many men. O

2. Out came the Laird of Lauderdale,
      Out frae the South Countrie,
    All for to court this pretty maid,
      Her bridegroom for to be.

3. He has teld her father and mither baith,
      And a' the rest o her kin,
    And has teld the lass hersell,
      And her consent has win.

4. Then came the Laird of Lochinton,
      Out frae the English border,
    All for to court this pretty maid,
      Well mounted in good order.

5. He's teld her father and mither baith,
      As I hear sindry say,
    But he has nae teld the lass her sell,
      Till on her wedding day.

6. When day was set, and friends were met,
      And married to be,
    Lord Lauderdale came to the place,
      The bridal for to see.

7. "O are you came for sport, young man,
      Or are you come for play?
    Or are you come for a sight o our bride,
      Just on her wedding day?"

8. "I'm nouther come for sport," he says,
      "Nor am I come for play;

But if I had one sight o your bride,
 I'll mount and ride away."

9.   There was a glass of the red wine
        Filld up them atween,
     And ay she drank to Lauderdale,
        Wha her true-love had been.

10. Then he took her by the milk-white hand,
        And by the grass-green sleeve,
     And he mounted her high behind him there,
        At the bridegroom he askt nae leive.

11. Then the blude run down by the Cowden Banks,
        And down by Cowden Braes,
     And ay she gard the trumpet sound,
        "O this foul, foul play."

12. Now a' ye that in England are,
        Or are in England born,
     Come nere to Scotland to court a lass,
        Or else ye'l get the scorn.

13. They haik ye up and settle ye by,
        Till on your wedding day,
     And gie ye frogs instead o fish,
        And play ye foul, foul play.

BONNY BABY LIVINGSTON (222)

This ballad, like several others (223, 224, 225), tells of a bride-
stealing, a common-enough happening even as late as the 18th century
on the rough Border. In some versions the girl gets back to her home
and lover; in others she dies, and her lover too in trying to rescue her.
     Text, Jamieson, ii, 135.

1.   O Bonny Baby Livingston
        Went forth to view the hay,
     And by it came him Glenlion
        Sta Bonny Baby away.

2.   O first he's taen her silken coat,
        And neest her satten gown,
     Syne rowd her in a tartan plaid,
        And hapd her round and rown.

3.   He has set her upon his steed
        And roundly rode away,

And neer loot her look back again
    The live-long summer's day.

4. He's carried her o'er hills and muirs
    Till they came to a Highland glen,
And there he's met his brother John,
    With twenty armed men.

5. O there were cows, and there were ewes,
    And lasses milking there,
But Baby neer anse lookd about,
    Her heart was filld wi care.

6. Glenlion took her in his arms,
    And kissd her, cheek and chin;
Says, "I'd gie a' these cows and ewes
    But ae kind look to win."

7. "O ae kind look ye neer shall get,
    Nor win a smile frae me,
Unless to me you'll favour shew,
    And take me to Dundee."

8. "Dundee, Baby? Dundee, Baby?
    Dundee you ne'er shall see
Till I've carried you to Glenlion
    And have my bride made thee.

9. "We'll stay a while at Auchingour,
    And get sweet milk and cheese,
And syne we'll gang to Glenlion,
    And there live at our ease,"

10. "I winna stay at Auchingour,
    Nor eat sweet milk and cheese,
Nor go with thee to Glenlion,
    For there I'll neer find ease."

11. Than out it spake his brother John,
    "O were I in your place,
I'd take that lady hame agina,
    For a' her bonny face.

12. "Commend me to the lass that's kind,
    Tho na so gently born;
And, gin her heart I coudna gain,
    To take her hand I'd scorn."

13. "O had your tongue now, John," he says,
    "You wis na what you say;
For I've lood that bonny face
    This twelve month and a day.

14. "And tho I've lood her lang and sair
  A smile I ne'er coud win;
Yet what I've got anse in my power
  To keep I think nae sin."

15. When they came to Glenlion castle,
  They lighted at the yate,
And out it came his sisters three,
  Wha did them kindly greet.

16. O they've taen Baby by the hands
  And led her oer the green,
And ilka lady spake a word,
  But bonny Baby spake nane.

17. Then out it spake her bonny Jean,
  The youngest o the three,
"O lady, dinna look sae sad,
  But tell your grief to me."

18. "O wherefore should I tell my grief,
  Since lax I canna find?
I'm stown frae a' my kins and friends,
  And my love I left behind.

19. "But had I paper, pen and ink,
  Before that it were day,
I yet might get a letter sent
  In time to Johny Hay."

20. O she's got paper, pen, and ink,
  And candle that she might see,
And she has written a broad letter
  To Johny at Dundee.

21. And she has gotten a bonny boy,
  That was baith swift and strang,
Wi philabeg and bonnet blue,
  Her errand for to gang.

22. "O boy, gin ye'd my blessing win
  And help me in my need,
Run wi this letter to my love,
  And bid him come wi speed.

23. "And here's a chain of good red gowd,
  And gowdn guineas three,
And when you've well your errand done,
  You'll get them for your fee."

24. The boy he ran oer hill and dale,
  Fast as a bird coud flee,

  And eer the sun was twa hours height
   The boy was at Dundee.

25. And when he came to Johny's door
   He knocked loud and sair;
  Then Johny to the window came,
   And loudly cry'd, "Wha's there?"

26. "O here's a letter I have brought,
   Which ye maun quickly read,
  And, gin ye woud your lady save,
   Gang back wi me wi speed."

27. O when he had the letter read,
   An angry man was he;
  He says, "Glenlion, thou shalt rue
   This deed of villany!

28. "O saddle to me the black, the black,
   O saddle to me the brown,
  O saddle to me the swiftest steed
   That eer rade frae the town.

29. "And arm ye well, my merry men a',
   And follow me to the glen,
  For I vow I'll neither eat nor sleep
   Till I get my love again."

30. He's mounted on a milk-white steed,
   The boy upon a gray,
  And they got to Glenlion's castle
   About the close of day.

31. As Baby at her window stood,
   The west wind saft did bla;
  She heard her Johny's well-kent voice
   Beneath the castle wa.

32. "O Baby, haste, the window jump!
   I'll kep you in my arm;
  My merry men a' are at the yate,
   To rescue you frae harm."

33. She to the window fixt her sheets
   And slipped safely down,
  And Johny catched her in his arms,
   Neer loot her touch the ground.

34. When mounted on her Johny's horse,
   Fou blithely did she say,
  "Glenlion, you hae lost your bride,
   She's aff wi Johny Hay."

35. Glenlion and his brother John
      Were birling in the ha,
   When they heard Johny's bridle ring,
      As first he rade awa.

36. "Rise, Jock, gang out and meet the priest,
      I hear his bridle ring;
   My Baby now shall be my wife
      Before the laverocks sing."

37. "O brother, this is not the priest;
      I fear he'll come o'er late;
   For armed men with shining brands
      Stand at the castle-yate."

38. "Haste Donald, Duncan, Dugald, Hugh!
      Haste, take your sword and spier!
   We'll gar these traytors rue the hour
      That e'er they ventured here."

39. The Highland men drew their claymores,
      And gae a warlike shout,
   But Johny's merry men kept the yate,
      Nae ane durst venture out.

40. The lovers rade the live-lang night,
      And safe gat on their way,
   And bonny Baby Livingston
      Has gotten Johny Hay.

41. Awa, Glenlion! fy for shame!
      Gae hide ye in some den!
   You've lettn your bride be stown frae you,
      For a' your armed men.

ROB ROY (225)

This ballad is very close to history. Read the account of the spirited affair in Scott's introduction to *Rob Roy*. The Rob Roy of the ballad is the fifth and youngest son of the Rob Roy of the novel. He was tried, condemned, and executed for the abduction in February, 1754.

Text, Kinloch, MSS., i, 343.

1. Rob Roy frae the Hielands cam
      Unto the Lawland border,
   And he has stown a ladie fair,
      To haud his house in order.

2. He guarded the house round about,
   Himsel went in and found her out,
     She hung close by her mither;
   Wi dolefu cries and watery eyes
     They parted frae each ither.

3. "Gang wi me, my dear," he says,
     "Gang and be my honey;
   Gang and be my wedded wife,
     I loe ye best o onie."

4. "I winna gang wi you," she says,
     "I winna be your honey;
   I winna be your wedded wife;
     Ye loe me for my money."

5. He gied na her na time to dress
     As ladies whan they're brides,
   But hurried her awa wi speed,
     And rowd her in his plaids.

6. He gat her up upon a horse,
     Himsel lap on ahind her;
   And they're awa to the Hieland hills;
     Her friends they canna find her.

7. As they gaed oure the Hieland hills,
     This lady aften fainted,
   Saying, "Wae be to my cursed gowd,
     This road to me invented!"

8. As they gaed oure the Hieland hills,
     And at Buchanan tarried,
   He bought to her baith cloak and goun,
     Yet she wadna be married.

9. Six held her up afore the priest,
     Four laid her in a bed, O.
   Maist mournfully she wept and cried
     Whan she bye him was laid, O.

10. "O be content, be content,
     Be content to stay, ladie;
   For now ye are my wedded wife
     Unto your dying day, ladie.

11. "Rob Roy was my father calld,
     M'Gregor was his name, ladie;
   And in a' the country whare he dwalt
     He exceeded ae in fame, ladie.

12. "He was a hedge unto his friends,
    A heckle to his faes, ladie;
And ilka ane that did him wrang,
    He beat him on the neis, ladie.

13. "I'm as bold, I am as bold
    As my father was afore, ladie;
Ilka ane that does me wrang
    Sall feel my gude claymore, ladie.

14. "There neer was frae Lochlomond west
    That eer I did him fear, ladie;
For, if his person did escape,
    I seizd upon his gear, ladie.

15. "My father delights in horse and kye,
    In sheep and goats and a', ladie,
And thee wi me and thirty merks
    Will mak me a man fu braw, ladie.

16. "I hae been in foreign lands,
    And servd the king o France, ladie;
We will get the bagpipes,
    And we'll hae a dance, ladie."

BONNY LIZIE BAILLIE (227)

This is a spirited and tuneful ballad even if it is a bit confused in its story. It seems to be founded on fact. Lizie Baillie was the daughter of Baillie of Castle Carey; she married Duncan Graham against her parents' wishes.

Text, Broadside, Maidment, *Scottish Ballads and Songs*, p. 13.

1. It fell about the Lambmass tide,
    When the leaves were fresh and green,
Lizie Bailie is to Gartartain gane,
    To see her sister Jean.

2. She had not been in Gartartain
    Even but a little while
Till luck and fortune happend her,
    And she went to the Isle.

3. And when she went into the Isle
    She met with Duncan Grahame;
So bravely as he courted her.
    And he convoyd her hame.

4. "My bonny Lizie Bailie,
    I'll row thee in my plaidie,

       If thou will go along with me
         And be my Highland lady."

5. "If I would go along with thee,
     "I think I were not wise;
  For I cannot milk cow nor ewe,
     Nor yet can I speak Erse."

6. "Hold thy tongue, bonny Lizie Bailie,
     And hold thy tongue," said he;
  "For any thing that thou does lack,
     My dear, I'll learn thee."

7. She would not have a Lowland laird,
     He wears the high-heeld shoes;
  She will marry Duncan Grahame,
     For Duncan wears his trews.

8. She would not have a gentleman,
     A farmer in Kilsyth,
  But she would have the Highland man,
     He lives into Monteith.

9. She would not have the Lowland man,
     Nor yet the English laddie,
  But she would have the Highland man,
     To row her in his pladie.

10. He took her by the milk-white hand,
     And he convoyed her hame,
  And still she thought, both night and day,
     On bonny Duncan Grahame.

11. "O bonny Duncan Grahame,
     Why should ye me miscarry?
  For, if you have a love for me,
     We'll meet at Castle Carry.

12. "As I came in by Dennie bridge,
     And by the holland-bush,
  My mother took from me my cloaths,
     My rings, ay and my purse.

13. "Hold your tongue, my mother dear,
     For that I do not care;
  For I will go with Duncan Grahame
     Tho I should ner get mair.

14. "For the first when I met Duncan Grahame
     I met with meikle joy,
  And many pretty Highland men
     Was there at my convoy."

15. And now he is gone through the muir,
    And she is through the glen.
    "O bonny Lizie Bailie,
    When will we meet again."

16. Shame light on these logerheads
    That lives in Castle Carry,
    That let away the bonny lass
    The Highland man to marry.

17. "O bonny Lizie, stay at home.
    The mother cannot want thee;
    For any thing that thou does lack,
    My dear, I'll cause get thee."

18. "I would not give my Duncan Grahame
    For all my father's land,
    Although he had three lairdships more,
    And all at my command."

19. And she's cast off her silken gowns,
    That she weard in the Lowland,
    And she's up to the Highland hills,
    To wear the gowns of tartain.

20. And she's cast off her high-heeld shoes,
    Was made of the gilded leather,
    And she's up to Gillecrankie,
    To go among the heather.

21. And she's cast off her high-heeld shoes,
    And put on a pair of laigh ones,
    And she's away with Duncan Grahame,
    To go among the brachans.

22. "O my bonny Lizie Bailie,
    Thy mother cannot want thee;
    And if thou go with Duncan Grahame
    Thou'll be a Gilliecrankie."

23. "Hold your tongue, my mother dear,
    And folly let thee be;
    Should not I fancie Duncan Grahame
    When Duncan fancies me?

24. "Hold your tongue, my father dear,
    And folly let thee be;
    For I will go with Duncan Grahame
    Fore all the men I see."

25. "Who is it that's done this turn?
    Who has done this deed?"

"A minister it's, father," she says,
"Lives at the Rughburn bridge."

26. "A minister, daughter?" he says,
"A minister for mister."
"O hold your tongue, my father dear,
He married first my sister."

27. "O fare you well, my daughter dear,
So dearly as I lovd thee.
Since thou wilt go to Duncan Grahame,
My bony Lizie Bailie."

28. "O fare you well, my father dear,
Also my sister Betty;
O fare you well, my mother dear,
I leave you all compleatly."

GLASGOW PEGGIE (228)

Text, Sharpe's *Ballad Book*, p. 40.

1. "As I cam in by Glasgow town,
The Highland troops were a' before me,
And the bonniest lass that eer I saw,
She lives in Glasgow, they ca her Peggie.

2. "I wad gie my bonnie black horse,
So wad I my gude grey naigie,
If I were twa hundred miles in the north,
And nane wi me but my bonnie Peggie."

3. Up then spak her father dear,
Dear wow! but he was wondrous sorrie;
"Weel may ye steal a cow or a yowe,
But ye dare nae steal my bonnie Peggie."

4. Up then spak her mother dear,
Dear wow! but she spak wondrous sorrie;
"Now since I have brought ye up this length,
Wad ye gang awa wi a Highland fellow?"

5. He set her on his bonnie black horse,
He set himsel on his gude gray naigie,
And they have ridden oer hills and dales,
And he's awa wi his bonnie Peggie.

6. They have ridden oer hills and dales,
They have ridden oer mountains many,

Until they cam to a low, low glen,
 And there he's lain down wi his bonnie Peggie.

7. Up then spak the Earl of Argyle,
 Dear wow! but he spak wondrous sorrie;
"The bonniest lass in a' Scotland
 Is off and awa wi a Highland fellow!"

8. Their bed was of the bonnie green grass,
 Their blankets war o the hay sae bonnie;
He folded his philabeg below her head,
 And he's lain down wi his bonnie Peggie.

9. Up then spak the bonny Lowland lass,
 And wow! but she spak wondrous sorrie;
"I'se warrant my mither wad hae a gay sair heart
 To see me lien here wi you, my Willie."

10. "In my father's house there's feather-beds,
 Feather-beds, and blankets mony;
They're a' mine, and they'll sune be thine,
 And what needs your mither be sae sorrie, Peggie?

11. "Dinna you see yon nine score o kye,
 Feeding on yon hill sae bonnie?
They're a' mine, and they'll sune be thine,
 And what needs your mither be sorrie, Peggie?

12. "Dinna ye see yon nine score o sheep,
 Feeding on yon brae sae bonnie?
They're a' mine, and they'll sune be thine,
 And what needs your mither be sorrie for ye?

13. "Dinna ye see yon bonnie white house,
 Shining on yon brae sae bonnie?
And I am the Earl of the Isle of Skye,
 And surely my Peggie will be ca'd a lady."

EARL CRAWFORD (229)

A ballad of tragedy over a series of misunderstandings. There may be some basis in fact for the story here. The eleventh Earl of Crawford married Lilias Drummond of Stobhall in 1574.

Text, Christie's *Traditional Ballad Airs,* i, 290 ff.

1. O we were sisters, sisters seven,
 We were a comely crew to see,
And some got lairds, and some got lords,
 And some got knichts o hie degree,

And I mysel got the Earl o Crawford,
    And wasna that a great match for me.

2. It was a fifteen that I was married,
        And at sixteen I had a son;
    And wasna that an age ower tender
        For a lady to hae her first-born.
    And wasna, etc.

3. But it fell ance upon a day
        I gaed into the garden green,
    And naebody was therein walking
        But Earl Crawford and his young son.

4. "I wonder at you, ye Earl Crawford,
        I wonder at you wi your young son;
    Ye daut your young son m..r than your Lillie;
        I'm sure you got na him your lane."

5. He turned about upon his heel,
        I wite an angry man was he;
    Says, "If I got nae my young son my lane,
        Bring me here the one that helpet me."

6. "O hold your tongue, my Earl Crawford,
        And a' my folly lat it be;
    There was nane at the gettin o oor son,
        Nae body only but you and me."

7. He set her on a milk-white steed,
        Her little son her before;
    Says, "Ye maun gae to bonny Stobha,
        For ye will enter my yates no more."

8. When she cam to her father's bowers,
        She lichtit low down on the stane,
    And wha sae ready as her auld father
        To welcome Lady Lillie in?

9. "O how's a' wi you, my daughter Lillie,
        That ye come here sae hastilie?
    And how's a' wi' the Earl o Crawford,
        That he didna send a boy wi thee?"

10. "O haud your tongue now, my old father,
        And ye'll lat a' your folly be;
    For ae word that my merry mou spak
        Has parted my good lord and me."

11. "O haud your tongue, my daughter Lillie,
        And a' your follies lat them be;

   I'll double your portion ten times ower,
    And a better match I'll get for thee."

12. "O haud your tongue now, my old father,
    And a' your folly lat it be;
   I wouldna gie ae kiss o Crawford
    For a' the goud that ye can gie.

13. "Whare will I get a bonny boy,
    That's willin to win meat and fee,
   Wha will gae on to Earl Crawford
    An see an's heart be fawn to me?"

14. When he cam to the yates o Crawford,
    They were a' sitting down to dine:
   "How comes it now, ye Earl Crawford,
    Ye arena takin Lady Lillie hame?"

15. "Ye may gae tell her Lady Lillie,
    And ye maun neither lee nor len,
   She may stay in her father's bowers,
    For she'll not enter my yates again."

16. When he cam back to her father's yates,
    He lichtit low down on his knee:
   "What news, what news, my bonny boy?
    What news, what news hae ye to me?"

17. "I'm bidden tell you, Lady Lillie—
    I'm bidden neither to lee nor len—
   She may stay in her father's bowers,
    For she'll not enter my yates again."

18. She stretched out her lily hand,
    Says, "Adieu, adieu to ane and a.
   Adieu, adieu to Earl Crawford."
    Wi that her sair heart brak in twa.

19. Then dowie, dowie her father raise up,
    And dowie, dowie the black put on,
   And dowie, dowie he mounted the brown,
    And dowie, dowie sat thereon.

20. And dowie rade to the yates o Crawford,
    And when to Crawford's yates he came,
   They were a' dressd in the robes o scarlet,
    Just gaun to tak Lady Lillie hame.

21. "Ye may cast aff your robes o scarlet—
    I wyte they set you wondrous weel—
   And now put on the black sae dowie,
    And come and bury your Lady Lill."

22.   He took his hat into his hand,
          And laid it low down by his knee:
      "An it be true that Lillie's dead,
          The sun shall nae mair shine on me."

RICHIE STORY (232)

The versions of this ballad fall into two groups: those that make the footman a real footman and those in which he is a nobleman in disguise. Lillias Fleming eloped with her father's footman, Richard Storry 1673(?). Her family procured him a place in the custom service. Probably the ballad echoes this event.

Text, Motherwell's MS., p. 426.

1.   The Earl of Wigton had three daughters,
          Oh and a waly, but they were unco bonnie.
     The eldest of them had the far brawest house,
          But she's fallen in love with her footman-laddie.

2.   As she was a walking doun by yon river-side,
          Oh and a wally, but she was unco bonnie.
     There she espied her own footman,
          With ribbons hanging over his shoulders sae bonnie.

3.   "Here's a letter to you, madame,
          Here's a letter to you, madame;
     The Earl of Hume is waiting on,
          And he has his service to you, madame."

4.   "I'll have none of his service," says she,
          "I'll have none of his service," says she,
     "For I've made a vow, and I'll keep it true,
          That I'll marry none but you Ritchie."

5.   "O say not so again, madame,
          O say not so again, madame;
     For I have neither lands nor rents
          For to keep you on, madam."

6.   "I'll live where e'er you please, Ritchie,
          I'll live where eer you please, Ritchie,
     And I'll be ready at your ca',
          Either late or early, Ritchie."

7.   As they went in by Stirling toun,
          O and a wally, but she was unco bonnie.
     A' her silks were sailing on the ground,
          But few of them knew of Ritchie Story.

8. As they went in by the Parliament Close,
        O and a wally, but she was unco bonnie.
    All the nobles took her by the hand,
        But few of them knew she was Ritchie's lady.

9. As they came in by her goodmother's yetts,
        O and a wally, but she was unco bonnie.
    Her goodmother bade her kilt her coats,
        And muck the byre with Ritchie Storie.

10. "Oh, may not ye be sorry, madame,
        Oh, may not ye be sorry, madame,
    To leave a' your lands at bonnie Cumbernaud,
        And follow home your footman-laddie?"

11. "What need I be sorry?" says she,
        "What need I be sorry?" says she,
    "For I've gotten my lot and my heart's desire,
        And what Providence has ordered for me."

THE EARL OF ABOYNE (235)

There seems to be no foundation in fact for the story here told. One version makes the lady his betrothed, not his wife. As a matter of fact, the first Earl of Aboyne did marry an Irvine (17th century).

Text, Kinloch MSS., v, 351.

1. The Earl of Aboyne he's courteous and kind,
        He's kind to every woman,
    And the Earl of Aboyne he's courteous and kind,
        But he stays ower lang in London.

2. The ladie she stood on her stair-head,
        Beholding his grooms a coming;
    She knew by their livery and raiment so rare
        That their last voyage was from London.

3. "My groms all, ye'll be well in call,
        Hold all the stables shining;
    With a bretther o degs ye'll clear up my nags,
        Sin my gude Lord Aboyne is a coming.

4. "My minstrels all, be well in call,
        Hold all my galleries ringing;
    With music springs ye'll try well your strings,
        Sin my gude lord's a coming.

5. "My cooks all, be well in call,
        Wi pots and spits well ranked;

And nothing shall ye want that ye call for,
   Sin my gude Lord Aboyne's a coming.

6. "My chamber-maids, ye'll dress up my beds,
   Hold all my rooms in shining;
With Dantzic waters ye'll sprinkle my walls,
   Sin my good lord's a coming."

7. Her shoes was of the small cordain,
   Her stockings silken twisting;
Cambrick so clear was the pretty lady's smock,
   And her stays o the braided sattin.

8. Her coat was of the white sarsenent,
   Set out wi silver quiltin,
And her gown was o the silk damask,
   Set about wi red gold walting.

9. Her hair was like the threads of gold,
   Wi the silk and sarsanet shining,
Wi her fingers sae white, and the gold rings sae grite,
   To welcome her lord from London.

10. Sae stately she steppit down the stair,
   And walkit to meet him coming;
Said, "O ye'r welcome, my bonny lord,
   Ye'r thrice welcome home from London."

11. "If this be so that ye let me know,
   Ye'll come kiss me for my coming,
For the morn should hae been my bonny wedding-day
   Had I stayed the night in London."

12. Then she turned her about wi an angry look,
   O for such an a sorry woman.
"If this be so that ye let me know,
   Gang kiss your ladies in London."

13. Then he looked over his left shoulder
   To the worthie companie wi him;
Says he, "Isna this an unworthy welcome
   The we've got, coming from London."

14. "Get yer horse in call, my nobles all,
   And I'm sorry for yer coming,
But we'll horse, and awa to the bonny Bog o Gight,
   And then we'll go on to London."

15. "If this be Thomas, as they call you,
   You'll see if he'll hae me with him;
And nothing shall he be troubled with me
   But myself and my waiting-woman."

16. "I've asked it already, lady," he says,
    "And your humble servant, madam;
    But one single mile he winna lat you ride
    Wi his company and him to London."

17. A year and mare she lived in care,
    And doctors wi her dealin,
    And with a crack her sweet heart brack,
    And the letters is on to London.

18. When the letters he got, they were all sealed in black,
    And he fell in a grievous weeping;
    He said, "She is dead whom I loved best
    If I had but her heart in keepin."

19. Then fifteen o the finest lords
    That London could afford him,
    From their hose to their hat, they were all clad in black,
    For the sake of her corpse, Margaret Irvine.

20. The furder he gaed, the sorer he wept,
    Come keping her corpse, Margaret Irvine,
    Until that he came to the yetts of Aboyne,
    Where the corpse of his lady was lying.

LORD SALTOUN AND AUCHANACHIE (239)

Text, Buchan, ii, 133.

1. "Auchanachie Gordon is bonny and braw,
    He would tempt any woman that ever he saw;
    He would tempt any woman, so has he tempted me,
    And I'll die if I getna my love Auchanachie."

2. In came her father, tripping on the floor,
    Says, "Jeanie, ye're trying the tricks o a whore;
    Ye're caring for them that cares little for thee;
    Ye must marry Salton, leave Auchanachie.

3. "Auchanachie Gordon, he is but a man;
    Altho he be pretty, where lies his free land?
    Salton's lands they lie broad, his towers they stand hie,
    Ye must marry Salton, leave Auchanachie.

4. .   .   .   .
    .   .   .   .
    "Salton will gar you wear silk gowns fring'd to thy knee,
    But ye'll never wear that wi your love Auchanachie."

5. "Wi Auchanachie Gordon, I would beg my bread

Before that wi Salton I'd wear gowd on my head,
Wear gowd on my head, or gowns fring'd to the knee;
And I'll die if I getna my love Auchanachie.

6. "O Salton's a valley lies low by the sea,
    He's bowed on the back, and thrawin on the knee;"

    .   .   .   .

    .   .   .   .

7. "O Salton's a valley lies low by the sea;
    Though he's bowed on the back and thrawin on the knee
    Though he's bowed on the back and thrawin on the knee,
    The bonny rigs of Salton they're nae thrawin tee."

8. "O you that are my parents to church may me bring,
    But unto young Salton I'll never bear a son;
    For son or for daughter, I'll ne'er bow my knee,
    And I'll die if I getna my love Auchanachie."

9. When Jeanie was married, from church was brought hame,
    When she wi her maidens sae merry shoud hae been,
    When she wi her maidens sae merry shoud hae been,
    She's called for a chamber, to weep there her lane.

10. "Come to your bed, Jeanie, my honey and my sweet,
    For to stile you mistress I do not think it meet."
    "Mistress or Jeanie, it is a' ane to me,
    It's in your bed Salton, I never will be."

11. Then out spake her father, he spake wi renown;
    "Some of you that are maidens, ye'll loose aff her gown;
    Some of you that are maidens, ye'll loose aff her gown;
    And I'll mend the marriage wi ten thousand crowns."

12. Then ane of her maidens they loosed aff her gown,
    But bonny Jeanie Gordon she fell in a swoon;
    She fell in a swoon low down by their knee;
    Says, "Look on, I die for my love Auchanachie."

13. That very same day Miss Jeanie did die,
    And hame came Auchanachie hame frae the sea;
    Her father and mither welcomed him at the gate;
    He said, "Where's Miss Jeanie, that she's nae here yet?"

14. The forth came her maidens, all wringing their hands,
    Saying, "Alas for your staying sae lang frae the land.
    Sae lang frae the land, and sae lang on the fleed.
    They've wedded your Jeanie, and now she is dead."

15. "Some of you, her maidens, take me by the hand,
    And show me the chamber Miss Jeanie died in."

He kissd her cold lips, which were colder than stane,
And he died in the chamber that Jeanie died in.

THE RANTIN LADDIE (240)

Another ballad with a difficult history; the story does not seem to belong to any of the Lords of Aboyne. There are American versions very like the English, and, in addition, one printed here in which the story element is practically gone.

Text A, Johnson's *Museum,* p. 474; B, traditional in Maine, Barry, p. 303.

A.

1. "Aften hae I playd at the cards and the dice,
    For the love of a bonnie rantin laddie,
    But now I maun sit in my father's kitchen-neuk
    And balow a bastard babie.

2. "For my father he will not me own,
    And my mother she neglects me,
    And a' my friends hae lightlyed me,
    And their servants they do slight me.

3. "But had I a servant at my command,
    As aft times I've had many,
    That wad rin wi a letter to bonie Glenswood,
    Wi a letter to my rantin laddie."

4. "O is he either a laird or a lord,
    Or is he but a cadie,
    That ye do him ca sae aften by name
    Your bonie, bonie rantin laddie?"

5. "Indeed he is baith a laird and a lord,
    And he never was a cadie,
    But he is the Earl o bonie Aboyne,
    And he is my rantin laddie."

6. "O ye'se get a servant at your command,
    As aft times ye've had many,
    That sall rin wi a letter to bonie Glenswood,
    A letter to your rantin laddie."

7. When Lord Aboyne did the letter get,
    O but he blinket bonie!
    But or he had read three lines of it
    I think his heart was sorry.

8. "O wha is this daur be sae bauld
    Sae cruelly to use my lassie?

    .   .   .   .

    .   .   .   .

9. "For her father he will not her know,
    And her mother she does slight her,
    And a' her friends hae lightlied her,
    And their servants they neglect her.

10. "Go raise to me my five hundred men,
    Make haste and make them ready,
    With a milk-white steed under every ane,
    For to bring hame my lady."

11. As they cam in thro Buchanshire,
    They were a company bonie,
    With a gude claymor in every hand,
    And O but they shin'd bonie.

B.

1. Aft hae I played at the cards an' dice
    For the love o' a rantin' laddie, O,
    But noo I maun sit in the ingle neuk,
    An' by-lo a bastard babbie O.

Refrain

Sing hush-a-by, an' hush-a-by,
   An' hush-a-by-lo babbie, O,
O hush-a-by, an' hush-a-by,
   An' hush-a-by, wee babbie O.

Sing hush-a-by, an' hush-a-by,
   An' hush-a-by-lo babbie, O,
O had your tongue, ma ain wee wean,
   An A gae a sook o' the pappie, O.

JAMES HARRIS (THE DAEMON LOVER) (243)

A ballad widely spread in England, Scotland, Ireland, and America.
It is the story of a revenant who before his death had been a mariner
espoused to a fair maid. When he does not return after three years,
she marries a carpenter (ship carpenter in England and house carpenter in America) and has children. Then the revenant comes; the lady
departs with him over the sea but is drowned when the strange ship
and its crew of dead men founders. It is interesting to contrast the

English version here (A) with the Celtic (C). As usual, the Scotch and Irish give the story more dramatic and romantic color.

Text A, Pepys *Ballads,* iv, 101; B, *The Rambler's Garland,* 1785; C, traditional in Scotland, Scott, ii, 427; D, American broadside, c. 1860, reprinted in *JAF,* 18:207.

A.

1. There dwelt a fair maid in the West,
    Of worthy birth and fame,
   Neer unto Plimouth, stately town,
    Jane Reynolds was her name.

2. This damsel dearly was belovd
    By many a proper youth,
   And what of her is to be said
    Is known for very truth.

3. Among the rest a seaman brave
    Unto her a wooing came;
   A comely proper youth he was,
    James Harris calld by name.

4. The maid and young man was agreed,
    As time did them allow,
   And to each other secretly
    They made a solemn vow,

5. That they would ever faithfull be
    Whilst Heaven afforded life;
   He was to be her husband kind,
    And she his faithfull wife.

6. A day appointed was also
    When they was to be married;
   But before these things were brought to pass
    Matters were strangely carried.

7. All of you that faithfull lovers be
    Give ear and hearken well,
   And what of them became at last
    I will directly tell.

8. The young man he was prest to sea,
    And forcëd was to go;
   His sweet-heart she must stay behind,
    Whether she would or no.

9. And after he was from her gone
    She three years for him staid,
   Expecting of his coming home,
    And kept herself a maid.

10. At last news came that he was dead
    Within a forraign land,
    And how that he was buried
    She well did understand,

11. For whose sweet sake the maiden she
    Lamented many a day,
    And never was she known at all
    The wanton for to play.

12. A carpenter that livd hard by,
    When he heard of the same,
    Like as the other had done before,
    To her a wooing came.

13. But when that he had gained her love
    They married were with speed,
    And four years space, being man and wife,
    They loveingly agreed.

14. Three pritty children in this time
    This loving couple had,
    Which made their father's heart rejoyce,
    And mother wondrous glad.

15. But as occasion servd, one time
    The good man took his way
    Some three days journey from his home,
    Intending not to stay.

16. But, whilst that he was gone away,
    A spirit in the night
    Came to the window of his wife,
    And did her sorely fright.

17. Which spirit spake like to a man,
    And unto her did say,
    "My dear and onely love," quoth he,
    "Prepare and come away.

18. "James Harris is my name," quoth he,
    "Whom thou didst love so dear,
    And I have traveld for thy sake
    At least this seven year.

19. "And now I am returnd again,
    To take thee to my wife,
    And thou with me shalt go to sea,
    To end all further strife."

20. "O tempt me not, sweet James," quoth she,
    "With thee away to go;

If I should leave my children small,
 Alas! what would they do?

21. "My husband is a carpenter,
  A carpenter of great fame;
 I would not for five hundred pounds
  That he should know the same."

22. "I might have had a king's daughter,
  And she would have married me;
 But I forsook her golden crown,
  And for the love of thee.

23. "Therefore, if thou'lt thy husband forsake,
  And thy children three also,
 I will forgive thee what is past,
  If thou wilt with me go."

24. "If I forsake my husband and
  My little children three,
 What means hast thou to bring me to,
  If I should go with thee?"

25. "I have seven ships upon the sea;
  When they are come to land,
 Both marriners and marchandize
  Shall be at thy command.

26. "The ship wherein my love shall sail
  Is glorious to behold;
 The sails shall be of finest silk,
  And the mast of shining gold."

27. When he had told her these fair tales,
  To love him she began,
 Because he was in human shape,
  Much like unto a man.

28. And so together away they went
  From off the English shore,
 And since that time the woman-kind
  Was never seen no more.

29. But when her husband he come home
  And found his wife was gone,
 And left her three sweet pretty babes
  Within the house alone,

30. He beat his breast, he tore his hair,
  The tears fell from his eyes,
 And in the open streets he run
  With heavy doleful cries.

31. And in this sad distracted case
    He hangd himself for woe
Upon a tree near to the place;
    The truth of all is so.

32. The children now are fatherless,
    And left without a guide,
But yet no doubt the heavenly powers
    Will for them well provide.

B.

1. "Well met, well met, my own true love,
    Long time I have been seeking thee;
I am lately come from the salt sea,
    And all for the sake, love, of thee.

2. "I might have had a king's daughter,
    And fain she would have married me;
But I've forsaken all her crowns of gold,
    And all for the sake, love, of thee."

3. "If you might have had a king's daughter,
    I think you much to blame;
I would not for five hundred pounds
    That my husband should hear the same.

4. "For my husband is a carpenter,
    And a young ship-carpenter is he,
And by him I have a little son,
    Or else, love, I'd go along with thee.

5. "But if I should leave my husband dear,
    Likewise my little son also,
What have you to maintain me withal,
    If I along with you should go?"

6. "I have seven ships upon the seas,
    And one of them brought me to land,
And seventeen mariners to wait on thee,
    For to be, love, at your command.

7. "A pair of slippers thou shalt have,
    They shall be made of the beaten gold,
Nay and be lin'd with velvet soft,
    For to keep thy feet from cold.

8. "A gilded boat thou then shall have,
    The oars shall gilded be also,
And mariners to row thee along,
    For to keep thee from thy overthrow."

9. They had not been long upon the sea
      Before that she began to weep:
   "What, weep you for my gold?" he said,
      "Or do you weep for my fee?

10. "Or do you weep for some other young man
       That you love much better than me?"
    "No, I do weep for my little son,
       That should have come along with me."

11. She had not been upon the seas
       Passing days three or four
    But the mariner and she were drowned,
       And never heard of more.

12. When tidings to old England came
       The ship-carpenter's wife was drownd,
    He wrung his hands and tore his hair,
       And grievously fell in a swoon.

13. "Oh cursed be those mariners!
       For they do lead a wicked life;
    They ruind me, a ship-carpenter,
       By deluding away my wife."

C.

1. "O where have you been, my long, long love,
      This long seven years and mair?"
   "O I'm come to seek my former vows
      Ye granted me before."

2. "O hold your tongue of your former vows,
      For they will breed sad strife;
   O hold your tongue of your former vows
      For I am become a wife."

3. He turnd him right and round about,
      And the tear blinded his ee:
   "I wad never hae trodden on Irish ground,
      If it had not been for thee.

4. "I might hae had a king's daughter,
      Far, far beyond the sea;
   I might have had a king's daughter,
      Had it not been for love o thee."

5. "If ye might have had a king's daughter,
      Yer sel ye had to blame;
   Ye might have taken the king's daughter,
      For ye kend that I was nane.

6.   "If I was to leave my husband dear,
    And my two babes also,
  O what have you to take me to,
    If with you I should go?"

7.   "I hae seven ships upon the sea—
    And the eighth brought me to land—
  With four-and-twenty bold mariners,
    And music on every hand."

8.   She has taken up her two little babes,
    Kissd them baith cheek and chin:
  "O fair ye weel, my ain two babes,
    For I'll never see you again."

9.   She set her foot upon the ship,
    No mariners could she behold;
  But the sails were o the taffetie,
    And the masts o beaten gold.

10. She had not sailed a league, a league,
    A league but barely three,
  When dismal grew his countenance,
    And drumlie grew his ee.

11. They had not saild a league, a league,
    A league but barely three,
  Until she espied his cloven foot,
    And she wept right bitterlie.

12. "O hold your tongue of your weeping," says he,
    "Of your weeping now let me be;
  I will shew you how the lilies grow
    On the banks of Italy."

13. "O what hills are yon, yon pleasant hills,
    That the sun shines sweetly on?"
  "O yon are the hills of heaven," he said,
    "Where you will never win."

14. "O whaten a mountain is yon," she said,
    "All so dreary wi frost and snow?"
  "O yon is the mountain of hell," he cried,
    "Where you and I will go."

15. He strack the tap-mast wi his hand,
    The fore-masts wi his knew,
  And he brake that gallant ship in twain,
    And sank her in the sea.

D.

THE DEMON LOVER

1. "Well met, well met, my own true love,
      Well met, well met!" cried he,
    "For I've just returned from the Salt Sea,
      And all for the love of thee!"

2. "I might have married the King's daughter, dear,—"
      "You might have married her," cried she,
    "For I am married to a House-Carpenter,
      And a fine young man is he!"

3. "If you will forsake your House-Carpenter,
      And go along with me,
    I will take you to where the grass grows high,
      On the banks of old Tennessee!"

4. "If I forsake my House-Carpenter,
      And go along with thee,
    What have you got to keep me upon,
      And keep me from misery?"

5. Says he, "I've got six ships at sea,
      All sailing to dry land,
    One hundred and ten of your own countrymen,
      Love, they shall be at your command!"

6. She took her babe upon her knee
      And kissed it one, two and three,
    Saying, "Stay at home, my darling sweet babe,
      And keep your father's company!"

7. They had not sailed four weeks or more,
      Four weeks, or scarcely three,
    When she thought of her darling sweet babe at home,
      And she wept most bitterly.

8. Says he, "Are you weeping for gold, my love,
      Or are you weeping for fear,
    Or are you weeping for your House-Carpenter,
      That you left and followed me?"

9. "I am not weeping for gold," she replied,
      "Nor am I weeping for fear,
    But I am weeping alonge for my sweet little babe,
      That I left with my House-Carpenter."

10. "Oh, dry up your tears, my own true love,
      And cease your weeping," cried he,

"For soon you'll see your own happy home,
    On the banks of old Tennessee!"

11. They had not sailed five weeks or more,
        Five weeks, or scarcely four,
    When the ship struck a rock and sprang a leak,
        And they never were seen any more.

12. A curse be on the sea-faring men,
        Oh, cursed by their lives,
    For while they are robbing the House-Carpenter,
        And coaxing away their wives.

JAMES HATLEY (244)

A traditional ballad of Scotland of the 17th century.
    Text, MS. Scott, materials for *Border Minstrelsy*.

Notes

    10/3. remnant of the ordeal by battle; God gives the victory to
the innocent man.

1. It happened once upon a time,
        When the king he was from home,
    Sir Fenwick he has stolen his jewels,
        And laid the blame on James Hatley.

2. James Hatley was in prison strong,
        A wait he was condemned to die;
    There was not one in all the court
        To speak one word for James Hatley.

3. No one but the king's daughter,
        A wait she loved him tenderlie;
    She's stolen the keys from her father's head,
        And gaed and conversed wi James Hatley.

4. "Come, tell to me now, James," she said,
        "Come, tell to me if thou hast them stolen,
    And I'll make a vow, and I'll keep it true,
        Ye shall never be the worse of me."

5. "I have not stolen them, lady," he said,
        "Nor as little it was intended by me;
    Sir Fenwick he has stolen them himself;
        A wait he has laid the blame on me."

6. "One asking, one asking, father dear,
        One asking, one asking grant to me,

For I never asked one in my life;
    I am sure you cannot but grant it to me."

7. "Weel ask it, weel ask it, daughter dear,
    Ask it, and it granted shall be;
If it should be my hole estate,
    Naesaid, naesaid, it shall not be."

8. "I want none of your gold, father,
    And I want none of your fee;
All that I ask, father dear,
    Is the life of James Hatley."

9. "Weel ask it, weel ask it, daughter dear,
    Weel ask it, and it answerëd shall be;
For I'll make a vow, and I'll keep it true,
    James Hatley shall never hangëd be."

10. "Another asking, father dear,
    Another asking grant to me;
Let Fenwick and Hatley go to the sword,
    And let them try their verity."

11. "'T is weel askëd, daughter dear,
    'T is weel asked, and it granted shall be;
For e'er the morn or twelve o'clock
    They both at the point of sword shall be."

12. James Hatley was fifteen years old,
    Sir Fenwick he was thirty-three;
But James lap about, and he struck about,
    Till he's gaen Sir Fenwick wounds three.

13. "Hold up, hold up, James Hatley," he cry'd,
    "And let my breath go out and in;
For I have stolen them myself,
    More shame and disgrace it is to me."

14. Up and spake an English lord,
    And O but he spake haughtily.
"I would reather given my whole estate
    Before ye had not hanged James Hatley."

15. But up and spake a Scottish lord,
    And O but he spake boldly.
"I would reather hae foughten among blood to the knees
    Before ye had hanged James Hatley."

16. Up and spake the king's eldest son,
    "Come hame, James Hatley, and dine wi me;
For I've made a vow, I'll keep it true,
    Ye's be my captain by land and by sea."

17.   Up and spake the king's daughter,
         "Come home, James Hatley, and dine wi me;
       For I've made a vow, I'll keep it true,
         I'll never marry a man but thee."

YOUNG ALLAN (245)

A somewhat confused account of a boat race in which Young Allan
has boasted that his ship can outsail any ship on the sea. In the race
which follows, all the ships are lost in the storm that comes up except
that of Young Allan which is saved by a bonny boy who takes the
helm and brings the ship safe to land. Stanza 21 in which the ship is
addressed directly suggests epic formulas. Especially in Scandinavian
ballad and saga are ships directly addressed.

Text, traditional in Scotland, Buchan, ii, 11.

1.   All the skippers o Scarsburgh
         Sat drinking at the wine;
       There fell a rousing them amang,
         On an unseally time.

2.   Some there rousd their hawk, their hawk,
         And some there rousd their hound,
       But Young Allan rousd his comely cog,
         As she stood on dry ground.

3.   "There's nae a ship in Scarsburgh
         Will sail the seas wi mine,
       Except it be the Burgess Black,
         Or than the smack calld Twine.

4.   "There's nae a ship amang you a'
         Will sail alang wi me,
       But the comely cog o Hecklandhawk,
         And Flower o Yermanie,
       And the Black Snake o leve London;
         They are a' gane frae me."

5.   Out it speaks a little wee boy
         Stood by Young Allan's knee;
       "My master has a coal-carrier
         Will take the wind frae thee.

6.   "She will gae out under the leaf,
         Come in under the lee,
       And nine times in a winter night
         She'll turn the wind wi thee."

7. When they had wagerd them amang
    Full fifty tuns o wine,
Besides as mickle gude black silk
    As clathe their lemans fine,

8. When all the rest went to the tows,
    All the whole night to stay,
Young Allan he went to his bower,
    There with his God to pray.

9. "There shall nae man gang to my ship
    Till I say mass and dine,
And take my leave o my lady;
    Gae to my bonny ship syne."

10. Then they saild east on Saturday,
    On Sunday sailëd west;
Likewise they sailed on Monday
    Till twelve, when they did rest.

11. At midnight dark the wind up stark,
    And seas began to rout,
Till Allan and his bonny new ship
    Gaed three times witherlands about.

12. "O," sighing says the Young Allan,
    "I fear a deadly storm;
For mony a heaving sinking sea
    Strikes sair on my ship's stern.

13. "Where will I get a little wee boy
    Will take my helm in hand
Till I gang up to my tapmast
    And see for some dry land?"

14. "O waken, waken your drunken men,
    As they lye drunk wi wine;
For when ye came thro Edinbro town
    Ye bought them sheen o ben.

15. "There was nae shoe made for my foot,
    Nor gluve made for my hand;
But never theless, my dear master,
    I'll take your helm in hand
Till ye gang to the tall tapmast
    And look for some dry land.

16. "And here am I, a little wee boy
    Will take your helm in han
Till ye gang up to your tapmast,
    But, master, stay not lang."

17. "I cannot see nae day, nae day,
    Nor nae meathe can I ken;
But mony a bonny feather-bed
    Lyes floating on the faem,
And the comely cog o Normanshore,
    She never will gang hame."

18. The comely cog o Nicklingame
    Came sailing by his hand;
Saye, "Gae down, gae down, ye gude skipper,
    Your ship sails on the sand."

19. "Come down, come down, my gude master,
    Ye see not what I see;
For thro and thro our comely cog
    I see the green haw sea."

20. "Take fifty ells o gude canvas
    And wrap the ship a' round;
And pick her weell, and spare her not,
    And make her hale and sound."

21. "If ye will sail, my bonny ship,
    Till we come to dry land,
For ilka iron mail in you,
    Of gowd there shall be ten."

22. The ship she listend all the while,
    And, hearing of her hire,
She flew as swift threw the saut sea
    As sparks do frae the fire.

23. The first an shore that they came till,
    They ca'd it Howdoloot;
Wi drums beating and cannons shouting,
    They held our gude ship out.

24. The next an shore that they came till,
    They ca'd it Howdilee;
Wi drums beating and fifes playing,
    They bare her to the sea.

25. The third an shore that they came till,
    They ca'd it Howdilin;
Wi drums beating and pipes playing,
    They towd our gude ship in.

26. The sailors walkd upon the shore,
    Wi their auld baucheld sheen,
And thanked God and their Lady,
    That brought them safe again.

27.   "For we went out o Scarsburgh
            Wi fifty ships and three;
        But nane o them came back again
            But Young Allan, ye see."

28.   "Come down, come down, my little wee boy,
            Till I pay you your fee;
        I hae but only ae daughter,
            And wedded to her ye'se be."

THE GREY COCK (248)

This ballad has lost its original point in the Child versions. The original story told of the visit of a ghost or of a revenant to her beloved. She tells the cock not to crow before day and he will be handsomely rewarded; for as soon as the cock crows all the dead must be back in their graves. See Barry's note to this ballad in *British Ballads from Maine,* p. 310.

Text A represents the early form of the ballad from P. W. Joyce, *Old Irish Folk Music and Songs,* p. 219; B, Herd, p. 324.

A.

1. "Oh, you're welcome home again," said the young man to his love,
        "I am waiting for you many a night and day.
    You are tired, you are pale," said this young man to his dear:
        "You must never again go away."
    "I must go away," she said, "when the little cock will crow,
        For here they will not let me stay;
    But if I had my wish, Oh, my darling," she said,
        "This night should never, never be day."

2. "Oh, my pretty, pretty cock, oh, my handsome little cock,
        I pray you will not crow before day;
    And your comb shall be made of the very beaten gold,
        And your wings of the silver so grey!"
    But, oh, this pretty cock, this handsome little cock,
        He crew full an hour too soon:
    "Oh, my true love," she said, "it is time for me to part,
        It is now the going down of the moon!"

3. "And where is your bed, my dearest dear?" he said,
        "And where are your white holland sheets?
    And where are your maidens, my dearest love," he said,
        "That wait on you while you are asleep?"
    "The clay is my bed, my dearest dear," she said,
        "The shroud is my white holland sheet;

The worms and creeping things are my waiting maids,
    To wait on me whilst I am asleep."

B.

1.   "O saw ye my father? or saw ye my mother?
    Or saw ye my true-love John?"
  "I saw not your father, I saw not your mother,
    But I saw your true-love John.

2.   "It's now ten at night, and the stars gie nae light,
    And the bells they ring ding, dang;
  He's met wi some delay that causeth him to stay,
    But he will be here ere lang."

3.   The surly auld carl did naething but snarl,
    And Johny's face it grew red;
  Yet, tho he often sighd, he neer a word replied
    Till all were asleep in bed.

4.   Up Johny rose, and to the door he goes,
    And gently tirlëd the pin;
  The lassie taking tent unto the door she went,
    And she opend and let him in.

5.   "And are ye come at last? and do I hold ye fast?
    And is my Johny true?"
  "I hae nae time to tell, but sae lang's I like mysell
    Sae lang will I love you."

6.   "Flee, flee up, my bonny grey cock,
    And craw whan it is day;
  Your neck shall be like the bonny beaten gold,
    And your wings of the silver grey."

7.   The cock prov'd false, and untrue he was,
    For he crew an hour o'er soon;
  The lassie thought it day when she sent her love away,
    And it was but a blink of the moon.

AULD MATRONS (249)

A Scotch ballad with much admixture of elements from the Robin
Hood ballad tradition.
  Text, Buchan, ii, 238.

1.   My love she is a gentlewoman,
    Has her living by the seam,

I kenna how she is provided
   This night for me and my foot-groom.

2. He is gane to Annie's bower-door,
    And gently tirled at the pin:
  "Ye sleep, ye wake, my love Annie,
    Ye'll rise and lat your true-love in."

3. Wi her white fingers lang and sma
    She gently lifted up the pin;
  Wi her arms lang and bent
    She kindly caught sweet Willie in.

4. "O will ye go to cards or dice?
    Or will ye go to play?
  Or will ye go to a well made bed,
    And sleep a while till day?"

5. "I winna gang to card nor dice,
    Nor yet will I to play;
  But I will gang to a well made bed,
    And sleep a while till day.

6. "My love Annie, my dear Annie,
    I would be at your desire;
  But wae mat fa the auld Matrons,
    As she sits by the kitchen fire."

7. "Keep up your heart, Willie," she said,
    "Keep up your heart, dinna fear;
  It's seven years, and some guid mair,
    Sin her foot did file the flear."

8. They hadna kissd nor love clapped,
    As lovers when they meet,
  Till up it raise the auld Matrons,
    Sae well's she spread her feet.

9. O wae mat fa the auld Matrons,
    Sae clever's she took the gate.
  And she's gaen ower yon lang, lang hill,
    Knockd at the sheriff's yate.

10. "Ye sleep, ye wake, my lord?" she said.
    "Are ye not your bower within?
  There's a knight in bed wi your daughter,
    I fear she's gotten wrang."

11. "Ye'll do ye down thro Kelso town,
    Waken my wall-wight men;
  And gin ye hae your wark well dune
    I'll be there at command."

12. She's done her down thro Kelso town,
  Wakend his wall-wight men;
 But gin she had her wark well done
  He was there at command.

13. He had his horse wi corn fodderd,
  His men armd in mail;
 He gae the Matrons half a merk
  To show them ower the hill.

14. Willie sleepd, but Annie waked
  Till she heard their bridles ring;
 Then tapped on her love's shoulder,
  And said, "Ye've sleepit lang."

15. "O save me, save me, my blessd lady,
  Till I've on my shooting-gear;
 I dinna fear the king himsell,
  Tho he an's men were here."

16. Then they shot in, and Willie out,
  The arrows graz'd his brow;
 The maid she wept and tore her hair,
  Says, "This can never do."

17. Then they shot in, and he shot out,
  The bow brunt Willie's hand;
 But aye he kissd her ruby lips,
  Said, "My dear, thinkna lang."

18. He set his horn to his mouth,
  And has blawn loud and shrill,
 And he's calld on his brother John,
  In Ringlewood he lay still.

19. The first an shot that Lord John shot,
  He wound fifty and fifteen;
 The next an shot that Lord John shot,
  He ca'd out the sheriff's een.

20. "O some o you lend me an arm,
  Some o you lend me twa;
 And they that came for strife this day,
  Take horse, ride fast awa.

21. "But wae mat fa yon, auld Matrons,
  An ill death mat ye die!
 I'll burn you on yon high hill-head,
  Blaw your ashes in the sea."

HENRY MARTYN (250)

This ballad is directly derived, it would seem, from "Andrew Barton."
The name Henry Martyn may even be a corruption of Andrew Barton.

Text from tradition by S. Baring-Gould, Child, iv, 393.

1. In merry Scotland, in merry Scotland
     There lived brothers three;
   They all did cast lots which of them should go
     A robbing upon the salt sea,

2. The lot it fell on Henry Martyn,
     The youngest of the three;
   That he should go rob on the salt, salt sea,
     To maintain his brothers and he.

3. He had not a sailed a long winter's night,
     Nor yet a short winter's day,
   Before that he met with a lofty old ship,
     Come sailing along that way.

4. O when she came by Henry Martyn,
     "I prithee now, let us go."
   "O no! God wot, that, that will I not,
     O that will I never do.

5. "Stand off! stand off!" said Henry Martyn,
     "For you shall not pass by me;
   For I am a robber all on the salt seas,
     To maintain us brothers three.

6. "How far, how far," cries Henry Martyn,
     "How far do you make it?" said he;
   "For I am a robber all on the salt seas,
     To maintain us brothers three."

7. For three long hours they merrily fought,
     For hours they fought full three;
   At last a deep wound got Henry Martyn,
     And down by the mast fell he.

8. 'T was broadside to the broadside then,
     And a rain and hail of blows,
   But the salt sea ran in, ran in, ran in,
     To the bottom then she goes.

9. Bad news, bad news for old England,
     Bad news has come to the town,

For a rich merchant's vessel is cast away,
  And all her brave seaman drown.

10. Bad news, bad news through London street,
      Bad news has come to the king,
    For all the brave lives of the mariners lost,
      That are sunk in the watery main.

THE KITCHIE-BOY (252)

This ballad is based on motifs made common by the various versions
of "King Horn" in both its romance and ballad forms.
  Text, traditional in Scotland, Buchan, i, 145.

1. Earl Richard had but ae daughter,
      A maid o birth and fame;
    She loved her father's kitchen-boy
      The greater was her shame.

2. But she could ne'er her true-love see,
      Nor with him could she talk,
    In towns where she had wont to go,
      Nor fields where she could walk.

3. But it fell ance upon a day
      Her father went from home;
    She's calld upon the kitchen boy
      To come and clean her room.

4. "Come sit ye down by me, Willie,
      Come sit ye down by me;
    There's nae a lord in a' the north
      That I can love but thee."

5. "Let never the like be heard, lady,
      Nor let it ever be;
    For if your father get word o this
      He will gar hang me hie."

6. "O ye shall ne'er be hangd, Willie,
      Your blude shall neer be drawn;
    I'll lay my life in pledge o thine
      Your body's ne'er get wrang."

7. "Excuse me now, my comely dame,
      No langer here I'll stay;
    You know my time is near expir'd,
      And now I must away.

8. "The master-cook will on me call,
     And answered he must be;
   If I am found in bower with thee,
     Great anger will there be."

9. "The master-cook will on you call,
     But shall not answerd be;
   I'll put you in a higher place
     Than any cook's degree.

10. "I have a coffer full of gold,
      Another of white monie
    And I will build a bonny ship,
      And set my love to sea.

11. "Silk shall be your sailing-clothes,
      Gold yellow is your hair,
    As white like milk are your twa hands,
      Your body neat and fair."

12. This lady, with her fair speeches,
      She made the boy grow bold,
    And he began to kiss and clap,
      And on his love lay hold.

13. And she has built a bonny ship,
      Set her love to the sea,
    Seven score o brisk young men
      To bear him companie.

14. Then she's taen out a gay gold ring,
      To him she did it gie:
    "This will mind you on the ladie, Willie,
      That's laid her love on thee."

15. Then he's taen out a piece of gold,
      And he brake it in two:
    "All I have in the world, my dame,
      For love I give to you."

16. Now he is to his bonny ship,
      And merrily taen the sea;
    The lady lay oer castle-wa,
      The tear blinded her ee.

17. They had not saild upon the sea
      A week but barely three
    When came a prosperous gale of wind,
      On Spain's coast landed he.

18. A lady lay o'er castle-wa,
      Beholding dale and down,

And she beheld the bonny ship
  Come sailing to the town.

19. "Come here, come here, my maries a',
       Ye see not what I see;
     For here I see the bonniest ship
       That ever sail'd the sea.

20. "In her there is the bravest squire
       That e'er my eyes did see;
     All clad in silk and rich attire,
       And comely, comely's he.

21. "O busk, O busk, my maries all,
       O busk and make ye fine;
     And we will on to yon shore-side,
       Invite yon squire to dine."

22. "Will ye come up to my castle
       Wi me and take your dine?
     And ye shall eat the gude white bread,
       And drink the claret wine."

23. "I thank you for your bread, lady,
       I thank you for your wine;
     I thank you for your kind offer,
       But now I have not time."

24. "I would gie all my land," she says,
       "Your gay bride were I she;
     And then to live on a small portion
       Contented I would be."

25. "She's far awa frae me, lady,
       She's far awa frae me
     That has my heart a-keeping fast,
       And my love still she'll be."

26. "But ladies they are unconstant,
       When their loves go to sea,
     And she'll be wed ere ye gae back;
       My love, pray stay wi me."

27. "If she be wed ere I go back,
       And prove sae false to me,
     I shall live single all my life;
       I'll ne'er wed one but she."

28. Then she's taen out a gay gold ring,
       And gae him presentlie:
     "'Twill mind you on the lady, young man,
       That laid her love on thee."

29. "The ring that's on my mid-finger
    Is far dearer to me,
Tho yours were o the gude red gold,
    And mine the metal free."

30. He viewd them all, baith neat and small,
    As they stood on the shore,
Then hoist the mainsail to the wind,
    Adieu, for evermore!

31. He had not saild upon the sea
    A week but barely three
Until there came a prosperous gale,
    In Scotland landed he.

32. But he put paint upon his face,
    And oil upon his hair,
Likewise a mask above his brow,
    Which did disguise him sair.

33. Earl Richard lay oer castle-wa,
    Beholding dale and down,
And he beheld the bonny ship
    Come sailing to the town.

34. "Come here, come here, my daughter dear,
    Ye see not what I see;
For here I see the bonniest ship
    That ever saild the sea.

35. "In her there is the bravest squire
    That e'er my eyes did see;
O busk, O busk, my daughter dear,
    Come here, come here, to me.

36. "O busk, O busk, my daughter dear,
    O busk, and make ye fine,
And we will on to the shore-side,
    Invite yon squire to dine."

37. "He's far awa frae me, father,
    He's far awa frae me
Who has the keeping o my heart,
    And I'll wed nane but he."

38. "Whoever has your heart in hand,
    Yon lad's the match for thee,
And he shall come to my castle
    This day and dine wi me."

39. "Will ye come up to my castle
    With me and take your dine?

And ye shall eat the gude white bread,
    And drink the claret wine."

40. "Yes, I'll come up to your castle
    With you and take my dine,
For I would give my bonny ship
    Were your fair daughter mine."

41. "I would give all my lands," he said,
    "That your bride she would be;
Then to live on a small portion
    Contented would I be."

42. As they gaed up from yon sea-strand
    And down the bowling-green,
He drew the mask out-oer his face,
    For fear he should be seen.

43. He's done him down from bower to bower,
    Likewise from bower to ha,
And there he saw that lady gay,
    The flower out-oer them a'.

44. He's taen her in his arms twa,
    And haild her courteouslie:
"Excuse me, sir, there's no strange man
    Such freedom use with me."

45. Her father turnd him round about,
    A light laugh then gave he:
"Stay, I'll retire a little while,
    Perhaps you may agree."

46. Now Willie's taen a gay gold ring,
    And gave her presentlie;
Says, "Take ye that, ye lady fair,
    A love-token from me."

47. "O got ye't on the sea sailing?
    Or got ye't on the sand?
Or got ye't on the coast of Spain,
    Upon a dead man's hand?"

48. "Fine silk it was his sailing-clothes,
    Gold yellow was his hair;
It would hae made a hale heart bleed
    To see him lying there.

49. "He was not dead as I pass by,
    But no remeid could be;
He gave me this token to bear
    Unto a fair ladie.

50. "And by the marks he has descrybed
         I'm sure that you are she;
     So take this token of free will,
         For him you'll never see."

51. In sorrow she tore her mantle,
         With care she tore her hair:
     "Now since I've lost my own true-love,
         I'll neer love young men mair."

52. He drew the mask from off his face,
         The lady sweetly smiled:
     "Awa, awa, ye fause Willie!
         How have you me beguiled?"

53. Earl Richard he went thro the ha,
         The wine-glass in his hand,
     But little thought his kitchen-boy
         Was heir oer a' his land.

54. But this she kept within her heart,
         And never told to one
     Until nine months they were expir'd,
         That her young son came home.

55. She told it to her father dear;
         He said, "Daughter, well won;
     You've married for love, not for gold,
         Your joys will neer be done."

LORD WILLIAM, OR, LORD LUNDY (254)

Text, Motherwell, p. 307.

1. Sweet William's gone over seas,
        Some unco lair to learn,
    And our gude Bailie's ae dochter
        Is awa to learn the same.

2. In one broad buke they learned baith,
        In one broad bed they lay;
    But when her father came to know
        He gart her come away.

3. "It's you must marry that Southland lord,
        His lady for to be;
    It's ye maun marry that Southland lord,
        Or nocht ye'll get frae me."

4. "I must marry that Southland lord,
   Father, an it be your will;
   But I rather it were my burial-day,
   My grave for to fill."

5. She walked up, she walked down,
   Had none to make her moan,
   Nothing but the pretty bird
   Sat on the causey-stone.

6. "If thou could speak, wee bird," she says,
   "As weell as thou can flee,
   I would write a long letter
   To Will ayont the sea."

7. "What thou wants wi Will," it says,
   "Thou'll seal it with thy ring,
   Tak a thread o silk and anither o twine,
   About my neck will hing."

8. What she wanted wi Willie
   She sealed it wi a ring,
   Took a thread of silk, another o twine,
   About its neck did hing.

9. The bird flew high, this bird flew low,
   This bird flew owre the sea,
   Until it entered the same room
   Wherein was Sweet Willie.

10. This bird flew high, this bird flew low,
    Poor bird, it was mistaen.
    It let the letter fa on Baldie's breist,
    Instead of Sweet William.

11. "Here's a letter, William," he says,
    "I'm sure it's not to me;
    And gin the morn gin twelve o'clock
    Your love shall married be."

12. "Come saddle to me my horse," he said,
    "The brown and a' that's speedie,
    And I'll awa to Old England,
    To bring home my ladie."

13. Awa he gaed, awa he rade,
    Awa wi mickle speed;
    He lichtit at every twa miles' end,
    Lichtit and changed his steed.

14. When she entered the church-style,
    A tear was in her ee;

But when she entered the church-door
    A blythe sicht did she see.

15.   "O hold your hand, you minister,
    Hold it a little wee,
  Till I speak wi the bonnie bride,
    For she's a friend to me.

16.   "Stand off, stand off, you braw bridegroom,
    Stand off a little wee;
  Stand off, stand off, you braw bridegroom
    For the bride shall join wi me."

17.   Up and spak the bride's father,
    And an angry man was he:
  "If I had pistol, powther and lead,
    And all at my command,
  I would shoot thee stiff and dead
    In the place where thou dost stand."

18.   Up and spoke then Sweet William,
    And a blithe blink from his ee:
  "If ye neer be shot till I shoot you,
    Ye'se neer be shot for me.

19.   "Come out, come out, my foremost man,
    And lift my lady on;
  Commend me all to my good-mother,
    At night when ye gang home."

WILLIE'S FATAL VISIT (255)

This ballad is largely pieced from "The Grey Cock," "Sweet William's Ghost," "Clerk Saunders," "Auld Matrons," "Clyde's Water," and probably others.

Text, Buchan's *Ballads of the North of Scotland,* ii, 259.

1.   'T was on an evening fair I went to take the air,
    I heard a maid making her moan;
  Said, "Saw ye my father? Or saw ye my mother?
    Or saw ye my brother John?
  Or saw ye the lad that I love best,
    And his name it is Sweet William?"

2.   "I saw not your father, I saw not your mother,
    Nor saw I your brother John;
  But I saw the lad that ye love best,
    And his name it is Sweet William."

3. "O was my love riding? or was he running?
        Or was he walking alone?
    Or says he that he will be here this night?
        O dear, but he tarries long."

4. "Your love was not riding, nor yet was he running,
        But fast was he walking alone;
    He says that he will be here this night to thee,
        And forbids you to think long."

5. Then Willie he has gane to his love's door,
        And gently tirled the pin:
    "O sleep ye, wake ye, my bonny Meggie,
        Ye'll rise, lat your true love in."

6. The lassie being swack ran to the door fu snack,
        And gently she lifted the pin,
    Then into her arms sae large and sae lang
        She embraced her bonny love in.

7. "O will ye gang to the cards or the dice,
        Or to a table o wine?
    Or will ye gang to a well-made bed,
        Well coverd wi blankets fine?"

8. "O I winna gang to the cards nor the dice,
        Nor yet to a table o wine;
    But I'll rather gang to a well-made bed,
        Well coverd wi blankets fine."

9. "My braw little cock, sits on the house tap,
        Ye'll craw not till it be day,
    And your kame shall be o the gude red gowd,
        And your wings o the siller grey."

10. The cock being fause untrue he was,
        And he crew an hour ower seen;
    They thought it was the gude day-light,
        But it was but the light o the meen.

11. "Ohon, alas!" says bonny Meggie then,
        "This night we hae sleeped ower lang."
    "O what is the matter?" then Willie replied,
        "The faster then I must gang."

12. Then Sweet Willie raise, and put on his claise,
        And drew till him stockings and sheen,
    And took by his side his berry-brown sword,
        And ower yon lang hill he's gane.

13. As he gaed ower yon high, high hill,
        And down yon dowie den,

Great and grievous was the ghost he saw,
 Would fear ten thousand men.

14. As he gaed in by Mary kirk,
 And in by Mary stile,
Wan and weary was the ghost
 Upon sweet Willie did smile.

15. "Aft hae ye travelld this road, Willie,
 Aft hae ye travelld in sin;
Ye neer said sae muckle for your saul
 As My Maker bring me hame.

16. "Aft hae ye travelld this road, Willie,
 Your bonny love to see;
But ye'll never travel this road again
 Till ye leave a token wi me."

17. Then she has taen him Sweet Willie,
 Riven him frae gair to gair,
And on ilka seat o Mary's kirk
 O Willie she hang a share;
Even abeen his love Meggie's dice,
 Hang's head and yellow hair.

18. His father made moan, his mother made moan,
 But Meggie made muckle mair;
His father made moan, his mother made moan,
 But Meggie reave her yellow hair.

ALISON AND WILLIE (256)

Even Child could not unravel Stanza 7.
 Text, Buchan's MSS., i, 231.

1. "My luve she lives in Lincolnshire,
 I wat she's neither black nor broun,
But her hair is like the thread o gowd,
 Aye an it waur weel kaiméd doun."

2. She's pued the black mask owre her face,
 An blinkit gaily wi her ee:
"O will you to my weddin come,
 An will you bear me gude companie?"

3. "I winna to your weddin come,
 Nor will I bear you gude companie,
Unless you be the bride yoursell,
 An me the bridegroom to be."

4. "For me to be the bride mysel,
        An you the bonnie bridegroom to be—
    Cheer up your heart, Sweet Willie," she said,
        "For that's the day you'll never see.

5. "Gin you waur on your saiddle set,
        An gaily ridin on the way,
    You'll hae nae mair mind o Alison
        Than she waur dead an laid in clay."

6. When he was on his saiddle set,
        An slowly ridin on the way,
    He had mair mind o Alison
        Than he had o the licht o day.

7. He saw a hart draw near a hare,
        An aye that hare drew near a toun,
    An that same hart did get a hare,
        But the gentle knicht got ne'er a toun.

8. He leant him owre his saiddle-bow,
        An his heart did brak in pieces three;
    Wi sighen said him Sweet Willie,
        "The pains o luve hae taen hald o me."

9. .   .   .   .

    There cam a white horse an a letter,
        That stopped the wedding speidilie.

10. She leant her back on her bed-side,
        An her heart did brak in pieces three;
    She was buried an bemoaned,
        But the birds waur Willie's companie.

BURD ISABEL AND EARL PATRICK (257)

Text, Kinloch MSS., i, 211.

1. There is a stane in yon water,
        It's lang or it grow green;
    It's a maid that maks her ain fortune,
        It'll never end its leen.

2. Burd Bell was na full fyfteen
        Till to service she did gae;
    Burd Bell was na full sixteen
        Till big wi bairn was scho.

*   *   *   *   *   *   *   *

3. "Burd Bell she is a gude woman,
  She bides at hame wi me;
  She never seeks to gang to church,
  But bides at hame wi me."

4. It fell ance upon a day
  She fell in travail-pain;
  He is gane to the stair-head
  Some ladies to call in.

5. "O gin ye hae a lass-bairn, Burd Bell,
  A lass-bairn though it be,
  Twenty ploughs bot and a mill
  Will mak ye lady free.

6. "But gin ye hae a son, Burd Bell,
  Ye'se be my wedded wife,

  .   .   .   .

  .   .   .   .

7. The knichts they knack their white fingers,
  The ladies sat and sang,
  T was a' to cheer bonnie Burd Bell,
  She was far sunk in pain.

          *   *   *   *   *   *

8. Earl Patrick is to his mither gane,
  As fast as he could hie:
  "An askin, an askin, dear mither,
  An askin I want frae thee.

9. "Burd Bell has born to me a son;
  What sall I do her wi?"
  "Gie her what ye like, Patrick,
  Mak na her your ladie."

10. He has gane to bonnie Burd Bell,
  Hir heart was pressd wi care:

  .   .   .   .

  .   .   .   .

11. "My father will dee, bonnie Burd Bell,
  My mither will do the same,
  And whan ye hear that they are gane
  It's then I'll bring ye hame."

12. Earl Patrick's bigget to her a bour,
  And strawn it round wi sand;
  He coverd it wi silver on the outside,
  Wi the red gowd within.

13. It happened ance upon a day
    She was kaiming his yellow hair,

   .   .   .   .   .

    .   .   .   .   .   .

14. "Your father is dead, Earl Patrick,
    Your mither is the same;
And what is the reason, Earl Patrick,
    You winna tak me hame?"

15. "I've bigget to you a bonnie bour,
    I've strawn it round wi sand;
I've coverd it wi silver on the outside,
    Wi gude red gowd within.

16. "If e'er I marry anither woman,
    Or bring anither hame,
I wish a hundred evils may enter me,
    And may I fa oure the brim!"

17. It was na very lang after this
    That a duke's dochter he's wed,
Wi a waggon fu of gowd

   .   .   .   .   .   .

18. Burd Bell lookit oure her castle-wa,
    And spied baith dale and down,
And there she saw Earl Patrick's aunt
    Come riding to the town.

19. "What want ye here, Earl Patrick's aunt?
    What want ye here wi me?"
"I want Earl Patrick's bonnie young son;
    His bride fain wad him see."

20. "I wad like to see that woman or man,
    Of high or low degree,
That wad tak the bairn frae my foot
    That I ance for bowd my knee."

    *   *   *   *   *   *

21. "Burd Bell, she's the bauldest woman
    That ever I did see."
"It's I'll gang to bonnie Burd Bell,
    She was never bauld to me."

22. Burd Bell lookit oure her castle-wa,
    Behaulding brave dale and down,
And there she spied him Earl Patrick
    Slowly riding to the town.

23. "What said ye to my great-grand-aunt

     .   .   .   .

  .   .   .   .

    .   .   .   .

24. "I said nathing to your great-grand-aunt
    But I will say to thee:
I wad like to see the woman or man,
    Of high or low degree,
That wad tak the bairn frae my foot
    I ance for bowd my knee.

25. "O dinna ye mind, Earl Patrick,
    The vows ye made to me,
That a hundred evils wad enter you
    If ye provd fause to me?"

26. He's turnd him richt and round about,
    His horse head to the wind,
The hundred evils enterd him,
    And he fell oure the brim.

LORD THOMAS STUART (259)

Text, Maidement, *North Countrie Garland,* p. 1.

1. Thomas Stuart was a lord,
    A lord of mickle land;
He used to wear a coat of gold,
    But now his grave is green.

2. Now he has wooed the young countess,
    The Countess of Balquhin,
An given her for a morning-gift
    Strathboggie and Aboyne.

3. But women's wit is aye willful,
    Alas that ever it was sae.
She longed to see the moning-gift
    That her gude lord to her gae.

4. When steeds were saddled an weel bridled,
    An ready for to ride,
There came a pain on that gude lord,
    His back, likewise his side.

5. He said, "Ride on, my lady fair,
    May goodness be your guide;

For I'm sae sick an weary that
    No farther can I ride."

6.   Now ben did come his father dear,
      Wearing a golden band;
    Says, "Is there nae leech in Edinburgh
      Can cure my son from wrang?"

7.   "O leech is come, an leech is gane,
      Yet, father, I'm aye waur;
    There's not a leech in Edinbro
      Can death from me debar.

8.   "But be a friend to my wife, father,
      Restore her to her own;
    Restore to her my morning-gift,
      Strathboggie and Aboyne.

9.   "It had been gude for my wife, father,
      To me she'd born a son;
    He would have got my lands an rents,
      Where they lie out an in.

10.   "It had been gude for my wife, father,
      To me she'd born an heir;
    He would have got my lands an rents,
      Where they lie fine an fair."

11.   The steeds they strave into their stables,
      The boys couldn't get them bound;
    The hounds lay howling on the leech,
      Cause their master was behind.

12.   "I dreamed a dream since late yeatreen,
      I wish it may be good,
    That our chamber was full of swine,
      An our bed full of blood."

13.   I saw a woman come from the West,
      Full sore wringing her hands,
    And aye she cried, "Ohon, alas!
      My good lord's broken bands."

14.   As she came by my good lord's bower,
      Saw mony black steeds an brown:
    "I'm feared it be mony unco lords
      Havin my love from town."

15.   As she came by my gude lord's bower,
      Saw mony black steeds an grey:
    "I'm feared it's mony unco lords
      Havin my love to the clay."

LORD THOMAS AND LADY MARGARET (260)

Text, Motherwell's MS., p. 407.

1. Lord Thomas is to the hunting gone,
     To hunt the fallow deer;
   Lady Margaret's to the greenwood shaw,
     To see her lover hunt there.

2. He has looked over his left shoulder,
     To see what might be seen,
   And there he saw Lady Margaret,
     As she was riding her lane.

3. He called on his servants all,
     By one, by two, by three:
   "Go hunt, go hunt that wild woman,
     Go hunt her far from me."

4. They hunted her high, they hunted her low,
     They hunted her over the plain,
   And the red scarlet robes Lady Margaret had on
     Would never be mended again.

5. They hunted her high, they hunted her low,
     They hunted her over the plain,
   Till at last she spy'd a tall young man,
     As he was riding alane.

6. "Some relief, some relief, thou tall young man,
     Some relief I pray thee grant me,
   For I am a lady deep wronged in love,
     And chased from my own countrie."

7. "No relief, no relief, thou lady fair,
     No relief will I grant unto thee
   Till once thou renounce all the men in the world
     My wedded wife for to be."

8. Then he set her on a milk-white steed,
     Himself upon a gray,
   And he has drawn his hat over his face,
     And chearfully they rode away.

9. Lady Margaret was at her bower-window,
     Sewing her silken seam,
   And there she spy'd like a wandering bodie,
     Lord Thomas begging alane.

10. "Some relief, some relief, thou lady fair,
    Some relief, I pray thee grant me,
For I am a puir auld doited carle,
    And banished from my ain countrie."

11. "No relief, no relief, thou perjured man,
    No relief will I grant unto thee;
For oh, if I had thee within my bower,
    There hanged dead thou would be."

12. "No such thing, Lady Margaret," he said,
    "Such a thing would never be;
For with my broadsword I would kill thy wedded lord,
    And carry thee far off with me."

13. "Oh no, no! Lord Thomas," she said,
    "Oh, no such things must be;
For I have wine in my cellars,
    And you must drink with me."

14. Lady Margaret then called her servants all,
    By one, by two, by three:
"Go fetch me the bottles of blude-red wine,
    That Lord Thomas may drink with me."

15. They brought her the bottles of blude-red wine,
    By one, by two, by three,
And with her fingers long and small
    She poisond them all three.

16. She took the cup in her lilly-white hand,
    Betwixt her finger and her thumb,
She put it to her red rosy lips,
    But never a drop went down.

17. Then he took the cup in his manly hand,
    Betwixt his finer and his thumb,
He put it to his red rosy lips,
    And so merrily it ran down.

18. "Oh, I am wearied drinking with thee, Margaret;
    I am wearied drinking with thee."
"And so was I," Lady Margaret said,
    "When thou hunted thy hounds after me."

19. "But I will bury thee, Lord Thomas," she said,
    "Just as if thou wert one of my own;
And when that my good lord comes home
    I will say thou's my sister's son."

LADY ISABEL (261)

Text, Buchan, i, 129.

1. 'T was early on a May morning
       Lady Isabel combd her hair;
   But little kent she or the morn
       She woud never comb it mair.

2. 'T was early on a May morning
       Lady Isabel rang the keys;
   But little kent she or the morn
       A fey woman she was.

3. Ben it came her step-mother,
       As white's the lily flower:
   "It's tauld me this day, Isabel,
       You are your father's whore."

4. "O them that tauld you that, mother,
       I wish they neer drink wine;
   For if I be the same woman
       My ain sell drees the pine.

5. "And them that's tauld you that, mother,
       I wish they neer drink ale;
   For if I be the same woman
       My ain sell drees the dail."

6. "It may be very well seen, Isabel,
       It may be very well seen;
   He buys to you the damask gowns
       To me the dowie green."

7. "Ye are of age and I am young,
       And young amo my flowers;
   The fairer that my claithing be,
       The mair honour is yours.

8. "I hae a love beyond the sea,
       And far ayont the faem;
   For ilka gown my father buys me,
       My ain luve sends me ten."

9. "Come ben, come ben now, Lady Isabel,
       And drink the wine wi me;
   I hae twa jewels in ae coffer,
       And ane o them I'll gie ye."

10. "Stay still, stay still, my mother dear,
        Stay still a little while,
    Till I gang into Maykirk;
        It's but a little mile."

11. When she gaed on to Maykirk,
        And into Mary's quire,
    There she saw her ain mother
        Sit in a gowden chair.

12. "O will I leave the lands, mother?
        Or shall I sail the sea?
    Or shall I drink this dowie drink
        That is prepar'd for me?"

13. "Ye winna leave the lands, daughter,
        Nor will ye sail the sea,
    But ye will drink this dowie drink
        This woman's prepar'd for thee.

14. "Your bed is made in a better place
        Than ever hers will be,
    And ere ye're cauld into the room
        Ye will be there wi me."

15. "Come in, come in now, Lady Isabel,
        And drink the wine wi me;
    I hae twa jewels in ae coffer,
        And ane o them I'll gie ye."

16. "Stay still, stay still, my mother dear,
        Stay still a little wee,
    Till I gang to yon garden green,
        My Maries a' to see."

17. To some she gae the broach, the broach,
        To some she gae a ring;
    But wae befa her step-mother,
        To her she gae nae thing.

18. "Come in, come in now, Lady Isabel,
        And drink the wine wi me;
    I hae twa jewels in ae coffer,
        And ane o them I'll gie ye."

19. Slowly to the bower she came,
        And slowly enterd in,
    And being full o courtesie,
        Says, "Begin, mother, begin."

20. She put it till her cheek, her cheek,
        Sae did she till her chin,

   Sae did she till her fu fause lips,
    But never a drap gaed in.

21. Lady Isabel put it till her cheek,
    Sae did she till her chin,
   Sae did she till her rosy lips,
    And the rank poison gaed in.

22. "O take this cup frae me, mother,
    O take this cup frae me;
   My bed is made in a better place
    Than ever yours will be.

23. "My bed is in the heavens high,
    Amang the angels fine;
   But yours is in the lowest hell,
    To drie torment and pine."

24. Nae moan was made for Lady Isabel
    In bower where she lay dead,
   But a' was for that ill woman,
    In the fields mad she gaed.

LADY DIAMOND (264)

Stories of fathers who kill their daughters' lovers, of husbands who kill their wives' lovers and taunt the survivor with the head, or heart, or body of the lover abound over Europe and Asia. Often the lover's heart is served up to the survivor as a dish at the table. The most famous of these stories is "Rosiglione," *Decameron,* iv, 9, probably the source of this ballad.

1. There was a king, and a very great king,
    And a king of meikle fame;
   He had not a child in the world but ane,
    Lady Daisy was her name.

2. He had a very bonnie kitchen-boy,
    And William was his name;
   He never lay out o Lady Daisy's bower,
    Till he brought her body to shame.

3. When een-birds sung, and een-bells rung,
    And a' men were boune to rest,
   The king went on to Lady Daisy's bower,
    Just like a wandering ghaist.

4. He has drawn the curtains round and round,
    And there he has sat him down;

"To whom is this, Lady Daisy," he says,
    "That now you gae so round?"

5.   "Is it to a laird? or is it to a lord?
        Or a baron of high degree?
    Or is it William, my bonnie kitchen-boy?
        Tell now the truth to me."

6.   "It's no to a laird, and it's no to a lord,
        Nor a baron of high degree;
    But it's to William, your bonnie kitchen-boy:
        What cause hae I to lee?"

7.   "O where is all my merry, merry men,
        That I pay meat and fee,
    That they will not take out this kitchen-boy,
        And kill him presentilie?"

8.   They hae taen out this bonnie kitchen-boy,
        And killd him on the plain;
    His hair was like the threads o gold,
        His een like crystal stane;
    His hair was like the threads o gold,
        His teeth like ivory bane.

9.   They hae taen out this bonnie boy's heart,
        Put it in a cup o gold;
    "Take that to Lady Daisy," he said,
        "For she's impudent and bold."
    And she washd it with the tears that ran from her eye
        Into the cup of gold.

10.   "Now fare ye weel, my father the king,
        You hae taen my earthly joy;
    Since he's died for me, I'll die for him,
        My bonnie kitchen-boy."

11.   "O where is all my merry, merry men,
        That I pay meat and wage,
    That they could not withold my cruel hand,
        When I was mad with rage?

12.   "I think nae wonder, Lady Daisy," he said,
        "That he brought your body to shame;
    For there never was man of woman born
        Sae fair as him that is slain."

THE HEIR OF LINNE (267)

This is a variant of the common spendthrift-knight motif in folk story, found widely in Europe and in Asia. Basically it is the story of a man who wastes his inheritance and then through advice left by his father or by the help of someone he is kind to (like The Grateful Dead) he gains it all back again. It was a popular broadside ballad subject, a typical example of which is "The Drunkard's Legacy." "The Sea Captain," an analogous ballad from North Carolina, *JAF,* 28:156, is included here for comparison.

Text, Buchan's MSS., i, 40.

1. "The bonny heir, and the well-faird heir,
      And the weary heir o Linne,
    Yonder he stands at his father's yetts,
      And naebody bids him come in.

2. "O see for he gangs, an see for he stands,
      The weary heir o Linne.
    O see for he stands on the cauld casey,
      And nae an bids him come in.

3. "But if he had been his father's heir,
      Or yet the heir o Linne,
    He wadna stand on the cauld casey,
      Some an woud taen him in."

4. "Sing ower again that sang, nourice,
      The sang ye sung just now."
    "I never sung a sang in my life
      But I woud sing ower to you.

5. "O see for he gangs, an see for he stands,
      The weary heir o Linne.
    O see for he stands on the cauld casey,
      An nae an bids him come in.

6. "But if he had been his father's heir,
      Or yet the heir o Linne,
    He woudna stand on the cauld casye,
      Some an woud taen him in.

7. "When his father's lands a selling were,
      His claise lay well in fauld,
    But now he wanders on the shore,
      Baith hungry, weet, and cauld."

8. As Willie he gaed down the town,
      The gentlemen were drinking;

Some bade gie Willie a glass, a glass,
 And some bade him gie nane,
Some bade gie Willie a glass, a glass,
 The weary heir o Linne.

9. As Willie he came up the town,
 The fishers were a' sitting;
Some bade gie Willie a fish, a fish,
 Some bade gie him a fin,
Some bade gie him a fish, a fish,
 And lat the palmer gang.

10. He turned him right and round about,
 As will as a woman's son,
And taen his cane into his hand,
 And on his way to Linne.

11. His nourice at her window lookd,
 Beholding dale and down,
And she beheld this distressed young man
 Come walking to the town.

12. "Come here, come here, Willie," she said,
 "And rest yoursel wi me;
I hae seen you in better days,
 And in jovial companie."

13. "Gie me a sheave o your bread, nourice,
 And a bottle o your wine,
And I'll pay you it a' ower again,
 When I'm the laird o Linne."

14. "Ye'se get a sheave o my bread, Willie,
 And a bottle o my wine,
But ye'll pay me when the seas gang dry,
 For ye'll neer by heir o Linne."

15. Then he turnd him right and round about,
 As will as woman's son,
And aff he set, and bent his way,
 And straightway came to Linne.

16. But when he came to that castle,
 They were set down to dine;
A score o nobles there he saw,
 Sat drinking at the wine.

17. Then some bade gie him beef, the beef,
 And some bade gie him the bane;
And some bade gie him naething at a',
 But lat the palmer gang.

18. Then out it speaks the new-come laird,
    A saucy word spake hee;
"Put round the cup, gie my rival a sup,
    Let him fare on his way."

19. Then out it speaks Sir Ned Magnew,
    Ane o young Willie's kin;
"This youth was ance a sprightly boy
    As ever lived in Linne."

20. He turned him right and round about,
    As will as woman's son,
Then minded him on a little wee key,
    That his mother left to him.

21. His mother left him this little wee key
    A little before she died;
And bade him keep this little wee key
    Till he was in maist need.

22. Then forth he went, these nobles left,
    All drinkin' in the room,
Wi walking rod intill his hand,
    He walked the castell roun.

23. There he found out a little door,
    For there the key slipped in,
And there he got as muckle red gowd
    As freed the lands o Linne.

24. Back through the nobles then he went,
    A saucy man was then:
"I'll take the cup frae this new-come laird,
    For he neer bade me sit down."

25. Then out it speaks the new-come laird,
    He spake wi mock an jeer;
"I'd gie a seat to the laird o Linne,
    Sae be that he were here.

26. "When the lands o Linne a selling were,
    A' men said they were free;
This lad shall hae them frae me this day,
    If he'll gie the third pennie."

27. "I take ye witness, nobles a',
    Guide witnesses ye'll be;
I'm promisd the lands o Linne this day,
    If I gie the third pennie."

28. "Ye've taen us witness, Willie," they said,
    "Guide witnesses we'll be.

But the lands o Linne who likes,
    They'll neer be bought by thee."

29. He's done him to a gaming-table,
    For it stood fair and clean;
There he tauld down as much rich gowd
    As freed the lands o Linne.

30. Thus having done, he turnd about,
    A saucy man was he.
"Take up your monie, my lad," he says,
    "Take up your third pennie.

31. "Aft hae I gane wi barefeet cauld,
    Likewise wi legs full bare,
And mony days walkd at these yetts
    Wi muckle dool and care.

32. "But now my sorrow's past and gane,
    And joy's returned to me,
And here I've gowd enough forbye,
    Ahin this third pennie."

33. As Willie he gaed down the town,
    There he crawd wonderous crouse;
He calld the may afore them a',
    The norice o the house,

34. "Come here, come here, my nurse," he says,
    "I'll pay your bread and wine;
Seas ebb and flow as they wont to do,
    Yet I'm the laird o Linne."

35. As he gaed up the Gallowgate port,
    His hose abeen his sheen;
But lang ere he came down again
    Was convoyed by lords fifeteen.

THE SEA-CAPTAIN

1. There was a sea captain lately come to shore,
His ragged apparel like one that was poor.

2. "What news, what news, dear Johnny, what news have you
    brought to me?"
"It's bad news, madam, I have brought to thee.

3. "Our ship had a broken voyage and all was lost," said he:
"And all the rest of our merry men got drownded at sea.

4. "Call down your daughter Polly, and set her down by me;
We'll drink and drown all sorrow, and married we will be."

5. "My daughter Polly's busy and cannot come to thee,
And neither can I trust you for one bowl or three."

6. Then poor Johnny smiled and hung down his head.
"Go light the candle and show me the bed."

7. "My green beds are all full and have been this week,
And therefore poor Johnny his lodging may seek."

8. "Pray, tell me what I owe you, and that I will pay;
Pray, tell me what I owe you, and without delay."

9. "Here's fifty of the new score and something of the old."
Then poor Johnny pulled out both hands full of gold.

10. When the old hag saw the money, then she began to rue;
Said, "Come back, dear Johnny, I have not done with you.

11. "If you were in earnest, I was only in a jest;
Upon my reputation I love you the best.

12. "For my green beds are all empty and have been for a week,
For you and my daughter Polly to take a pleasant sleep."

13. "No, I won't lie in your green beds, I'd rather lie in the street;
For when I had no money, out of doors I was kicked.

14. "Now I've got money plenty, I'll make the tavern roar;
With ale and beer and brandy I'll drink about galore."

THE EARL OF MAR'S DAUGHTER (270)

The bird lover is general in the folklore of all peoples; ballads using this theme are found in Danish, Swedish, in the Faroes, all derived, it would seem, from semiliterary versions, such as Marie de France's *Lai d' Yonec.*

Text, Buchan, i, 49.

1. It was intill a pleasant time,
     Upon a simmer's day,
   The noble Earl of Mar's daughter
     Went forth to sport and play.

2. As thus she did amuse hersell,
     Below a green aik tree,
   There she saw a sprightly doo
     Set on a tower sae hie.

3. "O Cow-me-doo, my love sae true,
     If ye'll come down to me,
   Ye'se hae a cage o guid red gowd
     Instead o simple tree.

4. "I'll put gowd hingers round your cage,
  And siller round your wa;
I'll gar ye shine as fair a bird
  As ony o them a'."

5. But she hadnae these words well spoke,
  Nor yet these words well said,
Till Cow-me-doo flew frae the tower
  And lighted on her head.

6. Then she has brought this pretty bird
  Hame to her bowers and ha,
And made him shine as fair a bird
  As ony o them a'.

7. When day was gane, and night was come,
  About the evening tide,
This lady spied a sprightly youth
  Stand straight up by her side.

8. "From whence came ye, young man?" she said;
  "That does surprise me sair;
My door was bolted right secure,
  What way hae ye come here?"

9. "O hold your tongue, ye lady fair,
  Lat a' your folly be;
Mind ye not on your turtle-doo
  Last day ye brought wi thee?"

10. "O tell me mair, young man," she said,
  "This does surprise me now;
What country hae ye come frae?
  What pedigree are you?"

11. "My mither lives on foreign isles,
  She has nae mair but me;
She is a queen o wealth and state,
  And birth and high degree.

12. "Likewise well skilld in magic spells,
  As ye may plainly see,
And she transformd me to yon shape,
  To charm such maids as thee.

13. "I am a doo the live-lang day,
  A sprightly youth at night;
This aye gars me appear mair fair
  In a fair maiden's sight.

14. "And it was but this verra day
  That I came ower the sea;

Your lovely face did me enchant;
I'll live and dee wi thee."

15. "O Cow-me-doo, my live sae true,
Nae mair frae me ye'se gae."
"That's never my intent, my luve,
As ye said, it shall be sae."

16. "O Cow-me-doo, my luve sae true,
It's time to gae to bed."
"Wi a' my heart, my dear marrow,
It's be as ye hae said."

17. Then he has staid in bower wi her
For sax lang years and ane,
Till sax young sons to him she bare,
And the seventh she's brought hame.

18. But aye as ever a child was born
He carried them away,
And brought them to his mither's care,
As fast as he coud fly.

19. Thus he has staid in bower wi her
For twenty years and three;
There came a lord o high renown
To court this fair ladie.

20. But still his proffer she refused,
And a' his presents too;
Says, "I'm content to live alane
Wi my bird, Cow-me-doo."

21. Her father sware a solemn oath
Amang the nobles all,
"The morn, or ere I eat or drink,
This bird I will gar kill."

22. The bird was sitting in his cage,
And heard what they did say;
And when he found they were dismist,
Says, "Wae's me for this day!

23. "Before that I do langer stay,
And thus to be forlorn,
I'll gang unto my mither's bower,
Where I was bred and born."

24. Then Cow-me-doo took flight and flew
Beyond the raging sea,
And lighted near his mither's castle,
On a tower o gowd sae hie.

25.   As his mither was wauking out,
      To see what she coud see,
And ther she saw her little son,
      Set on the tower sae hie.

26.   "Get dancers here to dance," she said,
      "And minstrells for to play;
For here's my young son, Florentine,
      Come here wi me to stay."

27.   "Get nae dancers to dance, mither,
      Nor minstrells for to play,
For the mither o my seven sons,
      The morn's her wedding-day."

28.   "O tell me, tell me, Florentine,
      Tell me, and tell me true,
Tell me this day without a flaw,
      What I will do for you."

29.   "Instead of dancers to dance, mither,
      Or minstrells for to play,
Turn four-and-twenty wall-wight men
      Like storks in feathers gray;

30.   "My seven sons in seven swans,
      Aboon their heads to flee;
And I mysell a gay gos-hawk,
      A bird o high degree."

31.   Then sichin said the queen hersell,
      "That thing's too high for me."
But she applied to an auld woman,
      Who had mair skill than she.

32.   Instead o dancers to dance a dance,
      Or minstrells for to play,
Four-and-twenty wall-wight men
      Turnd birds o feathers gray;

33.   Her seven sons in seven swans,
      Aboon their heads to flee;
And he himsell a gay gos-hawk,
      A bird of high degree.

34.   This flock o birds took flight and flew
      Beyond the raging sea,
And landed near the Earl Mar's castle,
      Took shelter in every tree.

35.   They were a flock o pretty birds,
      Right comely to be seen:

    The people viewd them wi surprise,
       As they dancd on the green.

36. These birds ascended frae the tree
       And lighted on the ha,
  And at the last wi force did flee
       Amang the nobles a'.

37. The storks there seized some o the men,
       They coud neither fight nor flee;
  The swans they bound the bride's best man
       Below a green aik tree.

38. They lighted next on maidens fair,
       Then on the bride's own head,
  And wi the twinkling o an ee
       The bride and them were fled.

39. There's ancient men at weddings been
       For sixty years or more,
  But sic a curious wedding-day
       They never saw before.

40. For naething coud the companie do,
       Nor naething coud they say
  But they saw a flock o pretty birds
       That took their bride away.

41. When that Earl Mar he came to know
       Where his dochter did stay,
  He signd a bond o unity,
       And visits now they pay.

THE SUFFOLK MIRACLE (272)

This is the only version in English of one of the most dramatic stories of Europe. The English ballad is a late broadside and not a very good one. It is interesting to study the American versions against the background of the English, for they are better motivated and generally superior. Burger's "Lenore" is the most important literary telling of this story. This story is widespread among the Slavs, though it seems to have originated in Greece. The basic idea of the story, so perverted in the English, tells of two lovers separated by the death of the man, her grief, his restlessness in the grave, his coming back to carry her (usually on a wild ride through the night) to his grave, her escape, though not without leaving a bit of her dress, handkerchief, etc., with him, her death when the token is discovered in his grave.

Text A, 17th-century broadside, Rawliston Wood, Bodleian, E 25,

fol. 83; B, traditional in Ireland via Vermont, printed in *Bulletin,*
5:7.

A.

1. A wonder stranger ne'r was known
   Then what I now shall treat upon.
   In Suffolk there did lately dwell
   A farmer rich and known full well.

2. He had a daughter fair and bright,
   On whom he plac'd his chief delight;
   Her beauty was beyond compare,
   She was both virtuous and fair.

3. A young man there was living by,
   Who was so charmëd with her eye
   That he could never be at rest,
   He was with love so much possest.

4. He made address to her, and she
   Did grant him love immediately;
   Which when her father came to hear,
   He parted her and her poor dear.

5. Forty miles distant was she sent,
   Unto his brother's, with intent
   That she should there so long remain
   Till she had chang'd her mind again.

6. Hereat this young man sadly grievd,
   But knew not how to be relievd;
   He sighd and sobd continually
   That his true love he could not see.

7. She by no means could to him send
   Who was her heart's espousëd friend;
   He sighd, she grievd, but all in vain,
   For she confin'd must still remain.

8. He mournd so much that doctor's art
   Could give no ease unto his heart;
   Who was so strangely terrified,
   That in short time for love he dyed.

9. She that from him was sent away
   Knew nothing of his dying-day,
   But constant still she did remain;
   To love the dead was then in vain.

10. After he had in grave been laid
    A month or more, unto this maid

He comes about the middle of the night,
Who joyd to see her heart's delight.

11. Her father's horse, which well she knew,
Her mother's hood and safeguard too,
He brought with him to testifie
Her parent's order he came by.

12. Which when her unckle understood,
He hop't it would be for her good,
And gave consent to her straightway
That with him she should come away.

13. When she was got her love behind,
They passd as swift as any wind,
That in two hours, or little more,
He brought her to her father's door.

14. But as they did this great haste make,
He did complain his head did ake;
Her handkerchief she then took out,
And tyed the same his head about.

15. And unto him she thus did say:
"Thou art as cold as any clay;
When we come home, a fire wee'l have."
But little dreamt he went to grave.

16. Soon were thy at her father's door,
And after she ne'r see him more,
"I'le set the horses up," then he said,
And there he left this harmless maid.

17. She knockt, and strait a man he cryed,
"Who's there?" "'T is I," she then replyed;
Who wondred much her voice to hear,
And was possest with dread and fear.

18. Her father he did tell, and then
He stared like an affrighted man.
Down stairs he ran, and when he see her,
Cry'd out, "My child, how cam'st thou here?"

19. "Pray, sir, did you not send for me,
By such a messenger?" said she:
Which made his hair stare on his head,
As knowing well that he was dead.

20. "Where is he?" then to her he said;
"He's in the stable," quoth the maid.

"Go in," said he, "and go to bed;
I'le see the horse well littered."

21.   He stared about, and there could hee
No shape of any mankind see,
But found his horse all on a sweat;
Which made him in a deadly fret.

22.   His daughter he said nothing to,
Nor no one else, though well they knew
That he was dead a month before,
For fear of grieveing her full sore.

23.   Her father to his father went
Who was deceasd, with this intent,
To tell him what his daughter said;
So both came back unto this maid.

24.   They askd her, and she still did say
'T was he that then brought her away;
Which when they heard they were amaz'd,
And on each other strangely gaz'd.

25.   A handkerchief she said she tyed
About his head, and that they tryed;
The sexton they did speak unto,
That he the grave would then undo.

26.   Affrighted then they did behold
His body turning into mould,
And though he had a month been dead,
This kerchief was about his head.

27.   This thing unto her then they told,
And the whole truth they did unfold;
She was thereat so terrified
And grievd, she quickly dyed.

28.   Part not true love, you rich men, then;
But, if they be right honest men
Your daughters' love, give them their way,
For force oft breeds their lives' decay.

B.

1.   There was a squire lived in this town,
He was a squire of high renown;
He had one daughter, a beauty bright,
And the name he called her was his "Heart's Delight."

2.   When her father came this to know,
He sent his daughter far away,

Sends her over fifty miles or more
To detain her of her wedding day.

3. One night as she was for her bed bound,
   As she was taking out her gown,
   She heard the knock and the deadly sound,
   "Loosen those bonds, love, that we have bound."

4. "I have your horse and your mother's cloak,
   And your father's orders to take you home."
   She dressed herself in rich attire,
   And rid away with her Heart's Desire.

5. As she got on, with him behind,
   They rode far faster than any wind,
   And every mile he would sigh and say
   "O my jewel, my head it aches."

6. A Holland handkerchief she then took out
   And tied his head with it around;
   She kissed his lips and she then did say,
   "O my love, you're colder than any clay."

7. When they came to her father's gate,
   "Come down, my jewel," this young man said,
   "Come down, my darling, and go to bed,
   And I'll see your horse in his stable led."

8. When she came to her father's hall,
   "Who's there, who's there?" her father called.
   "It is I, dear father; did you send for me
   By such a messenger?" naming he.

9. Her father, knowing this young man being dead,
   He tore his grey hair down from his head,
   He wrung his hands and he wept full sore,
   And this young man's darling cried more and more.

10. The next day to the grave they went,
    And although this young man had been nine months dead,
    He still wore the Holland handkerchief
    Around his head.

KING EDWARD THE FOURTH AND A TANNER OF TAMWORTH (273)

This story of a king or noble person, unrecognized, coming to a chance encounter with one of his subjects and the humor that grows out of the situation is a common one in Europe. Such stories are told of

Charlemagne, Alfred, Edward III, Henry II, etc. "Rauf Coilyear"
is an excellent example of a prose account of such a story. This ballad
is late 15th or early 16th century.

Text, Pepys, ii, 129.

1. In summer time, when leaves grew green,
        and birds were singing on every tree,
    King Edward would a hunting ride,
        some pastime for to see.

2. Our king he would a hunting ride,
        by eight o'clock of the day,
    And well was he ware of a bold tanner,
        cam riding on the way.

3. A good russet coat the tanner had on,
        fast buttoned under his chin,
    And under him a good cow-hide,
        and a mare of four shilling.

4. "Now stand you here, my good lords all,
        under this trusty tree,
    And I will wend to yonder fellow,
        to know from whence came he.

5. "God speed, God speed," then said our king;
        "Thou art welcome, good fellow," quoth he;
    "Which is the way to Drayton Basset
        I pray thee shew to me."

6. "The ready way to Drayton Basset,
        from this place as thou dost stand,
    The next pair of gallows thou comst to
        thou must turn up on thy right hand."

7. "That is not the way," then said our king,
        "the ready way I pray thee shew me."
    "Whether thou be thief or true man," quoth the tanner,
        "I'm weary of thy company.

8. "Away, with a vengeance," quoth the tanner,
        "I hold thee out of thy wit,
    For all this day have I ridden and gone,
        and I am fasting yet."

9. "Go with me to Drayton Basset," said our king,
        "no daintyes we will lack;
    We'l have meat and drink of the best,
        and I will pay the shot."

10. "Godamercy for nothing," said the tanner,
        "thou shalt pay for no dinner of mine;

I have more groats and nobles in my purse
    then thou hast pence in thine."

11. "God save your goods," then said the king,
    "and send them well to thee."
"Be thou thief or true man," quoth the tanner,
    "I am weary of thy company.

12. "Away, with a vengeance," quoth the tanner,
    "of thee I stand in fear;
The apparrell thou wearst on thy back
    may seem a good lord to wear."

13. "I never stole them," said our king,
    "I swear to thee by the rood."
"Thou art some ruffian of the country,
    thou rid'st in the midst of thy good."

14. "What news dost thou hear?" then said our king,
    "I pray what news do you hear?"
"I hear no news," answered the tanner,
    "but that cow-hides be dear."

15. "Cow-hides? cow-hides?" then said our king,
    "I marvell what they be."
"Why, art thou a fool," quoth the tanner,
    "look, I have one under me."

16. "Yet one thing now I would thee pray,
    so that thou wouldst not be strange;
If thy mare be better then my steed,
    I pray thee let us change."

17. "But if you needs with me will change,
    as change full well may ye,
By the faith of my body," quoth the tanner,
    "I look to have boot of thee."

18. "What boot wilt thou ask?" then said our king,
    "what boot dost thou ask on this ground?"
"No pence nor half-pence," said the tanner,
    "but a noble in gold so round."

19. "Here's twenty good groats," then said the king,
    "so well paid see you beg."
"I love thee better then I did before,
    I thought thou hadst nere a peny.

20. "But if so be we needs must change,
    as change thou must abide,

Though thou hast gotten Brock my mare,
    thou shalt not have my cow-hide."

21.   The tanner took the good cow-hide,
     that of the cow was hilt,
    And threw it upon the king's saddle,
     that was so fairly guilt.

22.   "Now help me, help me," quoth the tanner,
     "full quickly that I were gone,
    For when I come home to Gillian my wife
     she'l say I'm a gentleman."

23.   The king took the tanner by the leg,
     he girded a fart so round.
    "You'r very homely," said the king,
     "were I aware, I'd laid you o th' ground."

24.   But when the tanner was in the king's saddle
     astonëd then he was;
    He knew not that the stirrops that he did wear,
     whether they were gold or brass.

25.   But when the steed saw the black cow-tale wag,
     for and the black cow-horn,
    The steed began to run away,
     as the divel the tanner had born.

26.   Untill he came unto a nook,
     a little beside an ash;
    The steed gave the tanner such a fall
     his neck was almost brast.

27.   "Take thy horse again, with a vengeance," he said,
     "with me he shall not abide."
    "It is no marvell," said the king, and laught,
     "he knew not your cow-hide.

28.   "But if that we needs now must change,
     as change that well we mought,
    I'le swear to you plain, if you have your mare,
     I look to have some boot."

29.   "What boot will you ask?" quoth the tanner,
     "What boot will you ask on this ground?"
    "No pence nor half-pence," said our king,
     "but a noble in gold so round."

30.   "Here's twenty good groats," said the tanner,
     "and twenty more I have of thine;
    I have ten groats more in my purse,
     we'l drink five of them at the wine."

31. The king set a bugle-horn to his mouth,
   that blew both loud and shrill,
And five hundred lords and knights
   came riding over a hill.

32. "Away, with a vengeance," quoth the tanner,
   "with thee I'le no longer abide;
Thou art a strong thief, yonder be thy fellows,
   they will steal away my cow-hide."

33. "No, I protest," then said our king,
   "for so it may not be;
They be the lords of Drayton Basset,
   come out of the North Country."

34. But when they came before the king
   full low they fell on their knee;
The tanner had rather than a thousand pound
   he had been out of his company.

35. "A coller! a coller!" then said the king,
   "coller!" then did he cry;
Then would he have given a thousand pound
   he had not been so nigh.

36. "A coller? a coller?" then quoth the tanner,
   "it is a thing which will breed sorrow;
For after a coller commeth a halter,
   and I shall be hanged tomorrow."

37. "No, do not fear," the king did say;
   "for pastime thou hast shown me,
No coller nor halter thou shalt have,
   but I will give thee a fee.

38. "For Plompton Park I will give thee,
   with tenements three beside,
Which is worth three hundred pound a year,
   to maintain thy good cow-hide."

39. "Godamercy, Godamercy," quoth the tanner;
   "for this good deed thou hast done,
If ever thou comest to merry Tamworth,
   thou shalt have clouting-leather for thy shone."

OUR GOODMAN (274)

This ballad, one of the most popular of the humorous ballads, has in modern times become completely ribald. It is known throughout Europe. Several broadside versions turn the tables on the unfaithful wife, telling of the husband striking her: "Here are the blows your mammie sent to ye."

Text, Herd's MSS., ii, 140.

1.   Hame came our goodman,
      And hame came he,
  And then he saw a saddle-horse,
      Where nae horse should be.

2.   "What's this now, goodwife?
      What's this I see?
  How came this horse here,
      Without the leave o me?"

    Spoken: "A horse?" quo she.
      "Ay, a horse," quo he.

3.   "Shame fa your cuckold face,
      I'll mat ye see!
  'T is naething but a broad sow,
      My minnie sent to me."

    "A broad sow?" quo he.
    "Ay sow," quo she.

4.   "Far hae I ridden,
      And farer hae I gane,
  But a sadle on a sow's back
      I never saw nene."

5.   Hame came our goodman,
      And hame came he;
  He spy'd a pair of jack-boots,
      Where nae boots should be.

6.   "What's this now, goodwife?
      What's this I see?
  How came these boots here,
      Without the leave o me?"

    "Boots?" quo she.
    "Ay, boots," quo he.

7.   "Shame fa your cuckold face,
      And i'll mat ye see!
  It's but a pair of water-stoups,
      My minnie sent to me."

"Water-stoups?" quo he.
"Ay, water-stoups," quo she.

8. "Far hae I ridden,
    And farer hae I gane,
But siller spurs on water-stoups
    I saw never nane."

9. Hame came our goodman,
    And hame came he,
And he saw a sword,
    Whare a sword should na be.

10. "What's this now, goodwife?
    What's this I see?
How came this sword here,
    Without the leave o me?"

    "A sword?" quo she.
    "Ay, a sword," quo he.

11. "Shame fa your cuckold face,
    I'll mat ye see!
It's but a porridge-spurtle,
    My minnie sent to me."

    "A spurtle?" quo he.
    "Ay, a spurtle," quo she.

12. "Far hae I ridden,
    And farer hae I gane,
But siller-handed spurtles
    I saw never nane."

13. Hame came our goodman,
    And hame came he;
Ther he spy'd a powderd wig,
    Where nae wig shoud be.

14. "What's this now, goodwife?
    What's this I see?
How came this wig here,
    Without the leave o me?"

    "A wig?" quo she.
    "Ay, a wig," quo he.

15. "Shame fa your cuckold face,
    And i'll mat you see!

'T is naething but a clocken-hen,
  My minnie sent to me."

"Clocken-hen?" quo he.
"Ay, clocken-hen," quo she.

16. "Far hae I ridden,
        And farer hae I gane,
      But powder on a clocken-hen
        I saw never nane."

17. Hame came our goodman,
        And hame came he,
      And there he saw a muckle coat,
        Where nae coat shoud be.

18. "What's this now, goodwife?
        What's this I see?
      How came this coat here,
        Without the leave o me?"

"A coat?" quo she.
"Ay, a coat," quo he.

19. "Shame fa your cuckold face,
        I'll mat he see!
      It's but a pair o blankets,
        My minnie sent to me."

"Blankets?" quo he.
"Ay, blankets," quo she.

20. "Far hae I ridden,
        And farer hae I gane,
      But buttons on blankets
        I never saw nane."

21. Ben went our goodman,
        And ben went he,
      And there he spy'd a sturdy man,
        Where nae man shoud be.

22. "What's this now, goodwife?
        What's this I see?
      How came this man here,
        Without the leave o me?"

"A man?" quo she.
"Ay, a man," quo he.

23. "Poor blind body,
    And blinder mat ye be!
It's a new milking-maid,
    My mither sent to me."

"A maid?" quo he.
"Ay, a maid," quo she.

24. "Far hae I ridden,
    And farer hae I gane,
But lang-bearded maidens
    I never saw nane."

GET UP AND BAR THE DOOR (275)

Many variations of this story exist in the literature of Europe and Asia. The ballad is doubtless based on some prose version like that told in Straparola's *Tales*, First story, Eighth day. In an Arabian tale the characters are a bridegroom and his bride. The usual situation applies, and the usual compact is made. Neither speaks, though thieves steal every thing in the place, and even strip the clothes from the two without a protest. The next day the police discover them. When they can get no word out of the pair they are about to decapitate them, beginning with the bridegroom. Only then does the wife cry out: "Spare him." The bridegroom joyfully shouts: "You have lost; now close the door."

Text, Pinkerton, *Select Scottish Ballads*, ii, 150.

1. It fell about the Martinmas time,
    And a gay time it was then,
When our goodwife got puddings to make,
    And she's boild them in the pan.

2. The wind sae cauld blew south and north,
    And blew into the floor;
Quoth our goodman to our goodwife,
    "Gae out and bar the door."

3. "My hand is in my hussyfskap,
    Goodman, as ye may see;
An it shoud nae be barrd this hundred year,
    It's no be barrd for me."

4. They made a paction tween them twa,
    They made it firm and sure,
That the first word whaeer shoud speak,
    Shoud rise and bar the door.

5.   Then by there came two gentlemen,
      At twelve o clock at night,
    And they could neither see house nor hall,
      Nor coal nor candle-light.

6.   "Now whether is this a rich man's house,
      Or whether it is a poor?"
    But neer a word ane o them speak,
      For barring of the door.

7.   And first they ate the white puddings,
      And then they ate the black;
    Tho muckle thought the goodwife to hersel,
      Yet neer a word she spake.

8.   Then said the one unto the other,
      "Here, man, tak ye my knife;
    Do ye tak aff the auld man's beard,
      And I'll kiss the goodwife."

9.   "But there's nae water in the house,
      And what shall we do than?"
    "What ails ye at the pudding-broo,
      That boils into the pan?"

10.   O up then started our goodman,
      An angry man was he:
    "Will ye kiss my wife before my een,
      And scad me wi pudding-bree?"

11.   Then up and started our goodwife,
      Gied three skips on the floor:
    "Goodman, you've spoken the foremost word,
      Get up and bar the door."

THE WIFE WRAPT IN WETHER'S SKIN (277)

This ballad sung to a rollicking tune has long been a favorite in England and America. Like the preceding it is an example of a ballad being made from a popular prose tale. The prototype here is probably *A merry jeste of a shrewde and curste wyfe lapped in Morrelles skin for her good behauyour.* (See W. C. Hazlitt, *Early Popular Poetry,* iv, 179.)

Text A, Jamieson, i, 319; B, Alexander Whitelaw, *A Book of Scottish Songs* (1844), p. 333; C, traditional in Indiana, *JAF,* 48:309.

A.

1. She wadna bake, she wadna brew,
      Hollin, green hollin
   For spoiling o her comely hue.
      Bend your bow, Robin

2. She wadna wash, she wadna wring,
   For spoiling o her gay goud ring.

3. Robin he's gane to the fald
   And catched a weather by the spauld.

4. And he has killed his weather black
   And laid the skin upon her back.

5. "I darena pay you, for your kin,
   But I can pay my weather's skin.

6. "I darena pay my lady's back,
   But I can pay my weather black."

7. "O Robin, Robin, lat me be,
   And I'll a good wife be to thee.

8. "It's I will wash, and I will wring,
   And never mind my gay goud ring.

9. "It's I will bake, and I will brew,
   And never mind my comely hue.

10. "And gin ye thinkna that eneugh,
    I'se tak the goad and I'se ca the pleugh.

11. "Gin ye ca for mair whan that is doon,
    I'll sit i the neuk and I'll dight your shoon."

B.

1. There was a wee cooper who lived in Fife,
      Nickity, nackity, noo, noo, noo
   And he has gotten a gentle wife,
      Hey Willie Wallacky, how John Dougall,
      Alane, quo Rushety, roue, roue, roue

2. She wadna bake, nor she wadna brew,
   For the spoiling o her comely hue.

3. She wadna card, nor she wadna spin,
   For the shaming o her gentle kin.

4. She wadna wash, nor she wadna wring,
   For the spoiling o her gouden ring.

5.   The cooper's awa to his woo-pack
     And has laid a sheep-skin on his wife's back.

6.   "It's I'll no thrash ye, for your proud kin,
     But I will thrash my ain sheep-skin."

7.   "Oh, I will bake, and I will brew,
     And never mair think on my comely hue.

8.   "Oh, I will card, and I will spin,
     And never mair think on my gentle kin.

9.   "Oh, I will wash, and I will wring,
     And never mair think on my gouden ring."

10. A' ye wha hae gotten a gentle wife
     Send ye for the wee cooper of Fife.

C.

There was an old man who lived in the West,
　　Dan — doodle — dan,
He had an old woman who was none of the best,
　　Dan — doodle — dan.
Her old man came in from the plow, saying, "Old woman, is dinner
　　ready now?"
Sing lorum clorum clan a clish a ma clingo.

"There's a piece of cold meat upon the shelf,"
　　Dan — doodle — dan,
"If you want any better, you can cook it yourself,"
　　Dan — doodle — dan.
"There's a piece of cold meat upon the shelf; if you want any more,
　　you can cook it yourself."
Sing lorum clorum clan a clish a ma clingo.

This old man jumped into the sheepfold,
　　Dan — doodle — dan,
And gathered a wether right by the wool,
　　Dan — doodle — dan.
He stretched it over his old woman's back, and made the hickory go
　　"Whickety-whack."
Sing lorum clorum clan a clish a ma clingo.

THE FARMER'S CURST WIFE (278)

This ballad has had wide popularity in America, where it has developed some half dozen variations on the basic story. The original story
probably had to do with a compact between the farmer and the devil

under the terms of which the devil was to help him plow his fields in return for the soul of a member of the family. The farmer is relieved when the wife and not the son is chosen.

Text A, Dixon, p. 210; B, traditional in Maine, Barry, p. 330.

A.

1. There was an old farmer in Sussex did dwell,
        Whistle refrain
   There was an old farmer in Sussex did dwell,
   And he had a bad wife, as many knew well.
        Whistle refrain

2. Then Satan came to the old man at the plough:
   "One of your family I must have now.

3. "It is not your eldest son that I crave,
   But it is your old wife, and she I will have."

4. "O welcome, good Satan, with all my heart,
   I hope you and she will never more part."

5. Now Satan has got the old wife on his back,
   And he lugged her along, like a pedlar's pack.

6. He trudged away till they came to his hall-gate;
   Says he, "Here, take in an old Sussex chap's mate."

7. O then she did kick the young imps about;
   Says one to the other, "Lets try turn her out."

8. She spied thirteen imps all dancing in chains,
   She up with her pattens and beat out their brains.

9. She knocked the old Satan against the wall:
   "Let's turn her out, or she'll murder us all."

10. Now he's bundled her up on his back amain,
    And to her old husband he took her again.

11. "I have been a tormentor the whole of my life,
    But I ne'er was tormented so as with your wife."

B.

1. There was an old man who owned a small farm,
        Scrath-a-fillee, fillee, filiddle, filum,
   And he had no oxen to carry it on,
        Scrath-a-fillee, fillee, filiddle, filum.

2. He yokes his hogs right onto the plow,
   And down comes the Devil, saying, "How are you now?"

3. "Devil, O Devil, are you after my life?"
    "O, no, I'm after your darned ugly wife."

4. "Take her, O take her, with all of my heart,
    And I hope to the Lord you never will part."

5. The Devil he slung her across his back
    And to Hell he went flipperty crack.

6. She saw the Devil preparing his chains,
    And she up with her foot and kicked out his brains.

7. A little wee devil looked over the wall
    And said, "Take her away, or she'll murder us all."

8. The Devil he slung her across his back,
    And, like an old fool, went carrying her back.

9. He carried her right to the man with the plow,
    And said, "You dumb beast, I won't have you now."

10. "My dear old wife, you have done well,
    For you've killed all the devils and rent over Hell."
        Scrath-a-fillee, fillee, filiddle, filum.

THE CRAFTY FARMER (283)

Stories and ballads in which a highwayman is outwitted were very
popular. The reversal of the situation plot is always dramatic. Compare "The Yorkshire Bite," a secondary ballad thrown off by this.
    Text, Maidment, *Scottish Ballads and Songs*, p. 208.

1. The song that I'm going to sing,
        I hope it will give you content,
    Concerning a silly old man,
        That was going to pay his rent.

2. As he was riding along,
        Along all on the highway,
    A gentleman-thief overtook him,
        And thus to him did say.

3. "Well overtaken!" said the thief,
        "Well overtaken!" said he;
    And "Well overtaken!" said the old man,
        "If thou be good company."

4. "How far are you going this way?"
        Which made the old man for to smile;
    "By my faith," said the old man,
        "I'm just going two mile.

5. "I'm a poor farmer," he said,
    "And I farm a piece of ground,
And my half-year's rent, kind sir,
    Just comes to forty pound.

6. "And my landlord has not been at home,
    I've not seen him this twelvemonth or more,
Which makes my rent be large;
    I've to pay him just fourscore."

7. "Thou shouldst not have told any body,
    For thieves there's ganging many;
If any should light on thee,
    They'll rob thee of thy money."

8. "O never mind," said the old man,
    "Thieves I fear on no side,
For the money is safe in my bags,
    On the saddle on which I ride."

9. As they were riding along,
    The old man was thinking no ill,
The thief he pulled out a pistol
    And bid the old man stand still.

10. But the old man provd crafty,
    As in the world there are many;
He threw his saddle oer the hedge,
    Saying, Fetch it, if thou'lt have any."

11. The thief got off his horse,
    With courage stout and bold,
To search for the old man's bag,
    And gave him horse to hold.

12. The old man put's foot i the stirrup
    And he got on astride;
To its side he clapt his spur up,
    You need not bid the old man ride.

13. "O stay!" said the thief, "O stay!
    And half the share thou shalt have."
"Nay, by my faith," said the old man,
    "For once I have bitten a knave."

14. The thief he was not content,
    But he thought there must be bags;
He out with his rusty old sword
    And chopt the old saddle in rags.

15. When he came to the landlord's house,
    This old man he was almost spent;

　　　　Saying, "Come, show me a private room
　　　　　And I'll pay you a whole year's rent.

16.　"I've met a fond fool by the way,
　　　　I swapt horses and gave him no boot;
　　　But never mind," said the old man,
　　　　"For I got the fond fool by the foot."

17.　He opend this rogue's portmantle,
　　　　It was glorious to behold;
　　　There were three hundred pounds in silver,
　　　　And three hundred pounds in gold.

18.　And as he was riding home,
　　　　And down a narrow lane,
　　　He espied his mare tied to a hedge,
　　　　Saying, "Prithee, Tib, wilt thou gang hame?"

19.　When he got home to his wife
　　　　And told her what he had done,
　　　Up she rose and put on her clothes,
　　　　And about the house did run.

20.　She sung, and she sung, and she sung,
　　　　She sung with a merry devotion,
　　　Saying, "If ever our daughter gets wed,
　　　　It will help to enlarge her portion."

THE YORKSHIRE BITE
(Cf. Child, 283.)

Text, traditional in America, *JAF*, 45:30.

1.　"Come down, come down," said the farmer to his son,
　　"To make you some money" (and his name was John.)
　　"Here's a cow you can take her to the fair.
　　She's in good order and it's her I can spare."
　　Like tothers — tothers —
　　Come — a — ran — tan — e — o.

2.　He took that cow and he started to the fair;
　　Hadn't been gone long till he met with a man;
　　Hadn't been gone long till he met with a man;
　　He sold that cow for six pounds of tan.
　　etc.

3.　He went down to the bar-room to get him a drink;
　　The money was paid right down in chink;
　　There was a lady all dressed so fine;

She sewed that money in his coat line.
etc.

4. The boy got out and he started for his home;
The robbers they mounted and they come following on.
"If you are going down the road for a few miles,
Hop on behind and we'll both take a ride."
etc.

5. Hadn't been gone more than a mile that way
Till robbers said, "I'll tell you in plain;
It's your money I want without any strife;
If I don't get it, I'll end your sweet life."
etc.

6. The boy ran his hands in his pockets and pulled his money out.
In a high patch of weeds he strew it all about
And the robber jumped off to pick up the loss
And the boy jumped in the saddle and rode off with the horse.
etc.

7. "Come back, come back," the robber he roared;
"Come back, come back," the robber he roared;
"Come back, come back," the robber he roared;
"I'll give you your own and ten thousand more."
etc.

8. The boy rode on to the old man's door;
The old man came out with a stamp on the floor;
Said, "Son, oh, son, ain't it a curse,
That our old cow's turned off to a horse?"
etc.

9. The boy run his hand in his pocket and begun to unfold;
He had ten thousand in silver and gold;
The old man begin to puff and he begin to swell.
"Daddy, don't you think I sold your cow well?"
etc.

THE GEORGE ALOE AND THE SWEEPSTAKE (285)

This ballad from the end of the 16th or the beginning of the 17th century was probably based on an actual occurrence. Compare the American "High Barbary," p. 777.

Text, Percy Papers.

1. The George Aloe and the Sweepstakes too,
   With hey, with ho, for and a nony no

They were two merchant-men, a sailing for Safee.
   Along the course of Barbary

2. The George Aloe to anchor came,
   But the jolly Sweepstake kept on her way.

3. They had not sayled leagues two or three
   Before they spyed a sail upon the sea.

4. "O hail, o hail, you lusty gallants,
   From whence is your good ship and whither is she bound?"

5. "O we are some merchant-men, sailing for Safee."
   "And we be French rebels, a roving on the sea.

6. "O hail, O hail, you English dogs, hail!"
   "Then come aboard, you French dogs, and strike down your sail!"

7. "Amain, amain, you gallant Englishmen."
   "Come, you French swades, and strike down your sails."

8. They laid us aboard on the starboard side,
   And they overthrew us into the sea so wide.

9. When tidings to the George Aloe came
   That the jolly Sweepstakes by a Frenchman was tane,

10. "To top, to top, thou little ship-boy,
   And see if this French man-of-war thou canst descry."

11. "A sail, a sail, under your lee,
   Yea, and anchor under her bough."

12. "Weigh anchor, weigh anchor, O jolly boatswain,
   We will take theis Frenchman if we can."

13. We had not sailed leagues two or three
   But we met the French man-of-war upon the sea.

14. "All hail, all hail, you lusty gallants,
   Of whence is your fair ship, and whither is she bound?"

15. "O we are merchant-men, and bound for Safee."
   "And we are Frenchmen, roving upon the sea.

16. "Amain, amain, you English dogs!"
   "Come aboard, you French rogues, and strike your sails."

17. The first shot the George Aloe shot,
   It made the Frenchmen's hearts sore afraid.

18. The second shot the George Aloe did afford,
   He struck the main-mast over the board.

19. "Have mercy, have mercy, you brave Englishmen,"

"O what have you done with our brethren on shore?"
    As they sailed.

20. "He laid them aboard on the starboard side,
    And we threw them into the sea so wide."

21. "Such mercy as you have shewed unto them,
    Even the like mercy shall you have again."

22. We laid them aboard on the larboard side,
    And we threw them into the sea so wide.

23. Lord, how it grieved our hearts full sore
    To see the drowned Frenchmen float along the shore!

24. Now, gallant seamen all, adieu,
      With hey, with ho, for and a nony no
    This is the last news that I can write to you.
      To England's coast from Barbary.

THE SWEET TRINITY OR THE GOLDEN VANITY (286)

This story of Sir Walter Raleigh's ship was especially popular in the United States where many versions yet abound. Many changes of detail have been made, as well as many changes in name. All versions seem to stem from a late 17th-century broadside.

Text A, Pepys, *Ballads,* iv, 196; B, Ebsworth, *Roxburghe Ballads,* vi, 419; C, traditional in Maine, Barry, p. 339.

A.

1. Sir Walter Raleigh has built a ship,
    In the Neather-lands
  Sir Walter Raleigh has built a ship,
    In the Neather-lands
  And it is called The Sweet Trinity,
  And was taken by the false gallaly.
    Sailing in the Low-lands.

2. "Is there never a seaman bold
    In the Neather-lands
  Is there never a seaman bold
    In the Neather-lands
  That will go take this false gallaly,
    And to redeem The Sweet Trinity?"

3. Then spoke the little ship-boy;
    In the Neather-lands
  Then spoke the little ship-boy;

In the Neather-lands
"Master, master, what will you give me
And I will take this false gallaly,
And release The Sweet Trinity?"
    Sailing, etc.

4. "I'll give thee gold, and I'le give thee fee,
    In the Neather-lands
I'll give thee gold and I'le give thee fee,
    In the Neather-lands
And my eldest daughter thy wife shall be."
    Sailing, etc.

5. He set his breast, and away he did swim,
Until he came to the false gallaly.

6. He had an augor fit for the nonce,
The which will bore fifteen good holes at once.

7. Some ware at cards, and some at dice,
Until the salt water flashd in their eyes.

8. Some cut their hats, and some cut their caps,
For to stop the salt-water gaps.

9. He set his breast, and away did swim,
Until he came to his own ship again.

10. "I have done the work I promised to do,
For I have sunk the false gallaly,
And released The Sweet Trinity.

11. "You promised me gold, and you promised me fee,
Your eldest daughter my wife she must be."

12. "You shall have gold, and you shall have fee,
But my eldest daughter your wife shall never be."
    For sailing, etc.

13. "Then fare you well, you cozening lord,
Seeing you are not so good as your word."
    For sailing, etc.

14. And thus I shall conclude my song,
    Of the sailing in the Low-lands
Wishing all happiness to all seamen both old and young.
    In their sailing in the Low-lands.

B.

1. "I have a ship in the North Countrie,
And she goes by the name of The Golden Vanity;

I'm afraid she will be taken by some Turkish gallee,
    As she sails on the Low Lands Low."

2.   Then up starts our little cabin-boy,
    Saying, "Master, what will you give me if I do them destroy?"
    "I will give you gold, I will give you store,
    You shall have my daughter when I return on shore,
        If ye sink them in the Low Lands Low."

3.   The boy bent his breast and away he jumpt in;
    He swam till he came to this Turkish galleon,
        As she laid on the Low Lands Low.

4.   The boy he had an auger to bore holes two at twice;
    While some were playing cards, and some were playing dice,
    He let the water in, and it dazzled in their eyes,
        And he sunk them in the Low Lands Low.

5.   The boy he bent his breast and away he swam back again,
    Saying, "Master take me up, or I shall be slain,
        For I have sunk them in the Low Lands Low."

6.   "I'll not take you up," the master he cried;
    "I'll not take you up," the master replied;
    "I will kill you, I will shoot you, I will send you with the tide,
        I will sink you in the Low Lands Low."

7.   The boy he swam round all by the starboard-side;
    They laid him on the deck, and it's there he soon died;
    Then they sewed him up in an old cow's-hide,
    And they threw him overboard, to go down with the tide,
        And they sunk him in the Low Lands Low.

C.

THE GOLDEN VANITY

1.   'Twas all on board a ship down in a southern sea,
    And she goes by the name of the "Golden Vanity";
    I'm afraid that she'll be taken by this Spanish crew,
        As she sails along the Lowlands,
        As she sails along the Lowlands low.

2.   Then up speaks our saucy cabin boy, without fear or joy,
    Saying, "What will you give me, if I will her destroy?"
    "I'll give you gold and silver, my daughter fine and gay,
        If you'll destroy her in the Lowlands,
        If you'll sink her in the Lowlands low."

3.   The boy filled his chest and so boldly leaped in,
    The boy filled his chest and then began to swim;

He swam alongside of the bold Spanish ship,
And he sank her in the Lowlands,
And he sank her in the Lowlands low.

4. Some were playing cards and some were playing dice,
And some were in their hammocks sleeping very nice;
He bored two holes into her side, he let the water in,
And he sank her in the Lowlands,
And he sank her in the Lowlands low.

5. The boy then swam back unto our good ship's side,
And being much exhausted, bitterly he cried;
"Captain, take me in, for I'm going with the tide,
And I'm sinking in the Lowlands,
And I'm sinking in the Lowlands low."

6. "I will not take you in," our captain then replied,
"I'll shoot you and I'll stab you and I'll sink you in the tide,
And I'll sink you in the Lowlands,
And I'll sink you in the Lowlands low."

7. The boy then swam around next the larboard side,
And being more exhausted, bitterly he cried,
"Messmates, take me in, for I'm going with the tide,
And I'm sinking in the Lowlands,
And I'm sinking in the Lowlands low."

8. They hove the boy a rope and they hoisted him on deck,
They laid him on the quarter deck, the boy here soon died;
They sewed him up in a canvas sack, they hove him in the tide,
And they buried him in the Lowlands,
So they buried him in the Lowlands low.

CAPTAIN WARD AND THE RAINBOW (287)

This would seem to be a fairly accurate account of the fight with the pirate John Ward. He was captured and hanged c. 1610. Some of the American versions tell a slightly different story in making Ward offer his services to the king and then when he is scorned turn pirate and attack English ships only to be taken and hanged.

Text, *Bagford Ballads,* i, 65.

1. Strike up, you lusty gallants, with musick
and sound of drum
For we have descryed a rover, upon the sea
is come;
His name is Captain Ward, right well it doth
appear,

There has not been such a rover found out this
thousand year.

2. For he hath sent unto our king, the sixth of
January,
Desiring that he might come in, with all his
company:
"And if your king will let me come till I my
tale have told,
I will bestow for my ransom full thirty tun of
gold."

3. "O nay! O nay!" then said our king, "O
nay! this may not be,
To yield to such a rover my self will not agree;
He hath deceivd the French-man, likewise the
King of Spain,
And how can he be true to me that hath been
false to twain?"

4. With that our king provided a ship of worthy
fame,
Rainbow she is called, if you would know her
name;
Now the gallant Rainbow she rowes upon the
sea,
Five hundred gallant seamen to bear her company.

5. The Dutch-man and the Spaniard she made
them for to flye,
Also the bonny French-man, as she met him on
the sea:
When as this gallant Rainbow did come where
Ward did lye,
"Where is the captain of this ship?" this gal-
lant Rainbow did cry.

6. "O that am I," says Captain Ward, "there's
no man bids my lye,
And if thou art the king's fair ship, thou art
welcome unto me."
"I'le tell thee what," says Rainbow, "our king
is in great grief
That thou shouldst lye upon the sea and play
the arrant thief,

7. "And will not let our merchants ships pass as
they did before;

Such tydings to our king is come, which
  grieves his heart full sore,"
With that this gallant Rainbow she shot, out of
  her pride.
Full fifty gallant brass pieces, charged on every
  side.

8. And yet these gallant shooters prevailed not a
    pin,
  Though they were brass on the out-side, brave
    Ward was steel within;
  "Shoot on, shoot on," says Captain Ward,
    "your sport well pleaseth me,
  And he that first gives over shall yield unto
    the sea.

9. "I never wrongd an English ship, but Turk
    and King of Spain,
  For and the jovial Dutch-man as I met on the
    main.
  If I had known your king but one two years
    before,
  I would have savd brave Essex life, whose
    death did grieve me sore.

10. "Go tell the King of England, go tell him thus
    from me,
  If he reign king of all the land, I will reign
    king at sea."
  With that the gallant Rainbow shot, and shot,
    and shot in vain.
  And left the rover's company, and returnd
    home again.

11. "Our royal king of England, your ship's re-
    turnd again,
  For Ward's ship is so strong it never will be
    tane."
  "O everlasting!" says our king, "I have lost
    jewels three,
  Which would have gone unto the seas and
    brought proud Ward to me.

12. "The first was Lord Clifford, Earl of Cumber-
    land;
  The second was the lord Mountjoy, as you
    shall understand;
  The third was brave Essex, from field would
    never flee;

Which would a gone unto the seas and brought
proud Ward to me."

THE MERMAID (289)

Details are lacking in the various versions of this ballad, but the supposition is that the ship was sailing on a tragic voyage because she sailed on a Friday and because the men sighted a mermaid—both bad omens. The old belief was that the mermaid lured men to their destruction. The song was very popular in the United States in oral tradition and as a popular song. This ballad became the basis for a children's game and play party song.

Text, *Glasgow Lassies Garland*, B. M. 11621, c.3. 18th century.

1. As we lay musing in our beds,
     So well and so warm at ease,
   I thought upon those lodging-beds
     Poor seamen have at seas.

2. Last Easter day, in the morning fair,
     We was not far from land,
   Where we spied a mermaid on the rock,
     With comb and glass in hand.

3. The first came up the mate of our ship,
     With lead and line in hand,
   To sound and see how deep we was
     From any rock or sand.

4. The next came up the boatswain of our ship,
     With courage stout and bold:
   "Stand fast, stand fast, my brave lively lads,
     Stand fast, my brave hearts of gold!"

5. Our gallant ship is gone to wreck,
     Which was so lately trimmd;
   The raging seas has sprung a leak,
     And the salt water does run in.

6. Our gold and silver, and all our cloths,
     And all that ever we had,
   We forced was to heave them overboard,
     Thinking our lives to save.

7. In all, the number that was on board
     Was five hundred and sixty-four,
   And all that ever came alive on shore
     There was but poor ninety-five.

8. The first bespoke the captain of our ship,
　　　And a well-spoke man was he.
"I have a wife in fair Plymouth town,
　　　And a widow I fear she must be."

9. The next bespoke the mate of our ship,
　　　And a well-bespoke man was he.
"I have a wife in fair Portsmouth,
　　　And a widow I fear she must be."

10. The next bespoke the boatswain of our ship,
　　　And a well-bespoke man was he.
"I have a wife in fair Exeter,
　　　And a widow I fear she must be."

11. The next bespoke the little cabbin-boy,
　　　And a well-bespoke boy was he.
"I am as sorry for my mother dear
　　　As you are for your wives all three.

12. "Last night, when the moon shin'd bright,
　　　My mother had sons five,
But now she may look in the salt seas
　　　And find but one alive."

13. "Call a boat, call a boat, you little Plymouth boys,
　　　Don't you hear how the trumpets sound?
For the want of our boat our gallant ship is lost,
　　　And the most of our merry men is drownd."

14. Whilst the raging seas do roar,
　　　And the lofty winds do blow,
And we poor seamen do lie on the top,
　　　Whilst the landmen lies below.

JOHN OF HAZELGREEN (293)

In spite of the fact that this ballad has a rather wide popularity in England and America in folk tradition, it seems very literary and highly artificial, especially the versions in which the lady comes to know John in a dream and so fall in love with him. Scott's *Jock of Hazeldeen* was based on one of the versions of this ballad.

Text A, Elizabeth Cochrane's MS., p. 126; B, traditional in New Brunswick, *Bulletin,* 3:9; C, traditional in Virginia, Sharp, i, 294.

A.

1. Into a sweet May morning,
　　　As the sun clearly shone,
I heard a propper damsell

Making a heavy moan;
Making a heavy moan,
　I marvelled what she did mean,
And it was for a gentleman,
　Sir John of Hasilgreen.

2.　"What aileth thee now, bony maid,
　　To mourn so sore into the tide?
O happy were the man," he sayes,
　"That had thee to his bride,
To ly down by his side;
　Then he were not to mean."
But still she let the tears down fall
　For pleasant Hasilgreen.

3.　"O what for a man is Hasilgreen?
　　Sweet heart, pray tell to me."
"He is a propper gentleman,
　Dwels in the South Countrie;
With shoulders broad and arms long,
　And comely to be seen;
His hairs are like the threads of gold,
　My pleasant Hasilgreen."

4.　"Now Hasilgreen is married,
　　Let all this talking be."
"If Hasilgreen be married,
　This day then woe to me;
For I may sigh and sob no more,
　But close my weeping een,
And hold my peace and cry no more
　But dy for Hasilgreen."

5.　"Will you let Hasilgreen alone,
　　And go along with me?
I'll marry you on my eldest son,
　Make you a gay lady."
"Make me a gay lady?" she says,
　"I am a maid too mean;
I'll rather stay at home," she cries,
　"And dy for Hasilgreen."

6.　He takes this pretty maid him behind
　　And fast he spurred the horse,
And they're away to Bigger toun,
　Then in to Biggar Cross.
Their lodging was far sought,
　And so was it foreseen;

But still she let the tears doun fall
For pleasant Hasillgreen.

7. He's ta'en this pretty maid by the hand,
   And he is doun the toun;
   He bought for her a pettycoat,
   Yea, and a trailing goun;
   A silken kell fitt for her head,
   Laid oer with silver sheen;
   But still she let the tears doun fall
   For pleasant Hasilgreen.

8. He's taen this bony mey him behind,
   And he is to the Place,
   Where there was mirth and merryness,
   And ladyes fair of face,
   And ladyes fair of face,
   Right seemly to be seen,
   But still she let the tears doun fall
   For pleasant Hasilgreen.

9. Young Hasilgreen ran hastilie
   To welcome his father dear:
   He's ta'en that pretty maid in his arms,
   And kist off her falling tear:
   "O bony mey, now for thy sake
   I would give rent and rien:
   I would give all my father's lands
   To have thee in Hasilgreen."

10. "O hold your tongue now, son," he sayes,
    "Let no more talking be;
    This maid has come right far from home
    This day to visit thee.
    This day should have been your wedding-day,
    It shall be thy bridall-een,
    And thou's get all thy father's lands,
    And dwell in Hasillgreen."

B.

JOHN OF HASELGREEN

1. "Why weep, 'e by the tide, Ladye,
   Why weep 'e by the tide?
   I'll wed ye tae my youngest son,
   An' ye sall be his bryde;
   An' ye sall be his bryde, Ladye,
   Sae comely tae be seen";

But aye she loot the tear doon fa'
For Jock o' Hazeldean.

2. "O, what na man is Hazeldean?
I pray ye, tell tae me."
"O there is na a finer man
In a' the sooth countree;
His step is first in peaceful ha'
His sword in battle keen.
But aye she loot the tear doon fa'
For Jock o' Hazeldean.

3. .   .   .   .
.   .   .   .
Young Frank is chief of Errington
An' Lord of Langly Dale.
.   .   .   .
.   .   .   .
.   .   .   .
.   .   .   .

4. The church was decked at morning tide,
An' dame an' knight were there;
Wi' armour bright an' managed hawk
An' palfrey fresh an' fair;
They sought her baith by bower an' ha',
The ladye wasna seen—
She's ower the borders an' awa
Wi' Jock o' Hazeldean!

C.

1. While riding down that greenwood road
There sat a lady who mourned,
And all of her lamentation was,
It was John of Hazelgreen.

2. You are welcome with me, kind Miss,
You are welcome with me, said he,
And you may have my oldest son
A husband for to be.

3. O I don't want your oldest son,
He's neither lord nor king.
I intend to be the bride of none
But John of the Hazelgreen.

4. For he's tall and his shoulders broad,
He's the lord of all our kin,

His hair hangs down like the links of gold,
He's John of the Hazelgreen.

5. While riding down that lengthy lane,
        That lane that leads to town,
    O up stepped John of the Hazelgreen
        And holped his lady down.

6. Forty times he kissed her ruby lips,
        And forty times he kissed her chin,
    And forty times he kissed her ruby lips
        And let his lady in.

THE BROWN GIRL (295)

This has many elements that are common to other and better ballads
(cf. "Lord Thomas and Fair Ellinor," "Sweet William's Ghost,"
"Clerk Saunders," "Barbara Allen," "The Unquiet Grave"). But as
Child says, ". . . in the point of the proud and unrelenting character
of the Brown Girl it is original."

In America a large group of ballads variously titled tell the same
general story, though they are far removed from this ballad verbally.
Many scholars, however, classify them under "The Brown Girl."

Text A, traditional in England, transcribed by S. Baring-Gould,
Child, v, 167; B, traditional in Virginia, Sharp, i, 245.

A.

1. "I am as brown as brown can be,
        And my eyes as black as sloe;
    I am brisk as brisk can be,
        And wild as forest doe.

2. "My love he was so high and proud,
        His fortune too so high,
    He for another fair pretty maid
        Me left and passed me by.

3. "Me did he send a love-letter,
        He sent it from the town,
    Saying no more he loved me,
        For that I was so brown.

4. "I sent his letter back again,
        Saying his love I valued not,
    Whether that he would fancy me,
        Whether that he would not.

5. "When that six months were overpassd,
        Were overpassd and gone,

Then did my lover, once so bold,
    Lie on his bed and groan.

6. "When that six months were overpassd,
    Were gone and overpassd,
O then my lover, once so bold,
    With love was sick at last.

7. "First sent he for the doctor-man."
    "You, doctor, me must cure;
The pains that now do torture me
    I can not long endure."

8. "Next did he send from out the town,
    O next did send for me;
He sent for me, the brown, brown girl
    Who once his wife should be.

9. "O ne'er a bit the doctor-man
    His sufferings could relieve;
O never an one but the brown, brown girl
    Who could his life reprieve."

10. Now you shall hear what love she has
    For this poor love-sick man,
How all one day, a summer's day,
    She walked and never ran.

11. When that she came to his bedside,
    Where he lay sick and weak,
O then for laughing she could not stand
    Upright upon her feet.

12. "You flouted me, you scouted me,
    And many another one;
Now the reward is come at last,
    For all that you have done."

13. The rings she took from off her hands,
    The rings by two and three.
"O take, O take these golden rings,
    By them remember me."

14. She had a white wand in her hand,
    She strake him on the breast:
"My faith and troth I give back to thee,
    So may thy soul have rest."

15. "Prithee," said he, "Forget, forget,
    Prithee forget, forgive;
O grant me yet a little space,
    That I may be well and live."

16.　"O never will I forget, forgive,
　　　　So long as I have breath;
　　　　I'll dance above the green, green grave
　　　　Where you do lie beneath."

B.

1.　There was a rich lady, from England she came,
　　　Fine Sally, fine Sally, fine Sally by name,
　　　And she had more money than the king could possess,
　　　And her wit and her beauty was worth all the rest.

2.　There was a poor doctor who lived hard by,
　　　And on this fair damsel he cast his eye.
　　　Fine Sally, fine Sally, fine Sally, says he,
　　　Can you tell me the reason our love can't agree?
　　　I don't hate you, Billy, nor no other man,
　　　But to tell you I love you I never can.

3.　Fine Sally took sick and she knew not for why,
　　　And she sent for this young man that she was to deny.
　　　He says: Am I the doctor that you have sent for,
　　　Or am I the young man that you once did deny?
　　　Yes, you are the doctor can kill or can cure
　　　And without your assistance I'm ruined, I'm sure.

4.　Fine Sally, fine Sally, fine Sally, says he,
　　　Don't you remember when you slighted me?
　　　You slighted me highly, you used me with scorn,
　　　And now I reward you for what's passed and gone.

5.　What's passed and gone, love, forget and forgive,
　　　And spare me a while longer in this wide world to live.
　　　I don't want you, Sally, in the durance of my breath,
　　　But I'll dance on your grave when you're laid in the earth.

WALTER LESLY (296)

Text, Buchan, ii, 139.

1.　On the second of October, a Monday at noon,
　　　In came Walter Lesly, to see his proper one;
　　　He set a chair down by her side, and gently sat her by,
　　　Says, "Will ye go to Conland, this winter-time to lye?"

2.　He's taen a glass into his hand, inviting her to drink,
　　　But little knew she his meaning, or what the rogue did think;

Nor what the rogue did think, to steal the maid away;
"Will ye go to Conland, this winter-time to lye?"

3. When they had taen a glass or two, and all were making merry,
In came Geordy Lesly, and forth he did her carry;
Then upon high horseback sae hard's he did her tye,
"Will ye go to Conland, this winter-time to lye?"

4. Her mother she came to the door, the saut tears on her cheek,
She coudna see her daughter, it was for dust and reek;
It was for dust and reek the swords they glancd sae high.
"Will ye go to Conland, this winter-time to lye?"

5. When they came to the ale-house, the people there were busy;
A bridal-bed it was well made, the supper well made ready;
When the supper down was set, baith plum-pudding and pie.
"And will ye go to Conland, this winter-time to lye?"

6. When they had eaten and well drunken, and a' man bound for bed,
The laddie and the lassie in ae chamber were laid;
He quickly stript her to the smock, and gently laid her bye,
Says, "Will ye go to Conland, this winter-time to lye?"

7. But Walter being weary, he fell fast asleep,
And then the lassie thought it fet to start up till her feet;
To start up till her feet, and her petticoats to tye,
"We'll go no more to Conland, the winter-time to lye."

8. Then over moss and over muir sae cleverly she ran,
And over hill and over dale, without stockings or shoon;
The men pursued her full fast, wi mony shout and cry,
Says, "Will ye go to Conland, the winter-time to lye."

9. "Wae to the dubs o Duffus land, that eer they were sae deep;
They've trachled a' our horsemen and gart our captain sleep;
And gart our captain sleep, and the lassie win away,
And she'll go no more to Conland, the winter-time to lye."

10. "I'd rather be in Duffus land, selling at the ale,
Before I was wi Lesly, for a' his auld meal;
For a' his auld meal, and sae mony comes to buy;
I'll go no more to Conland the winter-time to lye.

11. "I'd rather be in Duffus land, dragging at the ware,
Before I was wi Lesly, for a' his yellow hair;
For a' his yellow hair, and sae well's he can it tye;
I'll go no more to Conland, this winter-time to lye."

12. It was not for her beauty, nor yet her gentle bluid,
But for her mither's dollars, of them he had great need;

Of them he had great need, now he maun do them by,
For she'll go no more to Conland, this winter-time to lye.

EARL ROTHES (297)

Text, Kinloch MSS., i, 333.

1. "O Earl Rothes, an thou wert mine,
        And I were to be thy ladie,
    I wad drink at the beer, and tipple at the wine,
        And by my bottle with any."

2. "Hold thy tongue, sister Ann," he says,
        "Thy words they are too many;
    What wad ye do wi sae noble a lord,
        When he has so noble a ladie?

3. "O I'll pay you your tocher, Lady Ann,
        Both in gear and money,
    If ye'll forsake Earl Rothes's companie,
        And mind that he has a ladie."

4. "I do not value your gold," she says,
        "Your gear it's no sae readie;
    I'll neer forsake Earl Rothes's companie
        And I don't gie a fig for his ladie."

5. "I'll keep ye i the castle, Lady Ann,
        O servants ye shall hae monie;
    I'll keep ye till ye're safely brocht to bed,
        And I'll mak you a marquis's ladie."

6. "I do not value your castle," she says,
        "Your servants are no sae readie;
    Earl Rothes will keep me till I'm brocht to bed,
        And he'll mak me a marquis's ladie."

7. "Woe be to thee, Earl Rothes," he says,
        "And the mark o the judge be upon thee,
    For the using o this poor thing sae,
        For the using my sister so badly.

8. "When I'm come to the years of a man,
        And able a sword to carry,
    I'll thrust it thro Earl Rothes' bodie
        For the using my sister sae badly.

9. "Fare thee well, Lady Ann," he says,
        "No longer will I tarry;

You and I will never meet again,
Till we meet at the bonny town o Torry."

YOUNG PEGGY (298)

Text, Kinloch, p. 153.

1. "O whare hae ye been, Peggy?
    O whare hae ye been?"
   "I the garden amang the gilly-flowrs,
    Atween twal hours and een."

2. "Ye've na been there your leen, Peggy,
    Ye've na been there your leen;
   Your father saw you in Jamie's arms,
    Atween twal hours and een."

3. "Tho my father saw me in Jamie's arms,
    He'll see me there again;
   For I will sleep in Jamie's arms
    When his grave's growin green."

4. "Your Jamie is a rogue, Peggy,
    Your Jamie is a loun,
   For trysting out our ae dochter,
    And her sae very young."

5. "Lay no the wyte on Jamie, mither,
    The blame a' lies on me;
   For I will sleep in Jamie's arms
    When your een winna see."

6. Now she has to her ain bouer gane;
    He was waiting there him leen.
   "I'm blythe to see ye, Jamie, here,
    For we maunna meet again."

7. She's tane the wine-glass in her hand,
    Pourd out the wine sae clear;
   Says, "Here's your health and mine, Jamie,
    And we maun meet na mair."

8. She has tane him in her arms twa,
    And gien him kisses five;
   Says, "Here's your health and mine, Jamie,
    I wish weel mote ye thrive."

9. "Your father has a bonnie cock,
    Divides the nicht and day,

And at the middle watch o the nicht
　　In greenwud ye'll meet me."

10.　Whan bells war rung, and mass was sung,
　　　And a' men boun for bed,
　　She's kilted up her green claithing,
　　　And met Jamie in the wud.

11.　Whan bells war rung, and mass was sung,
　　　About the hour o twa,
　　It's up bespak her auld father,
　　　Says, "Peggy is awa!"

12.　"Ga saddle to me the black, the black,
　　　Ga saddle to me the grey."
　　But ere they wan to the tap o the hill
　　　The wedding was a' bye.

THE TROOPER AND MAID (299)

This is one of a group of soldier-maiden ballads, all telling more or less the same story. In America the song was popular in two basic forms, the one close to the English given here; in the other the trooper becomes evasive about marrying the lady or refuses entirely.

Text, Buchan, i, 230.

1.　One evening as a maid did walk,
　　　The moon was shining clearly,
　　She heard a trooper at the gates,
　　　She thought it was her dearie.
　　She's taen his horse then by the head,
　　　And led him to the stable,
　　And gien to him baith corn and hay,
　　　To eat what he was able.
　　　　　Bonny lass, gin I come near you,
　　　　　　Bonny lass, gin I come near you,
　　　　　I'll gar a' your ribbons reel,
　　　　　　Bonny lass, or eer I lea you.

2.　She's taen the trooper by the hand,
　　　And led him to the table,
　　And furnishd him wi bread and cheese,
　　　To eat what he was able.
　　She's taen the wine-glass in her hand,
　　　Poured out the wine sae clearly;
　　"Here is your health an mine," she cried,
　　　"And ye're welcome hame, my deary!

3. "A glass o wine for gentlemen,
   And bonny lads for lasses,
And bread and cheese for cavaliers,
   And corn and hay for asses."
Then she went but and made his bed,
   She made it like a lady,
And she coost aff her mankie gown,
   Says, "Laddie, are you ready?"

4. Then he coost aff his big watch-coat,
   But and his silken beaver,
A pair o pistols frae his side,
   And he lay down beside her.
"Bonny lassie, I am wi you now,
   Bonny lassie, I am wi you,
But I'll gar a' your ribbons reel,
   Bonny lassie, ere I lea you."

5. The trumpet sounds thro Birldale,
   Says, "Men and horse, make ready;"
The drums do beat at Staneman hill,
   "Lads, leave your mam and daddie."
The fifes did play at Cromley banks,
   "Lads, leave the lewes o Fyvie;"
And then the trooper he got up,
   Says, "Lassie, I must lea you.

6. "Bonny lassie, I maun lea you now,
   Bonny lassie, I maun lea you;
But if ever I come this road again,
   I will come in and see you."

7. She's taen her gown out-ower her arms,
   And followed him to Stirling,
And aye the trooper he did say,
   "O turn ye back, my darling.
"Or when will we twa meet again?
   Or when will you me marry?"
"When rashin rinds grow gay gowd rings,
   I winna langer tarry."

8. "O when will we twa meet again?
   Or when will you me marry?"
"When heather-knaps grow siller taps,
   I winna langer tarry."
"O when will we twa meet again?
   Or when will you me marry?"
"When heather-cows grow owsen bows,
   I winna langer tarry."

9.   "O when will we twa meet again?
         Or when will you me marry?"
      "When cockle-shells grow siller bells,
         I winna langer tarry."
      "O when will we twa meet again?
         Or when will you me marry?"
      "When apple-trees grow in the seas,
         I winna langer tarry."

10.   "O when will we twa meet again?
         Or when will you me marry?"
      "When fishes fly, and seas gang dry,
         I winna langer tarry."
      "O when will we twa meet again?
         Or when will you me marry?"
      "When frost and snaw shall warm us a',
         I winna langer tarry."

11.   "Yestreen I was my daddie's dow,
         But an my mamy's dawtie;
      This night I gang wi bairn to you,
         Wae's me that I eer saw thee!"
      "Yestreen ye were your daddie's dow,
         But an your mammie's dawtie;
      But gin ye gang wi bairn to me,
         You may rue that eer you saw me.

12.   "O turn back, my bonny lass,
         And turn back, my dearie;
      For the Highland hills are ill to climb,
         And the bluidy swords woud fear ye."

THE HOLY NUNNERY (303)

Text, Buchan, i, 193.

1.   Fair Annie had a costly bower,
         Well built wi lime and stane,
      And Willie came to visit her,
         Wi the light o the meen.

2.   When he came to Annie's bower-door,
         He tirled at the pin:
      "Ye sleep ye, wake ye, Fair Annie,
         Ye'll open, lat me come in."

3.   "O never a fit," says Fair Annie,
         "Till I your errand ken;"

"My father's vowd a vow, Annie,
    I'll tell you when I'm in.

4. "My father's vowed a rash vow,
    I darena marry thee;
    My mither's vowed anither vow,
    My bride ye'se never be."

5. "If ye had tauld me that, Willie,
    When we began to woo,
    There was naithing in this warld wide
    Shoud drawn my love to you.

6. "A nun, a nun," said Fair Annie,
    "A nun will I be then;"
    "A priest, a priest," said Sweet Willie,
    "A priest will I be syne."

7. She is gane to her father,
    For mither she had nane;
    And she is on to her father,
    To see if she'd be a nun.

8. "An asking, an asking, father dear,
    An asking ye'll grant me;
    That's to get to the holy nunnery,
    And there to live or die."

9. "Your asking's nae sae great, daughter,
    But granted it shall be;
    For ye'se won to the holy nunnery,
    There to live or die."

10. Then they gaed on, and farther on,
    Till they came to the yate;
    And there they spied a maiden porter,
    Wi gowd upon her hat.

11. "An asking, asking, maiden porter,
    An asking ye'll grant me;
    If I'll won to the holy nunnery,
    There to live or die."

12. "Your asking's nae sae great, lady,
    But granted it shall be;
    For ye'se won to the holy nunnery,
    There to live or die.

13. "But ye maun vow a vow, lady,
    Before that ye seek in;
    Never to kiss a young man's mouth
    That goes upon the grun.

14. "And ye must vow anither vow,
      Severely ye must work;
    The well-warst vow that ye're to vow,
      Is never to gang to kirk."

15. "I will vow a vow," she said,
      "Before that I seek in;
    I neer shall kiss a young man's mouth
      That goes upon the grun.

16. "And I will vow anither vow,
      Severely I will work;
    The well-warst that I'm to vow
      Is never gang to kirk."

17. For seven years now Fair Annie,
      In the holy nunnery lay she,
    And seven years Sweet Willie lay,
      In languish like to die.

18. "Is there nae duke nor lord's daughter,
      My son, can comfort thee,
    And save thee frae the gates o death?
      Is there nae remedie?"

19. "There is nae duke nor lord's daughter,
      Mother, can comfort me,
    Except it be my love, Annie,
      In the holy nunnery lies she."

20. They've dressd Sweet Willie up in silk,
      Wi gowd his gown did shine,
    And nane coud ken by his pale face
      But he was a lady fine.

21. So they gaed on, and farther on,
      Till they came to the yate,
    And there they spied a maiden porter,
      Wi gowd upon her hat.

22. "An asking, an asking, maiden porter,
      An asking ye'll grant me;
    For to win in to the holy nunnery,
      Fair Annie for to see."

23. "Your asking's nae sae great, lady,
      But granted it shall be;
    Ye'se won into the holy nunnery,
      Fair Annie for to see.

24. "Be she duke's or lord's daughter,
      It's lang sin she came here."

Fair Annie kent her true love's face;
Says, "Come up, my sister dear."

25. Sweet Willie went to kiss her lips,
    As he had wont to do;
    But she softly whispered him,
    "I darena this avow."

THE BITTER WITHY

"The Bitter Withy" was first reported by Frank Sidgwick in *Notes and Queries*, Series 10, No. 83. This is really a carol ballad, belonging in the same category as "The Cherry Tree Carol." Like "The Cherry Tree Carol," "The Bitter Withy" is based on a legend of Christ, found in hagiographic literature. The legend of Christ and the bridge of sunbeams was widely known. It appears not only in religious but also in pictorial art. See G. H. Gerould, "The Ballad of the Bitter Withy," *PMLA*, xxiii:141–167; Phillips Barry, "The Bridge of Sunbeams," *JAF*, xxvii:79–89; *JFSS*, iv:29–47.

Text, *Notes and Queries, loc. cit.*

1. As it fell out on a Holy day
   The drops of rain did fall, did fall,
   Our Saviour asked leave of His mother Mary
   If he might go play at ball.

2. "To play at ball my own dear Son,
   It's time You was going or gone,
   But be sure let me hear no complaint of You
   At night when You do come home."

3. It was upling scorn and downling scorn,
   Oh, there He met three jolly jerdins
   Oh, there He asked the three jolly jerdins
   If they would go play at ball.

4. "Oh, we are lords' and ladies' sons,
   Born in bower or in hall,
   And you are but some poor maid's child
   Born'd in an ox's stall."

5. "If you are lords' and ladies' sons,
   Born'd in bower or in hall,
   Then at the very last I'll make it appear
   That I am above you all."

6. Our Saviour built a bridge with the beams of the sun,
   And over He gone, He gone He.

And after followed the three jolly jerdins,
    And drowned they were all three.

7.   It was upling scorn and downling scorn
    The mothers of them did whoop and call,
  Crying out, "Mary mild, call back your Child,
    For ours are drowned all."

8.   Mary mild, Mary mild, called home her Child,
    And laid our Saviour across her knee,
  And with a whole handful of bitter withy
    She gave Him slashes three.

9.   Then He says to His mother, "Oh! the withy, oh! the withy.
    The bitter withy that causes me to smart, to smart,
  Oh! the withy it shall be the very first tree
    That perishes at the heart."

THE HOLY WELL (SWEET JESUS)

This carol ballad should be associated with "The Bitter Withy" and the "Cherry Tree Carol." It is old and widely known in England. See *JFSS*, iv:26, v:i, for several versions and detailed discussion.
Text, William Howitt, *Rural Life in England*.

1.   Honour the leaves, and the leaves of life
    Upon this blest holiday,
    When Jesus asked His mother dear,
    Whether He might go to play.

2.   "To play! to play!" said the blessed Mary,
    "To play, then get you gone;
    And see there be no complaint of you,
    At night when you come home."

3.   Sweet Jesus, He ran into yonder town,
    As far as the Holy well,
    And there He saw three as fine children
    As ever eyes beheld,

4.   He said, "God bless you every one,
    And sweet may your sleep be;
    And now, little children, I'll play with you,
    And you shall play with me."

5.   "Nay, nay, we are lords' and ladies' sons,
    Thou art meaner than us all;
    Thou art but a silly fair maid's child,
    Born in an oxen's stall."

6. Sweet Jesus He turned himself about,
   Neither laugh'd, nor smiled, nor spoke,
   But the tears trickled down His pretty little eyes,
   Like waters from the rock.

7. Sweet Jesus He ran to His mother dear,
   As fast as He could run:
   "O mother, I saw three as fine children,
   As ever were eyes set on,

8. "I said, 'God bless you every one,
   And sweet may your sleep be—
   And now little children, I'll play with you,
   And you shall play with me.'

9. " 'Nay,' said they, 'we're lords' and ladies' sons,
   Thou art meaner than us all,
   For Thou art but a poor fair maid's child,
   Born in an oxen's stall,' "

10. "Then," said she, "go down to yonder town,
    As far as the Holy well,
    And there take up those infants' souls,
    And dip them deep in hell."

11. "O no! O no!" sweet Jesus cried,
    "O no! that never can be;
    For there are many of those infants' souls
    Crying out for the help of Me."

OVER YONDER'S A PARK (CORPUS CHRISTI)

This most scholars would probably classify as a lyric rather than a ballad. It certainly is lyrical but it possesses too that dramatic intensity that belongs to ballad. It was sung as a carol. Whether it is a ballad or not, the two versions here printed give us opportunity to compare a certainly 15th-century piece with a 19th century version of the same. The first is in a Middle English MS., a commonplace book belonging to a London tradesman, Richard Hill, who, one would guess, copied it from contemporary singers. The other is one of several versions that have been secured from singers in England in the 19th century. The ballad is certainly allegorical or at least symbolic, with apparent references to the Holy Grail legends. For an attempt to interpret these ballads, see Annie Gilchrist, *JFSS*, iv:52 ff.

Text A, from 15th-century MS., *Notes and Queries*, September 2, 1905; B, from the singing of a boy in Staffordshire, England, 1862.

A.

Lully, lulley, lully, lulley,
The faucon hath born my make away. (refrain)

1. He bare him up, he bare him down,
   He bare him into an orchard brown.

2. In that orchard there was an halle,
   That was hangèd with purpill and pall.

3. And in that hall there was a bede,
   It was hangèd with gold so rede.

4. And in that bed there lithe a knight,
   His woundès bleding day and night.

5. By that bede side kneleth a may,
   And she wepeth both night and day.

6. And by that bede side there standeth a stone,
   Corpus Christi wreten there on.

B.

1. Over yonder's a park which is newly begun,
   All bells in Paradise I hear them ring,
   Which is silver on the outside and gold within,
   And I love sweet Jesus above a thing.

2. And in that park there stands a hall,
   Which is covered all over with purple and pall.

3. And in that hall there stands a bed.
   Which is hung all round with silk curtains red.

4. And in that bed there lies a knight,
   Whose wounds they do bleed by day and by night.

5. At that bed side there lies a stone,
   Which is our blessed Virgin Mary then kneeling on.

6. At that bed's foot there lies a hound,
   Which is licking the blood as it daily runs down.

7. At that bed's head there grows a thorn,
   Which was never so blossomed since Christ was born.

THE BOLD FISHERMAN

Miss Broadwood is certainly right in suggesting that this ballad is a transmuted version of a once more-fully developed story. It seems probable too that the original was a medieval allegory embodying the

"River, the Sea, the Royal Fisher, the three Vestures of Light (or Robes of Glory) the Recognition and Adoration by the illuminated and humble Soul—free Pardon, the mystical union of the Bride to the Bridegroom in the House of the Father . . . familiar elements" in church mystical literature. (See *JFSS*, v:132.) On the other hand, it may well be that this ballad told a realistic story like "The Knight and the Shepherd's Daughter" (110).

Text, *JFSS*, v:132.

1. As I walked out one May morning,
    When May was all in bloom,
    Oh there I spied a bold fisherman,
    Come fishing all alone.

2. I said to this bold fisherman
    "How come you fishing here?"
    "I'm fishing for your own sweet sake
    All down the river clear."

3. He drove his boat towards the side,
    Which was his full intent,
    Then he laid hold of her lily-white hand
    And down the stream they went.

4. Then he pulled off his morning gown
    And threw it over the sea,
    And there she spied three robes of gold
    All hanging down his knee.

5. Then on her bended knees she fell
    "Pray, sir, pray pardon me
    For calling you a fisherman
    And a rover down the sea!"

6. "Rise up, rise up, my pretty fair maid,
    Don't mention that to me,
    For not one word that you have spoke
    Has the least offended me.

7. "Then we'll go to my father's hall,
    And married we will be,
    And you shall have your fisherman
    To row you on the sea."

8. Then they went to his father's house,
    And married now they be,
    And now she's got her fisherman
    To row her down the sea.

THE BLIND BEGGAR OF BEDNALL (BETHNAL) GREEN

The Percy *Folio* contains the earliest version of this ballad. In the *Reliques* Percy combined it with parts of another ballad and worked in a song through which the Blind Beggar reveals himself as Henry de Mountfort, son and heir of the Earl of Leicester, supposed to have been slain in the Battle of Evesham in 1265. This revelation, coming after the Blind Beggar has matched Betsey's suitor two guineas for one to the sum of ten thousand pounds, makes her suitor agree that she is worthy of him. The version in the *Reliques* is very long; it is in two fitts, 268 lines.

This ballad is found in the early collections, in the song books and in at least one broadside, and it is frequently found in oral tradition in England, but rather rarely in America.

Stanza 8 condenses part of the story to the point of obscurity. The Blind Beggar tells the suitor that he will match him two guineas to one. He does so until the young man has exhausted his store; whereupon the Beggar says he will add more to buy Betsey a gown.

Text, *JFSS*, i:202.

1. It's of a blind beggar, and he lost his sight,
   He had but one daughter, most beautiful bright.
   "Shall I seek my fortune, dear father?" said she.
   The favour was granted to pretty Betsey.

2. She set out for London, as I have heard say,
   And arrived in Bloomford that very same day,
   And when she came there unto my lord's house
   So handsomely admired was pretty Betsey.

3. She had not been there no length of time
   Before a young lord a-courting her came.
   "Your clothes shall be linèd with jewels," said he,
   "If you will but love me, my pretty Betsey."

4. "It's all for to do it I am willing," said she,
   "You must first ask the father of pretty Betsey."
   "Then who is your father? Pray tell unto me,
   That I may go with you your father to see."

5. "My father is every day to be seen,
   He is called the Blind Beggar of Bethlem Green,
   He is called the Blind Beggar. God knows," says she,
   "He has been a good father to his daughter Betsey."

6. "If you're a blind beggar's daughter you won't do for me
   A blind beggar's daughter my lady sha'n't be!

A blind beggar's daughter my lady sha'n't be!"
So scornfully turned from his pretty Betsey.

7. Then up spake a young Squire, with riches enough:
   "If she's a blind beggar's daughter she's never the worse.
   Your clothes shall be linèd with jewels," said he,
   "If you will but love me, my pretty Betsey."

8. "Your daughter's not clothed so fine as she shall be,
   For it's I will drop guineas for you, my girl."
   He droppèd these guineas till they dropp'd on the ground,
   He droppèd till he droppèd ten thousand pound.

9. "Dear honoured father, I've dropped all my store,
   I've dropped all my riches and I can't drop no more.
   But grant me your daughter, and that's all I crave,
   That I might be married to pretty Betsey."

10. "Oh take her, and make her your lady so bright:
    There's many a rich lord will owe you great spite,
    And, when you are married, I will lay her down
    Ten thousand bright guineas to buy her a gown."

11. It's Billy and Betsey to church they did go,
    It's Billy and Betsey they cut a fine show.
    The most beautiful creature that ever was seen
    Was the Blind Beggar's daughter of Bethlem Green.

ANNAN WATER

This ballad was first printed as a broadside, then by Scott "from tradition" in the *Minstrelsy,* ii, 138 (1802). The ballad is referred to in Allan Ramsay's *Tea-Table Miscellany* and by Allan Cunningham's *Songs of Scotland.* Cunningham said that he had heard it sung and that it had many variations. Child is skeptical about it as a folk ballad of very long standing; one would certainly question stanza 14.

Text, Scott, ii, 138.

1. "Annan water's wading deep,
       And my love Annie's wondrous bonny,
   And I am laith she suld weet her feet,
       Because I love her best of ony.

2. "Gar saddle me the bonny black,
       Gar saddle sune, and make him ready,
   For I will down the Gatehope-Slack,
       And all to see my bonny ladye."

3. He has loupen on the bonny black,
       He stirrd him wi the spur right sairly;

But, or he wan the Gatehope-Slack,
   I think the steed was wae and weary.

4. He has loupen on the bonny grey,
   He rade the right gate and the ready;
I trow he would neither stint nor stay,
   For he was seeking his bonny ladye.

5. O he has ridden oer field and fell,
   Through muir and moss, and mony a mire;
His spurs o steel were sair to bide,
   And frae her fore-feet flew the fire.

6. "Now, bonny grey, now play your part,
   Gin ye be the steed that wins my deary,
Wi corn and hay ye'se be fed for aye,
   And never spur sall make you wearie."

7. The grey was a mare, and a right good mare,
   But when she wan the Annan water
She couldna hae ridden a furlong mair
   Had a thousand merks been wadded at her.

8. "O boatman, boatman, put off your boat,
   Put off your boat for gowden money!
I cross the drumly stream the night,
   Or never mair I see my honey."

9. "O I was sworn sae late yestreen,
   And not by ae aith, but by many;
And for a' the gowd in fair Scotland
   I dare na take ye through to Annie."

10. The ride was stey, and the bottom deep,
   Frae bank to brae the water pouring,
And the bonny grey mare did sweat for fear,
   For she heard the water-kelpy roaring.

11. O he has poud aff his dapperpy coat,
   The silver buttons glanced bonny;
The waistcoat bursted aff his breast,
   He was sae full of melancholy.

12. He has taen the ford at that stream tail;
   I wot he swam both strong and steady;
But the stream was broad, and his strength did fail,
   And he never saw his bonny ladye!

13. "O wae betide the frush saugh wand!
   And wae betide the bush of brier!
It brake into my true-love's hand,
   When his strength did fail, and his limbs did tire.

14. "And wae betide ye, Annan Water,
        This night that ye are a drumlie river!
    For over thee I'll build a bridge,
        That ye never more true love may sever."

WILLIAM GLEN

This is a broadside widely known under several names, of which "Bonnie Annie" and "Sir William Gower" are the most common. The ballad is based on the common folk belief that a ship in peril of the sea and storms is probably carrying a criminal and that casting the wrongdoer overboard will cause the storm to abate. A number of ballads turn on this belief: "William Guiseman," "The Factor's Garland," a Danish ballad, "Sir John Rimord's Son's Shrift." Scott refers to this ballad and quotes from it in *The Pirate* (chap. 36).

Text, Christie's *Traditional Ballad Airs,* i, 241.

1. There was a ship, and a ship of fame,
    Launch'd off the stocks, bound to the main,
    With a hundred bold and brisk young men,
    Well pick'd and chosen every one.
    And William Glen was our captain's name,
    He was a tall and a brisk young man;
    As bold a sailor as went to sea,
    And we were bound for High Barbary.

2. On the first of April we did set sail,
    Blest with a sweet and a prosperous gale;
    They all fell sick but sixty-three,
    As we did sail to High Barbary.
    One night our captain lay in his sleep,
    And there came a voice, as if from the deep:—
    "Prepare you and your brave company;
    To-morrow night you must lodge with me."

3. This waken'd the captain in a fright,
    It was the third watch of the night,
    And for the boatswain he did call,
    And told him of his secrets all:—
    "I slew a lord in Straffordshire,
    All for the love of a lady fair;
    And though the king has pardon'd me,
    He's daily in my company."

4. "Oh! worthy captain, since it is so,
    I pray you let no body know;
    Keep you the secret in your breast,

And pray that you may get some rest."
But soon the sea did rage and roar,
We never thought to see the shore;
Our ship was wash'd both fore and aft,
Till only a few on board were left.

5.　Our foremost man at the helm stood,
And was swept off by the raging flood,
Crying for mercy on us all,
As to the bottom he did fall.
Our boatswain, then, he did declare,
That our captain was a murderer,
Which so enraged our whole ship's crew,
That overboard they the captain threw.

6.　Our treacherous captain being gone,
Immediately there was a calm;
The wind was calm'd, so was the sea,
And we arriv'd at High Barbary.
When to High Barbary we did come,
Our dismal state we to them made known:
Then all young sailors I pray beware,
And never sail with a murderer!

THE GOSPORT TRAGEDY

This ballad, first recorded in the Roxburghe Collection (see Ebsworth, viii, 143), certainly influenced, if it did not indeed furnish the pattern for, many of the "murdered lady" ballads. It has obvious affiliations with "William Glen." Usually, however, the murderer is a ship's carpenter. In some versions it is just the sight of the ghost of the murdered girl that causes the murderer's death. See *JAF,* 20:261; Brown Collection, *North Carolina Folklore,* ii:234.

Text A, Ebsworth, *Roxburghe Ballads;* B, E. C. Ball, Virginia, as sung to Alan Lomax.

A.

1.　In fair Worcester City and in Worcestershire,
A handsome young damsel she lived there.
A handsome young man he courted her to be his dear,
And he was by trade a ship carpenter.

2.　Now the King wanted seamen to go on the sea,
That caused this young damsel to sigh and say,
"O William, O William, don't you go to sea,
Remember the vows that you made to me."

3. It was early next morning before it was day,
   He went to his Polly, these words he did say:
   "O Polly, O Polly, you must go with me,
   Before we are married my friends for to see."

4. He led her through groves and valleys so deep
   And caused this young damsel to sigh and to weep:
   "O William, O William, you have led me astray,
   On purpose my innocent life to betray."

5. "It's true, it's true," these words he did say,
   "For all the long night I've been digging your grave,"
   The grave being open, the spade standing by,
   Which caused this young damsel to sigh and to cry.

6. "O William, O William, O pardon my life,
   I never will covet to be your wife,
   I will travel the world over to set you quite free,
   O pardon, O pardon, my baby and me."

7. "No pardon I'll give, there's no time for to stand,"
   So with that he had a knife in his hand,
   He stabb'd her heart till the blood it did flow,
   Then into the grave her fair body did throw.

8. He covered her up so safe and secure,
   Thinking no one would find her he was sure,
   Then he went on board to sail the world round,
   Before that the murder could ever be found.

9. It was early one morning before it was day,
   The captain came up, these words he did say,
   "There's a murderer on board, and he it lately has done,
   Our ship is in mourning and cannot sail on."

10. Then up stepp'd one: "Indeed it's not me,"
    Then up stepp'd another the same he did say.
    Then up starts young William to stamp and to swear:
    "Indeed it's not me, sir, I vow and declare."

11. As he was turning from the captain with speed
    He met his Polly, which made his heart bleed;
    She stript him and tore him, she tore him in three,
    Because he had murdered her baby and she.

B.

1. "Pretty Polly, pretty Polly, come go 'long with me,
   Pretty Polly, pretty Polly come go 'long with me,
   Before we get married some pleasure to see."

2. She got up behind him and away they did go,
   She got up behind him and away they did go,
   Over the hills to the valley so low.

3. They went up a little farther and what did they spy?
   They went up a little farther and what did they spy?
   A new-dug grave and a spade lying by.

4. He stobbed her to the heart, her heart blood it did flow,
   He stobbed her to the heart, her heart blood it did flow,
   And into the grave pretty Polly did go.

5. He threw somethin' over her and turned to go home,
   He threw somethin' over her and turned to go home,
   Leaving nothing behind him but the girl left to mourn.

6. Gentlemen and ladies, I'll bid you farewell,
   Gentlemen and ladies, I'll bid you farewell,
   For killin' pretty Polly will send my soul to Hell.

MOLLY BAWN

This ballad is known under many names: "Molly Bond," "Molly Van," "Vaughn," "Whan," "The Shooting of His Dear." It occurs as a broadside in both England and America. It is still sung in both countries.

Text, *JAF* (Kentucky), xxx:359.

1. Come all you young men who handle a gun,
   Be warned of shooting after the down sun.
   A story I'll tell you; it happened of late,
   Concerning Mollie Bond, whose beauty was great.

2. Mollie Bond was out walking, a shower came on;
   She sat under a beech tree the showers to shun.
   Jim Random was out hunting, a hunting in the dark;
   He shot at his true love and missed not his mark.

3. With a white apron pinned round her he took her for a swan;
   He shot and killed her; it was his Molly Bond.
   He ran to her; these words to her he said,
   And a fountain of tears on her bosom he shed.

4. Saying "Molly, dear Molly, you're the joy of my life.
   I always intended to make you my wife."
   Jim ran to his uncle with his gun in his hand,
   Saying, "Uncle, dear uncle, I've killed Mollie Bond."

5. Up stepped his dear uncle with lock's all so gray;
   Saying, "Stay at home, Jimmie, and do not run away.

Stay in your own country till your trial comes on:
You shall not be molested, if it costs me my farum."

6. The day of Jimmie's trial Mollie's ghost did appear,
Saying to the jury, "Jim Random, come clear!
With my apron pinned around me he took me for a swan.
He shot and killed me and now I am gone."

A SWEETHEART IN THE ARMY

The following two songs illustrate the popular returned-lover theme
so common in romance and ballad. Such ballads both in print and in
tradition are prevalent in England, Scotland, and America. In America there is usually the lack of recognition and consequently the testing
of the girl. The proof of identity is the token, often a broken token of
which each lover retains half. See examples of such ballads in Belden
beginning on p. 148, and compare "Hind Horn," "The Demon
Lover," "Lord William," "The Kitchie Boy," and "Katherine Jaffy."

Text A, from tradition in Aberdeenshire, about 1750, Christie,
Traditional Ballad Airs, i, 264; B, traditional in Kentucky, *JAF,*
xxii:67.

A.

1. A fair maid in a garden walking,
    A young man chanced her to see;
   He went up to her and thus address'd her,
    "Pretty maiden, could you fancy me?"
   Then first with smiling, and then reviling,
    She said, "Young man, what want ye with me?
   For I am neither to woo nor marry,
    Nor yet a servant girl to fee.

2. "I'm just a poor and forsaken maiden,
    And this makes many laugh at me;
   Tho' I had a true love once of my own,
    But it's seven years since he went to sea."
   "If it's seven years since he went to sea, may,
    Then surely he has forgotten thee;
   Or long ere now he would have wrote you,
    Were he not drowned in the sea."

3. "Where'er he be I did love him dearly;
    If he be dead I do wish him rest;
   For of all the young men that e'er I saw,
    I must declare that I lov'd him best."
   "Oh, don't you see yon bonny lands, may,
    So bonny as they lie in and out?

Oh, don't you see yon bonny castle,
 The stormy winds do blow about?

4. "Oh, don't you see this bonny garden,
 Set about wi' the flowers so fine?
Will you forsake your single sailor,
 And go yonder, and you'll be mine."
"I would not have your bonny castle,
 Were my single sailor now come home,
Nor all your lands and all your rents, sir,
 Tho' you count them up in a high sum."

5. He said, "I will no longer feign now,
 It's a pity true love should be cross'd,
I am your poor and single sailor,
 By the raging sea, you thought was lost."
"If you are my poor and single sailor,
 Your shape and colour do not agree;
But in long absence he might have changed,
 It's seven years since I did him see."

6. He pull'd his hand out of his bosom,
 His pretty fingers were long and small,
And show'd the ring they exchang'd between them,
 And, when she saw it, she down did fall.
He took her up into his arms,
 "I hope, my love, you are none the worse;
I am your poor and single sailor,
 That the raging sea has often cross'd."

7. Then he went to a priest directly,
 He thought it would end all the strife;
And the next morning they were married,
 And now she is her rich sailor's wife.

B.

1. A neat young lady at work in the garden,
 A gay young soldier came riding by.
He stepped up to this neat young lady
 And says, "Kind Miss, won't you marry me?"

2. "You're not a man of fancy honor,
 You're not the man I was taking you to be,
Imposing on a neat young lady,
 Saying, 'Kind Miss, won't you marry me?'

3. "I have a true love in the army,
 He's been gone for seven long years;

And if he's gone for seven years longer,
No man on earth can marry me."

4. "Perhaps he's dead, perhaps he's drowned,
Perhaps he's on some battlefield slain,
Perhaps he's stolen some fair girl and married her,
Perhaps you'll never see him again."

5. "If he's dead I hope he's happy,
Or if he's on some battlefield slain,
Or if he has stolen some fair girl and married her,
I love that girl for loving him."

6. He drew his hands all out of his pockets,
And his fingers both neat and small;
And the rings that shone upon them,
Beneath her feet he let them fall.

7. She picked them up on her little fingers;
The kisses she gave them was one, two, three,
Saying, "Is this my little single soldier,
Returning home to marry me?"

YOUNG EDWIN IN THE LOWLANDS LOW

This was a very popular broadside ballad widely sung over England, Scotland, and Ireland. Imported early to America, it has spread from New England and the Maritimes to the deep South. An early English and an American version are given here for comparison.

Text A, *JFSS*, iii:266; B, *JAF*, xxxv:421 (Kentucky).

A.

1. Come, all you wild young people, and listen to my song,
While I will unfold concerning gold, that guides so many wrong.
Young Emma was a servant maid and loved a sailor bold,
He ploughed the main much gold to gain, for his Love as we've been told.

2. As Emma she did daily mourn since Edwin first did roam,
When seven years were past and gone, then Edwin hailed his home.
He went unto young Emma's house to her much gold to show,
What he had gained upon the main, above the Lowlands Low.

3. Her father kept a public inn, it stood down by the sea,
Says Emma, "You can enter in and there this night can be;
I'll meet you in the morning, don't let my parents know
Your name it is young Edwin that ploughed the Lowlands Low."

4. As Emma she lay sleeping, she had a frightful dream,
   She dreamt her Love stood weeping and blood pour'd in a stream;
   She rose up in the morning and to her friends did go,
   Because she loved him dearly that ploughed the Lowlands Low.

5. "Oh, mother, where's the stranger come here last night to lay?"
   "Oh, he is dead, no tales can tell," her father he did say.
   "Then father, cruel father, you will die a public show,
   For murdering of my Edwin, that ploughed the Lowlands Low."

6. Says Emma, "I will wander down by the stormy seas,
   Where Edwin he lies under who once did brave the breeze.
   The shells that in the ocean are rolling to and fro
   Reminds me of my Edwin that ploughed the Lowlands Low.

7. "The fishes of the ocean swim o'er my lover's breast,
   His body rolls in motion, I hope his soul's at rest.
   How cruel was my parents to prove his overthrow,
   And take the gold from one so bold that ploughed the Lowlands
   Low."

8. As many a day she passed away and tried to ease her mind,
   Crying, "Oh, my friends, my Love is gone and I, poor girl, be-
   hind."
   Her friends were broken-hearted, to Bedlam forced to go,
   Their shrieks were for young Edwin that ploughed the Lowlands
   Low.

B.

1. Sweet Mary was a servant girl;
   She loved a sailor boy
   Who ploughed the main much gold to gain
   Down in the Lowlands Low.

2. "My father keeps a public house
   Down by the seaside shore,
   And you can enter there today
   And there all night may stay.

3. "I'll meet you in the morning here;
   Don't let my parents know
   Your name, young Edward dear,
   Who ploughs the Lowlands Low."

4. Young Edward he set down to drinking there
   Till time to go to bed,
   But little was he thinking then
   What soon would crown his head.

5. Young Edward rose and went to bed;
   Had scarcely gone to sleep,
   When Mary's cruel father bold
   Into his room did creep.

6. He killed him there and dragged him
   Down the seaside shore;
   He sent his body bleeding
   Down to the Lowland Low.

7. Sweet Mary she lay sleeping,
   She dreamed a frightful dream
   She dreamed she saw her lover's blood
   Flowing in a stream.

8. She rose, put on her clothes,
   Just at the break of day;
   "Father, where is that young man
   Who came last night to stay?"

9. "He's dead, he's dead, no tales to tell;
   His gold will make a show."
   "You've killed the one that loved me,
   The one that loved me so.

10. "My true-love is in the ocean,
    The waves roll o'er his breast,
    His body is in motion,
    I hope his soul's at rest."

IN BRUNTON TOWN

This ballad is a cognate, if not a derivative, of the story widely known as "Isabella and the Pot of Basil" (Boccaccio, *Decameron,* iv, 5; Keats, "Isabella, or the Pot of Basil"). *JFSS* prints several versions with the music, collected in England (*JFSS,* i:160; ii:42; v:123). Close variants occur under the names of "The Murdered Servant-Man," "The Constant Farmer's Son," "The Bramble Briar," "Over High Hills and Lonely Mountains." Though it must have existed as a broadside in England, none has been found. The only printed version, except those made directly from singers, is an American broadside which seems to derive from tradition rather than from an earlier printed version.

Text, *JAF,* xlvi:25.

1. In seaboard town there was a merchant,
   He had two sons and a daughter fair;
   And prettiest boy was bounden to him
   And to him he was the same.

2. Late one night they was silent a courting,
   Her brother's heard what they did say:
   "That long courtship shall soon be ended
   By forcing you into your grave."

3. They rose next morning early starting,
   Hunting these three men did go
   Over high hills and lonely mountains,
   And then into the place of woe.

4. Late that night while they was returning,
   She asked, "Where is the servant man?
   Oh brothers, you seem to whisper lowly,
   Oh, brothers, do tell me if you can."

5. "We lost him in some suits (?) of hunting,
   The face of him you no more shall see;
   What makes you seem so much affronted?
   Why do you examine me?"

6. Late that night while she was returning,
   His ghost to her bedside appeared;
   His face was badly bruised and bleeding,
   His cheeks all in his blood was smeared.

7. "Weep not for me, my dearest jewel,
   To weep for me 'tis all in vain;
   Go straight way to yon ditch of briars,
   There you find me dead and slain."

8. She rose next morning early starting,
   Hunting that dear boy of hers;
   She went till she came to the ditch of briars,
   And there she found him dead and slain.

9. His face was bloody as the butcher,
   Tears in his eyes like salty brine.
   She kissed his cold pale cheeks a crying,
   Saying "This dear boy was a friend of mine."

10. "Now since my brothers have been so cruel,
    As to force your dear sweet life away,
    One grave shall serve us both together,
    While I have breath with you I'll stay."

11. For three days she fasted o'er him,
    Until her heart was filled with woe;
    "I feel sharp hunger creeping o'er me,
    Homeward, or die, I'm bound to go."

12. Late that night while she was returning,
    Her brothers asked where she had been:

"Go way, go way, you cruel murderers
For this dear boy you have slain."

13. Now to get rid of the cruel murder
Was to sail across the deep blue sea.
The wind did blow and it ain't no wonder
And they (?) blew them both into their graves.

THE GREENLAND WHALE FISHERY

This is an old English broadside of the early 19th century. Brought to America early, it has been constantly reworked to fit local ships and voyages.
Text, Broadside, Pitts, London.

1. We can no longer stay on shore,
Since we are so deep in debt,
So a voyage to Greenland we will go
Some money for to get, brave boys.

2. Now when we lay at Liverpool
Our good-like ship to man,
'Twas there our names were all written down
And we're bound for Greenland, brave boys.

3. It was eighteen hundred and twenty-four
On March the twenty-third,
We hoisted our colors up to the masthead
And for Greenland bore away, brave boys.

4. But when we came to Greenland,
Our good-like ship to moor,
O then we wished ourselves back again,
With our friends upon the shore, brave boys.

5. The boatswain went up to the masthead,
With his spyglass in his hand,
"Here's a whale, a whale, a whale," he cried,
"And she blows at every spring, brave boys."

6. The captain on the quarter deck,
A very good man was he,
"Overhaul, overhaul, your boat tackle fall,
And launch your boats to sea, brave boys."

7. The boats being launched and the hands got in,
The whale fishes appeared in view.
Resolved was the whole boat's crew
To steer where the whale fish blew, brave boys.

8. The whale being struck and the line paid out,
   She gave a flash with her tail,
   She capsized the boat and lost five men
   Nor did we catch the whale, brave boys.

9. Bad news unto our captain brought,
   That we had lost 'prentice boys,
   He hearing of this dreadful news
   The colors down did haul, brave boys.

10. The losing of this whale, brave boys,
    Did grieve his heart full sore,
    But the losing of his five brave men
    Did grieve him ten times more, brave boys.

11. Come, weigh your anchors, my brave boys,
    For the winter stars I see,
    It is time we should leave this cold country
    And for England bear away, brave boys.

12. For Greenland is a barren place,
    Neither light nor day is to be seen,
    Naught but snow and ice where the whale fish blow,
    And the daylight seldom seen, brave boys.

VAN DIEMAN'S LAND

Van Dieman's Land is Tasmania, so named by its discoverer, Tasman, in honor of the Dutch governor of the East Indies. This ballad was very popular in Ireland and was generally known in England and Scotland. It reflects the practice of transporting criminals to Australia as colonists. Transportation to Tasmania obtained only between 1803 and 1839. This suggests that the ballad was composed early in the 19th century.

Text as sung to M.E.L. by Jack Keogh, Flatrock, Newfoundland, 1951.

1. Come all ye boys of Liverpool I'd have you to beware,
   When ye go a huntin with your dog and gun and snare,
   Watch for the land keeper; keep your dog at your command,
   And think on all the sorrow going to Van Dieman's Land.

2. We had two Irish lads on board, Jimmie Murphy and Pat Malone,
   And they were both the best friends that any man could own.
   The land keeper, he caught them and from old England land
   They were fourteen years transported to plough Van Dieman's Land.

3. We had an Irish girl on board, Mary Brophy was her name,
   And she was sent from Liverpool, for a playing of the game.
   She took the captain's fancy and he married her out of hand
   And the best usage she gave us, going to Van Dieman's Land.

4. The first day that they landed us all on that fateful shore,
   The planters gathered round us, full twenty score or more;
   They led us round like horses and sold us out of hand,
   And yoked us to the plow, me boys, to plow Van Dieman's Land.

5. As I lay in the bed one night a dreamin all alone,
   I dreamed I was in Liverpool down by a purling stream,
   With my true-love beside me, and her at my command,
   I awoke all broken-hearted, lying in Van Dieman's Land.

AMERICAN BALLADS

BY ORIGIN OR ADOPTION

PAUL JONES

Two ballads concerning Paul Jones are still in tradition. One tells of an expedition of Jones in the *Ranger;* and the other, the one printed here, of an engagement between the *Bon Homme Richard* and the *Serapis* convoying a fleet of forty sails off Flambough Head.

Text, from tradition as recorded by Lewis Chappell, *Folk Songs of Roanoke and the Albemarle,* p. 48.

1. Our forty-gun frigate from Baltimore came,
   Her guns mounted forty, the *Richard* by name,
   Went cruising the channel of old England land,
   With a noble commander, Paul Jones was the man.
   Hurrah! our country forever, hurrah!

2. We had not sailed long before we espied
   A large forty-four and a twenty close by;
   Those warships vessels full laden in store,
   Our captain pursued them on bold Europe's shore.
   Hurrah! etc.

3. At the hour of twelve Pierce he came alongside;
   With a loud speaking trupet, "Whence come you?" I cried;
   "Quick, give me an answer, I've hailed you before,
   Or at this very instant a broadside I'll pour."
   Hurrah! etc.

4. When the broadside was sent by those brave Englishmen,
   Like bold buckskin heroes we returned it again.
   Hurrah! etc.

5. We fought them five glasses, five glasses so hot,
   Till sixty bold seamen lie dead on the spot
   And seventy more lie bleeding in gore
   How fierce our loud cannons on the Richard did roar.
   Hurrah! etc.

6. Our gunner got frightened and to Paul Jones he came:
   Our ship is a-sinking, likewise in a flame;
   Paul Jones he smiled in the height of his pride,
   Saying, "This day I'll conquer or sink alongside."
   Hurrah! etc.

LOVEWELL'S FIGHT

Mrs. Eckstorm thought that this ballad was composed by Benjamin Franklin, uncle of the better-known Benjamin Franklin, about the time of the events it describes. It was printed in 1725 by James Franklin in Boston as a broadside and thence went into tradition. For many years it was "the best loved song in New England." Two versions of the ballad have been recorded—one here printed from a source not noticed before, Thomas Church, *The History of King Phillips' War,* 1829. This version is in seven-stress quatrains, rhyming in couplets, a common old ballad meter. The other version is in three stress quatrains, rhyming in ab, cb.

> "Of Worthy Captain Lovewell
> My purpose is to sing,
> How willingly he served
> His country and his king."

The ballad celebrates the fight between the colonists under Captain John Lovewell of Dunstable, Mass., against the Indians at Pigwacket, near present Fryeburg, Maine. It is interesting and instructive to compare this "border ballad" of America with such ballads in England and Scotland, especially for details and in relation to history. Like the English ballads, "Lovewell's Fight" does not tell a very accurate story; in fact, Mrs. Eckstorm shows that there was deliberate manipulation of the facts by Parson Symmes to cover up a scandal in connection with the affair. Lovewell and his men were animated largely by the reward of one hundred pounds for each scalp taken; in the three months before this fight they had made twelve hundred pounds.

Notes

2/1. eight: the battle was fought on May 9th.   2/4. Saco Pond.
5/4. Parson Symmes says that Ensign Wyman shot him, and that Mr. Frye, the Chaplain, and another scalped him.   16/2. Lieutenant Robins was left on the field with two loaded guns so that "when the Indians came on the next day to scalp him, he could kill at least one more." Frye, Harvard, 1723, was the Chaplain.   17/4. Wyman was commissioned Captain during the week of May 16th. He was the real hero of the affair, having saved the colonists from a disastrous defeat.
18/1. Paugus was known to the men personally. Notes in Church, from which these notes are taken, say that he was killed by John Chamberlain in a single combat after Paugus had challenged him to a fight to the death. The story is probably an invention of Symmes to glorify Chamberlain.

1.   Of worthy Captain Lovewell, I purpose now to sing,
     How valiantly he served his country and his King;

He and his valiant soldiers, did range the woods full wide,
And harships they endured to quell the Indians' pride.

2. 'Twas nigh unto Pigwacket, on the eight day of May,
   They spied a rebel Indian soon after break of day;
   He on a bank was walking, upon a neck of land,
   Which leads into a pond as we're made to understand.

3. Our men resolv'd to have him and travell'd two miles round,
   Until they met the Indian, who boldly stood his ground;
   Then spake up Captain Lovewell, "Take you good heed," says
      he,
   "This rogue is to decoy us, I very plainly see.

4. "The Indians lie in ambush, in some place nigh at hand,
   In order to surround us upon this neck of land;
   Therefore we'll march in order, and each man leave his pack,
   That we may briskly fight them when they make their attack."

5. They came unto this Indian, who did them thus defy,
   As soon as they came nigh him, two guns he did let fly,
   Which wounded Captain Lovewell, and likewise one man more,
   But when this rogue was running, they laid him in his gore.

6. Then having scalp'd the Indian, they went back to the spot,
   Where they had laid their packs down, but there they found
      them not,
   For the Indians having spy'd them, when they them down did
      lay,
   Did seize them for their plunder, and carry them away.

7. These rebels lay in ambush, this very place hard by,
   So that an English soldier did one of them espy,
   And cried out "Here's an Indian," with that they started out,
   As fiercely as old lions, and hideously did shout.

8. With that our valiant English, all gave a loud huzza,
   To shew the rebel Indians they fear'd them not a straw;
   So now the fight began, and as fiercely as could be,
   The Indians ran up to them, but soon were forc'd to flee.

9. Then spake up Captain Lovewell, when first the fight began,
   "Fight on my valiant heroes! You see they fall like rain."
   For as we are inform'd, the Indians were so thick,
   A man could scarcely fire a gun and not some of them hit.

10. Then did the rebels try their best our soldiers to surround,
    But they could not accomplish it, because there was a pond,
    To which our men retreated and covered all the rear,
    The rogues were forc'd to flee them, altho' they skulk'd for fear.

11.   Two logs there were behind them, that close together lay,
      Without being discovered, they could not get away;
      Therefore our valiant English, they travell'd in a row,
      And at a handsome distance as they were wont to go.

12.   'Twas 10 o'clock in the morning, when first the fight begun,
      And fiercely did continue until the setting sun,
      Excepting that the Indians, some hours before 'twas night,
      Drew off into the bushes and ceased awhile to fight.

13.   But soon again returned, in fierce and furious mood,
      Shouting as in the morning, but yet not half so loud;
      For as we are informed, so thick and fast they fell,
      Scarce twenty of their number at night did get home well.

14.   And that our valiant English, till midnight there did stay,
      To see whether the rebels would have another fray;
      But they no more returning, they made off towards their home,
      And brought away their wounded as far as they could come.

15.   Of all our valiant English, there were but thirty-four,
      And of the rebel Indians, there were about four score.
      And sixteen of our English did safely home return,
      The rest were killed and wounded, for which we all must
         mourn.

16.   Our worthy Captain Lovewell among them there did die,
      They killed Lt. Robins, and wounded good young Frye,
      Who was our English chaplain; he many Indians slew,
      And some of them he scalp'd when bullets round him flew.

17.   Young Fullam too I'll mention, because he fought so well,
      Endeavouring to save a man, a sacrifice he fell;
      But yet our valiant Englishmen in fight were ne'er dismay'd,
      But still they kept their motion, and Wyman's Captain made,

18.   Who shot the old chief Paugus, which did the foe defeat,
      Then set his men in order, and brought off the retreat;
      And braving many dangers and hardships in the way,
      They safe arriv'd at Dunstable, the thirteenth day of May.

BRAVE WOLFE

This ballad, one of two different versions based on Wolfe's death at
Quebec, is still in current tradition in New York state. Wolfe was engaged to be married to Katherine Lowther at the time of his death.
During the siege of Quebec Wolfe was mortally ill, and knowing his
condition he begged the physician to give him stimulants so that he
could lead his men in the battle. He was wounded three times and

died of the wounds September 13, 1779. The poem for all its transmission by folk is still stiff with literary starch.

Text A, from New York and printed by Harold Thompson in *Body, Boots and Britches*, p. 323; B as sung to M.E.L. by George Pullen, Rappahannock County, Virginia.

A.

1. Cheer up, ye young men all, let nothing fright you;
   Though at your love's pursuits, let that delight you;
   Don't let your fancy move when come to trial,
   Nor let your courage fail at the first denial.

2. "Bad news has come to town, bad news has carried;
   Bad news is whispered round—my love is married.
   I'll away to the wars of France where cannon rattle,
   Myself I will advance in the front of battle.

3. "I would go tell my love I'm going to leave her,
   Down to the wars of France I'm bound forever;
   But whene'er I go to speak, my tongue doth quiver,
   So I dare not tell my mind when I am with her.

4. "Here is a ring of gold, if you'll accept it;
   Here, here is a ring of gold, long time I've kept it.
   Whene'er you the posy read, think of the giver.
   Madam, remember me; I'm done forever."

5. So then this gallant youth took to the ocean
   To free America from its commotion.
   We landed at Quebec with all our party,
   The city to attack, being brave and hearty.

6. Brave Wolfe drew up his men in a line most pretty
   On the plains of Abraham just before the city.
   Not far distant from that place the French did meet us,
   With double our number of men resolved to beat us.

7. Brave Wolfe and Montcalm like brothers talked,
   And lovingly between their armies walked,
   Till each one took his post as they retired;
   Brave Wolfe took his leave and for death prepared.

8. Till each one took his post as they retired.
   So then this numerous host began their fire,
   When shot down from his horse fell this brave hero.
   We do lament his loss in words of sorrow.

9. He lifted up his head as he lay dying;
   The French their ranks had broke, and the troops were flying.
   He lifted up his head while the drum did rattle,
   And to his army said, "How goes the battle?"

10. His aide-de-camp replied: "All in our favor.
　　　Quebec will fall a prize, nothing can save her;
　　　She'll fall into our hands with all her treasure."
　　　So then replies brave Wolfe, "I die with pleasure."

B.

1. Cheer up, all you young men,
　　Let noth-in' fright you,
　　When e'er objections rise,
　　Let it delight you!
　　Don't let your courage fail,
　　When you come to trial,
　　Nor let your fancy move
　　At the first denial.

2. I went to see my love,
　　Thinkin' to win her,
　　I went to see my love,
　　Not to delude her.
　　When e'er I went to speak
　　My tongue did quiver,
　　I dare not speak my mind
　　While I was with her.

3. Love, here's a ring of gold,
　　Long time I've kept it,
　　Love, here's a ring of gold,
　　If you'll keep it.
　　When you the posy read
　　Think of the giver,
　　Darling, remember me,
　　I'm undone forever.

4. An' then this youth
　　Took to the ocean,
　　To free America
　　From the French invasion.
　　He landed at Quebec
　　With all his party,
　　The city to attack,
　　brave an hearty.

5. Brave Wolfe drew up his men
　　In a line so pretty,
　　On the plains of Abraham
　　Before the city.
　　A distance from the town
　　Come the French to meet them,

With double number men
Resolved for to beat them.

6. Brave Wolfe an' General Montcalm
    Together walked,
    Betwixt their armies both
    Together talked.
    Brave Wolfe says to Montcalm,
    It's our country's fate, sir,
    On your honor I depend,
    I'm the one who takes her.

7. Then each one took his post
    At their retire,
    An' then this numerous host
    Began their fire.
    'Twas an instant from his horse
    Fell this brave hero,
    An' all lament his loss
    In tears of sorrow.

8. The French they seemed to break
    With colors flyin',
    Brave Wolfe he seemed to wake
    Yet he was dyin',
    He raised up his head
    Where the cannons rattled,
    An' to his army said
    How goes the battle?

9. His army then replied,
    All in our favor,
    Quebec an' all her pride,
    Nothin' can save her.
    She'll fall into our hands
    With all her treasure!
    At last, said brave Wolfe,
    I die with pleasure.

SPRINGFIELD MOUNTAIN

This is one of the most widespread and varied of original American ballads. On August 7, 1761, one Timothy Myrick, son of Lieutenant Thomas Myrick of Wilberham, formerly Springfield Mountain, Mass., died of a rattlesnake bite. This ballad is based on that event; exactly when the song was composed and by whom is still unsettled. Some scholars think it was made almost immediately after the event; others, notably Barry, put it not earlier than "the second quarter of the last century." Barry distinguished four distinct types of "Spring-field Mountain," which he calls respectively (1) the Myrick type; (2) the Curtis type; (3) the Sally type; (4) the Molly type. The first two are based on the names of the young man as given in the ballad, and the last two on the names of his supposed sweetheart. The last two types are definitely of professional stage tradition; they went from the stage and printed form back into folk tradition. Today all four types are found with many cross variations. For details see Phillips Barry's discussion in various numbers of the *Bulletin of the Folk-song Society of the Northeast*.

The present texts are from New England as printed in the *Bulletin* (text I in vol. vii; text II in vol. viii; text III in vol. x; text IV in vol. xi).

I
(The Myrick Type)

1. On Springfield Mountain there did dwell
   a likely youth 'twas known full well,
   Left'ts Merrick's only Son,
   A likely youth near twenty-one.

2. One Friday Morning he did go
   down to the Meadow for to mow;
   Hee mowed around and he did feel
   a poisoning Serpent at his heel.

3. When he received this deadly wound
   He dropped his Scythe upon the ground
   and straight for Home was his intent,
   calling aloud Still as he went.

4. 't was all around his voice was heard
   but unto him no friend appeared;
   They thought he did Some workman call
   but Timothy alone must fall.

5. At length his careful Father went
   to seek his Son in discontent
   and there his only Son he found
   Dead as a Stone lay on the ground.

6. 't was the Seventh of August year 61
   this fatal accident was done.
   May this a warning be to all
   to be prepared when God shall call.

7. Who knows but that his blessed feet
   are treading the Celestial Street,
   the brightest Angels bowing round
   Jehovah and his golden crown.

II
(The Curtis Type)

1. On Springfield Mountain there did dwell
   A likely youth and known full well—
   A likely youth of twenty one,
   Leftenant Curts's only son—
      Only son, only son, only son—
      Leftenant Curts's only son.

2. One Monday morning he did go
   Down to the meadow for to mow.
   He mowed all day. At last he feels
   A pison sarpent bite his heels.
      Bite his heels, bite his heels, bite his heels—
      A pison sarpent bite his heels.

3. He laid his scythe upon the ground—
   He laid it down and looked around
   To see if nobody he couldn't espy
   To carry him home that he might die—
      That he might die, that he might die, that he might die—
      To carry him home that he might die.

4. He looked around, but looked in vain,—
   No one was there to ease his pain;
   So he made up his mind his time had come,
   And laid his head on a cold stun—
      On a cold stun, a cold stun, a cold stun—
      And laid his head on a cold stun.

5. So this young man gave up the ghost,
   And forth to Abraham's bosom did post
   Out of the meadow he came to mow,
   With nobody by to see him go,
      To see him go, see him go, see him go,
      With nobody by to see him go.

III
(The Sally Type)

1. On Springfield Mountain there did dwell,
   A lovely youth I knew full well;
      Ri tuga nuga nay, ru tuga nuga nay,
      Ri tuga nuga nuga nuga, na di O.

2. He took his scythe and off did go,
   Down in the meadow for to mow.

3. And as he mowed across the field,
   A poisonous serpent bit him on the heel.

4. They bore him to his Sally dear,
   Which made him feel so deuced queer.

5. "Why, Johnny dear, why did you go
   Down to the meadow for to mow?"

6. "Why, Sally dear, and didn't you know,
   'Twas Daddy's grass and it had to be mowed?"

7. At last he died, gave up the ghost,
   To Moses' bosom he did post.

8. Now young and old, a warning take,
   And shun the bite of a rattlesnake.

IV
(The Molly Type)

1. On Springfield mountain there did dwell
   A comely youth I knew full well,
    Ri tu ri nu, ri tu di na,
    Ri tu di nu, ri tu di na.

2. One Monday morning he did go
   Down in the meadow for to mow.

3. He scarce had mow-ed half the field,
   When a PESKY SARPENT bit his heel.

4. He took his scythe and with a blow
   He laid the pesky Sarpent low.

5. He took the Sarpent in his hand,
   And straitway went to Molly Bland.

6. Oh Molly, Molly, here you see
   The Pesky Sarpent what bit me.

7. Now Molly had a ruby lip
   With which the pizen she did sip.

8. But Molly had a rotten tooth,
   Which the Pizen struck and kill'd 'em both.

9. The neighbors found that they were dead,
   So laid them both upon one bed.

10. And all their friends both far and near
    Did cry and howl they were so dear.

11. Now all you maids a warning take,
    From Molly Bland and Tommy Blake.

12. And mind when you're in love, don't pass
    Too near to patches of high grass.

YOUNG CHARLOTTE

This ballad is based on an event that occurred in 1840. The ballad or part of it was composed by Seba Smith, a well-known journalist, and published in *The Rover* in 1843, under the title, "A Corpse Going to a Ball." W. L. Carter, a poet of Benson, Vermont, perhaps added stanzas; at any rate he must have associated the ballad with its western tune, for he certainly took it west when he joined the Mormons there. The song is very common among the lumbermen and is consequently found throughout the lumbering region. The lumbermen sing it to an Irish tune. It is interesting that one of Mrs. Eddy's informants told her that the incident occurred to one Charlotte Dills in 1862 at Auburn, Indiana, and added that the lady had two brothers who were lawyers and one who was a minister! Others likewise report independent knowledge of the tragedy; a Vermonter who furnished one of the texts said that the event occurred on a New Year's Eve in Vermont and that he knew the people; the New York text is from Fern Bishop, whose grandmother taught it to her and said that it had happened in Jefferson County, New York. All of this illustrates how information about traditional songs gets confused.

Text as sung by Mrs. Tiny Gaunt, Rappahannock County, Virginia to M.E.L., 1948.

1. Young Charlotte lived on a mountain side,
   In a wild and lonely spot;
   There was no other dwelling for five miles 'round
   Except her father's cot.

2. Her father owned the social board,
   And she was light and fair,
   And many a cold and winter night
   Young swains would gather there.

3. 'Twas New Year's Eve, the sun was low,
   Joy beamed in her mild blue eyes;
   And she sat and waited until Young Charles
   Came dashing swiftly by.

4. "Oh, daughter, dear!" the mother cried,
   "This blanket around you fold,
   For 'tis a dreadful night abroad
   And you'll take your death of cold."

5. "Oh, no! Oh, no!" the daughter cried,
   And she laughed like a gypsy queen;
   "To ride in a blanket all muffled up
   I never shall be seen.

6. "My silken cloak is quite enough,
   You know it's lined throughout;
   Besides I have a silken scarf
   To wrap my neck about."

7. Cloak and bonnet she put on,
   They stepped into the sleigh,
   And o'er hills and valley down
   For many a mile away.

8. In a village not more than fifty miles away,
   There's a royal ball tonight,
   The air is deathly freezing cold,
   But their hearts were young and light.

9. "Such a night," says Charles, "I never knew,
   My reins I scarce can hold;"
   Young Charlotte spoke in a frozen voice,
   "I am growing very cold."

10. He cracked his whip, he urged his team
    Much faster than before;
    Five miles in silence they rode on
    And neither spoke a word.

11. "How fast," said Charles, "this frosty ice
    Keeps gathering on my brow;"
    Young Charlotte spoke in a broken tone,
    "I am growing warmer now."

12. They drove up to the ball-room door
    He gave his hand to her
    "Why sit you like a monument
    That hath no power to stir?"

13. He asked her once, he asked her twice,
    Still she answered not a word;
    He asked her the third time then
    And still she never stirred.

14. He took her hand in his, and God,
    It was cold as any stone!
    He pulled the robe off her brow
    And the cold stars on her shone.

15. He then did kneel down by her side
    And kissed her marble brow;

"My once, my own intended bride,
You never more shall know."

16. He bore her out into the sleigh
And with her quickly drove he home,
And when he reached the cottage door
Oh, how her parents mourned.

17. They mourned the loss of their daughter dear
And Charles mourned o'er his doom,
He mourned until his heart did break
They sleep soundly in one tomb.

THE LITTLE MOHEE

This is an American ballad. Barry argues that it originated as a
"land" ballad of the love of an Indian girl for a white settler and was
then made over by sailors into a sailor's song. *Mohee* could be the
name of the Indian tribe, Miami of Ohio, and later be applied to the
Island of Maui (pronounced Mohee) in the Sandwich group. The
ballad has a number of variants, among which are several locating the
action in New Orleans.

Text from Mrs. David Kendall, Rappahannock County, Virginia,
as sung to M.E.L., 1947.

1. As I was a-roaming for pleasure one day,
For love's recreation, with thoughts far away;
As I sat amusing myself on the grass,
There stepped up beside me a fair Indian lass.

2. She sat down beside me, and taking my hand,
Said, "I know you're a stranger, and in a strange land;
But if you will follow, you're welcome to come,
For I live by myself in a snug little home."

3. The sun was just sinking just o'er the blue sea
As I walked along with this little Mohee;
Together we rambled, together we roamed,
Till we came to the cot in a cocoanut grove.

4. In the kindest of manners, she said unto me,
"If you will consent, Sir, to stay here with me,
No more to go roaming o'er all the blue sea,
I'll teach you the language of the little Mohee."

5. "Ah, no, my fair maiden, this never can be,
For I have a sweetheart in my own country;

And I'll not forsake her in her poverty,
For she's just as fair as the little Mohee."

6. The last time I saw her, 'twas down on the sand,
    As I was a-leaving, she waved me her hand,
    Saying, "When you get back to the maid that you love,
    Remember the lass in the cocoanut grove."

7. Now I'm safe landed on my native shore
    With friends and relations around me once more;
    As I gaze around me, there's none whom I see
    That I can compare with my pretty Mohee.

8. And the girl that I trusted proved untrue to me,
    So I'll turn my course backward, far o'er the blue sea;
    I'll turn my course backward, from here will I flee,
    I'll go spend my days with my little Mohee.

LOST JIMMIE WHALEN

This ballad, it would seem, is a genuine American product, for no European version exists so far as I can discover. The ballad lives in tradition in the Maritimes and in Maine. Barry suggests that the revenant is returning from "the Irish under-water other world." It seems rather, in view of lines 2/3–4, that he was drowned and that he is rising from his grave under the river. How insipid and cheaply sentimental this story of a revenant appears beside "The Unquiet Grave" or "The Wife of Usher's Well."

Text from Maine and printed in *Bulletin,* 11.

1. As lonely I strayed by the banks of the river,
    I was watching the sunbeams as evening drew nigh;
    As onward I rambled, I spied a fair damsel;
    She was weeping and wailing with many a sigh.

2. Crying for one who now lies a-sleeping,
    She was crying for one that no mortal could save;
    As the dark-rolling waters that roll all around him,
    As onward they sweep towards young Jimmie's grave.

3. "Darling," she cried, "won't you come to my bosom,
    And give me sweet kisses as oft times you gave?
    You promised to meet me, my darling, this evening—
    O come to me, Jimmie dear, come from your grave!"

4. Slowly there rose from the depths of the waters,
    A vision of splendor more bright than the sun;
    With robes of crimson around him were shining;
    For to speak to this fair maid, these words he began.

5. "Why have you called me from realms of glory,
   Back to this world I soon have to part?
   To fold you again in my strong, loving arms,
   For to see you once more, I have come from my grave."

6. "Oh, hard were my struggles from the wild, rushing waters,
   That encircled around me on every side;
   And the last thought I had was of God—darling,
   I was hoping one day that you'd sure be my bride."

7. "Jimmie," she cried, "won't you tarry here with me,
   And never, no never, no more from me part?
   Then take me away with you, Jimmie, my darling,
   For to sleep with you, down in your cold silent grave!"

8. "Darling," he says, "you are asking a favor
   Which no mortal person can grant unto thee;
   For death is the dagger that keeps us asunder,
   And wide is the gulf lies between you and me."

9. "Still, as you wander alone by the waters,
   I will ever be near you to guide and to save;
   I will ever endeavor to keep you from danger,
   I will guide you, my darling, from my silent grave."

10. "Adieu," then he said, and he vanished before her;
    And straight to the skies he did seem for to go;
    Leaving this fair maid alone and distracted,
    A-weeping and wailing in sorrow alone.

11. As she sank down on the ground she was standing,
    With the deepest of sorrow, these words she did say:
    "My darling," she cried, "O my lost Jimmie Whalen,
    I will sigh till I die by the side of your grave."

THE DROWSY SLEEPER

This is a very interesting ballad with a wide range in time and space
(see C. R. Baskerville, *PMLA*, xxxiv:565). It basically takes the
form of a dialogue between a lover and his mistress at her bedroom
window, he asking her to get her parents' consent to their marriage.
It ends in a variety of ways: her father may appear on the scene; the
lover may enter and spend the night with the lady; he may get a denial and go away disconsolate; or he may stab himself. Broadsides of
this exist in England and America.

Text A, traditional in Kentucky and printed in *JAF*, xx:260; B,
Christie, *Traditional Ballad Airs*, i, 225.

1. "Wake up, wake up, you drowsy sleeper,
   Wake up, wake up, it's almost day;
   How can you bear to sleep and slumber
   When your own true love is going away?"

2. "Who's this, who's this at my bedroom window,
   Calling so earnestly for me?"
   "Lie low, lie low, it's your own true lover;
   Awake, arise, and pity me.

3. "O love, go and ask your mother
   If my bride you ever can be;
   And if she says no, come back and tell me,
   It's the very last time I'll trouble thee."

4. "I dare (not) go and ask my mother
   If your bride I can ever be;
   Go your way and court another,"
   She whispered low in her true love's ear.

5. "O love, go and ask your father,
   If my bride you ever can be;
   If he says no, come back and tell me,
   It's the very last time I'll trouble thee."

6. "I dare (not) go and ask my father,
   For he is on his bed of rest,
   And in his arms he holds a weapon
   To kill the one I love the best."

7. "O, Mary, Mary, loving Mary,
   My heart is almost broke for you;
   From North Carolina to Pennsylvania
   I'll spend my hours and days with you.

8. "I'll move my boat to some other river,
   And by its waters I'll sit down;
   I'll eat nothing but green willow,
   I'll drink nothing but my tears."

9. "Come back, come back, you distracted lover,
   Come back, ...
   And I'll forsake, I'll forsake father and mother,
   Forsake them all and go with you."

B.

"Oh, I will put my ship in order,
And I will set her to the sea;
And I will sail to yonder harbour,
To see if my love will marry me."

He sailed eastward; he sailed westward;
He sailed far, far by sea and land;
By France and Flanders, Spain and Dover,
He sail'd the world all round and round,

Till he came to his love's sweet bower,
It was to hear what she would say.
"Awake, awake, ye lovely sleeper,
The sun is spreading the break of day."
"Oh, who is this at my bower window,
That speaks so lovingly to me?"
It is your own true constant lover,
That would now have some words with thee.

"Oh, ye will now go to your father,
And see if he'll let you my bride be;
If he denies you come and tell me,
'Twill be the last time I'll visit thee."
"My father is in his chamber sleeping,
Now taking to him his natural rest,
And at his hand there lies a letter,
That speaketh much to thy dispraise."

"To my dispraise, love?" "To thy dispraise, love."
"To my dispraise! How can that be?
I never grieved you nor deceived you,
I fear, my love, you're forsaking me.
But you will now go to your stepmother,
And see if she'll let you my bride be;
If she denies you come and tell me,
'Twill be the last time I'll visit thee."

"My mother is in her bower dressing,
And combing down her yellow hair;
Begone, young man, you may court another,
And whisper softly in her ear."
Then hooly, hooly raise up his lover,
And quickly put her clothing on;
But ere she got the door unlocked
Her true lover now was gone.

"Oh, are ye gone, love? Are ye gone, love?
Oh, are ye gone, and now left me?
I never grieved you, nor yet deceiv'd you,
But now I fear you are slighting me."
"The fish shall fly, love; the sea shall dry, love,
The rocks shall melt wi' the sun;
The blackbird shall give over singing,
Before that I return again."

"Oh, are you gone, love? Are you gone, love?
Oh, are you gone, and left me now?
It was not me; it was my stepmother,
That spoke to you from her bower window."
He turned him right and round so quickly,
Says, "Come with me, my lovely one,
And we'll be wed, my own sweet lover,
And let them talk when we are gone."

THE SILVER DAGGER

No printed version of this purely American ballad has been found, in spite of its literary touches. It is known widely throughout the South and West. Stanzas drift from it into "The Drowsy Sleeper." Randolph, *Ozark Folksongs,* ii, 55, records one version which ends with this "particularly touching" substitution for the rose and briar motif:

"A double coffin was directed,
Their hands placed on each other's breast,
An' now the lovers lie asleepin'
Together in eternal rest."

Text from the singing of Mrs. Tiny Gaunt, Rappahannock County, Virginia, to M. E. L. in 1948.

1. Young men and maids, pray lend attention
   Of these few lines I'm going to write,
   Of a young youth, no name I'll mention,
   Who courted a damsel, a beauty bright.

2. When his old parents came to know this,
   They strove to part them day and night;
   They strove to part him from his jewel,
   "She's poor, she's poor," they often cried.

3. Down on his bended knees he pleaded,
   Crying, "Father, mother, pity me!
   She is my own, my dearest jewel
   What's this world without her to be?"

4. She turned her back unto the city,
   She walked the green fields and meadows around;
   She walked unto some fair broad waters
   And under a shady grove sat down.

5. She picked up her silver dagger,
   Pierced it through her snow-white breast;

She said these words and gave a stagger;
"Farewell true love! I'm going to rest."

6. Her love, being out upon the water,
    Chanced to hear her dying groan;
He ran, he ran like one distracted:
    "I am ruined, I'm lost, I am left alone."

7. She opened her coal-black eyes upon him
    Saying, "O true love, you've come too late!
But meet me on the old road Zion,
    Where all our joys will be complete."

8. He picked up the bloody dagger,
    Pierced it through his tender heart:
Let this be a sad and woeful warning
    To all true lovers that have to part.

THE FAIR MAID BY THE SEASHORE

A widespread story in ballad and folk tale tells of a ship captain luring a lady on board a vessel and then sailing away with her. See Grimm's "The Faithful Servitor" and many references to that story. This story rather belongs to the tradition in which the lady escapes by one route or another. The American ballad found largely on the eastern seaboard is certainly drawn from a British broadside. For more discussion see *Bulletin*, vii:12, whence this text comes.

1. There was a fair lady far crossed in love,
    Far crossed in love as it were, O;
Nothing could she find to ease her fair mind,
    Than to stray all along the sea shore, O,
    Than to stray all along the sea shore.

2. There was a sea captain a-ploughing the deep,
    A-ploughing the deep as it were, O,
Nothing could he find to ease his sad mind,
    Than to sail all along the sea shore, O.

3. "I shall die, I shall die," the sea captain he cried,
    "If I don't get that lady so fair, O;
What will I not give to my jolly seamen,
    If they'll bring that fair damsel on board, O!"

4. "O, I have got silver and I have got gold,
    And I have got costly a ware, O;
All these I will give to my jolly seamen,
    If they'll bring this fair damsel on board, O."

5. With many persuasions she came on board,
      The captain he welcomed her there, O ;
   He welcomed her down to the cabin below,
      Saying, "Fare thee well, sorrow and care, O !"

6. She sang him a song, it was at his request,
      She sang it so sweet and so fair, O ;
   She sang it so sweet, so neat and complete,
      That she sang the sea captain to sleep, O.

7. Then she robbed him of silver, she robbed him of gold,
      She robbed him of costly a ware, O ;
   And the captain's broadsword she used for an oar,
      And she paddled her boat to the shore, O.

8. "O were my men sleeping, or were my men mad,
      Or were my men sunk in despair, O,
   That that lady so gay should thus run away,
      When the captain he welcomed her there, O ?"

9. "No, your men were not sleeping, your men were not mad,
      Your men were not sunk in despair, O ;
   I deluded your crew and likewise yourself too,
      And again I'm a maid on the shore, O !"

WILLIE LEONARD
OR THE LAKE OF COLD FINN

Barry very rightly remarks that this ballad is a "popular ballad in
every sense in which Child and his successors have understood the
phrase." It came to America from Ireland as a broadside, but since
has become traditional, variants being reported from Newfoundland
to New York state. 'n Ireland the song is still traditional. The complete story, no longer quite clear in the American versions, tells of
Willie being lured by a mermaid to the lake and drowned. One of the
Maine versions suggests that it was to a vanishing island that she
lured him. Cf. the following two stanzas which stand in place of
stanza 3 of the version here printed:

   Young Willie stripped off to swim the lake round ;
   He swam to an island, and came to dry ground,
      Saying, "Comrade, my comrade, don't venture to come in,
   For there's depth and false water in the Lake of Cool Finn."

   He went in again to swim it once more ;
   He swam it most over, but could not find dry ground,
      Saying, "Comrade, loyal comrade, I feel very weak,"
   And these were the last words Willie Lanard did speak.

Text from New Brunswick, printed in *Bulletin,* viii.

1. It was early Monday morning Willie Leonard arose,
   And straight to his comrade, young Leonard did go;
   Saying, "Arise, loyal comrade, and let nobody know,
   It's a fine summer morning, and a-bathing we will go."

2. They walked and they talked till they came to a lane,
   And the first one they met was a keeper of game;
   Saying, "Go back, Willie Leonard, do not venture in,
   For there's deep and false water in the Lake of Cold Finn."

3. Willie stripped off his clothes and he swam the lake around,
   He swam to an island, but not to dry ground;
   "Go back, loyal comrade, do not venture in,
   For there's deep and false water in the Lake of Cold Finn!"

4. It was early next morning Willie's sister arose,
   And straight to the bedchamber of her mother she goes;
   "Oh, mother, dear mother, I had a strange dream,
   I dreamed I saw Willie in a cold watery stream!"

5. It was early next morning Willie's mother was there,
   A-wringing of her hands and a-tearing of her hair;
   "Oh, murder, oh, murder,—was there nobody nigh,
   That would venture their life for my own darling boy?"

6. It was early next morning Willie's uncle was there,
   And he swam around the lake like a man in despair;
   "Was he surely drowned, or did he fall in?
   For there's deep and false water in the lake of Cold Finn!"

7. The day of Willie's funeral will be a grand sight,
   There will be four and twenty young men all dressed up in white;
   They will follow his remains till it's laid in the clay,
   They will (bid) young Willie adieu, and they will all march
   away.

8. For to see Willie's mother, it would grieve your heart sore,
   And to see Willie's sweetheart, it would grieve your heart more,
   For every fine morning he would her salute,
   With his pinks and red roses and fine garden fruit.

MARY OF THE WILD MOOR

That this song should be so popular in both England and America from the last half of the 19th century is indicative of the level of the general taste of the times. It was in and out of tradition, being printed in dozens of broadsides and collections. The air to which it was sung may have had something to do with keeping it alive.

Text from Iowa, published in *MAF*, xxix:28.

1. One night the wind it blew cold,
    Blew bitter across the wild moor;
    Young Mary she came with her child
    Wand'ring home to her own father's door;
    Crying, "Father, oh! pray let me in,
    Take pity on me I implore!
    Or the child at my bosom will die
    From the winds that blow 'cross the wild moor.

2. "Oh, why did I leave this fair cot
    Where once I was happy and free;
    Doomed to roam without friends or home—
    Oh! Father, take pity on me."
    But her father was deaf to her cries,
    Not a voice nor a sound reached the door;
    But the watch-dog did bark, and winds
    Blew bitter across the wild moor.

3. Oh, how must her father have felt
    When he came to the door in the morn!
    There he found Mary dead, and the child
    Fondly clasped to its dead mother's form.
    How in frenzy he tore his grey hairs,
    As on Mary he gazed at the door;
    For that night she had perished and died
    From the winds that blew 'cross the wild moor.

4. The father in grief pined away,
    The child to the grave was soon borne,
    And no one lives there to this day
    For the cottage to ruin has gone.
    The villagers point out the spot
    Where a willow droops over the door.
    Saying, "There Mary perished and died
    From the winds that blew 'cross the wild moor."

THE LITTLE FAMILY

This doubtless goes back to an English stall ballad. It is found in America in only one version and with few variations of text. It seems to survive in America through the South and the Middle West.

Text as sung by Mrs. Tiny Gaunt, Rappahannock County, Virginia, to M.E.L. 1948.

1. There was a little family
   Who lived in Bethany;
   Two sisters and a brother
   Composed this family.

2. With praying and with singing,
   Like angels in the sky,
   At morning and at evening,
   They raised their voices high.

3. They lived in peace and pleasure
   Though poor for years and years,
   Although they laid up treasure
   Beyond this vale of tears.

4. Though poor and without money,
   Their kindness made amend;
   Their house was always open
   To Jesus and his friend.

5. And thus they lived so happy,
   So poor, so kind, so good.
   Their brother grew afflicted
   And rudely throwed in bed.

6. Poor Martha and poor Mary,
   They wept aloud and cried;
   But still he grew no better,
   But lingered on and died.

7. The Jews came to the sisters,
   Put Lazreth in the tomb,
   And tried for them to comfort,
   And drive away their gloom.

8. When Jesus heard these tidings,
   Though in a distant land,
   How swiftly did he travel
   To join this lonely band!

9. When Martha saw him coming,
   She met him on his way;
   She told him that her brother
   Had died and passed away.

10. He cheered and he blessed her,
    He told her not to weep,
    For in him was the power
    To wake him from his sleep.

11. When Mary saw him coming,
    She ran and met him too,

And at his feet fell weeping,
Rehearsed the tale of woe.

12. When Jesus saw her weeping,
He fell a-weeping too;
He wept until they showed him
Where Lazreth was in tomb.

13. He rolled away the cover,
He looked upon the grave,
He prayed unto his Father,
His loving friend to save.

14. Then Lazreth in full power
Came from the gloomy mound,
And in full strength and vigor
He walked upon the ground.

15. Now if we but love Jesus,
And do his holy will,
Like Martha and like Mary,
He'll always use us well.

16. From death he will redeem us,
And take us to the skies,
Where we will reign forever,
Where pleasure never dies.

THE SAILOR BOY

This is a broadside very popular in the South, Virginia to the Mississippi, and in England and Scotland. It varies considerably as stanzas drift to and from other songs. It is a good example of a ballad about to lose all narrative and become lyric like "On Top of Old Smoky."

Text from Ohio as printed in *JAF*, xxxv:410.

1. Weary are the hours of a sailor boy;
Its cause, its cause, is to weep and to mourn,
Its cause, its cause, is to weep and to mourn,
For the sake of the lover that never will return.
Its cause, its cause, is to weep and mourn
For the sake of the lover that never will return.

2. Black is the color of my true-lover's hair,
His resemblance is the lily's fair,
To tell, to tell, will give me joy,
For none will I have but my sweet sailor boy.

3. Father, father, build me a boat,
   That I may on the ocean float;
   And every ship that I sail by,
   There I'll inquire for my sweet sailor boy.

4. As I sailed down from Spain,
   I saw three ships sail over the main,
   I hailed a happy captain as he passed by,
   And there I inquired for sweet Willy boy.

5. "Captain, captain, tell me true,
   Doth sweet Willy sail with you?
   To tell, to tell, 'twill give me joy,
   For none will I have but sweet Willy boy."

6. "O fair lady! I'll tell you true,
   He was drowned in the gulf below;
   On Eroc Isle as we passed by,
   There we left your sweet sailor boy."

7. She dashed her boat against a rock,
   I thought the lady's heart was broke,
   She wrung her hands and tore her hair,
   Just like a lady in despair.

8. "Bring me a chair to sit upon,
   And pen and ink to write it down."
   At the end of every line she dropped a tear,
   At the end of every verse cried, "Oh, my dear!"

9. "Dig my grave both wide and deep;
   Put a marble stone at my head and feet,
   And on my breast a turtle dove,
   To show the world that I did love."

THE BUTCHER BOY

In spite of its likeness to British stall ballads, "The Cruel Father" and "There's an Ale House in Yonder Town," "The Butcher Boy" seems to be American in origin. (See Belden, *Ballads and Songs*, p. 202.)

Text from Ohio, printed in *JAF*, xxix:169.

Notes

3/3–4. should read:
> "Their gold will melt; their silver fly;
> In time of need they're poor as I."

7/3–4. intrusive; the last two lines of stanza 5 should start stanza 6, etc.

1. New Jersey city where I did dwell,
   A butcher's boy I loved so well;
   He courted me my heart away,
   And then with me he would not stay.

2. There is a man in this same town,
   Where my love goes and sits him down,
   And there he takes strange girls on his knee,
   And tells to them what he did to me.

3. It's grief and pain to tell you why:
   Because they had more gold than I.
   But in time of need she will be as poor as I.

4. I went upstairs to make my bed,
   And nothing to my mother said.
   My mother she came up to me;
   "Oh, what's the matter, my daughter dear?"

5. O mother dear, it's, don't you know,
   It's grief and pain and sorrow, woe.
   Go get me a chair to sit me on,
   A pen and ink to write it down;
   And every line she dropped a tear,
   Calling home her Willie dear.

6. And when her father he came home,
   He says: "Where's my daughter gone?"
   He went up stairs, the door he broke;
   And there she hung upon a rope.

7. He took his knife and cut her down,
   And in her breast these words he found:
   "Oh! what a silly maid was I,
   To hang myself for a butcher's boy!

8. "Go dig my grave both wide and deep,
   Place marble stone at my head and feet,
   And on my breast a turtle dove,
   To show this world that I died for love."

THE WAGONER'S LAD

This ballad came to America as a broadside from England but it was immediately accepted by the folk in the South where it has long been a traditional song. It has thrown off numerous variants, of which the most popular is a version of "Old Smoky." Here again can be observed the process of an old ballad losing its story element and becoming lyric.

Text A, traditional in Kentucky, printed in *JAF,* xx:268; B, traditional in North Carolina, printed in *JAF,* xxviii:159.

A.

1. "I am a poor girl, and my fortune is bad;
    I have long time been courted by the wagoner's lad
    He courted me duly by night and by day,
    And now for to leave me he is going away.

2. "Your wagon's to grease, your bill is to pay;
    Come seat yourself beside me so long as you stay."
    "My wagon's done greased, my whip's in my hand;
    So fare you well, Nancy, I have no time to stand.

3. "I am a loving lad, and I can love long,
    I can love an old sweetheart till a new one comes on;
    I can hug them and kiss them and keep them at ease,
    Or I can turn my back upon them and court who I please."

4. "So hard is the fortune of poor womankind,—
    They are always objected, always confined;
    They are controlled by their parents until they are made wives,
    And slaves for their husbands the rest of their lives.

5. "I'll build me a castle on the mountains so high,
    Where the wild geese can see me as they pass me by,
    Where the wild geese can hear me my cries and my groans,—
    Be kind to the wagoner so far from his home."

6. "At the top of yon mountain, where my love's castle stands,
    It is dressed in green ivy from the top to the end;
    At the foot of yon mountain, where the wide ocean runs,
    We will commence our music and the firing of guns."

B.

OLD SMOKY

1. On the top of old Smoky all covered in snow
    I lost my true lover by sparking too slow.

2. Sparking is a pleasure, parting is a grief,
    And a false hearted lover is worse than a thief.

3. A thief will only rob you, will take what you have,
    And a false-hearted lover will take you to the grave.

4. The grave will only decay you, turn you to dust;
    There's not one boy in a hundred a poor girl can trust.

5. They will tell you they love you to give your heart ease,
   And as soon as your back's upon them they'll court who they
   please.

6. "It's raining, it's hailing; that moon gives no light;
   Your horses can't travel this dark lonesome night.

7. "Go put up your horses, feed them some hay;
   Come and set down here by me, love, as long as you stay."

8. "My horses are not hungry, they won't eat your hay:
   So farewell, my little darling! I'll feed on my way.

9. "I will drive on to Georgia, write you my mind;
   My mind is to marry, love, and leave you behind.

10. "Your parents is against me; mine is the same;
    If I'm down on your book, love, please rub off my name."

11. "I go upon old Smoky on the mountain so high,
    Where the wild birds and the turtle-dove can hear my sad cry."

12. "As sure as the dew drops grows on the green corn,
    Last night I were with her, but to-night she is gone."

THE BANKS OF DUNDEE

This is widely popular as a broadside and in the songsters; it is also
found generally in tradition both in the Old World and in America.
Another song, "The Banks of (Sweet) Dundee," is a sequel, telling
of the reunion of the lovers.

Text from Missouri, printed by Belden, p. 137.

1. Oh, Willie was a plowboy
   Whom Mary loved full well;
   Down in her uncle's garden
   The story of love to tell.
   There was a wealthy squire
   Who often came to see;
   But Mary loved the plowboy
   On the banks of a-Dundee.

2. Oh, the uncle and squire were a-riding,
   Out riding one day,
   And the uncle to the squire
   These bold words did say:
   "Young William is her favorite.
   We'll tie him to a tree,
   Unless in private we kill him
   On the banks of a-Dundee.

3. They taken William a prisoner
   Upon a certain day.
   He boldly fought for liberty,
   But there was three to one.
   The blood was flowing freely;
   "Pray kill me not," said he,
   "But I'll die for the love of Mary
   On the banks of a-Dundee."

4. Oh, Mary was one day walking,
   Lamenting her lost love.
   She met the wealthy squire
   Down in her uncle's grove.
   He threw his arms around her
   And loving words did say;
   But she fired and killed the squire
   On the banks of a-Dundee.

5. Her uncle, hearing a noise,
   Did hasten to the grove,
   Saying, "Since you have killed the squire
   I'll give you your death wound."
   "Stand back, stand back with vengeance," she cried,
   Then the trigger she drew
   And her uncle she slew
   On the banks of a-Dundee.

WILLIE RILEY

This Irish ballad has been very popular from the 18th century to the present. It is still fairly common in oral tradition and has been long in print in popular song books and ballad sheets. From Jamaica an interesting Negro *cante-fable* version has been collected.

Text A, as sung to M.E.L. by William Sutton, who has "been singing it over 60 years," Newfoundland, 1951; B, *cante-fable* version, Jamaica, *PMLA*, xxix:476.

A.

1. "O, rise up, Willie Riley, and come along with me.
   I mean to go with you and leave this counteree,
   To leave my father's dwelling house, his houses and free land."
   And away went Willie Riley, and his dear Colleen Bawn.

2. They go by hills and mountains and by an lonesome plain,
   To over shady groves and valleys all dangers to refrain;
   But her father followed after with a well-armed band,
   And taken was poor Riley and his dear Colleen Bawn.

3. It's in the cold, cold irons his hands and feet are bound;
   "I'm handcuffed like a murderer and tied unto the ground,
   But all the toil and slavery I'm willing for to stand,
   Still hoping to be succeeded by my dear Colleen Bawn."

4. The jailer's son to Riley go and thus to him did say:
   "O, get up, Willie Riley; you must appear this day,
   For great Squire Follard's anger you never can withstand;
   I'm afraid you'll suffer sorely for your dear Colleen Bawn."

5. Now Willie's dressed from top to toe all in a suit of green;
   His hair hangs o'er his shoulders most glorious to be seen.
   He's tall and straight and comely as any could be found;
   He's fit for Follard's daughter, were she heiress to a crown.

6. "This is the news, young Riley, last night that I did hear,—
   That lady's oath will hang you, or else will set you clear."
   "If that be so," said Riley, "that pleasure I will stand,
   Still hoping to be succeeded by my dear Colleen Bawn."

7. The judge he said, "This lady being in her tender youth,
   If Riley has deluded her, she will declare the truth."
   Then like a moving beauty bright before him she did stand:
   "You're welcome here, my heart's delight, my dear Colleen
   . Bawn."

8. "O gentlemen," Squire Follard said, "with pity look on me.
   This villyan came amongst us to disgrace our family,
   And by his base contrivance this villany was planned.
   If I don't get satisfaction, I'll quit this Irish land."

9. The lady with a tear began and thus replied she:
   "The fault is none of Riley's; the blame lies all on me.
   I forced him for to leave his place and come along with me;
   I loved him out of measure, which wrought our destiny."

10. Out spoke the noble Fox, at the table he stood by:
    "O gentlemen, consider on this extremity,—
    To hang a man for love it's murder you may see;
    To spare the life of Riley, let him leave this counteree."

11. "Good my lord, he stole from her her diamonds and her rings,
    Gold watch and silver buckles and many precious things,
    Which cost me in bright guineas more than five hundred pounds.
    I'll have the life of Riley should I lose ten thousand pounds."

12. "Oh, good my lord, I gave them him as tokens of true love,
    And when we are a-parting he will them all remove.

If you've got them, Riley, pray send them home to me."
"I will, my loving lady, with many thanks to thee."

13. "They are a ring among them I allow yourself to wear
With thirty locket diamonds well set in silver fair,
And as a true-love token, wear it on your right hand,
That you'll think on my poor broken heart when you're in a
foreign land."

14. Then out spake the noble judge, "You may let the prisoner go.
The lady's oath has cleared him, as the jury all may know.
She has released her own true love, she has renewed his name;
May her honor bright gain high estate and her offspring rise to
fame."

B.

SWEET RILEY

Anansi son name Stan'-up-stick. As Anansi poor, Stan'-up-stick don'
notice him. An' Stan'-up-stick buy a gold ring give him daughter
Absa; de ring cost a t'ousen' pound; it cut wid dimon' brooches an'
spliced wid hair. An' de daughter give it to a gentleman name William Riley. When Stan'-up-stick see William Riley wid de ring, he
sing,

> There is a ring I give my daughter,
> It cost a t'ousan' pound.
> It cut with di'mon brooches
> An' splic-ed with my hair.

De daughter sing,

> If you have them now, sweet Riley,
> Pray send them back to me.

William sing,

> O yes my general lady,
> With many a thank to you.
> Wear it upon your right han'
> An' think upon my broken heart
> When you are in foreign lan'.

Riley said, "My hands an' feet are chained to the ground like a murderer!" Lady sings,

> Come justice of the jury,
> Come plead the case for Riley
> And let his bond-es free!
> For he never stole my jewels,
> I will swear to all about;
> For I gave them to sweet Riley
> For token of true love.

Stan'-up-stick, he rise an' sing,
>> This ring, I give it my daughter,
>> It cost a t'ousan' pound.

Anansi come up an' say, "God! a you love me, so med Stan'-up-stick loss his t'ousan' pound!"

ONE MORNING IN MAY
(THE NIGHTINGALE)

This charming ballad descends from the 17th-century Roxborough ballad, "The Nightingale's Song." In America it exists only in oral tradition, where it preserves its delicacy of wit and pastoral charm. The device of the double entendre between lovers is very old in literature, as Belden points out in the headnote to his text.

Text from Missouri as printed by Belden, pp. 242–243.

1. One morning, one morning, one morning in May
    I spied a fair couple a-making their way.
    One was a lady so bright and so fair,
    And the other was a soldier, a gay cavalier.

2. "Oh, where are you going, my pretty fair maid?
    Oh, where are you going, sweet lady?" he said.
    "I'm going," said she, "to the banks of the stream,
    To see the waters gliding, hear the nightingales sing."

3. They had not been there but an hour or two
    Till out of his satchel a fiddle he drew.
    He played her a love-song caused the valleys to ring.
    "Hark, hark!" says the lady, "hear the nightingales sing!"

4. "Oh, now," says the soldier, "'tis time to give o'er."
    "Oh, no," says the lady, "just play one tune more;
    For I'd rather hear the fiddle, or one tug on the string,
    Than to see the waters gliding, hear the nightingales sing.

5. "Oh, now," says the lady, "it's won't you marry me?"
    "Oh no," says the soldier, "that never can be!
    I've a wife in Low Flanders, with children twice three;
    And two and the army's too many for me!

6. "I'll go home to Flanders and stay there one year.
    In place of pure water I'll drink wine and beer.
    And if ever I return, 'twill be in the spring
    When the waters are gliding and the nightingales sing."

7. Come all ye fair damsels, take warning from me.
    Never place your affections on a green willow tree;

For the leaves they will wither like flowers in the spring
While the waters are a-gliding and the nightingales sing.

8. Come all ye fair damsels, take warning from me,
Never place your affections on a soldier so free.
For he'll love you and leave you without any ring
To rock your young baby, hear the nightingales sing!

BRENNAN ON THE MOOR

This broadside was popular in Ireland, England, and America. It has
a better than broadside ring but is definitely of broadside origin, being
frequently printed. William Brennan was a real highwayman, executed in Cork, Ireland, in 1804. The obvious influence of Robin Hood
and other outlaw ballads is apparent. Printed broadsides from as early
as 1840 survive.

Text from Missouri and printed by Belden, p. 284.

1. 'T is of a fearless Irishman
The story I will tell;
His name was Willie Brennan,
In Ireland he did dwell.
'Twas in the Cumberland Mountains
He commenced his wild career,
And many a wealthy nobleman
Before him shook with fear.

2. A brace of loaded pistols
He carried night and day;
He never robbed a poor man
Upon the king's highway,
But when he'd taken from the rich
Like Durban and Black Bess,
He always divided
With the widow in distress.

3. Now Willie met with a packman
By the name of Julius Bunn.
They traveled on together
Till day began to dawn.
When Julius found his money gone,
Likewise his watch and chain,
He encountered Billy Brennan
And robbed him back again.

4. Now Willie finding the packman
As good a man as he,
He took him on the king's highway

A companion for to be.
Then Julius threw his pack away
Without any more delay
And proved a faithful comrade
Unto his dying day.

5. One day upon the king's highway
    As Willie sat him down,
    He met the mayor of Cortial
    One mile outside of town.
    The mayor knew his features,
    And "I think, young man," said he,
    "Your name is Billy Brennan.
    You must come along with me."

6. Now Willie's wife she being in town
    Provisions for to buy,
    When she saw her Willie
    She began to weep and cry.
    You ought to seen the token—
    As soon as Willie spoke
    She handed him a blunderbuss
    From underneath her cloak.

7. Now of this loaded blunderbuss
    The truth I'll unfold;
    He made the mayor to tremble
    And robbed him of his gold.
    A hundred pounds were offered
    For his apprehension there.
    His horse, saddle, and bridle
    To the mountains he did tear.

8. Now Willie being an outlaw
    Upon the mountain high,
    With infantry and cavalry
    To catch him they did try.
    He laughed at them, he scoffed at them
    Till at last he has to say
    "A false-hearted young girl
    Did beastly me betray."

9. 'Twas in the town of Tipperary,
    The county of Claymore,
    That Willie and his comrade
    Were made to suffer sore;
    They lay out in the briers
    That grew up in an open field,
    And they received twelve wounds
    Before it's they would yield.

10. Now Willie he was taken,
   With strong irons he was bound,
   They took him to the Commeral jail
   Where strong walls did him surround.
   The jury found him guilty
   And the judge made this reply:
   "For robbing on the king's highway
   You are condemned to die."

11. "Here's to my wife and children,
   Who long may mourn for me;
   Here's to my aged father,
   Who has shed tears for me;
   Here's to my aged mother,
   Who tore her locks and cried,
   Saying, 'Twere better, Billie Brennan,
   In your cradle you had died.' "

FATHER GRUMBLE

The first print of this widely circulated ballad was evidently by Allan Cunningham in *Songs of Scotland,* 1825, though analogues appear earlier. Many variations of Father Grumble's chores exist from text to text, but all texts have the same basic situation, one that likewise frequently occurs in folk tales. See Kittredge's notes to this text in *JAF,* xxvi:364, for details of similar ballads. Most versions end with this stanza:

Then the old man swore by the point of his nose
And all the stars in heaven
That his wife could do more work in one day
Than he could do in seven.

Text from Kansas as reported to Louise Pound and printed in *JAF,* xxvi:365.

1. Father Grumble he did say,
   As sure as the moss round a tree,
   That he could do more work in a day
   Than his wife could do in three, three,
   Than his wife could do in three.

2. Then Mother Grumble she did say,
   "O what's the row now?
   You can stay in the house and work,
   And I will follow the plow, plow,
   And I will follow the plow.

3.   "But don't forget the jar of cream
     That stands within the frame, frame;
   And don't forget the fat in the pot,
     Or it will all go into flame, flame;
   And don't forget the fat in the pot,
     Or it will all go into flame.

4.   "Don't forget the muley-cow,
     For fear she will go dry, dry;
   And don't forget the little pigs
     That lie within the sty, sty;
   And don't forget the little pigs
     That lie within the sty.

5.   "Don't forget the speckled hen,
     For fear she'll lay astray, astray;
   And don't forget the skein of yarn
     That I spin every day, day;
   And don't forget the skein of yarn
     That I spin every day."

6.   He went to churn the jar of cream
     That stood within the frame, frame;
   And he forgot the fat in the pot,
     And it all went into flame, flame;
   And he forgot the fat in the pot,
     And it all went into flame.

7.   He went to milk the muley-cow,
     For fear she would go dry, dry;
   She reared, she kicked, she faunched, she flinched,
     She hit him over the eye, eye;
   She reared, she kicked, she faunched, she flinched,
     She hit over the eye.

8.   He went to watch the speckled hen,
     For fear she'd lay astray, astray;
   And he forgot the skein of yarn
     That she spun every day;
   And he forgot the skein of yarn
     That she spun every day.

9.   Old Father Grumble coming in
     And looking very sad, sad,
   Old Mother Grumble clapped her hands
     And said that she was very glad, glad;
   Old Mother Grumble clapped her hands
     And said that she was very glad.

THE FOX

This ballad has long been famous in English tradition. As early as the latter part of the 18th century it had become a nursery ballad and in the 19th century in America it was appropriated by the Negroes to become one of their favorite songs.

Text traditional in America, printed *MAF*, xxix:43.

1. A hungry fox went out one night—
   He begged the moon to give him light
   For he had many miles to trot that night
   Before he could reach 'is dinno,
   Dinno, dinno. Before he could reach 'is dinno.

2. Soon he reached the farmer's yard;
   The ducks and geese declared it hard;
   Their nerves were shaken and rest was marred
   By a visit by Mister Foxo,
   Foxo, Foxo. A visit by Mister Foxo.

3. He grabbed the black duck by the neck
   And flung him all across his back;
   The black duck cried out, "Quack, quack, quack,"
   And his heels hung dangling downo,
   Downo, downo. And his heels hung dangling downo.

4. Old Lady Slipper-slopper jumped out of bed,
   Hoist up the window and thrust out her head,
   Crying, "John, John, John, the black duck's gone;
   The fox is off to his dinno."
   Dinno, dinno. The fox is off to his dinno.

5. John ran up on the hill
   And blew a blast both loud and shrill.
   Said the fox, "That's pretty music still
   I would rather be off to my dinno."
   Dinno, dinno. I would rather be off to my dinno.

6. Master fox trotted off to his den,
   To his dear little foxes, eight, nine, ten;
   Showing the luck of a good fat duck
   And his legs hang dangling downo,
   Downo, downo. And his legs hang dangling downo.

7. Master fox and his hungry wife
   Ate very well without fork and knife;
   They never had a better meal in all their life
   And the little ones slicked the boneso,
   Boneso, boneso. And the little ones slicked the boneso.

BETSY FROM PIKE

This ballad was sung in the days of '49 on the western migrations. Who composed it and when are unknown. It is in *Put's Golden Songster*, 1858, and is widely known in oral tradition.

Text from Missouri as printed by Belden, p. 344.

1. Oh, don't you remember sweet Betsy from Pike,
   Who crossed the big mountains with her lover Ike,
   With two yoke of oxen, a large yellow dog,
   A tall shanghai rooster and one spotted hog?
           Eli compoly compoli copelia
           Eli compoly com copleria
           Eli compoly com petheria
           Eli compoly com petheria.

2. One evening quite early they camped on the Platte,
   Close by the roadside on a green shady flat,
   Where Betsy shore-footed lay down to repose.
   With wonder she gazed on his Pike County nose.

3. The shanghai ran off and the cattle all died;
   The last piece of bacon that morning was fried.
   Poor Ike was discouraged, and Betsy was mad;
   The dog wagged his tail and looked wonderfully sad.

4. At length the old wagon came down with a crash
   And out on the prairie rolled all kinds of trash;
   A few little baby-clothes done up with great care
   Looked rather suspicious, though all on the square.

5. They went by Salt Lake to enquire the way,
   When Brigham declared sweet Betsy should stay.
   Betsy got frightened and ran like a deer,
   And Brigham stood pawing the ground like a steer.

6. They next reached the desert, where Betsy gave out
   And down in the sand she lay rolling about.
   Poor Ike, half discouraged, looked on with surprise,
   Saying, "Betsy, get up; you will git sand in your eyes."

7. At length they arrived on a very high hill,
   With wonder looked down upon old Placerville.
   Ike sighed, and he said, when he cast his eyes down,
   "Betsy, my darling, we've got to Hangtown."

8. This Pike County couple attended a dance,
   And Ike wore a pair of his Pike County pants;

Betsy was dressed up with ribbons and rings;
Says Ike, "You're an angel, but where is your wings?"

9. A miner says, "Betsy, won't you dance with me?"
"I will that, old hoss, if you don't make too free.
Don't dance me too hard; if you want to know why,
Doggone you, I'm chockful of strong alkali."

10. This Pike County couple got married, of course,
And Ike became jealous, obtained a divorce.
Betsy, well satisfied, cried with a shout,
"Goodby, you big lummix, I'm glad you backed out."

JOE BOWERS

Belden calls this the most popular of the Gold Rush songs and goes
on to say that according to H. C. Merwin (*Life of Bret Harte,*
p. 60) it was written by one Frank Swift from Pike County, Missouri. The other claimant is John Woodward, who is supposed to
have written it for Johnson's minstrels of San Francisco. It was frequently printed in the song books and is widespread in oral tradition,
having been adopted by cowboys, lumbermen, and Confederate soldiers.

Text from Missouri as printed in Belden, p. 342.

1. My name is Joe Bowers;
I've got a brother Ike;
I came from old Missouri,
All the way from Pike.
I'll tell you why I left thar
And why I came to roam
And leave my poor old mammy
So far away from home.

2. I used to court a gal thar,
Her name was Sally Black.
I axed her if she'd marry me;
She said it was a whack.
Says she to me, "Joe Bowers,
Before we hitch for life,
You ought to get a little home
To keep your little wife."

3. "Oh, Sally, dearest Sally,
Oh, Sally, for your sake
I'll go to California
And try to raise a stake."
Says she to me, "Joe Bowers,

You are the man to win;
Here's a kiss to bind the bargain,"
And she hove a dozen in.

4. When I got in that country
   I hadn't nary red,
   I had such wolfish feelings
   I wished myself 'most dead;
   But the thought of my dear Sally
   Soon made them feelings git,
   And I whispered hope to Bowers—
   I wish I had 'em yit.

5. At length I went to mining,
   Put in my biggest licks,
   Came down upon the boulders
   Just like a thousand bricks!
   I worked both late and early,
   In rain, in sun, in snow—
   I was working for my Sally;
   It was all the same to Joe.

6. At length I got a letter
   From my dear brother Ike,
   It came from old Missouri
   All the way from Pike;
   It brought to me the darndest news
   That ever you did hear.
   My heart is almost burstin',
   So pray excuse this tear.

7. It said that Sal was false to me,
   Her love for me had fled,
   She'd got married to a butcher—
   The butcher's hair was red.
   And more than that, the letter said—
   It's enough to make me swear—
   That Sally had a baby;
   The baby had red hair.

8. Now I've told you all
   About this sad affair,
   'Bout Sally marrying a butcher,
   That butcher with red hair.
   But whether 'twas a boy or gal child
   The letter never said;
   It only said the baby's hair
   Was inclined to be red.

JESSE JAMES

The most famous outlaw in American folk tradition is most certainly Jesse James. He is hardly a Robin Hood, for even in the ballads he lacks the swashbuckling, romantic qualities of the earlier outlaw hero. But many ballads are sung about him and his story is growing. Most of the Jesse James ballads center around the last dramatic episode of his life. It was a hot day, Jesse took off his coat and vest; and then remarking to Robert Ford, one of his men, that he should not be seen with his guns strapped around him, he took the guns off and placed them on the bed. He got up on a chair to dust or straighten a picture. Then Robert Ford shot him in the back, hoping to get the ten-thousand-dollar reward offered by Governor Crittendon for Jesse dead or alive. Belden thought that all Jesse James ballads sprang from one basic pattern and that they bore the refrain: *That dirty little coward* (etc.) . . . and that it was probably the work of a Negro convict.

Text A, from North Carolina, printed in *JAF*, xxii:246; B and C from Missouri, printed by Belden, pp. 403 and 402.

A.

1. Yes, I went down to the depot
   Not many days ago: they followed on behind,
   And I fell upon my knees, and I offered up the keys
   To Frank and his brother, Jesse James.

2. Poor Jesse James, poor Jesse James,
   He robbed that Danville train;
   Yes, the dirty little coward, he shot Mr. Howard,
   An' they laid poor Jesse in his grave.

3. Frank says to Jesse, not many days ago,
   "Let's rob that Danville train."
   An' Jesse says to Frank, "We'll take it as we go,
   For we may not be hyar any more."

   Poor Jesse James, etc.

4. Jesse was a man, an' he travelled over the land,
   With his sword an' his pistol to his side.
   Robert Ford watched his eye an' shot him on the sly,
   An' they laid poor Jesse in his grave.

   Poor Jesse James, etc.

5. Yes, Jesse had a wife, the darlin' of his life,
   An' the children all was brave.

Robert Ford watched his eye an' shot him on the sly,
An' they laid poor Jesse in his grave.

6. It was on Friday night, the moon was shinin' bright,
An' Jesse was standin' 'fore his glass,
Robert Ford's pistol ball brought him tremblin' from the wall,
An' they laid poor Jesse in his grave.

Poor Jesse James, etc.

7. Well, the people of the West, when they heard of Jesse's death,
They wondered how he come to die.
Robert Ford watched his eye an' shot him on the sly,
An' they laid poor Jesse in his grave.

B.

1. Jesse James was one of his names, another it was Howard.
He robbed the rich of every stitch. You bet, he was no coward.

2. His mother she was elderly, his father was a preacher,
Though some do say, I can't gainsay, his mother was his teacher.

3. Her strong right arm it came to harm. Detectives blew it off, sir,
And killed her son, the youngest one. No wonder such she'd
scoff, sir.

4. My Jesse dear, your mother here has taught more than she
ought ter,
For Robert Ford, I pledge my word, has marked you for his
slaughter.

5. For robbing trains Bob had no brains, unless Jess plainly showed
him.
Our governor for peace or war explained this for to goad him.

6. So Robert Ford he scratched his gourd, and then he said "I'll
go you,
Give me a price that's something nice, and then, by gee, I'll
show you!"

7. Then Governor C. he laughed with glee and fixed a price to
suit him.
And Bob agreed, with ready speed, to find Jess James and shoot
him.

8. And then he did as he was bid and shot Jess in the back, sir,
Then ran away on that same day, for cash he did not lack, sir.

9. He did his best to live out west, but no one was his friend there.
"You've killed your cousin," they went buzzin', however free
he'd spend there.

10. And then one day, the papers say, Bob Ford got his rewarding:
   A cowboy drunk his heart did plunk. As you do you'll git according.

C.

1. Jesse James was a lad that killed many a man.
   He robbed the Danville train.
   But that dirty little coward that shot Mr. Howard
   Has laid poor Jesse in the grave.

2. It was Robert Ford, that dirty little coward,
   I wonder how he does feel;
   For he ate of Jesse's bread and slept in Jesse's bed
   And laid poor Jesse in the grave.

Chorus
Poor Jesse had a wife to mourn for his life,
His children they were brave;
But that dirty little coward that shot Mr. Howard
And laid poor Jesse in the grave!

3. It was his brother Frank who robbed the Gallatin bank
   And carried the money from the town.
   It was at this very place they had a little chase,
   For they shot Capt. Sheets to the ground.

4. They went to the crossing not very far from here,
   And there they did the same;
   With the agent on his knees he delivered up the keys
   To the outlaws Frank and Jesse James.

5. It was on Wednesday night, the moon was shining bright,
   They robbed the Glenville train.
   The people they did say, for many miles away,
   It was robbed by Frank and Jesse James.

6. It was on Saturday night, Jesse was at home,
   Talking with his family brave.
   Robert Ford came along like a thief in the night
   And laid poor Jesse in the grave.

7. The people held their breath when they heard of Jesse's death
   And wondered how he ever came to die.
   It was one of the gang called little Robert Ford,
   He shot poor Jesse on the sly.

8. This song was made by Billy Gashade
   As soon as the news did arrive.
   He said there is no man with the law in his hand
   Can take Jesse James when alive.

JOHN HENRY

America has produced a real ballad hero in John Henry. He is, in every sense, a folk hero and a creation of the ballad muse. No one knows for certain whether such a man lived or not, but it makes little difference, for today he lives as a hero and an ideal. John Henry was a steel driving man; that is, he struck the drill which his shaker held to drill holes in rocks for the dynamite charges. Most of the ballads center around a great contest between John Henry and a steam drill. The contest was supposed to take place during the construction of the C. & O. tunnel at Big Bend, West Virginia. John Henry beat the steam drill but died of the effort. But this is all ballad story; there is no evidence outside the ballad that such a contest ever took place.

Many ballads have been composed about John Henry. The earliest one to find its way into print is a broadside signed by W. T. Blankenship, unfortunately undated but evidently from the latter part of the 19th century. This broadside is probably not the original John Henry ballad; rather it was worked out of traditional ballads of an older date. The some sixty other John Henry ballads are all from oral tradition. Professor Guy B. Johnson, who has collected over fifty such ballads and songs, has noted that three elements persist; these are represented by stanzas 1, 7, and 11 in version A below. A study of such persistent elements shows that the traditional versions most certainly stem from a single archetype. In addition to the ballads, several John Henry work songs, hammer songs, are found. It may be that they represent the oldest tradition of John Henry and that the ballads are built on them. See Guy B. Johnson, *John Henry,* and Lewis W. Chappell, *John Henry, a Folklore Study,* for details and texts of ballads.

Texts from Johnson, A from p. 101, B from p. 89.

A.

1. When John Henry was a little boy,
    Sitting upon his father's knee,
    His father said, "Look here, my boy,
    You must be a steel driving man like me,
    You must be a steel driving man like me."

2. John Henry went upon the mountain,
    Just to drive himself some steel.
    The rocks was so tall and John Henry so small,
    He said lay down hammer and squeal,
    He said lay down hammer and squeal.

3. John Henry had a little wife,
    And the dress she wore was red;
    The last thing before he died,

He said, "Be true to me when I'm dead,
Oh, be true to me when I'm dead."

4. John Henry's wife ask him for fifteen cents,
And he said he didn't have but a dime,
Said, "If you wait till the rising sun goes down,
I'll borrow it from the man in the mine,
I'll borrow it from the man in the mine."

5. John Henry started on the right-hand side,
And the steam drill started on the left.
He said, "Before I'd let that steam drill beat me down,
I'd hammer my fool self to death,
Oh, I'd hammer my fool self to death."

6. The steam drill started at half past six,
John Henry started the same time.
John Henry struck bottom at half past eight,
And the steam drill didn't bottom till nine,
And the steam drill didn't bottom till nine.

7. John Henry said to his captain,
"A man, he ain't nothing but a man,
Before I'd let that steam drill beat me down,
I'd die with the hammer in my hand,
Oh, I'd die with the hammer in my hand."

8. John Henry said to his shaker,
"Shaker, why don't you sing just a few more rounds?
And before the setting sun goes down,
You're gonna hear this hammer of mine sound,
You're gonna hear this hammer of mine sound."

9. John Henry hammered on the mountain,
He hammered till half past three,
He said, "This big Bend Tunnel on the C. & O. road
Is going to be the death of me,
Lord! is going to be the death of me."

10. John Henry had a little baby boy,
You could hold him in the palm of your hand.
The last words before he died,
"Son, you must be a steel driving man,
Son, you must be a steel driving man."

11. John Henry had a little woman,
And the dress she wore was red,
She went down the railroad track and never come back,
Said she was going where John Henry fell dead,
Said she was going where John Henry fell dead.

12.   John Henry hammering on the mountain,
        As the whistle blew for half past two,
      The last word I heard him say,
        "Captain, I've hammered my insides in two,
      Lord, I've hammered my insides in two."

B.

 1.   John Henry was a railroad man,
        He worked from six 'till five,
      "Raise 'em up bullies and let 'em drop down,
        I'll beat you to the bottom or die."

 2.   John Henry said to his captain:
        "You are nothing but a common man,
      Before that steam drill shall beat me down,
        I'll die with my hammer in my hand."

 3.   John Henry said to the Shakers:
        "You must listen to my call,
      Before that steam drill shall beat me down,
        I'll jar these mountains till they fall."

 4.   John Henry's captain said to him:
        "I believe these mountains are caving in."
      John Henry said to his captain: "Oh Lord!
        That's my hammer you hear in the wind."

 5.   John Henry he said to his captain:
        "Your money is getting mighty slim,
      When I hammer through this old mountain,
        Oh Captain will you walk in?"

 6.   John Henry's captain came to him
        With fifty dollars in his hand,
      He laid his hand on his shoulder and said:
        "This belongs to a steel driving man."

 7.   John Henry was hammering on the right side,
        The big steam drill on the left,
      Before that steam drill could beat him down,
        He hammered his fool self to death.

 8.   They carried John Henry to the mountains,
        From his shoulder his hammer would ring,
      She caught on fire by a little blue blaze
        I believe these old mountains are caving in.

 9.   John Henry was lying on his death bed,
        He turned over on his side,

And these were the last words John Henry said
"Bring me a cool drink of water before I die."

10. John Henry had a little woman,
Her name was Pollie Ann,
He hugged and kissed her just before he died,
Saying, "Pollie, do the very best you can."

11. John Henry's woman heard he was dead,
She could not rest on her bed,
She got up at midnight, caught that No. 4 train,
"I am going where John Henry fell dead."

12. They carried John Henry to that new burying ground
His wife all dressed in blue,
She laid her hand on John Henry's cold face,
"John Henry I've been true to you."

JOHN HARDY

John Hardy is often confused with John Henry, and a drift back and forth of elements from both groups of songs occurs. John Hardy was also a steel driver but his end was inglorious. He shot a man in a gambling quarrel and was executed for the murder on January 19, 1894. See discussion of John Hardy and ballads about him by John Harrington Cox, *JAF*, xxxii:505–521.

Text A from tradition in West Virginia, printed *JAF*, xxxii:518. B has a remarkable kinship to some of the simple and stark old English ballads; it is from North Carolina and is printed in *JAF*, xxii:247.

A.

1. John Hardy was a little farmer boy,
Sitting on his father's knee;
Says he, "I fear the C. & O. Road
Will be the ruination of me, poor boy!
Will be the ruination of me."

2. John Hardy got to be a desperate man,
Carried a pistol and a razor every day;
Shot a nigger through the heel in a Chinese camp,
And you ought of seen that nigger get away, poor boy!
And you ought of seen that nigger get away.

3. John Hardy's mother ran up to him,
Saying, "Son, what have you done?"
"I murdered a man in a Chinese camp,

And now I'm sentenced to be hung, poor boy!
And now I'm sentenced to be hung."

4. John Hardy's father went to the judge,
   Saying, "What do you think will be done?"
   The judge he answer with a quick reply,
   "I'm afraid John Hardy will be hung, poor boy!
   I'm afraid John Hardy will be hung."

5. John Hardy was standing in a dice-room door,
   He didn't have a nickel to his name;
   Along came a yaller gal, threw a dollar on the board,
   Saying, "Deal John Hardy in the game, poor boy!"
   Saying, "Deal John Hardy in the game."

6. John Hardy was standing in a railroad-station,
   As drunk as he could be:
   A policeman came up and took him by the arm,
   "John Hardy, come along with me, poor boy!
   John Hardy, come along with me."

7. "Oh, who will shoe your pretty little feet,
   And who will glove your hands,
   And who will kiss your sweet rosy lips,
   When I'm in a foreign land, poor boy!
   When I'm in a foreign land?"

8. "My father will shoe my pretty little feet,
   My mother will glove my hands;
   John Hardy will kiss my sweet rosy lips,
   When he comes from a foreign land, poor boy!
   When he comes from a foreign land."

9. John Hardy married a loving wife,
   And children he had three:
   He called to him his oldest son,
   Saying, "Son, make a man like me, poor boy!"
   Saying, "Son, make a man like me."

10. John Hardy married a loving wife,
    And children he had three:
    He cared no more for his wife and child
    Than the rocks in the bottom of the sea, poor boy!
    Than the rocks in the bottom of the sea.

B.

1. John Hardy was a mean an' disperated man,
   He carried two guns ever' day,

He shot a man in New Orlean Town,
John Hardy never lied to his gun, poor boy.

2. He's been to the east and he's been to the west,
   An' he's been this wide world round,
   He's been to the river an' been baptized,
   An' he's been on his hangin' grounds, poor boy.

3. John Hardy's father was standin' by,
   Sayin', "Johnie, what have you done?"
   He murdered a man in the same ole town,
   You ought to see John Hardy gittin' away, poor boy.

4. John Hardy's mother come weepin' around
   Cryin', "Johnie, what have you done?"
   "It's all for the sake of her I love."
   An' they run John Hardy back in jail, poor boy.

FRANKIE AND ALBERT (JOHNNIE)

Frankie and Albert and John Henry are the finest of the original American folk ballads. The dramatic focus, the gapped structure, the starkness of the action, the original phraseology, and the power of the refrain all combine to make this a great narrative song. Its origin and authorship are still disputed; we are not even sure whether it is originally Negro or not. Negroes everywhere sing it, usually the protagonists are Negro, and there are many touches of Negro style. If the Negro did not originate it, he certainly worked on many versions of it. We don't even know how old the song is. Barry (see *Bulletin* 10:24) thinks that it was made about a murder committed by one Frankie Silver in North Carolina in 1831 (a Frankie Silver ballad is extant, though it shows only general resemblance to this story). Other characters have been identified as Frankie and Albert, the most common being Frankie Baker and Allen Britt. This Frankie killed Britt in St. Louis in 1899, but the Frankie and Albert ballads are certainly older than 1899. (For full details see Randolph, ii, 126; Belden, p. 330). "Johnnie" is substituted for "Albert" in 1911 by a vaudeville team who used this song on the stage.

Many texts exist in tradition, with much variation in stanza and diction. The two here are from North Carolina and printed in *JAF*, xlv:142.

A.

1. Frankie was a good girl
   As everybody knows;
   She paid a hundred dollar bill

For Albert a suit of clothes,
Just because she loved him so.

2. Frankie took them to him;
Albert put them on,
Went stepping off down the broad highway,
Saying, "By, by, Honey, I'm gone
For I'm your man who won't treat you right."

3. Frankie went to the beer shops
And called for a glass of beer,
Saying to the bar-room keeper,
"Have you seen little Albert here?"
"Oh, no, no, Frankie, no."

4. The keeper turned to Frankie,
Says, "Frankie I told you a lie;
He left here about an hour ago
With a girl he called Alice Fry;
I know he's your man; he won't treat you right."

5. Frankie went to the bar-room;
She called for a glass of gin,
Saying to the burie-be,
"I'm going to get drunk again;
I'll kill my man, who won't treat me right."

6. Frankie went down the broadway,
With a razor in her hand:
"Stand back all you loving girls;
I'm hunting my gamblin man;
I'll kill my man, who won't treat me right."

7. She went down to the pool room;
She looked in the pool room door,
And there she spied the man she loved,
A-sitting in the middle of the floor,
Saying, "I'm your man who won't treat you right."

8. "Come to me, little Albert,
I'm calling through no fun;
If you don't come to the one loves you,
I'll shoot you with my old gun;
For you're my man, who won't treat me right."

9. Albert went behind the counter;
He fell upon his knees—
Look right up into Frankie's face,
Saying, "Frankie, don't shoot me please,
For I'm your man who won't treat you right."

10. Frankie got up next morning,
    About nine o'clock.
    She picked up that forty-four gun,
    And fired the fatal shot,
    She killed her man, who wouldn't treat her right.

11. "Turn me over, Frankie,
    Turn me over slow;
    Turn me over on my left side;
    Those bullets hurt me so.
    You've killed your man who wouldn't treat you right."

12. People all said to Frankie:
    "Little girl, why don't you run?
    Don't you see that chief police
    With a forty-four smokeless gun?
    You've killed your man who wouldn't treat you right."

13. Frankie went down to the river;
    She marched from bank to bank;
    "I've done all I could for a gambling man
    And yet I got no thanks
    For killing my man who wouldn't treat me right."

14. Frankie went to the funeral;
    She rode in a rubber tired hack;
    When they lowered him into the grave,
    She screamed, "He'll never come back,
    He'll never come back, he'll never come back."

15 Frankie had two children,
    A boy and a girl;
    She told them if they ever saw their papa,
    They would see him in another world.
    She killed her man who wouldn't treat her right.

16. Frankie sat in the court-room,
    Fanning with an electric fan.
    Whispering to her sister, she said,
    "Never love a gambling man,
    For all you do, he won't treat you right."

17. Judge said to the jury:
    "Jury, I cannot see,
    Though Frankie has killed the man she loved,
    Why she should not go free
    For killing her man who wouldn't treat her right."

18. Frankie walked out on the scaffold,
    As brave as a girl could be,

Saying, "Judge, you tried me
Murder in the first degree,
For killing my man, who wouldn't treat me right."

19. Now little Frankie is buried;
She's sleeping by Albert's side;
Albert was a gambling man,
And Frankie was his bride;
She killed her man, who wouldn't treat her right.

B.

1. Frankie and Johnnie were lovers.
Oh, ho, how they did love!
Swore to be true to each other
As true as the stars up above.
He was her man; he wouldn't do her wrong.

2. Frankie went down to the corner
Just for a bucket of beer.
Said, "Mr. Bartender,
Has my loving Johnnie been here?
He's my man; he won't do me wrong."

3. "Frankie, I'll cause you no trouble;
Frankie, I'll tell you no lie;
Your lover left here about an hour ago
With a girl named Nellie Bly.
He's your man but he's doing you wrong."

4. Frankie looked over the transom;
There to her great surprise—
There on a couch sat her Johnnie
Making love to Nellie Bly.
He was her man, but he done her wrong.

5. Frankie pulled back her kimona,
Drew out her little forty-four turuute; (toot root toota)
Three times she shot
Right through that hard wood door—
Killed her man 'cause he done her wrong.

6. "Frankie, come turn me over;
Come turn me over slow;
Your bullet in my left side;
Oh, how it hurts me so!
You killed your man 'cause he done you wrong."

7. Bring on your rubber tired horses;
Bring on your rubber tired hack.

Taking my man to the grave yard
And I'm not going to bring him back.
I killed my man 'cause he done me wrong.

8. Frankie went to the warden.
Said, "What are you going to do?"
The warden said to Frankie;
"It's the electric chair for you.
You've killed your man 'cause he done you wrong."

9. Frankie went to the policeman.
Said, "I don't want to live another day.
Lock me up in a dungeon
And throw the key away.
I've killed my man 'cause he done me wrong."

10. This story has no moral;
This story has no end;
This story goes right on to show
There's not no good in men.
She killed her man 'cause he done her wrong.

STAGOLEE

Along with John Henry, Stagolee has developed as a hero of the Negro. Stagolee is more the bad-man hero than is John Henry. He is so bad in one version that the devil won't have him in hell. His career in general is more fantastic and exaggerated than that of John Henry. Many stories exist about him, all pretty much in the vein of the Paul Bunyan stories. He is the subject also of a number of folk songs.

Texts A and B from the collection of Howard W. Odum as printed in *JAF*, xxiv :288.

A.

1. Stagolee, Stagolee, what's dat in yo' grip?
Nothin' but my Sunday clothes, I'm goin' to take a trip,
O dat man, bad man, Stagolee done come.

2. Stagolee, Stagolee, where you been so long?
I been out on de battle fiel' shootin' an' havin' fun,
O dat man, bad man, Stagolee done come.

3. Stagolee was a bully man, an' ev'y body knowed,
When dey seed Stagolee comin', to give Stagolee de road,
O dat man, bad man, Stagolee done come.

4. Stagolee started out, he give his wife his han',
"Good-by darlin', I'm goin' to kill a man."
etc.

5. Stagolee killed a man an' laid him on de flo',
What's dat he kill him wid? Dat same ole fohty-fo'.

6. Stagolee killed a man an' laid him on his side,
What's dat he kill him wid? Dat same ole fohty-five.

7. Out of house an' down de street Stagolee did run,
In his hand he held a great big smokin' gun.

8. Stagolee, Stagolee, I'll tell you what I'll do,
If you'll git me out'n dis trouble I'll do as much for you.

9. Ain't it a pity, ain't a shame?
Stagolee was shot, but he don't want no name.

10. Stagolee, Stagolee, look what you done done,
Killed de best ole citerzen; now you'll hav' to be hung.

11. Stagolee cried to de jury an' to de judge: Please don't take my life,
I have only three little children an' one little lovin' wife,
O dat man, bad man, Stagolee done come.

B.

I got up one mornin' jes' 'bout four o'clock;
Stagolee an' big bully done have one finish' fight:
What 'bout? All 'bout dat raw-hide Stetson hat.

Stagolee shot Bully; Bully fell down on de flo',
Bully cry out: "Dat fohty-fo' hurts me so."
Stagolee done killed dat Bully now.

Sent for de wagon, wagon didn't come,
Loaded down wid pistols an' all dat gatlin' gun,
Stagolee done kill dat Bully now.

Some giv' a nickel, some giv' a dime,
I didn't give a red copper cent, 'cause he's no friend o' mine,
Stagolee done kill dat Bully now.

Carried po' Bully to cemetery, people standin' 'round,
When preacher say Amen, lay po' body down,
Stagolee done kill dat Bully now.

Fohty dollah coffin, eighty dollah hack,
Carried po' man to cemetary but failed to bring him back,
Ev'y body been dodgin' Stagolee.

LOOKIN' FOR THE BULLY OF THE TOWN

Each town had its bad man—the bully. And he is bully until someone successfully disputes his right. Here is the story of the challenge to the bully in a spirited, characteristically Negro ballad. It was recorded by Howard W. Odum and published in *JAF*, xxiv:293.

1. Monday I was 'rested, Tuesday I was fined,
   Sent to chain gang, done serve my time,
   Still I'm lookin' for that bully of this town.

2. The bully, the bully, the bully can't be found,
   If I fin' that bully, goin' to lay his body down,
   I'm lookin' for that bully of this town.

3. The police up town they're all scared,
   But if I fin' that bully, I goin' to lay his body 'way,
   For I'm lookin' for that bully of this town.

4. I'm goin' down on Peter Street;
   If I fin' that bully, will be bloody meet,
   For I'm lookin' for that bully of this town.

5. I went down town the other day,
   I ask ev'ybody did that bully come this way,
   I wus lookin' for that bully of this town.

6. Oh, the gov'ner of this State offer'd one hundred dollars reward,
   To any body's arrested that bully boy,
   I sho' lookin' for dat bully of this town.

7. Well, I found that bully on a Friday night,
   I told that bully I's gwine to take his life,
   I found dat bully of this town.

8. I pull out my gun an' begin to fire,
   I shot that bully right through the eye,
   An' I kill that bully of this town.

9. Now all the wimmins come to town all dressed in red,
   When they heard that bully boy was dead,
   An' it was the last of that bully of this town.

VILLKINS AND HIS DINAH

There is a serious form of this ballad, "Willkins and Dinah," "Jimmie and Dinah" (see *JAF*, xxix:190; xxxv:419) on which the comic parody widely found in copy books and the like is based. The parody originated on the stage and was sung by comic actors. It was printed as early as 1860.

The text that follows, "Jimmie and Dinah," is from Ohio and is published in *JAF*, xxxv:418; B, the "Dutch" version, is from Iowa and is published in *MAF*, xxix:54.

A.

1. In Cumberland city, as you shall all hear,
   There lived a young damsel both comely and fair,
   Her name was Diana, scarce fifteen years old,
   And she had to her position (portion?) a large sum of gold.

2. Besides an estate, when her father did die,
   Which caused many a young man to court the lady;
   Among the whole number sweet Jimmy was one,
   Who strove for to make this fair damsel his own.

3. Hand in hand together they used for to walk,
   To hear the small birds sing, and sweetly they'd talk;
   He said, "My Diana, sweet, innocent maid,
   My lovely Diana, my heart you've betrayed."

4. In two or three weeks after, her father did say,
   "Go dress yourself up in your best rich array,
   For I've a knight for you worth thousands a year,
   And he says he will make you his joy and his dear."

5. "To wed with any young man I don't feel inclined,
   To wed with any old man I won't be confined.
   Besides, I'm too young, and I pray you, therefore,
   To let me live single one year or two more."

6. "O stubborn daughter! Oh, what do you mean?
   Go dress yourself up, no more fit to be seen."
   In this wretched condition this maid was forced out,
   And she went a-roving the groves all about.

7. She went to yonder bower where the small birds sing sweet,
   Where she and her Jimmy they used for to meet;
   She sat herself down by the side of a tree,
   And a strong dose of poison ended her misery.

8. She had not been there one half-hour, I'm sure,
   Till Jimmy came roving the groves o'er and o'er;
   He espied his Diana, a note laying by,
   And in it she told him "'Tis for you I die."

9. He kissed her cold clay lips ten thousand times o'er;
   "I'm robbed of my jewel; I'm robbed of my store."
   He fell on his sword like a lover so brave;
   Now Jimmy and Diana both lie in one grave.

B.

1. There was a rich Dutchman
   In New York did dwell;
   He had a fine daughter
   The truth for to tell.

2. Her name was Katrina,
   As sweet as a rose,
   And she had a large fortune
   In the hands of old Mose.

3. As Katrina was drinking buttermilk one day,
   Her father came to her thus he did say,
   "Now hurry up, Katrina, the parlor go to,
   There's a young man waits to go riding with you."

4. "O, father, why don't they some other girls find?
   To ride with these people I don't feel inclined.
   They drive the buggy so fast they make me feel weak,
   And I want to get married mit Hans Dunder next week."

5. Then her father got mad and he swore his God damn
   She never should marry mit any young man;
   "If you like dis Hans Dunder then go take his bags
   And with his hooks and his baskets go help gather rags."

6. Then away to the kitchen Katrina ran saying,
   "I'll eat me my breakfast so fast as I can;
   Then I'll travel away since I can't be his wife."
   But 'twas by this thing that Katrina lost her life.

7. For as she was eating a big bologna sausage
   It stuck in her throat and stopped up the passage;
   She tried hard to breathe but by grief overcome
   Her head it rolled round and she fell very much numb.

8. Now as Hans Dunder chanced to pass by the door,
   He saw his Katrina lying dead on the floor;
   The big bologna sausage lay there by her side
   And he said, "I'll be damned 'twas by this thing she died."

9. Now all you young fellers take warning from me,
   Be careful whose girl you go for to see;
   And all you young ladies what court in the passage,
   Think of Hans and Katrina and the big bologna sausage.

THE BANKS OF GASPEREAUX

This excellent American (New Brunswick, Nova Scotia, Maine) ballad one would think should be more widely found. Barry thinks that it may be one of the oldest of the woods' songs. The Gaspereaux is a river in New Brunswick. The whole ballad has a distinct shanty-boy flavor. Cf. the last stanza to the "Little Brown Bulls."

Text from Maine, printed by Barry in *Bulletin*, v:13.

1. Come all you jolly lumbermen, I'd have you for to know
   The Yankees they'll return no more to drive the Gaspereaux;
   You told them all the lies you could; you were their bitter foe;
   Bad luck attend those wild galoots who live on Gaspereaux.

2. You thought to scare those Americans and fill their hearts with
      fear,
   You told them they could not get out their lumber the first year;
   But our boss he says, "My brave boys, we'll let those galpins
      know,—"
   And in seven days with his boys so brave, he drove the Gaspe-
      reaux.

3. One of the natives and a daughter, and she was handsome too,
   And she was much admired by one of the Yankee crew;
   Because she wore a purple dress and a red apron also,
   They called her Robin Redbreast on the banks of Gaspereaux.

4. The first time that I saw this bird she filled me with surprise,
   To see such a charming creature appear before my eyes;
   I watched her with amazement to see where she did go;
   She flew into my arms on the banks of Gaspereaux.

5. I says, "My pretty fair one, come go along with me,
   And I will show you a short cut across this counteree;
   I'll dress you up in rich apparel and to the church we'll go,
   And we'll leave these dismal scenes behind on the banks of Gas-
      pereaux."

6. "O no, O no," this fair maid says, "I cannot leave my home,—
   My sisters, they'd lament for me, and papa he would moan;
   But you go and ask my papa, and to the church we'll go,
   And I'll be your kind companion on the banks of Gaspereaux."

7. The next was to the old man and that without delay,
   "I wish to wed your daughter,—an answer, sir, I pray."
   "O yes, O yes," the old man says, "but from me she can't go.
   She can be your kind companion on the banks of Gaspereaux."

8. "O no, O no," the young man says, "this place I cannot bear,

We'll go unto the state of Maine, and we'll be happy there."
"O no, O no," the old man says, "It's from me she can't go,
Why can't you live contented on the banks of Gaspereaux?"

9. "It's now, my lovely Robin, it's you and I must part!"
   And little did they know the grief and woe that lay at his trou-
      bled heart;
   For her hair hung down in ringlets, while the tears from her
      eyes did flow,
   When she parted with her own true love on the banks of Gas-
      pereaux.

10. Now these true lovers parted and sorely they complain,
    For one lives in Gaspereaux and the other in the state of Maine;
    The state we roam all over and we'll ramble to and fro,
    And we'll think of lovely Robin on the banks of Gaspereaux.

11. It's now our lumber's rafted and going to St. John,
    And when that we get it there, we'll put it in the pond;
    We'll drink our health to Robin, the Stars and Stripes also,
    Likewise those kind old people we left in Gaspereaux.

THE JAM ON GERRY'S ROCK

This most famous of all shanty-boy ballads is found nearly all over the
United States carried by the lumbermen. Two versions exist, an eastern and a western. The eastern version, originating probably in
Maine, is the cruder and seemingly the older. The name of lady in
this version varies: Miss Carrow, Miss Clark, etc. In this version too,
the head of Monroe is found, not the body. In an interesting essay
which tells much of the ballad collector's method and problems, "The
Pursuit of a Ballad Myth," *Minstrelsy of Maine*, pp. 176–198, Mrs.
Eckstorm tells a long story of her search for the sources and the authorship of this famous ballad. Since she found neither, probably
neither will ever be found. One would hazard a guess that it was
originally a Maine ballad and that it was composed in the late century.
   Text from *The Maine Sportsman* (1904), No. 125, reported from
tradition.

1. Come all of you bold shanty boys, and list while I relate
   Concerning a young shanty boy and his untimely fate,
   Concerning a young river-man, so manly, true and brave;
   'Twas on the jam at Gerry's Rock he met a watery grave.

2. It was on Sunday morning as you will quickly hear,
   Our logs were piled up mountains high, we could not keep them
      clear.

Our foreman said, "Turn out brave boys, with heart devoid of
    fear;
We'll break the jam on Gerry's Rock and for Eganstown we'll
    steer."

3. Now some of them were willing while others they were not,
For to work on jams on Sunday they did not think we ought;
But six of our Canadian boys did volunteer to go
And break the jam on Gerry's Rock with the foreman, young
    Monroe.

4. They had not rolled off many logs when they heard his clear
    voice say:
"I'd have you boys be on your guard for the jam will soon give
    way."
These words were scarcely spoken when the mass did break and
    go,
And it carried off those six brave youths and their foreman, Jack
    Monroe.

5. When the rest of our brave shanty boys the sad news came to
    hear
In search of their dead comrades to the river they did steer;
Some of the mangled bodies a-floating down did go,
While crushed and bleeding near the bank was that of young
    Jack Monroe.

6. They took him from his watery grave, brushed back his raven
    hair;
There was one fair girl among them whose sad cries rent the
    air—
There was one fair form among them, a maid from Saginaw
    town,
Whose moans and cries rose to the skies for her true love who'd
    gone down.

7. Fair Clara was a noble girl, the river-man's true friend;
She lived with her widowed mother dear, down at the river's
    bend;
The wages of her own true love the "boss" to her did pay,
And the shanty boys for her made up a generous purse next day.

8. They buried him with sorrow deep, 'twas on the first of May;
"Come all of you, bold shanty boys, and for your comrade pray!"
Engraved upon a hemlock-tree that by the grave did grow,
Was the name and date of the sad, sad fate of the shanty boy,
    Monroe.

9. Fair Clara did not long survive, her heart broke with her grief,
And scarcely two months afterward death came to her relief.

And when the time had passed away and she was called to go,
Her last request was granted, to be laid by young Monroe.

10. Come all of you bold shanty boys, I would have you call and see
Those green mounds by the riverside, where grows the hemlock-
tree.
The shanty boys cleared off the wood by the lovers there laid
low—
'Twas the handsome Clara Vernon and her true love, Jack
Monroe.

CANADAY I. O.
(THE BUFFALO SKINNERS)

These ballads belong to a group of songs that show a remarkable development. In 1853 one Ephraim Braley composed the ballad "Canaday I. O.," adapting it from an old English sea song, "Canada I. O.,"
printed in *The Forget Me Not Songster,* New York, 1847, and
widely circulated in Maine. This song in turn was based on "Cale-
donia," a song in *The Caledonian Garland.* "Canaday I. O." in its
turn begot three songs: (1) a Pennsylvania song, "The Jolly Lumberman" or "Colley's Run I. O." (see Shoemaker, *Penna. Minstrelsy,*
p. 86), (2) "Michigan I. O.," widely current among the lumbermen
in Michigan (see Rickably, p. 41), (3) "The Buffalo Skinners," a
western reworking of "Canaday I. O." Both "Canaday I. O." and
"The Buffalo Skinners" are printed here for comparison. Lomax
quotes Kittredge as saying that "The Buffalo Skinners" is the greatest of the western ballads.

Text of "Canaday I. O." from Maine and printed by Mrs. Eckstorm in *Bulletin* vi:10, whence the notes given above, and that of
"The Buffalo Skinners" from Allan Lomax, *Folk Songs U.S.A.,* p.
175.

THE BUFFALO SKINNERS

1. 'Twas in the town of Jacksboro in the year of '73,
When a man by the name of Crego came stepping up to me,
Saying, "How do you do, young fellow, and how would you like
to go
And spend one summer pleasantly on the range of the buffalo?"

2. It's me being out of employment, boys, to old Crego I did say,
"This going out on the buffalo range depends upon the pay.
But if you will pay good wages, give transportation, too,
I think, sir, I will go with you to the range of the buffalo."

3. It's now our outfit was complete, seven able-bodied men,
With navy six and needle gun our troubles did begin;

Our way, it was a pleasant one, the route we had to go,
Until we crossed Pease River on the range of the buffalo.

4. It's now we've crossed Pease River, our troubles have begun,
The first damned tail I went to rip, it's how I cut my thumb!
The water was salty as hell-fire, the beef I could not go,
And the Indians waited to pick us off, while skinning the buffalo.

5. Our hearts were cased with buffalo hocks, our souls were cased
with steel,
And the hardships of that summer would nearly make us reel.
While skinning the damned old stinkers, our lives they had no
show,
For the Indians waited to pick us off on the hills of Mexico.

6. The season being near over, boys, old Crego, he did say
The crowd had been extravagant, was in debt to him that day.
We coaxed him and we begged him, but still it was no go—
So we left his damned old bones to bleach on the range of the
buffalo.

7. Oh, it's now we've crossed Pease River and homeward we are
bound,
No more in that hell-fired country shall ever we be found.
Go home to our wives and sweethearts, tell others not to go,
For God's forsaken the buffalo range and the damned old buffalo.

CANADAY I. O.

1. Come all ye jolly lumbermen, and listen to my song,
But do not get discouraged, the length it is not long,
Concerning of some lumbermen, who did agree to go
To spend one pleasant winter up in Canada I O.

2. It happened late one season in the fall of fifty-three,
A preacher of the gospel one morning came to me;
Said he, "My jolly fellow, how would you like to go
To spend one pleasant winter up in Canada I O?"

3. To him I quickly made reply, and unto him did say:
"In going out to Canada depends upon the pay.
If you will pay good wages, my passage to and fro,
I think I'll go along with you to Canada I O."

4. "Yes, we will pay good wages, and will pay your passage out,
Provided you sign papers that you will stay the route;
But if you do get homesick and swear that home you'll go,
We never can your passage pay from Canada I O."

5. "And if you get dissatisfied and do not wish to stay,
We do not wish to bind you, no, not one single day;

You just refund the money we had to pay, you know,
Then you can leave that bonny place called Canada I O."

6. It was by his gift of flattery he enlisted quite a train,
   Some twenty-five or thirty, both well and able men;
   We had a pleasant journey o'er the road we had to go,
   Till we landed at Three Rivers, up in Canada I O.

7. But there our joys were ended, and our sorrows did begin;
   Fields, Phillips and Norcross they then came marching in;
   They sent us all directions, some where I do not know,
   Among those jabbering Frenchmen up in Canada I O.

8. After we had suffered there some eight or ten long weeks
   We arrived at headquarters, up among the lakes;
   We thought we'd find a paradise, at least they told us so,
   God grant there may be no worse hell than Canada I O!

9. To describe what we have suffered is past the art of man,
   But to give a fair description I will do the best I can;
   Our food the dogs would snarl at, our beds were on the snow,
   We suffered worse than murderers up in Canada I O.

10. Our hearts were made of iron and our souls were cased with steel,
    The hardships of that winter could never make us yield;
    Fields, Phillips and Norcross they found their match, I know,
    Among the boys that went from Maine to Canada I O.

11. But now our lumbering is over and we are returning home,
    To greet our wives and sweethearts and never more to roam,
    To greet our friends and neighbors; we'll tell them not to go
    To that forsaken G__ D__ place called Canaday I O.

THE LITTLE BROWN BULLS

According to one of Rickaby's informants, this ballad was composed "in Mort Douglas's camp in northern Wisconsin in 1872 or '73." It was in this camp that the contest took place. As Rickaby points out, the characteristic leaping technique of the ballad in passing over antecedent material to come to the climax deprives us of the account of what must have been an epic struggle.

Text from Nova Scotia as sung by John Kenny to M. E. L., 1936.

1. Not a thing on the river McCluskey did fear
   As he swung his goad-stock o'er the big speckled steers;
   They were long, fat and thick, girt in eight foot and three—
   "Ha! Ha!" said McCluskey, "the laddies for me."
   Darry down, down, down, darry down.

2. The next came bold Gordon, whose skidding was full;
    He would bet two to one on his little brown bulls;
    They were short, thick, and soggy, girt in six foot and nine,
    "Not fit," said McCluskey, "to handle our pine."
        Darry down etc.

3. Oh, three to the thousand our contract did call,
    Our skidding was good and our lumber was tall;
    McCluskey he swore to do the day full,
    He'd skid two to one, to the little brown bulls,

4. "Oh, no" said bold Gordon, "that trick you can't do,
    Though I very well know you've the pets of the crew;
    But mind you, my boy, you'll do the day full
    If you skid a log more than the little brown bulls."

5. A day was appointed and soon did draw nigh
    With twenty-five dollars their fortunes to try;
    All eager and anxious next morning was found,
    While judges and scalers appeared on the ground.

6. The first came McCluskey, with a whoop and a roar,
    And his big speckled steers with a cud in their jaw;
    "It's chewing your cud, boys, and keep your jaw full,
    And we'll easily beat them, the little brown bulls."

7. The next came bold Gordon, a pipe in his jaw,
    And the little brown bulls with a cud in their maw;
    But little we thought, as we saw them come down,
    A hundred and forty they would swing around.

8. Said McCluskey to Sandy: "Now strip to the skin,
    We'll dig them a hole and we'll shove 'em therein;
    We'll teach the damned Yankees to fear the brave Scot,
    We'll mix them a dose, boy, and give it to them hot."

9. Says Gordon to Griffin, with blood in his eye:
    "This day we will conquer McCluskey or die."
    Says Kennebec John: "My boy, never fear;
    You ne'er shall be beat by the big speckled steers."

10. The sun it went down and our foreman did say:
     "Come in, lads, come in; it's enough for the day;
     We've counted and scaled for each man and his team,
     And we very well know just which one tips the beam."

11. When supper was over McCluskey appears
     With a belt ready made for his big speckled steers;
     He meant to conduct it according to law,
     So he went and tore up his new mackinaw.

12. "Hold on," said our scaler, "hold on for awhile,
    For your big speckled steers are behind just a mile;
    You've skidded a hundred and ten and no more,
    While Gordon has beat you full ten and a score."

13. Then the shanty did ring and McCluskey did swear,
    By the handfuls he tore out his long yellow hair.
    He stepped up to Gordon; "The colors we'll pull,"
    Saying, "Here, take the belt for your little brown bulls."

14. Here's a health to bold Gordon and Kennebec John,
    For the best day's work on the river ever done.
    So fill up your glasses and fill them up full
    And we'll all drink our health for the little brown bulls.

HIGH BARBARY

This spirited sea ballad is distantly related to Child 285, "The George
Aloe and the Sweepstake." It has been in and out of tradition both in
England and America since the early 18th century. In America it was
regularly printed in the songsters, though its circulation in oral tradi-
tion continued independently. The following from *The American
Songster* is the usual last stanza, omitted from this traditional version.

> For better than two hours this battle lasted as you see,
> Blow high, blow low and so sail'd we,
> The ship it was their coffin, and their grave it was the sea,
> Cruising down the coast of Barbary.

Text from *British Ballads of Maine,* p. 413, from oral tradition.

1. There were two lofty ships from Old England came,
      Blow high, blow low, and so sailed we;
   One was the Queen of Russia and the other Prince of Wales,
      Cruising down along the coast of the High Barbaree.

2. "Aloft there, aloft!" our jolly boatswain cried,
      Blow high, blow low, and so sailed we;
   "Look ahead, look astern, look aweather, look alee,
      Look down along the coast of the High Barbaree."

3. "There's nought upon the stern, there's nought upon the lee,"
      Blow high, blow low, and so sailed we;
   "But there's a lofty ship to windward and she's sailing fast and
      free,
      Sailing down along the coast of the High Barbaree."

4. "Oh, hail her, oh, hail her!" our gallant captain cried,
      Blow high, blow low and so sailed we;

"Are you a man-of-war, or a privateer," said he,
"Cruising down along the coast of the High Barbaree?"

5. "Oh, I'm not a man-of-war, nor a privateer," said he,
Blow high, blow low, and so sailed we;
"But I'm a salt-sea pirate a-looking for a fee,
Cruising down along the coast of the High Barbaree."

6. Oh, 'twas broadside to broadside a long time we lay,
Blow high, blow low, and so sailed we,
Until the Queen of Russia shot the pirate's mast away,
Cruising down along the coast of the High Barbaree.

7. "Oh, quarter, oh, quarter!" those pirates then did cry
Blow high, blow low, and so sailed we,
But the quarter that we gave them, we sunk them in the sea,
Cruising down along the coast of the High Barbaree.

THE FLYING CLOUD

This ballad from Irish or English broadside sources was very popular in America, especially among sailors who sang it as a forecastle song, and also among lumbermen, carried to them as were many other narratives of the sea by sailors working the woods in the winter when the sea was inhospitable. The song is older than the famous clipper ship, *The Flying Cloud,* and has nothing to do with her, except that her name may have supplanted another name in the ballad. Two distinct stories seem to be joined in this ballad: a story of slaving and a story of piracy. It is very possible that two once-separate ballads are here joined.

Text from the singing of Dale Potter, Maine, to Horace P. Beck, 1947.

Notes

1/3. Waterford is in Ireland, as is Trymore. 1/4. Eirings: Erin's.

1. My name is Edward Holland
As you may understand
I belong to the county of Waterford
Near Eirings happy land

2. When I was young and in my prime
And fortune on me smiled
My parents rared me tenderly
I being their only child

3. My father bound me to a trade
In Waterford's own town

He bound me to a cooper there
By the name of William Brown

4. I served my master faithfully
For eighteen months or more
Till I shipped aboard of the Ocean Queen
Bound down for Bermuda's shore

5. When we arrived at Bermuda shore
I fell in with a Capting More.
The commander of the Flying Cloud
And belonging to Trymore.

6. He questioned and cross questioned me
On a slaving voyage to go
To the burning shores of Africa
Where the sugar cane does grow.

7. Now three or four weeks after this
We arrived at the African shore
And eighteen hundred of those poor souls
From their native land we bore.

8. We would march them on our quarterdecks
And store them down below.
It was eighteen inches to a man;
It was what they had to go.

9. We sailed away without delay
With our cargo of slaves.
It would been better for them poor souls
Had they been in their graves.

10. The plaguey fever came aboard
Swept half of them away
We dragged their dead bodies on deck
And threw them in the sea.

11. Now two or three weeks after this
We arrived at Bermuda shore
Where we sold them to the planters there
To be slaves for ever more.

12. The rye and coffee fields to hoe
Beneath the burning sun
For to live a long and dreary life
'Till their career was run.

13. Now when our slaving money was all gone
We put to sea again.
When Capting More he came on deck
And said to us his men.

14. "There is gold and silver to be had
    If you will agree with me.
    We will hoist aloft pirate flag
    And scour the raging sea."

15. Now they all agreed excepting five
    And those we had to land.
    Two of them being Boston boys,
    Two more from Newfoundland.

16. The other being an Irish man
    Belonging to Trymore.
    I wish to God I had joined those five
    And went with them on shore.

17. Now we robbed and plundered many the ship
    Down on the Spanish Main
    Caused many the widow and orphan child
    In sorrow to remain.

18. We would march them on their quarterdecks
    Give them a watery grave
    For the saying of that Capting More
    That a dead man tells no tales.

19. Now chased were we by many the ship
    Both frigates and liners too.
    It was all in vain astern of us
    Their bomb shells they did throw.

20. It was all in vain astern of us
    Their cannons roared aloud.
    It was all in vain for to ever try
    For to catch the Flying Cloud.

21. Now the Flying Cloud was a Spanish ship
    Five thousand tons or more.
    She would easily outsail any ship
    Coming out of Baltimore.

22. Her sails were as white as the driven snow
    On them there were no stains.
    With a forty-nine brass pounded gun
    She would carry an after main.

23. Now the Flying Cloud was as fine a ship
    As ever swam the sea.
    Or ever spread a main top sail
    Before a pleasant breeze.

24. Now often have I watched that ship
    As she went sailing by

With her royal galyants spread aloft
Above the canvas high.

25. Now a Spanish ship, the man of war
Her dungeon hove in view.
She fired a shot across our deck
As a signal to heave to.

26. But to her we paid no attention
As before a pleasant breeze
Till a chance shot cut our mainmast down
We then soon fell behind.

27. We cleared our decks for action
As she ranged up alongside.
And soon acrost our quarterdecks
There flowed a crimson tide.

28. We fought till Capting More was slain
And eight of our men
Till a bombshell set our ship on fire
We were forced to surrender then.

29. It's now to Newgate we are brought
Bound down in iron bands
For the murdering and plundering of many the ship
Down on the ocean strands.

30. It's drinking and bad company
That's made a wretch of me.
Come all young men a warning take
Bid a curse to the pirate sea.

FIFTEEN SHIPS ON GEORGE'S BANKS

The Fisherman's Memorial and Record Book, according to Mrs. Eckstorm, recounts the story of this gale. It happened February 24, 1862. Fifteen vessels and crews of 120 men were lost, leaving 70 widows and 140 fatherless children. The ballad exists in several forms and is still to be found in tradition. George's Banks are famous fishing banks off Nova Scotia.

Text from Maine and printed by Mrs. Eckstorm in *Minstrelsy of Maine,* p. 281.

1. Come all you bold, undaunted ones,
Who brave the winter cold,
And you that sail on George's Banks
Where thousands have been lost.

2. Come all you sad and grieving mothers,
   And wives and sweethearts too,
   Likewise you loving sisters
   Who bade them last adieu.

3. 'Twas on the first of February,
   In eighteen sixty-two,
   Three vessels sailed from Gloucester
   With each a hearty crew.

4. The course they steered was east-south-east,
   Cape Ann passed out of sight;
   They anchored on the Banks that night,
   With everything all right.

5. The thoughts of home and loving friends
   Did fill their hearts full sore,
   For well convinced were all those men
   They'd see their homes no more.

6. No tongue can e'er describe the sea,
   The sky was thick with snow;
   Fifteen sails did founder there,
   And down to bottom go.

7. One hundred and forty-nine brave men,
   So lately left their land,
   Now sleep beneath the George's Banks,
   Those rough and shifting sands.

8. One hundred and seventy children
   Those men have left on shore,
   With seventy mournful widows
   Their sorrows to endure.

9. I hope they will be reconciled
   And not give up to grief,
   There is a widow's God above,
   And He will give relief.

10. There were many in the army,
    And in the navy too,
    Who mourn and grieve in private,
    Who will sympathize with you.

11. You will at times think of home,
    Of days that's past and gone,
    When by their sides their husbands sat,
    And cheerful was their song.

12. So now adieu to George's Banks,
    That place I now despise,

For many a storm I've braved out there,
And heard the widows cry.

13. So bid adieu to George's Banks,
Dry up your tearful eyes,
Prepare to meet your God above,
And dwell beyond the sky.

THE AVONDALE MINE DISASTER

This ballad is probably the best known of the mine disaster ballads.
It recounts the story of the terrible tragedy when fire struck in the
Avondale mine near Wilkes-Barre, Pennsylvania, in 1869. The ballad
as a broadside was written by an unknown ballad maker at that time.
It went immediately into tradition and is now found far and wide.
Text, *Penna. Songs and Legends,* ed. Korson, p. 386.

1. Good Christians all, both great and small,
I pray you lend an ear,
And listen with attention while
The truth I will declare;
When you hear this lamentation
'Twill cause you to weep and wail,
About the suffocation
In the mines of Avondale.

2. On the sixth day of September,
Eighteen sixty-nine,
Those miners all then got a call
To go work in the mine;
But little did they think that (day)
That death would soon prevail
Before they would return again from
The mines of Avondale.

3. The women and their children,
Their hearts were filled with joy
To see their men go to their work
Likewise every boy;
But a dismal sight in broad daylight,
Soon made them turn pale,
When they saw the breaker burning
O'er the mines of Avondale.

4. From here and there and everywhere,
They gathered in a crowd,
Come tearing off their clothes and hair,
And crying out aloud—

"Get out our husbands and our sons,
 Death he's going to steal
Their lives away without delay
 In the mines of Avondale."

5. But all in vain, there was no hope
 One single soul to save,
For there is no second outlet
 From the subterranean cave.
No pen can write the awful fright
 And horror that prevailed,
Among those dying victims,
 In the mines of Avondale.

6. A consultation then was held.
 'Twas asked who'd volunteer
For to go down this dismal shaft
 To seek their comrades dear;
Two Welshmen brave, without dismay,
 And courage without fail,
Went down the shaft, without delay,
 In the mines of Avondale.

7. When at the bottom they arrived,
 And thought to make their way,
One of them died for want of air,
 While the other in great dismay,
He gave a sign to hoist him up,
 To tell the dreadful tale,
That all were lost forever
 In the mines of Avondale.

8. Every effort then took place
 To send down some fresh air;
The men that next went down again
 They took of them good care;
And traversed through the chambers,
 And this time did not fail
In finding those dead bodies
 In the mines of Avondale.

9. Sixty-seven was the number
 That in a heap were found.
It seemed that they were bewailing
 Their fate underneath the ground;
They found the father with his son
 Clasped in his arms so pale.
It was a heart-rending scene
 In the mines of Avondale.

10.   Now to conclude, and make an end,
      Their number I'll pen down—
    A hundred and ten of brave strong men
      Were smothered underground;
    They're in their graves till the last day,
      Their widows may bewail,
    And the orphan's cries they rend the skies
      All around through Avondale!

THE LEXINGTON MURDER

This is typical of many murder ballads. It is found under various names, such as "The Lexington Girl," "The Wexford Girl," "The Oxford Girl," and "The Lexington Miller." All stem ultimately from British broadsides of the 18th century by way of American printed broadsides. Here, along with a traditional version from North Carolina (*JAF,* xlvi:29), is a broadside from the Harvard collection of broadsides, "The Lexington Miller."

1.   My tender parents brought me up, providing me full well,
    And in the city of Lexington they put me in the mill;
    And there I spied a fair young maid, and on her I cast my eye;
    I asked her if she'd marry me and she believed a lie.

2.   We went into her sister's house about eight o'clock one night;
    Not one time did the creature think at her I had a spite.
    I asked her for to take a walk a little ways away,
    That she and I might have a talk about our wedding day.

3.   We walked along, we talked along, to a lonely desert place,
    I drew a stick from off the fence and struck her in the face;
    Down on her bended knee she fell and loud for mercy cried,
    "For Heaven's sakes don't murder me, I'm not prepared to die."

4.   But little did I pay to her, I only struck her more,
    Until I saw that innocent blood which I could not restore;
    I ran my hands through her cold black hair and I tried to cover
      my sins,
    I drug her to the river's bank and there I plunged her in.

5.   As I returned back to my mill, I met my servant John,
    He asked me why I looked so sad and yet so badly one.
    I lit my candle and went to bed expecting to take a rest
    It seemed as if the flames of hell were burning at my breast.

    Young men and boys, take warning from this and unto your lover
      be true,
    Don't never let the devil get the upper hand of you.

THE LEXINGTON MILLER

1. Come all you men and maidens dear, to you I will relate.
    Pray lend an ear and you shall hear concerning my sad fate,
    My parents brought me up with care, provided for me well,
    And in the town of Lexington employ'd me in a mill.

2. 'Twas there I 'spied a comely lass, she cast a winning eye,
    I promis'd I would marry her if she would but comply.
    I courted her about six months, which caused us pain and woe;
    'Twas folly brought us into a snare, and it prov'd our overthrow.

3. Her mother came to me one day as you shall understand,
    Begging that I would appoint a day, and marry her at hand;
    It was about one month from Christmas; O, cursed be that day,
    The devil put in my heart to take her life away.

4. I was perplex'd on every side, no comfort could I find
    Then for to take her life away, my wicked heart inclin'd;
    I went unto her sister's house at eight o'clock at night,
    And she, poor soul, little thought or knew I ow'd her any spite.

5. I said, come go along with me, out door a little way,
    That you and I may both agree upon our wedding day,
    Then hand in hand I led her on, down to some silent place;
    I took a stake out of the fence, and struck her on the face.

6. Now she upon her knees did fall, and most heartily did cry,
    Saying, kind sir, don't murder me for I am not fit to die;
    I would not harken unto her cries, but laid it on the more,
    Till I had taken her life away, which I could not restore.

7. All in the blood of innocence, my trembling hands have dy'd,
    All in the blood of her who should have been my lawful bride;
    She gave a sigh and bitter groan, and cast a wishful look,
    I took her by the hair of the head and flung her in the brook.

8. Now straight unto the Mill I went, like one that's in a maze,
    And first I met was my servant boy, who deeply on me gaz'd;
    How came that blood upon your hands, likewise on your clothes?
    I instantly made reply, "'Twas bleeding of the nose." '

9. I called for a candle, the same was brought to me.
    And when the candle I had light, an awful sight I see;
    Now straightway unto bed I went, thinking relief to find,
    It seemed as if the plagues of hell, were lodg'd within my mind.

10. Next day her body was search'd for, but it could not be found,
    Then I was in my chamber seized, and in my chains were bound.
    In two or three days after, this fair maid she was found,

Came floating by her mother's house, that was near Wenton-
town.

11. Her sister swore against me, she said she had no doubt,
'Twas I took her life away, as 'twas I that led her out.
It's now my end comes hastening on, and death approaches nigh,
And by my own confession I am condemn'd to die.

Now fare you well to Lexington, where my first breath I drew,
I warn all men and maidens, to all their vows prove true.

FAIR FLORELLA OR
THE JEALOUS LOVER

Many ballads varying in details and language but keeping the same
general story pattern as this are found all over America. Fair Florella
(she is also called Louella, Ella, Lena, Ellen, Nina, Abbey, Emma,
Alice) is evidently based on an English broadside, "The Murder of
Betsy Smith," early 19th century. "Florella," or "The Jealous Lover,"
furnished a pattern for many ballads based on real murders, like
"Mary Phagan," "Pearl Bryan," "Nellie Cropsey."
Text A from New England as printed *JAF*, xxii:370; B from
Virginia as sung by Mrs. Tiny Gaunt to M.E.L., 1937.

A.

1. Down by yon weeping willow,
Where flowers so sweetly bloom,
There sleeps the fair Florilla,
So silent in her tomb.

2. She died not broken hearted,
Nor sickness e'er befell,
But in one moment parted
From all she loved so well.

3. One night the moon shone brightly,
And gentle zephyrs blew,
Up to her cottage lightly
Her treacherous lover drew.

4. He says, "Come let us wander,
In those dark woods we'll stray,
And there we'll sit and ponder
Upon our wedding-day."

5. "Those woods look dark and dreary,
I am afraid to stray,
Of wandering I am weary,
So I'll retrace my way."

6. "Those woods, those gentle zephyrs,
   Your feet no more will roam,
   So bid adieu forever
   To parents, friends, and home."

7. Down on her knees before him
   She begged for her life,
   When deep into her bosom
   He plunged that hateful knife.

8. "O William! I'll forgive you,"
   Was her last dying breath,
   Her pulses ceased their motion,
   Her eyes were closed in death.

9. Down by yon weeping willow,
   Where flowers so sweetly bloom,
   There sleeps that fair Florilla,
   So silent in her tomb.

B.

1. Down in a lonesome valley
   Where the modest violets bloom,
   There's where my sweetheart Ella
   Lies mouldering in the tomb.

2. One eve when the moon was shining
   And the stars were shining too,
   A-lightly to her cottage
   The jealous lover flew.

3. Saying, "Come my love, let's wander
   In these wild woods so gay.
   While wandering there we'll ponder
   And name our wedding day."

4. "Oh, the night is growing dreary
   And I'm afraid to stay,
   For I am growing weary
   I would like to retrace my way."

5. "Retrace your way, no never!
   From me you cannot flee
   So bid farewell forever
   Fair Ella, you must die!"

6. Down on her knees before him
   She pleaded for her life,
   "What have I done, dear Henry,
   That you should take my life?

7. "You know that I've always been faithful
   And would have been your wife."
   But deep into her bosom
   He plunged the fatal knife.

8. "Oh Henry, I'll forgive you,"
   Were her last dying words
   "I never have deceived you."
   And she closed her eyes in death.

9. The birds sang in the morning
   So solemn was the sound.
   A stranger found her body
   On the cold and silent ground.

10. Come all young men and maidens
    And warning here take heed,
    Don't put your trust in young men
    Or you astray they may lead.

PEARL BRYAN

Ballads bearing the title "Pearl Bryan" appear as a variation of "The Jealous Lover" and also as a separate composition. The second type was based on an actual murder—that of one Pearl Bryan—who was murdered by a Scot Jackson and Alonzo Walling about January 29, 1896. Her headless body was found near Fort Thomas, Kentucky. Several versions in different meters in addition to the Jealous Lover type are found.

Text from Indiana and printed by Brewster, *Ballads and Songs from Indiana*, p. 285. For details of the crime see *JAF*, xlii:301.

1. Now, ladies, if you'll listen, a story I'll relate
   What happened near Fort Thomas in the old Kentucky state.
   'T was late in January this awful deed was done
   By Jackson and by Walling; how cold their blood did run!

2. How bold these cruel villains to do this awful deed,
   To ride away Pearl Bryan when she to them did plead!
   The driver tells the story of how Pearl Bryan did moan
   From Cincinnati to the place where the cruel deed was done.

3. But little did Pearl's parents think when she left her happy home
   That their own dear darling daughter would ne'er return again.
   We know her dear old parents their fortune they would give
   If Pearl could just return home a happy life to live.

4. The driver was the only one could tell her awful fate,
   Of poor Pearl far away from home in the old Kentucky state;

A farmer passing by next day her lifeless form he found,
A-lying . . . where her blood had stained the ground.

5.   Pearl Bryan left her parents on a dark and gloomy day;
     She went to meet the villain in a spot not far away.
     She thought it was the lover's hand that she could trust each day;
     Alas, it was a lover's hand that took her life away!

6.   Young ladies, now take warning; young men are so unjust;
     It may be your best lover, but you know not whom to trust.
     Pearl died away from home and friends, out on that lonely spot;
     Take heed; take heed! believe me, girls; don't let this be your lot!

COLONEL SHARP

This ballad is based on a killing that took place in Frankfort, Kentucky, in 1824. The dramatic story begot many ballads and a number of novels, stories, and plays, of which the most popular are Poe's *Politian,* William Simms' two novels, *Charlemont* and *Beauchampe,* C. F. Hoffman's *Greyslaer,* Charlotte Barnes' *Octavia Bragaldi,* Chivers' *Conrad and Eudora* (a verse drama), and finally Robert Penn Warren's *World Enough and Time,* 1950.

The details are as given in the ballad except that the two tried to commit suicide by poison; the wife died from the effects of the poison shortly after the husband was executed.

Text from tradition in North Carolina, printed in *JAF,* xxviii:166–168.

1.   Gentlemen and Ladies, I pray you lend an ear;
     A very sad story you now shall quickly hear;
     It was of a bold young lawyer lived in Kentucky state
     Who on his own true lovyer with patience he did wait.

2.   She told him she would marry him if he would avenge her heart
     Of injury had been done her by one said Colonel Sharpe,
     She said he had seduced her and brought her spirits low
     "And without some satisfaction no pleasures can I know."

3.   It's "Oh, my dearest Jewel, that's pleasant talk to me.
     To kill the man who injured you I really do feel free;
     For I never could expect you for to become my wife
     Until I did attack him and surely take his life."

4.   He had made some preparations and on to Frankfort went;
     To kill this noble Colonel it was his whole intent.
     He took him out to one side and gave to him a knife.
     He said, "I cannot fight you if this lady be your wife."

5. He went down to Frankfort all on the very next day.
   He hunted Frankfort over, and Sharpe had gone away.
   He turned to his lovyer and told her what he'd done,
   And both agreed within themselves they'd let him longer run.

6. She made a mask of black silk and put it on his head;
   So they might think he was some negro as he ran from the bed.
   He slipped along most secretly till he came to Colonel Sharpe;
   Called him from his bed chamber and stabbed him to his heart.

7. And then this Colonel's friends they all came flocking round.
   .   .   .   .
   And wasn't it most sorrowful to see him bleed and die,
   And leave his little children and his poor wife to cry?

8. And then his dearest lovyer turned to his loving wife,
   Says, "Oh, my dearest Jewel, I've took that Colonel's life.
   And now we will prepare ourselves and to Missouri run,
   And I hope we'll be more happier than when we first begun."

9. She said, "Oh, my dearest Jewel, just do as you please;
   You've took me out of trouble and set me at my ease."
   This couple was followed after and back was fetched again.
   He was tried by judge and jury, and guilty he was found.
   They carried him to the jail house and in it he was bound.

10. Then he called for pen and ink to write all around,
    "I want this whole world to know what I have done:
    I've killed this noble Colonel that injured my poor wife
    And always will protect her as long as I have life.

11. "My dear old father, don't you trouble me;
    And my dear old mother, don't grieve nor cry for me;
    For the laws of old Kentucky say I must shortly die
    And leave my little brothers and sisters here to cry."

12. Then he says, "Oh, my dearest Jewel, come stay awhile with me,
    For I shortly must leave you to go to eternity.
    May the heavens bless you while here on earth you stay,
    And all my friends protect you and help you on your way."

13. She says, "My dearest Jewel, I'll stay awhile with you;
    The reasons of your troubles were all becaused by me."
    She says, "I will stay with you while here on earth you stay,
    And when you're persecuted lie with you in the clay."

14. She ground her penknife, she ground it keen and sharp;
    While he was talking to her she stabbed it to her heart;
    She gave it to her own true-love, he undertook the same;
    The very second blow he made she stopped it with her hand.

15. Perhaps there's some one here who'd wish to know their names.
     It was Andy Bowens Beecher and Andy Cooker's dame.
     And wasn't it surprising that they behaved so brave,
     And in each other's bosom lay mouldering in the grave?
     Was ever a transaction that caused so much blood
     Was ever a true-hearted man more constant to his love?

HENRY GREEN

Henry Green is typical of the broadside murder ballads of the North-east, as "The Jealous Lover-Florella-Pearl Bryan" was of the South and West. The ballad records the murder of Mary Wyatt Green by Henry Green, her husband of less than a week. The murder occurred in February, 1845. For details and a facsimile copy of one of the broadsides see Lewis Jones, "Folksongs of Mary Wyatt and Henry Green," *Bulletin,* 12. Many verses were written about this affair and published in local papers.

Text from Vermont and printed in *Bulletin,* xii:16.

1. Come, listen to my tragedy, good people, young and old;
    An awful story you shall hear, 'twill make your blood run cold;
    Concerning a fair damsel; Mary Wyatt was her name—
    She was poisoned by her husband, and he hung for the same.

2. Mary Wyatt she was beautiful, not of a high degree,
    And Henry Green was wealthy, as you may plainly see;
    He said, "My dearest Mary, if you'll become my wife,
    I will guard you and protect you, through all this gloom of life."

3. "O Henry, I would marry you, I would give my consent,
    But before that we'd been married long, I fear you would re-
    pent;
    Before that we'd been married long, you'd make me a disgrace,
    Because I'm not as rich as you, which oft times is the case."

4. "O Mary, dearest Mary, how can you grieve me so?
    I'll vow and 'clare by all that's fair, I always will prove true;
    But unless you consent to become my wife, you'll surely end my
    life,
    For no longer do I wish to live, unless you are my wife."

5. Believing what he said was true, she then became his wife,
    But little did she think, poor girl, that he would end her life;
    O little did she think, poor child, and little did she expect
    That he would end her precious life he'd just sworn to protect.

6. They had not been married but a week or two, when she was
    taken ill,

Great doctors were sent for, to try their powerful skill;
Great doctors were sent for, but none of them could save,
And soon it was proclaimed she must go to her grave.

7. O when her brothers heard of this, straightway to her did go,
Saying, "Sister dear, you're dying, the doctors tell us so";
Saying, "Sister dear, you're dying, your life is at an end";
Saying, "Haven't you been poisoned by the one you call your
friend.

8. "I'm on my deathbed lying. I know that I must die,
I know I'm going before my God, and the truth I won't deny;
I know my Henry's poisoned me—dear brother, for him send,
For I love him now as dearly as when he was my friend."

9. When Henry heard those tidings, straightway to his wife to see,
Saying "Mary, my dearest Mary, was you ever deceived in me?"
Three times she called "Dear Henry," then, and sank into a
swoon;
He gazed on her indifferently, and in silence left the room.

10. "Now Henry has deceived me,—how my poor heart is wrung!
But when I'm dead and buried, O don't have poor Henry hung!
I freely have forgiven him—" and she turned upon her side;
"In Heaven meet me, Henry!" and she sweetly smiled and died.

NAOMI (OMIE) WISE

This murder ballad follows the usual pattern: a girl is murdered because the man who has seduced her does not want to marry her. About
1808 Jonathan Lewis murdered Naomi Wise by drowning her in
Deep River, North Carolina. See *Folk Ballads from North Carolina*
(Frank Brown Collection, ii, 690) for the documented story.

Text A from Virginia, Belden, 323; B from Kentucky, *JAF*,
xx:265.

A.

1. Come all you young people, I pray you draw near,
A sorrowful ditty you quickly shall hear.
The truth I will tell you about Omie Wise,
How Omie was deceived by Lewis's lies.

2. Come all ye pretty fair maids take warning from me,

.   .   .   .

Let this be a warning to all who pass by
That you be not deceived by Lewis's lie.

3. He promised to wed her at Adam's springs.
Some money he'd give her and other fine things.

  Neither of them he gave her but flattered the case,
   Saying, "We will be married; will be no disgrace."

4. He said he'd go with her right straight to the town,
  There they would be married, in union be bound.
 He took her on behind him and away they did go
  Till they came to the banks where the river did flow.

5. "Now, Omie, poor Omie, I'll tell you my mind;
  I intend for to drown you and leave you behind."
 "Have mercy, have mercy!" poor Omie did cry,
  Saying, "I'm a poor rebel and not fit to die."

6. "No mercy I'll have," this hero did cry,
  "In the bottom of the river your body shall lie."
 "Have mercy, have mercy, and spare me my life!
  Let me go rejected and not be your wife."

7. This hero did choke her, as we understand,
  And threw her in the river below the mill dam.
 Some count this high treason; but oh! what a crime
  To murder poor Omie and leave her behind!

8. Now Omie is missing, as we all do know,
  And down to the river a-hunting they go.
 They found her a-floating on the water so deep,
  Which caused many people to sigh and to weep.

9. The people they gathered to behold a great sight.
  They left her on the shores all the dark stormy night.
 The next day a-following the inquest was held.
  No doubt but the jury their minds they could tell.

B.

1. The first time he came to see me,
  He told me he loved me well;
 The next time he came to see me,
  He told me he'd use me well.

2. He promised to meet me at Adams' spring;
  For the money that he'd give all other fine things.

3. Instead of the money he flattered the case;
  If we were to get married it would be no disgrace.

4. "Come jump up behind me and away we will go,
  Down by the side of Siota, where the waters o'erflow.

5. "O Oma, Oma, let me tell you my mind;
  My mind is to drown you and leave you behind."

6. "O Lewis, O Lewis, pray spare me my life,
   And I will deny you and not be your wife."

7. He kicked her and he stamped her, he threw her in the deep;
   He mounted his pony and rode in full speed.

8. The screams of poor Oma followed after him so nigh,
   Saying, "I am a poor rebel not fitting to die."

9. She was missing one evening, next morning was found
   In the bottom of Siota below the milldam.

10. They took as a prisoner, condemned to die,
    He owned he was the man that killed poor Oma Wise.

GLOSSARY

BIBLIOGRAPHY

RECORDINGS

GLOSSARY

(Only unusual forms and meanings are given.)

a aye

a of; at

a bye past

a wait, a wat, a wete I know; truly

abeen falling down over

aboard, laid us aboard laid alongside of us

abon, abone, aboon above

aboun about; on

abowthe about

abune above

abyde endure (it)

acward see *awkward*

ae ever

aevery hungry

again in turn

agast, nothing of him agast not at all concerned about him

(of) age old

ageyn toward

aȝon upon

ahın in addition to, over and above

aik oak

ain own; *ain sell* own self

airn iron

airt point of the compass; *ride the airt of* ride in the direction of

aits oats

alide related

amain strike sails; *sound amain* battle stations on the double

amain vigorously

ambellet gait of horse (Both legs on one side move simulta-neously, making for easy riding. Women's horses were trained in this gait.)

American leather morocco made from American horsehides under patent of 1799 (Child)

amo among

an one; redundant after numerals and superlatives, e.g., *firstan town*

an on; if

ance once

ancyents ensigns

and if

angel a coin worth about 10s.

an's if his

anse once

answery answer

ant and

ap descendant of

ar, are ere

archborde for *hachebord,* side of ship(?); perhaps a piece of timber across a ship's stern, carrying the name

(in) arms arm in arm

artillery device for discharging any weapon; loosely, the weapon

arwe arrow

as has

asay tried

aught a bairn had a child

auld old, eldest; term of endearment, as in *auld son*

ava of all

avow own

aw all
awa away
awenden thought
awet find out; know
awkward unexpected, unusual, backhanded
ayen again
ayont beyond
ayre heir
ay's ye wash you are always washing

ba ball
bacon i.e., poor fare compared with the wedding feast
bad paused, stopped
bade ordered
baffled disgraced
bags of bread food bags
bait feed
bale trouble
ballup crotch
balow croon to, sing a lullaby to
balys troubles
ban curse; hinge; bone; hem; band; bond
ban to bound
ban bound, chained
ban-dog fighting dog, tracking dog
bane death; bone
bangisters outlaws
barm lap
barn-well read *barn; well* is intrusive
barne man
basnites helmets
bassonnettes helmets
batts blows
baucheld destitute, down at the heels; a *bauchle* is an old shoe worn down at the heels
bauld bold; assertive
baun curse
bauning cursing
bayliff sheriff's officer who serves writs; a constable
baylye mayor

be that when
be to and al be on by two and also by one
beames downfall heavy timbers to drop from topcastle of vessel to deck of attacker
bearing arrow long straight arrow for distance shooting
beaver beaver hat
bed offered
Bedlam Bethlehem; Bedlam Hospital was a hospital for the insane in London
bedone bedecked
bed-stock bedstead
bedyng bidding
beerly great
befalle befitted (?)
befforen before, earlier
beft beat; beaten
begeck, give them a begeck make a fool of them
beheard heard; overheard
behind out of sight
behint behind
behynde to follow after
being since
beliue immediately
Belly Blind a household familiar, a helpful dwarf-like creature
ben in, within; inner room
benbow bow, bent bow, i.e., strung; ready to shoot
bend the turn of the way
benison blessing
bent coarse, rushlike grass, thought to protect against the evil eye; combined with broom, a plant widely used as a specific against witches, it made a powerful charm
bent field covered with bent
bent his breast and swam bent to the water so that he was in a horizontal position
bent took

benty line the edge of the bent grass field

ber bore

berdys birds

berne fighting man

bescrow curse

beshrew to wish a curse upon

bespoke well spoken

bestand help

bestead in phrase *hard bestead,* hard situated; badly treated

bestride walk through

bete help

bete better

bether, betur better

betide befall; happen to

bets boots

bett kindled

better advantage

bey buy; by

bier complaint

bierly (beerly) handsome

bigget built

biggin mansion

bigly splendid, well appointed

(forest) bill a weapon with a broad, hook-shaped blade fixed to a long handle

billie, billy brother, friend, buddy

bird, burd damsel, young lady

birk birch (Birch was often associated with the dead.)

birl drink, ply with drink

birled drank

birlin drinking

birtled cut up

bite soe lowe fight unfairly

blacke water deep water (in contrast to wan water?)

blaewort cornflower

blan, blane, blanne stopped

blate silly

blee color

blin stop

blink gleam, look

blinkit looked

block bargain

blood iron instrument used in bloodletting

bloschoms blossoms

blutter dirty

bobs jerks, swing, dances

bocking vomiting

bode offer; waited for

bode wordes message of heavy portent

bodkin long pin for fastening the hair

boer bower

bolt arrow

boltys short-shafted arrows

bon bone

boot something in addition

boote help

boris boar's

borrow ransom, rescue

boskyd made ready

bot, boot, bote help

bot and and also

bote unless

bottys butts, targets usually set on rising ground; hence the ground itself, place where the targets were fixed

boughing door corrupt form of bower door

bouk body

boulster bolster

boun boon

bound made ready

boune make ready

bouted bolted, i.e., white flour

bow bough; elbow

bowd my knee bent my knee

bowen ready

bowhes boughs

bowing birk bending birch

bown, bowne, bowen ready

bownd bounded

bowndyn made ready; dead (fig.)

bowne make ready

bowr chamber, room

bowr woman maid

bowynd (*boun*) made ready; went

boys bows

boyt both

bra handsome

brachans bracken, ferns

brae forehead

braid open; long

brain in phrase *gaed brain* went insane

branches brooches

brand sword

branded reddish brown

braw fine, pleasant; brave, handsome

brawn muscle, calf of leg

bray, bra, brae hill, banks

bread breadth; *three pence bread* the breadth of three-pence

bred bread

bree brow

breed cause; *breed thy pain* cause you suffering

breeden breed

breek thigh back pocket of his breeches

breeks breeches

breiks breeches

bretther o degs probably corrupt, but it seems to mean, with cloth and torn rags

breyde rushed; *with a breyde* in a rush

brig bridge

brim sea cliff

brisk splendidly attired

broad brood

broad arrow an arrow with a barbed head for close in-shooting, in contrast to *bearing arrow*

broked black and white, pied

broken men outlaws

brook enjoy, pledge, endure

broom a common shrub of several varieties, especially the *planta genista* of history and legend

broom cow piece of broom

brunt burnt

brusten burst

bryk breeches

bryttled cut up

bryttlyng carving

buckler shield

bugge brig

bully friend, companion

burd see *bird*

burn brook

burning burnished

busk dress, prepare; *busk and boun* is a cliché, both parts of which mean practically the same thing

buskt made ready

buss clump, bush

but outside, outer room; *but and ben* outer room and inner

but unless

but cask, especially wine cask holding 126 gallons

but an and also

but even only

but if unless

b'w'ye be with you

by buy; be; concerning

by, aby pay for

byckarte harried; killed

byddys abides

bydeene successively

byre cow stable

byste beast

bystode pressed

ca drive; *ca'd* drove

cadie steward, workman

camovine camomile

can (for *gan?*) did

cankerdly crossly

cannilie cautiously

capull-hyde horsehide

carbuncle a stone that was thought to have various magical properties *care-bed* bed of worry, sickbed

carel, carril, carl, churl peasant

carket necklace

carline old woman

carp talk; sing to the harp

carpe off care tell sad stories

carping talking, faultfinding

casey causeway

cast plan, venture

cause take me cause me to be taken

causey-stone paving stone

cavil lot

cawker one who calculates horoscopes

cawte cunning

cerstyn Christian

certyl kirtle, shirt

cesererea imitation of the sound of bells

chaffare merchandise

chaffing dish a brazier-like vessel heated by charcoal and used to boil water or cook food, or to heat cauterizing instruments

chafts jaws

chain yeards pieces of chain to serve as missiles

chamer chamber

channerin fretting

chap or ca knock or call

chappit knock, rap

chays hunting range

chear well to cheerful at the prospects of

cheek and chin kissed her on the cheek and lips

cheffe head; chief

chepe bargain for; *chepyd* bargained for

chere cheer, entertainment

cherishing cheering

chess jess, strap

cheys choose

child, chiel child, young man

chin for *gin*, latch

chiven a kind of fish; *play the*

chiven run off at the slightest provocation

church style the stile in the fence around the churchyard

chylderin fellows

claise clothes

claithes clothes

clang clang of handcuffs

clap tap, knock

clap embrace, kiss

clappit caress

clare probably mistaken for *close*

claymore double-edged sword of the Highlanders

cleading clothing

cleed clothe

clef cleaved

cleffe cleave

clepyn was called, named

clever skillfully

clipping embracing, kissing

cloathe garment

clock cripple, straggler

clocken-hen setting hen

cloke-lap the lower edge of the cloak

close, closs courtyard

(in) close in extremities

close parler enclosed room

cloth-yard old measure of cloth, 27 inches; *clothyard shaft* an arrow a clothyard long, the longest arrow used

clouted patched

cloutie patched

clouting leather mending leather

cnistes knights

cod pillow; *cods* husks with which pillows and beds were stuffed

coerlets coverlets

coffer case, trunk

coft bought

cog boat

cold knew; could

collayne Cologne (steel)

comely fitting, decorous

command commission, credentials

complete competently, in a finished manner

comyn aʒon came upon

comyn-bell town bell, alarm bell

coost accosted; cast

coot ankle

cop head

corbies crows

cordain Cordovan

corn grain

cornet the lowest commissioned officer in the cavalry

cors curse

corsaire battle horse

cot cottage

coulter, colter knife, cutting blade of a plow

countenance encouragement

courting exchanging of courtesies

cousin relative

couth knew, was able; customary

covant contract; *covant comes out* term of office expires

covenant term of office

cow cut

cowtale cow's tail attached to the hide

coy disdainful; quiet

coyn a corner, a projecting point

crab-tree crab-apple tree

crack talk, boast

cracked bragged

cramasie crimson

crawd crowed

crawn crowed

cressawntes crescents

crew crowd

crey cry

(cam) cripple came hobbling like a cripple

cristus natus est Christ is born

croodlin cooing

crooked bent, hunched over

crookt crippled

crost opposed, circumvented

crouse merrily

crowne head

crowt wrinkle

cumbrous clumsy; in 186/41 the reference is to the leg irons

cunning skill; mystery

curch kerchief, head covering

curious elaborate, well wrought

curn quantity; package

curst turne job for which he is cursed

curtal friar a friar wearing a short gown; *curtal dog* one with its tail cut off

dae doe

dag-durk stabbing dagger

dail, doel, dole distress; *dress the dole* endures the hurt

dale dole, a place where alms were dispensed to beggars

dame prior

dandoo Child conjectures that this is *dun doe*

dang struck, beat

Danzig waters gold water

dapperpy of several colors, plaid

darena dare not

daunton daunt, subdue

daut caress, love

dawtie, dautie darling

day die, dead

dead death

dear wow exclamation used for emphasis or surprise

dearsome costly

dede, deed, dead, dɣid, died death

deerlye dight splendidly fitted out

deft well-groomed, neat

degree rank, position; *bear no degree* have no standing

deil, diel devil

dele part

delicate delightful, charming

deluded bewitched

den vale, glade

dere injury

designs intends; is destined

deythe prepared

dice church seat

did off took off

dight clean, polish; dress; winnow

dight ornamented

din noise

dinne trouble

dip deep

diuel's mouth public, like the wide-open devil's mouth depicted on church windows (Child citing Skeat)

do me thy hawkes deliver to me

doen her to betaken her

doited stupid; doting

doo dove

dool grief

dought was able

dow, dou dove

dowie sad

dowy sad, dreary

doyt doth

dragging at the ware dragging up seaweed for fertilizer

draw up take up

draw well well from which water was drawn, in contrast to a spring from which water was dipped

drawn by dale and downe dragged over dale and down at the tail of a horse

dre endure; be able

dread doubt

(gie a) dreel to put to flight

drees suffers

dressing board table on which food was prepared

(be that it) drewe by the time that it became

(can) drie is able

drift drove

drive the Gaspereaux drive logs down the Gaspereaux

drou strike

drumlie murky, gloomy

drussie drowsy

drye stand; hold out

dryfyng driving

drywyng driving

dub slough, pond

duckers divers

du3ty doughty

dule distress, sorrow

dumpes distress

dun dark brown

dung beat, beaten; broke

dwell hesitate

dyght brought; ordained

dynte blow

e only

Earl Martial probably the marshall-in-hall is meant; other versions read the *earl marshall*

earthen lake shroud of earth

eartly earthly

ease in phrase *ill at ease,* sick, hurt

ee awe

een one; I

effen even

eild age

ell unit of cloth measure, 45 inches

eme uncle

emys uncles

end its leen come to an end by itself

enes cunnes any kind of

eneuch enough

eney every

entertain enlist in service

envye harm; ill will

esk lizard

esquire eldest son of knight

eueryche each

euyn evening

eylde yield; *eylde het the* recompense thee for it

eyls else
eylyt aileth
eyne eyes
eyre years
eyþer either

fa fall, fall on
face boldness
fact evidence
fadge clumsy woman
faem foam, waves, sea
(*but*) *fail* without fail, certainly
fail-dyke wall of turf
fain pleased
fairlie wonder
faith and troth pledged friendship, blood brotherhood
fallow's deed Child suggests felon's deed
falyf fallow
fame foam, sea
fang thong; coil of rope; trap
fankit entangled; penned, sheathed
farder farther
fared favored
farleys new things, marvels
farrow cow a cow which in a given season is giving milk though she has not produced a calf that year
fashes troubles
fat what
faucheon (falchion) a short sword with a slightly curved point
(*in*) *fauld* neatly pressed
fawken falcon
fawn fallen
fayne pleased
fayned imagined
feale fail
fear frightened; *fearder, feardest*
fee property; pay
fee fated, doomed
feed feud

feid feud
feire mate, spouse
feires fellows
fell skin, hide
fells high pasture land
felon traitor
fend(*e*) fiend
fer far
fere companion, company; *in fere* together
ferly strange
fesh fetch
fet opportune
fette fetch
fey fated, marked by death
feyre fair, clear
ffaine pleased
ffarbod forbid; *godys ffarbod* God forbid
ffarley strange, wonderful
ffay faith
ffayne glad, pleased
ffend protest
ffetteled made ready
ffettle make ready
ffey (121/74) probably a mistake; cf. stanza 75
ffeyffe five
ffeyne fine
ffoder tun or hogshead
fforefend forbid
ffre free; of vague and indefinite meaning—of noble birth, well brought up, beautiful, valorous, etc.; often little more than a rime word
ffroe from
file defile; feel
filinge defiling
filled followed
finikin beautiful; beautifully appareled
fiste fight
fit foot, feet
fit section of a story or poem
flake flame
flaps blows
flaw lie

flear, fleer floor
flee fly
fleed flood
flesse flesh
flex flax
fleych flesh, meat, game
flied frightened
flinders pieces
flo arrow
fond silly
for because of
for to in phrase *for to bind,* for to be bound
forby, forbye aside, apart, near by
forehammer sledge-hammer
foret toward
forfaulted forfeited
forfee lee bow; see *formast* for 245/5
forfoughten tired through fighting
forlorn, forlorne lost; abandoned; killed
formast, gang in at your formast . . . your forlee she'll cross before your bows, sail around, and come abreast of your lee bow
forn fared well
fothe foot
forward compact
fou full
fou a unit of measure of some 3 bushels
foulys birds
four-nooked sheet four-cornered sheet
foure-eared fool twice an ass
free gracious, fine—any positive quality; often little more than a rime word; cf. mod. Eng. *nice*
freke fellow
freyke brave man
fringed grey gray horse with long mane
frisk leap, dance

frith wood
frush brittle
ful of flud at the height of flood
full and by close hauled
full fro from him
furs furrows
fynde probably *fyne,* end

ga gall
gad, gaud bar
gae go; gave
gae so round i.e., have become pregnant
gaed went; also occasionally, gone
gaes goes
gaffe gave
gain going
gallaly galley
galoot a weak or silly fellow
galpins for *galopins* (?), errand boy, page
game joke
gang go, walk
gang by haulds walk with the aid of hand holds
gar cause, make
gard, gart caused, made
gare, gaire a gore, triangular piece of cloth inserted in a garment to give width at the bottom. Such a piece was often thought to have magic powers and was often used to cast a spell. *gaire to gair* side to side; *down at the gaire* (*gore*) at the knee
garl gravel
garlande a circlet set on a wand as a target
garrd caused
garre me ones to dyne even give me my dinner (to say nothing of a fight)
garrett watchtower, lookout
gars me greet makes me weep
gart caused to
gaule red

gay give

gear, gere merchandise; affair; equipment

geere will sway affair will turn out

geldynges gresse fat geldings

(*marry*) *gep with a wenion* expression of contempt: *gep* get up; *wenion* a curse on you

gereamarsey thank you; gramercy

geue over give over, abandon

gey gay

gie give

giein giving

gier property, cattle

gif, giffe if

gillore galore

gin toward; around (of time); if

girded let out

girdle griddle; belt

girds hoops

glamer spell; charm

glamourie charm

glanced shone

glancing flashing

glasse ship lantern

glasses glasses for measuring time; *fought them five glasses* fought them five half hours; the nautical glass ran for one half hour

glau(v)e a short knife or sword fixed on the end of a pole

glede, gleed glowing coal

glee glove

gleid squint-eyed, cross-eyed

glent dashed

gleuves gloves

gloom frown

glytteryde gleamed

god, goods provisions

god amarsey thank you

godde in phrase *that a godde,* that's a good one

go(e) move

golett part of hood that covers the neck

good went

good ben, good benison (?) good blessing (Child's conjecture)

gorgett any of a variety of ruff or neckpiece

gorney journey

goud gold

gowan daisy

gowany covered with daisies

gowd gold

graff a short stick

graie dogs perhaps Eng. gray, but probably O.N. *grey,* dog; cf. greyhounds. Such dogs were used to run down deer.

graine fork of a tree

graith adorn, dress

graithd clad in armor

graithed equipped

grat lamented; wept

gravat cravat

greece in phrase *of greece,* fat

greeme young man

greet cry

greete grit, sand

greetin weeping

gret greet; greeted

gret chepe very cheap

gret hedid large hooded (?)

grevis groves

grewhound greyhound; see *graie dogs*

grey (*meal*) barley meal

grite great

grith free conduct, amnesty

groat English coin worth about fourpence

groom man

grounden sharpened

ground-oak oak sapling

grownede ground

grumly in a sullen manner; savage

grun ground

grype griffon

gryte grit; large, great

gudeman husband

gueed good

guide treat

guinea gold 22-carat gold from which guineas were coined

guns mounted forty she carried 40 mounted guns

gurious grim

gyde, I shall be the munkis gyde I shall dispose of the monk

gynnyst to brede (?) Kittredge would emend, *gynnyst to wede*, to go mad

gyst gettest; givest

ha, hae have; hall

habit garb

hachebord stern rather than gunwale; see *archborde*

hached inlaid, engraved

haches hatch, hatch opening

had hold

haffe have

haik ye up hang up as on a frame; *haik* in Scots is a frame for drying cheese, holding hay, etc.; hence Hang ye up or confine you as on a haik

hail completely

hailing rushing

halch greet, salute

hall hull

hallow seat holy seat, dwelling of a holy one

hals bane neck bone

halyde hauled

hambellet amble

hand handle; *near hand* about

hand for hand equal; in a fair fight

handsome convenient

hansell reward, present; *hansell ffor the mare* the more you buy the more presents you get

hantyd frequented

hap cover; *hapd* covered

hap quilt

harbengers king's officers who made arrangements for the king's entertainment on the road

harniss armor

harp and carp sing songs or romances to the accompaniment of the harp

hart male red deer over five years old; *hart of greece* fat hart

hase throat, neck

haud hold, keep

haulds by holding; *gang by haulds* walk by assisting with the hands

hause-bane neck bone

hautyd come frequently

haw blue

hawt aught

hay, view the hay take a walk

haylle whole

hayt hath

he high

he they (115/4)

head to behead

headit beheaded

heal hail

heans hens

hear here

heather-cow tips of heather; heather crow

heather-knaps heather-covered hills

heckle comb for separating flax fiber

hedge protections

hee high

heel came off sign of bad luck

heie high

height are called

heiste named

held up (*child*) i.e., accepted it as his

hem them

hend noble

hent, hente caught, took

her their

her lane alone

herkens listen to, attend (the common minstrel bid for attention)

herry harry

het eat; it; hot

hett bid

hette called

heved head

hewene heaven

hey high

heyt war howte term used to drive horses, "get up!"

hie, hye haste

high-colld fashioned to tie above the knee

hight named

hight promise

hilt flayed; stripped

hin, hine young, courteous, well bred

hind (*n*), youth; (*adj.*), courteous, well born

hingers hinges

hinny honey

hire charter money, increase, wages

ho, hoo who

hode hat

hog sheep

hoky-gren blanketed fire

hold house, settlement

holde keeping

holidame holy relic

holland linen cloth made in Holland

holland-bush holly

Hollans Dutch

hollen, hollin holly

holpe helped

holtes woods

holydame a mild oath

hondrith hundred

honey-mark mole, love spot

hongut hanged

hook shepherd's crook

horsing mounting of horses

hos us

hotys oats

hough joint

houm river plain

houp hollow between hills

houzle communion; to administer the sacrament

hoved tarried

how hollow, a low land

howket hacked

howre our

howt struck, dug

hoy a northern island; an exclamation, especially in *a*(*o*)*hoy!*

huggell embrace

huly slowly

humming causing the head to hum (said of liquor)

huner hundred

hunt's ha hunting lodge

husbondes farmers

hussyfskap work (housewifery)

hy high; on, by; erect

hye haste

hyer higher

hyght high

hyght promised

hynde female deer

i in

i feth in faith

I aye

I wiss, i wys, i-wysse indeed, certainly

iacke coat of mail

ibouht=*iboust* bought

ic, ich I

icnowe I know

iflawe flayed

ilk in that ilk; at that same moment

ilka each, either

ilkone each one

ill upon worse back worse and worse back (there), worse piled on worse

im am

in as

inne lodging

innocent half-witted
inow enough
into from; in (not implying motion); unto
invented come upon, find; *this road for me's invented* I'm forced to go
Iove Jove
ir are
is his
I'se I shall
itake taken
ith with, in the
ither one another, other

jack, iacketts canvas vest or coat studded with metal for protection
jack boot a large boot reaching over the knee and so serving as armor
jaw wave
jelly jolly, handsome
jelly-flower gillyflower, probably the garden pink
jerdins fellows(?); other versions have dons, jorrans, children
jerkin a close-fitting coat, common in 16th and 17th centuries
jilt flirt
jimp slender
jo sweetheart
jobbing thrusting, billing
jow stroke
juber ju Negro dance

kale cabbage
kechone kitchen
keepe guard
keist cast
kell net cap
kemp warrior
ken know
kep catch
kepe care for; *kepe I be* care I to be
kettrin Highland brigand

kiest cast, tied
kilt tuck up
kimmer gossip, liar; witch
kin, a kin kind every kind
kirk church (north and south); the established church of Scotland
kirtle (man's) waistcoat; (woman's) slip, petticoat, short mantle, etc.
kist chest
kitchen-neuk kitchen corner
knet knotted
knew, knie knee
knife-less without use of knife
knop blow, bump
know, knoe hill
knyȝt a champion, one devoted to the service of another; said of Jesus
knyled kneeled
kod quoth
kye cattle, often milk cows
kyst cast

lack low, mean
laid lodged
laigh low; low land
laigh-calld low cut
lain long in remained at home, not gone on raids
laine conceal
lair lore
laird landowner with considerable property
lairy miry, boggy
lake sheet, shroud; *earthen lake* shroud of earth
lakkyt lacketh
lamar amber
Lamasse August 1, church festival in celebration of Peter's chains
land-sergeant officer in charge of the soldiers guarding the Border
lane, lain alone, lone; (with pronoun) *my lane* me alone;

your lane you alone, by yourself, etc.

langsome tedious

lanyne lie

lap edge of coat

lap leaped

lapp wrap

lauch laugh

lavede a blode swam in blood

lavrock lark

lawing reckoning, lodging, account; *clear your lawing* pay your account

lax relief

lay meadow

lay (nautical) bring into the wind

lay by put behind, outsail

lay to apply vigorously, check

layed aimed

layn lie; *withouten layn* true

lazer leper

lead (186/30) roof

lead (184/26) lead their horses

leade vat

leaf luff, weather

leal, leel faithful, true

leaned lay concealed

lear information

lease=leash pack

leasing lying

leath loath

leaugh low

leber rather

ledde took

lee lone

lee fallow

leech leash

lee-lang livelong

leen, its leen itself; *(your) leen* yourself, alone

leenes leaves

leffe beheynde stay behind

left'ts lieutenants

leman sweetheart, beloved

len deceive; conceal

lene lend

lent a blow give a blow

lesse false

let hinder

leugh low, lower part. *For leugh o Liddesdale* evidently means: he was from lower Liddesdale

leve lovely; an epithet associated with London that became a ballad cliché

leve dear

leven grassy glade

lever rather, more pleasant

ley land not being cultivated

leygh laughed

leythe light

lichtit alighted

lidder lazy

lie, lye live, reside

lieugh low

lig lie

light dismounted

lighted of alighted from

lighter delivered of a child

lightly treat with disrespect, hold lightly

lily, lilly, lillie lovely, charming; often has no more force than *nice* in mod. Eng. colloquial usage

limmer a mongrel hound, a low depraved person; *limmer loon* damn fool

lin(n) river, stream

lin stop

Lincoln green Lincoln green, a favorite color of huntsmen and outlaws and of woodsmen in general; Lincoln produced most of the dyed goods of this color, hence the name

ling tall grass; also heath

lingcan, lingean body

liquor to drench; to beat bloody

list desire

lither wicked, bad

(can) lo look

(deep) load drunk

locked fastened

Locksly name given by the Queen to Robin Hood. According to some traditions he was born at Locksly in Nottinghamshire

lode heavily

loder louder

lodging-maill lodging bill

lodly loathy

loe love, value

logeed quartered

lome cripple, lame one

long of þe because of you

longes lungs

loo love

loof palm of hand

looked him round about examined him all over

lookid looked up, sought out

loot let

looted bent

loset loosed

lotten permitted

loukynge expectations

loun, loon fellow of low rank, rascal

loup leaped

louted bowed

louys loves

loverd lord

lovy lovely

low, lowe hill; fire, flame

low, lowe laughed

low, lowe, bite soe lowe (167/66) fight unfairly

lucettes pikes

luppen leaped

lust desire

lustely spiritedly

lusty beautiful, delightful; pregnant

lute let

lyed accused him of lying

lyff-tenant lieutenant

lyke wake body watching, wake

lyne linden

lyne stream water

lyth and listen give ear and listen (typical ballad opening formula)

lyþ lieth

lyvar liver

made to seke caused search to be made

mae more

magger in the phrase *in magger of,* in spite of

mailison curse

maill rent

make mate

(to) make to be made

makys mates

male coat of mail

malicen curse

maney band of followers

manhood deeds of valor

mankie kind of cloth

mansworn perjured

many ae many a one

marchandise business, dealing

march-man a man of the Border between England and Scotland

march-parti neighborhood of the Border

mare more

maries ladies

mark coin worth 7s.

(thy) mark I will not shun I will not avoid being thy target

markyd market; marquis

marrow mate

marry geþ see *geþ*

mary waiting maid, companion

marynmas Martinmas

mast mayest

masterless without a rider

masteryes feats of skill

mat may

matrons woman (*sing.*)

maukie kind of woolen cloth from Flanders

maun must

maut malt beer

may maid

meakle much

me bitaiste committed to me

meal earth

meal flour; *leather meal* flour bag; *meal-pack* meal bag

meane lament

meany company

mear mare

meathe landfall

meatriff full of food

medys midst

meed heart, mood

meen moon

meikle great

mell maul, hammer

mellison curse

mense compensation

menyice, menyie retainers

merchandyes booty

merked, marked took aim at

mervaile marvel

me stende that one should stone

methe meat

mettle courageous

met-yard measuring stick carried to measure distance in archery

meythe might

mickle much, great

mild, myld gentle, meek, compassionate

mill mile

mind remembered

minnie mother

mirk dark

miscarry fail

mister need

misters sorts of

mold earth

monand moaning

mood soul, courage

moody-hill molehill.

morning-gift gift to a bride on the morning after her marriage

morning tyde time of the morning

mort signal given on the hunting horn to denote that the animal has been killed.

moss swamp

most must

mot may; make

mote might; *mote if thi leman be* if I might be thy sweetheart

motion, his body's in motion drifting out with the tide

mou mouth

muck the byre clean manure out of the stable

muckle much

muckle coat greatcoat

muir moor

muley-cow hornless cow

muse wonder

muskadine spiced wine

my me

myȝth might

myllan Milan steel

mylner miller

mynde mind, consciousness; *were in her mynde* were conscious

myneyeple corruption of *manople* (Child, quoting Skeat), gauntlet

mysaunter mischance

naesaid refused

napkin scarf, handkerchief

nar nor, than

near-hand almost

needle-work lace embroidery

neen none

neis nose

neist next

nelle = *ne wille* will not

nere ear; *They nere* Thine ear (that is, if he's good, he can bend the bow until the string is opposite his right ear, his left arm extended)

nere were it not

neuk nook

newfangle fickle, capricious

next nighest
ney neigh
nice neigh
nice ignorant; silly
nie nigh
niest next, nearest, close to
nip bit
nobellys coin worth about 6s.
noble excellent, choice
nones cunnes lihte no kind of reward
nook bit
nook corner
nooked cornered
norish nursing
note, notte nut
nourice, nourris nurse
nout neat, cattle
nouþer neither
nul will not

of off, by, from
of age old
off of
office ceremony
ohon and alake exclamation of sorrow
oke graff stick, sapling
on one
on of
on hyght aloud
on slepe asleep
on thre in three parts, a cliché; today we would say cleft it in two
onfowghten without fighting
on's on his
op up
or ere
orderly fittingly
o't of it
oth of the
operis others, of the other
ought owed
ousen oxen
out of hand immediately
owar hour

ower-word repeated word, refrain
owsen oxen
owsen-bows oxen yokes
owt o hand immediately
owtlay outlaw

pa, pall fine cloth such as that used in coronation robes; cloak
paction compact
palffrey small riding horse
pallions pavilions, tents
palmer pilgrim, but often tramp. Strictly a pilgrim who has visited the Holy Land and brought a palm leaf to place on the altar of his priest's church; a wandering mendicant friar
pap nipple
paramour lover, little meaning in 5/4/2, where it should mean sweets to eat or drink
part share, portion; place
partakers helpers
parti, upon a parti aside
pastes pastries
pat pot, hole in river
patten thick-soled wooden shoe
pavage, pavag, pawage road tax, passage tax
pay beat
peel pond
peerls poor people
pellettes bullets
pen knife see *wee pen knife;* a penknife was a small knife used to sharpen quill pens
(third) pennie third part
penny-fee penny tip
pens pence
perte part of standard or heraldic shield
pestilett a small pistol
peysse peace
philabey kilt
pick coat with pitch
pike pick
pike-staff a can with an iron

head capable of serving as a weapon; carried by beggars and pilgrims

pin, pin'd pinned; the pin of metal or wood was fastened to a thong which passed through a hole in the door to the outside. When the pin was inserted in the latch, the door could be opened by pulling the thong on the outside. The door could be secured by removing the pin from the latch. Anyone wanting to enter then pulled on the thong and so rattled the pin, calling the inmates' attention to the visitor. Sometimes the pin was inserted in a small hole above the latch so that the latch could not be lifted, thus pinning the door

pinder an officer whose duty is to impound cattle or sheep that have strayed, and to enforce laws against trespassing in general on the lands of the manor

pine suffering

pinfold pound for cattle and sheep seized for trespassing

pinnace a small sloop-rigged boat often used as a tender

piteous paltry, poor

plaguy vexatious

plate jack plate armor

platen pieces

played at the glove a game consisting of spearing at the glove rather than the usual ring

played clang made a clanging noise on account of his handcuffs

played o'er played the better

play-feres playfellows

plea quarrel

plough of land amount of land one plowman can cultivate

plumnet pommel or knob on the hilt of a sword

pock bag

polle pull

polle het op to they nere pull it up to thine ear, i.e., bend the bow until the arm is full outstretched and consequently the string is opposite the right ear

porridge-spurtle stirring rod

portmantle portmanteau; a traveling case originally carried behind a saddle; hence, cylindrical

posy a verse of poetry inscribed in a ring, etc.; a motto or epigram

pot pool

potewer pouch

pottle tankard

powd pulled

prate speak

preke wand used as a mark in shooting

presentlye immediately

prest ready, freely

prevelye privately

pricke target, usually a wand, a thin stick

pricked spurred

pride exuberance of animal spirits, mettle

prime first canonical hour, i.e., first hour after sunrise

prin pin

prithee pray thee

privately secretly

process happenings

proper well formed, handsome

prosperous strong

prove proof; *armour of proue* arrow-proof armor

pu pull

pudding-bros pudding broth

pudding-pricks skewers

puggish ragged, thieves' attire

pulde pulled

putten down hanged, throttled

pype a measure of wine, averaging 126 gallons

quarter-staff a weapon made from a pole 6½ feet long. The user grasped it with one hand in the middle and the other one quarter way (hence the name). In combat the user shifted his hand between the two quarters, giving the staff a circular motion and making it difficult for an adversary to avoid a blow

quat what

queet ankle

quequer quiver

querry, quarry refuse parts of a game animal collected in its skin and given to the hunting dogs; any product of the chase

queyt requite

quiere, quire choir; *Mary's quire* choir of St. Mary's church

quit requited, repaid

quite relinquish

quyrry see *querry*

quyte revenged

rack a ford

rader redder

radly quickly

rae roe

rake advance, walk

rakeing walking, moving

rang the keys played the spinet

rank violent, wild

ranke turn

ranked behaved

rantin jovial, high-spirited; dissipated

rappit knocked

rarely a word of very general meaning, useful as a rime word

rashin rush

rashin rinds rasher rinds

rathes fourth part of the year

rawstye by the roote rusty at the end

ray prepare, array; track

raysse raid, riding

reacheles on reckless about

read interpret, explain

read rode

reade advise

readie certain

reaveld tangled

reaving destroying

red rid

red clear

red, rede advice; *do after my rede* follow my advice

redding kaim a large toothed comb for the hair

reek smoke

reel dance merrily

reesin rousing, boasting, praising

reest, roast roost

reet root

refrain leave

regis king royal highness

reiver, riever robber

rekeles without fear or restraint

renoun authority

rent reigned

require ask for

resemblance face (only in the sense of likeness, image)

rid red

rid at the ring a game of skill in which the rider attempts to pick off a suspended ring with his rod or lance as he rides past at full speed

riggin ridge

right (*adv.*) right off, immediately; (*adj.*) proper

rigs ridge

rin run

rinds bark

ring the circle of dancers; *fill the ring* fill often means follow; here, rather, make up the ring dance

ripe clear or clean out

rise twig, branch

rive break, tear

river comb Child conjectures *river* as a corruption of ivory

roc rock

rod, rad sidepiece for a stretcher

roddins the red berries of the mountain ash; rats

rode, rood; be the rode by the cross

roo deer

rottons rats

round in phrase *gae so round,* are pregnant

roundelay a song in which some element, usually the refrain, is continually repeated

rousing bragging

rout roar; blow

routh plenty

row wrap

(on a) row in a line

rowd wrapped, rolled

row-footed rough footed

rowght company

rowght see *ryall*

royal bone meaning uncertain; Skeat suggests ivory or walrus

rudd reddens

rugge back

rule bewailing

rung roar

rung staff

ryall, royall kingly, royal; *ryall in rowght* royal army men

ryȝth aright

rynde cut, strike; *rynde and rent* flayed

sae so

safer saffron

saft lightly (186/36)

saint blessed

sair sorely

sakeless innocent

sall shall

sanchopis fork, codpiece

sark shirt

sarsanet fine thin silk

sat salt

sat . . . a dynt inflicted a blow

saugh willow; *saugh-bush* willow bush

saught meat for St. Peter begged meat in the name of St. Peter

saut salt

sauyour see took the sacrament

saw so

sawten attack; assaulted

say saw

scaith hurt

scaler one who measures (scales) logs to determine the number of board feet

scales sequins worn as head ornaments

scarlet red uniform of the king's men, a garb of gentlemen in contrast to the Lincoln green of the outlaw

scere-thorsday Thursday before Easter

scharpper sharper

schette shot

schetyng shooting

scho she

scholde should

schoote hys horse drove his horse away

schrewde treacherous; cursed

scop head

scoup fly

scouth space

screffe sheriff; *screffeys* sheriffs

scroggs underbrush

soug expiate

se saw

sea-ground bottom of the sea

securly surely

seen soon

seke search; *to seke* at a loss

selchie, selkie, silkie seal

seld sold

selling were being sold

sembled assembled, met

semblyde assembly

sen sent

sertan, in sertan surely

service love; duty

set because

set his brest set his breast to the water, i.e., swam

set op put up

seth saith

sett well aim well

settle by set aside

setts is fated

seyng complaining

shank edge of a hill

share part

shathmont unit of measurement from tip of thumb to wrist; six inches

shaw thicket

shawes woods

shear several

sheave slice

shee shoe

sheen o ben shoes of heavy leather

sheene bright, beautiful

sheerless without use of scissors

shete a peny shoot for a penny as prize

sheyne see *sheene*

shiffted his roome changed his position

shift change, resource

shivers pieces; *to shivered* broken all to pieces

shogged moved

shot reckoning

shot window a small window, often part of a bow window or a window on stairs

shotten spent, darted

showr, shower twinge of pain, throe

shradds groves

shreeuen shriven

shroggs thin saplings used as targets

sic such

siccer safely, securely

sichin sighing

sicke such

side (*adj.*) wide, distant; (*n.*) edge, bounding line

siller silver

silly simple, harmless, mean

silver wood birch wood

simple poor

skidding drawing a log from the place where it was felled to the river; *skidding was full* was expert at skidding

skinkled sparkled

skips dance steps

skorne humiliation, mockery

slack a pass or intervale between two hills

slade ditch, ravine

slae, sloe plum

slae-thorn sloe thorn.

sleight stealth

slight destroy

sliken slack, quench

slily slyly, craftily

slough-hounds bloodhounds

sma small; *sma holland* finely woven linen

smirling suppressed

smoldereth smothereth

snack quickly

sneed snood

sned cut

snell bitter cold

snooded put up in a snood, net, or band

socht sought

soggy (oxen) dull, spiritless

solem day feast day

sorrow sad

soþe truth; *for soþe* forsooth

south sweet

sowt, sought looked about

soyt sooth, truth

spait flood

spare stop, refrain

sparr bar

spauld shoulder

spear ask, inquire of

spec   spoke

spede   drive to ruin

speed   ability, opportunity

speer   inquire

speir   ask

spendyd   placed in the rest, made ready (Skeat)

spight   spite

splent   plate armor

spole   shoulder

sprente   spurted

spring   lurch, rise out of the water

spulyie   destroy

spurne   conflict

spurtle   spoon, stirring stick

spyrr   ask

in the spyt   in spite of

sta   steal, stole; stall

stabbed   searched; *stabbed the house*   searched as if prodding with an instrument; cf. *They stabbed the feather bed all round* (Child, iv, 152)

staff   stout stick

stage   stag

stage, at a stage   from above

staking   cutting into stakes

stap   stop, live

stark and strong   strong (ballad cliché; both words mean about the same thing)

starkest   strongest

stean   stone, stone seat

stear   stir

steed   stood

steer   move, go; stern

stele   pulled the arrow to its head

stelld   placed; stole

stern   stars; light

sterre   star

steuen   voice, time; *unsett steuen*   unappointed time

stey   steep

stick   in phrase *drew the stick,* struck with a goad

stickd   stabbed

stile   call

stime   gleam of light

stint   stop

stirred . . . mast   broke out no flags in identification or greeting

St. Mary Knott   hamstring, i.e., cut the Achilles tendon

stock   uncouth fellow; the outer side of the bed

stock to stone   (cliché) stock, a block, a log; hence, something lifeless and senseless; cf. the common ballad and romance cliché *stocks and stones*

stone   unit of weight, 14 to 16 lbs.

store   plenty

stot   young ox

stounde   time

stour   fight

stown   stolen

stowre   strong

straiks   blows, strokes (of sword)

strait   immediately

stratlins   stridings

straucht   straightway

strave   to be restive (see *strive, NED*)

streak   stretch

stream-tail   lower end of ford where the water rushes over

streen   yestreen

streght   straight

streikit   stretched out, laid out

strinkled   sprinkled

striped   stropped, sharpened

stubborn   quarrelsome

studdiest   sturdiest

stude   place

stye   alley

style   refers to a deer's carrying its head high

stynttyde   stopped

styrande   disturbing, stirring

suar   sure

such on   such a number

sud   should; *sudna*   should not

sugar - candy rock sugar in brandy or whiskey, rock and rye

suit sweet

sulle sell

sumner (*adj.*) one summer's growth

supply help; *supply me* aid me

swack light-footed

swade good for nothing

swades soldiers

swakked struck with sword

swapped struck

swapte struck

sway turn out

sweavens dreams

sweer slow to part with money

sweven dream

swikele wicked

swire neck

sworn extracted an oath not to work against him

sworn to pledged to go

syde low hanging

sydis side

sygnets ornaments

syke marsh, ditch

syn since

syne then, since

taen taken; grasped; shook

tail, gave him the tail tied him on facing the horse's tail

take up call off

taken mee sworne taken my parole

talbott kind of dog

tan, pounds of tan error for *pounds ten* (shillings)

tane taken

taps tops

tear ever

tell pay

tene harm

tent heed

tet, teet lock of horse's mane

thame, thane then

þau though

þe (*pro.*) thee; (*def. art.*) the

the thrive

the the, they

the suffer, endure

theek thatch

þen than

there that

there as where, wherever

thes, this, thys thus

theuys thieves

thimber thick through

thirst bird, probably the thristle-thrush

thirty merks (225) about £2, which has little point; the other versions have amounts, such as 20,000 pounds

þo those

þorne thorn

thos this

thoule endure

thou's should be *thou'll,* thou shall, or *thou pu's,* thou pullest

þowt thought

thrast pressed

thraw twist, move

thrawin twisted

three-fold o'er a tree form constructed by analogy with two-fold over a tree (staff), i.e., bent double

three times asked banns must be published for three successive periods

thrien thrice

thrild rattled

þritti thirty

throly actively, purposefully, stubbornly

throuch through

through an thro the bonny ship her seams had so opened that they could see through them

throw shoot

throwout through

þrumme a bag or pouch made of coarse threads, used especially to hold arrows *thye* thigh

tide time

tidings, tiddings news

tiend tribute

tift puff

till while, to

tine, tyne lose

tinkled at the ring supplants *tirled at the pin* in many late ballads, knocked on the knocker

tint lost

tippld slow and steady drinking; the usual meaning hardly fits with galore (125/34)

tirled at the pin pulled or shook the door fastening to attract attention

tithyngus news

to even to, including; two; for

tobreke break to pieces

tocher toucher, dowry

to-handle two-handed

toke put

tolbooth jail

told(e) counted

tone the one

toom empty

topcastle a platform erected at the heads of the masts for use in working the sails; also (167/27) a place where heavy beams were kept ready to drop on an enemy vessel

torne turns

tortyll-tree, trystill tree place of rendezvous

to-towe (emphatic) too, too

touting blowing (horn)

tows drinking; tavern

trachled tired out

tree staff, club

tree wood; cross

trenchen, trenchen tree truncheon

trew believe; trust

trews trousers (227), i.e., not kilts

treyffe thrive

tristil-tree trysting tree, i.e., rendezvous

trought pledge

trow think

trowet troth

true-love, trulove plighted love, betrothed one, true love

truff turf

trusyd laced

tryst to entice, to cause to come

trysting paying court, enticing

tua two

tun cask of varying size, but usually 252 wine gallons

turmentowres tormentors

turtle-doo turtledove

twa fold bent double; *twa-fold ower his steed* doubled over his horse—head on one side, legs on the other

twain separate

twal twelve; *twal hours* noon

twine thread

twine part with, deprive

twinn (in) apart, in twain

twinn part with, deprive; *separate in twinn* apart

twyned deprived

tyde time; *in tyde* now

ull shall

unbeen not closed in

unbetthought him bethought himself of

unbigged unbuilt

unco extraordinary, unknown, strange; (*adv.*) unusually, very

uncouth unknown

unseally unlucky

unset steven unappointed time

unshorn uncut

until to

upling scorn, downling scorn other versions have *upling call, uplane call*. The best explanation of these difficult terms is, I feel, that of Gomme: on holidays ball games took place in each town between the two parts of the town, the uptowners and the downtowners. One object of the game was to kick the ball into the opponent's territory. The two teams were called variously uptowners, downtowners, up streeters, down streeters. It is an easy step to upling and downling to designate them.

ure our

vallow not the feed value not the feud (which this will cause), i.e., don't be concerned about it

vanward vanguard

veiwe yew

verament truly

veretye truth

virr vigor

virgis verdigris

vow exclamation of surprise

wa wall; would

wad pledge; would

wadded blue

wadded at wagered on

wae mat fa may woe overtake

wael choice

waft weft, woof

wait in phrase *a wait*, I know, indeed

walking-rod cane

walker fuller

wall (well) sea a deep in the sea; *green wall sea* the green waters of the deep

wallace wight one of Wallace's men; Sir William Wallace (d. 1305) is a national hero of Scotland

wallowt drooped, whitened

wall-wight, well-wight stalwart, brave

walting welting, edging

waly exclamation with no specific meaning

wan colorless, pallid; *drink wan water* pallid water, in contrast with wine

wan, wan water dark, and so suggesting deep

wan to arrived at

wand twig, sprout; *white willow wand* staff used by merchants instead of an ensign

wane large number

wannelled wavered, staggered

wanton free, frolicksome; *Wanton Brown* name of horse

wantonly spiritedly

wap toss

wappid flapped

war aware; worse

waran sponsor

wardles worlds

ware sea weed

ware on aware of

warison, waryson reward

warld is room space of the whole world

warning surety

warr aware

warrant safeguard

warsle wrestling

warstan worst

was wash

wast wist

water-kelpy water sprite

water-stoup water bucket

waught draft

waur were; worse

(after the) way upon the way

we with

weal clasp

wean child

wear were

wearit wearied, troubled

weate I wit, I think

weather castrated male sheep

wed fine, forfeit; pledge

wedden pledge; wedding

wee pen knife may derive from

weapon knife; *weapon knife* (pronounced weepen knife) occurs

weed, weede garment, clothing

weel good; *for my weel* for my good or advantage

weel-warst very worst

welde would

well see *wall*

well-kent well known

well-wight see *wall-wight*

wen win; go

wend go to

werion curse

we's we shall

west known

wet know

weynde wind

whaten what a, what sort of

whatten what kind of

whidderand whizzing

while period of time

white monie silver

whute whistle

whyll that the, until they

wi with; why

wicht strong

wicker willow

wicket gate

wid with

widifu, widdiefu, widifuls outlaw; *widdie filler* i.e., destined for a *widdie*, halter

wierd weird; fate

wife woman

wight strong; fellow

wightdom weight

wilfu willful

wilful of my way lost

will bewildered

wimon woman

win (*hay*) make, i.e., turn until it is dry; go

wind in phrase *take wind from*, outsail, get between another vessel and the wind

wind blow

wing and wing nautical term

designating sailing before the wind, one sail out on the starboard and one on the port; in a schooner the mainsail is set on one side and the foresail on the other

wiss wish

wiste knew

wit mind; *out of thy wit* out of your mind

wite blame

witherlands contrary way

withy willow

wittering knowledge, information

wod, wode mad

wode woods

wol, wolle will

won go

wonder wondrous; wonderfully

wone plenty; *gode wone* goodly number

wons dwells

woo wool

woo he be woe be on him

woodbine the common honeysuckle, regarded as having magical properties; it was used not only as a charm against witches but by witches to bespell

woodcock (*beware thy eye*) fool (from the bird's reputation for folly; Child). May it not rather mean: watch out for Robin's shooting? A woodcock is so difficult a target that it takes an expert to hit it

woode mad

wooden knife corruption of wood knife, woodsman's knife

woodweele wood thrush

woon dwell

wordy worthily

wots knows

wou how

wouche harm; evil

wow anger, distress; exclamation of surprise, admiration

wrack ruin

wreck vengeance

wreke avenged

wring, wring their hands grieve

wrist ankle

wrocken avenged

wrongeous unjust

wrthe worthy

wud wood

wyȝth wight, fellow

wyld deer

wynne joy

wynnes spreads out to dry

wyrke work

wyte blame

xal, xul shall

xalt shalt

y (ae) one; every

ȝare ready

yate gate

ȝates gates

ych each

ȝe ye

ye you (*sing.*, polite form)

yede, yeed, yeede went

yef if

ye-faith in faith

yeffell evil

yeldyde surrendered

ȝelpe boast

ȝeluer more yellow

ȝemen yeomen

yend yon

yes, ye'se ye shall

yett if; gate

ȝete ate

ȝeue give

yeuer ever

yode went; walked

ȝoman yeoman

yonders yonder

ȝone yon

youd went

yowe ewe

ȝouyn given

BIBLIOGRAPHY
(A selected list of books for further study of the ballad)

I. BALLAD BIBLIOGRAPHIES

Child, F. J., *English and Scottish Popular Ballads,* 5 vols., Boston, 1882–1898. Extensive bibliographies.

Coffin, Tristram P., *The British Traditional Ballad in North America,* Philadelphia, 1950. Bibliography and discussion.

Dean-Smith, Margaret, *A Guide to English Folk Song Collections, 1822–1952,* Liverpool, 1954. Very valuable index and discussions.

Ford, W. C., "Broadside Ballads . . . Printed in Massachusetts, 1639–1800," *Publications of the Massachusetts Historical Society,* vol. 75, 1922. Check list of broadsides and other early pieces.

Gable, J. Harris, *A Bibliography of Robin Hood,* Lincoln, 1939.

Haywood, Charles, *A Bibliography of North American Folklore and Folksong,* New York, 1951.

Henry, M. E., *A Bibliography for the Study of American Folk Songs,* London, 1937.

Laws, G. Malcolm, Jr., *Native American Balladry,* Philadelphia, 1950. Bibliography and discussion.

Library of Congress, Music Division, *Check-List of Recorded Songs to July 1940* (mimeograph), Washington, 1942.

Mattfeld, Julius, *The Folk Music of the Western Hemisphere; A List of References in the New York Public Library,* New York Public Library Bulletin, 1925.

Pound, Louise, *Folk-Song of Nebraska and the Central West, a Syllabus,* Nebraska Academy of Sciences, *Publications,* vol. 9, 1915.

Shearin, H. G., and Combs, J., *A Syllabus of Kentucky Folk-Songs,* Lexington, 1911.

II. PERIODICALS CONTAINING BALLADS AND DISCUSSION OF BALLAD

Bulletin of the Folk-Song Society of the Northeast, Numbers 1–12, Cambridge, Mass., 1930–1937.

Journal of American Folklore, Philadelphia, 1888–   . Invaluable; many collections of ballads, articles discussing ballads, music, bibliography. Annual bibliography of folklore including ballad.

Journal of the Folk-Song Society, 1899–1936. Continued as *Journal of Folk-Dance and Song Society (JFSS).* Invaluable reference, full of discussion of ballads, texts, music, bibliography.

Midwest Folklore, 1951–

New York Folklore Quarterly, 1945–
Southern Folklore Quarterly, University of Florida, 1937–
Texas Folklore Society, *Publications,* 1916–
Western Folklore, 1942–

III. HISTORY AND CRITICISM OF BALLAD

Bronson, Bertrand H., *The Traditional Tunes of the Child Ballads,* Princeton, 1959. Two volumes of this important work have appeared (1964), covering ballads 1-113; invaluable for study of ballad tunes.

Campbell, John C., *The Southern Highlander and His Home,* New York, 1921.

Chambers, E. K., "The Close of the Middle Ages," *The Oxford History of English Literature,* Oxford, 1945, vol. 2, part 2. One chapter on the ballad.

Chappell, L. W., *John Henry: A Folklore Study,* Jena, 1933.

Entwistle, William, *European Balladry,* Oxford, 1939.

Gerould, Gordon H., *The Ballad of Tradition,* Oxford, 1932.

Hart, Walter M., *Ballad and Epic,* Boston, 1907.

Henderson, T. F., *The Ballad in Literature,* Cambridge, 1912.

Hendren, J. W., *A Study of Ballad Rhythm,* Princeton, 1936.

Hodgart, M. J. C., *The Ballads,* London, 1950.

Hustvedt, Sigurd B., *Ballad Books and Ballad Men,* Cambridge, Mass., 1930.

Hustvedt, Sigurd B., *Ballad Criticism in Scandinavia and Great Britain During the Eighteenth Century,* London, 1916.

Johnson, G. B., *John Henry: Tracking Down a Negro Legend,* Chapel Hill, 1929.

χ Ker, W. P., *On the History of Ballads, 1100–1500* (Proceedings of the British Academy, vol. 4), London, 1910.

Leach, Maria (ed.), *Dictionary of Folklore, Mythology and Legend,* New York 1950. Many articles on the ballad.

Lomax, John, *Adventures of a Ballad Hunter,* New York, 1947.

Mackenzie, W. R., *The Quest of the Ballad,* Princeton, 1919.

χ Pound, Louise, *Poetic Origins and the Ballad,* New York, 1921.

Randolph, Vance, *The Ozarks: An American Survival of Primitive Society,* New York, 1931.

Scott, Sir Walter, *Minstrelsy of the Scottish Border,* ed. T. F. Henderson, 4 vols., New York, 1902.

Sharp, C. J., *English Folksong, Some Conclusions,* London, 1907.

Sidgwick, F., *The Ballad,* London, 1914.

Smith, Reed, *South Carolina Ballads,* Cambridge, Mass., 1928.

χ Steenstrup, J. O. H. R., *The Medieval Popular Ballad,* trans. Cox, Boston, 1914.

Stewart, G. R., *The Technique of English Verse,* New York, 1930.

Wells, E. K., *The Ballad Tree,* New York, 1950.

Wilgus, D. K., Anglo-American Folksong Scholarship since 1898, Rutgers Press, 1959.

Wimberly, L. C., "Death and Burial Lore in the English and Scottish Popular Ballad," *University of Nebraska Studies in Language, Literature and Criticism*, No. 8, 1927.

Wimberly, L. C., *Folklore in the English and Scottish Ballads*, Chicago, 1928.

Wimberly, L. C., "Minstrelsy, Music and Dance in the English and Scottish Popular Ballads," *University of Nebraska Studies in Language, Literature and Criticism*, No. 4, 1921.

IV. BALLAD COLLECTIONS

(Many contain melodies, bibliographies, history, and criticism)

Ashton, J., *A Century of Ballads*, London, 1887.

Ashton, J., *Modern Street Ballads*, London, 1888.

Ashton, J., *Real Sailor Songs*, London, 1891.

Aytoun, W. E., *The Ballads of Scotland*, Edinburgh, 1858.

Barbeau, M., and Sapir, E., *Folk Songs of French Canada*, New Haven, 1925.

Baring-Gould, S., and Sheppard, H. F., *A Garland of Country Song*, London, 1895.

Baring-Gould, S., and Sheppard, H. F., *Songs and Ballads of the West*, London, 1891; revised ed., C. Sharp, (ed.), 1905.

Barry, Phillips, *The Maine Woods Songster*, Cambridge, 1939.

Barry, Phillips, Eckstorm, F. H., and Smyth, M. W., *British Ballads from Maine*, New Haven, 1929.

Beck, E. C., *Songs of the Michigan Lumberjacks*, Ann Arbor, 1942.

Belden, H. M. (ed.), *Ballads and Songs Collected by the Missouri Folk-Lore Society*, Columbia, 1940.

Botkin, B. A., *The American Play Party Song*, Lincoln, 1937.

Brewster, P. G., *Ballads and Songs of Indiana*, Bloomington, 1940.

Broadwood, L., *English Traditional Songs and Carols*, London, 1908.

Broadwood, L., and Fuller-Maitland, J. A., *English Country Songs*, London, 1893.

Bruce, J. C., and Stokoe, John, *Northumbrian Minstrelsy*, Newcastle-upon-Tyne, 1882.

Buchan, Peter, *Ancient Ballads and Songs of the North of Scotland*, 2 vols., Edinburgh, 1828, 1875.

Buchan, Peter, *Gleanings of Scotch, English and Irish Scarce Old Ballads*, Peterhead, 1825.

Butterworth, G., *Folksongs from Sussex*, London and Boston, 1912.

Cambiaire, C. P., *East Tennessee and Western Virginia Mountain Ballads*, London, 1935.

Chappell, Louis W., *Folksongs of Roanoke and the Albemarle*, Morgantown, West Virginia, 1939.

Chappell, W., *Popular Music of the Olden Time*, London, 1858.

Chappell, W., and Ebsworth, J. W. (eds.), *Roxburghe Ballads*, 9 vols., London, 1871–1899.

Chase, Richard, *Traditional Ballads, Songs, and Games*, Chapel Hill, 1935.

Child, F. J., *English and Scottish Popular Ballads*, 5 vols., Boston, 1882–1898.

Christie, W., *Traditional Ballad Airs*, 2 vols., Edinburgh, 1876–1881.

Clark, Andrew (ed.), *The Shirburn Ballads*, Oxford, 1907.

Clawson, W. H., *The Geste of Robin Hood*, Toronto, 1909.

Colcord, J. C., *Roll and Go, Songs of American Sailor Men*, Indianapolis, 1924; reissue, 1938.

Combs, Josiah, *Folk-Songs du Midi des Etats-Unis*, Paris, 1925.

Combs, Josiah, *Folk-Songs from the Kentucky Highlands*, New York, 1939.

Cox, J. H., *Folk-Songs of the South*, Cambridge, Mass., 1925.

Creighton, Helen, *Songs and Ballads from Nova Scotia*, Toronto, 1933.

Creighton, Helen, and Senior, D. H., *Traditional Songs from Nova Scotia*, Toronto, 1950.

Cromek, R. H., *Select Scottish Songs with Critical Observations and Biographical Notices by Robert Burns*, 2 vols., London, 1810.

Davis, A. K., *Traditional Ballads of Virginia*, Cambridge, Mass., 1929.

Dean, Michall, *The Flying Cloud and One Hundred and Fifty Other Old Time Songs and Ballads*, Virginia, Minn., 1922.

Dixon, J. H., *Ancient Poems, Ballads and Songs of the Peasantry of England*, London, 1846.

Doerflinger, William, *Shantymen and Shantyboys*, New York, 1951.

Ebsworth, J. W. (ed.), *Bagford Ballads*, London, 1878.

Eckstorm, F. H., and Smyth, M. W., *The Minstrelsy of Maine*, Boston, 1927.

Eddy, Mary O., *Ballads and Songs from Ohio*, New York, 1939.

Evans, T., *Old Ballads*, 2 vols., 1777; 4 vols., R. H. Evans (ed.), 1810.

Eyre-Todd, G., *Ancient Scots Ballads*, London, 1895.

Finger, Charles J., *Frontier Ballads*, New York, 1927.

Firth, C. H., *Ballads Relating to America*, Oxford, 1915.

Firth, C. H., *Naval Songs and Ballads*, London, 1908.

Flanders, Helen H., and others, *The New Green Mountain Songster*, New Haven, 1939.

Flanders, Helen H., and Brown, G., *Vermont Folk-Songs and Ballads*, Brattleboro, 1931.

Fuson, H. H., *Ballads of the Kentucky Highlands*, London, 1931.

Gardner, E. E., and Chickering, G. J., *Ballads and Songs of Southern Michigan*, Ann Arbor, 1939.

Gibson, J. M., *Canadian Folksongs*, London, 1927.

Gomme, A. B., and Sharp, C. J., *Children's Singing Games*, 5 vols., London, 1909 ff.

Gray, Roland P., *Songs and Ballads of the Maine Lumberjacks*, Cambridge, Mass., 1924.

Greene, Richard L., *The Early English Carols*, Oxford, 1935.

Greenleaf, E. B., and Mansfield, G. Y., *Ballads and Sea Songs of Newfoundland*, Cambridge, Mass., 1933.

Greig, Gavin, *Folk-Song in Buchan and Folk-Song of the North-East*, Reprint, Hatboro, Pa., 1963.

Greig, Gavin, *Last Leaves of Traditional Ballads*, Aberdeen, 1925.

Hales, J. W., and Furnivall, F. J., *Bishop Percy's Folio Manuscript*, 3 vols., London, 1867–1868.

Henry, M. E., *Folk Songs from the Southern Highlands*, New York, 1938.

Herd, D., *Ancient and Modern Scottish Songs*, 2 vols., Edinburgh, 1776.

Hill, Geoffry, *Wiltshire Folk-Songs and Carols*, Bournemouth, 1904.

Hudson, A. P., *Folksongs of Mississippi and Their Background*, Chapel Hill, 1936.

Hughes, H., *Irish Country Songs*, London, 1915.

Jamieson, R., *Popular Ballads and Songs from Tradition*, Edinburgh, 1806.

Jewett, Sophie, *Folk Ballads from Southern Europe*, New York, 1913.

Jewitt, L. (ed.), *The Ballads and Songs of Derbyshire*, London, 1867.

Johnson, Guy B., *John Henry*, Chapel Hill, 1929.

Johnson, J., *The Scots Musical Museum*, 6 vols., Edinburgh, 1787–1803; also later eds.

Joyce, P. W., *Ancient Irish Music*, Dublin, 3rd ed., 1882.

Karpeles, Maud, *Folk Songs from Newfoundland*, Oxford, 1934.

Kidson, Frank, *Traditional Tunes*, Oxford, 1891.

Kinloch, G. R., *Ancient Scottish Ballads*, London, 1827.

Korson, G. G., *Coal Dust on the Fiddle*, Philadelphia, 1943.

Korson, G. G., *Minstrels of the Mine Patch*, Philadelphia, 1938.

Korson, G. G. (ed.), *Pennsylvania Songs and Legends*, Philadelphia, 1949.

Korson, G. G., *Songs and Ballads of the Anthracite Miners*, New York, 1927.

Laing, David (ed.), *A Ballad Book. By Charles Kirkpatrick Sharpe, Esq., 1823*, reprinted Edinburgh, 1880.

Linscott, E. H., *Folk Songs of Old New England*, New York, 1939.

Lochlainn, C. O., *Irish Street Ballads*, London, 1939.

Lomax, John, *Cowboy Songs and Other Frontier Ballads*, New York, 1910, revised, 1938.

Lomax, John and Alan, *Folk Song U.S.A.*, New York, 1949; reprint, 1953.

Lomax, John and Alan, *Negro Folk Songs as Sung by Leadbelly*, New York, 1936.

Mackenzie, William R., *Ballads and Sea Songs from Nova Scotia*, Cambridge, Mass., 1928.

Maidment, J., *Scottish Ballads and Songs*, Edinburgh, 1859.

Maidment, J., *Scottish Ballads and Songs, Historical and Traditionary*, 2 vols., Edinburgh, 1868.

McGill, J., *Folk Songs of the Kentucky Mountains*, New York, 1917.

Memoirs of the American Folklore Society; see especially:

    Vol. 3. *Bahama Songs and Stories.*
     "   10. *Spanish-American Folk Songs.*
     "   16. *Folklore of the Sea Islands, South Carolina.*
     "   18. *Folklore of Maryland.*
     "   21. *Jamaica Folklore.*
     "   24. *Folklore from Nova Scotia.*
     "   26. *Folklore of the Antilles.*
     "   29. *Folklore from Iowa.*

Morris, Alton C., *Folksongs of Florida*, Gainesville, 1950.

Motherwell, William, *Minstrelsy, Ancient and Modern*, 2 vols., Glasgow, 1827; Boston, 1846.

Neeser, Robert W., *American Naval Songs and Ballads*, New Haven, 1938.

Newell, W. H., *Games and Songs of American Children*, New York, 1903.

O'Conor, Manas, *Old Time Songs and Ballads of Ireland*, New York, 1901.

Odum, H. W., and Johnson, G. B., *Negro Workaday Songs*, Chapel Hill, 1926.

Odum, H. W., and Johnson, G. B., *The Negro and His Songs*, Chapel Hill, 1925.

Olrik, Axel, *A Book of Danish Ballads*, trans. E. M. Smith-Dampier, Princeton, 1939.

Ord, J., *The Bothy Songs and Ballads of Aberdeen, Banff, and Moray, etc.*, Paisley, 1930.

Percy, Thomas, *Reliques of Ancient English Poetry*, London, 4th ed., 1794.

Petrie, G., *The Complete Collection of Irish Music*, London, 1902.

Pound, Louise, *American Ballads and Songs*, New York, 1922.

Prior, R. C. A. (trans.), *Ancient Danish Ballads*, 3 vols., Edinburgh, 1860.

Quiller-Couch, Arthur T. (ed.), *The Oxford Book of Ballads*, Oxford, 1910.

Ramsay, A., *The Ever Green*, 2 vols., Edinburgh, 1724.

Ramsay, A., *The Tea-Table Miscellany*, 4 vols., Edinburgh, 1724.

Randolph, Vance, *Ozark Folk Songs*, 4 vols., Columbia, Missouri, 1947–50. Major collection, with full bibliography and discussion of many ballads.

Ravenscropt, Thomas, *Melismata; Musicall Phansies*, London, 1611.

Richardson, E. P., *American Mountain Songs*, New York, 1927.

Rickaby, Franz, *Ballads and Songs of the Shanty Boy*, Cambridge, Mass., 1926.

Ritson, J., *Ancient Songs, from the Time of King Henry the Third to the Revolution*, London, 1790.

Ritson, J., *Pieces of Ancient Popular Poetry*, London, 1791.

Ritson, J., *Robin Hood, a Collection of Ancient Poems, Songs, and Ballads . . .*, 2 vols., London, 1795.

Ritson, J., *Scottish Song*, 2 vols., London, 1794.

Rollins, Hyder E., *Cavalier and Puritan*, New York, 1923.

Rollins, Hyder E., *The Pepys Ballads*, 9 vols., Cambridge, Mass., 1929–1932.

Rollins, Hyder E., *The Phoenix Nest*, Cambridge, Mass., 1931.

Sandburg, Carl, *The American Songbag*, New York, 1927; 2nd ed., 1952.

Sandys, William, *Christmas Carols, Ancient and Modern*, London, 1833.

Sargent, Helen C., and Kittredge, G. L., *The English and Scottish Popular Ballads*, Boston, 1904. A one-volume abridgment of Child's *English and Scottish Popular Ballads*.

Scarborough, D., *A Song Catcher in the Southern Mountains*, New York, 1937.

Scarborough, D., *On the Trail of Negro Folk-Songs*, Cambridge, Mass., 1925.

Sharp, C. J., *English Folk Carols*, London, 1911.

Sharp, C. J., *English Folk Songs from the Southern Appalachians*, M. Karpeles (ed.), 2 vols., London, 1932, 1952.

Sharp, C. J., *One Hundred English Folk Songs*, Boston, 1916.

Sharp, C. J., and Marson, C. L., *Folk Songs from Somerset*, 3 vols., London, 1904.

Sharp, C. J., and others, *Folk Songs of England*, 5 Books, 1908–1912.
1. Dorset by H. E. D. Hammond.
2. Eastern Counties by R. V. Williams.
3. Hampshire by G. B. Gardiner.
4. Various Counties by C. J. Sharp.
5. Sussex by W. P. Merrick.

Shay, Frank, *Deep Sea Chantys*, London, 1925.

Shearin, H. G., *British Ballads in the Cumberland Mountains*, Sewanee, Tenn., 1911.

Shoemaker, H. W., *Mountain Minstrelsy of Pennsylvania*, Philadelphia, 1931.

Shoemaker, H. W., *North Pennsylvania Minstrelsy*, Altoona, 1923.

Sidgwick, F., *Popular Ballads of the Olden Times*, 4 vols., London, 1903–1912.

Smith, Reed, *South Carolina Ballads*, Cambridge, Mass., 1928.

Thompson, H. W., *Body, Boots and Britches*, Philadelphia, 1940.

Tozer, F., *Fifty Sailors' Songs and Chanties*, London, n.d.

Whall, W. B., *Sea Songs and Shanties*, London, 1926, 1930.

White, N. I., *American Negro Folk Songs*, Cambridge, Mass., 1928.

Williams, A., *Folk Songs of the Upper Thames*, London, 1923.

Work, J. W., *Folk Song of the American Negro*, Nashville, 1915.

Wyman, Lorraine, and Brockway, Howard, *Lonesome Tunes*, New York, 1916.

SELECTED LIST OF BALLAD RECORDINGS
(* indicates recordings especially recommended for authenticity.)

By far the most important and authentic ballad recordings are those issued by the Folk Music Section of the Library of Congress, Archive of American Folk Song (AAFS). These are field recordings with no editing, arranging, or intrusive instrumental accompaniments. Records and albums of folk songs are available only direct from the Library. An indispensable source of information for any user of recorded folk music is *A List of American Folksongs Currently Available on Records,* a compilation of The Archive of American Folksong of The Library of Congress (Government Printing Office). The 176-page list of titles, with an index to performers, contains references to all items available from commercial producers and the Library as of the first part of 1953.

The Avondale Mine Disaster, L of C, AAFS 76, Album 16.*

Barbara Allan, L of C, AAFS 66, Album 14.*
 L of C, AAFS 2, Album 1.*
 A. R. Summers, Columbia 408.
 Richard Dyer-Bennett, Asch 461.

Blue Mountain Lake, Frank Warner, Disc 611; Elektra LP 3.*

The Boll Weevil, Huddie Ledbetter, Musicraft M-31.*
 Tony Kraber, Keynote K 104; Mercury LP, MG 20,008.
 Bill Bonyun, Folkways FP 2.
 Terry Gilkynson, Decca 5263.
 Carl Sandburg, Lyrichord LL 4.

The Boston Burglar, L of C, AAFS 67, Album 14.*

Brave Wolf, Frank Warner, Hudson Valley Songs, Disc 611.*
 Madrigal Singers, Columbia 329.

Brennan on the Moor, Burl Ives, Stinson LP 1.

The Broken Token (Sweetheart in the Army), AAFS 104, Album 21.*

The Brookfield Murder, Earl Rogers, Musicraft M 68.

Buffalo Skinners, Woodie Guthrie, Stinson-Asch Album 360.
 Bill Bender, Asch A 410.

The Butcher Boy, Henry Lee, Folkways FP 251.

Captain Wedderburn's Courtship (riddle part), Burl Ives, Columbia C-103.
 Tom Scott, Signature S-5.

The Cherry Tree Carol, AAFS 66, Album 14.*
 A. R. Summers, Columbia 408. Folkways FP 61.
 J. J. Niles, Victor M 718.

Claude Allen, L of C, AAFS 35, Album 7.*
Corpus Christi Carol, Roycroft Records 157.
The Cruel Brother, A. R. Summers, Folkways FP 64.
The Cruel Mother, Shep Ginandes, Elektra JH 508-A.
The Death of Queen Jane, AAFS 104, Album 21.*
   J. J. Niles, Victor M 824.
   Isla Cameron, H.M.V. B 10111.*
The Derby Ram, Richard Dyer-Bennett, Mercury LP MG-20007.
   Bascom Lunsford, Brunswick BL 59001: Decca-Brunswick B
     1024.*
   L of C, AAFS 59, Album 12.*
The Drowsy Sleeper, Tom Glazer, Mercury LP MG 20007.
   Carter Family, Decca 5612.
   Kelly Harrell, Vic. 20,280.
Earl Brand, AAFS 60, Album 12.*
Edward, AAFS 57, Album 12.*
   Shep Ginandes, Elektra JH 508-B.
   Adolf Stark and Aino Karelia, Velisurmaaj (Finnish), Asch 560.
The Elfin Knight, Wallace House, Asch UN 203.
Eppie Morrie, Ewan MacColl, H.M.V. B 10260.*
The False Knight upon the Road, AAFS 104, Album 21.
The Farmer's Curst Wife, AAFS 1, Album 1.*
   Mrs. Texas Gladden, Disc 737.*
   Richard Dyer-Bennett, Decca 10; DLP 5046.
   Burl Ives, Columbia C-186.
   Sam Eskin, Folkways 1020.
   A. R. Summers, Folkways FP 21B.
Father Grumble, AAFS 70, Album 14.*
Frankie and Albert, Huddie Ledbetter, Musicraft M-31.
Geordie, A. R. Summers, Folkways FP 64.
The Golden Vanity, AAFS 31, Album 7.*
   Pete Seeger, Commodore CR-11.
   Almanac Singers, General 20.
   Shep Ginandes, Elektra JH 508-A.
   Carter Family, Columbia 20333.
   Sam Eskin, Staff 1.
   Richard Dyer-Bennett, Vox 632; Mercury MG-20007.
The Greenland Fishery, John and Lucy Allison, Keynote K 102.
   Hermes Nye, Folkways FP 37.
The Gypsy Laddie, AAFS 2, Album 1.*
   I. G. Greer, Parlaphone 3195.*
   Jean Ritchie, Elektra LP 2.*
Henry Martin, Burl Ives, Stinson LP 1.
   Phillip Tanner, Columbia 372-M.
House Carpenter, see James Harris.
Jam on Gerry's Rocks, Seeger, Folkways FP 3.
   Earl Rogers, Musicraft M-68.

James Harris, AAFS 1, Album 1.*
  Clarence Ashley, Columbia 15654.
  Richard Dyer-Bennett, Keynote K-108; Mercury MG 20007.
  Henry Lee, Folkways FP 251.
  A. R. Summers, Folkways FP 64.*
Jesse James, Bill Bonyun, Folkways FP 2.
  Brownie McNeil, album available from the singer, Trinity University, San Antonio, Texas.
John Hardy, Huddie Ledbetter, Musicraft 311; Disc 660.*
  Henry Lee, Folkways FP 251.
  Burl Ives, Columbia CL 6058.
  Buel Kazee, Brunswick 144.
  Carter Family, Bluebird 6033.
John Henry, AAFS 15, Album 3.*
  Huddie Ledbetter, Asch A-343.*
  Josh White, Decca A-447.
  Dave Macon, Decca-Brunswick B 1024.
  Sam Eskin, Folkways 1020.
  Richard Dyer-Bennett, Asch 461; Remington 199-34.
  Bascom Lunsford, *et el.,* Brunswick BL 59001.
  Legend of John Henry, Folkways LA 8.
  Tom Scott, Signature S-5.
  Josh White, Decca DL 5082.
King Henry V's Conquest of France, Jean Ritchie, New Records NRLP 2005.
Lady Isabel and the Elf Knight, Richard Dyer-Bennett, Decca A-573.
Lamkin, AAFS 34, Album 7.*
  Shep Ginandes, Folk Songs, Elektra JH 508.*
The Lincolnshire Poacher, Richard Dyer-Bennett, Keynote 108; Mercury MG 20007.
The Little Brown Bulls, Sam Eskin, Folkways FP 19.*
  AAFS 5, Album 1.*
The Little Mohee, Burl Ives, Columbia CL 6058; Columbia C-186.*
  Buel Kazee, Brunswick 156.
  J. J. Niles, Victor M-604.
Little Musgrave, J. J. Niles, Victor M-824.
  Shep Ginandes, Elektra JH 508.*
Lord Bateman, AAFS 56, Album 12.*
  Joseph Taylor, H.M.V. 2972.*
  Shep Ginandes, Elektra JH 508.
Lord Lovel, Frank Warner, Elektra JH 504 A.
Lord Randal, Ewan MacColl, H.M.V. B 10259.*
  Burl Ives, Columbia C-186; CL 6058.
  Jaques Gordon, Decca A-270.
  Sam Eskin (Croodin Doo) Staff, FM 1.*
  Shep Ginandes (Welsh), Elektra, 508-B.
  Richard Dyer-Bennett, Remington, 199-44.

Lord Thomas and Fair Annet, AAFS 33, Album 7.*

Shep Ginandes, Elektra JH 508 B.

The Lowlands of Holland, AAFS 103, Album 21.*

The Maid Freed from the Gallows, A. R. Summers, Columbia 408.*

Ledbetter, Musicraft M-31.

Mary Hamilton, Isla Cameron, H.M.V. B 10111.*

AAFS 32, Album 7.*

A. R. Summers, Columbia 408.

Montcalm and Wolfe, Frank Warner, Disc 611.

Naomi Wise, AAFS 57, Album 12.*

Al Craver, Columbia 15053-D.

Old Smoky, AAFS 69, Album 14.*

Burl Ives, Columbia C-103.

On the Banks of Sweet Dundee, George Edwards, Asch 560.*

Our Goodman, AAFS 60, Album 12.*

The Oxford Girl, AAFS 57, Album 12.*

Pretty Polly, AAFS 3, Album 1.

Lunsford, *et al.,* Brunswick BL 59001.

Riddles Wisely Expounded, AAFS 4, Album 1.*

Isla Cameron, H.M.V. 10110.*

Burl Ives, Decca A-431 ; Columbia CL 6109.

Sir Lionel (Old Bangum), A. R. Summers, Columbia 408.*

Richard Dyer-Bennett, Keynote K-108.

Bentley Ball, Columbia 90055.

Sir Patrick Spens, Ewan MacColl, H.M.V. B 10260.*

Springfield Mountain, Sam Eskin, Staff FM 1.*

Burl Ives, Columbia CL 6058.

Old Harp Singers, Musicraft 41.

American Ballad Singers, Victor P-41.

Stackolee, Woodie Guthrie, Stinson LP 7.

Lunsford, *et al.,* Brunswick BL 59001.

Henry Lee, Folkways FP 251.

Sweet Betsy from Pike, Bill Bender, Asch A-410.

Burl Ives, Columbia CL 6109.*

Cisco Houston, Folkways FP 22.

The Three Ravens, Richard Dyer-Bennett, Asch 461.

The Two Brothers, AAFS 32, Album 7.*

Shep Ginandes, Elektra JH 508.

The Two Sisters, AAFS 33, Album 7.*

A. R. Summers, Columbia 408.

Richard Hayward, Decca G-20234.

Richard Dyer-Bennett, Remington 199-34.

The Unquiet Grave, A. R. Summers, Folkways FP 64.*

Van Dieman's Land, Ewan MacColl, H.M.V. B 10259.*

Villikens and His Dinah, Richard Dyer-Bennett, Decca A-573 ; Decca
DL-5046.

The Wagoner's Lad, Henry Lee, Folkways FP 251.
  Buel Kazee, Brunswick 213.
The Wife of Usher's Well, AAFS 34, Album 7.*
  A. R. Summers, Columbia 408.
  J. J. Niles, Victor M 824.
  Buell Kazee, Decca-Brunswick B-1024; Brunswick 212.
  Shep Ginandes, Elektra JH 508.*
The Wife Wrapped in Wether's Skin, Burl Ives, Columbia C-103.*
  Richard Dyer-Bennett, Remington 199-34.
The Wild Barbaree (cf. Child 285), AAFS 103, Album 21.*
  Burl Ives, Columbia CL 6144.
  Almanac Singers, General 20.
  Seeger, *et al.*, Commodore CR 11.
Young Charlotte, AAFS 68, Album 14.*

Since 1950 many more important ballad recordings have been made. Note especially the long playing records released by the Folk Music Section of the Library of Congress. Many of these are new releases. Note for study of ballad variants in text and tune, Charles Seeger's L. of C. Record *Barbara Allen* with texts and detailed analysis. For full list of L. of C. recordings send for their catalogue. Invaluable for the teacher of ballad is Lloyd, A. L. and MacCall, Ewan, *The English and Scottish Popular Ballads and the Great British Ballads,* ed. K. Goldstein, 5 vols., Riverside 12-621, etc. and reissue by Washington. Here are 72 traditional ballads, sung traditionally. Valuable notes.

For other ballad record listings see the "Discography" in Appendix 2 of D. K. Wilgus, *Anglo-American Folksong Scholarship*, etc. and the forthcoming complete folksong discography compiled by Kenneth Goldstein and D. K. Wilgus.

INDEX OF TITLES

(Italics indicate main entries.)